ACCA

Paper P2 INT/UK

Corporate Reporting

Complete Text

British library cataloguing-in-publication data

A catalogue record for this book is available from the British Library.

Published by:
Kaplan Publishing UK
Unit 2 The Business Centre
Molly Millars Lane
Wokingham
Berkshire
RG41 2QZ

ISBN: 978-0-85732-666-9

Printed and bound in Great Britain

Acknowledgements

We are grateful to the Association of Chartered Certified Accountants and the Chartered Institute of Management Accountants for permission to reproduce past examination questions. The answers have been prepared by Kaplan Publishing.

KAPLAN

Contents

Paper Introduction

How to Use the Materials

The nature of the P2 **Corporate Reporting** exam, is that of a 'pillar topic'. This means that students will need a good understanding of the basics of accounting as covered initially in F3 and then in F7.

The ACCA website www.accaglobal.com includes a useful FAQ section. Within this section the examiner recommends:

> *'It is important that students have done some pre-course work such as attempting as homework a past F7 exam as appropriate revision before starting work on P2. This message applies equally to students who have attempted and passed F7 and to those who have gained an exemption from F7'.*
>
> *P2 examiner – ACCA website*

These Kaplan Publishing learning materials have been carefully designed to make your learning experience as easy as possible and to give you the best chances of success in your examinations.

The product range contains a number of features to help you in the study process. They include:

(1) Detailed study guide and syllabus objectives

(2) Description of the examination

(3) Study skills and revision guidance

(4) Complete text or essential text

(5) Question practice

The sections on the study guide, the syllabus objectives, the examination and study skills should all be read before you commence your studies. They are designed to familiarise you with the nature and content of the examination and give you tips on how to best to approach your learning.

The **complete text or essential text** comprises the main learning materials and gives guidance as to the importance of topics and where other related resources can be found. Each chapter includes:

• The **learning objectives** contained in each chapter, which have been carefully mapped to the examining body's own syllabus learning objectives or outcomes. You should use these to check you have a clear understanding of all the topics on which you might be assessed in the examination.

- The **chapter diagram** provides a visual reference for the content in the chapter, giving an overview of the topics and how they link together.

- The **content** for each topic area commences with a brief explanation or definition to put the topic into context before covering the topic in detail. You should follow your studying of the content with a review of the illustration/s. These are worked examples which will help you to understand better how to apply the content for the topic.

- **Test your understanding** sections provide an opportunity to assess your understanding of the key topics by applying what you have learned to short questions. Answers can be found at the back of each chapter.

- **Summary diagrams** complete each chapter to show the important links between topics and the overall content of the paper. These diagrams should be used to check that you have covered and understood the core topics before moving on.

- **Question practice** is provided through this text.

Icon Explanations

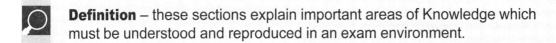 **Definition** – these sections explain important areas of Knowledge which must be understood and reproduced in an exam environment.

Key Point – identifies topics which are key to success and are often examined.

New – identifies topics that are brand new in papers that build on, and therefore also contain, learning covered in earlier papers.

Expandable Text – within the online version of the work book is a more detailed explanation of key terms, these sections will help to provide a deeper understanding of core areas. Reference to this text is vital when self studying.

Test Your Understanding – following key points and definitions are exercises which give the opportunity to assess the understanding of these core areas. Within the work book the answers to these sections are left blank, explanations to the questions can be found within the online version which can be hidden or shown on screen to enable repetition of activities.

Illustration – to help develop an understanding of topics and the test your understanding exercises the illustrative examples can be used.

Exclamation Mark – this symbol signifies a topic which can be more difficult to understand, when reviewing these areas care should be taken.

Tutorial note – included to explain some of the technical points in more detail.

Footsteps – helpful tutor tips.

On-line subscribers

Our on-line resources are designed to increase the flexibility of your learning materials and provide you with immediate feedback on how your studies are progressing.

If you are subscribed to our on-line resources you will find:

(1) On-line referenceware: reproduces your Complete or Essential Text on-line, giving you anytime, anywhere access.

(2) On-line testing: provides you with additional on-line objective testing so you can practice what you have learned further.

(3) On-line performance management: immediate access to your on-line testing results. Review your performance by key topics and chart your achievement through the course relative to your peer group.

Ask your local customer services staff if you are not already a subscriber and wish to join.

Paper introduction

Paper background

The aim of ACCA Paper P2 (INT), **Corporate reporting**, is to apply knowledge and skills and to exercise professional judgement in the application and evaluation of financial reporting principles and practices in a range of business contexts and situations.

Objectives of the syllabus

- Discuss the professional and ethical duties of the accountant.
- Evaluate the financial reporting framework.
- Advise on and report the financial performance of entities.
- Prepare the financial statements of groups of entities in accordance with relevant accounting standards.
- Explain reporting issues relating to specialised entities.
- Discuss the implications of changes in accounting regulation on financial reporting.
- Appraise the financial performance and position of entities.
- Evaluate current developments.

Core areas of the syllabus

- The professional and ethical duty of the accountant.
- The financial reporting framework.
- Reporting the financial performance of entities.
- Financial statements of groups of entities.
- Specialised entities and specialised transactions.
- Implications of changes in accounting regulation on financial reporting.
- The appraisal of financial performance and position of entities.
- Current developments.

Approach to INT and UK syllabus elements

Due to the alignment of the UK and INT syllabus elements one text has been produced to address both variants. Both streams apply the principles of International Financial Reporting Standards (IFRS).

The international variant has been used as the basis of the text. Any variances relevant only to the UK syllabus (such as the Companies Act 2006) have been included at the end of the relevant chapter in expandable text boxes headed "UK syllabus focus". All test your understandings (where appropriate) have also been appended to reflect any UK-specific variations.

In principle, the variances consist of the additional requirement to discuss and apply the key differences between UK GAAP and IFRS.

Syllabus objectives

We have reproduced the ACCA's syllabus below, showing where the objectives are explored within this book. Within the chapters, we have broken down the extensive information found in the syllabus into easily digestible and relevant sections, called Content Objectives. These correspond to the objectives at the beginning of each chapter.

Syllabus learning objective / Chapter

A THE PROFESSIONAL AND ETHICAL DUTIES OF THE ACCOUNTANT

1 Professional behaviour and compliance with accounting standards

(a) Appraise and discuss the ethical and professional issues in advising on corporate reporting.[3] **Ch. 7**

(b) Assess the relevance and importance of ethical and professional issues in complying with accounting standards.[3] **Ch. 7**

2 Ethical requirements of corporate reporting and the consequences of unethical behaviour

(a) Appraise the potential ethical implications of professional and managerial decisions in the preparation of corporate reports.[3] **Ch. 7**

(b) Assess the consequences of not upholding ethical principles in the preparation of corporate reports.[3] **Ch. 7**

3 Social responsibility

(a) Discuss the increased demand for transparency in corporate reports, and the emergence of non-financial reporting standards.[3] **Ch. 19**

(b) Discuss the progress towards a framework for environmental and sustainability reporting.[3] **Ch. `19**

B THE FINANCIAL REPORTING FRAMEWORK

1 The applications, strengths and weaknesses of an accounting framework

(a) Evaluate the valuation models adopted by standard setters.[3] **Ch. 8**

(b) Discuss the use of an accounting framework in underpinning the production of accounting standards.[3] **Ch. 8**

(c) Assess the success of such a framework in introducing rigorous and consistent accounting standards.[3] **Ch. 8**

2 Critical evaluation of principles and practices

(a) Identify the relationship between accounting theory and practice.[2] **Ch. 8**

(b) Critically evaluate accounting principles and practices used in corporate reporting.[3] **Ch. 8**

C REPORTING THE FINANCIAL PERFORMANCE OF ENTITIES

1 Performance reporting

(a) Prepare reports relating to corporate performance for external stakeholders.[3] **Ch. 9**

(b) Discuss the issues relating to the recognition of revenue.[3] **Ch. 9**

(c) Evaluate proposed changes to reporting financial performance.[3] **Ch. 9**

2 Non-current assets

(a) Apply and discuss the timing of the recognition of non-current assets and the determination of their carrying amounts including impairment and revaluations.[3] **Ch. 14**

(b) Apply and discuss the treatment of non-current assets held for sale.[3] **Ch. 14**

(c) Apply and discuss the accounting treatment of investment properties including classification, recognition and measurement issues.[3] **Ch. 14**

(d) Apply and discuss the accounting treatment of intangible assets including the criteria for recognition and measurement subsequent to acquisition and classification.[3] **Ch. 14**

3 Financial instruments

(a) Apply and discuss the recognition and derecognition of financial assets and financial liabilities.[2] **Ch. 16**

(b) Apply and discuss the classification of financial assets and financial liabilities and their measurement.[2] **Ch. 16**

(c) Apply and discuss the treatment of gains and losses arising on financial assets and financial liabilities.[2] **Ch. 16**

(d) Apply and discuss the treatment of impairment of financial assets.[2] **Ch. 16**

(e) Account for derivative financial instruments, and simple embedded derivatives.[2] **Ch. 16**

(f) Outline the principle of hedge accounting and account for fair value hedges and cash flow hedges including hedge effectiveness.[2] **Ch. 16**

4 Leases

(a) Apply and discuss the classification of leases and accounting for leases by lessors and lessees.[3] **Ch. 15**

(b) Account for and discuss sale and leaseback transactions.[3] **Ch. 15**

5 Segment reporting

(a) Determine the nature and extent of reportable segments.[3] **Ch. 12**

(b) Specify and discuss the nature of segment information to be disclosed. [3] **Ch. 12**

6 Employee benefits

(a) Apply and discuss the accounting treatment of short term and long term employee benefits.[3] **Ch. 10**

(b) Apply and discuss the accounting treatment of defined contribution and defined benefit plans.[3] **Ch. 10**

(c) Account for gains and losses on settlements and curtailments.[2] **Ch. 10**

(d) Account for the 'Asset Ceiling' test and the reporting of actuarial gains and losses.[2] **Ch. 10**

7 Income taxes

(a) Apply and discuss the recognition and measurement of deferred tax liabilities and deferred tax assets.[3] **Ch. 18**

(b) Determine the recognition of tax expense or income and its inclusion in the financial statements.[3] **Ch. 18**

8 Provisions, contingencies, events after the reporting date

(a) Apply and discuss the recognition, derecognition and measurement of provisions, contingent liabilities and contingent assets including environmental provisions.[3] **Ch. 17**

(b) calculate and discuss restructuring provisions.[3] **Ch. 17**

(c) Apply and discuss the accounting for events after the reporting date.[3] **Ch. 17**

(d) Determine and report going concern issues arising after the reporting date.[3] **Ch. 17**

9 Related parties

(a) Determine the parties considered to be related to an entity.[3] **Ch. 13**

(b) Identify the implications of related party relationships and the need for disclosure.[3] **Ch. 13**

10 Share-based payment

(a) Apply and discuss the recognition and measurement criteria for share-based payment transactions.[3] **Ch. 11**

(b) Account for modifications, cancellations and settlements of share-based payment transactions.[2] **Ch. 11**

11 Reporting requirements of small and medium-sized entities (SMEs)

(a) Outline the principal considerations in developing a set of accounting standards for SMEs.[3] **Ch. 20**

(b) Discuss solutions to the problem of differential financial reporting.[3] **Ch. 20**

(c) Discuss the reasons why the IFRS for SME's does not address certain topics.[3] **Ch. 20**

(d) Discuss the accounting treatments not allowable under the IFRS for SME's including the revaluation model for certain assets.[3] **Ch. 20**

(e) Discuss and apply the simplifications introduced by the IFRS for SMEs including accounting for goodwill and intangible assets, financial instruments, defined benefit schemes, exchange differences and associates and joint ventures.[3] **Ch. 20**

D FINANCIAL STATEMENTS OF GROUPS OF ENTITIES

1 Group accounting including statements of cash flow

(a) Apply the method of accounting for business combinations, including complex group structures.[3] **Ch. 1, 2 and 3**

(b) Apply the principles in determining the cost of a business combination. [3] **Ch. 1, 2 and 3**

(c) Apply the recognition and measurement criteria for identifiable acquired assets and liabilities and goodwill including step acquisitions. [3] **Ch. 1, 2 and 3**

(d) Apply and discuss the criteria used to identify a subsidiary and an associate.[3] **Ch. 1**

(e) Determine and apply appropriate procedures to be used in preparing group financial statements.[3] **Ch. 1, 2 and 3**

(f) Identify and outline the circumstances in which a group is required to prepare consolidated financial statements; the circumstances when a group may claim an exemption from the preparation of consolidated financial statements, and why directors may not wish to consolidate a subsidiary and where this is permitted.[2] **Ch. 1**

(g) Apply the equity method of accounting for associates[3] **Ch. 1**

(h) Outline and apply the key definitions and accounting methods which relate to interests in joint arrangements.[3] **Ch. 1**

(i) Prepare and discuss group statements of cash flows.[3] **Ch. 6**

2 Continuing and discontinued interests

(a) Prepare group financial statements where activities have been discontinued, or have been acquired or disposed in the period.[3] **Ch. 3**

(b) Apply and discuss the treatment of a subsidiary which has been acquired exclusively with a view to subsequent disposal.[3] **Ch. 3**

3 Changes in group structures

(a) Discuss the reasons behind a group reorganisation.[3] **Ch. 4**

(b) Evaluate and assess the principal terms of a proposed group reorganisation.[3] **Ch. 4**

4 Foreign transactions and entities

(a) Outline and apply the translation of foreign currency amounts and transactions into the functional currency and the presentational currency. [3] **Ch. 5**

(b) Account for the consolidation of foreign operations and their disposal.[2] **Ch. 5**

E SPECIALISED ENTITIES AND SPECIALISED TRANSACTIONS

1 Financial reporting in specialised, not-for-profit and public sector entities

(a) Apply knowledge from the syllabus to straightforward transactions and events arising in specialised, not-for-profit, and public sector entities.[3] **Ch. 20**

2 Entity reconstructions

(a) Identify when an entity may no longer be viewed as a going concern or uncertainty exists surrounding the going concern status.[2] **Ch. 20**

(b) Identify and outline the circumstances in which a reconstruction would be an appropriate alternative to a company liquidation.[2] **Ch. 20**

(c) Outline the appropriate accounting treatment required relating to reconstructions.[2] **Ch. 20**

F IMPLICATIONS OF CHANGES IN ACCOUNTING REGULATION ON FINANCIAL REPORTING

1 The effect of changes in accounting standards on accounting systems

(a) Apply and discuss the accounting implications of the first time adoption of a body of new accounting standards.[3] **Ch. 21**

2 Proposed changes to accounting standards

(a) Identify the issues and deficiencies which have led to a proposed change to an accounting standard.[2] **Ch. 22**

G THE APPRAISAL OF FINANCIAL PERFORMANCE AND POSITION OF ENTITIES

1 The creation of suitable accounting policies

(a) Develop accounting policies for an entity which meets the entity's reporting requirements.[3] **Ch. 23**

(b) Identify accounting treatments adopted in financial statements and assess their suitability and acceptability.[3] **Ch. 23**

2 Analysis and interpretation of financial information and measurement of performance

(a) Select and calculate relevant indicators of financial and non-financial performance.[3] **Ch. 23**

(b) Identify and evaluate significant features and issues in financial statements.[3] **Ch. 23**

(c) Highlight inconsistencies in financial information through analysis and application of knowledge.[3] **Ch. 23**

(d) Make inferences from the analysis of information taking into account the limitation of the information, the analytical methods used and the business environment in which the entity operates.[3] **Ch. 23**

H CURRENT DEVELOPMENTS

1 Environmental and social reporting

(a) Appraise the impact of environmental, social, and ethical factors on performance measurement.[3] **Ch. 19**

(b) Evaluate current reporting requirements in the area.[3] **Ch. 19**

(c) Discuss why entities might include disclosures relating to the environment and society.[3] **Ch. 19**

2 Convergence between national and international reporting standards

(a) Evaluate the implications of worldwide convergence with International Financial Reporting Standards.[3] **Ch. 21**

(b) Discuss the influence of national regulators on international financial reporting.[2] **Ch. 21**

3 Current reporting issues

(a) Discuss current issues in corporate reporting.[3] **Ch. 22**

The superscript numbers in square brackets indicate the intellectual depth at which the subject area could be assessed within the examination. Level 1 (knowledge and comprehension) broadly equates with the Knowledge module, Level 2 (application and analysis) with the Skills module and Level 3 (synthesis and evaluation) to the Professional level. However, lower level skills can continue to be assessed as you progress through each module and level.

The examination

Examination format

The syllabus is assessed by a three-hour paper-based examination. It examines professional competences within the corporate reporting environment.

Students will be examined on concepts, theories and principles and on their ability to question and comment on proposed accounting treatments.

Students should be capable of relating professional issues to relevant concepts and practical situations. The evaluation of alternative accounting practices and the identification and prioritisation of issues will be a key element of the paper. Professional and ethical judgement will need to be exercised, together with the integration of technical knowledge when addressing corporate reporting issues in a business context.

Global issues will be addressed via the current issues questions on the paper. Students will be required to adopt either a stakeholder or an external focus in answering questions and to demonstrate personal skills such as problem solving, dealing with information and decision making.

The paper also deals with specific professional knowledge appropriate to the preparation and presentation of consolidated and other financial statements from accounting data, to conform with accounting standards.

Section A will consist of one scenario based question worth 50 marks. It will deal with the preparation of consolidated financial statements including group statements of cash flows and with issues in financial reporting.

Students will be required to answer two out of three questions in Section B, which will normally comprise two questions which will be scenario or case-study based and one essay question which may have some computational element. Section B could deal with any aspects of the syllabus.

UK variant students will sit a similar format examination paper. However, the Examiner has indicated that the differences from the IFRS paper which may be examined in the UK variant of the paper will account for no more than 20% of that paper. The differences examined may be included within one or more questions in the examination paper.

	Number of marks
Section A	
Compulsory question	50
Section B	
Two from three 25-mark questions	50
	———
Total time allowed: 3 hours	100

Note that, in common with other ACCA Professional level papers, there will be a total of four professional marks available to candidates in each P2 examination paper. In the case of P2, the professional marks will be only available in section B, with two marks allocated to each of the three optional questions, with candidates required to attempt any two of those questions.

Study skills and revision guidance

This section aims to give guidance on how to study for your ACCA exams and to give ideas on how to improve your existing study techniques.

Preparing to study

Set your objectives

Before starting to study decide what you want to achieve – the type of pass you wish to obtain. This will decide the level of commitment and time you need to dedicate to your studies.

Devise a study plan

Determine which times of the week you will study.

Split these times into sessions of at least one hour for study of new material. Any shorter periods could be used for revision or practice.

Put the times you plan to study onto a study plan for the weeks from now until the exam and set yourself targets for each period of study – in your sessions make sure you cover the course, course assignments and revision.

If you are studying for more than one paper at a time, try to vary your subjects as this can help you to keep interested and see subjects as part of wider knowledge.

When working through your course, compare your progress with your plan and, if necessary, re-plan your work (perhaps including extra sessions) or, if you are ahead, do some extra revision/practice questions.

Effective studying

Active reading

You are not expected to learn the text by rote, rather, you must understand what you are reading and be able to use it to pass the exam and develop good practice. A good technique to use is SQ3Rs – Survey, Question, Read, Recall, Review:

(1) **Survey the chapter** – look at the headings and read the introduction, summary and objectives, so as to get an overview of what the chapter deals with.

(2) **Question** – whilst undertaking the survey, ask yourself the questions that you hope the chapter will answer for you.

(3) **Read** through the chapter thoroughly, answering the questions and making sure you can meet the objectives. Attempt the exercises and activities in the text, and work through all the examples.

(4) **Recall** – at the end of each section and at the end of the chapter, try to recall the main ideas of the section/chapter without referring to the text. This is best done after a short break of a couple of minutes after the reading stage.

(5) **Review** – check that your recall notes are correct.

You may also find it helpful to re-read the chapter to try to see the topic(s) it deals with as a whole.

Note-taking

Taking notes is a useful way of learning, but do not simply copy out the text. The notes must:

- be in your own words
- be concise
- cover the key points
- be well-organised
- be modified as you study further chapters in this text or in related ones.

Trying to summarise a chapter without referring to the text can be a useful way of determining which areas you know and which you don't.

Three ways of taking notes:

Summarise the key points of a chapter.

Make linear notes – a list of headings, divided up with subheadings listing the key points. If you use linear notes, you can use different colours to highlight key points and keep topic areas together. Use plenty of space to make your notes easy to use.

Try a diagrammatic form – the most common of which is a mind-map. To make a mind-map, put the main heading in the centre of the paper and put a circle around it. Then draw short lines radiating from this to the main sub-headings, which again have circles around them. Then continue the process from the sub-headings to sub-sub-headings, advantages, disadvantages, etc.

Highlighting and underlining

You may find it useful to underline or highlight key points in your study text – but do be selective. You may also wish to make notes in the margins.

Revision

The best approach to revision is to revise the course as you work through it. Also try to leave four to six weeks before the exam for final revision. Make sure you cover the whole syllabus and pay special attention to those areas where your knowledge is weak. Here are some recommendations:

Read through the text and your notes again and condense your notes into key phrases. It may help to put key revision points onto index cards to look at when you have a few minutes to spare.

Review any assignments you have completed and look at where you lost marks – put more work into those areas where you were weak.

Practise exam standard questions under timed conditions. If you are short of time, list the points that you would cover in your answer and then read the model answer, but do try to complete at least a few questions under exam conditions.

Also practise producing answer plans and comparing them to the model answer.

If you are stuck on a topic find somebody (a tutor) to explain it to you.

Read good newspapers and professional journals, especially ACCA's Student Accountant – this can give you an advantage in the exam.

Ensure you know the structure of the exam – how many questions and of what type you will be expected to answer. During your revision attempt all the different styles of questions you may be asked.

Further reading

Updated editions of the following publications are expected to be available from early 2013. Both publications will include content which deals with the requirements of International Financial Reporting Standards as examinable for 2013 examinations.

'A student's guide to International Financial Reporting Standards', by Clare Finch.

'A student's guide to Group Accounts' by Tom Clendon.

You can find further reading and technical articles within the student section of ACCA's website.

Technical update

This text has been updated to reflect Examinable Documents 2013 issued by ACCA. Specifically, this includes the most recently issued new and revised reporting standards and other examinable documents including:

- IFRS 9 Financial instruments

- IFRS 10 Consolidated financial statements

- IFRS 11 Joint Arrangements

- IFRS 12 Disclosure of involvement in other entities

- IFRS 13 Fair value measurement

- IAS 1 Amendment – presentation of items of other comprehensive income

- IAS 12 Income taxes

- IAS 19 Employee benefits

- IAS 27 Separate financial statements

- IAS 28 Investments in associates and joint ventures

- Management Commentary (Practice Statement 1)

- Conceptual Framework for Financial Reporting 2010

Current developments are included throughout the text in the relevant chapters. For example, chapter 16 includes information regarding continuing developments in the financial reporting of financial instruments and chapter 21 deals with the convergence process between IFRS and US GAAP.

Group accounting – basic groups

Chapter learning objectives

Upon completion of this chapter you will be able to:

- apply the method of accounting for business combinations (IFRS 10)
- apply the principles relating to the cost of a business combination
- apply the recognition and measurement criteria for identifiable acquired assets and liabilities and goodwill
- apply and discuss the criteria used to identify a subsidiary and an associate
- determine appropriate procedures to be used in preparing group financial statements
- apply the equity method of accounting for associates and joint ventures (IAS 28)
- outline and apply the key definitions and accounting methods that relate to interests in joint arrangements (IFRS 11)
- understand and discuss issues associated with disclosure of interests in other entities (IFRS 12)
- understand and discuss current issues in group accounting.

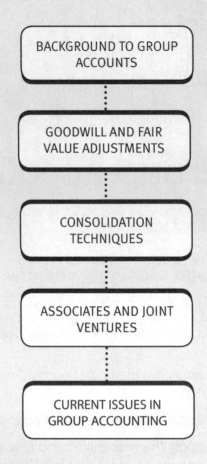

Background to group accounts

This chapter revises the basic principles of group accounting included within Paper F7 or equivalent previous studies, and introduces the new and amended requirements of IFRS 3 as revised in 2008, and IFRS 10 Consolidated Financial Statements as introduced in 2011.

In particular, the revision of IFRS 3 has meant significant changes as follows:

- new restrictions on what expenses can form part of the acquisition costs

- revision of the treatment of contingent consideration

- measurement of non-controlling interests (NCI) (the new name for minority interests) and the knock-on effect that this has on consolidated goodwill

- considerable guidance on recognising and measuring the identifiable assets and liabilities of the acquired subsidiary. in particular the illustrative examples discuss several intangibles, such as market-related, customer-related, artistic-related and technology-related assets

- accounting for step acquisitions (covered in chapter 3)
- clarifies that an entity must classify and designate all contractual arrangement at acquisition date, subject to two exceptions: leases and insurance contracts.

1 Overview of interests in other entities

The following diagram presents an overview of the varying types of interests in other entities, together with identification of applicable reporting standards.

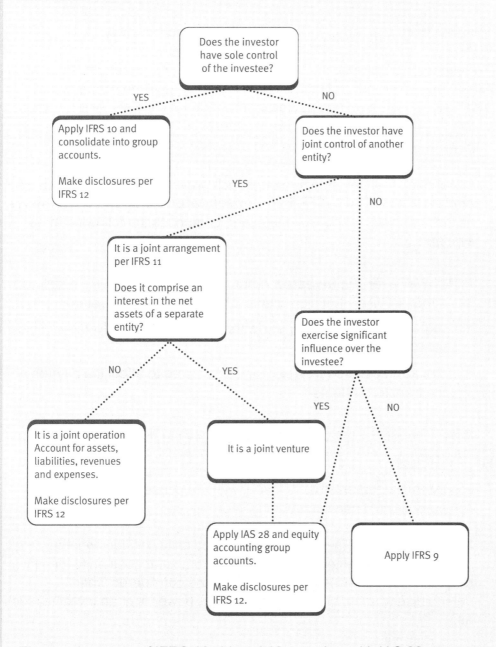

The requirements of IFRS 10, 11 and 12, together with IAS 28, are covered in this chapter. The requirements of IFRS 9 are covered in chapter 16 of this publication dealing with financial instruments.

2 Definitions

Definitions

IFRS 10 Consolidated Financial Statements amended some of the definitions and terminology relating to accounting for business combinations. Note that there is no change to the basic principles or mechanics of how to prepare group accounts, rather it is the application of the definition of control which has changed.

The current definitions are as follows:

A **parent** is an entity that controls one or more entities.

A **subsidiary** is an entity that is controlled by another entity.

Note that IFRS 10 refers to "investor" and "investee" to refer to situations where one entity may potentially control another, until the nature of that relationship is determined as being parent and subsidiary, or otherwise.

Definitions – further detail

In a change from the structural approach previously required by IAS 27, **control** is identified by **IFRS 10 Consolidated Financial Statements** as the sole basis for consolidation and comprises the following three elements:

- **power over the investee**, where the investor has current ability to direct activities that significantly affect the investee's returns;
- **exposure, or rights to, variable returns** from involvement in the investee; and
- **the ability to use power** over the investee to affect the amount of the investor's returns.

IFRS 10 adopts a principles-based approach to determining whether or not control is exercised in a given situation, which may require the exercise of judgement. One outcome is that it should lead to more consistent judgements being made, with the consequence of greater comparability of financial reporting information.

IFRS 10 states that investors should periodically consider whether control over an investee has been gained or lost. It goes on to identify a range of circumstances that may need to be considered when determining whether or not an investor has power over an investee, such as:

- exercise of the majority of voting rights in an investee;
- contractual arrangements between the investor and other parties;

- holding less than 50% of the voting shares, with all other equity interests held by a numerically large, dispersed and unconnected group;

- **potential voting rights** (such as share options or convertible loans) may result in an investor gaining or losing control at some specific date. For potential voting rights to be taken onto account when determining whether or not control is exercised at a particular point, they must be substantive, i.e. capable of being exercised. In the case of **protective rights,** holders of such rights would not normally have power over an investee, or be able to prevent another party from having power over that investee. Protective rights may apply, for example, when the holder of such rights has the right to approve the issue of new debt finance or approve the issue of additional equity shares, or the right of a lender to seize assets in the event of default – these rights will only apply in specified circumstances to protect the interests of that party;

- the exercise of power **as either a principal or as an agent**; in the latter case, power is exercised on behalf of someone else and control remains with the principal. Similarly, a principal will retain control even when it is delegated to an agent to act on their behalf;

- the nature of the investors relationship with other parties may enable that investor to exercise control over an investee. An example of this situation would be related parties as defined by IAS 24 who could be regarded as acting as agents on behalf of an investor to enable that investor to exercise control over an investee;

- the exercise of control over a portion of another entity could lead to consolidation of only part of a separate entity over which control is exercised. This is referred to in IFRS 10 as "**a silo**" and would still require that the IFRS 10 definition of control can be applied to distinguishable or ring-fenced assets and liabilities of that other entity.

The **non-controlling interest** is the equity in a subsidiary not attributable to a controlling investor. This was previously known as the minority interest.

Key points regarding group accounts

- International Financial Reporting Standards, together with legislation and regulation in many countries, require that group accounts are prepared when one entity controls one or more other entities.

- Control may be exercised in a number of ways, either directly or indirectly.

- As the parent and its subsidiaries are acting as a single unit (the group), the users of the accounts will only be able to make informed economic decisions if they have access to a set of financial statements that combines the results, assets and liabilities of all entities in the group.

- Consolidated accounts must exclude transactions between group members as their inclusion could inflate the assets and profits of individual entities.

- For the purposes of consolidated accounts all group members must use the same accounting policies and currencies.

- All group members should have the same financial reporting date as the parent. If this is not practical, there are two possible solutions to this problem:
  - prepare interim financial statements up to the group reporting date
  - use the most recent set of the subsidiary's own accounts. The date for these must be within three months before the group reporting date.

- There are a number of exemptions from consolidation which are considered elsewhere within this chapter.

Application of IFRS 10 control definition

Example 1:

An investor acquires 48 per cent of the voting rights of an investee. The remaining voting rights are held by thousands of shareholders, none individually holding more than 1 per cent of the voting rights. None of the shareholders has any arrangements to consult any of the others or make collective decisions. When assessing the proportion of voting rights to acquire, on the basis of the relative size of the other shareholdings, the investor determined that a 48 per cent interest would be sufficient to give it control.

In this case, on the basis of the absolute size of its holding and the relative size of the other shareholdings, the investor concludes that it has a sufficiently dominant voting interest to meet the power criterion without the need to consider any other evidence of power.

Example 2:

Investor A holds 40 per cent of the voting rights of an investee and twelve other investors each hold 5 per cent of the voting rights of the investee. A shareholder agreement grants investor A the right to appoint, remove and set the remuneration of management responsible for directing the relevant activities. To change the agreement, a two-thirds majority vote of the shareholders is required.

In this case, investor A concludes that the absolute size of the investor's holding and the relative size of the other shareholdings alone are not conclusive in determining whether the investor has rights sufficient to give it power. However, investor A determines that its contractual right to appoint, remove and set the remuneration of management is sufficient to conclude that it has power over the investee. The fact that investor A might not have exercised this right or the likelihood of investor A exercising its right to select, appoint or remove management shall not be considered when assessing whether investor A has power.

Exemptions for intermediate parent companies

An intermediate parent entity is an entity which has a subsidiary but is also itself a subsidiary of another entity. For example:

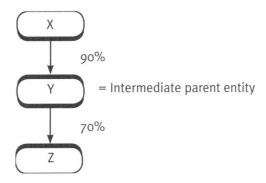

= Intermediate parent entity

IFRS 10 permits a parent entity not to present group financial statements provided all of the following conditions apply:

* it is a wholly-owned, or partially-owned subsidiary where owners of the non-controlling interest do not object to the non-preparation,

* its debt or equity instruments are not currently traded in a domestic or foreign market,

* it is not in the process of having any of its debt or equity instruments traded on a domestic or foreign market, and

* the ultimate parent entity produces consolidated financial statements that comply with IFRS and which are available to the public.

If this is the case, IAS 27 Separate Financial Statements (revised) requires that the following disclosures are made:

- the fact that consolidated financial statements have not been presented;

- a list of significant investments (subsidiaries, joint ventures and associates, etc.) including percentage shareholdings, principal place of business and country of incorporation; and

- the bases on which those investments listed above have been accounted for in its separate financial statements.

Particular situations

IFRS 10 and IAS 27 (revised) do not specify any other circumstances when subsidiaries must be excluded from consolidation. However, there may be specific circumstances that merit particular consideration as follows:

(a) **Severe long-term restrictions**

Consolidation is based on the concept of control as defined by IFRS 10; i.e. an entity is a subsidiary because the parent controls it. Previously, IAS 27 permitted exclusion from consolidation where the subsidiary was subject to long-term restrictions on the ability to transfer funds to the parent; this exclusion is no longer permitted as it may still be possible to control a subsidiary in such circumstances.

(b) **Acquired for resale**

A subsidiary acquired exclusively with a view to disposal within 12 months will probably meet the conditions in **IFRS 5 Non-current assets held for sale and discontinued activities** for classification as held for sale. If it does, it is accounted for under IFRS 5; the effect is that all its assets are presented as a single line item below current assets and all its liabilities are presented as a single line item below current liabilities. So it is still consolidated, but in a different way.

Note that when a subsidiary is acquired with a view to sale, there is a three-month period from the date of acquisition for it to meet the IFRS 5 criteria to be classified and accounted for as held-for-sale. Additionally, IFRS 5 requires measurement of assets held for sale to be at fair value less costs to sell; the consequence of this is that goodwill on acquisition is increased by the amount of costs to sell. Remember also that the net carrying value of assets held-for-sale are reclassified as current assets on the statement of financial position.

(c) **Materiality**

Accounting standards do not normally apply to immaterial items; therefore an immaterial subsidiary need not be consolidated. However, this would need to be kept under review from year to year, and the parent would need to consider each subsidiary to be excluded on this basis, both individually and collectively. Ideally, a parent should consolidate all subsidiaries which it controls in all accounting periods, rather than report changes in the corporate structure from one period to the next.

Invalid reasons to exclude a subsidiary from consolidation

In addition to the valid reasons to exclude a subsidiary from consolidation considered earlier, directors of the parent entity may seek to exclude a subsidiary from group accounts for several reasons as follows:

- The **subsidiary undertakes different activities** and/or operates in different locations, thus being distinctive from other members of the group. This is not a valid reason for exclusion from consolidation; indeed it could be argued that inclusion within the group accounts of such a subsidiary will enhance the relevance and reliability of the information contained within the group accounts. This will be further supported by disclosures required by e.g. IFRS 8 *Segment Reporting* to provide a full understanding of the financial position and performance of the group as a whole.

- The **subsidiary has made losses or has significant liabilities** which the directors would prefer to exclude from the group accounts to improve the overall reported financial performance and position of the group. This could be motivated, for example, by determination of directors' remuneration based upon group financial performance. This is not a valid reason for exclusion from consolidation.

- The directors may seek to **disguise the true ownership of the subsidiary**, perhaps to avoid disclosure of particular activities or events, or to avoid disclosure of ownership of assets. This could be motivated, for example, by seeking to avoid disclosure of potential conflicts of interest which may be perceived adversely by users of financial statements.

- The directors may seek to exclude a subsidiary from consolidation in order for the group to **disguise its true size and extent**. This could be motivated, for example, by trying to avoid legal and regulatory compliance requirements applicable to the group or individual subsidiaries. This is not a valid reason for exclusion from consolidation.

3 Non-controlling interest (NCI) and its impact on goodwill

IFRS 3 revised provides a choice in valuing the non-controlling interest at acquisition:

EITHER: OR:

Method 1 – 'the old method'	Method 2 – 'the new method'
NCI % × Fair value of the net assets of the subsidiary at the acquisition date	Fair value of NCI at date of acquisition. This is usually given in the question.

- **Method 1** is essentially the same as the calculation of the minority interest under the previous version of IFRS 3.

- Where an exam question requires the use of this method, it will state that 'it is group policy to value the non-controlling interest at its proportionate share of the fair value of the subsidiary's identifiable net assets'.

- **Method 2** requires that where shares are publicly traded, the fair value of the NCI is measured according to market prices. Where this is not the case other valuation techniques must be used.

- This method is known as the 'full goodwill' method, since 100% of goodwill is reflected in the group financial statements as an asset (with the NCI line then effectively including the proportion of goodwill relating to them).

- Where an exam question requires the use of this method, it will state that 'it is group policy to value the non-controlling interest using the full goodwill method'.

Note that, for any subsidiary, there should be a consistent accounting treatment of goodwill and non-controlling interest; both should both be accounted for either on a full basis or a proportionate basis respectively.

Note also that IFRS 3 permits the goodwill accounting policy to be selected and applied on an acquisition-by-acquisition basis. This means that, within the same group, some subsidiaries may be accounted for applying the full goodwill policy, whilst other subsidiaries may be accounted for applying the proportion of net assets basis.

In addition, note also that the acquirer has a period of time, up to one year from the date of acquisition, to finalise the accounting for a business combination. This may be necessary, for example, where accounting for a business combination is not yet complete by the end of a reporting period and provisional values have been used to measure any of the components required to compute goodwill, such as the fair value of identifiable net assets and liabilities acquired or non-controlling interest.

Consequently, any measurement period adjustment which relates to circumstances existing at the acquisition date will be reflected by an increase or decrease in the carrying value of goodwill. After the measurement period has expired, any revision to accounting for business combinations should be accounted for in accordance with IAS 8 (prior period adjustment). If a change does not qualify as a measurement period adjustment, it is included in current year profit or loss.

Non-controlling interest

Choice of method

The standard indicates that the method used should be decided on a transaction by transaction basis.

The upside of recognising full goodwill (method 2) is that assets on the statement of financial position will be increased.

The potential downside is that any future impairment of goodwill will be greater. However, goodwill impairment testing may be easier in that there is no need to gross up goodwill for partially owned subsidiaries.

Full goodwill method – valuation

Where the full goodwill method is chosen, the fair value of the NCI may differ from that of the controlling interest on a per-share basis. This is likely to be due to the inclusion of a control premium in the per-share fair value of the parent's controlling interest.

Subsequent measurement of the NCI

In subsequent years the NCI is increased by the proportion of post-acquisition retained earnings and any other reserves (e.g. revaluation reserve) due to the NCI. This is true regardless of which method is initially used to value the NCI.

In addition, an entity must attribute their share of total comprehensive income to the NCI even if this results in a deficit balance.

ED 2009/11 Improvements to IFRS issued in August 2009 clarifies that NCI measurement is based upon only those instruments which are entitled to share in the net assets of the acquired entity. Any other instruments which meet the definition of NCI in the entity should be measured at fair value or in accordance with the applicable IFRS.

Test your understanding 1 – Rosa

Rosa acquires 80% of the Parks's equity capital in a share-for-share exchange. Parks has issued equity capital comprising 100 shares, each of $1 nominal value.

The consideration that Rosa gives to acquire Parks is by making a two for one share issue when the share price of each Rosa share is $5.

At the date of acquisition the fair value of the net assets of Parks is $600 and the market value of a Parks share is $8.

Required:

(i) **Calculate the goodwill arising valuing the NCI using the proportion of the net assets method.**

(ii) **Calculate the goodwill arising valuing the NCI using the full goodwill method**

Illustration Malawi

Malawi has made an acquisition of 100% of the equity shares in Blantyre when the net assets of Blantyre were $80,000. The consideration that Malawi gave for the investment in the subsidiary Blantyre comprised:

(1) Cash paid $25,454

(2) Shares – Malawi issued 10,000 shares to the shareholders of Blantyre, each with a nominal value of $1 and a market value of $4.

(3) Deferred consideration – $20,000 is to be paid one year after the date of acquisition. The relevant discount rate is 10%.

(4) Contingent consideration – $100,000 may be paid one year after the date of acquisition. It is judged that there is only a 40% chance that this will occur. The fair value of this consideration can be measured as the present value of the expected value.

(5) Legal fees associated with the acquisition amounted to $15,000.

Required:

Calculate the goodwill arising on the acquisition of Blantyre.

Solution Malawi

The goodwill on acquisition of Blantyre is as follows:

Fair value of consideration paid:		$
Cash		25,454
Shares at fair value	10,000 × $4	40,000
Deferred consideration	$20,000 × 1/1.1	18,182
Contingent consideration	$100,000 × 40% × 1/1.1	36,364
		———
		120,000
Less: Fair value of net assets at acquisition		80,000
		———
		40,000
		———

Note – legal fees are expensed and not capitalised.

Fair value of net assets of acquiree

- In line with the original standard, IFRS 3 revised requires that the identifiable net assets of the subsidiary should be measured at their fair values at the date of acquisition.

- There are certain exceptions to this rule such as deferred tax and pension obligations, which are valued according to the relevant standard.

- Contingent liabilities that are present obligations arising from past events and can be measured reliably are recognised at fair value at the acquisition date. This is true even where an economic outflow is not probable.

- A provision for future operating losses cannot be created as this is a post-acquisition item. Similarly, restructuring costs are only recognised to the extent that a liability actually exists at the date of acquisition.

- The fair value exercise affects both the values given to the assets and liabilities acquired in the group statement of financial position and the value of goodwill.

Recognition of identifiable assets acquired and liabilities assumed

An asset is identifiable if:

- It is capable of disposal separately from the business owning it, or

- It arises from contractual or other legal rights, regardless of whether those rights can be sold separately.

The identifiable assets and liabilities of the acquiree (subsidiary) should be recognised at fair value where:

- They meet the definitions of assets and liabilities in the Conceptual Framework for Financial Reporting 2010 (previously the Framework document)

- And they are exchanged as part of the business combination rather than a separate transaction.

Items that are not identifiable or do not meet the definitions of assets or liabilities are subsumed into the calculation of purchased goodwill.

Fair value – exceptions

There are certain exceptions to the requirement to measure the subsidiary's net assets at fair value when accounting for business combinations:

- The assets and liabilities falling within the scope of IAS 12 Income Taxes, IAS 19 Employee benefits, IFRS 2 Share-based Payment and IFRS 5 Non-current assets held for sale and Discontinued Operations are required to be valued according to those standards;

- Leases are required to be classified on the basis of factors at the inception date rather than factors at the acquisition date of the subsidiary.

Intangible assets

Acquired intangible assets must always be recognised and measured; unlike the previous IFRS 3 there is no exception where reliable measurement cannot be ascertained.

KAPLAN PUBLISHING

Illustration Brussels

Brussels acquired 82% of Madrid

- At acquisition, the statement of financial position of Madrid showed issued equity capital of $3,000,000 and retained earnings of $3,255,000. Included in this total is freehold land with a book value of $400,000 (market value $958,000), a brand with a nil book value (fair value $500,000), plant and machinery with a book value of $1,120,000 and a fair value of $890,000. The fair value of all other assets and liabilities is approximately equal to book value.

- The directors of Brussels intend to close down one of the divisions of Madrid and wish to provide for operating losses up to the date of closure, which are forecast as $729,000.

- An investment in plant and machinery will be required to bring the remaining production line of Madrid up to date. This will amount to $405,000 in the next 12 months.

- The consideration comprised $4,000,000 cash, 1,500,000 shares with a nominal value of $1.00 and fair value of $1.50 each as well as further cash consideration of $400,000 to be paid one year after acquisition.

The discount rate is 10%.

Required:

Calculate the goodwill arising on consolidation using the proportionate share of the fair value of net assets method to value the NCI.

Solution Brussels

Goodwill on acquisition – proportionate basis:

	$	$
Consideration paid by parent		
Cash	4,000,000	
Shares at FV 1,500,000 × $1.50	2,250,000	
Deferred consideration		
400,000 × 1/1.1	363,636	
		6,613,636
NCI value at acquisition	18% x 7,083,000 (W1)	1,274,940
		7,888,576

Less: 100% of net assets at acquisition (W1)	(7,083,000)
Goodwill	805,576

(W1) Net assets at acquisition

	$
Issued equity capital	3,000,000
Retained earnings	3,255,000
Freehold land (958 – 400)	558,000
Brand	500,000
Plant and machinery (890 – 1,120)	(230,000)
	7,083,000

- The goodwill must be calculated on the basis of assets and liabilities that exist on the date of acquisition which means the provision for operating losses and investment in plant cannot be recognised.

- Deferred consideration is discounted to its present value at the date of acquisition.

Bargain purchases

Accounting treatment for bargain purchases is as follows:

- If the share of net assets acquired exceeds the consideration given, then 'negative goodwill' arises on acquisition.

- IFRS 3 revised requires that the fair values of the consideration and the net assets acquired are checked carefully to ensure that no errors have been made.

- After the checking exercise is complete, if there is still negative goodwill it should credited to profit or loss for the year immediately

Current assets

Inventory	13,800	12,400	7,200
Trade receivables	6,400	3,000	4,800
Total assets	96,500	36,200	48,000

Equity and liabilities

Equity shares of $1 each	20,000	8,000	8,000
Retained earnings			
– at 31 March 2007	32,000	12,000	22,000
– for year ended 31 March 2008	18,500	5,800	10,000
	70,500	25,800	40,000

Non-current liabilities

7% Loan notes	10,000	2,000	2,000
Current liabilities	16,000	8,400	6,000
	96,500	36,200	48,000

The following information is relevant:

(i) At the date of acquisition Sonia had an internally generated brand name. The directors of Pauline estimate that the value of this brand name has a fair value of $2 million, an indefinite life and has not suffered any impairment.

(ii) On 1 April 2007, Pauline sold an item of plant to Sonia at its agreed fair value of $5 million. Its carrying amount prior to the sale was $4 million. The estimated remaining life of the plant at the date of sale was five years (straight-line depreciation).

(iii) During the year ended 31 March 2008 Sonia sold goods to Pauline for $5.4 million. Sonia had marked up these goods by 50% on cost. Pauline had a third of the goods still in its inventory at 31 March 2008. There were no intra-group payables/receivables at 31 March 2008.

(iv) Pauline has a policy of valuing non-controlling interests at fair value at the date of acquisition. For this purpose the share price of Sonia at this date should be used. Impairment tests on 31 March 2008 concluded that neither consolidated goodwill or the value of the investment in Arthur have been impaired.

(v) The held for trading investments are included in Pauline's statement of financial position (above) at their fair value on 1 April 2007, but they have a fair value of $18 million at 31 March 2008.

(vi) No dividends were paid during the year by any of the companies.

Required:

Prepare the consolidated statement of financial position for Pauline as at 31 March 2008.

(25 marks)

Solution Pauline

Consolidated statement of financial position of Pauline as at 31 March 2008

	$000	$000
Assets		
Non-current assets:		
Property, plant and equipment		
(36,800 + 20,800 – 800 (W8))		56,800
Goodwill (W3)		
		10,000
Brand name		2,000
Investments – associate (W6)		21,000
– held for trading		18,000
		107,800
Current assets		
Inventory (13,800 + 12,400 – 600 URP (W7))	25,600	
Trade receivables	9,400	35,000
Total assets		142,800
Equity and liabilities		
Equity attributable to equity holders of the parent		
Equity shares of $1 each (W3)		23,000
Share premium (W3)	15,000	
Retained earnings (W5)	60,600	75,600
		98,600
Non-controlling interest (W4)		7,800
Total equity		106,400

KAPLAN PUBLISHING

Non-current liabilities

7% Loan notes (10,000 + 2,000)	12,000

Current liabilities (16,000 + 8,400)   24,400

Total equity and liabilities   142,800

Workings

(W1) **Group structure**

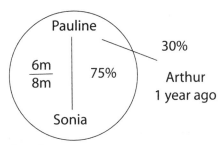

Pauline

6m / 8m   75%   30%

Arthur
1 year ago

Sonia

(W2) **Net assets – Sonia**

	At reporting date	At acquisition date
	$000	$000
Equity capital	8,000	8,000
Retained earnings	17,800	12,000
Fair value adj:		
Brand	2,000	2,000
PURP (W7)	(600)	
	27,200	**22,000**

Arthur

	At reporting date	At acquisition date
	$000	$000
Equity capital	8,000	8,000
Retained earnings	32,000	22,000
	40,000	30,000

(W3) Goodwill

	Sonia
Pauline – cost of investment	$000
– Share exchange [6,000 × 2/4 × $6]	18,000
– cash paid [6,000 × $1.25]	7,500
	———
	25,500
FV of NCI at acquisition (2m @ $3.25)	6,500
	———
	32,000
Less: 100% of NA at acquisition: (W2)	(22,000)
	———
Total goodwill	10,000
	———

Tutorial note:

The consideration given by Pauline for the shares of Sonia works out at $4.25 per share i.e. consideration of $25.50 million for 6 million shares. This is considerably higher than the market price of Sonia's shares ($3.25) before the acquisition. This probably reflects the cost of gaining control of Sonia. This is also why it is probably appropriate to value the NCI in Sonia at $3.25 each, because (by definition) the NCI does not have any control.

The 3 million shares issued by Pauline in the share exchange at a value of $6 each would be recorded as $1 per share as equity capital and $5 per share as premium giving an increase in equity capital of $3 million and a share premium of $15 million.

(W4) NCI

	$000
Fair value of NCI at acquisition (as above)	6,500
NCI share of post-acquisition profit	
(25% × (27,200 – 22,000)) (W2)	1,300
	———
	7,800
	———

(W5) Group retained earnings

	$000
100% Parent (32,000 + 18,500)	50,500
Professional costs written off	(1,000)
Gain on held for trading financial asset	5,000
75% Sonia post-acquisition reserves (75% × (27,200 – 22,000)) (W2))	3,900
30% Arthur post-acquisition reserves (30% × (40,000 – 30,000)) (W2))	3,000
Less PURP in plant(W8)	(800)
	60,600

(W6) Investment in associate

	$000
Cost (8,000 × 30% × $7.50)	18,000
Share post-acquisition profit (10,000 × 30%)	3,000
	21,000

(W7) PURP in inventory

The unrealised profit (PURP) in inventory is calculated as:

Intra-group sales are $5.4 million on which Sonia made a profit of $1,800,000 (5,400 × 50/150). One third of these are still in inventory of Pauline, thus there is an unrealised profit of $600,000.

(W8) PURP in PPE

The transfer of the plant creates an initial unrealised profit (PURP) of $1,000,000. This is reduced by $200,000 for each year (straight-line depreciation over 5 years) of depreciation in the post-acquisition period. Thus at 31 March 2008 the net unrealised profit is $800,000. This should be eliminated from Pauline's retained profits and from the carrying amount of the plant.

(W9) Held for trading financial asset

The gain on held for trading financial assets are classified as fair value through profit or loss and will be recognised in the statement of profit or loss for the year.

Test your understanding 2 – Borough High Street

Borough purchased shares in two entities, High and Street, as follows:

Borough High Street

	Date of acq'n	FV of the NCI at acq'n	Retained earnings at acq'n	Fair value of net assets at acq'n	Cost of invest- ment	No. of equity shares acquired
		$	$	$	$	
High	1 July 20X7	55,000	30,000	120,000	100,000	45,000
Street	1 July 20X7	N/R	25,000		21,000	10,500

Summarised accounts of three entities for the year ended 30 June 20X8 are as follows:

Statements of financial position:

	Borough	High	Street
Assets:	$	$	$
Tangible Non Current Assets	100,000	80,000	60,000
Investments	121,000	---	--
Inventory	22,000	30,000	15,000
Receivables	70,000	10,000	2,000
Cash at Bank	37,000	20,000	3,000
	350,000	140,000	80,000
Equity and liabilities			
Equity capital ($1 shares)	100,000	75,000	35,000
Retained earnings	200,000	50,000	40,000
Liabilities	50,000	15,000	5,000
	350,000	140,000	80,000

KAPLAN PUBLISHING

Statements of profit or loss and other comprehensive income.

	Borough $	High $	Street $
Revenue	500,000	200,000	100,000
Cost of sales	(300,000)	(140,000)	(60,000)
Gross profit	200,000	60,000	40,000
Administration costs	(50,000)	(10,000)	(10,000)
Operating profit	150,000	50,000	30,000
Interest	10,000	(10,000)	–
Profit before tax	160,000	40,000	30,000
Tax	(60,000)	(20,000)	(15,000)
Profit after tax	100,000	20,000	15,000

Note: there are no items of other comprehensive income.

Any excess of the fair value of net assets over their carrying values at the date of acquisition of High relates to tangible assets with a remaining estimated useful life of five years at that date. The fair values have not been incorporated into the accounting records of High. It is group policy to value the non-controlling interest using the full goodwill method. Goodwill has been subject to an impairment review and there is impairment to the extent of $7,000.

During the year Borough sold goods to High for $10,000 at a margin of 50%. At the year end the group had sold only 80% of these goods.

During the year Borough gave High substantial short-term loans – most of which was repaid shortly before the year-end. The final balance of $5,000 was paid on 10 July 20X8. The interest charged in High's statement of profit or loss and the interest receivable in Borough's statement of profit or loss represents interest on this loan.

Required:

Prepare the consolidated statement of profit or loss for the year ended 30 June 20X8 and consolidated statement of financial position as at 30 June 20X8.

Illustration 2 H, S & A

The following are the summarised accounts of H, S, and A for the year ended 30 June 20X8.

The shares in S and A were acquired on 1 July 20X5 when the retained earnings of S were $15,000 and the retained earnings of A were $10,000.

At the date of acquisition, the fair value of S's non-current assets, which at that time had a remaining useful life of ten years, exceeded the book value by $10,000.

During the year S sold goods to H for $10,000 at a margin of 50%. At the year-end H had sold 80% of the goods.

The group accounting policy is to measure the non-controlling interest of the subsidiary using the proportion of net assets method. At 30 June 20X8 the goodwill in respect of S had been impaired by 30% of its original amount, of which the current year loss was $1,200.

At 30 June 20X8 the investment in A had been impaired by $450, of which the current year loss was $150.

Statements of financial position

	H	S	A
	$	$	$
Tangible non-current assets	87,000	88,000	62,000
Shares in S: (80%)	92,000		
Shares in A: (30%)	15,000		
Current assets	97,000	40,000	9,000
	291,000	128,000	71,000
Equity capital ($1 shares)	200,000	75,000	35,000
Retained earnings	89,000	51,000	34,000
Liabilities	2,000	2,000	2,000
	291,000	128,000	71,000

Statements of profit or loss

	$	$	S
Revenue	500,000	200,000	100,000
Operating costs	(400,000)	(140,000)	(60,000)
Profit from operations	100,000	60,000	40,000
Tax	(23,000)	(21,000)	(14,000)
Profit after tax	77,000	39,000	26,000

Note: there were no items of other comprehensive income in the year.

Required:

Prepare the consolidated statement of profit or loss for the year ended 30 June 20X8 and consolidated statement of financial position as at 30 June 20X8.

Solution – H, S & A

Group statement of profit or loss for the year ended 30 June 20X8

	$
Revenue (500,000 + 200,000 -10,000 intra-group)	690,000
Operating costs (400,000 + 140,000 + 1,200 goodwill impairment –10,000 intra-group + 1,000 20X8 depreciation on FV adj + 1,000 PURP)	(533,200)
Profit from operations	156,800
Income from associate ((30% × 26,000) – goodwill impairment 150)	7,650
Profit before tax	164,450
Tax (23,000 + 21,000)	(44,000)
Profit for the period	120,450

Attributable to:

Equity holders of the parent	113,050
Non-controlling interest (20% × (39,000 – 1,000 20X8 depreciation on FV adj – 1,000 PURP)	7,400
	————
Profit for the financial year	120,450
	————

Note: there were no items of other comprehensive income in the year.

Consolidated statement of financial position as at 30 June 20X8

	$
Goodwill (W3)	8,400
Investment in associate (W6)	21,750
Tangible non-current assets	
(87,000 + 88,000 + 10,000 FV – 3,000 FV	
depreciation (W2))	182,000
Current assets (97,000 + 40,000 – 1,000 PURP (W2))	136,000
	————
	348,150
	————

	$
Equity share capital	200,000
Retained earnings (W5)	117,750
Non-controlling interest (W4)	26,400
Liabilities (2,000 + 2,000)	4,000
	————
	348,150
	————

Workings

(W1) Group structure

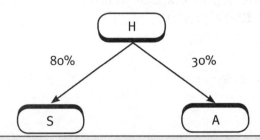

KAPLAN PUBLISHING

(W2) **Net assets**

	S Acq	Rep date
	$	$
Equity share capital	75,000	75,000
Retained earnings	15,000	51,000
Fair value adj	10,000	10,000
Depreciation (3/10 × FV adj)	–	(3,000)
URPS inventory (W7)		(1,000)
	100,000	132,000

(W3) **Goodwill – Proportionate share method**

	$
Consideration paid by parent	92,000
NCI value at acquisition (20% × 100,000)(W2)	20,000
	112,000
Less: 100% of net assets at acquisition (W2)	(100,000)
	12,000
Less: impairment loss – 30% thereof	(3,600)
	8,400

(W4) **Non-controlling interest on proportionate basis**

	$
NCI value at acquisition (W3)	20,000
NCI share of post-acquisition profit (20% × 32,000) (W2)	6,400
	26,400

(W5) Retained earnings

	$
Parent	89,000
Less: impairment:	
S (W3)	(3,600)
A (W6)	(450)
Group share post-acq retained earnings:	
S 80% × 32,000 (W2)	25,600
A 30% × (34,000 – 10,000)	7,200
	_____
	117,750
	_____

(W6) Investment in associate

	$
Cost	15,000
Share of increase in retained earnings	
30% × (34,000 – 10,000)	7,200
	_____
	22,200
Less: impairment	(450)
	_____
	21,750
	_____

(W7) Inter company trading

Subsidiary made sales to parent

		$
80% Group and 20% NCI		
Unrealised profit	10,000 × 20% × 50%	1,000
Dr group retained earnings	80% × 1,000	800
Dr NCI	20% × 1,000	200
Cr Inventory		1000

Note that as the unrealised profit on inventory has been earned by S. the consolidation adjustment required can be made in the net assets working at the reporting date.

5 IFRS 11 – Joint arrangements

IFRS 11 Joint Arrangements was issued in 2011 to replace IAS 31. IFRS 11 provides new or updated definitions to determine whether there is a joint arrangement and, if so, the nature of that arrangement together with associated accounting requirements. It adopts the definition of control as included in IFRS 10 (see elsewhere within this chapter) as a basis for determining whether there is joint control.

Definitions

Joint arrangements are defined as arrangements where two or more parties have joint control, and that this will only apply if the relevant activities require unanimous consent of those who collectively control the arrangement. They may take the form of either joint operations or joint ventures. The key distinction between the two forms is based upon the parties' rights and obligations under the joint arrangement.

IFRS 11 – further detail

Joint operations are defined as joint arrangements whereby the parties that have joint control have rights to the assets and obligations for the liabilities. Normally, there will not be a separate entity established to conduct joint operations. IFRS 11 requires that joint operators each recognise their share of assets, liabilities, revenues and expenses of the joint operation over which they have rights and obligations. This may consist of maintaining a joint operation account to record transactions undertaken on behalf of the joint operation, together with balances due to or from other parties to the joint operation.

Example of a joint operation

A and B decide to enter into a joint operation to produce a new product. A undertakes one manufacturing process and B undertakes the other. A and B have agreed that decisions regarding the joint operation will be made unanimously and that each will bear their own expenses and take an agreed share of the sales revenue from the product.

Joint ventures are defined as joint arrangements whereby the parties have joint control of the arrangement and have rights to the net assets of the arrangement. This will normally be established in the form of a separate entity to conduct the joint venture activities. The equity method of accounting must be used in this situation. The accounting policy choice of proportionate consolidation or equity accounting previously allowed by IAS 31 is no longer available; all interests in joint ventures must now be equity-accounted. IAS 28 deals with accounting for associates and joint ventures and is considered elsewhere within this chapter.

Example of a joint venture

A and B decide to set up a separate entity, C, to enter into a joint venture. A will own 55% of the equity capital of C, with B owning the remaining 45%. A and B have agreed that decision-making regarding the joint venture will be unanimous. Neither party will have direct right to the assets, or direct obligation for the liabilities of the joint venture; instead, they will have an interest in the net assets of entity C set up for the joint venture.

Joint control is defined as contractually agreed sharing of control of an arrangement which exists only when the decisions about the relevant activities require the unanimous consent of the parties sharing control. The key aspects of joint control are described as follows:

- Contractually agreed – contractual arrangements are usually, but not always, written, and provide the terms of the arrangement.

- Control and relevant activities – IFRS 10 describes how to assess whether a party has control, and how to identify the relevant activities.

- Unanimous consent – exists when the parties to an arrangement have collective control over the arrangement and no single party has control.

Accounting for joint arrangements

Joint operations

Arrangements defined as joint operations by IFRS 11 were previously classified as either jointly controlled operations or jointly controlled assets by IAS 31. In principle, there is no change for the accounting for such arrangements in accordance with IFRS 11. The individual financial statements of each joint operator will recognise:

- the assets that it controls and the liabilities that it incurs, and

- the expenses that it incurs, and

- share of the revenue that it earns from the sale of goods or services by the joint venture.

This may also include amounts due to and from the other joint operators.

As the income, expenses, assets and liabilities of the joint venture are included in the individual financial statements they will automatically flow through to the consolidated financial statements.

Joint ventures

Joint arrangements classified as joint ventures by IFRS 11 are accounted for in a separate entity. The individual financial statements of each joint venture party will recognise:

- the cost of the investment in the joint venture entity (e.g. the share capital subscribed for), and

- any returns received in the form of dividends from the joint venture entity.

In the consolidated financial statements, the interest in the joint venture entity will be equity-accounted as required by IAS 28. In principle, the accounting for a joint venture in consolidated financial statements is now identical to accounting for an associate.

In situations where there are transactions between a joint venture party and the separate joint venture entity, the joint venture party should recognise only that part of any gain attributable to the interests of the other joint venture parties – it cannot make a profit out of transactions with itself.

To the extent that a loss arises on transactions between a joint venture party and the separate joint venture entity, the full amount of the loss should be recognised as this is likely to reflect a fall in the net realisable value of a current asset and/or impairment of a non-current asset (investment in the joint venture entity).

Note that if an interest in a joint venture meets the definition of held for sale as specified in IFRS 5, it should be accounted for accordingly.

Illustration 3 - Joint operation - Blast

Blast has a 30% share in a joint operation; assets, liabilities, revenues and costs are apportioned on the basis of shareholding. The following information relates to the joint arrangement activity for the year ended 30 November 20X2:

- The manufacturing facility cost $30m to construct and was completed on 1 December 20X1 and is to be dismantled at the end of its estimated useful life of 10 years. The present value of this dismantling cost to the joint arrangement at 1 December 20X1, using a discount rate of 8%, was $3m.

- During the year ended 30 November 20X2, the joint operation entered into the following transactions:

  - goods with a production cost of $36m were sold for $50m

  - other operating costs incurred amounted to $1m

  - administration expenses incurred amounted to $2m.

Blast has only accounted for its share of the cost of the manufacturing facility, amounting to $9m. The revenue and costs are receivable and payable by the two other joint operation partners who will settle amounts outstanding with Blast after each reporting date.

Required:
Show how Blast will account for the joint operation within its financial statements for the year ended 30 November 20X2.

Solution - Blast

Profit or loss impact:	$m
Revenue ($50m × 30%)	15.000
Cost of sales ($36m × 30%)	(10.800)
Operating costs ($1m × 30%)	(0.300)
Depreciation (($30m + 3m) × 1/10 × 30%)	(0.990)
Administration expenses ($2m × 30%)	(0.600)
Finance cost ($3m × 8% × 30%)	(0.072)
	———
Share of net profit re joint operation (include in retained earnings within SOFP)	2.238
	———

Statement of financial position impact:	$m
Property, plant and equipment (amount paid = share of cost)	9.000
Dismantling cost ($3m × 30%)	0.900
Depreciation ($33m × 10% × 30%)	(0.990)
	———
	8.910
	———
Trade receivables (i.e. share of revenue due)	15.000
	———
Non-current liabilities:	
Dismantling provision (($3m × 30%) + $0.072)	0.972
	———
Current liabilities:	
Trade payables ($10.8m + $0.3m + $0.6m) (i.e. share of expenses to pay)	11.700
	———

KAPLAN PUBLISHING

Note that the various items should be classified under the appropriate headings within the statement of profit or loss for the year or statement of financial position as appropriate.

Note also that where there are amounts owed to and from a joint operating partner, it may be acceptable to show just a net amount due to or from each partner.

IFRS 12 Disclosure of Interests

IFRS 12 Disclosure of Interests in Other Entities

IFRS 12 was issued in May 2011 and is now the single source of disclosure requirements that were previously contained within IAS 27 (group accounts), IAS 28 (associates) and IAS 31 (joint ventures). This reporting standard has also extended the disclosure requirements to include additional information which is regarded as being helpful to users of financial statements, including:

- disclosure of significant assumptions and judgements made in determining whether an investor has control, joint control or significant influence over an investee

- disclose the nature, extent and financial effects of its interests in joint arrangements and associates

- additional disclosures relating to subsidiaries with non-controlling interests, joint arrangements and associates that are individually material,

- significant restrictions on the ability of the parent to access and use the assets or to settle the liabilities of its subsidiaries, and

- extended disclosures relating to "structured entities", previously referred to as special-purpose entities, to enable a full understanding of the nature of the arrangement and associated risks, such as the terms on which an investor may be required to provide financial support to such an entity.

IFRS 12 is effective for accounting periods commencing on or after 1 January 2013, but early adoption of IFRS 12 is permitted, either as an individual standard, or in conjunction with IFRS 10, IFRS 11, IFRS 12 and revised standards IAS 27 and IAS 28.

IAS 27 Separate financial statements

IAS 27 (revised) applies when an entity has interests in subsidiaries, joint ventures or associates and either elects to, or is required to, prepare separate non-consolidated financial statements.

Disclosures required when separate, non-consolidated, financial statements have been prepared by the parent entity:

*   the fact that exemption from consolidation has been used (usually as an intermediate holding company), together with the name, place of business and country of incorporation of the ultimate holding company who have prepared group financial statements in compliance with IFRS, and an address from which those financial statements can be obtained

*   in other cases than being an intermediate holding company, the fact that they are separate financial statements, together with the reason why separate financial statements have been prepared

*   a list of names, interests in equity capital and principal place of business for each significant subsidiary, associate and joint venture, including details of how they have been accounted for in the separate financial statements

If the financial statements are not consolidated, they must therefore present interests in other entities at cost or in accordance with IFRS 9 Financial Instruments.

In the previous version of IAS 27, disclosure requirements relating to group accounts where included within this reporting standard. These requirements have been transferred to IFRS 12 Disclosure of Interests in Other Entities which are considered elsewhere within this chapter.

Current issues in group accounting

Consolidation and investment entities

The issue of IFRS 10, 11 and 12 represents part of the response by the IASB and US FASB to the global financial crisis.

Following the issue of IFRS 10, IFRS 11 and IFRS 12 in May 2011, the first part of a joint project between the IASB and US FASB was completed. Both the IASB and US FASB believe that their respective requirements relating to defining control, together with accounting for subsidiaries, associates and joint arrangements are now substantially converged.

Part two of the project deals with the definition and accounting policies of investment entities. The IASB issued an ED 'Investment Entities' in August 2011 with the objective of defining an investment entity, and also specify the accounting treatment for such entities. In principle, an investment entity is one which invests in other entities to achieve capital appreciation and/or investment returns for its own investors. It is proposed that such entities should be exempt from the provisions of IFRS 10 and therefore do not consolidate any subsidiaries but, instead, measure investments in other entities at fair value through profit or loss. This arguably better represents the substance of the relationship between the two parties.

The proposals are based upon existing requirements in US GAAP which provide an exemption from consolidation and instead require that an investment entity measures investments in other entities that it controls to be measured at fair value.

Development work will focus upon the definition of an investment entity and ensuring that there appropriate disclosures are made so that users if financial statements understand the nature of the investment in another entity and the accounting treatment adopted.

The IASB and FASB propose six qualifying criteria that an entity must meet in order to be classified as an investment entity.

(1) The entity's nature is such that its only substantive activities are investing in multiple entities to achieve capital appreciation, earn investment income, or both.

(2) The entity's business purpose is investing to earn capital appreciation, investment income, or both and it makes an explicit commitment to investors about this.

(3) Investors own units of investments (e.g. shares or partnership interests) in the entity.

(4) The entity pools the funds it receives from its investors, so that the investors can benefit from professional investment management.

(5) The entity manages and evaluates the performance of its investments on a fair value basis.

(6) The entity provides financial information about its investment activities to its investors.

Those entities that meet the criteria for qualifying as an investment entity would be exempt from consolidating its subsidiaries in accordance with IFRS 10.

Key benefits expected to accrue from this development are greater transparency and understanding of accounting treatment adopted, improved relevance of information for investors in investment entities and increased convergence of accounting treatment between IFRS and US GAAP.

Business combinations under common control

Business combinations under common control are excluded from the requirements of IFRS 3. This project would deal with defining common control and to develop standard practice, in both the group and individual entity financial statements of the acquirer, for transactions and arrangements that arise for entities under common control. The project was paused in 2009.

Transition Guidance - Proposed amendments to IFRS 10

In December 2011 the IASB issued ED/2011/7 Amendments to IFRS 10, 11 and 12 - Transition Guidance. The key points are as follows:

- The date of initial application (DOIA) is defined as the beginning of the accounting period for which IFRS 10 is applied for the first time. Unless there has been early application of the IFRS 10 - 12, this will be for accounting periods beginning on or after 1 January 2013.

- At the DOIA an entity should consider whether the decision to consolidate another entity in accordance with IFRS 10 is different to that arrived at under previous regulation IAS 27 and SIC 12.

- If the decision to consolidate is unchanged upon application of IFRS 10 for the first time, no retrospective adjustments are required. In effect, this provides an element of retrospective relief from having to restate previous periods when control of a subsidiary was lost or disposed of during the accounting period immediately preceding the DOIA.

- If the decision is to now consolidate an entity upon application of IFRS 10 for the first time:
    - IFRS 3 should be applied at the date when the investor gained control based upon application of IFRS 10 criteria.

    - The entity should retrospectively adjust the financial statements for the accounting period immediately prior to the DOIA. If control was deemed to have been acquired at a date earlier than the start of the immediately preceding accounting period, any difference between the amounts recognised on consolidation and previous carrying amounts are accounted for as a prior period adjustment and adjusted in equity at the start of the accounting period immediately preceding the DOIA.

    - If the deemed date of acquisition was prior to revision of IFRS 3 and IAS 27 in 2008, an entity can choose to apply either the 2008 or 2004 version of those reporting standards.

KAPLAN PUBLISHING

- If the decision is to no longer consolidate an entity upon application of IFRS 10 for the first time:
  - The interest should be measured at the amount at which it would have been measured as if IFRS 10 had been effective, whether that be the date the interest was acquired or the date control was lost.
  - The entity should retrospectively adjust the financial statements for the accounting period immediately prior to the DOIA. If control was deemed to have been lost at a date earlier than the start of the immediately preceding accounting period, any difference between the amounts recognised on consolidation and previous carrying amounts would be accounted for as a prior period adjustment and adjusted in equity at the start of the immediately preceding accounting period.

- Additional points:
  - If an entity prepares comparatives for more than one accounting period, it need only make retrospective adjustments for the immediately preceding period. However, it must identify which earlier years' comparatives have not been restated.
  - If retrospective application of deemed acquisition or deemed disposal is not possible, it should be done at the start of the earliest accounting period for which it is practicable.
  - Transition relief in relation to IFRS 11 - relief from the disclosure requirements of IAS 8 para 28(f) restating each line item affected for the current and preceding period, including impact on earnings per share if relevant, for periods earlier than the immediately preceding accounting period.
  - Transition relief in relation to IFRS 12 - relief from disclosure of comparatives relating to unconsolidated structured entities for periods earlier than the immediately preceding accounting period.

UK syllabus focus

The ACCA UK syllabus contains a requirement that UK variant candidates should be able to discuss and apply the key differences between UK GAAP and IFRS GAAP. The accounting requirements of UK GAAP and IFRS GAAP are very similar in this area, but there are one or two differences.

You should approach questions using the standard approach of completing the five standard workings identified within chapter 1. However, there are some key similarities and differences:

- IFRS 10 states the requirements for control to be exercised, and therefore provide a basis for the requirement to prepare consolidated financial statements. Under UK GAAP, CA 2006 provides the definition of parent and subsidiary entity, which is then applied in UK FRS 2 to identify six situations where one entity may be the subsidiary of another as follows:

  - the parent owns a majority of the voting shares in the subsidiary,

  - the parent is a member (i.e. a shareholder) of the subsidiary and has the right to appoint or remove a majority of the directors,

  - the parent has the right to exercise dominant influence over the subsidiary based upon a control contract,

  - the parent is a member of the subsidiary and controls a majority of the voting rights based upon an agreement with other members,

  - the parent has the power to exercise dominant influence over the subsidiary, and

  - the parent and subsidiary is managed on a unified basis.

- Both UK GAAP and IFRS GAAP require consolidation when one entity acquires control of another; the basic mechanics of how this is achieved is similar under both sets of regulation. For example, UK FRS 7 and IFRS 3 both require that the fair value of the net assets at the date of acquisition be determined as a basis for calculation of goodwill.

- Under UK GAAP, goodwill, and therefore minority interest (non-controlling interest under IFRS GAAP) is calculated only on the cost of acquisition incurred by the parent entity; i.e. the **'proportionate or partial basis'** referred to within this publication. Therefore any group accounts questions using the proportionate basis for calculation of goodwill and non-controlling interest are appropriate for compliance with UK GAAP.

- Under UK GAAP, FRS 7 permits only separable **intangibles** to be capitalised upon acquisition; IFRS 3 requires intangibles to be recognised which are identifiable. Identifiable is defined by IFRS 3 as either separable or that arise from contractual or legal rights.

- Under UK GAAP, FRS 7 requires that where there are **provisional values for the fair value of any of the net assets acquired**, there is a time limit up to the date of approval of the financial statements for the year following the acquisition; in practice, this period could be up to two years, depending upon the date of acquisition and the reporting date of the group. This will affect both the cost of acquisition and goodwill.

- Under UK GAAP, FRS 7 requires that a reasonable estimate of the fair value of amounts expected to be payable in the future in respect of **contingent consideration** is made at the at the date of acquisition. This should be reviewed at each reporting date and the cost of investment (and therefore goodwill) revised accordingly until the final amounts payable are determined. Note that there is no time limit on the period in which deferred consideration which is contingent may be adjusted.

- Under UK GAAP, **goodwill is normally amortised over its expected useful** life in accordance with FRS 10, which contains a rebuttable presumption that the estimated useful life of goodwill is a maximum of twenty years. On occasion, examination questions have stated that goodwill is to be regarded as a permanent asset, subject to annual impairment review. This would bring the accounting treatment for goodwill into alignment with IFRS GAAP. Therefore, there will also be some value in working questions where the goodwill accounting policy is to regard it as a permanent asset, subject to an annual impairment review.

- Under UK GAAP, **costs of acquisition** (e.g. legal and professional fees incurred) are capitalised as part of the cost of the acquisition. This is not the case under IFRS GAAP.

- If **negative goodwill** arises on consolidation, it is capitalised within fixed assets as a 'negative asset' and released to profit or loss based upon the nature of what has given rise to that negative goodwill. For monetary assets and liabilities (e.g. receivables and payables etc), negative goodwill is released immediately to profit and loss. For non-monetary assets (e.g. non-current assets and inventories) it is released to profit and loss over the expected life of those assets.

- UK FRS 9 deals with accounting for associates and joint ventures. There are no major differences between UK FRS 9 and the requirements of IAS 28 (revised) and IFRS 11 issued in May 2011 dealing with associates and joint ventures and joint arrangements respectively. One minor detail is that in the group income statement, the **share of associates operating profit, interest and tax** are separately accounted for, rather than simply taking the share of associate profit after tax for the year. The end result is the same, but UK FRS 9 discloses additional detail.

- UK FRS 9 requires that the **gross equity method** is used when accounting for a joint venture. In effect, this is the same as the equity method used for associates but with additional disclosures. In the group statement of profit or loss, the investor's share of revenue from the joint venture should be separately disclosed before arriving at group revenue. In the group statement of financial position within non-current assets, the investor's share of the gross assets and of the gross liabilities of the joint venture should both be disclosed in arriving at the net carrying value of the joint venture at the reporting date. IFRS 11 and IAS 28 require that joint ventures are accounted for using the equity method.

- The Companies Act and FRS 2 identify reasons for the possible **exclusion of a subsidiary from consolidation** which can be summarised as follows:

Reason	FRS 2	Treatment
Immaterial	Not applicable	Exclude from consolidation as reporting standards do not apply to immaterial items, and such items are not required to be fairly stated in order for the financial statements to show a true and fair view.
Severe long-term restrictions in exercising control.	Mandatory exclusion	If restrictions in force at date of acquisition, initially recognise at cost. If restrictions come into force at a later date, equity account from date restrictions came into force. Consider the possible recognition of an impairment of the investment.
Interest held solely with a view to sale.	Mandatory exclusion	Recognise as a current asset at the lower of cost and NRV
Consolidation would only be possible following undue expense or delay in obtaining or preparing information.	Mandatory inclusion	Consolidate as normal
Dissimilar activities	Mandatory inclusion	Consolidate as normal. Additional disclosures would normally be provided per SSAP 25.

- **Exemption from the requirement to prepare consolidated accounts** (as opposed to exclusion of an individual subsidiary from group accounts – as above) is possible in each of the following circumstances:

    - the aggregate of all subsidiaries is considered to be immaterial (s405 CA 2006), or

    - it meets the definition of a small group, and includes no ineligible subsidiaries (s467 CA 2006) – see also chapter 20 for UK syllabus focus in relation to small and medium-sized entities), or

    - it is a wholly-owned intermediate parent company (s400-401 CA 2006) whose results are consolidated into a larger group, or

    - it is a non-wholly owned intermediate parent company, and there has not been a request to prepare consolidated accounts by non-group shareholders to prepare such accounts.

UK GAAP Question

Crash, Bang and Wallop

	Date of acquisition	Reserves at acq'n	FV of net assets at acq'n	Cost of investment	Equity shares acquired
		$	$	$	£
Bang	1 July 20X7	30,000	120,000	100,000	45,000
Wallop	1 July 20X7	25,000	70,000	30,000	10,500

Summarised accounts of three entities for the year ended 30 June 20X8 are as follows:

Statements of financial position:

	Crash $	Bang $	Wallop $
Non-current assets:			
Property plant and equipment	100,000	80,000	60,000
Investments	130,000		
Current assets:			
Inventory	10,000	30,000	15,000
Receivables	70,000	10,000	2,000
Cash at Bank	40,000	20,000	3,000
	350,000	140,000	80,000
Equity and liabilities:			
Equity share capital ($1 shares)	100,000	75,000	35,000
Retained earnings	200,000	50,000	40,000
Liabilities	50,000	15,000	5,000
	350,000	140,000	80,000

Income statements:

	$	$	$
Revenue	500,000	200,000	100,000
Cost of sales	(300,000)	(140,000)	(60,000)
Gross profit	200,000	60,000	40,000
Administration costs	(50,000)	(10,000)	(10,000)
Operating profit	150,000	50,000	30,000
Finance costs	10,000	(10,000)	–
Profit before tax	160,000	40,000	30,000
Tax	(60,000)	(20,000)	(15,000)
Profit after tax	100,000	20,000	15,000

The fair value adjustment in respect of Bang relates to tangible assets with a five-year life. The fair value adjustment in respect of Wallop relates to land. The fair values have not been incorporated.

During the year Crash sold goods to Bang for $10,000 at a margin of 50%. At the year end the group had sold only 80% of these goods.

During the year Crash gave Bang substantial short-term loans – most of which was repaid shortly before the year-end. The final balance of $5,000 was paid on 10 July 20X8. The interest charged in Bang's income statement and the interest receivable in Crash's profit and loss account represents interest on this loan.

It is group accounting policy to amortise goodwill over five years.

Required:

Prepare the consolidated statement of financial position at 30 June 20X8, together with the consolidated income statement for the year ended 30 June 20X8.

UK GAAP Answer

Crash Group income statement for the year ended 30 June 20X8

			$
Revenue	500,000 + 200,000	Less inter coy (10,000)	690,000
Cost of Sales	300,000 + 140,000	Less inter coy (10,000)	(439,600)
	Plus the PURP 1,000		
	Plus: g'will amort 5,600 (W3)		
	Plus: dep'n on the FVA 3,000		
Gross profit			250,400
Administration exps	50,000 + 10,000		(60,000)
Operating profit			190,400
Finance costs	All intercompany		nil
Income from Assoc.	(W8)		7,200

Profit before tax			197,600
Tax	60,000 + 20,000		(80,000)
Share of assoc tax	(30% x 15,000)		(4,500)
Profit after tax			113,100
Attributable to group	Bal fig		106,300
Attributable to NCI	(W9)		6,800
			113,100

Crash Group statement of financial position as at 30 June 20X8

			$
Non-current Assets			
Intangible – goodwill	(W3)		22,400
property, plant & equipment	100,000 + 80,000	**Plus** FVA 15,000 less dep'n (3,000) (W2)	192,000
Investment in Associate	(W7)		32,700
			247,100
Current Assets			
Inventory	10,000 + 30,000	Less PURP (w5) (1,000)	39,000
Receivables	70,000 + 10,000	Less intercompany (5,000)	75,000
Cash at bank	40,000 + 20,000		60,000 174,000
			421,100

			$
Equity and liabilities			
Equity share capital			100,000
Retained earnings	(W5)		206,300
Non-controlling interest (MI)	(W4)		54,800
Payables	50,000 + 15,000	Less intercompany (5,000)	60,000
			421,100

(W1) Group structure

Crash is the parent

Bang is a 60% subsidiary (45/75)

Wallop is a 30% associate (10.5/35)

Both acquisitions took place a year ago

(W2) Net assets

	Bang		Wallop	
	Acq	Y/e	Acq	Y/e
	$	$	$	$
Equity capital	75,000	75,000	35,000	35,000
Retained earnings	30,000	50,000	25,000	40,000
FVA	15,000	15,000	10,000	10,000
Dep'n on FVA		(3,000)		
	120,000	137,000	70,000	85,000

(W3) Goodwill

	Bang	Wallop
	$	$
Consideration paid	100,000	30,000
Less: 60% × 120,000 re Bang (W2)	(72,000)	
Less: 30% × 70,000 re Wallop (W2)		(21,000)
Goodwill at acquisition	28,000	9,000
Amortisation 1/5	(5,600)	(1,800)
Unamortised goodwill	22,400	7,200

(W4) NCI re Bang

	$
40% × 137,000	54,800

(W5) Group retained earnings

		$
Crash		200,000
Less PURP (W6)	Parent is the seller	(1,000)
Share of post-acquisition retained earnings:	(change in net assets)	
Bang 60% × (137,000 – 120,000) (W2)		10,200
Wallop 30% × (85,000 – 70,000) (W2)		4,500
Goodwill amortised – Bang (W3)		(5,600)
Goodwill amortised – Wallop (W3)		(1,800)
		206,300

(W6) Provision for unrealised profit

The parent is the seller so the parent's retained earnings are adjusted
20% × 10,000 = 2,000 (unsold goods) x 50% margin = 1,000

(W7) Investment in the associate – Wallop

EITHER:

	$
Cost	30,000
Share of increase in net assets (30% × (85–70) (W2))	4,500
Less: amortisation of premium on acquisition	(1,800)
	32,700

OR:

	$
Group share of net assets: 30% × 85,000 (W2)	25,500
Plus: unamortised premium on acquisition (W3)	7,200
	32,700

(W8) **Income from the associate**

	$
Group % of operating profit	9,000
Less: amortisation of premium (1/5 × 9,000) (W3)	(1,800)
	7,200

(W9) **NCI in the profit after tax**

	$
40% × (20,000 – *3,000)	6,800

*the depreciation on the fair value adjustment

6 Chapter summary

Background to group accounts

- Consolidated accounts show the results of the group
- Intercompany transactions and balances must be eliminated
- All companies in the group should use the same accounting policies and have the same reporting sheet date

Goodwill and fair value adjustments

- Goodwill is calculated as the excess of consideration + the NCI over the fair value of the net assets of the subsidiary
- The NCI is valued as either:
  - the NCI% × NAs of the subsidiary at reporting date OR
  - FV of the NCI at acquisition + NCI% × post acquisition movement in reserves
- All assets, liabilities and contingent liabilities at the acquisition date (including those not recognised in the subsidiary's financial statements) must be recognised at fair value

Consolidation techniques

- A methodical approach is the best way to complete a group accounting question
- The following workings should be used:
  - group structure
  - net assets
  - goodwill
  - non-controlling interest
  - group retained earnings

Associates and joint ventures

- Associates are accounted for using the equity method
- Joint ventures are accounted for according to the type of venture
- Joint ventures that are separate entities may be accounted for using the equity method in the same way as associates

Current issues in group accounting

- Consolidation
- Joint arrangements

Test your understanding answers

Test your understanding 1 – Rosa

(i) Goodwill calculation using the proportion of net assets method:

	$
Purchase consideration (2/1 × (80% × 100) = 160 × $5)	800
NCI value at acquisition (20% × 600)	120
	920
Less: fair value of all identifiable net assets at acquisition (per net assets working)	(600)
Prop goodwill at acquisition	320
Less: impairment to date (if applicable)	(X)
Goodwill to consolidated statement of financial position	320

(i) Goodwill calculation using the full goodwill method:

	$
Purchase consideration (2/1 × (80% × 100) = 160 × $5)	800
NCI value at acquisition**(20% × 100 × $8)	160
	960
Less: fair value of all identifiable net assets at acquisition (per net assets working)	(600)
Goodwill at acquisition	360
Less: impairment to date (if applicable)	(X)
Goodwill to consolidated statement of financial position	360

**if full goodwill method adopted, NCI value = FV of NCI at date of acquisition; this will normally be given in a question.

**if proportionate basis adopted, NCI value = NCI% of net assets at acquisition (per net assets working).

The cost of the investment that Rosa (the parent) has made in the Parks (the subsidiary) is the fair value of the consideration given. This is the fair value of the shares that Rosa has issued.

Test your understanding 2 – Borough High Street

Borough Group statement of profit or loss for the year ended 30 June 20X8

			$
Revenue	500,000 + 200,000	Less inter coy (10,000)	690,000
Cost of Sales	300,000 + 140,000	Less inter coy (10,000)	(441,000)
	Plus the PURP 1,000	Add dep'n on the FVA 3,000	
	G'will impaired 7,000		
			———
Gross profit			249,000
Administration exps	50,000 + 10,000		(60,000)
			———
Operating profit			189,000
Interest	All intercompany		nil
Income from Ass.	(W8)		4,500
			———
Profit before tax			193,500
Tax	60,000 + 20,000		(80,000)
			———
Profit after tax			113,500
			———
Attributable to owners of parent	Bal fig		109,500
Attributable to NCI	(W9)		4,000
			———
			113,500
			———

There were no items of other comprehensive income in the year.

Borough Group statement of financial position as at 30 June 20X8

Non Current Assets			$
Intangible	(W3)		28,000
Tangible	100,000 + 80,000	Add: FVA 15,000 less dep'n 3,000 (W2)	192,000
Investment in Associate	(W7)		25,500
Current Assets			
Inventory	22,000 + 30,000	Less PURP (W5) (1,000)	51,000
Receivables	70,000 + 10,000	Less interco (5,000)	75,000
Cash at bank	37,000 + 20,000		57,000
			428,500
Equity capital			100,000
Retained earnings	(W5)		209,500
Non-controlling interest	(W4)		59,000
Total equity			368,500
Liabilities	50,000 + 15,000	Less inter co (5,000)	60,000
			428,500

(W1) Group structure

Borough is the parent

High is a 60% subsidiary (45/75)

Street is a 30% associate (10.5/35)

Both acquisitions took place a year ago

(W2) Net assets

	High Acq	Rep date
	$	$
Equity capital	75,000	75,000
Retained earnings	30,000	50,000
FVA	15,000*	15,000
Dep'n on FVA		(3,000)
*bal fig	120,000	137,000

(W3) Goodwill – Full goodwill (fair value) method

		High
		$
Consideration paid		100,000
FV of NCI at acq		55,000
		155,000
Less: 100% of net assets at acquisition (W2)		(120,000)
Total goodwill at acquisition		35,000
Impairment	Group (60% × $7,000)	(4,200)
	NCI (40% × $7,000)	(2,800)
		(7,000)
Unimpaired goodwill		28,000

(W4) Non-controlling interest (full basis)

	$
Fair value of NCI at acquisition (given)	55,000
NCI % of post-acquisition retained earnings (40% × 17,000)	6,800
NCI share of goodwill impairment (W3)	(2,800)
Total unimpaired goodwill	59,000

(W5) Group retained earnings

		$
Parent		200,000
Less PURP (W5)	Parent is the seller (change in net assets)	(1,000)
Share of post-acquisition retained earnings:		
High 60% × (137,000 – 120,000) (W2)		10,200
Street 30% × (40,000 – 25,000)		4,500
Group share of goodwill impairment (W3)		(4,200)
		209,500

(W6) Provision for unrealised profit

The parent is the seller so the parent's retained earnings are adjusted
20% × 10,000 = 2,000 (unsold goods) × 50% margin = 1,000

(W7) Investment in the associate

	$
Cost	21,000
Share of increase in retained earnings (30% × (40,000 – 25,000))	4,500
	25,500

(W8) Income from the associate

		$
Group % of the profit after tax	(30% × 15,000)	4,500

(W9) Non-controlling interest in the profit after tax

	$
40% × (20,000 – *3,000)	6,800
Less: NCI share of goodwill impairment (W3)	(2,800)
	4,000

*the depreciation charge for the year on the fair value adjustment

Complex groups

Chapter learning objectives

Upon completion of this chapter you will be able to:

Determine appropriate procedures to be used in preparing group financial statements:

- apply the method of accounting for business combinations, including complex group structures (vertical and D-shaped/mixed groups)
- apply the recognition and measurement criteria for identifiable acquired assets and liabilities and goodwill including step acquisitions
- determine the appropriate procedures to be used in preparing group financial statements.

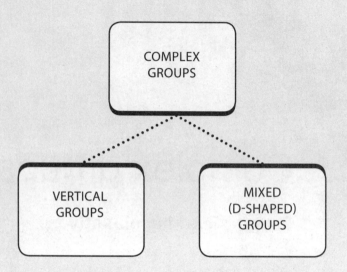

1 Complex group structures

Complex group structures exist where a subsidiary of a parent entity owns a majority shareholding in another entity which makes that other entity also a subsidiary of the parent entity.

Complex structures can be classified under two headings:

- vertical groups
- mixed groups.

2 Vertical groups

Definition

A **vertical group** arises where a subsidiary of the parent entity holds shares in a further entity such that control is achieved. The parent entity therefore controls both the subsidiary entity and, in turn, its subsidiary (often referred to as a sub-subsidiary entity). Look at the two situations:

Situation 1:	**Situation 2:**
H	H
owns 90% of	owns 70% of
S	S
who, in turn, owns 80% of	who, in turn, owns 60% of
T	T

In both situations, H controls both S and also T - there is a vertical group comprising three entities. H has a controlling interest in entity S. S has a controlling interest in entity T. H is therefore able to exert control over T by virtue of its ability to control S.

The normal consolidation principles and workings will be applied to consolidate a vertical group. Goodwill must be calculated and non-controlling interests recognised for each subsidiary in the group. Particular care will be needed to apply the holding entity (H in the two situations above) effective interest in the sub-subsidiary (T in the two situations above) in the workings.

The narrative which follows explains and illustrates how the group effective interest and non-controlling effective interest in a sub-subsidiary is determined, together with workings to calculate goodwill, NCI and group retained earnings as required. There is also explanation to determine when the sub-subsidiary becomes a member of the group for consolidation.

Consolidation

Where a parent entity owns a controlling interest in a subsidiary, which in turn owns a controlling interest in a sub-subsidiary, then the group accounts of the ultimate parent entity must include the underlying net assets and earnings of both the subsidiary and the sub-subsidiary entities.

Thus, both entities that are controlled by the parent are consolidated.

The basic techniques of consolidation are the same as seen previously, although calculations of goodwill and the non-controlling interest become slightly more complicated.

Effective shareholding and non-controlling interest

In the two situations identified opposite, H has a **direct** interest in S and an **indirect** interest in T (exercised via S's holding in T).

In situation 1, H has an **effective** interest of only 72% (90% × 80%) in T. Nevertheless, T is a sub-subsidiary of H because H has a controlling interest in S and S has a controlling interest in T. As H has an effective interest in T of 72%, it follows that the non-controlling interest in T is 28%. This can be analysed as follows:

	%
Owned by outside shareholders in T	20
Owned by outside shareholders in H (100% – 90%) × 80%	8
	——
Effective non-controlling interest in T	28
	——

Similarly, in situation 2, H has an **effective** interest of just 42% (70% × 60%) in T. Nevertheless, T is a sub-subsidiary of H because H has a controlling interest in S and S has a controlling interest in T. As H has an effective interest in T of 42%, it follows that the non-controlling interest in T is 58%. This can be analysed as follows:

	%
Owned by outside shareholders in T	40
Owned by outside shareholders in H (100% – 70%) × 60%)	18
	——
Effective non-controlling interest in T	58
	——

The group effective interest in T will be used within the goodwill and group reserve calculations for the sub-subsidiary.

In situation 2, do not be put off by the fact that the effective group interest in T is less than 50%, and that the effective non-controlling interest in T is more than 50%. The effective interest calculations are the result of a two-stage acquisition and are used to simplify the consolidation workings.

Group reserves

Only the group or effective percentage of each of the reserves of the sub-subsidiary are included within group reserves. Often the only reserve will be retained earnings, but there could be others, such as revaluation reserve.

Date of acquisition

The date of acquisition of each subsidiary is the date on which H gains control. If S already held T when H acquired S, treat S and T as being acquired on the same day. Consider the following situations to determine when the sub-subsidiary company, T, becomes a member of the H group::

(1) H acquired control of S on 1 January 2004; S subsequently acquired control of another entity, T, on 1 July 2006.

(2) H acquired control of S on 1 July 2006; S had already acquired control of another entity, T, on 1 January 2004.

In the first situation, T does not come under the control of H until S acquires shares in T – i.e. on 1 July 2006. In the second situation, H cannot gain control of T until S acquires shares in T on 1 July 2006.

To identify the date that the sub-subsidiary becomes a member of the group, include the dates of share purchases within your group structure when answering questions: the key date will be the later of the two possible dates of acquisition.

The following examples consider situations where:

(1) the subsidiary is acquired by the parent first; the subsidiary later acquires the sub-subsidiary, and

(2) the parent acquires the subsidiary that already holds the sub-subsidiary.

Illustration 1 - Vertical group 1

The draft statements of financial position of David, Colin and John, as at 31 December 20X4, are as follows:

	D	C	J		D	C	J
	$000	$000	$000		$000	$000	$000
Sundry assets	280	180	130	Equity capital	200	100	50
				Retained earnings	100	60	30
Shares in subsidiary	120	80		Liabilities	100	100	50
	400	260	130		400	260	130

You ascertain the following:

• David acquired 75,000 $1 shares in Colin on 1 January 20X4 when the retained earnings of Colin amounted to $40,000. At that date, the fair value attributable to the non-controlling interest in Colin was valued at $38,000.

• Colin acquired 40,000 $1 shares in John on 30 June 20X4 when the retained earnings of John amounted to $25,000; they had been $20,000 on the date of David's acquisition of Colin. At that date, the fair value of the non-controlling interest in John (both direct and indirect), based upon effective shareholdings, was valued at $31,000.

• Goodwill has suffered no impairment.

Required:

Produce the consolidated statement of financial position of the David group at 31 December 20X4. It is group policy to use the full goodwill method.

Solution vertical group 1

Step 1 – Group structure

Draw a diagram of the group structure and set out the respective interests of the parent entity and the non-controlling interests, distinguishing between direct (D) and indirect (I) interests. You may find it useful to include on the diagram the dates of acquisition of the subsidiary and the sub-subsidiary.

David
  | 75% acquired 1 Jan X4
Colin
  | 80% acquired 30 June X4
John

Group and Non Controlling interests

	Colin	John
Group interest	75%	60% (75% × 80%)
Non Controlling interest	25%	40% (25% × 80%)
	100%	100%

Step 2 - Start with the **net assets** consolidation working as normal.

Care must be taken in determining the date for the split between post-acquisition and pre-acquisition retained earnings. The relevant date will be that on which David (the parent company) acquired control of each entity:

- Colin: 1 January 20X4

- John: 30 June 20X4

Therefore, the information given regarding John's retained earnings at 1 January 20X4 is irrelevant in this context.

	$000
Colin: NCI FV at acquisition	38
Colin NCI share of post-acq'n retained earnings (25% × 20,000)	5
Less: NCI share of cost of investment in John (25% × 80,000)	(20)
	23
John: NCI FV at acquisition	31
John NCI share of post acq'n retained earnings (40% × 5,000)	2
	56

Step 5 - Group retained earnings

	$000
David	100
Colin 75% × 20,000 (post-acquisition retained earnings)	15
John 60% × 5,000 (post-acquisition retained earnings)	3
	118

Note that again, only the group or effective interest of 60% is taken of the post-acquisition retained earnings of John.

Step 6 - Summarised group SOFP for the David group at 31 December 20X4

	$
Goodwill (18,000 + 16,000)	34,000
Sundry assets (280,000 + 180,000 + 130,000)	590,000
	624,000

Net assets of subsidiaries

	Colin		John	
	At acq'n	At rep date	At acq'n	At rep date
	$	$	$	$
Equity capital	100,000	100,000	50,000	50,000
Reserves	40,000	60,000	25,000	30,000
	140,000	160,000	75,000	80,000

Step 3 - Goodwill

- A separate calculation is required to determine goodwill for each subsidiary.

- For the sub-subsidiary, goodwill is calculated from the perspective of the ultimate parent entity (David) rather than the immediate parent (Colin). Therefore, the effective cost of John is only David's share of the amount that Colin paid for John, i.e. $80,000 × 75% = $60,000.

	Colin	John	
	$000	$000	
Cost of investment in subsidiary	120	60	(i.e. 75% × 80,000)
Fair value of NCI	38	31	
	158	91	
FV of net assets (W2)	(140)	(75)	
	18	16	

Step 4 - Non-controlling interest

When taking the non-controlling share of Colin's net assets, an adjustment must be made to take out the cost of investment in John that is included in the net assets of Colin.

In the group statement of financial position, the cost of investment is replaced by including all the net assets of John, so no investment must remain.

The non-controlling interest in Colin are entitled to their (indirect) share of the net assets of John, but they receive these by virtue of the effective interest that will be used to calculate the non-controlling interest in John.

Equity and liabilities:	
Equity capital	200,000
Retained earnings (Step 5)	118,000
	―――
	318,000
Non-controlling interest (Step 4)	56,000
	―――
Total equity	374,000
Liabilities (100,000 + 100.000 + 50,000)	250,000
	―――
	624,000
	―――

Illustration 2 – Vertical group 2

The draft statements of financial position of Daniel, Craig and James as at 31 December 20X4 are as follows:

	D	C	J		D	C	J
	$000	$000	$000		$000	$000	$000
Sundry assets	180	80	80	Equity capital	200	100	50
Shares in subsidiary	120	80		Retained earnings	100	60	30
	―	―	―		―	―	―
	300	160	80		300	160	80
	―	―	―		―	―	―

- Craig acquired 40,000 $1 shares in James on 1 January 20X4 when the retained earnings of James amounted to $25,000.

- Daniel acquired 75,000 $1 shares in Craig on 30 June 20X4 when the retained earnings of Craig amounted to $40,000 and those of James amounted to $30,000.

It is group policy to value the non-controlling interest using the proportion of net assets method.

Required:

Produce the consolidated statement of financial position of the Daniel group at 31 December 20X4.

Solution vertical group 2

Solution

Assets:	$000
Goodwill (W3) (15 + 12)	27
Assets (180 + 80 + 80)	340
	─────
	367
	─────

Equity and liabilities:	$000
Equity capital	200
Retained earnings (W5)	115
NCI (W4)	52
	─────
	367
	─────

(W1) Group structure

Draw a diagram of the group structure and set out the respective interests of the parent entity and the non-controlling interests, distinguishing between direct (D) and indirect (I) interests. You may find it useful to include on the diagram the dates of acquisition of the subsidiary and the sub-subsidiary.

Daniel
| 75% acquired 30 Jun X4
Craig
| 80% acquired 1 Jan X4
James

The relevant acquisition date for both entities is the date that they both joined the Daniel group, i.e. 30 June 20X4.

KAPLAN PUBLISHING

(W2) Net assets for each subsidiary – remember correct date of acquisition

	Craig		James	
	Acq'n date	Rep date	Acq'n date	Rep date
	$	$	$	$
Share capital	100,000	100,000	50,000	50,000
Reserves	40,000	60,000	30,000	30,000
	140,000	160,000	80,000	80,000

(W3) Goodwill – proportionate basis

	Craig $000		James $000
Cost of investment	120	(75% × 80,000)	60
FV of NCI at acquisition:			
(25% × 140,000) (W2)	35	(40% × 80,000) (W2)	32
	155		92
FV of NA at acquisition (W2)	(140)		(80)
Goodwill	15		12

(W4) NCI

Craig:	$000	$000
FV of NCI at acquisition:(25% × 140,000) (W2)	35	
Share of post-acq'n RE ((25% × (160,000 – 140,000) (W2)	5	40

James:		
FV of NA at acquisition: (40% × 80,000) (W2)	32	
Share of post-acq'n RE ((40% × (80,000 – 80,000) (W2)	–	32
Less: NCI% of cost of investment by C in J (25% × 80,000)		(20)
		52

(W5) **Group retained earnings**

	$000
Daniel	100
Craig (75% × 20) (post-acquisition retained earnings)	15
James (no post-acquisition retained earnings)	–
	___
	115
	___

Test your understanding 1 – H, S & T

The following are the statements of financial position at 31 December 20X7 for H group companies:

	H	S	T
	$	$	$
45,000 shares in S	65,000		
30,000 shares in T		55,000	
Sundry assets	280,000	133,000	100,000
	_____	_____	_____
	345,000	188,000	100,000
	_____	_____	_____
Equity share capital ($1 shares)	100,000	60,000	50,000
Retained earnings	45,000	28,000	25,000
Liabilities	200,000	100,000	25,000
	_____	_____	_____
	345,000	188,000	100,000
	_____	_____	_____

The inter-company shareholdings were acquired on 1 January 20X1 when the retained earnings of S were $10,000 and those of T were $8,000. At that date, the fair value of the non-controlling interest in S was $20,000. The fair value of the total non-controlling interest (direct and indirect) in T was $50,000. It is group policy to value the non-controlling interest using the full goodwill method. At the reporting date, goodwill is fully impaired and had been written off in an earlier year.

Required:

Prepare the consolidated statement of financial position for the H group at 31 December 20X7.

Test your understanding 2 – Grape, Vine and Wine

Grape purchased 40,000 of the 50,000 $1 shares in Vine on 1 July 20X5, when the retained earnings of that entity were $80,000. At that time, Vine held 7,500 of the 10,000 $1 shares in Wine. These had been purchased on 1 January 20X5 when Wine's retained earnings were $65,000. On 1 July 20X5, Wine's retained earnings were $67,000.

At 1 July 20X5, the fair value of the non-controlling interest in Vine was $27,000, and that of Wine (both direct and indirect) was $31,500.

Statements of financial position of the three entities at 30 June 20X6 were as follows:

	Grape	Vine	Wine
	$000	$000	$000
Investment	110	60	
Sundry assets	350	200	120
Net assets	460	260	120
Equity share capital	100	50	10
Retained earnings	210	110	70
Liabilities	150	100	40
	460	260	120

Required:

Prepare the consolidated statement of financial position for Grape group at 30 June 20X6. It is group policy to value the non-controlling interest using the full goodwill method.

3 Mixed (D-shaped) groups

Definition

In a mixed group situation the parent entity has a direct controlling interest in at least one subsidiary. In addition, the parent entity and the subsidiary together hold a controlling interest in a further entity.

e.g.

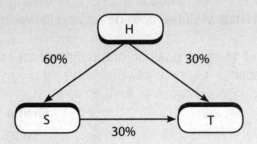

- H controls 60% of S; S is therefore a subsidiary of H.

- H controls 30% of T directly and another 30% indirectly via its interest in S. T is therefore a sub-subsidiary of the H group. H has control of 60%, either directly or indirectly, of the shares in T and is therefore able to control it.

Date of acquisition

As with the vertical group structure considered earlier in this chapter, identify the dates of the respective share purchases to help determine the date when the entity at the bottom of the group (often, but not always a sub-subsidiary) becomes a member of the group. Using the example of H, S & T above, if dates of share purchases are added as follows:

Suppose H acquired a 60% interest in S on 1 January 2004, and acquired its 30% interest on the same date. S subsequently acquired its 30% interest in T on 1 July 2006.

Initially, from 1 January 2004, H exercises significant influence over T as an associate entity. It is only from 1 July 2006 that H has access to more than 50% of the voting power in T; T is therefore consolidated into the H group accounts as a subsidiary from 1 July 2006.

Alternatively, suppose H acquired a 60% interest in S on 1 January 2006, and acquired its 30% interest on the same date. S acquired its 30% interest in T on 1 July 2004.

Initially, from 1 January 2004, S exercises significant influence over T as an associate entity. It is only from 1 July 2006 that H has access to more than 50% of the voting power in T; T is therefore consolidated into the H group accounts from 1 July 2006.

Further detail on mixed groups

Note that the definition of a mixed group does not include the situation where the parent and an associate together hold a controlling interest in a further entity.

E.g.

H owns 35% of S, S owns 40% of W and H owns 40% of W.

This is **not** a mixed group situation. Neither S nor W is a member of the H group, although S and W may both be 'associates' of H.

H's interest in W might be calculated as before as (35% × 40%) + 40% = 54%. Although H has an arithmetic interest in W that is more than 50%, it does not have parent entity control of W, as it does not control S's 40% stake in W.

Consolidation

All three entities in the above mixed group are consolidated.

The approach is similar to dealing with sub-subsidiaries, i.e. an effective interest is computed and used to allocate share capital and retained earnings.

From the example above:

S	Group share	60%	
	NCI		40%
T	Group share		
	Direct	30%	
	Indirect 60% of 30%	18%	
		─────	
	Total	48%	
	NCI		52%

All consolidation workings are the same as those used in vertical group situations, with the exception of goodwill.

The **goodwill** calculation for the sub-subsidiary differs in that two elements to cost must be considered, namely:

- the cost of the parent's direct holding

- the parent's percentage of the cost of the subsidiary's holding (the indirect holding).

Illustration 3 – Mixed (D-shaped) groups

The statements of financial position of H, S and M as at 31 December 20X5 were as follows:

	H	S	M
	$	$	$
45,000 shares in S	72,000		
16,000 shares in M	25,000		
12,000 shares in M		20,000	
Sundry assets	125,000	120,000	78,000
	222,000	140,000	78,000
Equity share capital ($1 shares)	120,000	60,000	40,000
Retained earnings	95,000	75,000	35,000
Liabilities	7,000	5,000	3,000
	222,000	140,000	78,000

All shares were acquired on 31 December 20X2 when the retained earnings of S amounted to $30,000 and those of M amounted to $10,000.

It is group accounting policy to value non-controlling interest on a proportionate basis.

Required:

Prepare the statement of financial position for the H group at 31 December 20X5.

Solution

Group statement of financial position – H group at 31 December 20X5

	$
Intangible – goodwill (4,500 + 8.750) (W3)	13,250
Sundry assets (125,000 + 120,000 + 78,000)	323,000
	336,250

	$
Equity and liabilities:	
Equity share capital	120,000
Retained earnings (W5)	144,375
Non-controlling interest (W4)	56,875
Total equity	321,250
Liabilities (7,000 + 5,000 + 3,000)	15,000
	336,250

(W1) Determine group structure:

In S: 45,000 / 60,000 × 100% =

75%

In M

Direct	16,000 / 40,000 × 100% =	40.0%
Indirect	75% × 12,000 / 40,000 × 100% =	22.5%

62.5%

(W2) Net assets

	S		M	
	At acq'n	At rep date	At acq'n	At rep date
(W2) Net assets of $ & M	$	$	$	$
Equity capital	60,000	60,000	40,000	40,000
Retained earnings	30,000	75,000	10,000	35,000
	90,000	135,000	50,000	75,000

(W3) **Goodwill re S & M**

	$			$
Cost of investment	72,000	Direct		25,000
		Indirect	(75% × 20)	15,000
FV of NCI at acq'n (25% × 90)			(37.5% × 50)	18,750
	22,500			
	———			———
	94,500			58,750
Less: FV of NA at acq'n (W2)				
	(90,000)			(50,000)
	———			———
	4,500			8,750
	———			———

(W4) **Non-controlling interest**

		$
S – FV of NCI at acq'n		22,500
NCI share of post acq'n retained earnings	(25% × (135,000 – 90,000)) (W2)	11,250
M – FV of NCI at acq'n	37.5% × $50,000 (W2)	18,750
Share of post acq'n retained earnings	(37.5% × (75,000 – 50,000)) (W2)	9,375
Less: NCI share of S cost of investment in M	(25% × $20,000)	(5,000)
		———
		56,875
		———

(W5) **Retained earnings**

	$
H	95,000
S – (75% × (135,000 – 90,000)) (W2)	33,750
M – (62.5% × (75,000 – 50,000)) (W2)	15,625
	———
	144,375
	———

Test your understanding 3 – T, S & R

The following are the summarised statements of financial position of T, S and R as at 31 December 20X4.

	T	S	R
	$	$	$
Non-current assets	140,000	61,000	170,000
Investments	200,000	65,000	–
Current assets	20,000	20,000	15,000
	360,000	146,000	185,000
Equity shares of $1 each	200,000	80,000	100,000
Retained earnings	150,000	60,000	80,000
Liabilities	10,000	6,000	5,000
	360,000	146,000	185,000

On 1 January 20X3 S acquired 35,000 ordinary shares in R at a cost of $65,000 when the retained earnings of R amounted to $40,000.

On 1 January 20X4 T acquired 64,000 shares in S at a cost of $120,000 and 40,000 shares in R at a cost of $80,000. The retained earnings of S and R amounted to $50,000 and $60,000 respectively on 1 January 20X4. The fair value of the NCI in S at that date was $27,000. The fair value of the whole (direct and indirect) NCI in R was $56,000. The non-controlling interest is measured using the full goodwill method. At the reporting date, goodwill has not been impaired.

Required:

Prepare the consolidated statement of financial position of the T group as at 31 December 20X4.

UK syllabus focus

The ACCA UK syllabus contains a requirement that UK variant candidates should be able to discuss and apply the key differences between UK GAAP and IFRS GAAP. The accounting requirements of UK GAAP and IFRS GAAP are very similar in this area, but there are one or two differences.

You should approach questions using the approach of completing the five standard workings identified within chapter 1. Rather than step acquisition as detailed within this chapter, UK GAAP students should, instead, think in terms of **piecemeal acquisitions**. Each time an additional share purchase is made, there should be incremental adjustments to goodwill and group reserves. This means that a net assets working is required at the date of each additional share purchase as illustrated in the following question. Any subsequent remeasurement of a fair value adjustment will be treated as a revaluation.

UK GAAP Question

On 1 January 20X2, Drew acquired 25,000 shares in Karin for $80,000, and obtained significant influence at that date. At that date, the fair value of land owned by Karin exceeded its book value at that date by $10,000 and the balance on retained earnings was £45,000.

On 1 January 20X4, Drew acquired a further 40,000 shares in Karin for $150,000 and obtained control at that date. The fair value of the land had increased to $40,000 and the balance on retained earnings was $60,000.

None of the fair value increases had been reflected in the books of Karin.

Goodwill is amortised over five years.

The statements of financial position of both entities at 31 December 20X8 were as follows:

	Drew	Karin
	$m	$m
Investment in Karin	230,000	
Non-current assets	275,500	100,000
Current assets	215,100	103,000
	720,600	203,000

Equity and liabilities	$m	$m
$1 equity shares	100,000	100,000
Share premium	200,000	
Retained earnings	415,600	100,000
Trade payables	5,000	3,000
	720,600	203,000

Required:

Prepare the group statement of financial position as at 31 December 20X8.

UK GAAP Answer

The Drew group statement of financial position as at 31 December 20X8:

	$m
Non-current assets (275,000 + 100,000 + 40,000 FVA)	415,500
Current assets (215,100 + 103,000)	318,100
	733,600

Equity and liabilities:	$m
$1 equity shares	100,000
Share premium	200,000
Revaluation reserve (W6)	7,500
Retained earnings (W5)	334.100
Non-controlling interest (W5)	84,000
Trade payables (5,000 + 3,000)	8,000
	733,600

(W1) Group structure

Drew

25% at 1 Jan X2 – associate
40% at 1 Jan X4
65% from 1 Jan X4 – consolidate

Karin

(W2) **Net assets**	Net assets 1 Jan X2	Net assets 1 Jan X4	Net assets 31 Dec X8
	$m	$m	$m
Equity capital	100,000	100,000	100,000
Retained earnings	45,000	60,000	100,000
FVA - land	10,000	40,000	40,000
	155,000	200,000	240,000

(W3) **Goodwill**	1 Jan X2	1 Jan X4
	$m	$m
Cost of investment	80,000	150,000
share of net assets acquired:		
1 Jan X2: 25% × 155,000 (W2)	(38,750)	
1 Jan X4: 40% × 200,000 (W2)		(80,000)
Goodwill fully amortised by reporting date	41,250	70,000

Note that goodwill has been calculated on an incremental basis for the purchase made on 1 January 20X4, as the investment in Karin changes from being an associate to a subsidiary. Even if there was a further purchase of shares, taking the total group shareholding to, say, 80%, the same approach would be adopted.

(W4) **Non-controlling interest at reporting date**	$m
35% × 240,000 (W2)	84,000

Note that NCI is based upon the NCI% at the reporting date.

(W5) **Group retained earnings**	$m
Drew	415,800
Karin: (25% × (100,000 – 45,000))	13,750
Karin: (40% × (100,000 – 60,000))	16,000
Less: goodwill amortisation	
(41,250 + 70,000) (W3)	(111,250)
	334,100

Note that the group share of post-acquisition reserves is calculated for each separate acquisition.

(W6) **Revaluation reserve**	$m
25% × 40,000 – 10,000 (W2)	7,500

Note that this arises as there has been a remeasurement of the fair value of land at the date of the second purchase of shares.

4 Chapter summary

Complex Groups:
where a subsidiary of a parent entity owns all or part of a shareholding, which makes another entity also a subsidiary of the parent entity

Vertical groups:
where a subsidiary of the parent company holds shares in a further company such that control is achieved:

- consolidate all companies from date P achieved control
- use effective group interest in subsidiary for goodwill, reserves and non-controlling interest calculatons

Mixed (D-shaped) groups:
where the parent entity has a direct controlling interest in at least one subsidiary. In addition, the parent entity and the subsidiary together hold a controlling interest in a further entity:

- consolidate all companies
- use effective group interest in subsidiary for goodwill, reserves and non-controlling interest calculations
- two elements to cost of subsidiary in goodwill calculation

Test your understanding answers

Consolidated statement of financial position as at 31 December 20X7

	$
Sundry net assets (280,000 + 133,000 + 100,000)	513,000

Equity and liabilities

	$
Equity share capital	100,000
Retained earnings (W5)	39,938
NCI (W4)	48,062
Liabilities (200,000 + 100,000 + 25,000)	325,000
	513,000

(W1) **Group structure**

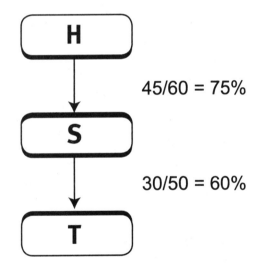

H

45/60 = 75%

S

30/50 = 60%

T

Consolidation	%	
S: Group share	75%	
NCI	25%	
T: Group share 75% of 60%	45%	
NCI	55%	(40% directly plus (25% × 60% =) 15% indirectly)

(W2) Net assets

	S		T	
	At acq'n	At rep date	At acq'n	At rep date
	$	$	$	$
Equity capital	60,000	60,000	50,000	50,000
Retained earnings	10,000	28,000	8,000	25,000
	70,000	88,000	58,000	75,000

(W3) Goodwill

	S	T
	$	$
Consideration paid	65,000	55,000
FV of NCI	20,000	50,000
Indirect Holding Adjustment (25% × $55,000)		(13,750)
	85,000	91,250
FV of NA at acquisition	(70,000)	(58,000)
Goodwill at acquisition	15,000	33,250
Less: allocation of impairment based upon shareholdings		
Group share (75%:45%)	(11,250)	(14,962)
NCI share (25%:55%)	(3,750)	(18,288)
Goodwill at reporting date	Nil	Nil

(W4) Non-controlling interest

	$
S – FV at date of acquisition	20,000
S – NCI share of post-acq'n retained earnings (25% × 18,000)	4,500
T – FV at date of acquisition	50,000
T – NCI share of post-acq'n retained earnings (55% × 17,000)	9,350
Indirect Holding Adjustment (25% × 55,000)	(13,750)
	70,100
Less NCI share of goodwill impairment re S & T (3,750 + 18,288) (W3)	(22,038)
Total for CSFP	48,062

(W5) Consolidated retained earnings

	$
Retained earnings of H	45,000
Group share of post-acquisition retained earnings or change in net assets	
S (75% × 18,000)	13,500
T (45% × 17,000)	7,650
Goodwill impaired (11,250 + 14,962) (W3)	(26,212)
	39,938

Consolidated statement of financial position as at 30 June 20X6

	$
Goodwill (7,000 + 2,500 (W3))	9,500
Sundry assets (350,000 + 200,000 + 120,000)	670,000
	679,500

Equity and liabilities	$
Equity share capital	100,000
Retained earnings (W5)	235,800
Non-controlling interest (W4)	53,700
Liabilities (150,000 + 100,000 + 40,000)	290,000
	679,500

(W1) Group structure

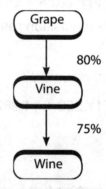

Consolidation		%
Vine	Group share	80%
	NCI	20%
Wine	Group share 80% of 75%	60%
	NCI	40%
	(25% directly plus (20% × 75% =) 15% indirectly)	

(W2) Net assets

	Vine		Wine	
	At acq'n	At reporting date	At acq'n	At reporting date
	$	$	$	$
Equity capital	50,000	50,000	10,000	10,000
Retained earnings	80,000	110,000	67,000	70,000
	130,000	160,000	77,000	80,000

The acquisition date for both entities is the date they joined the Grape group, i.e. 1 July 20X5.

(W3) Goodwill – full basis

	Vine	Wine
	$	$
Consideration paid	110,000	60,000
FV of NCI	27,000	31,500
Indirect holding adjustment (20% × $60,000)		(12,000)
	137,000	79,500
FV of net assets at acquisition (W2)	(130,000)	(77,000)
Goodwill – full basis	7,000	2,500

(W4) Non-controlling interest

	$
V – FV of NCI at date of acquisition	27,000
V – NCI share of post acq'n retained earnings (20% × 30,000)	6,000
W – FV of NCI at date of acquisition	31,500
W – NCI share of post acq'n retained earnings (40% × 3,000)	1,200
Indirect Holding Adjustment (20% × 60,000)	(12,000)
	53,700

(W5) **Consolidated retained earnings**

	$
Retained earnings of Grape	210,000
Group share of post-acquisition retained earnings	
V (80% × $30,000)	24,000
W (60% × $3,000)	1,800
	————
	235,800
	————

Test your understanding 3 – T, S & R

T consolidated statement of financial position as at 31 December 20X4

	$
Intangible fixed assets: goodwill (17,000 + 28,000(W3))	45,000
Non-current assets (140,000 + 61,000 + 170,000)	371,000
Current assets (20,000 + 20,000 + 15,000)	55,000
	————
	471,000
	————

	$
Equity share capital	200,000
Group retained earnings (W5)	171,600
	————
	371,600
Non-controlling (W4)	78,400
Liabilities (10,000 + 6,000 + 5,000)	21,000
	————
	471,000
	————

(W1) Group structure

T has a controlling interest in both S and R as follows:

Interest in S			**Interest in R**		
T	80%	T – direct		40%	
		T – indirect (80% × 35%)		28%	68%
NCI	20%	NCI			32%
	_____				_____
	100%				100%
	_____				_____

(W2) Net assets of S and R

	S		**R**	
	At acq'n	**At rep date**	**At acq'n**	**At rep date**
	$	$	$	$
Equity share capital	80,000	80,000	100,000	100,000
Retained earnings	50,000	60,000	60,000	80,000
	_____	_____	_____	_____
	130,000	140,000	160,000	180,000
	_____	_____	_____	_____

T's acquisition date for both entities is 1 January 20X4.

(W3) Goodwill – S Fair value (full goodwill) method

	$
Consideration paid	120,000
FV of NCI	27,000
	_____
	147,000
FV of net assets at acquisition (W2)	(130,000)
	_____
Total Goodwill	17,000
	_____

Goodwill – R

	$
Direct purchase consideration	80,000
Indirect purchase consideration (80% × 65,000)	52,000
Fair value of NCI at acquisition	56,000
	188,000
FV of net assets at acquisition (W2)	(160,000)
Full goodwill	28,000

(W4) Non-controlling interest

	$
S – FV of NCI at acquisition	27,000
S – 20% × (140,000 – 130,000) (W2)	2,000
Less NCI share of S cost of investment in R (20% × 65,000)	(13,000)
R – FV of NCI at acquisition	56,000
R – 32% × (180,000 – 160,000) (W2)	6,400
Total NCI to SOFP	78,400

(W5) Group retained earnings

	$
T	150,000
S 80% × (140,000 – 130,000) (W2)	8,000
R 68% × (180,000 – 160,000) (W2)	13,600
	171,600

KAPLAN PUBLISHING

Change in a group structure

Chapter learning objectives

Upon completion of this chapter you will be able to:

- prepare group financial statements where activities have been acquired, discontinued or have been disposed of in the period

- discuss and apply the treatment of a subsidiary that has been acquired exclusively with a view to subsequent disposal

- discuss and apply the treatment for transactions between equity holders where either additional shares have been purchased, or shares have been disposed of, without any change in control.

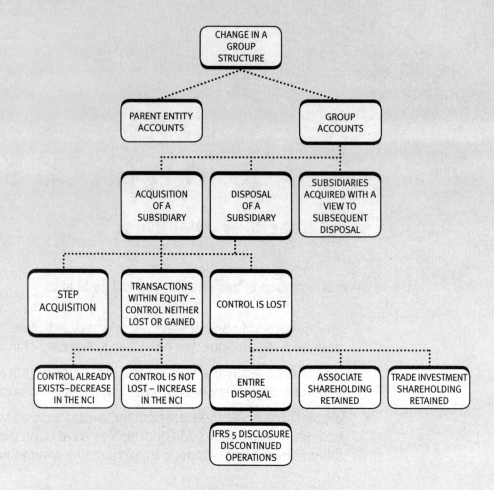

1 Acquisition of a subsidiary

Remember that a parent entity acquires control of a subsidiary from the date that it obtains a majority shareholding. If this happens mid-year, then it will be necessary to pro-rata the results of the subsidiary for the year to identify the net assets at the date of acquisition.

Illustration 1 – Tudor - mid-year acquisition of a subsidiary

On 1 July 2004 Tudor purchased 1,600,000 of 2,000,000 equity shares of $1 each in Windsor for $10,280,000. On the same date it also acquired 1,000,000 of Windsor's 10% loan notes. At the date of acquisition the retained earnings of Windsor were $6,150,000. The summarised draft statement of profit or loss and other comprehensive income for each entity for the year ended 31 March 2005 was as follows.

	Tudor	Windsor
	$000	$000
Revenue	60,000	24,000
Cost of sales	(42,000)	(20,000)
Gross profit	18,000	4,000
Distribution costs	(2,500)	(50)
Administration expenses	(3,500)	(150)
Profit from operations	12,000	3,800
Interest received/(paid)	75	(200)
Profit before tax	12,075	3,600
Tax	(3,000)	(600)
Profit for the year	9,075	3,000
Retained earnings b'fwd	16,525	5,400

There were no items of other comprehensive income in the year.

The following information is relevant:

(1) The fair values of Windsor's assets at the date of acquisition were mostly equal to their book values with the exception of plant, which was stated in the books at $2,000,000 but had a fair value of $5,200,000. The remaining useful life of the plant in question was four years at the date of acquisition. Depreciation is charged to cost of sales and is time apportioned on a monthly basis.

(2) During the post-acquisition period Tudor sold Windsor some goods for $12 million. The goods had originally cost $9 million. During the remaining months of the year Windsor sold $10 million (at cost to Windsor) of these goods to third parties for $13 million.

(3) Revenues and expenses should be deemed to accrue evenly throughout the year.

(4) Tudor has a policy of valuing non-controlling interests using the full goodwill method. The fair value of non-controlling interest at the date of acquisition was $2,520,000.

(5) The fair value of goodwill was impaired by $300,000 at the reporting date.

Required:

Prepare a consolidated statement of profit or loss for Tudor group for the year to 31 March 2005.

Solution Tudor

Tudor group statement of profit or loss for the year ended 31 March 2005:

	Tudor	Windsor (9/12)	Adjusts	Group SOCI
	$000	$000		$000
Revenue	60,000	18,000	(12,000)	66,000
Cost of sales	(42,000)	(15,000)	12,000	
URPS (W4)	(500)			(46,100)
FVA adjust dep'n (W2)		(600)		
Gross profit				19.900
Distribution costs	(2,500)	(38)		(2,538)
Administration expenses	(3,500)	(112)		
Goodwill impairment (W3)			(300)	(3,912)
Profit from operations				13,450
Interest received	75		(75)	–
Interest paid		(150)	75	(75)
Profit before tax				13,375
Tax	(3,000)	(450)		(3,450)
Profit after tax for the year		1,650		9,925
NCI – take 20% of 1,650		330		
Less: NCI goodwill impairment (300 × 20%)		(60)		
				270
Group share of profit after tax – bal fig				9,655
				9,925

There were no items of other comprehensive income in the year.

(W1) Group structure – Tudor owns 80% of Windsor

- the acquisition took place three months into the year

- nine months is post-acquisition

(W2) Net assets

	Acq'n date	Rep date
	$000	$000
Equity capital	2,000	2,000
Retained earnings	6,150	8,400
	8,150	10,400
FVA – PPE	3,200	3,200
FVA – dep'n adjust 3,200/48 × 9		(600)
	11,350	13,000

(W3) Goodwill

	Windsor
	$000
Cost of investment	10,280
FV of NCI at acquisition	2,520
	12,800
FV of net assets at acquisition (W2)	(11,350)
Total goodwill at acquisition	1,450
Impaired during year	(300)
Unimpaired goodwill	1,150

(W4) URPS of parent company

$2,000 × (33.33/133.33 = $500)

2 Step acquisitions

Step acquisitions

- A step acquisition occurs when the parent (investing) entity acquires control over the subsidiary (investeee) in stages. This is achieved by buying blocks of shares at different times.

- Amendments to IFRS 3 and IAS 27 mean that acquisition accounting (accounting for recognition of goodwill and non-controlling interests) is only applied at the date when control is achieved.

- Any pre-existing equity interest in an entity is accounted for according to:

  - IFRS 9 in the case of simple investments

  - IAS 28 in the case of associates and joint ventures

  - IFRS 11 in the case of joint arrangements other than joint ventures

- At the date when equity interest is increased and control achieved:

  (1) re-measure the previously held equity interest to fair value

  (2) recognise any resulting gain or loss in profit or loss for the year

  (3) calculate goodwill and non-controlling interest on either a partial (i.e. proportionate) or full (i.e. fair value) basis in accordance with IFRS 3 Revised. The cost of acquiring control will be the fair value of the previously held equity interest plus the cost of the most recent purchase of shares at acquisition date.

- If there has been re-measurement of any previously held equity interest that was recognised in other comprehensive income, any changes in value recognised in earlier years are now reclassified from equity to profit or loss.

- The situation of a further purchase of shares in a subsidiary after control has been acquired (for example taking the group interest from 60% to 75%) is regarded as a transaction between equity holders; goodwill is not recalculated. This situation is dealt with separately within this chapter.

KAPLAN PUBLISHING

Illustration 2 – Ayre and Byrne

Ayre holds a 10% investment in Byrne at $24,000 in accordance with IFRS 9. On 1 June 20X7, it acquires a further 50% of Byrne's equity shares at a cost of $160,000.

On this date fair values are as follows:

- Byrne's net assets – $200,000
- The non-controlling interest – $100,000
- The 10% investment – $26,000

Note: the non-controlling interest is to be valued using the full goodwill method.

Required:

How do you calculate the goodwill arising in Byrne?

Solution Ayre and Byrne

(W1) Group Structure

Ayre

60% (10% + 50%)

Byrne

Note – due to step acquisition – revalue the investment – take gain or loss to profit or loss for the year – i.e. an increase in carrying value from $24,000 to $26,000.

Dr Investment	2,000
Cr Profit on remeasurement	2,000

(W2) Net assets

	At date of acquisition 1 June 20X7
Net assets	200,000

(W3) Goodwill – fair value (full goodwill) method

	$
Purchase consideration (26,000 + 160,000)	186,000
FV of NCI at acquisition date	100,000
	286,000
Total Goodwill	**86,000**

Test your understanding 1 – Major and Tom

The statements of financial position of two entities, Major and Tom as at 31 December 20X6 are as follows:

	Major $000	Tom $000
Investment	160	
Sundry assets	350	250
	510	250
Equity share capital	200	100
Retained earnings	250	122
Liabilities	60	28
	510	250

> Major acquired 40% of Tom on 31 December 20X1 for $90,000. At this time the retained earnings of Tom stood at $76,000. A further 20% of shares in Tom was acquired by Major three years later for $70,000. On this date, the fair value of the existing holding in Tom was $105,000. Tom's retained earnings were $100,000 on the second acquisition date, at which date the fair value of the non-controlling interest was $90,000. It is group policy to value the non-controlling interest on a full fair value basis.
>
> **Required:**
>
> **Prepare the consolidated statement of financial position for the Major group as at 31 December 20X6.**

3 Disposal scenarios

During the year, one entity may sell some or all of its shares in another entity.

Possible situations include:

(1) the disposal of all the shares held in the subsidiary

(2) the disposal of part of the shareholding, leaving a residual holding after the sale, which is regarded as an associate

(3) the disposal of part of the shareholding, leaving a residual holding after the sale, which is regarded as a trade investment

(4) the disposal of part of the shareholding, leaving a controlling interest after the sale

4 Investing entity's accounts

Gain to investing entity

In all of the above scenarios, the gain on disposal in the investing entity's accounts is calculated as follows:

	$
Sales proceeds	X
Carrying amount (usually cost) of shares sold	(X)
	X
Tax – amount or rate given in question	(X)
Net gain to parent	X

The gain would often be reported as an exceptional item; if so, it must be disclosed separately on the face of the parent's statement of profit or loss for the year in arriving at profit before tax.

Tax on gain on disposal

The tax arising as a result of the disposal is always calculated based on the gain in the investing entity's accounts, as identified above.

The tax calculated forms part of the investing (parent) entity's total tax charge. As such this additional tax forms part of the group tax charge.

 ## 5 Group accounts

In the group accounts the accounting for the sale of shares in a subsidiary will depend on whether or not the transaction causes control to be lost, or whether control is still retained following the disposal.

Where control is lost, there will be a gain or loss to the group which must be included in the group statement of profit or loss for the year. Additionally, there will be derecognition of the assets and liabilities of the subsidiary disposed of, together with elimination of goodwill and non-controlling interest from the group accounts. The income statement of the subsidiary will be consolidated up to the date of disposal.

Where control is of the subsidiary is retained, there is no gain or loss to be recorded in the group accounts. Instead, the transaction is regarded as one between equity holders, with the end result being an increase in non-controlling interest. The group continues to recognise the goodwill, assets and liabilities of the subsidiary at the year end, and consolidates the statement of profit or loss and other comprehensive income of the subsidiary for the year.

Accounting for a disposal where control is lost

- Where control **is lost** (i.e. the subsidiary is completely disposed of or becomes an associate or investment), the parent:
  - Recognises
    - the consideration received
    - any investment retained in the former subsidiary at fair value on the date of disposal

- Derecognises
  - the assets and liabilities of the subsidiary at the date of disposal
  - unimpaired goodwill in the subsidiary
  - the non-controlling interest at the date of disposal (including any components of other comprehensive income attributable to them)
  - Any difference between these amounts is recognised as an exceptional gain or loss on disposal in the group accounts.
  - In the group income statement, it will also be necessary to pro-rata the results of the subsidiary for the year into pre-disposal for consolidation, and post-disposal for accounting as an associate or simple investment as appropriate.

Where control of a subsidiary has been lost, the following template should be used for the calculation of the gain or loss on disposal:

		$m
Disposal proceeds		X
FV of retained interest		X
		–––
		X
Less interest in subsidiary disposed of:		
Net assets of subsidiary at disposal date	X	
Unimpaired goodwill at disposal date	X	
Less: carrying value of NCI at disposal date	(X)	
	–––	
		(X)
		–––
Pre-tax gain/loss to the group		X
		–––

Presentation in the group statement of profit or loss when control is lost:

Exceptional Gain

The gain to the group would often be reported as an exceptional item, i.e. presented as an exceptional item on the face of the statement of profit or loss after operating profit.

There are two ways of presenting the results of the disposed subsidiary:

(i) **Time-apportionment line-by-line**

In the group income statement, where the sale of the subsidiary has occurred during the year, basic consolidation principles will only allow the income and expenses of the subsidiary to be consolidated up to the date of disposal. The traditional way is to time apportion each line of the disposed subsidiary's results in the same way that a subsidiary's results that had been acquired part way through the year would be consolidated.

(ii) **Time-apportioned and a discontinued operation**

If however the subsidiary that has been disposed qualifies as a discontinued operation in accordance with "IFRS 5 Accounting for Non-current Assets held for sale and discontinued operations", then the pre-disposal results of the subsidiary are aggregated and presented in a single line on the face of the statement of profit or loss immediately after profit after tax from continuing operations.

A discontinued operation is a component of an entity that either has been disposed of or is classified as held for sale, and:

- represents a separate major line of business or geographical area of operations,

- is part of a single co-ordinated plan to dispose of a separate major line of business or geographical area of operations, or

- is a subsidiary acquired exclusively with a view to resale and the disposal involves loss of control.

Associate time-apportioned

Further if the disposal means control is lost but it leaves a residual interest that gives that the parent significant influence, this will mean that in the group statement of profit or loss there will be an associate to account for, for example if a parent sells half of its 80% holding to leave it owning a 40% associate. Associates are accounted for using equity accounting and as the associate relationship will only be relevant from the date of disposal it will be time apportioned in the group statement of profit or loss.

6 Group accounts – entire disposal

Entire disposal

Illustration 3 – Rock – entire disposal

Rock has held a 70% investment in Dog for two years. Rock is disposing of this investment. Goodwill has been calculated using the full goodwill method. No goodwill has been impaired. Details are:

	$
Cost of investment	2,000
Dog – Fair value of net assets at acquisition	1,900
Dog – Fair value of the non-controlling interest at acquisition	800
Sales proceeds	3,000
Dog – Net assets at disposal	2,400

Required:

Calculate the profit/loss on disposal.

(a) In Rock's individual accounts

(b) In the consolidated accounts

Rock is subject to tax at the rate of 25%.

Solution Rock

(a) **Gain to Rock plc**

	$
Sales proceeds	3,000
Cost of shares sold	(2,000)
Gain on disposal	1,000
Tax charge against Rock at 25%	250

(b) Consolidated accounts

	$	$
Sales proceeds		3000
Net assets at disposal	2,400	
Unimpaired goodwill (W1)	900	
Less: carrying value of NCI at disposal date:		
FV of NCI at acquisition	800	
NCI % of post-acq'n retained earnings:		
30% × (2,400 – 1,900)	150 (950)	
		(2,350)
Gain to group before tax		650
Tax charge on gain made by Rock (as above)		250

(W1) Goodwill

	$
Cost of investment	2,000
FV of NCI at acquisition	800
	2,800
FV of net assets at acquisition	(1,900)
Total Goodwill	900

Test your understanding 2 – Snooker

Snooker purchased 80% of the shares in Billiards for $100,000 when the net assets of Billiards had a fair value of $50,000. Goodwill was calculated using the proportion of net assets method amounting to $60,000 and has not suffered any impairment to date. Snooker has just disposed of its entire shareholding in Billiards for $300,000, when the net assets were stated at $110,000. Tax is payable by Snooker at 30% on any gain on disposal of shares.

KAPLAN PUBLISHING

Required:

- **Calculate the gain or loss arising to the parent entity on disposal of shares in Billiards.**

- **Calculate the gain or loss arising to the group on disposal of the controlling interest in Billiards.**

Test your understanding 3 – Padstow

Padstow purchased 80% of the shares in St Merryn four years ago for $100,000. On 30 June it sold all of these shares for $250,000. The net assets of St Merryn at acquisition were $69,000 and at disposal, $88,000. Fifty per cent of the goodwill arising on acquisition had been written off in an earlier year. The fair value of the non-controlling interest in St Merryn at the date of acquisition was $15,000. It is group policy to account for goodwill using the full goodwill method.

Tax is charged at 30%.

Required:

What profits/losses on disposal are reported in Padstow's statement of profit or loss and in the group statement of profit or loss?

IFRS 5 Discontinued operations

Where an entity has disposed of its entire holding in a subsidiary that represents a separate major line of business or geographical area of operations, that subsidiary will meet the IFRS 5 definition of a discontinued operation.

The Examiner may therefore require you to present the group accounts in accordance with this standard.

IFRS 5 is included within this text in the chapter dealing with non-current assets and inventories.

7 Group accounts disposal – subsidiary to associate

This situation is where the disposal results in the subsidiary becoming an associate, e.g. 90% holding is reduced to a 40% holding.

After the disposal the income, expenses, assets and liabilities of the ex-subsidiary can no longer be consolidated on a line by line basis; instead they must be accounted for under the equity method, with a single amount in the statement of profit or loss and other comprehensive income for the share of the post tax profits for the period after disposal and a single amount in the statement of financial position for the fair value of the investment retained plus the share of post-acquisition retained earnings.

Consolidated statement of profit or loss and other comprehensive income

- Pro rate the subsidiary's results up to the date of disposal and :
    - consolidate the results up to the date of disposal as a subsidiary
    - equity account for the results after the date of disposal as an associate

- Include the group gain or loss on disposal of subsidiary.

Consolidated statement of financial position

- Equity account by reference to the year-end holding, based upon the fair value of the associate holding at date of initial recognition plus group share of profit or loss of associate from date of recognition to reporting date.

Illustration 4 – Thomas and Percy

Thomas disposed of a 25% holding in Percy on 30 June 20X6 for $125,000. A 70% holding in Percy had been acquired five years prior to this. Thomas uses the full goodwill method in accordance with IFRS 3 revised. Goodwill was impaired and written off in full prior to the year of disposal. Details of Percy are as follows:

	$
Net assets at disposal date	340,000
Fair value of a 45% holding at 30 June 20X6	245,000

If the carrying value of NCI is $80,000 at the date of the share disposal, what gain on disposal is reported in the Thomas Group accounts for the year ended 31 December 20X6?

Ignore tax.

Solution Thomas and Percy

Thomas Group – answer

(W1) Group Structure

Thomas	70%	Thomas
	(25%)	
75%	———	45%
	45%	
Percy		Percy
Subsidiary		Associate
× 6/12		× 6/12

Gain or loss to the group on disposal

		$
Proceeds		125,000
FV of retained interest		245,000
		———
		370,000
Net assets recognised at disposal	340,000	
Less: NCI at disposal date	(80,000)	(260,000)
	———	———
Group gain on disposal		110,000
		———

OR

	$
Proceeds – 25% interest disposed	125,000
45% retained interest at fair value	245,000
30% NCI	80,000
	———
	450,000
100% Net assets at date of disposal	(340,000)
	———
GAIN ON DISPOSAL	110,000

Test your understanding 4 – Hague

Hague has held a 60% investment in Maude for several years, using the full goodwill method to value the non-controlling interest. Half of the goodwill has been impaired prior to the date of disposal of shares by Hague. Details are as follows:

	$000
Cost of investment	6,000
Maude – Fair value of net assets at acquisition	2,000
Maude – Fair value of a 40% investment at acquisition date	1,000
Maude – Net assets at disposal	3,000
Maude – FV of a 30% investment at disposal date	3,500

Required:

(a) **Assuming a full disposal of the holding and proceeds of $10 million, calculate the profit/loss arising:**

    (i)   **in Hague's individual accounts**

    (ii) **in the consolidated accounts.**

    Tax is 25%.

(b) **Assuming a disposal of half the holding and proceeds of $5 million:**

    (i)   **calculate the profit/loss arising in the consolidated accounts**

    (ii) **explain how the residual holding will be accounted for.**

    Ignore tax.

Test your understanding 5 – Kathmandu

The statements of profit or loss of Kathmandu and Nepal for the year ended 31 December 20X9 were as follows:

	Kathmandu group	Nepal
	$	$
Revenue	553,000	450,000
Operating costs	(450,000)	(400,000)
Operating profits	103,000	50,000
Dividends receivable	8,000	–
Profit before tax	111,000	50,000
Tax	(40,000)	(14,000)
Profit after tax	71,000	36,000
Retained earnings b/f	100,000	80,000
Profit after tax	71,000	36,000
Dividend paid	(25,000)	(10,000)
Retained earnings c/f	146,000	106,000

There were no items of other comprehensive income during the year.

Additional information

- The accounts of the Kathmandu group do not include the results of Nepal.

- On 1 January 20X5 Kathmandu acquired 70% of the shares of Nepal for $100,000 when the fair value of Nepal's net assets were $110,000. Nepal has equity capital of $50,000. At that date, the fair value of the non-controlling interest was $40,000.

- Nepal paid its 20X9 dividend in cash on 31 March 20X9.

- Goodwill is to be accounted for based upon the fair value of non-controlling interest. No goodwill has been impaired.

- Kathmandu has other subsidiaries participating in the same activities as Nepal, and therefore the disposal of Nepal shares does not represent a discontinued operation per IFRS 5.

Required:

(a) (i) Prepare the group statement of profit or loss for the year ended 31 December 20X9 for the Kathmandu group on the basis that Kathmandu plc sold its holding in Nepal on 1 July 20X9 for $200,000. This disposal is not yet recognised in any way in Kathmandu group's statement of profit or loss.

(ii) Compute the group retained earnings at 31 December 20X9.

(iii) Explain and illustrate how the results of Nepal are presented in the group statement of profit or loss in the event that Nepal represented a discontinued activity per IFRS 5.

Ignore tax on the disposal.

(b) (i) Prepare the group statement of profit or loss for the year ended 31 December 20X9 for the Kathmandu group on the basis that Kathmandu sold half of its holding in Nepal on 1 July 20X9 for $100,000 This disposal is not yet recognised in any way in Kathmandu group's statement of profit or loss. The residual holding of 35% has a fair value of $100,000 and leaves the Kathmandu group with significant influence.

(ii) Compute the group retained earnings at 31 December 20X9.

Ignore tax on the disposal.

8 Group accounts – Disposal with trade investment retained

This situation is where the subsidiary becomes a trade investment, e.g. 90% holding is reduced to a 10% holding.

Consolidated statement of profit or loss

- Pro rate the subsidiary's results up to the date of disposal and then:
  - consolidate the results up to the date of disposal
  - only include dividend income after the date of disposal.

- Include the group gain on part disposal.

Consolidated statement of financial position

- Recognise the residual holding retained as an investment, measured at fair value in accordance with IFRS 9.

9 Disposal where control is not lost (increase in NCI)

From the perspective of the group accounts, where there is a sale of shares but the parent still retains control then, in essence, this is an increase in the non-controlling interest.

For example if the parent holds 80% of the shares in a subsidiary and sells 5%, the relationship remains one of a parent and subsidiary and as such will remain consolidated in the group accounts in the normal way, but the NCI has risen from 20% to 25%. In effect, the NCI have bought an increased interest in the total carrying value of the subsidiary in the group accounts from the controlling group.

Where there is such an increase in the non-controlling interest:

- No gain or loss on disposal is calculated
- No adjustment is made to the carrying value of goodwill
- The difference between the proceeds received and change in the non-controlling interest is accounted for in shareholders' equity as follows:

	$
Cash proceeds received	X
NCI % increase × (NAs at date of change + unimpaired goodwill of sub)	(X)
Difference to equity (increase or decrease)	X

Note that the difference taken to equity could either be an increase or decrease, depending upon the detail of any given situation

No loss of control – Juno

Until 30 September 20X7, Juno held 90% of Hera. On that date it sold a 10% interest in the equity capital for $15,000. At the date of share disposal, the carrying value of net assets and goodwill of Juno were $100,000 and $20,000 respectively.

How should the disposal transaction be accounted for in the Juno Group accounts?

Solution Juno

	$
Cash proceeds	15,000
Increase in NCI: 10% × (100,000 + 20,000)	12,000
	——
Increase in equity	3,000
	——

There is no gain or loss to the group as there has been no loss of control. Note that, depending upon the terms of the share disposal, there could be either an increase or decrease in equity.

Disposal with no loss of control

In this situation, the subsidiary remains a subsidiary, albeit the shareholding is reduced, e.g. 90% holding is reduced to a 60% holding.

Consolidated statement of profit or loss and other comprehensive income

- Consolidate the subsidiary's results for the whole year.

- Calculate the non-controlling interest relating to the periods before and after the disposal separately and then add together:

- e.g. (X / 12 × profit × 10%) + (Y / 12 × profit × 40%)

Consolidated statement of financial position

- Consolidate as normal, with the non-controlling interest valued by reference to the year-end holding

- Take the difference between proceeds and the change in the NCI to shareholders' equity as previously discussed.

Test your understanding 6 – David and Goliath

David has owned 90% of Goliath for many years and is considering selling part of its holding, whilst retaining control of Goliath.
At the date of considering disposal of part of the shareholding in Goliath, the NCI has a carrying value of $7,200 and the net assets and goodwill have a carrying value of $70,000 and $20,000 respectively.

(i) David could sell 5% of the Goliath shares for $5,000 leaving it holding 85% and increasing the NCI to 15%, or

(ii) David could sell 25% of the Goliath shares for $20,000 leaving it holding 65% and increasing the NCI to 35%.

Required:

Calculate the difference arising that will be taken to equity for each situation

10 Subsidiaries acquired exclusively with a view to subsequent disposal

IFRS 5: non-current assets held for sale and discontinued operations

- A subsidiary acquired exclusively with a view to resale is not exempt from consolidation.

- But if it meets the criteria in IFRS 5:
  - it is presented in the financial statements as a disposal group classified as held for sale. This is achieved by amalgamating all its assets into one line item and all its liabilities into another
  - it is measured, both on acquisition and at subsequent reporting dates, at fair value less costs to sell. (IFRS 5 sets down a special rule for such subsidiaries, requiring the deduction of costs to sell. Normally, it requires acquired assets and liabilities to be measured at fair value).

- The criteria include the requirements that:
  - the subsidiary is available for immediate sale
  - it is likely to be disposed of within one year of the date of its acquisition.
  - the sale is highly probable.

- A newly acquired subsidiary which meets these held for sale criteria automatically meets the criteria for being presented as a discontinued operation.

Illustration: IFRS 5

David acquires Rose on 1 March 20X7. Rose is a holding entity with two wholly-owned subsidiaries, Mickey and Jackie. Jackie is acquired exclusively with a view to resale and meets the criteria for classification as held for sale. David's year-end is 30 September.

On 1 March 20X7 the following information is relevant:

- the identifiable liabilities of Jackie have a fair value of $40m
- the acquired assets of Jackie have a fair value of $180m
- the expected costs of selling Jackie are $5m.

On 30 September 20X7, the assets of Jackie have a fair value of $170m.

The liabilities have a fair value of $35m and the selling costs remain at $5m.

Discuss how Jackie will be treated in the David Group financial statements on acquisition and at 30 September 20X7.

Solution

On acquisition the assets and liabilities of Jackie are measured at fair value less costs to sell in accordance with IFRS 5's special rule.

	$m
Assets	180
Less selling costs	(5)
	175
Liabilities	(40)
Fair value less costs to sell	135

At the reporting date, the assets and liabilities of Jackie are remeasured to update the fair value less costs to sell.

	$m
Assets	170
Less selling costs	(5)
	165
Liabilities	(35)
Fair value less costs to sell	130

The fair value less costs to sell has decreased from $135m on 1 March to $130m on 30 September. This $5m reduction in fair value must be presented in the consolidated statement of profit or loss as part of the single line item entitled 'discontinued operations'. Also included in this line items is the post-tax profit or loss earned/incurred by Jackie in the March – September 20X7 period.

The assets and liabilities of Jackie must be disclosed separately on the face of the statement of financial position. Below the subtotal for the David group's current assets Jackie's assets will be presented as follows:

	$m
Non-current assets classified as held for sale	165

Below the subtotal for the David group's current liabilities Jackie's liabilities will be presented as follows:

	$m
Liabilities directly associated with non-current assets classified as held for sale	35

No other disclosure is required.

11 Further purchase by group after control obtained (decrease in NCI)

From the perspective of the group accounts where there is a purchase of more shares in a subsidiary then, in essence, this is not an acquisition – it is a decrease in the non-controlling interest.

For example if the parent holds 80% of the shares in a subsidiary and buys 5% more the relationship remains one of a parent and subsidiary and as such will be remain consolidated in the group accounts in the normal way, but the NCI has decreased from 20% to 15%.

Where there is such a decrease in the NCI:

- There is no change in the goodwill asset

- No gain or loss arises as this is a transaction within equity i.e. with the NCI

- A difference will arise that will be taken to equity and is determined in the following proforma. The difference taken to equity may be an increase or decrease, depending upon the detail of any given situation.

	$
Cash paid	X
Decrease in NCI (prop'n decrease in NCI × NCI at date of decrease)	X
	—
Difference to equity (increase or decrease)	X
	—

Test your understanding 7 – Gordon and Mandy

Gordon has owned 80% of Mandy for many years.

Gordon is considering acquiring more shares in Mandy, which will decrease the NCI. The NCI of Mandy currently has a carrying value of $20,000, with the net assets and goodwill having a value of $125,000 and $25,000 respectively.

Gordon is considering the following two scenarios:

(i)   Gordon could buy 20% of the Mandy shares leaving no NCI for $25,000, or

(ii) Gordon could buy 5% of the Mandy shares for $4,000 leaving a 15% NCI.

Required:

Calculate the difference arising that will be taken to equity for each situation

UK syllabus focus

The ACCA UK syllabus contains a requirement that UK variant candidates should be able to discuss and apply the key differences between UK GAAP and IFRS GAAP. As with other areas of group accounts, the accounting requirements of UK GAAP and IFRS GAAP are very similar in this area, but there are one or two differences.

You should approach questions using the approach of completing the five standard workings identified within chapter 1 as far as they are required. Normally a net assets working is required at the date of any disposal of shares (whether or not control has been lost), together with identification of any unamortised goodwill at that date. Normally, any change in share ownership by the parent company will result in an incremental addition or reduction in goodwill.

UK GAAP requires that, where there is a **partial disposal**, a gain or loss on that disposal should be calculated and included in profit or loss for the year. The gain or loss calculated must include a share of goodwill disposed of. This will apply whether or not there has been a loss of control of the subsidiary. Any residual holding of shares is not restated to fair value; it continues to be carried at cost.

In contrast, IFRS 10 distinguishes between disposals which result in either a loss of control or control continues to be exercised. If control has been lost, a gain or loss on disposal is calculated and any residual holding is remeasured to fair value. If control continues to be exercised, it is regarded as a transaction between equity holders (i.e. group and NCI) with an adjustment made within the statement of changes in equity; it is not a gain or loss situation.

UK GAAP requires that, where there is a **subsequent purchase of shares** in a subsidiary having gained control at an earlier date, there is an incremental calculation of additional goodwill arising on that transaction. IFRS 10 requires that goodwill is recognised initially at the date control is acquired and is not restated for the effect of any subsequent purchase of shares. In effect, IFRS 10 requires that any additional purchase of shares is regarded as a transaction between equity holders with an adjustment made within the statement of changes in equity.

UK GAAP Question 1

Parker purchased 80% of the shares in Tramp four years ago for $100,000. On 30 June it sold all of these shares for $250,000. The net assets of Tramp at acquisition were $69,000 and at disposal, $88,000. Half of the goodwill arising on acquisition had been amortised by the date of the share disposal.

Tax is charged at 30%.

Required:

What profits/losses on disposal are reported in Parker's income statement and in the group income statement?

UK GAAP Answer 1

(a) **Gain to Parker**

	$000
Sales proceeds	250
Cost of shares sold	(100)
Gain on disposal	150
Tax at 30%	(45)
Net gain on disposal	105

(b) **Consolidated accounts**

	$000
Sales proceeds	250.0
Share of net assets sold (88,000 × 80%)	(70.4)
Goodwill disposed of (W1)	(22.4)
Gain on disposal	157.2
Tax (per parent)	(45.0)
Net gain on disposal	112.2

(W1) Goodwill

	$000
Cost of investment	100.0
Group share of FV of net assets at acquisition (80% × 69)	(55.2)
	44.8
Impaired to extent of 50%	(22.4)
Unamortised goodwill at disposal date	22.4

Normally the parent entity profit is greater than the group profit, by the share of the post-acquisition retained earnings now disposed of. In this case the reverse is true, because the $22,400 amortisation of goodwill already recognised exceeds the $15,200 ((88,000 – 69,000) × 80%) share of post acquisition profits.

UK GAAP Question 2

Barker has held a 60% investment in Corbett for several years. Forty per cent of the goodwill arising on acquisition has been amortised. A disposal of the investment has taken place as follows:

	$000
Cost of investment	6,000
Corbett – Fair value of net assets at acquisition	2,000
Corbett – Net assets at disposal	3,000

Required:

(a) **Assuming a full disposal of the holding and proceeds of $10 million, calculate the profit/loss arising:**

    (i) **in Barker's individual accounts**

    (ii) **in the group accounts.**

    Tax is 25%.

(b) **Assuming a disposal of half the holding and proceeds of $5 million:**

    (i) **calculate the profit/loss arising in the group accounts**

    (ii) **explain how the residual holding will be accounted for.**

    Ignore tax.

UK GAAP Answer 2

(W1) Goodwill

	$000
Cost of investment	6,000
Less: (60% × 2,000)	1,200
	4,800
Amortised (40%)	(1,920)
Goodwill not yet amortised	2,880

Full disposal of shares

Gain in Barker's individual accounts

	$000
(a) (i) Sale proceeds	10,000
Less Cost of shares sold	(6,000)
Gain to parent	4,000
Tax at 25% × 4,000	(1,000)
	3,000

Full disposal of shares – gain in Barker's Group accounts

	$000
Sale proceeds	10,000
Less: group %age of net assets at disposal (60% × 3,000)	(1,800)
Less: goodwill not yet amortised	(2,880)
Gain before tax	5,320
Tax per part (a)(i)	(1,000)
	4,320

(b) (i) **Disposal of half of the holding to leave a residual shareholding:**

	$000
Disposal proceeds	5,000
Less: %age of net assets at disposal (30% × 3,000)	(900)
Less: goodwill not yet written off (30 / 60 × 2,880)	(1,440)
	2,660

(ii) After the date of disposal, the residual holding will be equity accounted, with amounts in the income statement for the share of the profit before tax and share of the tax charge for the year included in the group income statement. Initial recognition on the group statement of financial position will comprise the remaining cost of investment retained, plus remaining balance of goodwill not yet amortised or disposed of.

UK GAAP Question 3

The income statements for the year ended 31 December 20X9 are as follows:

	Kathmandu group	Doha
	$	$
Revenue	553,000	450,000
Operating costs	(450,000)	(400,000)
Operating profits	103,000	50,000
Dividends receivable	8,000	–
Profit before tax	111,000	50,000
Tax	(40,000)	(14,000)
Profit after tax	71,000	36,000
Retained earnings b/f	100,000	80,000
Profit after tax	71,000	36,000
Dividend paid	(25,000)	(10,000)
Retained earnings c/f	146,000	106,000

Additional information

- The accounts of the Kathmandu group do not include the results of Doha.

- On 1 January 20X5 Kathmandu acquired 70% of the equity of Doha for $100,000 when the fair value of Doha's net assets were $120,000. Doha has equity share capital of $50,000.

- Doha paid its 20X9 dividend in cash on 31 March 20X9.

- Goodwill has an indefinite life, and has suffered no impairment to date.

- Kathmandu has other subsidiaries participating in the same activities as Doha, and therefore the disposal of Doha shares does not represent a discontinued operation per FRED 32.

Required:

(a) (i) Prepare the consolidated income statement for the year ended 31 December 20X9 for the Kathmandu group on the basis that Kathmandu plc sold its holding in Doha on 1 July 20X9 for $200,000. This disposal is not yet recognised in any way in Kathmandu group's profit and loss account.

(ii) Compute the group retained earnings at 31 December 20X9.

(iii) Explain and illustrate how the results of Doha are presented in the group income statement in the event that Doha represented a discontinued activity per FRED 32 (equivalent of IFRS 5).

Ignore tax on the disposal.

(b) (i) Prepare the group income statement for the year ended 31 December 20X9 for the Kathmandu group on the basis that Kathmandu sold half of its holding in Doha on 1 July 20X9 for $200,000 This disposal is not yet recognised in any way in Kathmandu group's income statement. The residual holding of 35% leaves the Kathmandu group with significant influence.

(ii) Compute the group retained earnings at 31 December 20X9.

Ignore tax on the disposal.

UK GAAP Answer 3

(a) (i) Consolidated income statement – full disposal

	Kathmandu group	Doha	Group
	$		$
Revenue	553,000	(6/12 × 450,000)	778,000
Operating costs	450,000	(6/12 × 400,000)	(650,000)
			─────────
Operating profit			128,000
Dividend	8,000 less inter-co (70% × 10,000)		1,000
Profit on disposal (W3)			87,400
			─────────
Profit before tax			216,400
Tax	40,000	(6/12 × 14,000)	(47,000)
			─────────
Profit after tax			169,400
			─────────
Attributable to:			
Equity holders of Kathmandu (β)			164,000
NCI		(30% × 36,000 × 6/12)	5,400
			─────────
			169,400
			─────────

(ii) Group retained earnings at 31 December 20X9 – full disposal

	$
Brought forward:	
Kathmandu	100,000
Group % of Doha's post acquisition retained earnings b/f	
(70% × (130,000 (W1) – 120,000) (per Q))	7,000
	107,000
Profit for year per consolidated income statement	164,000
Less Dividend paid	(25,000)
Retained earnings carried forward	246,000

(iii) Treatment of Doha as a discontinued activity per FRED 32 (equivalent to IFRS 5)

	Kathmandu group	Group
	$	$
Revenue	553,000	553,000
Operating costs	450,000	(450,000)
Operating profit		103,000
Dividend	8,000 less inter-co (70% × 10,000)	1,000
Profit on disposal (W3)		87,400
Profit before tax		191,400
Tax	40,000	(40,000)
Profit after tax – continuing operations		151,400
Discontinued operations ($36,000 × 6/12)		18,000
		169,400
Attributable to:		
Equity holders of Kathmandu (β)		164,000
NCI		5,400
		169,400

Notice that the post-tax results of the subsidiary up to the date of disposal are presented as a one-line entry in the group income statement. There is no line-by-line consolidation of results when this method of presentation is adopted.

(b) (i) **group profit and loss account – part disposal with residual interest**

	Kathmandu group	Doha	Group
	$		$
Revenue	553,000	(6 / 12 × 450,000)	778,000
Operating costs	450,000	(6 / 12 × 400,000)	(650,000)
Operating profit			128,000
Dividend	8,000 less inter-co (70% × 10,000)		1,000
Income from associate	(35% × 50,000 × 6 / 12)		8,750
Profit on disposal (W3)			143,700
Profit before tax			281,450
Tax	40,000	(6 / 12 × 14,000)	(47,000)
– re associate		(35% x 14,000 × 6/12)	(2,450)
Profit after tax			232,000
Attributable to:			
Kathmandu (β)			226,600
NCI		(30% × 36,000 × 6/12)	5,400
			232,000

(ii) **Group retained earnings at 31 December 20X9 – part disposal**

	$
Brought forward	
Kathmandu	100,000
Group % of Doha's post acquisition retained earnings b/f	
(70% × (130,000 (W1) – 120,000) (per Q))	7,000
	———
	107,000
Group income per consolidated income statement	226,600
Less Dividend paid	(25,000)
	———
	308,600
	———

Workings

(W1) Net assets – Doha

	Net assets at disposal	Net assets b/f
	$	$
Equity share capital	50,000	50,000
Retained earnings b/f	80,000	80,000
Retained earnings for year: 6/12 × 36,000	18,000	
Less Dividend	(10,000)	–
	———	———
	138,000	130,000
	———	———

(W2) Goodwill

Cost to parent	100,000
Group share of FV of net assets at date of acquisition (70% × 120,000)	(84,000)
	———
Unimpaired goodwill	16,000
	———

(W3) **Profit on disposal**

Full disposal (a)(i)

	$
Proceeds	200,000
Less: Net assets disposed of (70% × 138,000) (W1)	(96,600)
Less: Goodwill disposed of (70/70 × 16,000) (W1)	(16,000)
Profit on disposal	87,400

Part disposal (b)(i)		$
Proceeds		200,000
Less: net assets disposed of:	(35% × 138,000) (W1)	(48,300)
Less: goodwill disposed of:	(35/70 × 16,000) (W2)	(8,000)
		143,700

UK GAAP Question 4

H acquired investments as follows:

Entity	Date	Cost	Percentage acquired	Issued equity capital	Reserves at acq'n	Goodwill on acq'n
		$000		$000	$000	$000
S	20X0	110,000	80%	100,000	12,000	20,400
W	20X5	60,000	60%	70,000	10,000	12,000

H sold 5% of the issued shares in W on 13 March 20X9 for $12 million. Goodwill on acquisition has been fully amortised.

W's reserves at 1 January 20X9 were $25 million.

Summarised income statements for the year ended 31 December 20X9 were as follows:

	H	S	W
	$000	$000	$000
Profit before tax	100,000	80,000	30,000
Tax	(35,000)	(28,000)	(10,500)
Profit after tax	65,000	52,000	19,500

Required:

Prepare the income statement for the H group for the year ended 31 December 20X9.

Ignore tax.

UK GAAP Answer 4

Calculation of group gain or loss on disposal of shares in W:

Note that, H still retains control of W after the disposal. Therefore, consolidate the results of W for the year and time-apportion the calculation of NCI share of profit in W for the year.

(W1) Group gain or loss on disposal:

		$000
Disposal proceeds		12,000
Net assets of S at date of disposal:		
Issued share capital	70,000	
Reserves brought forward	25,000	
Profit for year to date of disposal: (3/12 × $19,500)	4,875	
Apply %age of share capital disposed of – 5%	99,875	(4,994)
Group gain on disposal before tax		7,006

H Group

Group income statement for the year ended 31 December 20X9:

		$000
Group gain or loss on disposal:		
Group operating profit	(100,000 + 80,000 + 30,000)	210,000
Profit on disposal of continuing operations (W1)		7,006
Profit before tax		217,006
Tax	(35,000 + 28,000 + 10,500)	(73,500)
Profit after tax for the year on continuing operations		143,506
Amount attributable to NCI:		
S:	(20% × 52,000)	10,400
W:	(3/12 × 40% × 19,500)	1,950
W:	(9/12 × 45% × 19,500)	6,581
		18,931
Amount attributable to group (bal fog)		124,575
		143,506

12 Chapter summary

```
                        ┌──────────────────────┐
                        │      DISPOSALS       │
                        └──────────────────────┘
```

Parent entity accounts
Gain:

Proceeds	X
Cost	(X)
Tax	(X)
	X

Group accounts gain
- No gain or loss where no loss of control
- If control is lost, calculate gain as:

proceeds		X
FV of any interest retained		X
Net assets of sub at disposal	X	
Goodwill	X	
NCI at disposal	(X)	
		(X)
		(X)

Step Acquisitions:
Parent acquires control over subsidiary in stages.

At date of acquiring control, revalue existing equity holding to FV and recognise gain or loss in equity. Goodwill calculated as normal at date control is acquired

Acquisition of further shares after control is acquired are accounted for in equity. Goodwill is not remeasured.

Whole shareholding disposal of SCI/IS: consolidate to disposal and show group gain
B/S: subsidiary's net assets not included

IFRSs
Disclosure discontinued operations

No loss of control
SCI/IS: consolidate for full year, calculate NCI pre and post disposal
SFP: consolidate as normal with NCI based on year end holding, account for gain or loss to NCI in equity

Associate shareholding retained
SCI/IS: consolidate to date of disposal, then equity account, show gain
SFP: equity account at year end based on FV of associate shareholding at disposal

Trade investment shareholding retained
SCI/IS: consolidate to date of disposal, then include dividend income, show gain
SFP: Record retained investment at fair value at disposal date

Subsidiaries acquired with a view to subsequent disposal must consolidate present as disposal group; measure at lower of CV and FV - selling costs

KAPLAN PUBLISHING

Test your understanding answers

Test your understanding 1 – Major and Tom

Consolidated statement of financial position for Major as at 31 December 20X6

	$
Goodwill (W3)	65,000
Sundry assets (350,000 + 250,000)	600,000
	———
	665,000
	———

	$
Equity and liabilities	
Equity share capital	200,000
Retained earnings (W5)	278,200
Non-controlling interest (W4)	98,800
Liabilities (60,000 + 28,000)	88,000
	———
	665,000
	———

(W1) Group structure

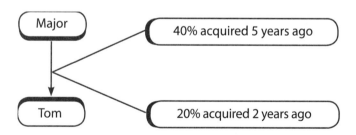

Therefore, Tom becomes a subsidiary of Major from December 20X4.

The investment will need to be revalued

Dr Investment 15,000
(105,000 – 90,000)
Cr Profit   15,000

(W2) Net assets

	At Acquisition 20X4	At Reporting date
	$	$
Share capital	100,000	100,000
Retained earnings	100,000	122,000
	200,000	222,000

(W3) Goodwill

	$
Consideration paid by parent	175,000
(105,000 + 70,000)	
FV of NCI (given)	90,000
	265,000
Less: FV of NA at acquisition (W2)	(200,000)
	65,000

(W4) Non-controlling interest

	$
FV at acquisition date	90,000
NCI % of post-acquisition retained earnings	
(40% × $22,000)	8,800
	98,800

(W5) Group Retained earnings

	$
Major	250,000
Gain on remeasurement	15,000
Tom 60% × (222,000 – 200,000)	13,200
	278,200

Test your understanding 2 – Snooker

(a) Gain to Snooker

	$000
Sales proceeds	300
Cost of shares sold	(100)
	____
Gain on disposal	200
Tax at 30%	(60)
	____
Net gain on disposal	140
	____

(b) Consolidated accounts

		$000
Proceeds		300
FV of retained interest		NIL
		____
		300
Less interest in subsidiary disposed of:		
Net assets of subsidiary at disposal date	110	
Unimpaired goodwill at disposal date	60	
Less: NCI carrying value at disposal date (W1)	(22)	
	____	
		(148)
		____
		152
		____
Tax on gain as per Snooker (part (a))		(60)
		____

(W1) NCI at disposal date

		$000
NCI % of net assets at acquisition	(20% × 50)	10
NCI % of increase in net assets to disposal date	(20% × (110 – 50))	12
		____
		22
		____

Test your understanding 3 – Padstow

(a) Gain to Padstow

	$000
Sales proceeds	250
Cost of shares sold	(100)
Gain on disposal	150
Tax at 30%	(45)
Net gain on disposal	105

(b) Consolidated accounts

		$000
Sales proceeds		
Carrying value of subsidiary at disposal date:		
Net assets at disposal date – given	88.0	
Unimpaired goodwill at disposal date (W1)	23.0	
	111.0	
Less: CV of NCI at disposal (W2)	(14.2)	
		(96.8)
Pre-tax gain on disposal for group accounts		153.2
Tax charge on parent for group accounts (per parent in part (a)		(45.0)

(W1) Goodwill

	$000
Cost of investment	100.0
FV of NCI at acquisition	15.0
	115.0
FV of net assets at acquisition	(69.0
Full goodwill at acquisition	46.0

Goodwill impaired to extent of 50%

Group share – 80%	(18.4)	
NCI share – 20%	(4.6)	(23.0)
Unimpaired goodwill at disposal date		23.0

(W2) NCI at disposal date

	$000
FV at date of acquisition	15.0
NCI % of post-acq'n retained earnings (20% × (88.0 – 69.0))	3.8
NCI % of impairment (W1)	(4.6)
	14.2

Normally the parent entity profit is greater than the group profit, by the share of the post-acquisition retained earnings now disposed of. In this case the reverse is true, because the $23,000 impairment loss already recognised exceeds the $15,200 ((88,000 – 69,000) × 80%) share of post acquisition retained earnings.

Test your understanding 4 – Hague

(W1) **Goodwill**

	$000
Cost of investment	6,000
FV of the NCI at date of acquisition	1,000
	7,000
FV of NA at acquisition (given)	(2,000)
Total goodwill	5,000
Impaired (50%)	(2,500)
Unimpaired goodwill	2,500

(W2) **NCI at disposal date**

	$000
FV at date of acquisition	1,000
NCI share of post-acquisition retained earnings (40% × (3,000 – 2,000))	400
Less: NCI share of goodwill impairment (40% × 2500)	(1,000)
	400

Full disposal of shares

Gain in Hague's individual accounts

	$000
(a) (i) Sale proceeds	10,000
Less Cost of shares sold	(6,000)
Gain to parent	4,000
Tax at 25% × 4,000	(1,000)
	3,000

Full disposal of shares – gain in Hague Group accounts

		$000
Sale proceeds		10,000
FV of retained interest		nil
CV of subsidiary at disposal:		
Net Assets	3,000	
Unimpaired goodwill (W1)	2,500	
	———	
	5,500	
Less: NCI at disposal date (W2)	(400)	
	———	(5,100)
		———
Gain before tax		4,900
Tax per part (a)(i)		(1,000)
		———
		3,900
		———

(b) (i) Disposal of half of the holding to leave a residual shareholding:

	$000	$000
Disposal proceeds		5,000
FV of retained interest		3,500
		———
		8,500
CV of subsidiary at disposal date:		
Net assets	3,000	
Unimpaired goodwill (W1)	2,500	
	———	
	5,500	
Less: FV of NCI at disposal date (W2)	(400)	
	———	(5,100)
		———
		3,400
		———

(ii) After the date of disposal, the residual holding will be equity accounted, with a single amount in the statement of profit or loss for the share of the post-tax retained earnings for the period after disposal and a single amount in the statement of financial position for the fair value at disposal date of the investment retained plus the group share of post-acquisition retained earnings.

Test your understanding 5 – Kathmandu

(a) (i) Consolidated statement of profit or loss – full disposal

	Kathmandu group	Nepal	Group
	$		$
Revenue	553,000	(6 / 12 × 450,000)	778,000
Operating costs	450,000	(6 / 12 × 400,000)	(650,000)
			————
Operating profit			128,000
Dividend	8,000 less inter-co (70% × 10,000)		1,000
Profit on disposal (W4)			80,400
			————
Profit before tax			209,400
Tax	40,000	(6 / 12 × 14,000)	(47,000)
			————
Profit after tax			162,400
			————
Attributable to:			
Equity holders of Kathmandu (β)			157,000
Non-controlling interest		(30% × 36,000 × 6/12)	5,400
			————
			162,400
			————

There were no items of other comprehensive income during the year.

(ii) Group retained earnings at 31 December 20X9 – full disposal

	$
Brought forward	
Kathmandu	100,000
Group % of Nepal's post acquisition retained earnings b/f	
(70% × (130,000 (W1) – 110,000) (per Q))	14,000
	114,000
Profit for year per consolidated statement of profit or loss	157,000
Less Dividend paid	(25,000)
Retained earnings carried forward	246,000

(iii) Group statement of profit or loss – discontinued operations presentation

	Kathmandu group	Group
	$	$
Revenue	553,000	553,000
Operating costs	450,000	(450,000)
Operating profit		103,000
Dividend	8,000 less inter-co (70% × 10,000)	1,000
Profit before tax		104,000
Tax		(40,000)
Profit after tax – continuing operations		64,000
Discontinued operations	($36,000 × 6/12) + (80,400 (W4))	98,400
		162,400

Attributable to:		
Equity holders of Kathmandu (β)		157,000
Non-controlling interest	(30% × 36,000 × 6/12)	5,400
		162,400

There were no items of other comprehensive income during the year.

Notice that the post-tax results of the subsidiary up to the date of disposal are presented as a one-line entry in the group statement of profit or loss. There is no line-by-line consolidation of results when this method of presentation is adopted.

(b) (i) Consolidated statement of profit or loss – part disposal with residual interest

	Kathmandu group	Nepal	Group
	$		$
Revenue	553,000	(6 / 12 × 450,000)	778,000
Operating costs	450,000	(6 / 12 × 400,000)	(650,000)
Operating profit			128,000
Dividend	8,000 less inter-co (70% × 10,000)		1,000
Income from associate	(35% × 36,000 × 6 / 12)		6,300
Profit on disposal (W4)			80,400
Profit before tax			215,700
Tax	40,000	(6 / 12 × 14,000)	(47,000)
Profit after tax			168,700

There were no items of other comprehensive income during the year.

Attributable to:		
Equity holders of Kathmandu (β)		163,300
Non-controlling interest	(30% × 36,000 × 6 / 12)	5,400
		168,700

(ii) Group retained earnings at 31 December 20X9 – part disposal

	$
Brought forward	
Kathmandu	100,000
Group % of Nepal's post acquisition retained earnings b/f	
(70% × (130,000 (W1) – 110,000) (per Q))	14,000
	————
	114,000
Group income per consolidated profit or loss statement	163,300
Less Dividend paid	(25,000)
	————
	252,300
	————

Alternatively:

	$
Kathmandu c/fwd	146,000
Parent gain on disposal of shares	
($100,000 – (50% × $100,000))	50,000
Gain on remeasurement of residual holding	
($100,000 – $50,000)	50,000
Share of associate profit (6/12 × 35% × $36,000)	6,300
	————
	252,300
	————

Workings

(W1) **Net assets – Nepal**	Net assets at disposal	Net assets b/f
	$	$
Share capital	50,000	50,000
Retained earnings		
B/f	80,000	80,000
6 / 12 × 36,000	18,000	
Less Dividend	(10,000)	–
	————	————
	138,000	130,000
	————	————

(W2) Goodwill

	$
Cost to parent	100,000
FV of NCI at date of acquisition	40,000
	140,000
FV of net assets at date of acquisition (per question)	110,000
Unimpaired goodwill	30,000

(W3) NCI at disposal date

FV of NCI at date of acquisition	40,000
NCI share of post-acquisition retained earnings (30% × (138,000 – 110,000)	8,400
	48,400

(W4) Profit on disposal

Full disposal (a)(i)	$	$
Proceeds		200,000
Net assets recorded prior to disposal		
Net assets	138,000	
Full goodwill – unimpaired	30,000	
	168,000	
NCI at date of disposal (W3)	(48,400)	
		(119,600)
Profit on disposal to group statement of profit or loss		80,400

Part disposal (b)(i)

Proceeds		100,000
FV of retained interest (per question)		100,000
		200,000
Net assets recorded prior to disposal:		
Net assets	138,000	
Unimpaired goodwill at disposal date	30,000	
	168,000	
NCI at date of disposal (W3)	(48,400)	
		(119,600)
profit on disposal to group statement of profit or loss		80,400

Test your understanding 6 – David and Goliath

(i) **Sale of 5% of Goliath shares**

	$
Cash proceeds	5,000
Increase in NCI (5% × (70,000 + 20,000)	(4,500)
Increase in equity	500

(ii) **Sale of 25% of Goliath shares**

	$
Cash proceeds	20,000
Increase in NCI (25% × (70,000 + 20,000)	(22,500)
Decrease in equity	(2,500)

Note that in both situations, Goliath remains a subsidiary of David after the sale of shares. There is no gain or loss to the group – the difference arising is taken to equity. Goliath would continue to be consolidated within the David Group like any other subsidiary; there is no change to the carrying value of goodwill. The only impact will be the calculation of NCI share of retained earnings for the year – this would need to be time-apportioned based upon the NCI percentage pre- and post-disposal during the year.

Test your understanding 7 – Gordon and Mandy

(i) **Purchase of 20% of Mandy shares**

	$
Cash paid	25,000
Decrease in NCI ((20% / 20%) × 20,000)	20,000
Decrease in equity	5.000

(ii) **Purchase of 5% of Mandy shares**

	$
Cash paid	4,000
Decrease in NCI ((5% / 20%) × 20,000)	5,000
Increase in equity	1,000

4

Group reorganisations

Chapter learning objectives

Upon completion of this chapter you will be able to:

- discuss the reasons behind a group reorganisation
- evaluate and assess the principal terms of a proposed group reorganisation.

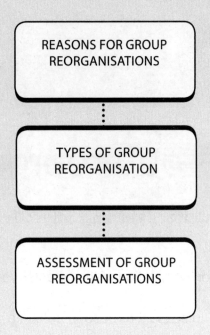

Definition of a group reorganisation

A group reorganisation (or restructuring) is any of the following:

(a) the transfer of shares in a subsidiary from one group entity to another

(b) the addition of a new parent entity to a group

(c) the transfer of shares in one or more subsidiaries of a group to a new entity that is not a group entity but whose shareholders are the same as those of the group's parent

(d) the combination into a group of two or more companies that before the combination had the same shareholders

(e) the acquisition of the shares of another entity that itself then issues sufficient shares so that the acquired entity has control of the combined entity.

Reasons for a reorganisation

There are a number of reasons why a group may wish to reorganise. These include the following.

- A group may wish to list on a public stock exchange. This is usually facilitated by creating a new holding company and keeping the business of the group in subsidiary entities.

- The ownership of subsidiaries may be transferred from one group company to another. This is often the case if the group wishes to sell a subsidiary, but retain its trade.

- The group may decide to transfer the assets and trades of a number of subsidiaries into one entity. This is called divisionalisation and is undertaken in order to simplify the group structure and save costs. The details of divisionalisation are not examinable at P2.

- The may be corporate tax advantages to reorganising a group structure, particularly if one or more subsidiaries within the group is loss-making.

- The group may split into two or more parts; each part is still owned by the same shareholders but is not related to the other parts. This is a demerger and is often done to enhance shareholder value. By splitting the group, the value of each part is realised whereas previously the stock market may have undervalued the group as a whole. The details of demergers are not examinable at P2.

- An unlisted entity may purchase a listed entity with the aim of achieving a stock exchange listing itself. This is called a reverse acquisition.

Types of group reorganisation

There are a number of ways of effecting a group reorganisation. The type of reorganisation will depend on what the group is trying to achieve.

New holding company

A group might set up a new holding entity for an existing group in order to improve co-ordination within the group or as a vehicle for flotation.

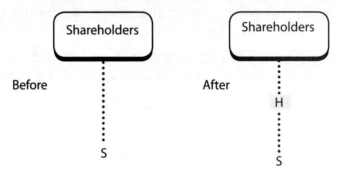

- H becomes the new holding entity of S.

- Usually, H issues shares to the shareholders of S in exchange for shares of S, but occasionally the shareholders of S may subscribe for shares in H and H may pay cash for S.

IFRS 3 excludes from its scope any business combination involving entities or businesses under 'common control', which is where the same parties control all of the combining entities/businesses both before and after the business combination.

As there is no mandatory guidance in accounting for these items, the acquisition method should certainly be used in examination questions.

IASB's common control project

You may be aware that the IASB is approaching the topic of business combinations in two phases. Phase I resulted in the issue of IFRS 3 revised, which states that:

- 'standard' business combinations must be accounted for using the acquisition method

- goodwill arising on consolidation is capitalised, not amortised, but subject to an annual impairment review.

Phase II is considering non-standard business combinations, e.g. combinations involving entities under common control, or combinations involving two or more mutual entities (such as mutual insurance companies). The project will examine the definition of common control and the methods of accounting for business combinations under common control in the consolidated and acquirer's individual financial statements. No firm decisions have yet been taken, but the IASB hopes to develop a standard in due course.

At April 2009. the progress of this project had still to be clarified by the IASB.

Change of ownership of an entity within a group

Change of ownership of an entity within a group

This occurs when the internal structure of the group changes, for example, a parent may transfer the ownership of a subsidiary to another of its subsidiaries.

The key thing to remember is that the reorganisation of the entities within the group should not affect the group accounts, as shareholdings are transferred from one company to another and no assets will leave the group.

The individual accounts of the group companies will need to be adjusted for the effect of the transfer.

The following are types of reorganisation:

(a) **Subsidiary moved up**

Before

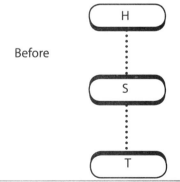

After

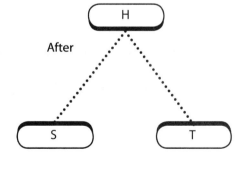

This can be achieved in one of two ways.

(a) S transfers its investment in T to H as a dividend in specie. If this is done then S must have sufficient distributable profits to pay the dividend.

(b) H purchases the investment in T from S for cash. In practice the purchase price often equals the fair value of the net assets acquired, so that no gain or loss arises on the transaction.

Usually, it will be the carrying value of T that is used as the basis for the transfer of the investment, but there are no legal rules confirming this.

A share-for-share exchange cannot be used as in many jurisdictions it is illegal for a subsidiary to hold shares in the parent company.

(b) **Subsidiary moved down**

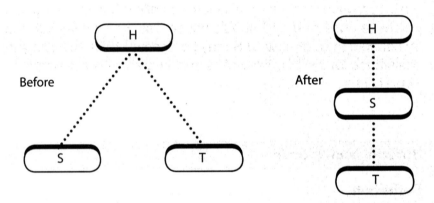

This reorganisation may be carried out where there are tax advantages in establishing a 'sub-group', or where two or more subsidiaries are linked geographically.

This can be carried out either by:

(a) a share-for-share exchange (S issues shares to H in return for the shares in T)

(b) a cash transaction (S pays cash to H).

(c) Subsidiary moved along

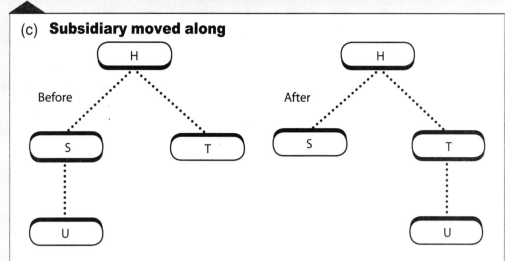

This is carried out by T paying cash (or other assets) to S. The consideration would not normally be in the form of shares because a typical reason for such a reconstruction would be to allow S to be managed as a separate part of the group or even disposed of completely. This could not be achieved effectively were S to have a shareholding in T.

If the purpose of the reorganisation is to allow S to leave the group, the purchase price paid by T should not be less than the fair value of the investment in U, otherwise S may be deemed to be receiving financial assistance for the purchase of its own shares, which is illegal in many jurisdictions.

Reverse acquisitions

Definition

A **reverse acquisition** occurs when an entity obtains ownership of the shares of another entity, which in turn issues sufficient shares so that the acquired entity has control of the combined entity.

Reverse acquisitions are a method of allowing unlisted companies to obtain a stock exchange quotation by taking over a smaller listed company.

For example, a private company arranges to be acquired by a listed company. This is effected by the public entity issuing shares to the private company so that the private company's shareholders end up controlling the listed entity. Legally, the public entity is the parent, but the substance of the transaction is that the private entity has acquired the listed entity.

Assessment of group reorganisations

Previous examination questions testing group reorganisations have provided a scenario with a group considering a number of reorganisation options. The questions have then asked for an evaluation and recommendation of a particular proposal.

In order to do this, you will need to consider the following:

- the impact of the proposal on the individual accounts of the group entities

- the impact of the proposal on the group accounts

- the purpose of the reorganisation

- whether there is any impairment of any of the group's assets

- whether any impairment loss should be recognised in relation to the investment in subsidiaries in the parent company accounts.

UK syllabus focus

The ACCA UK syllabus contains a requirement that UK variant candidates should be able to discuss and apply the key differences between UK GAAP and IFRS GAAP. As with other areas of group accounts, the accounting requirements of UK GAAP and IFRS GAAP are very similar in this area, but there are one or two differences.

UK GAAP **FRS 6 'Acquisitions and Mergers'** permits an **alternative to acquisition accounting** where a business combination takes place. In effect, rather than one entity gaining control of another, the business combination arises by virtue of a **pooling of assets and liabilities, together with the shareholders of the two or more entities, into one merged entity**. A key feature of the new combined entity is that neither party to the merger (or its' shareholders) will dominate or control the new combined entity – it is a genuine merger or pooling of interests.

UK FRS 6 para 2 defines a merger as:

" ...a business combination that results in the formation of a new reporting entity formed from the combining parties, in which the shareholders....come together ....for the mutual sharing of risks and benefits....in which no party....obtains control over any other..."

Where merger accounting is to be applied to a business combination, there are several pre-requisites as follows:

- the offer to the shareholders in the entities to be merged must be made to all shareholders and the consideration offered to them must comprise substantially of equity shares in the new combined entity. This ensures that each set of shareholders joining the merged entity will be substantially unchanged and each will retain an equity interest in the new entity, and there will be minimal loss of resources (cash paid or liabilities incurred) by the new merged entity.

- at least 90% of the nominal value of voting equity shares in each entity to be merged must be held by the new combined entity. This helps to ensure that a pooling of shareholders takes place, with no significant loss of shareholders from the merging entities to the new combined entity.

- any cash or non-equity consideration must account for no more than 10% of the nominal value of shares issued as part of the merger. This helps to preserve assets within the new combined entity.

- none of the individual parties in the new combined entity must dominate either the board of directors or the shareholders in that new entity. This helps to ensure that no one group dominates or controls the new entity, and that there is a genuine partnership or pooling of interests between the parties.

- there should be joint participation by the entities to be merged in establishing the management structure of the new combined entity, including participation in management thereafter.

- to ensure that no one party dominates a merger, there is a relative size test which presumes that one party will dominate the other if it is more than 50% larger than each of the other parties to the new combined entity.

- all shareholders in the new combined entity will share in future performance of that entity as a whole, rather than from only part of it.

The consequences of applying merger accounting are as follows:

- net assets are combined using carrying values, rather than fair values,

- retained earnings and other elements of equity are pooled, and make no distinction between pre- or post combination

- goodwill is not calculated, and

- the new combined entity is regarded as if it had always been in existence, rather than having come into being at a specified date of acquisition.

UK FRS 6 also deals with group reconstructions which are defined as any of the following arrangements:

(a) the transfer of a shareholding in a subsidiary from one group company to another;

(b) the addition of a new parent company to the group;

(c) the transfer of shares in one or more subsidiaries to a new company that is not a group company, but whose shareholders are the same as those of the group's parent;

(d) the combination into a group of two or more companies that before the combination had the same shareholders.

In effect, merger accounting of such group reconstructions will be permitted where the ultimate shareholders remain the same and where any non-controlling interest (i.e. minority interest) is unaffected.

1 Chapter summary

Reasons for group reorganisations
- Transfer of shares in a subsidiary from one group entity to another
- Addition of a new parent entity to a group
- Transfer of shares in one or more subsidiaries of a group to a new entity that is not a group entity, but whose shareholders are the same as those of the group's parent
- Combination into a group of two or more companies that before the combination had the same shareholders

Types of group reorganisations
- New holding company
- Change of ownership of an entity within the group
- Reverse acquisition

Assessment of group reorganisations
- Look for the effect on the group and individual financial statements
- Look for any impairment of assets in the group
- Look for any impairment of investments in the parent company

Group accounting – foreign currency

Chapter learning objectives

Upon completion of this chapter you will be able to:

- outline the principles for translating foreign currency amounts, including translations into the functional currency and presentation currency
- apply these principles
- account for the consolidation of foreign operations and their disposal.

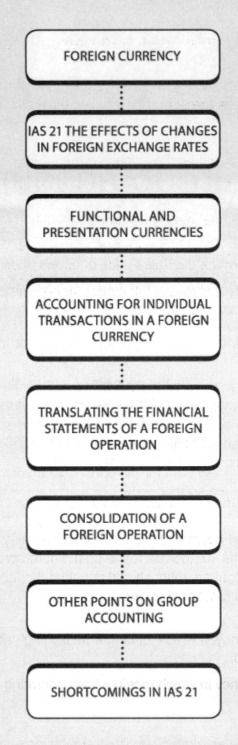

1 IAS 21 The effects of changes in foreign exchange rates

IAS 21 deals with:

- the definition of functional and presentation currencies
- accounting for individual transactions in a foreign currency
- translating the financial statements of a foreign operation.

Functional and presentation currencies

The **functional currency** is the currency of the primary economic environment where the entity operates. In most cases this will be the local currency.

An entity should consider the following when determining its functional currency.

- The currency that mainly influences sales prices for goods and services.
- The currency of the country whose competitive forces and regulations mainly determine the sales price of goods and services.
- The currency that mainly influences labour, material and other costs of providing goods and services.

The entity maintains its day-to-day financial records in its functional currency.

The **presentation currency** is the currency in which the entity presents its financial statements. This can be different from the functional currency, particularly if the entity in question is a foreign-owned subsidiary. It may have to present its financial statements in the currency of its parent, even though that is different from its own functional currency.

Functional and presentation currencies

The **functional currency** is the currency an entity will use in its day-to-day transactions. In addition to the points noted previously, IAS 21 also identifies that that an entity should consider the following factors in determining its functional currency:

- The currency in which funding from issuing debt and equity is generated.
- The currency in which receipts from operating activities are usually retained.

Let us consider an example to illustrate this point. Entity A operates in the UK. It sells goods throughout the UK and Europe with all transactions denominated in sterling. Cash is received from sales in sterling. It raises finance locally from UK banks with all loans denominated in sterling.

Looking at the factors listed above it is apparent that the functional currency for Entity A is sterling. It trades in this currency and raises finance in this currency.

Therefore Entity A would record its accounting transactions in sterling as its functional currency.

One complication in determining functional currency arises if an entity is a foreign operation. For example, if Entity A (from above) has a subsidiary Entity B located in Europe, Entity B will also have to determine its functional currency. The question arises as to whether this will be the same as the parent or will be the local currency where Entity B is located.

The factors that must be considered are:

- whether the activities of the foreign operation are carried out as an extension of the parent, rather than with a significant degree of autonomy

- whether transactions with the parent are a high or low proportion of the foreign operation's activities

- whether cash flows from the foreign operation directly affect the cash flows of the parent and are readily available for remittance to it

- whether cash flows from the activities of the foreign operation are sufficient to service existing debt obligations without funds being made available by the parent.

So, continuing with the example above, if Entity B operates as an independent operation, generating income and expenses in its local currency and raising finance in its local currency, then its functional currency would be its local currency and not that of Entity A. However, if Entity B was merely an extension of Entity A, only selling goods imported from Entity A and remitting all profits back to Entity A, then the functional currency should be the same as the parent. In this case Entity B would record its transactions in sterling and not its local currency.

Once a functional currency is determined it is not changed unless there is a change in the underlying circumstances that were relevant when determining the original functional currency.

IAS 21 states that whereas an entity is constrained by the factors listed above in determining its functional currency, it has a completely free choice as to the currency in which it presents its financial statements. If the **presentation currency** is different from the functional currency, then the financial statements must be translated into the presentation currency. For example, a group may have subsidiaries whose functional currencies are different to that of the parent. These must be translated into the presentation currency so that the consolidation procedure can take place.

KAPLAN PUBLISHING

2 Accounting for individual transactions designated in a foreign currency

Where an entity enters into a transaction denominated in a currency other than its functional currency, that transaction must be translated into the functional currency before it is recorded.

Examples of foreign currency transactions

Whenever a business enters into a contract where the consideration is expressed in a foreign currency, it will be necessary to translate that foreign currency amount at some stage into the functional currency for inclusion into its own accounts. Examples include:

- imports of raw materials

- exports of finished goods

- importation of foreign-manufactured non-current assets

- investments in foreign securities

- raising an overseas loan.

The exchange rate used to initially record transactions should be either:

- the spot exchange rate on the date the transaction occurred, or

- an average rate over a period of time, providing the exchange rate has not fluctuated significantly.

Cash settlement

When cash settlement occurs, for example payment by a receivable, the settled amount should be translated using the spot exchange rate on the settlement date. If this amount differs from that used when the transaction occurred, there will be an exchange difference.

Exchange differences on settlement

IAS 21 requires that exchange gains or losses on settlement of individual transactions must be recognised in profit or loss in the period in which they arise. However, IAS 21 is not definitive in stating where in profit or loss any such gains or losses are classified. It would seem reasonable to regard them as items of operating expense or income; however, other profit or loss headings may also be appropriate.

Illustration: exchange differences on settlement

On 7 May 20X6 a dollar-based entity sells goods to a German entity for € 48,000 when the rate of exchange was $1 = € 3.2.

To record the sale:

	$
Dr Receivable €48,000 @ 3.2	15,000
Cr Sales	15,000

On 20 July 20X6 the customer remitted a draft for € 48,000 when the rate of exchange was $1 = €3.17.

	$
Dr Bank € 48,000 @ 3.17	15,142
Cr Customer	15,000
Cr Profit or loss (exchange gain)	142

The $142 exchange gain forms part of the profit for the year.

Treatment of year-end balances

The treatment of any 'foreign' items remaining in the statement of financial position at the year-end will depend on whether they are classified as monetary or non-monetary:

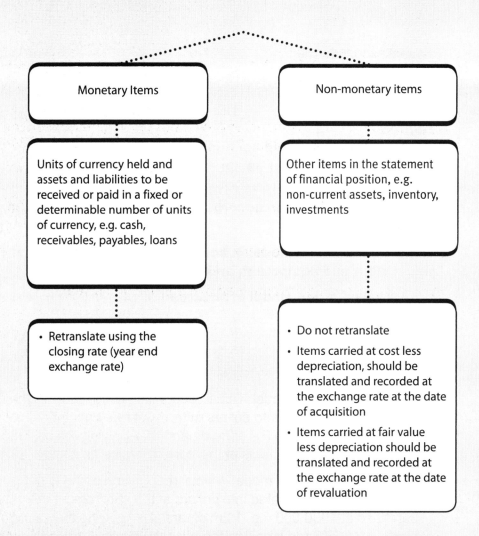

Note that if a non-monetary item is required to be restated to fair value at the reporting date (for example application of the fair value model in IAS 16 or IAS 40) it is first measured using the appropriate foreign currency at that date. This amount is then translated using the closing rate. Refer to Illustration1 within this chapter for application of this principle.

Exchange differences on retranslation of monetary items

As with exchange differences arising on settlement, IAS 21 requires that exchange differences arising on retranslation of monetary assets and liabilities must be recognised in profit or loss. IAS 21 is not specific under which heading(s) such exchange gains or losses should be classified. It would seem reasonable to regard them as items of operating income or operating expense as appropriate.

Illustration: Non-monetary items

On 1 July 20X5 Olympic, which has a functional and presentation currency of the dollar, purchased a plot of land in another country for 1.2 million dinars. At 30 June 20X6, the fair value of the plot of land was 1.5 million dinars.

Relevant exchange rates:	Dinars to $1
1 July 20X5	4
30 June 20X6	3

Required:
State how Olympic would account for the purchase of the plot of land if it is accounted for using:

(a) **the cost model in accordance with IAS 16 Property, plant and equipment,**

(b) **the valuation model in accordance with IAS 16 Property, plant and equipment, and**

(c) **the valuation model in accordance with IAS 40 Investment property.**

Answer

(a) IAS 16 PP&E cost model - initial recognition of the asset is the cost of the land translated into dollars at the spot rate on the date of purchase at $300,000 (i.e 1.2m dinars /4). Applying the cost model of IAS 16, the land remains at this carrying value at 30 June 20X6.

(b) IAS 16 PPE valuation model – initial recognition of the asset is the cost of the land translated into dollars at the spot rate on the date of purchase at $300,000 (i.e. 1.2m dinars /4). Applying the valuation model of IAS 16 requires that the asset is remeasured to fair value at the reporting date, and the valuation is then translated at the spot rate at the reporting date. At 30 June 20X6, the carrying value of the land will therefore be $500,000 (i.e. 1.5m dinars /3). The increase in the carrying value of the land of $200,000 (i.e. $500,000 - $300,000) will be reported as a revaluation gain in other comprehensive income for the year and a revaluation reserve included within other components of equity on the statement of financial position at the reporting date.

(c) IAS 40 Investment property – initial recognition of the asset is the cost of the land translated into dollars at the spot rate on the date of purchase at $300,000 (i.e. 1.2m dinars /4). Applying the valuation model of IAS 40 requires that the asset is remeasured to fair value at the reporting date, and the valuation is then translated at the spot rate at the reporting date. At 30 June 20X6, the carrying value of the land will therefore be $500,000 (i.e. 1.5m dinars /3). The increase in the carrying value of the land of $200,000 (i.e. $500,000 - $300,000) will be taken to profit or loss for the year ended 30 June 20X6.

The key point to note with each situation is that, as a non-monetary asset, IAS 21 does not require land to be remeasured or retranslated at each reporting date (i.e. applying the IAS 16 cost model). If other requirements from reporting standards apply (i.e. valuation models from either IAS 16 or IAS 40), valuation is required by the relevant standard, not the requirements of IAS 21.

Test your understanding 1 – Butler, Waiter and Attendant

(a) An entity, Butler, has a reporting date of 31 December. On 27 November 20X6 Butler plc buys goods from a Swedish supplier for SwK 324,000.

On 19 December 20X6 Butler plc pays the Swedish supplier in full.

Exchange rates were as follows:

27 November 20X6 $1 = SwK 11.15

19 December 20X6 $1 = SwK 10.93

Required:

Show how the expense and liability, together with the exchange difference arising, should be accounted for in the financial statements.

(b) An entity, Waiter, which has a reporting date of 31 December and the dollar ($) as its functional currency, borrows in the foreign currency of the Kram (K). The loan of K120,000 was taken out on 1 January 20X7. A repayment of K40,000 was made on 1 March 20X7.

The following rates of exchange are relevant:

	K1 to $
1 January 20X7	K1: $2
1 March 20X7	K1: $3
31 December 20X7	K1: $3.5

Required:

Show how the liability and the exchange difference will be represented in the year end financial statements.

(c) An entity, Attendant, which has a reporting date of 31 December and has the dollar ($) as its functional currency, purchased a plot of land overseas on 1 March 20X0. The entity paid for the land in the currency of the Rylands (R). The purchase cost of the land at 1 March 20X0 was R60,000. The value of the land at the reporting date was R80,000.

Rates of exchange were as follows:
1 March 20X0   R8 : $1
31 December 20X0 R10 :$1

Required:

Show how this transaction should be accounted for in the financial statements for the year ended 31 December 20X0:

- **if the land is carried at cost**

- **if the land is carried at valuation**

Test your understanding 2 – Highlight

Part (a)

Highlight is an entity whose functional currency is the dollar ($) and has an annual reporting date of 31 December. During the year ended 31 December 20X3, Highlight entered into a number of transactions with Exotic, an overseas entity who supplies plant and equipment. One particular transaction for the import of the machinery is denominated in Dinars (Dn), Exotic's functional currency, as follows:

1 July 20X3 Purchase of an item of plant on extended credit terms from Exotic Dn400,000
1 November 20X3 Cash payment to Exotic Dn180,000

Highlight has a policy of applying historical cost accounting and depreciating plant and equipment at the rate of 20% per annum. The item of plant and equipment is not expected to have any residual value at the end of its useful life.

Relevant exchange rates to $1 are as follows:	Dn
1 July 20X3	10.0
1 November 20X3	7.2
1 December 20X3	9.0
31 December 20X3	8.0

Required:

Prepare relevant extracts from the financial statements for the year ended 31 December 20X3 of Highlight to illustrate the effects of the above transactions.

Part (b)

During 20X3, Highlight also entered into a number of transactions with Eraser, an overseas customer; two particular contracts for the export of goods to Eraser are denominated in Dinars (Dn) as follows:
1 November 20X3 credit sales to Eraser on 3 months credit Dn360,000
1 December 20X3 credit sales to Eraser on 3 months credit Dn540,000

By 31 December 20X3, Highlight had received no payment from Eraser. As the receivables were still within their credit period, they were not regarded as being impaired.

Relevant exchange rates to $1 are as follows:	Dn
1 July 20X3	10.0
1 November 20X3	7.2
1 December 20X3	9.0
31 December 20X3	8.0

Required:

Prepare relevant extracts from the financial statements for the year ended 31 December 20X3 of Highlight to illustrate the effects of the above transactions.

3 Consolidation of a foreign operation

In principle, the same workings and accounting adjustments that may be required in any consolidation question could also be required when consolidating a foreign subsidiary. You should prepare a group structure, together with workings for net assets, goodwill, non-controlling interest and retained earnings as normal, plus additional workings necessary to deal with other accounting issues as required within a question.

However, there are three particular issues that must be dealt with when consolidating a foreign subsidiary as follows:

- Translation of the subsidiary's income and expenses in the statement of profit or loss and other comprehensive income into the presentation currency of the parent.

- Translation of the subsidiary's assets and liabilities in the statement of financial position into the presentation currency of the parent.

- Translation of goodwill on acquisition of the foreign subsidiary into the presentation currency of the parent.

The third issue arises as IAS 21 requires that goodwill is calculated using the functional currency of the subsidiary and then subject to annual retranslation at the closing rate at each reporting date. It follows that workings for net assets and goodwill should initially be prepared in the functional currency of the subsidiary, before translation of goodwill into the presentation currency of the parent at an appropriate point. Workings for non-controlling interest, group retained earnings and other components of equity will also include elements relating to the foreign subsidiary which will need to be translated into the parent entity's presentation currency as part of the consolidation exercise.

Translation of the financial statements of a foreign subsidiary

When a subsidiary entity's functional currency is different from the presentation currency of its parent, its financial statements must be translated into the parent's presentation currency prior to consolidation. The following exchange rates should be used in the translation:

Statement of profit or loss and other comprehensive income:

Income & expenses	) At the rate for each transaction or, as an approximation, the average rate for the year.
Other comprehensive income	)

Statement of financial position:

Assets and liabilities	) At the closing rate (i.e. rate at the reporting date)
Goodwill on acquisition	)

The equity capital and reserves of the foreign subsidiary are included in the net assets working compiled in the subsidiary's functional currency, which is then used as a basis for calculation of goodwill, non-controlling interest and reserves required for the group financial statements.

One point to note is that the subsidiary reserves, and any other items in the net assets working (such as fair value adjustments and associated depreciation or impairment), are clearly identified as being either pre-or post-acquisition.

The net assets working is extended to include a translation of net assets at the date of acquisition and at the reporting date. The $ value of post-acquisition reserves can then be identified as a balancing figure. Together with the identification of pre- and post-acquisition reserves, this helps to calculate the exchange difference arising on retranslation of net assets.

Exchange differences arising on consolidation of a foreign subsidiary

Exchange differences arise because items have been translated at different points in time at different rates of exchange as part of the procedure to consolidate a foreign subsidiary into group accounts. There are three components of this total exchange difference as follows:

1 Opening net assets	Net assets are restated from the closing rate at one reporting date to the closing rate at the next reporting date.
2 Retained profit for the year	Items of income and expense are translated at the average rate for the year for inclusion in the group statement of profit or loss and other comprehensive income for the year. The resultant retained profit is part of group reserves which is effectively translated at the closing rate for inclusion in the group statement of financial position.
3 Goodwill	Goodwill is restated from the closing rate at one reporting date to the closing rate at the next reporting date.

In practical terms, the exchange gain or loss on components (1) and (2) is effectively calculated as one item. The exchange gain or loss for the year on this item will be allocated between the group and non-controlling interest based upon their respective shareholdings.

Depending upon the accounting policy for goodwill, the exchange gain or loss for the year will be allocated between the group and non-controlling interest based upon either their respective shareholdings (full goodwill method) or solely to the group (proportionate goodwill method).

Calculation of foreign exchange gains and losses on retranslation

Pro-forma for calculation of annual exchange gain or loss on retranslation of net assets:

		Dinar (m)	Rate	$m
Opening net assets*	Translated at opening rate	X	Opening	X
	(i.e. closing rate at the previous reporting date)			
Profit (loss) for the year	Translated at average rate for each year**	X	Average	X
Exchange gain (loss) arising on retranslation of net assets		**Bal fig**		**X** **(X)**
Closing net assets	Translated at closing rate	X	Closing	X

Pro-forma for calculation of annual exchange gain or loss on retranslation of goodwill:

		Dinar (m)	Rate	$m
Opening goodwill*	Translated at opening rate (i.e. closing rate at the previous reporting date)	X	Opening	X
Impairment in the year	Translated at average rate for the year**	(X)	Average	(X)
Exchange gain (loss) arising on retranslation of goodwill		**Bal fig**		**X** **(X)**
Closing goodwill	Translated at closing rate	X	Closing	X

Note:* If it is the year of acquisition, the net assets and exchange rate at the date of acquisition will be used.

Note:** i.e. as used to translate income and expense in the statement of profit or loss.

How are the exchange gains and losses accounted for?

Group statement of total comprehensive income - the total of exchange gains and losses on retranslation of net assets and goodwill for the year are reported as an item of other comprehensive income annually. They are allocated between the group and non-controlling interest when reporting the group and non-controlling interest respective share of total comprehensive income.

Group statement of financial position – the non-controlling interest balance will include their share of the exchange gains or losses on retranslation of net assets and goodwill year-by-year. The group share of exchange gains and losses arising on retranslation are accumulated year-by-year and reported as a component of equity. In effect, the net balance at each reporting date represents an unrealised gain or loss for the group arising on an investment in a foreign subsidiary which will only be realised upon disposal of that subsidiary. At that point, the foreign exchange reserve will be recycled or reclassified to profit or loss and will form part of the reported profit or loss on disposal of a subsidiary.

Illustration 1 – Exchange differences

On 1 July 20X4, Hail, who has the $ as its functional and presentation currency, acquired eighty per cent of the equity share capital of Snow for cash consideration of $10 million.

Snow is based in a different country to Hail and has the dinar (Dr) as its functional currency. At the date of acquisition, Snow had issued equity capital of Dr5 million and retained earnings of Dr25 million. At that date, the carrying values of the separable net assets of Snow approximated to their fair values. The fair value of the non-controlling interest in Snow on 1 July 20X4 was Dr7.5 million

At the date of reporting date, Hail had retained earnings of $15 million and Snow had retained earnings of Dr43.5 million.

Relevant rates of exchange are as follows: .	Dr to $1
1 July 20X4	4.0
30 June 20X5	5.0
Average for the year	4.5

Required:

Calculate the following amounts that would be included in the Hail group financial statements for the year ended at 30 June 20X5:

(a) **Foreign exchange gain or loss on retranslation of net assets**

(b) **Foreign exchange gain or loss on retranslation of goodwill**

(c) **Non-controlling interest at 30 June 20X5**

(d) **Group retained earnings at 30 June 20X5**

(e) **Group foreign exchange reserve at 30 June 20X5**

(f) **Amount taken to other comprehensive income for the year ended 30 June 20X5**

Solution

(a) Foreign exchange gain or loss on retranslation of net assets:

	Acq'n date	Rep date	Rate	Rep date
	Dr000	Dr000		$000
Equity capital	5,000	5,000		
Pre-acquistion earnings	25,000	25,000		
		30,000	4.0	7,500
Post-acquisition earnings (43,500 – 25,000)		18,500	4.5	4,111
FX loss on retranslation of net assets			**Bal fig**	**(1,911)**
Allocate loss on retranslation as follows:	30,000	48,500	5.0	9,700
Group (80% × $1,911) = $1,529 loss				
NCI (20% × $1,911) = $382 loss				

(b) Foreign exchange gain or loss on retranslation of goodwill

	Dr000
Full goodwill in functional currency of subsidiary	
Cost to gain control $10m × 4	40,000
FV of NCI at acquisition	7,500
	47,500
FV of net assets at acquisition	(30,000)
Full goodwill at acquisition	17,500

Retranslation of goodwill:	Dr000	Rate	$000
Goodwill at acquisition	17,500	4.0	4,375
Impairment of goodwill in year	(N/A)	4.5	(N/A)
FX loss on retranslation of goodwill		**Bal fig**	**(875)**
	17,500	5.0	3,500

Allocate retranslation loss as follows:
Group (80% × $875) = $700 loss
NCI (20% × $875) = $175 loss

(c) Non-controlling interest at the reporting date:

	Dr000	Rate	$000
NCI at acquisition	7,500	4.0	1,875
NCI % of goodwill impairment in year	(N/A)	4.5	(N/A)
NCI % of proft for the year	3,700	4.5	822
(20% × Dr18,500) (part (a))			
NCI % of FX retranslation loss on retranslation of net assets (part (a))			(382)
NCI % of FX retranslation loss on goodwill (part (b))			(175)
			2,140

(d) Group retained earnings at the reporting date:

	Dr000	Rate	$000
Hail retained earnings per question			15,000
Group share of goodwill impairment in year	(N/A)	4.5	(N/A)
Group share of proft for the year	14,800	4.5	3,289
(80% × Dr18,500) (part (a))			
			18,289

(e) Group foreign exchange reserve at the reporting date

	$000
Group share of FX loss on retranslation of net assets (part (a))	(1,529)
Group share of FX loss on retranslation of goodwill (part (b))	(700)
	(2,229)

(f) Amount taken to other comprehensive income for the year

	$000
Total of FX loss on retranslation of net assets (part (a))	(1,911)
Total of FX loss on retranslation of goodwill (part (b))	(875)
	(2,786)

Illustration 2 – Consolidation of foreign subsidiary

On 1 July 20X1 H acquired 80% of ABC Inc, whose functional currency is KRs. The cost of gaining control was KR7,500. Their financial statements at 30 June 20X2 were as follows.

Statement of financial position

	H	ABC
Assets	$	KR
Investment in ABC	5,000	–
Non-current assets	10,000	3,000
Current assets	5,000	2,000
	20,000	5,000
Equity and liabilities	$	KR
Equity capital	6,000	1,500
Retained earnings	4,000	2,500
Liabilities	10,000	1,000
	20,000	5,000

Statement of profit or loss

	H	ABC
	$	KR
Revenue	25,000	35,000
Operating costs	(15,000)	(26,250)
Profit before tax	10,000	8,750
Tax	(8,000)	(7,450)
Profit for the year	2,000	1,300

Neither entity recognised any items of other comprehensive income in their individual accounts in the period.

The following information is applicable:

(i) At the date of acquisition the fair value of the net assets of ABC were KR6,000. The increase in the fair value is attributable to land that remains carried by ABC at its historical cost.

(ii) During the year H sold goods on cash terms for $1,000 to ABC.

(iii) On 1 June 20X2 H made a short-term loan to ABC of $400. The liability is recorded by ABC at the historic rate. The loan is recorded within current assets and liabilities as appropriate

(iv) The non-controlling interest is valued using the proportion of net assets method.

Exchange rates to $1.

	KR
1 July 20X1	1.50
Average rate	1.75
1 June 20X2	1.90
30 June 20X2	2.00

Required:

Prepare the group statement of financial position, together with the group statement of profit or loss and other comprehensive income for the year ended 30 June 20X2.

Solution

H & ABC Group statement of financial position

Assets:	$
Non-current assets	
Intangible – goodwill (W3)	1,350
Tangible (10,000 + ((KR3,000 + KR3,300(FVA)) /2.0))	13,150
	———
	14,500
Current assets (5,000 + (KR2,000 /2.0) – inter-co 400)	5,600
	———
	20,100
	———

Equity and liabilities		$
Share capital		6,000
Group reserves		
Retained earnings (W5)	4,576	
Group exchange differences (W7)	(1,322)	
		3,254
		9,254
Non-controlling interest (W4)		726
Total equity of the group		9,980
Liabilities (10,000 + ((KR1,000 + 40(W1)) /2.0) – inter-co 400)		10,120
		20,100

H Group – Statement of profit or loss and other comprehensive income for the year

	$
Revenue (25,000 + (35,000/1.75) – interco 1,000)	44,000
Operating costs (15,000 + ((26,250 + 40(W1) /1.75)) – interco 1,000)	(29,023)
Profit before tax	14,977
Tax (8,000 + (7,450 / 1.75))	(12,257)
Profit after tax	2,720

Other comprehensive income – amounts which may be recycled (i.e.reclassified) to profit or loss in subsequent periods:

Total exchange differences on translation of foreign operations ((450)(W3) + (1,090)(W6))	(1,540)
Total comprehensive income for the year	1,180

Profit for the year attributable to:

Owners of parent (β)	2,576
Non-controlling interest (20% × ((1,260 (W2)) /1.75))	144
	2,720

Total comprehensive income for the year attributable to:

Owners of parent (β)	1,254
Non-controlling interest (144 (as above) – 218)(W6))	(74)
	1,180

(W1) Group structure

```
                    H
                    |
NCI = 20% for full year       80%
                    |
                   ABC
```

Note (iii) accounting error to correct before translation

H has made a loan to ABC. ABC therefore has a liability outstanding at the reporting date of a monetary item denominated in foreign currency – this needs to be restated at the closing rate prior to translation at the year-end. Any gain or loss on translation is part of the operating results of ABC for the year.

1 June ABC received loan of $400 @ 1.9 = KR760

30 June restate loan at closing rate $400 @ 2.0 = KR800

i.e. increased liability and exchange loss of KR40 for ABC

(W2) Net assets of subsidiary in own functional currency

	KR	KR	
Equity capital	1,500	1,500	
Retained earnings	1,200	2,500	
FVA – land (bal fig)	3,300	3,300	
Exchange loss re short-term loan (W1)		(40)	
Movement in post acq'n retained earnings	6,000	7,260	1,260

(W3) Goodwill in ABC functional currency – proportionate basis

	KR
Investment in ABC $5,000 × 1.5	7,500
FV of NCI at acquisition (KR6,000 × 20%)	1,200
	8,700
Less: FV of NA at acquisition (W2)	(6,000)
Prop goodwill	2,700
– no impairment to date –	
closing rate @ 2.0 = $1,350 to SOFP	

The exchange gain (loss) arising on retranslation of goodwill is identified as follows:

	KR	Rate	$
Goodwill at acquisition (as above) at acquisition rate	2,700	1.5	1,800
Exchange gain (loss) on retranslation of goodwill			**bal fig (450) (W7)**
Goodwill at reporting date at closing rate	2,700	2.0	1,350

Note: all of the gain (loss) arising on retranslation will relate to the parent entity as goodwill has been accounted for using the proportion of net assets method.

(W4) NCI on proportionate basis

		KR	Rate	$
NCI at date of acquisition	(20%× 6,000) (W2)	1,200	1.50	800
NCI % of profit for the year	(20% × (7,260 – 6,000)) (W2)	252	1.75	144
NCI share of gain (loss) on retranslation of goodwill				N/A
NCI share of gain (loss) on retranslation of net assets	(W6)			(218)
To group SOFP				726

(W5) **Group retained earnings**

	KR	Rate	$
Parent			4,000
Group % of post-acq'n (80% × (KR7,260 - 6,000))	1,008	1.75	576
			4,576

Note that, when **group retained earnings** are calculated, the group share of the subsidiary's profit is translated at the average rate for the year.

(W6) **Gain or loss on retranslation of net assets**

	KR	Rate	$
Net assets at acquisition (W2)	6,000	1.5	4,000
Retained earnings for the year	1,260	1.75	720
Exchange gain (loss) arising on retranslation - bal fig			**(1,090)**
Net assets at reporting date	7,260	2.0	3,630

Note that, when the **retained earnings for the year of the subsidiary** are retranslated, the **average rate** for the year is used. The gain or loss on retranslation of net assets must then be allocated between the group and NCI based upon their respective shareholdings as follows:

			$
Group share	(80% × 1,090)	(W7)	(872)
NCI share	(20% × 1,090)	(W4)	(218)
			(1,090)

(W7) **Group foreign exchange reserve**

	$
Group share of exchange gain (loss) on retranslation of proportionate goodwill (W3)	(450)
Group share of exchange gain (loss) on retranslation of net assets (W6)	(872)
Group share of total exchange gains (losses) on retranslation to SOFP	1,322

Test your understanding 3 – Parent & Overseas

Parent is an entity that owns 80% of the equity shares of Overseas, a foreign entity that has the Shilling as its functional currency. The subsidiary was acquired at the start of the current accounting period on 1 January 20X7 when its reported reserves were 6,000 Shillings.

At that date the fair value of the net assets of the subsidiary was 20,000 Shillings. This included a fair value adjustment in respect of land of 4,000 Shillings that the subsidiary has not incorporated into its accounting records and still owns.

Parent wishes the presentation currency of the group accounts to be $. Goodwill, which is unimpaired at the reporting date, is to be accounted for using the full goodwill method. At the date of acquisition, the non-controlling interest in Overseas had a fair value of 5,000 Shillings.

Statements of financial position	Parent $	Overseas Shillings
Investment (20,999 shillings)	3,818	
Assets	9,500	40,000
	13,318	40,000
Equity and liabilities	$	Shillings
Equity capital	5,000	10,000
Retained earnings	6,000	8,200
Liabilities	2,318	21,800
	13,318	40,000

Statement of profit or loss for the year:

	Parent $	Overseas Shillings
Revenue	8,000	5,200
Costs	(2,500)	(2,600)
Profit before tax	5,500	2,600
Tax	(2,000)	(400)
Profit for the year	3,500	2,200

Neither entity recognised any other comprehensive income in their individual accounts in the period.

Relevant exchange rates (Shillings to $1) are:

Date	Exchange rate (Shillings to $1)
1 January 20X7	5.5
31 December 20X7	5.0
Weighted average for year	5.2

Required:

Prepare the consolidated statement of financial position at 31 December 20X7, together with a consolidated statement of profit or loss and other comprehensive income for the year ended 31 December 20X7

Test your understanding 4 – Saint & Albans

On the 1 July 20X1 Saint acquired 60% of Albans, whose functional currency is Ds. The financial statements of both entities as at 30 June 20X2 were as follows.

Statement of financial position at 30 June 20X2	Saint	Albans
Assets:	$	D
Investment in Albans	5,000	–
Loan to Albans	1,400	–
Tangible assets	10,000	15,400
Inventory	5,000	4,000
Receivables	4,000	500
Cash at bank	1,600	560
	27,000	20,460
Equity and liabilities	$	D
Equity capital ($1 / D1)	10,000	1,000
Share premium	3,000	500
Retained earnings	4,000	12,500
Non-current liabilities	5,000	5,460
Current liabilities	5,000	1,000
	27,000	20,460

Statement of profit or loss for the year ended 30 June 20X2	Saint	Albans
	$	D
Revenue	50,000	60,000
Cost of sales	(20,000)	(30,000)
Gross profit	30,000	30,000
Distribution and Administration expenses	(20,000)	(12,000)
Profit before tax	10,000	18,000
Tax	(8,000)	(6,000)
Profit for the year	2,000	12,000

Note: There were no items of other comprehensive income within the individual financial statements of either entity.

The following information is applicable.

(i) Saint purchased the shares in Albans for D10,000 on the first day of the accounting period. At the date of acquisition the retained earnings of Albans were D500 and there was an upward fair value adjustment of D1,000. The fair value adjustment is attributable to plant with a remaining five-year life as at the date of acquisition. This plant remains held by Albans and has not been revalued. No shares have issued since the date of acquisition.

(ii) Just before the year-end Saint acquired some goods from a third party at a cost of $800, which it sold to Albans for cash at a mark up of 50%. At the reporting date all the goods remain unsold.

(iii) On 1 June X2 Saint lent Albans $1,400. The liability is recorded at the historic rate within the non-current liabilities of Albans.

(iv) No dividends have been paid. Neither entity has recognised any gain or loss in reserves.

(v) Goodwill is to be accounted using the full goodwill method. An impairment review was performed and goodwill had reduced in value by 10% at 30 June 20X2. Impairment is to be charged to cost of sales. The fair value of the non-controlling interest at the date of acquisition was D5,000. The presentational currency of the group is to be the $.

Exchange rates to $1	D
1 July 20X1	2.00
Average rate	3.00
1 June 20X2	3.90
30 June 20X2	4.00

Required:

(1) **Prepare the group statement of financial position at 30 June 20X2**

(2) **Prepare the group statement of profit or loss and other comprehensive income for the year ended 30 June 20X2.**

Other points on group accounting

Disposal of a foreign entity

On the disposal of a foreign subsidiary, the cumulative exchange difference recognised as other comprehensive income and accumulated in a separate component of equity (because it was unrealised) becomes realised. The standard requires the exchange reserve to be recycled (i.e. reclassified) on the disposal of the subsidiary as part of the gain/loss on disposal.

Test your understanding 5 – LUMS Group

The LUMS group has sold its entire 100% holding in an overseas subsidiary for proceeds of $50,000. The net assets at the date of disposal were $20,000 and the carrying value of goodwill at that date was $10,000. The cumulative balance on the group foreign currency reserve is a gain of $5,000. Tax can be ignored.

Calculate the exceptional gain arising to the group on the disposal of the foreign subsidiary.

Equity accounting

The principles to be used in translating a subsidiary's financial statements also apply to the translation of an associate's.

Once the results are translated, the carrying amount of the associate (cost (at the closing rate) plus the share of post-acquisition retained earnings) can be calculated together with the group's share of the profits for the period and included in the group financial statements.

Shortcomings in IAS 21

There are a number of issues on which IAS 21 is either silent or fails to give adequate guidance.

(a) Under IAS 21 transactions should be recorded at the rate ruling at the date the transaction occurs (i.e. the date when the transaction qualifies for recognition in the accounts), but in some cases this date is difficult to establish. For example, it could be the order date, the date of invoice or the date on which the goods were received.

(b) IAS 21 states that average rates can be used if these do not fluctuate significantly, but what period should be used to calculate average rates? Should the average rate be adjusted to take account of material transactions?

(c) IAS 21 provides only limited guidance where there are two or more exchange rates for a particular currency or where an exchange rate is suspended. It has been suggested that companies should use whichever rate seems appropriate given the nature of the transaction and have regard to prudence if necessary.

(d) IAS 21 makes a distinction between the translation of monetary and non-monetary items, but in practice some items (such as progress payments paid against non-current assets or inventories, and debt securities held as investments) may have characteristics of both.

(e) Retranslating the opening reserves at the closing rate gives a difference that goes direct to reserves under the closing rate method. The reasoning behind this is that these exchange differences do not result from the operations of the group. To include them in profit or loss would be to distort the results of the group's trading operations. However, some commentators consider that all such gains and losses are part of a group's profit and should be recorded in profit or loss.

4 Chapter summary

```
┌─────────────────────────────┐
│      FOREIGN CURRENCY        │
└─────────────────────────────┘
              ⋮
┌─────────────────────────────┐
│     IAS 21 THE EFFECTS OF    │
│     CHANGES IN FOREIGN       │
│      EXCHANGE RATES          │
└─────────────────────────────┘
              ⋮
┌─────────────────────────────┐
│ Functional currency:        │
│ The currency of the primary │
│ economic environment where  │
│ the entity operates         │
│                             │
│ Presentation currency:      │
│ The currency in which the   │
│ entity presents its         │
│ financial statements        │
└─────────────────────────────┘
```

```
┌─────────────────────────────┐    ┌─────────────────────────────┐
│ Accounting for individual   │    │ Translating the financial   │
│ transactions in a foreign   │    │ statements of a foreign     │
│ currency                    │    │ operation                   │
│ • At transaction date       │    │ Statement of financial      │
│ • On settlement             │    │ position: translate at      │
│ • At reporting date         │    │ closing rate                │
└─────────────────────────────┘    │ Income statement: translate │
                                    │ at average rate             │
                                    │ Calculation of exchange     │
                                    │ difference                  │
                                    └─────────────────────────────┘
                                                   ⋮
                                    ┌─────────────────────────────┐
                                    │ Consolidation of a foreign  │
                                    │ operation                   │
                                    │ • Calculation of goodwill   │
                                    │ • Adjustment to cost of     │
                                    │   investment                │
                                    │ • Calculation of non-       │
                                    │   controlling interests     │
                                    └─────────────────────────────┘
                                                   ⋮
                                    ┌─────────────────────────────┐
                                    │ Other points on group       │
                                    │ accounting                  │
                                    │ • Disposal of foreign entity│
                                    │ • Equity accounting         │
                                    └─────────────────────────────┘
                                                   ⋮
                                    ┌─────────────────────────────┐
                                    │   Shortcomings in IAS 21    │
                                    └─────────────────────────────┘
```

Test your understanding answers

Test your understanding 1 – Butler, Waiter and Attendant

(a) Butler – Solution

27 November 20X6 Dr Purchases $29,058 Cr Payables $29,058	Translate transaction prior to recording:	324,000 / = $29,058 11.15

19 December 20X6	SwK 324,000 is paid. At 19 December rate this is:	324,000 / = $29,643 10.93
Dr Payables	$29,058 (being the payable created on 27 November)	
Dr Income statement	$585 i.e. exchange loss	
Cr Cash	$29,643	

$585 is an exchange loss arising because the functional currency ($) has weakened against the transaction currency (SwK) since the transaction occurred.

(b) Waiter – Solution

	Z	Rate	$
1 January 20X7 record liability	120,000	2.0	240,000
1 March 20X7 repay part of liability	(40,000)	3.0	(120,000)
Exchange loss – balancing figure – taken to income			160,000
31 December 20X7	80,000	3.5	280,000

The $160,000 is the loss that will be reported in income for the year. The liability is a monetary item and so has been retranslated at the closing rate. It will be reported in the statement of financial position as $280,000.

(c) **Attendant**

As the asset is a non-monetary item, it will not normally be subject to retranslation at the reporting date. If the land is carried at cost, the asset remains stated at $ cost translated at the rate ruling at the date of purchase as follows:

R60,000 divided by 8 = $7,500

If the revaluation model from either IAS 16 Property, plant and equipment or IAS 40 Investment property is applied, the asset must first be remeasured at the reporting date to fair value in Rylands. The revalued amount is then translated at the rate at the reporting date to provide the $ valuation for inclusion in the financial statements.

If IAS 16 is applied. the movement in carrying value of $500 is reported in other comprehensive income and taken to other components of equity in the statement of financial position. If IAS 40 is applied, the movement in carrying value of $500 is taken to profit or loss for the year.

	R	Rate	$
1 March 20X0 purchase land	60,000	8.0	7,500
Gain to profit or loss or equity as applicable.			500
31 December 20X0	80,000	10.0	8,000

Test your understanding 2 – Highlight

Part A

Both the purchase of plant and equipment and the associated payable are recorded using the rate ruling at the date of the transaction (i.e. Dn10 = $1), giving a value of $40,000. The part-payment made on 1 November is recorded using the rate applicable on that date, with the remaining dinar liability being restated in dollars at the closing rate at the reporting date. The exchange difference, in this case a loss, is identified as a balancing figure and is taken to profit or loss as an operating expense.

		Dn	Rate	Liability - $
1 July 20X3	Payable recorded	400,000	10.0	40,000
1 November 20X3	Part-payment made	(180,000)	7.2	(25,000)
				15,000
	Exchange loss - balancing figure			12,500
31 December 20X3	Payable outstanding	220,000	8.0	27,500

Plant and equipment, as a non-monetary item, is accounted for at historic cost and thus not revalued. As such it is not retranslated. To reflect six months of its five year life passing it is, of course, subject to depreciation. The depreciation charge is $4,000 (i.e. $40,000 × 1/5 × 6/12).

Extracts of the financial statements for the year ended 31 December 20X3 are as follows:

Statement of profit or loss:	$
Cost of sales (depreciation charge)	(4,000)
Operating expenses (exchange loss on retranslation of payable)	(12,500)

Statement of financial position:	
Property, plant and equipment (40,000 - 4,000)	36,000
Deficit on retained earnings (4,000 depreciation + 12,500 exchange loss)	(16,500)
Current liabilities	27,500

Part B

Each of the sales invoices denominated in Dn must be translated into $ using the spot rate on the date of each transaction. Each transaction will result in recognition of revenue and a trade receivable at each of the following amounts:

1 November X3 Dn360,000 / 7.2 = $50,000
1 December 20X3 Dn540,000 / 9.0 = $60,000

Both amounts remain outstanding at the reporting date and must be restated into $ using the closing rate of Dn8 = $1. The exchange difference, in this case a gain, is identified as a balancing figure and must be taken to profit or loss as an item of other operating income.

		Dn	Rate	Receivable - $
1 November 20X3	Receivable recorded	360,000	7.2	50,000
1 December 20X3	Receivable recorded	540,000	9.0	60,000
				‾‾‾‾
				110,000
	Exchange gain - balancing figure			2,500
		‾‾‾‾		‾‾‾‾
31 December 20X3	Receivable outstanding	900,000	8.0	112,500
		‾‾‾‾		‾‾‾‾

Extracts of the financial statements for the year ended 31 December 20X3 are as follows:

Statement of profit or loss:	$
Revenue (50,000 + 60,000)	110,000
Other operating income (exchange gain on retranslation of receivable)	2,500

Statement of financial position:	
Receivable	112,500
Retained earnings (2,500 exchange gain)	2,500

Test your understanding 3 – Parent & Overseas

Group statement of financial position

Note: the assets and liabilities of Overseas have been translated at the closing rate of 5.0 Shillings = $1.

		$
Goodwill	(W3)	1,200
Assets (9,500 + ((40,000 + 4000 FVA) / 5.0))		18,300
		19,500

		$
Equity and liabilities		
Equity capital		5,000
Retained earnings	(W5)	6,338
Group foreign exchange reserve	(W7)	392
		11,730
Non-controlling interest	(W4)	1,092
		12,822
Total equity of the group		12,822
Liabilities (2,318 + (21,800 / 5.0))		6,678
		19,500

Group statement of profit or loss and other comprehensive income for the year

Note: the income and expenses for Overseas have been translated at the average rate of 5.2 Shillings = $1

	$
Revenue (8,000 + (5,200 / 5.2)	9,000
Costs (2,500 + (2,600 / 5.2)	(3,000)
	————
Profit before tax	6,000
Tax (2,000 + (400 / 5.2)	(2,077)
	————
Profit for the year	3,923

Other comprehensive income which may be recycled (i.e. reclassified) to profit or loss in future years:

Total exchange gains on net investment of foreign subsidiary in the year (109 (W3) + 381 (W6))	490
	————
Total comprehensive income for the year	4,413
	————

Profit for the year attributable to:

Owners of Parent (β)	3,838
Non-controlling interest (20% × (2,200 / 5.2))	85
	————
	3,923
	————

Total comprehensive income attributable to:

Owners of Parent (β)	4,230
Non-controlling interest 85 (per PorL) + 22(W3) + 76(W6)	183
	————
	4,413
	————

Workings

(W1) Group structure

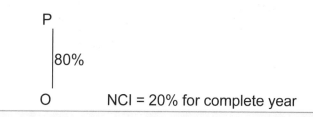

P

80%

O   NCI = 20% for complete year

(W2) **Net assets of subsidiary in functional currency**

	Acq'n date	Rep date	
	Shillings	Shillings	Shillings
Share capital	10,000	10,000	
Retained earnings	6,000	8,200	
Fair value adjustment – land	4,000	4,000	
Post-acquisition movement	20,000	22,200	2,200

(W3) **Full goodwill in subsidiary functional currency and retranslation summary**

	Shillings
Full goodwill:	
Cost of investment $3,818 @ 5.5	20,999
FV of NCI at acquisition	5,000
	25,999
FV of NA at acquisition (W2)	(20,000)
Full goodwill at acquisition	5,999
Translate at closing rate @ 5.0	$1,200

	Shillings	$
Exchange gain (loss) arising on retranslation of goodwill:		
Goodwill translated at rate at acquisition @ 5.5	5,999	1,091
Exchange gain (loss) arising on retranslation of goodwill	**bal fig**	**109**
Goodwill translated at closing rate @ 5.0	5,999	1,200

Allocate gain on retranslation of goodwill between group and NCI based upon respective shareholding:

Group 80% = $87 (W7).and NCI 20% = 22 (W4).

(W4) Non-controlling interest

	Shillings	Rate	$
NCI fair value at acquisition	5,000	5.5	909
NCI share of post-acquisition profit (20% × 2,200 (W2))	440	5.2	85
NCI share of exchange gain on retranslation of goodwill (W3)			22
NCI share of exchange gain on retranslation of net assets (W6)			76
			1,092

(W5) Retained earnings

	Shillings	$
Parent		6,000
Group share of post-acquisition profit (80% × 2,200 (W2))	1,760	
Translated at average rate @ 5.2		338
		6,338

Note that, for the calculation of **group share of subsidiary's profit**, the **average rate** of exchange is used.

(W6) Gain or loss arising on retranslation of net assets

	Shillings	Rate	$
Net assets at acquisition (W2)	20,000	5.5	3,636
Retained profit for the year (W2)	2,200	5.2	423
Exchange gain (loss) on retranslation of net assets	**bal fig**		**381**
Closing net assets	22,200	5.0	4,440

Note that the total gain (loss) on retranslation of net assets must be allocated between the group and NCI based upon their respective shareholdings as follows:

Group (80% × 381 = 305 (W7) and NCI (20% × 381 = 76 (W4)

(W7) **Group share of total exchange differences**

	$
Group share of retranslation of gain re goodwill (W3)	87
Group share of retranslation re net assets (W6)	305
	——
To SOFP	392
	——

Test your understanding 4 – Saint & Albans

Saint Group

Group statement of financial position at 30 June 20X2

The assets and liabilities of Albans have been translated at the closing rate of D4 = $1

				$
Goodwill (W3)				2,700
Loan to Albans	1,400		Interco (1,400)	Nil
Tangible assets	10,000	+ (15,400 + 1,000 (W2) − 200 (W2)) / 4		14,050
Inventory	5,000	+ 4,000 / 4	purp (W5) (400)	5,600
Receivables	4,000	+ 500 / 4		4,125
Cash at bank	1,600	+ 560 / 4		1,740
				——
				28,215
				——

	$
Equity capital	10,000
Share premium	3,000
Group net earnings (W5)	5,692
Group FX reserve (loss) (W7)	(2,773)
	——
	15,919

NCI (W4)	2,046

Total equity of the group	17,965

Non-current liabs   5,000   + (5,460 + 140) / 4   Interco (1,400)   5,000

Current liabilities   5,000   + 1,000/ 4   5,250

                                                28,215

Note: income and expenses of Albans translated at the average rate for the year of D3 = $1.

Group statement of profit or loss and other comprehensive income for the year ended 30 June 20X2

			$
Revenue	50,000 + (60,000 / 3)	Less Interco ($1,200)	68,800
Cost of sales	20,000 + ((30,000 + 200(W2) + 140(W2) + 1,200(W3)) / 3)	Less Interco ($1,200) purp $400	(29,714)
Gross profit			39,086
Admin exps	20,000 + (12,000 / 3)		(24,000)
Profit before tax			15,086
Tax	8,000 + (6,000 / 3)		(10,000)
Profit for the year:			5,086

Other comprehensive income - item that may be reclassified to profit or loss in future periods:

Total exchange difference arising on foreign operations (Goodwill (2,900) (W3) + net assets (1,722) (W6))	(4,622)
Total comprehensive income for the year	464

Profit for the year:	D	$
Attributable to Group - bal fig		3,691
Attributable to NCI - profit for the year	11,660	
Goodwill impaired in year	(1,200)	
Translate at ave rate @ 3 and take NCI share @ 40%	10.460	1,395
		5,086

		$	$
Total comprehensive income for the year:			
Attributable to Group - bal fig			918
Attributable to NCI - profit for the year as above		1,395	
NCI share of exchange gains (losses) on retranslation)			
(Goodwill (1,160) (W3) + net assets (689) (W6))		(1,849)	(454)
			464

(W1) **Group Structure**

Saint

| 60 % acquired one year ago – NCI = 40%

Albans

(W2) **Net assets of subsidiary in functional currency**

	At acquisition	Rep date	
	D	D	D
Equity capital	1,000	1,000	
Share premium	500	500	
Retained earnings	500	12,500	
Fair value adjustment – plant	1,000	1,000	
FVA – dep'n on plant (1/5)		(200)	
Exchange loss on loan		(140)	
Post acquisition movement	3,000	14,660	11,660

Exchange loss on loan received by Albans

Received 1 June X2 $1,400 @ 3.9 = D5,460

Non-current liability 30 June X2 $1,400 @ 4.0 = D5,600

Exchange loss Albans = D140 and increased non-current liability

(W3) **Full goodwill in functional currency of subsidiary**

	D
Cost to parent $5,000 @ 2	10,000
FV of NCI at acquisition	5,000
	15,000
FV of NA at acquisition (W2)	(3,000)
Full goodwill at acquisition	12,000
Impairment - 10%	(1,200)
Unimpaired goodwill at reporting date	10,800

The exchange gain (loss) arising on retranslation of goodwill is as follows:

	D	Rate	$
Full goodwill on acquisition	12,000	2.0	6,000
Impaired in year - 10%	(1,200)	3.0	(400)
Exchange gain (loss) arising on retranslation		**Bal fig**	**(2,900)**
Unimpaired goodwill at reporting date	10,800	4.0	2,700

The exchange loss on retranslation of goodwill is allocated between the group and NCI as follows:

Group: (60% × (2900)) = $1,740 (W7) and NCI (40% × (2900)) = $1,160 (W4)

(W4) **Non-controlling interest**

	D	Rate	$
FV at acquisition per question	5,000	2.0	2,500
NCI % of post-acquisition profit (40% × D11,660) (W2)	4,664	3.0	1,555
NCI % of goodwill impairment (40% × D1,200) (W3)	480	3.0	(160)
NCI % of retranslation loss on goodwill (W3)			(1,160)
NCI % of retranslation loss on net assets (W6)			(689)
To SOFP			2,046

(W5) Group retained earnings

	$
Parent retained earnings	4,000
Group share of goodwill impairment 60% × (D1,200 / 3) (i.e. average rate)(W3)	(240)
Group share of post-acq'n profit 60% × (D11,660 / 3) (i.e. average rate)	2,332
URPS on inventory (800 × 1.5 = 1,200 - 800 = 400)	(400)
	5,692

(W6) Exchange differences on retranslation of net assets

	D	Rate	$
Net assets at acquisition translated at historic rate	3,000	2.0	1,500
Profit for year translated at average rate for year	11,660	3.0	3,887
Exchange gain (loss) on retranslation of net assets		**bal fig**	**(1,722)**
Net assets at reporting date translated at closing rate	14,660	4.0	(3,665)

Allocate exchange loss between group and NCI based upon respective shareholdings:
Group: (60% × $1,722) = ($1,033) (W7)
NCI: (40% × $1,722) = ($689) (W4)

(W7) Group foreign exchange reserve

	$
Group % of exchange loss on retranslation of net assets (W6)	(1,033)
Group % of exchange loss on retranslation of goodwill (W3)	(1,740)
To Group SOFP	(2,773)

Test your understanding 5 – LUMS Group

	$	$
Proceeds		50,000
Net assets recorded prior to disposal:		
Net assets	20,000	
Goodwill	10,000	
	———	
		(30,000)
Realisation of the group exchange difference, reclassified to profit as part of the gain		5,000
		———
		25,000

6

Group statement of cash flows

Chapter learning objectives

Upon completion of this chapter you will be able to:

- prepare and discuss the group statement of cash flows.

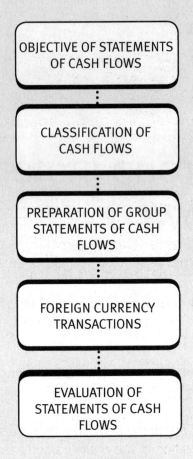

1 Objective of statements of cash flows

- IAS 7 **Statement of cash flows** provides guidance on the preparation of a statement of cash flow.

- The objective of a statement of cash flows is to provide information on an entity's changes in cash and cash equivalents during the period.

- The statement of financial position and statement of comprehensive income are prepared on an accruals basis and do not show how the business has generated and used cash in the accounting period.

- The statement of comprehensive income may show profits on an accruals basis even if the company is suffering severe cash flow problems.

- Statements of cash flows enable users of the financial statements to assess the **liquidity, solvency** and **financial adaptability** of a business.

Definitions:

- **Cash** consists of cash in hand and deposits repayable upon demand, less overdrafts. This includes cash held in a foreign currency.
- **Cash equivalents** are short-term, highly liquid investments that are readily convertible to known amounts of cash and are subject to an insignificant risk of changes in value.
- **Cash flows** are inflows and outflows of cash and cash equivalents.

2 Classification of cash flows

IAS 7 does not prescribe a specific format for the statement of cash flows, although it requires that cash flows are classified under three headings:

- cash flows from operating activities, defined as the entity's principal revenue earning activities and other activities that do not fall under the next two headings
- cash flows from investing activities, defined as the acquisition and disposal of long-term assets and other investments (excluding cash equivalents)
- cash flows from financing activities, defined as activities that change the size and composition of the entity's equity and borrowings.

Proforma statement of cash flow per IAS 7

	$	$
Operating activities		
Profit before tax		X
Add: interest payable		X
Less: Income from associate		(X)
Adjust for non-cash items dealt with in arriving at operating profit:		
Add: depreciation		X
Less: gain on disposal of subsidiary		(X)
Add: loss on disposal of subsidiary		X
Add: loss on impairment charged to PorL		X
Add: loss on disposal of non-current assets		X
Add: increase in provisions		X
		─────
		X
		─────

Changes in working capital:		
Increase in inventory		(X)
Increase in receivables		(X)
Decrease in payables		(X)
Cash generated		X
Interest paid		(X)
Taxation paid		(X)
Net cash Inflow(outflow) from operating activities		X
Investing activities		
Payments to purchase NCA	(X)	
Receipts from NCA disposals	X	
Net cash paid to acquire subsidiary	(X)	
Net cash proceeds from subsidiary disposal	X	
Dividend received from associate	X	
Interest received	X	
Net cash inflow(outflow) from investing activities	——	X(X)
Financing activities		
Proceeds from share issue	X	
Proceeds from loan or debenture issue	X	
Cash repayment of loans or debentures	(X)	
Finance lease repayments	(X)	
Equity dividend paid by parent	(X)	
Dividend paid to NCI	(X)	
Net cash inflow(outflow) from financing activities	——	X(X)
Increase(Decrease) in cash and equivalents for the year		X(X)
Cash and equivalents brought forward		X(X)
Cash and equivalents carried forward		X(X)

KAPLAN PUBLISHING

Classification of cash flows

Cash flows from operating activities

There are two methods of calculating the cash from operations.

- The **direct method** shows operating cash receipts and payments. This includes cash receipts from customers, cash payments to suppliers and cash payments to and on behalf of employees. The Examiner has indicated that the direct method is unlikely to be examined in detail, although you may be required to explain key similarities and differences between the two methods.

- The **indirect method** starts with profit before tax and adjusts it for non-cash charges and credits, to reconcile it to the net cash flow from operating activities.

IAS 7 permits either method; note that the standard encourages, but does not require, use of the direct method. The methods differ only in respect of derivation of the item 'net cash inflow from operating activities'. Subsequent inflows and outflows for investing and financing activities are the same. A comparison between the direct and indirect method to arrive at net cash inflow from operating activities is shown below.

Direct method:	$m	Indirect method:	$m
Cash receipts from customers	15,424	Profit before tax	6,022
Cash payments to suppliers	(5,824)	Depreciation charges	899
Cash payments to and on behalf of employees	(2,200)	Increase in inventory	(194)
Other cash payments	(511)	Increase in receivables	(72)
		Increase in payables	234
Net cash inflow from operating activities	6,889	Net cash inflow from operating activities	6,889

The principal advantage of the direct method is that it discloses operating cash receipts and payments. Knowledge of the specific sources of cash receipts and the purposes for which cash payments have been made in past periods may be useful in assessing and predicting future cash flows.

Under the **indirect method,** typically begin with profit before tax and then make adjustments for a number of items, the most frequently occurring of which are:

- depreciation or amortisation charges in the year
- impairment charged to profit or loss in the year
- profit or loss on disposal of non current assets
- change in inventory
- change in receivables
- change in payables.

Cash flows from investing activities

Cash flows to appear under this heading include:

- cash paid for property, plant and equipment and other non-current assets
- cash received on the sale of property, plant and equipment and other non-current assets
- cash paid for investments in or loans to other entities (excluding movements on loans from financial institutions, which are shown under financing)
- cash received for the sale of investments or the repayment of loans to other entities (again excluding loans from financial institutions).

Cash flows from financing activities

Financing cash flows mainly comprise receipts or repayments of principal from or to external providers of finance.

Financing **cash inflows** include:

- receipts from issuing shares or other equity instruments
- receipts from issuing debentures, loans, notes and bonds and from other long-term and short-term borrowings (other than overdrafts, which are normally included in cash and cash equivalents).

Financing **cash outflows** include:

- repayments of amounts borrowed (other than overdrafts)
- the capital element of finance lease rental payments
- payments to reacquire or redeem the entity's shares.

Interest and dividends

There are divergent and strongly held views about how interest and dividends cash flows should be classified. Some regard them as part of operating activities, because they are as much part of the day to day activities as receipts from customers, payments to suppliers and payments to staff. Others regard them as part of financing activities, the heading under which the instruments giving rise to the payments and receipts are classified. Still others believe they are part of investing activities, because this is what the long-term finance raised in this way is used for.

IAS 7 allows interest and dividends, whether received or paid, to be classified under any of the three headings, provided the classification is consistent from period to period.

The practice adopted in this workbook is to classify:

- interest received as a cash flow from investing activities
- interest paid as a cash flow from operating activities
- dividends received as a cash flow from investing activities
- dividends paid as a cash flow from financing activities.

Cash flows from operating activities

Calculation of net cash flow from operating activities

Profit before tax is computed on the accruals basis, whereas net cash flow from operating activities only records the cash inflows and outflows arising out of trading.

The main categories of items in the statement of profit or loss and other omprehensive income and on the statement of financial position that form part of the reconciliation between profit before tax and net cash flow from operating activities using the indirect method are:

- **Depreciation**.

    Depreciation is a non-cash cost, being a book write-off of capital expenditure. Capital expenditure will be recorded under 'investing activities' at the time of the cash outflow. Depreciation therefore represents an **addition** to reported profit in deriving cash inflow.

- **Profit/loss on disposal of non-current assets.**

  The cash inflow from such a disposal needs to be recorded under 'investing activities'. If the profit or loss on the sale has been included in profit before tax, an adjustment is necessary in computing operating cash flow. A loss on disposal is added to reported profit, while a profit on disposal is deducted from reported profit.

- **Statement of financial position change in inventories**

  Inventory at the reporting date represents a purchase that has not actually been charged against current profits. However, as cash was spent on its purchase or a payable incurred, it does represent an actual or potential cash outflow. The effect on the statement of cash flows of a change in inventories is:

  - an increase in inventory is a deduction from reported profit, because it requires financing

  - a decrease in inventory is an addition to reported profit, because the amount of financing required has fallen.

- **Statement of financial position change in receivables**

  A sale once made creates income irrespective of the date of cash receipt. If the cash has not been received by the reporting date, there is no cash inflow from operating activities for the current accounting period. Similarly, opening receivables represent sales of a previous accounting period, most of which will be cash receipts in the current period.

  The change between opening and closing receivables will thus represent the adjustment required to move from profit to net cash inflow. The reasoning is the same as for inventories. An increase in receivables is a deduction from reported profit. A decrease in receivables is an addition to reported profit.

- **Statement of financial position change in payables**

  A purchase represents the incurring of expenditure and a charge or potential charge to the profit or loss or other comprehensive income. It does not represent a cash outflow until paid. To the extent that a purchase results in a charge to profit or loss:

  - an increase in payables between two reporting dates is an addition to reported profit

  - a decrease in payables is a deduction from reported profit.

If the purchase does not result in a charge to profit or loss in the current year, the corresponding payable is not included in the reconciliation of profit to net cash inflow. For example, a payable in respect of a non-current asset is not included.

Income taxes

Cash flows arising from taxes on income should be separately disclosed as part of operating activities unless they can be specifically identified with financing or investing activities. It is reasonable to include income taxes as part of operating activities unless a question gives a clear indication to the contrary.

If income tax payments are allocated over more than one class of activity, the total should be disclosed by note.

The computation of income taxes paid may present a practical problem.

It is often convenient to arrive at the figure by means of a single tax working account into which all tax balances, whether current or deferred, are entered.

Sales tax

The existence of sales tax raises the question of whether the relevant cash flows should be reported gross or net of the tax element and how the balance of tax paid to, or repaid by, the taxing authorities should be reported.

The cash flows of an entity include sales tax where appropriate and thus strictly the various elements of the statement of cash flows should include sales tax. However, this treatment does not take into account the fact that normally sales tax is a short-term timing difference as far as the entity's overall cash flows are concerned and the inclusion of sales tax in the cash flows may distort the allocation of cash flows to standard headings.

In order to avoid this distortion and to show cash flows attributable to the reporting entity's activities, it is usual for amounts to be shown net of sales taxes and the net movement on the amount payable to, or receivable from, the taxing authority should be allocated to cash flows from operating activities unless a different treatment is more appropriate in the particular circumstances concerned.

Unusual items and non-cash transactions

Unusual cash flows

Where cash flows are unusual because of their size or incidence, sufficient disclosure should be given to explain their cause and nature.

For a cash flow to be unusual on the grounds of its size alone, it must be unusual in relation to cash flows of a similar nature.

Discontinued activities

Cash flows relating to discontinued activities are required by IFRS 5 to be shown separately, either on the face of the statement of cash flows or by note.

Major non-cash transactions

Material transactions not resulting in movements of cash should be disclosed in the notes to the statement of cash flows if disclosure is necessary for an understanding of the underlying transactions.

Consideration for transactions may be in a form other than cash. The purpose of a statement of cash flows is to report cash flows, and non-cash transactions should therefore not be reported in a statement of cash flows. However, to obtain a full picture of the alterations in financial position caused by the transactions for the period, separate disclosure of material non-cash transactions is also necessary.

Examples of non-cash transactions are:

- **the acquisition of assets by finance leases**

Finance leases are accounted for by the lessee capitalising the present value of the minimum lease payments (see later chapter). A liability and a corresponding asset are produced, which do not reflect cash flows in the accounting period. The statement of cash flows records the cash flow, i.e. the rentals paid, with the reduction in liability shown under financing. The interest element of the payment may be included in operating activities with only the portion of the payment which reduces the lease liability shown under financing activities.

- **the conversion of debt to equity**

If debt is issued with conversion rights attached it will be cancelled using an issue of shares and no cash flow will arise. The statement of cash flows is not affected.

- **the acquisition of a subsidiary by issue of shares**.

> If the purchase consideration on acquisition of a subsidiary is settled using a share for share exchange no cash flow will arise and the statement of cash flows is not affected.

3 Preparation of group statements of cash flows

So far in this chapter, we have revised the basics on statements of cash flows. You should be familiar with this from previous studies.

Group statements of cash flows add three extra elements:

- cash paid to non-controlling interests
- cash received from associates
- acquisition and disposal of subsidiaries.

Cash paid to non-controlling interests

- When a subsidiary that is not wholly owned pays a dividend, some of that dividend is paid outside of the group to the non-controlling interest.

- Such dividends paid to non-controlling interests should be disclosed separately in the statement of cash flows.

- To calculate the amount paid, reconcile the non-controlling interest in the statement of financial position from the opening to the closing balance. You can use a T-account to do this. This working remains the same whichever method is used to value the non-controlling interest.

Illustration: Non-controlling interest

The following information has been extracted from the consolidated financial statements of WG for the years ended 31 December:

	20X7	20X6
	$000	$000
NCI in consolidated net assets	780	690
NCI in consolidated profit after tax	120	230

Required:

What is the dividend paid to non-controlling interests in the year 20X6?

Solution

Steps:

(1) Set up a T-account or schedule for the NCI balance.

(2) Insert the opening and closing balances for net assets and the NCI share of profit after tax.

(3) Balance or reconcile the working.

(4) The balancing figure is the cash dividend paid to the NCI.

Non-controlling interests

	$000		$000
NCI derecognised re sub disposal	XX	NCI Balance b/fwd	690
Dividends paid (bal fig)	30	NCI recognised re acq'n of sub	XX
NCI Balance c/fwd	780	Share of profits in year	120
	———		———
	810		810
	———		———

Alternatively:

	$000
NCI bal b/fwd per opening SOFP	690
Add: NCI re sub acquired in year	XX
Add: NCI share of profit for the year	120
Less: NCI derecognised re sub disposed in year	(XX)
Cash dividend paid in year **(bal fig)**	(30)
	———
NCI bal c/fwd per closing SOFP	780
	———

Watch out for an acquisition or disposal of a subsidiary during the year. This will affect the NCI and will need to be taken account of in the T-account or schedule as indicated, showing the NCI that has been acquired or disposed of during the period.

Associates

Associates generate cash flows into or out of the group to the extent that:

* dividends are received out of the profits of the associate
* trading occurs between the group and associate
* further investment is made in the associate.

Associates are usually dealt with under the equity method of accounting and this terminology is used below. (This also applies to joint ventures as defined in IFRS 11 Joint Arrangements.)

Standard accounting practice

* The cash flows of any equity accounted entity should be included in the group statement of cash flows only to the extent of the actual cash flows between the group and the entity concerned, for example dividends received in cash and loans made or repaid.

Dividends

* Only dividends received represent a cash inflow. Dividends declared but unpaid represent an increase in group receivables.
* When reconciling group net cash inflow to group reported profit, the movement between opening and closing receivables must exclude dividends receivable from the associate so that dividends received can be shown in the statement of cash flows.
* Dividends received from associates should be included as a separate item in the group statement of cash flows.

Trading between group and associate

* Trading between the group and an associate will give rise to inter-entity balances in the group statement of financial position at the year end.
* The balances will be treated in the same way as any other trading receivables and payables, i.e. the movement between opening and closing balances forms part of the reconciliation between group profit and group net cash inflow from operating activities.

Change in investment in associate

A change in investment in the associate can arise when:

- an additional shareholding is purchased or part of the shareholding is sold

- loans are made to/from the associate or amounts previously loaned are repaid.

 Illustration: associate

The following information has been extracted from the consolidated financial statements of H for the year ended 31 December 20X1:

Group statement of profit or loss extract

	$000
Operating profit	734
Income from associate	68
Profit before tax	802
Tax on profit (including 20 in respect of associate)	(324)
Profit after tax	478

Show the relevant figures to be included in the group statement of cash flows for the year ended 31 December 20X1.

Group statement of financial position extracts

	20X1	20X0
	$000	$000
Investments in associates		
CV of interest in associate	466	456
Loan to associate	380	300
Current assets		
Receivables	260	190
Included within group receivables is the following amount:		
Current account with associate	40	70

Required:

Show the relevant figures to be included in the group statement of cash flows for the year ended 31 December 20X1.

Solution

When dealing with the dividend from the associate, the process is the same as we have already seen with the non-controlling interest.

Set up a schedule or T account or schedule and include all the balances that relate to the associate. When you balance or reconcile the account, the balancing figure will be the cash dividend received from the associate.

(W1) **Dividend received from associate**

Associate

	$000		$000
Balance b/d		Dividend received	
Share of net assets	456	(bal fig)	38
		Share of net assets	466
Share of profit after tax	48		
(68–20)	———		———
	504		504
	———		———

Alternatively:

	$000
Assoc bal b/fwd from opening SOFP	456
Add: share of profit after tax due from associate per PorL (68-28)	48
Cash dividend received **(bal fig)**	(38)
	———
Assoc bal c/fwd from closing SOFP	466
	———

Note that the current account with the associate remains within receivables and the loan made to the associate is accounted for separately.

Extracts from statement of cash flows

	$000
Cash flows from operating activities	
Profit before tax	802
Share of profit of associate	(68)
Investing activities	
Dividend received from associate (W1)	38
Loan to associate (380 – 300)	(80)

Acquisition and disposal of subsidiaries

Standard accounting practice

- If a subsidiary joins or leaves a group during a financial year, the cash flows of the group should include the cash flows of that subsidiary for the same period that the results of the subsidiary are included in the statement of profit or loss and other comprehensive income.

- Cash payments to acquire subsidiaries and receipts from disposals of subsidiaries must be reported separately in the statement of cash flows under investing activities. The cash and cash equivalents acquired or disposed of should be shown separately.

- A note to the statement of cash flows should show a summary of the effects of acquisitions and disposals of subsidiaries, indicating how much of the consideration comprised cash and cash equivalents, and the assets and liabilities acquired or disposed of.

Acquisitions

- In the statement of cash flows we must record the actual cash flow for the purchase, not the net assets acquired.

- The assets and liabilities purchased will not be shown with the cash outflow in the statement of cash flows.

- All assets and liabilities acquired must be included in any workings to calculate the cash movement for an item during the year. If they are not included in deriving the balancing figure, the incorrect cash flow figure will be calculated. This applies to all assets and liabilities acquired including the non-controlling interest.

Disposals

- The statement of cash flows will show the cash received from the sale of the subsidiary, net of any cash balances that were transferred out with the sale.

- The assets and liabilities disposed of are not shown in the cash flow. When calculating the movement between the opening and closing balance of an item, the assets and liabilities that have been disposed of must be taken into account in order to calculate the correct cash figure. As with acquisitions, this applies to all assets and liabilities and the non-controlling interest.

Foreign subsidiaries within the group

When accounting for a foreign subsidiary within a group, foreign exchange differences arise on retranslation of the opening net assets from the rate of exchange at that reporting date to the closing rate of exchange at the current reporting date. The exchange gains and/or losses on each of the individual net assets needs to be included in your workings to correctly determine cashflows and adjustments for inclusion in the group statement of cash flows. This will be considered in more detail elsewhere in this chapter, but the impact on working capital can be considered here.

Similarly, with the acquisition or disposal of a subsidiary during the year, you should be provided with a summary of the individual net assets acquired or disposed of which can be used when reconciling movements in assets and liabilities to identify relevant amounts to include in the group statement of cash flows.

Illustration: Acquisition / disposal of subsidiary

The following extracts from a group statement of financial position are presented below: During the year, one subsidiary was acquired and another disposed of, with details of working capital as summarised below:

	20X8 $000	20X7 $000	Sub acquired $000	Sub disposed $000
Inventory	74,666	53,019	4,500	6,800
Trade receivables	58,246	62,043	7,900	6,700
Trade payables	93,678	86,247	8,250	5,740

Required:

Calculate the movement on inventory, trade receivables and trade payables for inclusion in the group statement of cash flows.

Solution

The working capital balances brought forward and carried forward are not directly comparable - they need to be adjusted to make them comparable so that the resulting increase or decrease in each item of working capital can be included as an adjustment within the 'Operating activities' section of the statement of cash flows.

This can be achieved, including accounting for any foreign exchange gain or loss arising on retranslation of a foreign subsidiary (see later), by preparing a schedule as follows:

	Inventory	Trade rec'ables	Trade payables
	$000	$000	$000
Bal b/fwd	53,019	62,043	86,247
Add: sub acquired in year	4,500	7,900	8,250
Less:sub disposed in year	(6,800)	(6,700)	(5,740)
FX gain re foreign sub (Note 1)	XX	XX	(XX) (Note 2)
FX loss re foreign sub (Note 1)	(XX)	(XX)	XX (Note 2)
Sub-total	50,719	63,243	88,757
Bal c/fwd	74,666	58,246	93,678
Movement in the year	inc (23,947)	dec 4,897	inc 4,921
Impact on cash flow	Outflow	Inflow	Inflow

Note 1: Inclusion of foreign exchange gains and/or losses arising on retranslation of a foreign subsidiary are included within this template for illustrative purposes only. This will be considered in detail elsewhere within this chapter.

Note 2: Notice that a foreign exchange gain will reduce a liability and a foreign exchange loss will increase a liability.

Test your understanding 1 – Extracts

CASH FLOW EXERCISES

Calculate the cash flows given the following extracts from statements of financial position drawn up at the year ended 31 December 20X0 and 20X1.

(1)	20X0	20X1
	$	$
Non-current assets (CV)	100	250

During the year depreciation charged was $20, a revaluation surplus of $60 was recorded, non-current assets with a CV of $15 were disposed of and non-current assets acquired subject to finance leases had a CV of $30.

Required:

How much cash was spent on non-current assets in the period?

(2)	20X0	20X1
	$	$
Deferred tax	50	100
Income tax liability	100	120

The income tax charge was $180.

Required:

How much tax was paid in the period?

(3)	20X0	20X1
	$	$
Non-controlling interest	440	840

The group statement of profit or loss and other comprehensive income reported a non-controlling interest of $500.

Required:

How much was the cash dividend paid to the non-controlling interest?

(4)	20X0	20X1
	$	$
Non-controlling interest	500	850

The group statement of profit or loss and other comprehensive income reported a non-controlling interest of $600.

Required:

How much was the cash dividend paid to the non-controlling interest?

(5)	20X0	20X1
	$	$
Investment in associate undertaking	200	500

The group statement of profit or loss reported 'Income from Associate Undertakings' of $750.

Required:

How much was the cash dividend received by the group?

(6)	20X0	20X1
	$	$
Investment in associate undertaking	600	3200

The group statement of profit or loss reported 'Income from Associate Undertakings' of $4,000

In addition, during the period the associate revalued its non-current assets, the group share of which is $500.

Required:

How much was the cash dividend received by the group?

(7)	20X0	20X1
	$	$
Non-current asset (CV)	150	500

During the year depreciation charged was $50, and the group acquired a subsidiary with non-current assets of $200.

Required:

How much cash was spent on non-current assets in the period?

(8)	20X0	20X1
	$	$
Loan	2,500	1,000

The loan is denominated in an overseas currency, and a loss of $200 has been recorded on the retranslation.

Required:

How much cash was paid?

The group had the following working capital:

(9)	20X0	20X1
	$	$
Inventory	200	100
Receivables	200	300
Trade payables	200	500

During the period the group acquired a subsidiary with the following working capital.

Inventory	50
Receivables	200
Trade Payables	40

During the period the group disposed of a subsidiary with the following working capital.

Inventory	25
Receivables	45
Trade Payables	20

During the period the group experienced the following exchange rate differences.

Inventory	11	Gain
Receivables	21	Gain
Trade payables	31	Loss

Required:

Calculate the extract from the statement of cash flows for working capital.

Test your understanding 2 – AH Group

Extracts from the consolidated financial statements of the AH Group for the year ended 30 June 20X5 are given below:

AH Group: Consolidated statement of profit or loss for the year ended 30 June 20X5

	20X5
	$000
Revenue	85,000
Cost of sales	(60,750)
	————
Gross profit	24,250
Operating expenses	(5,650)
	————
Operating Profit	18,600
Finance cost	(1,400)
	————
Profit before disposal of property	17,200
Disposal of property (note 2)	1,250
	————
Profit before tax	18,450
Tax	(6,250)
	————
Profit for the period	12,200
	————
Attributable to:	
Non-controlling interest	405
Owners of the parent	11,795
	————
	12,200
	————

Note: There were no items of other comprehensive income during the year.

AH Group: Statement of financial position, with comparatives, at 30 June 20X5

		20X5		20X4
ASSETS	$000	$000	$000	$000
Non-current assets				
Property, plant and equipment	50,600		44,050	
Goodwill (note 3)	5,910		4,160	
		56,510		48,210
Current assets				
Inventories	33,500		28,750	
Trade receivables	27,130		26,300	
Cash	1,870		3,900	
		62,500		58,950
		119,010		107,160
Equity and liabilities	$000	$000	$000	$000
Equity shares @ $1 each	20,000		18,000	
Share premium	12,000		10,000	
Retained earnings	24,135		18,340	
		56,135		46,340
Non-controlling interest		3,875		1,920
Total equity		60,010		48,260
Non-current liabilities				
Interest-bearing borrowings		18,200		19,200
Current liabilities				
Trade payables	33,340		32,810	
Interest payables	1,360		1,440	
Tax	6,100		5,450	
		40,800		39,700
		119,010		107,160

Notes:

(1) Several years ago, AH acquired 80% of the issued equity shares of its subsidiary, BI. On 1 January 20X5, AH acquired 75% of the issued equity shares of CJ in exchange for a fresh issue of 2 million of its own $1 equity shares (issued at a premium of $1 each) and $2 million in cash. The net assets of CJ at the date of acquisition were assessed as having the following fair values:

	$000
Property, plant and equipment	4,200
Inventories	1,650
Receivables	1,300
Cash	50
Trade payables	(1,950)
Tax	(250)
	5,000

(2) During the year, AH disposed of a non-current asset of property for proceeds of $2,250,000. The carrying value of the asset at the date of disposal was $1,000,000. There were no other disposals of non-current assets. Depreciation of $7,950,000 was charged against consolidated profits for the year.

(3) Goodwill on acquisition relates to the acquisition of two subsidiaries. Entity BI was acquired many years ago, and goodwill relating to this acquisition was calculated on a proportion of net assets basis. Goodwill relating to the acquisition of entity CJ during the year was calculated on the full goodwill basis. On 1 January 20X5 when CJ was acquired, the fair value of the non-controlling interest was $1,750,000. Any impairment of goodwill during the year was accounted for within cost of sales.

Required:

Prepare the consolidated statement of cash flows of the AH Group for the financial year ended 30 June 20X5 in the form required by IAS 7 Statements of Cash Flows, and using the indirect method. Notes to the statement of cash flows are NOT required, but full workings should be shown.

Foreign currency transactions

It is likely that any statement of cash flows question will require you to deal with exchange gains and losses.

Individual entity stage

- Exchange differences arising at the individual entity stage are in most instances reported as part of operating profit. If the foreign currency transaction has been settled in the year, the cash flows will reflect the reporting currency cash receipt or payment and thus no problem arises.

- An unsettled foreign currency transaction will, however, give rise to an exchange difference for which there is no cash flow effect in the current year. Such exchange differences therefore need to be eliminated in computing net cash flows from operating activities.

- Fortunately this will not require much work if the unsettled foreign currency transaction is in working capital. Adjusting profit by movements in working capital will automatically adjust correctly for the non-cash flow exchange gains and losses.

Illustration: Foreign currency transactions: individual entity

The financial statements of A are as follows:

Statements of financial position at 31 December

	20X3	20X4
	$	$
Non-current assets	–	–
Current assets		
Inventory	300,000	300,000
Cash	335,000	595,000
	635,000	895,000

	$	$
Equity and liabilities	100,000	190,000
Foreign currency loan	235,000	245,000
Trade payables	300,000	460,000
	635,000	895,000
Capital and reserves	100,000	190,000
Foreign currency loan	235,000	245,000
Trade payables	300,000	460,000
	635,000	895,000
Capital and reserves	100,000	190,000
Foreign currency loan	235,000	245,000
Trade payables	300,000	460,000
	635,000	895,000

During the year, A purchased raw materials for Z200,000, recorded in its books as $100,000. By the year end A had settled half the debt for $48,000 and the remaining payable is retranslated at closing rate at $45,000.

These transactions are included in the purchase ledger control account, which is as follows:

Purchase ledger control

	$		$
Cash	743,000	Balance b/d	300,000
Exchange gains		Purchases	910,000
On settled transaction			
(50,000 – 48,000)	2,000		
On unsettled transaction			
(50,000 – 45,000)	5,000		
Balance c/d			
Foreign currency			
payable	45,000		
Other	415,000		
	1,210,000		1,210,000

Show the gross cash flows (i.e. cash flows under the direct method) from operating activities, together with a reconciliation of profit before tax to net cash flow from operating activities.

Solution

Statement of cash flows for the year

	$	$
Cash received from customers	1,003,000	
Cash payments to suppliers	743,000	
Net cash inflow from operations		260,000
Increase in cash		260,000

Note that because there is no change in inventory, cost of sales is the same as purchases.

Reconciliation of profit before tax to net cash inflow from operating activities

	$
Profit before tax	90,000
Exchange loss on foreign currency loan	10,000
Increase in payables	160,000
	————
Net cash inflow from operations	260,000
	————

Consolidated statements of cash flow

- The key to the preparation of a group statement of cash flows involving a foreign subsidiary is an understanding of the make-up of the foreign exchange differences themselves.

- None of the differences reflects a cash inflow/outflow to the group. The main concern, therefore, is to determine the real cash flows, particularly if they have to be derived as balancing figures from the opening and closing statements of financial position.

- If cash balances are partly denominated in a foreign currency, the effect of exchange rate movements on cash is reported in the statement of cash flows in order to reconcile the cash balances at the beginning and end of the period. This amount is presented separately from cash flows from operating, investing and financing activities.

Closing rate/net investment method

- Using the closing rate/net investment method, the exchange difference on translating the statements of the foreign entity will relate to the opening net assets of that entity (i.e. non-current assets, inventories, receivables, cash, payables and loans) and also to the difference between the average and the closing rates of exchange on translation of the result for the period.

- Under the closing rate/net investment method, translation exchange differences are disclosed as other comprehensive income and taken to other components of equity in the statement of financial position.

Care needs to be taken in two areas:

- **Analysis of non-current assets**

  Non-current assets may require analysis in order to determine cash expenditure. Part of the movement in non-current assets may reflect an exchange gain/loss.

- **Analysis of non-controlling interests**

  If non-controlling interests require analysis to determine the dividend paid to them, it must be remembered that they have a share in the exchange gain/loss arising from the translation of the subsidiary's accounts.

Illustration: Foreign currency transactions: groups

B Group recognised a gain of $160,000 on the translation of the financial statements of a 75% owned foreign subsidiary for the year ended 31 December 20X7. This gain is found to be made up as follows

	$
Gain on opening net assets:	
Non-current assets	90,000
Inventories	30,000
Receivables	50,000
Payables	(40,000)
Cash	30,000
	160,000

B Group recognised a loss of $70,000 on retranslating the parent entity's foreign currency loan. This loss has been disclosed as other comprehensive income and charged to reserves in the draft financial statements.

Consolidated statements of financial position as at 31 December

	20X7	20X6
	$000	$000
Non-current assets	2,100	1,700
Inventories	650	480
Receivables	990	800
Cash	500	160
	4,240	3,140
Share capital	1,000	1,000
Consolidated reserves	1,600	770
	2,600	1,770
Non-controlling interest	520	370
Equity	3,120	2,140
Long-term loan	250	180
Payables	870	820
	4,240	3,140

There were no non-current asset disposals during the year.

Consolidated statement of profit or loss for the year ended 31 December 20X7

	$000
Profit before tax (after depreciation of $220,000)	2,170
Tax	(650)
Group profit for the year	1,520
Profit attributable to:	
Owners of the parent	1,260
Non-controlling interest	260
Net profit for the period	1,520

Note:

The dividend paid during the year was $480,000.

Prepare a statement of cash flows for the year ended 31 December 20X7.

Solution

The first stage is to produce a statement of reserves so as to analyse the movements during the year.

Statement of reserves

	$000
Reserves brought forward	770
Group share of profit for the year	1,260
Dividend paid by B	(480)
Exchange gain	
(160,000 × 75%) – 70,000	50
	–––––
Reserves carried forward	1,600
	–––––

Statement of cash flows for the year ended 31 December 20X7

Cash flows from operating activities

	$000
Profit before tax	2,170
Depreciation charges	220
Increase in inventory (650 – 480 – 30)	(140)
Increase in receivables (990 – 800 – 50)	(140)
Increase in payables (870 – 820 – 40)	10
	–––––
Cash generated from operations	2,120
Income taxes paid	(650)
	–––––
Net cash from operating activities	1,470

Cash flows from investing activities

Purchase of non-current assets (W2)	(530)	
	–––––	–––––
		(530)

Cash flows from financing activities

Dividends paid to non-controlling interests (W1)	(150)
Dividends paid	(480)
	(630)
Exchange gain on cash	30
Increase in cash	340
Cash at 1 Jan 20X7	160
Cash at 31 Dec 20X7	500

Workings

(W1) Non-controlling interest

	$000		$000
Dividend paid (bal fig)	150	Balance b/d	370
Balance c/d	520	Total comprehensive income (Note)	300
	670		670

Note: i.e. NCI share of tax 260 + (25% × $160,000 exchange gain) = 300

(W2) Non-current assets

	$000		$000
Balance b/d	1,700	Depreciation	220
Exchange gain	90	Balance c/d	2,100
Additions (bal fig)	530	Exchange gain	
	2,320		2,320

KAPLAN PUBLISHING

Illustration 1 Changes in group with foreign exchange

The following are excerpts from a group's financial statements

	Opening balance	Closing balance
	$000	$000
Group statement of financial position extracts		
Non-current assets	400	500
Loans	600	300
Tax	300	200
Statement of profit or loss extracts		
Depreciation	50	
Loss on disposal of non-current asset (sold for $30,000)	10	
Tax charge	200	

During the accounting period, one subsidiary was sold, and another acquired. Extracts from the statements of financial position are as follows:

	Sold	Acquired
	$000	$000
Non-current assets	60	70
Loans	110	80
Tax	45	65

During the accounting period, the following net exchange gain arose in respect of overseas net assets:

	$000
Non-current assets	40
Loans	(5)
Tax	(5)

Required:

Calculate the group cash flows for non-current assets, loans and tax.

Solution

Non-current assets

	$000
Opening balance	400
Depreciation	(50)
Disposal (30 + 10)	(40)
Disposal of subsidiary	(60)
Acquisition of subsidiary	70
Exchange gain	40
	360
Cash acquisitions (bal figure)	140
Closing balance	500

Loans

Opening balance	600
Disposal of subsidiary	(110)
Acquisition of subsidiary	80
Exchange loss	5
	575
Therefore redemption	(275)
Closing balance	300

Tax

Opening balance	300
Charge for the year	200
Disposal of subsidiary	(45)
Acquisition of subsidiary	65
Exchange loss	5
	525
Therefore cash paid	(325)
Closing balance	200

Test your understanding 3 – Boardres

Set out below is a summary of the accounts of Boardres, a public limited company, for the year ended 31 December 20X7.

Consolidated statement of profit or loss and other comprehensive income for the year ended 31 December 20X7

	$000
Revenue	44,754
Cost of sales and other expenses	(39,613)
Income from associates	30
Finance cost	(305)
	————
Profit before tax	4,866
Tax:	(2,038)
	————
Profit for the period	2,828
Other comprehensive income: Items that may be reclassified to profit or loss in future periods	
Total exchange difference on retranslation of foreign operations (note 5)	302
	————
Total comprehensive income	3,130
	————
Profit for the year attributable to:	
Owners of the parent	2,805
Non-controlling interests	23
	————
	2,828
	————
Total comprehensive income for the year attributable to:	
Owners of the parent (2,805 + 302)	3,107
Non-controlling interests	23
	————
	3,130
	————

		$000
Summary of changes in equity for the year		
Equity b/f		14,164
Profit for year		2,805
Dividends paid		(445)
Exchange differences		302
Equity c/f		16,826

Consolidated statements of financial position at 31 December

	Note	20X7 $000	20X7 $000	20X6 $000	20X6 $000
Non-current assets					
Intangible assets – goodwill			500		–
Tangible assets	(1)		11,157		8,985
Investment in associate			300		280
			11,957		9,265
Current assets					
Inventories		9,749		7,624	
Receivables		5,354		4,420	
Short-term investments		1,543		741	
Cash at bank and in hand		1,013	17,659	394	13,179
			29,616		22,444
Equity and liabilities			$000		$000
Equity share capital @ $1			1,997		1,997
Share premium			5,808		5,808
Retained earnings			9,021		6,359
			16,826		14,164
Non-controlling interest			170		17

Total equity		16,996	14,181
Non-current liabilities:			
Loans		2,102	1,682
Provisions	(3)	1,290	935
Current liabilities:	(2)	9,228	5,646
		29,616	22,444

Notes to the accounts

(1) Tangible assets

Non-current asset movements included the following:

	$000
Disposals at carrying amount	305
Proceeds from asset sales	854
Depreciation provided for the year	907

(2) Current liabilities

	20X7	20X6
	$000	'000
Bank overdrafts	1,228	91
Trade payables	4,278	2,989
Tax	3,722	2,566
	9,228	5,646

(3) Provisions

	Pensions	Deferred taxation	Total
	$000	$000	$000
At 31 December 20X6	246	689	935
Exchange rate adjustment	29	–	29
Increase in provision	460	–	460
Decrease in provision	–	(134)	(134)
At 31 December 20X7	735	555	1,290

(4) Liberated

During the year, the company acquired 82% of the issued equity capital of Liberated for a cash consideration of $1,268,000. The fair values of the assets of Liberated were as follows:

	$000
Non-current assets	208
Inventories	612
Trade receivables	500
Cash in hand	232
Trade payables	(407)
Debenture loans	(312)
	833

(5) Exchange gains

Exchange gains on translating the financial statements of a wholly-owned subsidiary have been taken to equity and comprise differences on the retranslation of the following:

	$000
Non-current assets	138
Pensions	(29)
Inventories	116
Trade receivables	286
Trade payables	(209)
	302

(6) Non-controlling interest

The non-controlling interest is valued using the proportion of net assets method.

Required:

Prepare a statement of cash flows for the year ended 31 December 20X7.

4 Evaluation of statements of cash flows

Usefulness of the statement of cash flows

A statement of cash flows can provide information that is not available from statements of financial position and statements of comprehensive income.

(a) It may assist users of financial statements in making judgements on the amount, timing and degree of certainty of future cash flows.

(b) It gives an indication of the relationship between profitability and cash generating ability, and thus of the quality of the profit earned.

(c) Analysts and other users of financial information often, formally or informally, develop models to assess and compare the present value of the future cash flow of entities. Historical cash flow information could be useful to check the accuracy of past assessments.

(d) A statement of cash flow in conjunction with a statement of financial position provides information on liquidity, solvency and adaptability. The statement of financial position is often used to obtain information on liquidity, but the information is incomplete for this purpose as the statement of financial position is drawn up at a particular point in time.

(e) Cash flow cannot easily be manipulated and is not affected by judgement or by accounting policies.

Limitations of the statement of cash flows

Statements of cash flows should normally be used in conjunction with statements of profit and loss and other comprehensive income and statements of financial position when making an assessment of future cash flows.

(a) Statements of cash flows are based on historical information and therefore do not provide complete information for assessing future cash flows.

(b) There is some scope for manipulation of cash flows. For example, a business may delay paying suppliers until after the year-end, or it may structure transactions so that the cash balance is favourably affected. It can be argued that cash management is an important aspect of stewardship and therefore desirable. However, more deliberate manipulation is possible (e.g. assets may be sold and then immediately repurchased). Application of the substance over form principle should alert users of the financial statements to the true nature of such arrangements.

(c) Cash flow is necessary for survival in the short term, but in order to survive in the long term a business must be profitable. It is often necessary to sacrifice cash flow in the short term in order to generate profits in the long term (e.g. by investment in non-current assets). A substantial cash balance is not a sign of good management if the cash could be invested elsewhere to generate profit.

Neither cash flow nor profit provides a complete picture of an entity's performance when looked at in isolation.

UK syllabus focus

The ACCA UK syllabus contains a requirement that UK variant candidates should be able to discuss and apply the key differences between UK GAAP and IFRS GAAP. As with other areas of group accounts, the accounting requirements of UK GAAP and IFRS GAAP are very similar in this area; the basic mechanics of the workings required are the same. The only real distinctions relate to the flow-through of workings relating to goodwill and minority interest on a proportionate basis, together with the slightly different format under FRS 1.

Both of these points are illustrated in the question and answer which follow this narrative.

Under FRS 1, the starting point of the cash flow statement is operating profit for the year. This must be adjusted for items affecting operating profit, but for which there is not a matching cash flow, to arrive at cash flow on operating activities. There should also be a reconciliation between operating profit and net cash inflow from operating activities.

FRS 1 provides more precise definitions to apply when preparing a cash flow statement as follows:

- **Cash** is defined as in hand and deposits repayable on demand, less overdrafts repayable on demand. Deposits are repayable on demand if they can be withdrawn at any time without notice and without penalty or there is a notice period of less than twenty-four hours. These definitions include amounts designated in foreign currency.

- **Liquid resources** are defined as current asset investments held as being readily realisable, are disposable without curtailing or disrupting the business and are either convertible into known amounts of cash, or are traded in an active market. They are outside of the definition of cash as stated above, but are held to manage liquidity as opposed to being invested to earn returns.

Finally, the primary exemptions from the FRS 1 requirement to prepare a cash flow statement are as follows:

- companies who comply with the designation of being 'small' - refer to UK syllabus focus content within chapter 20 of this publication for detail on this definition. This will apply whether or not the company has decided to adopt the UK FRSSE.

- subsidiary companies who are 90% or more owned by their parent company, provided their cash flows are included within the cash flow statement for the group.

Consolidated cash flow statement for the year ended 31 December 20XX

	$000	$000
Reconciliation of operating profit to net cash flow from operating activities:		
Operating profit		X
Adjustment for non-cash items dealt with in arriving at operating profit:		
Depreciation		X
(Increase) Decrease in trade receivables		X(X)
(Increase) Decrease in inventory		X(X)
Increase (Decrease) in trade payables		X(X)
		___
Cash generated from operations		X
Dividends from associates		X
Returns on investments and servicing of finance:		
Interest paid	(X)	
Dividend paid to NCI	(X)	(X)
	___	
Taxation paid		(X)
Capital expenditure		
Cash purchases of PPE	(X)	
Proceeds from sale non-current assets	X	X(X)
		___

Acquisition/disposal of subsidiaries:

Net cash outflow upon subsidiary acquired	(X)	
Net cash inflow upon subsidiary disposed	(X)	X(X)

Equity dividend paid	(X)
Management of liquid resources	X(X)

Financing activities:

Long term loan received (repaid) in year	X(X)	
Finance lease payments	(X)	
Proceeds of share issue	X	X(X)

Net increase (decrease) in cash for the year	X(X)

UK GAAP Question

Extracts from the consolidated financial statements of the AH Group for the year ended 30 June 20X5 are given below:

AH Group: Consolidated income statement for the year ended 30 June 20X5

	20X5
	$000
Revenue	85,000
Cost of sales	(59,750)
Gross profit	25,250
Operating expenses	(5,650)
Operating Profit	19,600
Finance cost	(1,400)
Profit before disposal of property	18,200
Disposal of property (note 2)	1,250
Profit before tax	19,450
Tax	(6,250)
Profit for the period	13,200

Attributable to:

Non-controlling interest	655
Owners of the parent	12,545
	————
	13,200
	————

AH Group: Statement of financial position, with comparatives, at 30 June 20X5

	20X5			20X4
	$000	$000	$000	$000
Non-current assets:				
Property, plant and equipment	50,600		44,050	
Goodwill (note 3)	6,410		4,160	
	————		————	
		57,010		48,210
Current assets:				
Inventory	33,500		28,750	
Receivables	27,130		26,300	
Cash	1,870		3,900	
	————	62,500	————	58,950
		————		————
		119,510		107,160
		————		————

Equity and liabilities:				
	$000	$000	$000	$000
Equity capital @ £1 each	20,000		18,000	
Share premium	12,000		10,000	
Retained earnings	24,885		18,340	
	————		————	
		56,885		46,340
Non-controlling interest		3,625		1,920
		————		————
		60,510		48,260

Non-current liabilities:		
Loans	18,200	19,200
Current liabilities:		
Trade payables	33,340	32,810
Interest payable	1,360	1,440
Income tax	6,100	5,450
	119,510	107,160

Notes:

(1) Several years ago, AH acquired 80% of the issued equity shares of its subsidiary, BI. On 1 January 20X5, AH acquired 75% of the issued equity shares of CJ in exchange for a fresh issue of 2 million of its own $1 equity shares (issued at a premium of $1 each) and $2 million in cash. The net assets of CJ at the date of acquisition were assessed as having the following fair values:

	$000
Property, plant and equipment	4,200
Inventory	1,650
Trade receivables	1,300
Cash	50
Trade payables	(1,950)
Income tax	(250)
	5,000

(2) During the year, AH disposed of a property for proceeds of $2,250,000. The carrying value of the asset at the date of disposal was $1,000,000. There were no other disposals of fixed assets. Depreciation of $7,950,000 was provided in the year.

(3) Intangible assets comprise goodwill on acquisition of BI and CJ. Entity BI was acquired many years ago. Goodwill is accounted for as a permanent asset, and is unimpaired since acquisition.

Required:

Prepare the consolidated cash flow statement of the AH Group for the financial year ended 30 June 20X5 in the form required by FRS 1 using the indirect method. Notes to the statement of cash flows are NOT required, but full workings should be shown.

UK GAAP Answer

Consolidated cash flow statement for the year ended 30 June 20X5

	$000	$000
Reconciliation of operating profit to net cash flow from operating activities:		
Operating profit		19,600
Adjustment for non-cash items dealt with in arriving at operating profit:		
Depreciation		7,950
Decrease in trade receivables (27,130 – 26,300 – 1,300)		470
Increase in inventory (33,500 – 28,750 – 1,650)		(3,100)
Decrease in trade payables (33,340 – 32,810 – 1,950)		(1,420)
		────
Cash generated from operations		23,500
Dividends from associates		nil
Returns on investments and servicing of finance:		
Interest paid (W1)	(1,480)	
Dividend paid to NCI (W4)	(200)	(1,680)
		────
Taxation paid (W2)		(5,850)
Capital expenditure		
Purchase of PPE (W3)	(11,300)	
Proceeds from sale of property	2,250	(9,050)
		────
Acquisition/disposal of subsidiaries:		
Net cash impact of subsidiary acquired (2,000 – 50)		(1,950)

Equity dividend paid (W5)   (6,000)

Management of liquid resources   –

Financing activities:

    Long term loan repaid (18,200 – 19,200)   (1,000)

Net decrease in cash for the year (3,900 – 1,870)   (2,030)

Workings

(W1)

Interest paid

	$000		$000
Cash paid (bal figure)	1,480	Balance b/d	1,440
Balance c/d	1,360	IS for year	1,400
	2,840		2,840

(W2)

Income tax paid

	$000		$000
Cash paid (bal figure)	5,850	Balance b/d	5,450
		IS for year	6,250
Balance c/d	6,100	New subsidiary	250
	11,950		11,950

(W3)

Property, plant and equipment

	$000		$000
Balance b/d	44,050	Depreciation	7,950
New subsidiary	4,200	Disposals	1,000
Additions (bal figure)	11,300	Balance c/d	50,600
	59,550		59,550

(W4)

Non-controlling interest

	$000		$000
Dividend paid (bal figure)	200	Balance b/d	1,920
		NCI re CJ acquired (25% × 5,000)	1,250
Balance c/d	3,625	IS for year	655
	——		——
	3,825		3,825
	——		——

(W5)

Retained earnings

	$000		$000
Dividend paid (bal figure)	6,000	Balance b/d	18,340
Balance c/d	24,885	IS for year	12,545
	——		——
	30,885		30,885
	——		——

5 Chapter summary

Objective of statements of cash flows

- To provide information on changes in cash and cash equivalents
- To enable users to assess the liquidity, solvency and financial adaptability of a business

Classifications of cash flows

- No specific format for the cash flow in IAS 7
- IAS 7 only requires 3 headings:
  - Operating
  - Investing
  - Financing

Preparation of group statements of cash flows

- Three additional elements:
  - Cash paid to non-controlling interest
  - Cash received from associates
  - Acquisition and disposal of subsidiaries/ associates

Foreign currency transactions

- Individual company transactions are likely to have been settled in the year and no adjustment will be required
- Foreign subsidiary – exchange gains must be taken out of the statement of financial position movements as they are not cash

Evaluation of statements of cash flows

- Proivdes information not available in the statement of financial position and income statement
- Shows relationship between profitability and cash generating ability

Test your understanding answers

Test your understanding 1 – Extracts

(1)

Non-current assets (CV)

	$		$
Balance b/f	100	Depreciation	20
Revaluation	60	Disposals	15
Additions (bal fig)	125	Balance c/f	250
	285		285

Cash additions = 125 – finance lease additions of 30 = 95

(2)

Tax

	$		$
Tax paid (bal fig)	110	Balances b/fwd	
		DT	50
Balances c/fwd		CT	100
DT	100		
CT	120	Profit or loss	180
	330		330

(3)

Non-controlling interest

	$		$
		Balance b/f	440
Dividend paid (bal fig)	100	Profit or loss	500
Balance c/f	840		
	940		940

(4)

Non-controlling interest

	$		$
		Balance b/f	500
Dividend paid (bal fig)	250	Profit or loss	600
Balance c/f	850		
	1,100		1,100

(5)

Associate

	$		$
Balance b/f	200	Cash received (bal fig)	450
Profit or loss	750	Balance c/f	500
	950		950

(6)

Associate

	$		$
Balance b/f	600		
Profit or loss	4,000	Cash received (bal fig)	1,900
Revaluation	500	Balance c/f	3,200
	5,100		5,100

(7)

Non-current assets (CV)

	$		$
Balance b/f	150	Depreciation	50
New subsidiary	200		
Cash additions (bal fig)	200	Balance c/f	500
	550		550

KAPLAN PUBLISHING

(8)

Loan

	$		$
		Balance b/f	2,500
Cash paid (bal fig)	1,700	Exchange loss	200
Balance c/f	1,000		
	2,700		2,700

(9)

	$
Movement in inventory (W1)	136
Movement in receivables (W2)	76
Movement in payables (W3)	249

(W1) **Movement of inventory**

	$		$
B/f balance	200	C/f balance	100
Disposal	(25)	Acquisition	(50)
		Exchange gain	(11)
Revised b/f	175	Revised c/f	39

Movement therefore a decrease of 136

(W2) **Movement of receivables**

	$		$
B/f balance	200	C/f balance	300
Disposal	(45)	Acquisition	(200)
		Exchange gain	(21)
Revised b/f	155	Revised c/f	79

Movement therefore a decrease of 76

(W3) Movement of payables

	$		$
B/f balance	200	C/f balance	500
Disposal	(20)	Acquisition	(40)
		Exchange loss	(31)
	——		——
Revised b/f	180	Revised c/f	429
	——		——

Movement therefore an increase of 249

Test your understanding 2 – AH Group

Consolidated statement of cash flows for the year ended 30 June 20X5

	$000	$000
Operating activities		
Profit before tax		18,450
Adjustment		
Less: gain on disposal of property		(1,250)
Add: finance cost		1,400
Adjustment for non-cash items dealt with in arriving at operating profit:		
Depreciation		7,950
Decrease in trade and other receivables (27,130 – 26,300 – 1,300)		470
Increase in inventories (33,500 – 28,750 – 1,650)		(3,100)
Decrease in trade payables (33,340 – 32,810 – 1,950)		(1,420)
Goodwill impaired (W4)		1,000
		——
Cash generated from operations		23,500
Interest paid (W1)		(1,480)
Income taxes paid (W2)		(5,850)
		——
Net cash from operating activities		16,170

Investing activities

Acquisition of subsidiary net of cash acquired (2,000 – 50)	(1,950)	
Purchase of property, plant, and equipment (W3)	(11,300)	
Proceeds from sale of property	2,250	
Net cash used in investing activities		(11,000)

Financing activities

Repayment of long-term borrowings (18,200 – 19,200)	(1,000)	
Dividend paid by parent (W7)	(6,000)	
Dividends paid to NCI (W6)	(200)	
Net cash used in financing activities		(7,200)
Net decrease in cash and cash equivalents		(2,030)
Cash and cash equivalents at 1 July 20X4		3,900
Cash and cash equivalents at 30 June 20X5		1,870

Workings

(W1)

Interest paid

	$000		$000
Cash paid (bal figure)	1,480	Balance b/d	1,440
Balance c/d	1,360	Profit or loss	1,400
	2,840		2,840

(W2)

Income taxes paid

	$000		$000
Cash paid (bal figure)	5,850	Balance b/d	5,450
		Profit or loss	6,250
Balance c/d	6,100	New subsidiary	250
	———		———
	11,950		11,950
	———		———

(W3)

Property, plant and equipment

	$000		$000
Balance b/d	44,050	Depreciation	7,950
New subsidiary	4,200	Disposals	1,000
Additions (bal figure)	11,300	Balance c/d	50,600
	———		———
	59,550		59,550
	———		———

(W4) Goodwill re acquisition during year

		$000
Fair value of shares issued	Equity capital – NV	2,000
	Share premium	2,000
Cash paid		2,000
		———
		6,000
Fair value of NCI	per question	1,750
		———
		7,750
FV of net assets at acq'n	per question	5,000
		———
Full goodwill at acquisition		2,750
		———

(W5)

Goodwill

	$000		$000
Balance b/d	4,160	Impaired in year (bal fig)	1,000
Goodwill on sub acquired (W4)	2,750	Balance c/d	5,910
	6,910		6,910

(W6)

Non-controlling interest

	$000		$000
Dividend paid (bal figure)	200	Balance b/d	1,920
		NCI at fair value re CJ acquired	1,750
Balance c/d	3,875	Income statement	405
	4,075		4,075

(W7)

Retained earnings

	$000		$000
Dividend paid (bal figure)	6,000	Balance b/d	18,340
Balance c/d	24,135	Profit or loss	11,795
	30,135		30,135

Test your understanding 3 – Boardres

Statement of cash flows for the year ended 31 December 20X7

	$000	$000
Operating activities		
Profit before tax	4,866	
Interest payable	305	
Income from associate	(30)	
	———	
Operating profit	5,141	
Non-cash items		
Depreciation	907	
Goodwill (W7)	85	
Gain on disposal of assets (W1)	(549)	
Increase in pension provision	460	
	———	
	6,044	
Change in working capital		
Increase in inventory		
(9,749 – 7,624 – 612 acq – 116 ex diff)	(1,397)	
Increase in receivables		
(5,354 – 4,420 – 500 acq – 286 ex diff)	(148)	
Increase in payables		
(4,278 – 2,989 – 407 acq – 209 ex diff)	673	
	———	
	5,172	
Interest paid	(305)	
Tax paid (W2)	(1,016)	
	———	———
		3,851
Investing activities		
Purchase of non-current assets (W3)	(3,038)	
Proceeds on disposal	854	
Cash consideration paid on acquisition		
of subsidiary, net of cash acquired		
(1,268 – 232)	(1,036)	
Dividend received from associate (W4)	10	
	———	———
		(3,210)

Financing activities

Dividends paid	(445)
Dividends paid to NCI (W6)	(20)
Proceeds from debt issue (W5)	108

	(357)
Change in cash and cash equivalents	284
Opening cash and cash equivalents	
(394 + 741 – 91)	1,044
Closing cash and cash equivalents	
(1,013 + 1,543 – 1,228)	1,328

Workings

(W1) Proceeds of disposal of NCA

	$
Sales proceeds	854
CV	(305)
Profit on disposal	549

(W2)

Tax

	$		$
Cash	1,016	Balance b/f–CT	2,566
Balance c/f–CT	3,722	Balance b/f–DT	689
Balance c/f–DT	555	I/S	2,038
	5,293		5,293

(W3)

Non-current assets

	$		$
Balance b/f	8,985	Depreciation	907
Exchange gain	138	Disposal	305
Acquisition	208	Balance c/f	11,157
Cash	3,038		
	12,369		12,369

(W4)

Dividends from associates

	$		$
Balance b/f	280	Cash	10
Profit	30	Balance c/f	300
	310		310

(W5)

Debentures

	$		$
Balance c/f	2,102	Balance b/f	1,682
		Acquisition	312
		Cash	108
	2,102		2,102

(W6)

Non-controlling interest

	$		$
Cash	20	Balance b/f	17
Balance c/f	170	I/S	23
		Acquisition (18% × 833)	150
	190		190

(W7) **Goodwill – proportionate basis**

	$
Cost of investment	
Cost of investment	1,268
CV of NCI at acquisition (18% × 833)	150
	1,418
FV of net assets at acquisition	(833)
Goodwill at acquisition	585
Balance b/fwd	nil
	585
Amount written off (Bal fig)	(85)
Bal c/fwd per closing group SOFP	500

The professional and ethical duty of the accountant

Chapter learning objectives

Upon completion of this chapter you will be able to:

- appraise the ethical and professional issues in advising on corporate reporting

- assess the relevance and importance of ethical and professional issues in complying with accounting standards

- appraise the potential ethical implications of professional and managerial decisions in the preparation of corporate reports

- assess the consequences of not upholding ethical principles in the preparation of corporate reports.

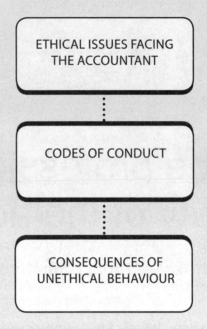

The ethical issues facing the accountant

Definition: Professional ethics are the principles and standards that underlie the responsibilities and conduct of a person in performing his/her function in a particular field of expertise.

Introduction

• Ethical principles are important in a business organisation as they set the tone for the culture and behaviour of employees and management.

• For example, a business's ethical aim may be to treat employees fairly and to be honest in all business transactions.

• The application of ethics can sometimes be intangible. Ethics is often described as 'doing the right thing' but this can mean different things to different individuals.

• After the accounting scandals in Enron, Worldcom, Parmalat and others, business ethics has become more prominent in the accounting world.

• As a result, many companies have an ethical code that sets out their ethical objectives. This can be a huge benefit for businesses, as employees tend to prefer to work for a company with good guidelines of moral behaviour, and customers and suppliers will prefer to deal with such a business.

Issues in advising on corporate reporting

- An audit is an independent examination of, and report on, the financial statements and therefore it is expected that the auditors are independent.

- However, there has always been an area of contention in the accountancy profession as to whether auditors can actually be independent when their clients pay for their services.

- Many audit fees are very high, for example, in 2000 Enron Corp paid Arthur Andersen US$25 million for the audit. It becomes very difficult for the auditor to say no to a client when such great sums of money are involved.

- There is a balance between agreeing with the client's accounting practices in order to keep the client, and allowing them to get away with dubious accounting practices and potentially being fined, not allowed to practise or even ending up in prison.

- Another independence issue is that accountancy firms complete non-audit work for their clients in addition to the audit. This work is often of a higher value than the audit and, again, makes it difficult for the auditor to be completely independent as they potentially could lose a great deal of fee income.

- Accountancy bodies such as the ACCA, the Institute of Chartered Accountants in England and Wales (ICAEW) and the Chartered Institute of Management Accountants (CIMA) are aware of this and issue codes of conduct and ethical guidelines that they require their members to comply with.

The preparation of accounting information

- Ethics in the preparation of business information starts in the individual entity with those responsible for preparing the entity's financial statements.

- A key role for professional accountants is to drive the ethics process from the bottom up, ensuring that the financial statements have been prepared in accordance with accounting standards and present a true and fair view.

- One of the issues in preparing financial information is the pressure that may be put on individuals by officers of the organisation who are acting unethically. If an individual's senior is asking him or her to prepare financial information in a misleading way, then it can be very difficult to speak up and refuse to do what is being asked for.

- In many cases, accountants know what they should do, but often there are adverse consequences for them if they take a stand. It takes a great deal of courage to speak out and potentially lose one's job for doing so.

- Ethical codes of conduct take into account the accountant and business and offer guidance on how to deal with ethical issues.

- Some accountancy bodies, such as the ICAEW and the CIMA, operate ethics helplines where members can phone for advice on ethical issues facing them.

Ethical conflicts of interest

Situations may arise in which an accountant might be asked to behave (or might be tempted to behave) in a way that conflicts with ethical standards and guidelines.

Conflicts of interest could relate to unimportant matters, but they might also involve fraud or some other illegal activity. Examples of such ethical conflicts of interest are as follows:

- There could be pressure from an overbearing supervisor, manager or director, adversely affecting the accountant's integrity.

- An accountant might mislead his or her employer as to the amount of experience or expertise they have, when in reality the expert advice of someone else should be sought.

- An accountant might be asked to act contrary to a technical or professional standard. Divided loyalty between the accountant's superior and the required professional standards of conduct could arise.

- A conflict of interest could arise when the employer publishes (or proposes to publish) misleading information that will benefit the employer, and may or may not benefit the accountant personally as well.

Resolution of ethical conflicts of interest

Conflicts of interest can arise in so many different ways that it would be difficult to provide a detailed set of guidelines for their resolution.

Accountants faced with conflicts should evaluate their significance. Unless they are so insignificant that they can be ignored, the accountant should consider the safeguards that are available for their elimination or reduction.

For example, it may be possible to:

- obtain advice from within the employing organisation, an independent professional adviser or a relevant professional body

- invoke a formal dispute resolution process within the employing organisation

- seek legal advice.

Ethical implications of preparing corporate reports

- Preparers of financial information must prepare that information honestly and fairly. Financial information may be relied upon by users of the financial statements, investors and potential investors, banks, suppliers, etc.

- Such information must be prepared in accordance with accounting standards so that it complies with current practice and presents a true and fair view.

- If financial information is not prepared in this manner, the risk is that is does not show a true and fair view of the performance and position of the entity and is misleading.

- Users who make decisions based on the information reported stand to lose out if it subsequently turns out that the entity is not what it seems.

- This was certainly the case in Enron who misstated five years of financial statements, reporting profits rather than losses. Shares in Enron became worthless and many investors and employees lost a lot of money.

ACCA Code of Professional Ethics

In common with other professional bodies, ACCA has an extensive rulebook of regulations, including requirements to uphold appropriate professional ethical standards. In terms of professional ethics, there will be a considerable degree of overlap and consistency with the ethical standards required and expected of professionals in a range of busines and other disciplines including accountancy, law, medicine and nursing.

The following information regarding fundamental ethical principles was extracted from the ACCA 2012 Rulebook. Student members of ACCA also agree to uphold these principles as part of their conditions of student membership of ACCA.

A professional accountant shall comply with the following fundamental principles:

(a) **Integrity** – to be straightforward and honest in all professional and business relationships.

(b) **Objectivity** – to not allow bias, conflict of interest or undue influence of others to override professional or business judgments.

(c) **Professional Competence and Due Care** – to maintain professional knowledge and skill at the level required to ensure that a client or employer receives competent professional services based on current developments in practice, legislation and techniques and act diligently and in accordance with applicable technical and professional standards.

(d) **Confidentiality** – to respect the confidentiality of information acquired as a result of professional and business relationships and, therefore, not disclose any such information to third parties without proper and specific authority, unless there is a legal or professional right or duty to disclose, nor use the information for the personal advantage of the professional accountant or third parties.

(e) **Professional behaviour** – to comply with relevant laws and regulations and avoid any action that discredits the profession.

The journals and magazines of professional instututes regularly include details of professional disciplinary proceedings brought against individual members who were believed to have fallen short of the high professional standards expected of them.

You should be prepared to apply and evaluate the relevance of each of these principles as required when dealing with ethical issues associated with the preparation of financial statements. In Paper P2, this is normally examined as part of the written content within the compulsory question in Section A of the examination paper. There is further detailed study of ethical issues within Paper P1 Governance, Risk and Ethics.

Sarbanes-Oxley

Sarbanes-Oxley

The Sarbanes-Oxley Act 2002 was introduced in the US after a series of corporate accounting scandals. Public trust in accounting and financial reporting practices was declining due to the number of scandals uncovered, such as those at – Enron, Worldcom and Tyco.

It has been described as 'corporate accountability legislation'. Unlike the UK, the US has taken a strong legislative and regulatory route for the achievement of good corporate governance.

The Act itself contains various specific requirements:

- The Act places personal responsibility for the accuracy of a company's financial statements on its chief executive officer (CEO) and the chief financial officer (CFO, the equivalent of the finance director in the UK).

- All companies with a US listing must provide a signed certificate to the Securities and Exchange Commission vouching for the accuracy of the company's financial statements, signed by the CEO and CFO. There must be such a certificate for each report containing financial information that is filed with the SEC by the company.

- The CEO and CFO are therefore required to take direct responsibility for the accuracy of their company's financial statements. (This requirement is more specific than the provisions in the UK Combined Code, under which the responsibility for preparing the financial statements and a going concern statement lies with the board as a whole.)

- This requirement applies to foreign companies with a US listing, as well as to US companies.

- The SEC also requires the CEO and CFO to certify in each quarterly and annual report:
  - the accuracy of the information in the report
  - the fairness of the financial information.

- The report should contain information about the effectiveness of the company's 'disclosure controls and procedures' and its internal controls over financial reporting. This should be covered by the certifications.

- The CEO and CFO must return bonuses to the company, including equity or incentive compensation awards, awarded to them in the preceding twelve months, if their company's financial statements are re-stated due to material non-compliance with accounting rules and standards.

Increased financial disclosures

The Act includes a number of provisions for greater or more rapid disclosure of financial information.

- In its financial reports, the company must disclose details about its off-balance sheet transactions and their material effects.

- Material changes should be disclosed on a 'rapid and current basis'. The Act gave responsibility to the SEC for making the detailed regulations. Material changes should include matters such as creating a new off-balance sheet transaction, a decision to make a one-off writing down charge, or the loss of a contract with a major customer.

Internal control report

Companies should include a report on 'internal control over financial reporting' in their annual report. This internal control report must:

- include a statement of management's responsibility for an adequate internal control system

- identify the framework used to evaluate internal control

- provide an assessment by management of the effectiveness of internal control and any material weakness.

In addition, there must be an annual evaluation of the internal controls by the company's external auditors, who must provide an 'attestation' about them.

In other words, the external auditors must provide a statement confirming that the internal controls are sufficiently effective.

Amendments

In 2007 the SEC amended the requirements of Sarbanes-Oxley in relation to the assessment of internal control as the current compliance was costly and time consuming.

The changes are principles-based and require management to design controls to prevent financial misstatement and assess their effectiveness according to a risk based review.

Audit committee

Stock exchanges are prohibited from listing the securities of any company that does not comply with certain audit committee requirements. These include the following:

- Every member of the audit committee should be independent.

- The audit committee must have responsibility for the appointment and compensation of the external auditors.

- The audit committee must have responsibility for the oversight of the work of the external auditors.

- The committee must establish procedures for whistleblowers who raise concerns about questionable accounting or auditing matters.

Auditors and the audit

Restrictions have been placed on the types of non-audit work that can be carried out by the audit firm for a client company. Prohibited services include:

- book-keeping services and other services related to the accounting records or financial statements of the company

- the design and implementation of financial information systems

- actuarial services

- valuation services

- internal auditing (outsourced)

- legal services

- management functions

- broker/dealer or investment advice services.

Tax services are specifically permitted by the Act, unless they come within a prohibited category of non-audit services.

There is a compulsory five-year rotation of both the lead audit partner and the concurring partner working on the audit of a corporate client.

It is illegal for the directors and officers of a company to coerce, manipulate, mislead or fraudulently influence an auditor, in the knowledge that such action, if successful, could make the financial statements materially misleading.

US stock exchange rules

Following the Sarbanes-Oxley Act and regulations by the SEC, the national securities exchanges in the US were required to develop corporate governance rules for companies whose shares are listed on the exchange. The rules drawn up by the New York Stock Exchange can be compared directly with a number of the principles and provisions in the UK Combined Code.

The majority of the board of directors should be independent directors. 'We believe requiring a majority of independent directors will increase the quality of board oversight and lessen the possibility of damaging conflicts of interest.' The definition of 'independent' is quite strict.

Example

The chief financial officer of Cardinal Bankshares, a Virginia company, raised concerns with his superiors about insider trading, faulty internal controls and irregularities in financial reporting. The company initiated an investigation into his whistle blowing allegations, but he became sufficiently concerned to call in a lawyer to give him legal representation.

The company sacked the individual, alleging that he had failed to comply in an internal audit, and he took his case to court under the Sarbanes-Oxley legislation.

The court ruled (March 2004) that the individual had been sacked because of his whistle blowing. It ordered the company to re-employ him with back-pay, to reimburse his legal fees and to pay damages.

This was the first reported case of the use in a court of the Sarbanes-Oxley legislation.

Consequences of unethical behaviour

The consequences of unethical behaviour in deliberately presenting incorrect financial information, or failing to audit such information properly, are severe. Many accountants have been fined or jailed for not fulfilling their professional duties.

Consequences for preparers of financial statements

As can be seen from the review of the Enron fraud in section 1, the consequences for deliberately preparing false accounting information and lying to the stock market brings severe penalties. The senior management at Enron were given long prison sentences and the fraud brought about the downfall of the company.

The consequences for individuals include:

- prison sentence
- fines or repayments of amounts fraudulently taken
- loss of professional reputation
- being prevented from acting as a director or officer of a public company in the future
- possibility of being expelled by professional accountancy body, if membership held.

It can be difficult to pluck up the courage to report fraudulent behaviour as the consequences for the individuals concerned can be frightening. These can include losing their job, losing their professional reputation in the firm, and being prevented from testifying in legal cases in the future.

Consequences for auditors of financial statements

The consequences for auditors can be as severe as those for the preparers of financial statements. They include:

- the audit firm being taken to court and charged with a criminal offence

- individual partners of the audit firm being banned from audit work

- loss of reputation leading to the loss of clients and income

- fines or compensation payable

- investigation by accounting body, such as ACCA or ICAEW.

Arthur Andersen, the Enron auditor, ceased operating because of the effect of the scandal. Clients moved to other audit firms and Arthur Andersen was prosecuted for obstructing the course of justice.

Ethical & professional issue

Question:

An entity is considering entering into a number of leasing agreements. It is aware of the required accounting treatment of leases based upon IAS 17, including how to distinguish between finance and operating leases.

The nature of the lease agreements is that the entity would take on substantially the risks and rewards associated with owning the assets concerned. However, the finance director of the entity is in discussion with the leasing company to establish whether, having agreed the terms and conditions of the leasing agreements, they would be willing to refer to the agreements as operating leases. If this was done, the entity would then regard the agreements as operating leases and would account for the leases on that basis. One possibility would be to have an initial lease period which would indicate that it was an operating lease, with a secondary lease period on advantageous terms so that it would be taken up by the entity.

Additionally, the finance director has heard that reporting standards dealing with leases may be revised, such that all leases will be accounted for in the same way. The finance director has therefore come to the conclusion that the current reporting standard need not be followed if it is expected to be replaced at some later date.

Required:

Discuss why an entity may seek to do this, explain the accounting treatment for leases and evaluate the ethical and professional issues arising from this situation.

Answer – Ethical and professional issue

An entity may seek to exclude liabilities from its statement of financial position in order to improve the view presented by the statement of financial position. Additionally, the annual depreciation charge on such assets, (which should be capitalised) and finance costs associated with the lease obligation will also be excluded from the statement of comprehensive income. There would also be operating lease rentals wrongly included within expenses.

If liabilities are excluded from the statement of financial position, accounting ratios such as measures of gearing will be misstated. This may be particularly important for current or potential providers of loan finance who may rely upon this financial information as a basis for their decision-making.

Similarly, performance and investment appraisal measures, such as return on capital employed and earnings per share may also be distorted, leading to inappropriate decisions being made by users of that financial information.

If the finance director is successful in achieving a misrepresentation of the leases, the financial statements may not show a true and fair view. The reliability of the financial statements would have been undermined. It would also result in a lack of comparability with financial information from other companies who have correctly applied the relevant reporting standard.

The requirements of IAS 17 are that leases which transfer substantially all of the risks and rewards of ownership are regarded as finance leases. Such leases should be capitalised as assets, and depreciated over their expected useful life to the business. The loan obligation should also be capitalised, with loan repayments and finance costs recognised over the lease term.

Any lease not meeting the definition of a finance lease is regarded as being an operating lease. The accounting treatment for operating leases is to regard them as rental agreements and spread the total payments associated with such leases over the lease period on a straight-line basis. There may be an accrual for amounts paid in advance or arrears at the reporting date.

The terms of the lease should be evaluated using the expected lease term, including any secondary term which is expected to taken up. Therefore, if the lease is classified and treated as an operating lease, it would be an inappropriate accounting treatment.

The finance director is likely to be a professionally qualified accountant. If this is the case, he or she will be bound by a professional and ethical code by virtue of their membership of a professional accountancy institute, such as ACCA. Failure to uphold the ethical and professional standards expected of a professional accountant may leave the individual concerned liable to criminal penalties if they have committed an offence or liable to civil action for damages if others suffered financial loss as a result of their action. In the content of being an employee, the finance director may face the possibility of disciplinary action, which could result in dismissal from their post.

In principle, reporting standards should be complied with if financial statements are to give a true and fair view. If departure from a reporting standard is done in order for the financial statements to show a true and fair view, this would be an unusual situation, and would need to be explained and justified in the supporting notes. The potential replacement of a reporting standard is not, in itself, a good enough reason not to apply the current standard, unless it has been formally withdrawn..

If the ACCA ethical guide is used as a basis for evaluating the actions of the finance director, issues of professional competence should be considered. It would be expected that the finance director is aware of, and understands the requirements of, IAS 17. Competence may be developed from a combination of practical work experience, technical expertise and professional qualification. Where an individual has achieved competence, this should be maintained by practical experience and Continuing Professional Development (CPD) which is mandatory for professionally qualified accountants.

Associated with competence is due care and skill in the performance of work or discharge of responsibilities. Application of due care and skill may be regarded as the application f competence. If the finance director did not perform his or her work with the required degree of care, they would be negligent in the performance of their duties.

A more insidious interpretation could be that the finance director is seeking to deliberately distort the financial information presented to others. This may be due to seeking personal gain, such as achieving a performance indicator used to determine eligibility for bonus payments. Such behaviour will call into question the professional integrity of the finance director if they knowingly misrepresent financial information they are responsible for.

Professional accountants should also be objective in performance of their work. This means that they should be free from bias and act in an open and honest manner in the performance of their work. Clearly, if integrity can be questioned, it is likely that objectivity will also be compromised and undermined.

A further issue is the perception of poor professional behaviour by the finance director. This will adversely affect the professional reputation of the individual concerned. Furthermore, it will undermine the professional reputation of qualified accountants generally in the eyes of the general public. By falling short of the high standards expected from a professionally qualified accountant, they leave themselves exposed to the possibility of disciplinary action by their institute.

If such an action is pursued and proven, the finance director may be liable to a range of disciplinary sanctions as follows:

- Warning or admonishment
- Fine
- Suspension of membership
- Exclusion from membership

Chapter summary

Ethical issues facing the accountant
- An accountant must be independent and must speak out if a client is following irregular accounting practices
- Accountants must follow the Codes of Ethics for the professional body of which they are a member
- Financial information must be prepared so that it meets accounting standards and shows a true and fair view/fair presentation of the financial position of the entity
- An employer may ask an accountant to act unethically by preparing the financial statements in a way that does not show the true picture

Codes of ethics

The principles in the ACCA Code of Ethics and Conduct are:
- Integrity
- Objectivity
- Professional competence and due care
- Confidentiality
- Professional behaviour

Consequences of unethical behaviour

The consequences of failing to act ethically are many and can be severe. They include:
- Prison sentence
- Fines or repayments of amounts taken fraudulently
- Loss of professional reputation
- Being prevented from acting in the same capacity in the future
- Investigation by professional accountancy body

8

The financial reporting framework

Chapter learning objectives

Upon completion of this chapter you will be able to:

- evaluate the consistency and clarity of corporate reports

- assess the insight into financial and operational risks provided by corporate reports

- discuss the usefulness of corporate reports in making investment decisions

- evaluate models adopted by standards setters

- discuss the use of the 2010 Conceptual Framework for Financial Reporting (2010 Framework) in the production of accounting standards

- assess the success of the 2010 Framework in introducing rigorous and consistent accounting standards

- identify the relationship between accounting theory and practice

- critically evaluate accounting principles and practices used in corporate reporting

- explain the reasons for the introduction of IFRS 13 Fair value measurement together with application of the key principles to determine fair value measurement in specific situations.

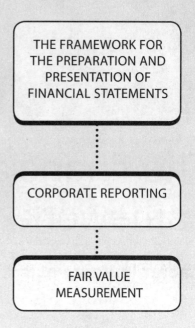

1 Conceptual Framework for Financial Reporting

This section briefly recaps the IASB's Framework, which was first published in 1989. This was examinable in earlier examination papers and should be familiar to you. You should be aware that this document has been subsumed into the Conceptual Framework for Financial Reporting 2010 and remains valid to the extent that it has not been replaced by new content.

The purpose of the Framework

The purpose of the Framework is to:

(a) assist in the development of future accounting standards and in the review of existing standards

(b) provide a basis for reducing the number of alternative accounting treatments permitted by international standards

(c) assist national standard setters in developing national standards

(d) assist preparers of financial statements in applying international standards and in dealing with issues not covered by international standards

(e) assist auditors in forming an opinion whether financial statements conform to international standards

(f) assist users of financial statements in interpreting the information contained in financial statements complying with international standards

(g) provide information about the IASB's approach to setting international standards.

The content of the Framework

Key points

- The objective of financial statements is to provide useful information to users.

- Financial statements complying with international standards should meet the common needs of most users. However, financial statements do not provide all the information that users may need because they concentrate on the financial effects of past events.

- The user groups of financial statements vary, including equity investors, employees, lenders, suppliers, customers, government and the public.

- The underlying assumptions of financial statements are the accrual basis and going concern.

Underlying assumption

The 2010 Framework identifies that there is one underlying assumption governing the preparation of financial statements:

Going concern

The going concern basis assumes that the entity has neither the need nor the intention to liquidate or curtail materially the scale of its operations. This is contained within chapter 4 para 1 of the 2010 Conceptual Framework and reflects the increasing emphasis upon the definition of an asset and liability for inclusion of items on the statement of financial position. Hence accruals of income and expense will still be recognised in the financial statements as long as they meet the definition of an asset or liability.

Previously accruals was also regarded as a fundamental assumption. Although it is still retained within chapter 1 para 17 of the 2010 Conceptual Framework it is no longer referred to as an underlying assumption.

2 Elements of the financial statements

The Framework identifies five elements of financial statements, which are currently retained within chapter 4 of the 2010 Conceptual Framework as follows:

An **asset** is a resource controlled by the entity as a result of past events and from which future economic benefits are expected to flow to the entity.

A **liability** is a present obligation of the entity arising from past events, the settlement of which is expected to result in an outflow from the entity of resources embodying economic benefits.

Equity is the residual interest in an entity's assets after deducting all its liabilities.

Income is the increase in economic benefits during an accounting period.

Expenses are decreases in economic benefits during an accounting period.

Recognition of the elements of financial statements

An item should be recognised in the financial statements if:

- it meets one of the definitions of an **element**
- it is probable that any future economic benefit associated with the item will flow to or from the entity
- the item can be measured at a monetary amount (cost or value) with sufficient reliability.

The recognition of assets and liabilities falls into three stages:

- initial recognition (e.g. the purchase of a non-current asset)
- subsequent remeasurement (e.g. revaluation of the above asset)
- derecognition (e.g. sale of the asset).

Derecognition

Derecognition occurs when:

- an event occurs that eliminates a previously recognised asset or liability (e.g. a trade receivable is irrecoverable)
- there is no longer sufficient evidence to support continued recognition. For example, a reorganisation provision may no longer be needed.

Measurement of the elements of financial statements

The Framework identifies four possible measurement bases, with no particular measurement basis stated as being preferred, as follows:

Historical cost

Assets are recorded at the amount of cash or cash equivalents paid to acquire them.

Liabilities are recorded at the proceeds received in exchange for the obligation, or at the amounts expected to be paid to satisfy the liability.

Current cost

Assets are carried at their current purchase price.

Liabilities are carried at the undiscounted amount currently required to settle them.

Realisable value

Assets are carried at the amount that could currently be obtained by an orderly disposal. Liabilities are carried at their settlement values – the amount to be paid to satisfy them in the normal course of business.

Although historical cost is the most common basis, the others are often used to modify historical cost. For example, inventories are usually carried at the lower of cost and net realisable value, investments may be carried at market value and pension liabilities are carried at their present value.

Present value

Assets are carried at the present discounted value of the future net cash inflows that the item is expected to generate in the normal course of business. Liabilities are carried at the present discounted value of the expected cash outflows necessary to settle them.

Assessment of the Framework

- The Framework provides a conceptual underpinning for IFRS.
- One of the objectives of the Framework is to provide a basis for the formulation of IFRS.
- By providing definitions of assets, liabilities, etc. and guidance on recognition and measurement, the Framework forms a basis for dealing with any accounting issues that arise which are not covered by accounting standards.
- The Framework's approach builds corporate reporting around the definitions of assets and liabilities and the criteria for recognising and measuring them in the statement of financial position.
- This approach views accounting from the perspective of the statement of financial position ('a balance sheet perspective'), whereas most companies would not consider the measurement and recognition of assets and liabilities as the starting point for the determination of profit.
- In many jurisdictions, the financial statements form the basis of dividend payments, the starting point for the assessment of taxation, and often the basis for executive remuneration. A balance sheet fair value system, which the IASB seems to favour, would have a major impact on the above elements.

3 Development of the Conceptual Framework

This is a long-term joint project between IASB and the US FASB, which was first agreed in 2004. The end point of the eight-stage project will be approval of a single, self-contained document which will create a foundation for the development of future accounting standards that are principles based, internally consistent and internationally converged. Ultimately, it will replace the Framework for the Preparation and Presentation of Financial Statements which was first published in 1989. As this project progresses and individual chapters are approved, the new Conceptual Framework for Financial Reporting 2010, published in September 2010, will be updated and the superseded provisions of the original Framework document, currently included as chapter 4, will be deleted.

The Conceptual Framework for Financial Reporting 2010 project has the following phases:

Phase A – objectives and qualitative characteristics

In September 2010, the IASB and FASB approved the following chapters of the 2010 Conceptual Framework:
Chapter 1 – The objective of general purpose financial reporting
Chapter 3 – Qualitative characteristics of useful financial information.

There is no significant change to the underlying objective of the 2010 Conceptual Framework in comparison with its predecessor – to provide financial information about the reporting entity that is useful to existing and potential investors, lenders and other creditors in making decisions about providing resources to the entity.

Consequently, existing and potential investors, lenders and other creditors need information to help them assess the prospects for future net cash inflows to an entity. Existing and potential investors, lenders and other creditors need information about the resources of the entity, claims against the entity, and how efficiently and effectively the entity's management and governing board* have discharged their responsibilities to use the entity's resources. Examples of such responsibilities include protecting the entity's resources from unfavourable effects of economic factors such as price and technological changes and ensuring that the entity complies with applicable laws, regulations and contractual provisions. Information about management's discharge of its responsibilities is also useful for decisions by existing investors, lenders and other creditors who have the right to vote on or otherwise influence management's actions.

Chapter 2 of the 2010 Conceptual Framework dealing with The Reporting Entity comprises Phase D of the project, which has not yet commenced. Until that occurs, the relevant parts of the original Framework document continue to apply.

There is a change within chapter 3 of the 2010 Conceptual Framework dealing with qualitative characteristics of useful financial information. There are two fundamental qualitative characteristics of relevance and faithful representation. If each of these characteristics is considered in turn:

Relevance:

Relevant financial information is regarded as information which is capable of making a difference in decisions made by users of that information. It will be regarded as being relevant if it has either predictive value and/or confirmatory value to a user.

Relevance is supported by materiality considerations. Information is regarded as material if its omission or misstatement could influence the decisions made by users of that information.

Faithful representation:

For financial information to be faithfully presented, it must be complete, neutral and free from error. Therefore, it must comprise information necessary for a proper understanding, it must be without bias or manipulation and clearly described.

In addition to the two fundamental qualitative characteristics, there are four enhancing characteristics which enhance the usefulness of information which is regarded as relevant and faithfully represented as follows:

Comparability:

Information is more useful if it can be compared with similar information about other entities, or even the same entity over different time periods. Consistency of methodology, approach or presentation helps to achieve comparability of financial information. Permitting different accounting treatments for similar items is likely to reduce comparability.

Verifiability

Verifiability of financial information provides assurance to users regarding its credibility and reliability. It means that different, knowledgeable and independent observers could reach consensus, although not necessarily complete agreement, that a particular presentation of an item or items is a faithful representation.

Timeliness

This means uses should have information within a timescale which is likely to influence their decisions.

Understandability

Appropriate classification, characterisation and presentation of information will help to make it understandable. For example, standard formats of information and standard accounting treatments help users to understand the information presented.

Notwithstanding the fundamental qualitative and enhancing qualitative characteristics of financial reporting information, it is important that costs incurred in reporting that information are outweighed by the benefits of providing that information. Ultimately, information which is relevant and faithfully represented leads to improved confidence in decisions made by users of that information and results in the more efficient working of the capital markets.

Phase B – elements and recognition

The objectives of this phase of the project are to refine and converge the IASB and FASB frameworks as follows:

- Revise and clarify the definitions of asset and liability.

- Resolve differences regarding other elements and their definitions.

- Revise the recognition criteria concepts to eliminate differences and provide a basis for resolving issues such as derecognition and unit of account.

Based upon progress to date, draft definitions are as follows:

- An asset of an entity is a present economic resource to which the entity has either a right or other access that others do not have

- A liability of an entity is a present economic obligation for which the entity is the obligor

The principal reasons for reviewing and potentially changing these definitions are as follows:

- The current definitions place too much emphasis on identifying the future inflow or outflow of economic benefits, instead of focusing on the item that presently exists, an economic resource or economic obligation.

- The current definitions place undue emphasis on identifying the past transactions or events that gave rise to the asset or the liability, instead of focusing on whether the entity has an economic resource or obligation at the reporting date.

- It is unclear how the current definitions apply to contractual obligations.

This phase of the project was last updated in March 2010.

Phase C – measurement

In July 2010 the IASB reached the following tentative decisions relating to the development of preliminary views for the measurement chapter of the Conceptual Framework:

Implications of the objective of financial reporting for measurement – The best way to satisfy the objective of financial reporting through measurement is to consider the effect of a particular measurement selection on all of the financial statements, instead of emphasising the statement of financial position over the statement of comprehensive income or vice versa.

General implications of the fundamental qualitative characteristics for measurement – Selection of bases of measurement should be related to the qualitative requirements that financial information should be relevant and faithfully presented.

Specific implications of the fundamental qualitative characteristics for historical cost and fair value – The objective of selecting a measurement for a particular item is to maximise the information about the reporting entity's prospects for future cash flows subject to the ability to faithfully represent it at a cost that is justified by the benefits.

What should the measurement chapter accomplish – The measurement chapter should list and describe possible measurements, arrange or classify the measurements in a manner that facilitates standard-setting decisions, describe the advantages and disadvantages of each measurement in terms of the qualitative characteristics of useful financial information, and discuss at a conceptual level how the qualitative characteristics and cost constraint should be considered together in identifying an appropriate measurement. Without prescribing specific measurements for particular assets and liabilities, the measurement chapter should discuss how its concepts might be applied to individual classes of assets and liabilities.

This phase of the project was last updated in November 2010.

Phase D – the reporting entity

An ED was issued in July 2010 dealing with this topic which will comprise chapter 2 of the 2010 Conceptual Framework. It is expected that this is likely to be either an individual entity or a combined group of entities under common control. This phase of the project was last updated in November 2010.

The following phases are not yet active:

Phase E – presentation and disclosure
Phase F – purpose and status
Phase G – application to not-for-profit entities
Phase H – remaining issues

4 Fair Value Measurement – IFRS 13

Introduction

The objective of IFRS 13 is to provide a single source of guidance for fair value measurement where it is required by a reporting standard, rather than it being spread throughout several reporting standards. There is now a uniform framework for measurement of fair value for entities around the world who apply either US GAAP or IFRS GAAP. IFRS 13 does not extend the use of fair value – it provides guidance on how it should be determined when an initial or subsequent fair value measurement is required by a reporting standard.

Note that IFRS 13 does not apply to share-based payment transactions accounted for by IFRS 2 Share-based Payment and IAS 17 Leases. IFRS 13 also does not apply to situations where different measurements are required, such as net realisable value or value in use which may be required by other reporting standards, such as IAS 2 Inventories and IAS 36 Impairment respectively.

IFRS 13 is effective for accounting periods commencing on or after 1 January 2013, with early adoption permitted.

Reasons for the issue of IFRS 13

*   To standardise the definition of fair value.

*   To help users by providing additional disclosures relating to how fair value has been determined.

*   To improve consistency of reported information; this will also help to reduce complexity in application of measurement of fair value.

*   To increase the extent of convergence between IFRS and US GAAP.

Definitions relevant to fair value

Fair value is defined as the price that would be received to **sell an asset or paid to transfer a liability in an orderly transaction** between market participants at the measurement date; i.e. it is an exit price, whether observable in an active market (level one inputs – see later), or estimated using a valuation technique (with the use of level 2 and/or level three inputs – see later).

Market participants comprise independent buyers and sellers who are informed and willing and able to enter into a transaction in the principal or the most advantageous market as appropriate. Fair value is the price that would apply between market participants, **whether observable in an active market** (use of level 1 inputs – see later), **or estimated using a valuation technique** (with the use of level 2 and 3 inputs – see later).

Fair value of an asset or a liability may be required to be measured in a variety of circumstances as follows:

(a) Fair value on a **recurring basis** arises when a reporting standard requires fair value to be measured on an ongoing basis. Examples of this include IAS 40 Investment Property, or IFRS 9 Financial Instruments which require some financial assets and liabilities to be measured at fair value.

(b) Fair value on a **non-recurring basis** arises when a reporting standard requires fair value to be measured at fair value only in certain specified circumstances. For example, IFRS 5 requires that assets classified as held for sale are measured at fair value.

(c) Fair value upon **initial recognition** arises when a reporting standard requires fair value to be measured upon initial recognition. For example, IFRS 3 Business Combinations (Revised) requires that the separable net assets of the acquired entity are measured at fair value to determine goodwill at acquisition.

The price paid to acquire an asset or received to assume a liability (i.e. an entry price) may (or may not) be fair value. If it is not, there should be an adjustment to fair value, with a gain or loss recognised immediately, or when specified by the relevant standard. In the case of a financial instrument, this may only be done when fair value is evidenced by a data from observable inputs (see later).

To determine whether fair value at initial recognition equals transaction price, an entity must consider factors specific to the transaction and factors specific to the asset or liability to be measured; – is there any evidence to suggest that the transaction may not be at fair value? One situation where the price paid to acquire an asset may not be a reliable indicator of fair value arises when the asset is purchased from a related party.

The basis of a fair value measurement

The following factors should be taken into consideration when measuring fair value:

(a) The asset or liability to be measured may be an **individual asset** (e.g. plot of land) **or liability, or a group of assets and liabilities** (e.g. a cash generating unit or business), depending upon exactly what is required to be measured.

(b) The measurement should reflect the price at which an orderly transaction between willing market participants would take place under current market conditions – i.e. **not a distress transaction**.

(c) The entity must determine the market in which an orderly transaction would take place. This will be the **principal market or, failing that, the most advantageous market** that an entity has access to at the measurement date. They will often, but not always, be the same.

(d) Unless there is evidence otherwise, the market that an entity would normally enter into is presumed to be the principal or most advantageous market.

(e) It is quite possible that different entities within a group or different businesses within an entity may have different principal or most advantageous markets, for example, due to their location.

(f) The valuation or measurement should reflect the **characteristics of the asset or liability** (age, condition, location, restrictions on use or sale etc) if they are relevant to market participants.

(g) It is not adjusted for **transaction costs** – they are not a feature of the asset or liability, but may be relevant when determining the most advantageous market. If location, for example, is a characteristic of the asset, then price may need to be adjusted for any costs that may be incurred to transport an asset to or from a market.

Principal or most advantageous market

Numerical Example

An asset is sold in two different active markets at different prices. An entity enters into transactions in both markets and can access the price in those markets for the asset at the measurement date as follows:

	Market 1	Market 2
	$	$
Price	26	25
Transactions cost	(3)	(1)
Transport cost	(2)	(2)
	___	___
Net price received	21	22
	___	___

If Market 1 is the principal market for the asset (i.e. the market with the greatest volume and level of activity for the asset), the fair value of the asset would be measured using the price that would be received in that market, after taking into account transport costs is ($26 – $2) $24. Transactions costs are ignored as they are not a characteristic of the asset.

If neither market is the principal market for the asset, the fair value of the asset would be measured using the price in the most advantageous market. The most advantageous market is the market that maximises the amount that would be received to sell the asset, after taking into account transaction costs and transport costs (i.e. the net amount that would be received in the respective markets).

Because the maximum net amount that the entity would receive is $22 in Market 2 ($25 – $3), the fair value of the asset would be measured using the price in that market ($25), less transport costs of $2, resulting in a fair value measurement of $23. Although transaction costs are taken into account when determining which market is the most advantageous market, the price used to measure the fair value of the asset is not adjusted for those costs (although it is adjusted for transport costs).

Valuation techniques

Valuation techniques should be used which are appropriate to the asset or liability at the measurement date and for which sufficient data is available, applying the fair value hierarchy to maximise the use of observable inputs as far as possible. IFRS 13 identifies three valuation approaches:

(1) Income approach – e.g. where estimated future cash flows may be converted into a single, current amount stated at present value.

(2) Market approach – e.g. where prices and other market-related data is used for similar or identical assets, liabilities or groups of assets and liabilities.

(3) Cost approach – e.g. to arrive at what may be regarded as current replacement cost to determine the cost that would be incurred to replace the service or operational capacity of an asset.

More than one valuation technique may be used in helping to determine fair value in a particular situation. Note that a change in valuation technique is regarded as a change of accounting estimate in accordance with IAS 8 which needs to be properly disclosed in the financial statements.

5 Fair value hierarchy

IFRS 13 establishes a hierarchy that categorises the inputs to valuation techniques used to measure fair value. As follows:

(a) **Level 1 inputs** comprise quoted prices ('observable') in active markets for identical assets and liabilities at the measurement date. This is regarded as providing the most reliable evidence of fair value and is likely to be used without adjustment.

(b) **Level 2 inputs** are observable inputs, other than those included within Level 1 above, which are observable directly or indirectly. This may include quoted prices for similar (not identical) asset or liabilities in active markets, or prices for identical or similar assets and liabilities in inactive markets. Typically, they are likely to require some degree of adjustment to arrive at a fair value measurement.

(c) **Level 3 inputs** are unobservable inputs for an asset or liability, based upon the best information available, including information that may be reasonably available relating to market participants.
An asset or liability is regarded as having been measured using the lowest level of inputs that is significant to its valuation.

Selection and use of inputs into valuation techniques

- Inputs into a valuation technique should be consistent with those which would be used by market participants, including control premiums or discounts for lack of control. Prices based upon bid-ask spreads should be the most representative of fair value from within that spread.

- Prices may be provided by third parties, such as brokers, but the prices must be determined in accordance with the requirements of IFRS 13; e.g. they may be regarded as either observable or unobservable data.

- If markets are not active, then further analysis of transactions actually taking place, and/or the prices, may be required. This may result in an adjustment of such prices to establish fair value.

Inputs to determine fair value

Examples of inputs used to determine fair value include:

	Asset or liability	Example
Level 1	Equity shares in a listed entity	Unadjusted quoted prices in an active market
Level 2	Finished goods inventory at a retail outlet	Price paid by retail customers
	Licence acquired as part of a business combination which as recently negotiated with an unrelated party	The royalty rate contained within the contract
	Cash generating unit	Valuation multiple from observed transactions involving similar businesses
	Building held and used	Price per square metre for the building from observable market data, such as observed transactions for similar buildings in similar locations.
Level 3	Interest rate swap	Adjustment made to a mid-market non-binding price using data that cannot be directly observed or corroborated
	Decommissioning liability assumed upon a business combination	Use of own data to make estimates of expected future cash outflows to fulfil the obligation used to estimate the present value of that future obligation.
	Cash-generating unit	Profit or cash flow forecast using own data.

Specific application principles

Non-financial assets

Fair value of a non-financial asset is based upon highest and best use of that asset that would maximise its value, based upon uses which are physically possible, legally permissible and financially feasible. This is considered from the perspective of market participants, even if they may use the asset differently. Current use of a non-financial asset is presumed to be its highest and best use, unless there are factors that would suggest otherwise.

- Used in combination with other assets – fair value of an asset will be based upon what would be received if the asset was sold to another market participant, and that the complementary assets and liabilities they needed for highest and best use would be available to them.

- Used on a stand-alone basis – the price that would be received to sell the asset to a market participant who would use it on a stand-alone basis.

In either situation, it is assumed that the asset is sold individually, rather than as part of a collection of assets and liabilities.

Example — Land

An entity acquires land in a business combination. In accordance with IFRS 3 (revised), this must be stated at fair value at the date of acquisition to help determine the value of goodwill at that date. The land is currently developed for industrial use as a site for a factory. Alternatively, the site could be developed into a block of residential flats which, based upon evidence relating to adjoining plots of a similar size, appears to be a practical use of the site.

The current use of land is presumed to be its highest and best use unless market or other factors suggest a different use. In this situation, there is a possible alternative use which should be considered as follows:

The highest and best use of the land would be determined by taking the higher measurement from the two possible outcomes:

(a) the value of the land as currently developed for industrial use (i.e. the land would be used in combination with other assets, such as the factory, or with other assets and liabilities).

(b) the value of the land as a vacant site for residential use, taking into account the costs of demolishing the factory and other costs (including the uncertainty about whether the entity would be able to convert the asset to the alternative use, such as legal and planning issues) necessary to convert the land to a vacant site (i.e. the land is to be used by market participants on a stand-alone basis).

Example – Research and development project

An entity acquires a research and development (R&D) project in a business combination. The entity does not intend to complete the project as, if completed, the project would compete with one of its own projects (to provide the next generation of the entity's commercialised technology). Instead, the entity intends to hold (i.e. lock up) the project to prevent its competitors from obtaining access to the technology. In doing this the project is expected to provide defensive value, principally by improving the prospects for the entity's own competing technology and preventing access by competitors to the technology.

To measure the fair value of the project at initial recognition, the highest and best use of the project would be determined on the basis of its use by market participants. For example, the highest and best use of the R&D project could be:

(a) **to continue development** if market participants would continue to develop the project and that use would maximise the value of the group of assets or of assets and liabilities in which the project would be used (i.e. the asset would be used in combination with other assets or with other assets and liabilities). The fair value of the project would be measured on the basis of the price that would be received in a current transaction to sell the project, assuming that the R&D would be used with its complementary assets and the associated liabilities and that those assets and liabilities would be available to market participants.

(b) **to cease development for competitive reasons** if market participants would lock up the project and that use would maximise the value of the group of assets or of assets and liabilities in which the project would be used. The fair value of the project would be measured on the basis of the price that would be received in a current transaction to sell the project, assuming that the R&D would be used (i.e. locked up) with its complementary assets and the associated liabilities and that those assets and liabilities would be available to market participants.

(c) **to cease development if market participants would discontinue its development**. The fair value of the project would be measured on the basis of the price that would be received in a current transaction to sell the project on its own (which might be zero).

Financial assets and financial liabilities – offsetting positions

If an entity manages a group of financial assets and liabilities within the scope of IFRS 9 Financial Instruments, which are measured at fair value based upon their net exposure to particular risks, then it is permitted to value the net exposure at fair value, provided this is in accordance with documented strategy and information is reported on this basis to key management.

Liabilities and equity instruments

Ideally, fair value is measured using quoted prices for identical instruments – i.e. level one observable inputs. If this is not possible, it may be possible to use prices in an inactive market – level two observable inputs. If this is not possible, a valuation model should be used e.g. present value measurement.

Note that any fair value measurement of a liability should include non-performance or default risk. This may be different for different types of liability held by an entity; for example, default risk for a secured loan is less than default risk of an unsecured loan at any point in time. Also, be aware that this risk may change over time as an entity may or may not encounter financial and other commercial difficulties.

Fair value measurement of a liability or equity instrument assumes that it is transferred at the measurement date, and that both a liability and/or equity instrument would remain outstanding, rather than being settled or redeemed.

When a quoted price is not available for such an item, an entity shall measure fair value from the perspective of a market participant who holds the identical item as an asset at the measurement date. If there are no such observable prices, then an alternative valuation technique must be used.

Measurement of liabilities

Consider two entities, A and B, who each have a legal obligation to pay $1000 cash to another entity, C, in ten years.

Entity A has an excellent credit rating and can borrow at 5 per cent, whereas Entity B has a lower credit rating and is able to borrow at 8 per cent. Entity A will receive approximately $614 in exchange for its promise (the present value of $1,000 in ten years using a discount factor of 5%). Entity B will receive approximately $463 in exchange for its promise (the present value of $1,000 in ten years using a discount factor of 8%).

The fair value of the liability to each entity (i.e. the proceeds) therefore incorporates that entity's credit standing

Disclosures

Disclosures should provide information that enables users of financial statements to evaluate the inputs and methods used to determine how fair value measurements have been arrived at.

The level in the three-tier valuation hierarchy should be disclosed, together with supporting details of valuation methods and inputs used where appropriate. As would be expected, more detailed information is required where there is significant use of level-three inputs to arrive at a fair value measurement to enable users of financial statements to understand how such fair values have been arrived at.

Disclosure should also be made when there is a change of valuation technique to measure an asset or liability. This will include any change in the level of inputs used to determine fair value of particular assets and/or liabilities.

Corporate reporting

Definition

Corporate reports aim to provide information about the resources and performance of the reporting entity to users of such reports.

Reporting corporate performance

- Traditional corporate reports include historical financial information regarding the operating and financial performance of the entity.

- Financial information and ratios can be supplemented by commentary on the performance and strategy of the company, such as the chairman's report.

- In recent years, non-financial information has become more prevalent. More and more users of financial information require information on an entity's policies towards the environment, employees and society.

- IFRSs do not require these non-financial reports, but many companies produce them voluntarily.

- Investors require up-to-date information and in this sense financial reports do not meet this need. By the time the information is published, it is already several months out of date.

- Up-to-date financial information is freely available to investors from online news and market-information companies, databases and financial statements.

Usefulness of corporate reporting

- Financial reports will always need to be produced to satisfy statutory requirements, such as filing accounts or for the preparation of tax returns.

- As the harmonisation of accounting standards takes place on a global scale, corporate reports become more comparable. This is particularly useful for investors who should be able to compare financial information from different entities that are located in different countries.

- The number of disclosures in financial statements is increasing and companies have to be more transparent in their reporting. Recent developments have continued this trend. For example, IFRS 8 **Segment reporting** (see chapter 13) requires segment information to be reported on the basis that information is reported to the management of an entity, thus showing how the company is structured and assessed internally.

- The IASB issued a Practice Statement (PS) in December 2010 **Management commentary** (see chapter 19) which is concerned with the adoption of a formal process of commentary on the performance of the business. Entities should disclose the nature of the business as well as its objectives, strategies results, prospects and performance measures. The PS is a non-binding framework for presentation of a management commentary which supports financial statements prepared in accordance with IFRS.

- It is in the interests of an entity to make its information as accessible to users as possible and many corporate reports include a great deal of information on strategy and activities of entities.

- Increased disclosure of non-financial information such as environmental and social reports is also a positive move for users of financial statements, who can see the progress the entity is making in certain areas.

Compliance with accounting standards

- Despite the number of accounting standards in issue and the requirement for accounts to present a true and fair view, there are still a number of companies that fail to comply with requirements of the standards.

- The Financial Reporting Review Panel (FRRP) in the UK has the aim of ensuring that both public and private companies comply with the Companies Act and accounting standards. It has expanded its role to assess financial statements prepared under IFRS in the UK.

- It has the authority to require the directors of a company to amend their financial statements to remove any departures from requirements.

- There is no equivalent under IFRS; individual countries are each responsible for policing compliance.

Question and answer

Question:

Although it may come as a surprise to many non-accountants, the accounting profession internationally has encountered a great deal of problems in arriving at robust definitions for the 'elements' of financial statements. Defining assets, liabilities, and gains and losses (income and expenditure) has been particularly problematical. These definitions form the core of any conceptual Framework that is to be used as a basis for preparing financial statements. It is also in this area that the International Accounting Standards Committee's Conceptual Framework for Financial Reporting 2010 (2010 Framework) has come in for some criticism.

It seems that the current accounting treatment of certain items does not (fully) agree with definitions in the 2010 Framework. A major objective of the 2010 Framework is to exclude from the statement of financial position items that are neither assets nor liabilities; and to make 'off balance sheet' assets and liabilities more visible by putting them on the statement of financial position whenever practicable.

(a) **Critically discuss the definition of assets and liabilities contained in the Framework**.

Your answer should explain the importance of the definitions and the relevance of each component of the definitions.

(b) Below is a series of transactions or events that have arisen in relation to Worthright. The company's year end is 31 March 20X1.

(i) Worthright has entered into two contracts. The first contract entails Worthright installing and maintaining a telephone system in a building owned by Cranbourne. The installation will be completed by June 20X1 and the contract will run for ten years. Worthright will receive a payment of $200,000 per annum. Worthright has installed many similar systems and it can reliably estimate that the annual cost of the contract will amount to $150,000 per annum.

In order to secure supplies, Worthright entered into a second contract agreeing to purchase 50,000 units of gas heating fuel per annum for the next five years at a price of $20 per unit. The contract, which is non-cancellable, was signed on 20 February 20X1. The supply of gas will commence on 1 September 20X1.

Since the contract was signed there have been several large discoveries of this type of gas field and as a consequence the market price of the gas has fallen to $14 per unit. This market price is expected to prevail for the whole of the period of Worthright's contract.

(ii) On 1 April 20X0 Worthright purchased a new office building at a cost of $1 million. The building has an estimated life of 50 years, but it contains a sophisticated air conditioning and heating system (included in the price of the building), which will require replacement every ten years at a cost of $100,000. Worthright intends to depreciate the building at $20,000 per annum and provide a further $10,000 each year to facilitate the replacement of the heating system

(iii) Worthright is approximately half way through a three-year contract to build a sugar refinery for Sweetness. The contract contains a severe penalty clause that would require Worthright to pay Sweetness $1.5 million if the contract is not completed by its due date of 30 September 20X2. Although the contract is currently on schedule, Worthright is not entirely confident that the penalty will be avoided. It therefore considers it prudent to provide for the penalty as a liability.

The refinery is being constructed under local building regulations, which require the builder of new properties to give a five-year warranty against defective materials and defective construction techniques. Worthright's past experience is that there are usually some warranty claims, but they are seldom of high value and in the past have been charged to the period in which they have arisen

(iv) Worthright undertakes a considerable amount of research and development work. Most of this work is done on its own behalf, but occasionally it undertakes this type of work for other companies. Before any of its own projects progress to the development stage, they are assessed by an internal committee, which carefully analyses all information relating to the project. This process has led to a very good record of development projects delivering profitable results. Despite this, Worthright deems it prudent to write off immediately all research and development work, including that which it does for other companies.

For the items (i) to (iv) above, discuss whether the transactions or events give rise to assets or liabilities; and describe how they should be recognised and measured under current International Accounting Standards and conventionally accepted practice.

Answer:

(a) **Importance of the definitions**:

The definitions of assets and liabilities are fundamental to the IASB's Conceptual Framework for Financial Reporting 2010. Apart from forming the obvious basis for the preparation of a statement of financial position, they are also the two elements of financial statements that are used to derive the other elements. Equity (ownership) interest is the residue of assets less liabilities. Gains and losses are changes in ownership interests, other than contributions from, and distributions to, the owners. In effect, a gain is an increase in an asset or a reduction of a liability whereas a loss is the reverse of this. Transactions with owners are defined in a straightforward manner in order to exclude them from the definitions of gains and losses.

Assets:

The IASB's 2010 Framework retains the definition of an asset from the 1979 Framework document and defines an asset as 'a resource controlled by an entity as a result of past events and from which future economic benefits are expected to flow to the entity'. This definition is similar to equivalent definitions in the USA and UK. The first part of the definition 'a resource controlled by an entity' is a refinement of the principle that an asset must be owned by the entity. This refinement allows assets that are not legally owned by an entity, but over which the entity has the rights that are normally conveyed by ownership, such as the right to use or occupy an asset, to be recognised as an asset of the entity.

The essence of this approach is that an asset is not the physical item that one might expect it to be, such as a machine or a building, but it is the right to enjoy the future economic benefits that the asset will produce (normally future cash flows). Perhaps the best known example of this type of arrangement is a finance lease. Control not only allows the entity to obtain the economic benefits of assets but also to restrict the access of others to them. Where an entity develops an alternative manufacturing process that reduces future cash outflows in terms of lower cost of production, this too can be an asset. Assets can also arise where there is no legal control. The Framework cites the example of 'know-how' derived from a development activity. Where an entity has the capacity to keep this a secret, the entity controls the benefits that are expected to flow from it.

Notably, other versions of the definition of an asset (e.g. in the USA) refer to future economic benefits being probable. This wording recognises that all future economic benefits are subject to some degree of risk or uncertainty. The IASB deals with the 'probable' issue by saying that future economic benefits are only 'expected' and therefore need not be certain.

Note that the development of the Conceptual Framework for Financial Reporting 2010 is part of a long-term project between the IASB and US FASB.

The reference to past events makes it clear that transactions arising after the reporting date that may lead to economic benefits cannot be treated as assets. The use of the word 'events' in this part of the definition recognises that it is not only transactions that can create assets or liabilities (see below), but other events such as 'legal wrongs' that may lead to damages claims. This aspect of the definition does cause some problems. For example, it could be argued that signing a profitable contract before the reporting date is an 'event' that gives rise to a future economic benefit. It is widely held that the justification for not recognising future profitable contracts as assets is that the rights and obligations under these contracts are equal (which is unlikely to be true) and also that the historical cost of 'signing' them is zero.

Liabilities:

The IASB retains the definition of a liability from the 1979 Framework document which defines a liability as 'a present obligation of the entity arising from past events which is expected to result in an outflow from the entity of resources embodying economic benefits'. The IASB stress that the essential characteristic is the 'present obligation'. Although the definition is complementary to that of assets, it is perceived as less controversial. Most other parts of the definition have the same meaning as in the definition of assets, e.g. the terms 'economic benefits' and 'past events'.

Most liabilities are legal or contractual obligations to transfer known amounts of cash, e.g. trade payables and loans. Occasionally they may be settled other than for cash such as in a barter transaction, but this still constitutes transferring economic benefits. It is necessary to consider the principles and definitions in the 2010 Framework alongside those of the IASB's IAS 37 **Provisions, contingent liabilities and contingent assets**. Within the Framework the IASB introduces the concept of obligations arising from 'normal business practice' being liabilities. One such example is rectifying faults in goods sold even when the warranty period has expired. IAS 37 explores this principle more fully and refers to them as 'constructive' obligations. These occur where an entity creates a valid expectation that it will discharge responsibilities that it is not legally obliged to. This is usually as a result of past behaviour, or by commitments given in a published statement (e.g. voluntarily incurring environmental costs).

Where the exact amount of a liability is uncertain it is usually referred to as a provision.

Obligations may exist that are not expected to require 'transfers of economic benefits'. These again are described in IAS 37 and are more generally known as contingent liabilities. For example, where a holding company guarantees a subsidiary's loan.

Similar to assets, costs to be incurred in the future do not represent liabilities. This is because either the entity has the ability to avoid the costs, or if it cannot (e.g. where a contract exists), then incurring the cost would be matched by receiving an asset of equal value.

(b) (i) This example illustrates the asymmetry of accepted practice in accounting for profits and losses. Most people would consider the first contract, which is going to be profitable, to be an asset. It results from a past event (the signing of the contract) and in all probability will result in future economic benefits. Indeed, there have been examples of companies that were unsuccessful in bidding for a contract actually buying the company that was awarded the contract. This presumably occurs because the contract is seen to be a valuable asset.

Despite the nature of this contract appearing to be an asset, Worthright would not be able to recognise it as such in its statement of financial position. As noted in (a) the IASB consider that an uncompleted contra ct has both rights and obligations that are in balance, as well as the fact that the transaction has no historic cost. So despite an expected income stream of $200,000 with associated costs of the $150,000 per annum (which are clearly not in balance), this contract cannot be shown as an asset.

The second contract, by contrast, appears to represent an obligation. The company is committed to purchasing goods for the next five years at a price that is above current market prices. It is not immediately obvious that this contract will result in future losses, but if the gas is to be consumed by Worthright, then the losses are an opportunity cost of $6 per unit of fuel. If the gas is to be sold on by Worthright then, given the fall in market prices, it is unlikely that it will be sold at a profit. It is therefore highly likely that this represents an onerous contract for which a liability should be provided. More information and analysis would be needed to determine the amount of the liability.

(ii) On first impressions there may appear to be a liability for the replacement of the air conditioning and heating system. If the company wishes to use the property for the whole of its life then it will certainly have to replace the system several times. The past event is the purchase of the building and replacing the system will involve the future transfer of economic benefits. However, this analysis misses the important point that the company is not committed to using the building; it could choose to sell it. Even if it does not sell the building, it does not have to replace the system.

(1) The solution to the treatment of the building lies in IAS 16 **Property, plant and equipment**. Para 13 states that in certain circumstances it is appropriate to allocate the total expenditure on an asset to its component parts and to account for them separately. The building and the air conditioning system should be treated as separate assets and depreciated over their relative lives. The depreciation of the building will be $18,000 per annum ($1 million – $100,000/50 years) and the depreciation of the heating system will be $10,000 per annum ($100,000/10 years). When this approach is adopted, it becomes clear that if Worthright were to make a provision for the replacement of the system, as well as depreciating it, it would be 'double charging' for the asset.

(2) There are two aspects to consider here: whether (i) the penalty clause and (ii) the warranty represent liabilities. Arguably they are both contingent liabilities in that it will be future uncertain events that will determine whether an outflow of future economic benefits will arise. A careful consideration of the 2010 Framework's definition of a liability would result in the view that the penalty clause is not a liability. This is because there is no past event. One may consider the signing of the contract to be the past event, but this does not cause the liability. It would be finishing the contract late that would cause a liability, and this has not yet occurred. In effect, the penalty costs can be avoided by performing the contract as it was agreed, i.e. on time. Avoidable costs are not liabilities.

The warranty, on the other hand, should be considered as a liability under the requirements of IAS 37 **Provisions, contingent liabilities and contingent assets**. The signing of the contract gives rise to this potential liability. It is difficult to quantify (as it is in the future and it may not happen) and it may not be material. In principle the company's current policy of charging warranty costs to the period in which they arise is incorrect. These costs should be matched with the benefits from the contract, i.e. its revenues/profits. Although most warranty costs may be relatively small amounts, it is possible that a large claim could arise. Worthright should provide, as part of the contract costs, the best estimate of the cost of the warranty over the period of the contract.

(iv) For many years, research and development costs have represented the classic dilemma of whether they are an asset or an expense. If they result in future economic benefits, they are assets; if not, they are expenses. Unfortunately, the resolution to this question (at the time of preparing financial statements) lies in the future and is therefore unknown. Empirical research in the USA some time ago showed that less than 5% of all research resulted in profitable products, and perhaps, surprisingly, most projects that progressed through to development did not prove to be profitable either. From this evidence, based on probabilities, most research and development is not an asset.

In the case of the development expenditure of Worthright, it appears that it may satisfy the criteria in IAS 38 **Intangible assets** to be treated as an intangible asset, particularly in view of Worthright's impressive track record on development projects. More details would have to be obtained in order to determine whether the expenditure does qualify as an asset. If it does, the company's existing policy would not be permitted under IAS 38, as this says that if the recognition criteria are met, the expenditure should be capitalised. It does not offer a choice. Interestingly, under USA standards, development, expenditure is always written off, and other domestic standards (including the UK) allow a choice.

The above only applies to Worthright's own development costs. The company also performs research and development for clients and here the case is different. Although it is conducting research and development, it is in fact carrying out contract work. The costs of this research and development should be matched with the revenues it will bring. To the extent it has been invoiced to clients, it should be recognised as cost of sales in profit or loss (not as research and development). Any unbilled costs should appear as a current asset under work in progress.

Current issues

Conceptual Framework for Financial Reporting 2010

This is a long-term project divided into several phases as identified earlier within this chapter. At September 2012, there has been little tangible progress on any of the project phases in the previous two years as other projects have taken priority.

Credit Risk in Liability Management (DP/2009/2)

Arguably, questions about the role of credit risk in liability measurement have generated more comment and controversy than any other aspect of fair value measurement. For example; should current measurements of liabilities (including fair value) incorporate the chance that an entity will fail to perform as required? If not, what are the alternatives?

An entity's credit standing affects the credit risk of its liabilities, but the effect may be different from one liability to another. For example, a liability which is secured against assets of the business has less credit risk than an entity's other liabilities. For those other liabilities, the credit risk of the entity translates directly to the credit risk of those liabilities. The IASB has stressed that it is the particular liability that is being measured, and the relevant credit risk is the risk associated with that liability, rather than all liabilities collectively.

The DP outlines the three most often-cited arguments in favour of including credit risk and the three most often-cited arguments against. This paper includes within its scope all current measurements of liabilities. Standard-setters have concluded that the fair value of a liability is a price and, thus, necessarily includes the credit standing of that liability. It does not follow that other current measurements of the liability should do so. Alternative current measurements of liabilities might include, for example:

- fulfilment value, as it is being developed in the IASBs joint project with FASB on insurance contracts;

- the value at which the liability could be settled with the counterparty;

- fair value, but excluding the effects of credit risk, and

- the value at which the liability could be transferred in a transaction permitted by industry regulators.

Just as there are several alternative current measures of a liability, there are several reasons why the reported amount of a liability might change. Some of those changes do not involve changes in credit risk, for example, changes in expected cash flows or currency exchange rates.

Some liability measurements have always included the effects of credit risk. Explicit consideration of the idea in standards and concepts is relatively recent.

In 2000 the FASB published Concepts Statement No 7 Using Cash Flow Information and Present Value in Accounting Measurements. That Statement described the role of present value in 'fresh start' measurements of the fair value of assets and liabilities. In doing so, it could not avoid the question of the entity's credit standing. Within that document, the FASB said 'The most relevant measure of a liability always reflects the credit standing of the entity obligated to pay'.

Development of this DP into a separate reporting standard has now stopped. The IASB has decided that, from October 2009, any continuing work on this topic will become part of the measurement phase of the development of the Conceptual Framework for Financial Reporting 2010. The work done to October 2009 will also be used to inform the development of other reporting standards dealing with measurement of liabilities – e.g. IFRS 9 Financial Instruments updated in October 2010 to include accounting for financial liabilities as part of the project to replace IAS 39 (refer to the chapter dealing with financial instruments).

UK syllabus focus

The ACCA UK syllabus contains a requirement that candidates should be able to discuss and apply the key differences between UK GAAP and IFRS GAAP. The accounting requirements of UK GAAP and IFRS GAAP are similar in this area; the key issues include the following:

The preparation of single company and group accounts in the UK is governed by the Companies Act 2006. The form and content of financial statements is specified in CA2006 and supplemented by IFRS or UK FRS (as applicable) to comply with the requirement that financial statements show a true and fair view.

Companies or groups must disclose the accounting framework used as the basis for the preparation of the financial statements. The normal expectation is that financial statements should comply with all relevant reporting standards to show a true and fair view. Where there has been departure from a reporting standard in order to give a true and fair view, this must be disclosed and explained within the financial statements.

For companies or groups listed on a stock exchange within the EU, they are obliged to prepare their annual financial statements in accordance with IFRS GAAP. Accounts for listed companies and groups should be filed at Companies House within six months of the annual reporting date. Typically, they will adopt a slightly different presentation style; the balance sheet is typically presented showing assets, together with equity and liabilities, rather than the net assets style of presentation normally adopted under UK GAAP. There are also some differences in terminology between the two frameworks as summarised below:

UK GAAP	**IFRS GAAP**
Balance sheet	Statement of financial position
Reserves	Equity
Profit and loss account	Statement of profit or loss
Statement of total recognised gains and losses	Other comprehensive income
Debtors	Receivables
Creditors	Payables
Corporation tax	Income tax
Turnover	Revenue
Minority interest	Non-controlling interest

Non-listed companies and groups can prepare and file their annual financial statements either in accordance with UK GAAP as regulated by the ASB, or in accordance with IFRS GAAP. For non-listed companies and groups, annual financial statements should be filed within nine months of the annual reporting date.

Chapter summary

The framework
- Underpins accounting standards
- Characteristics of useful information are:
  - relevant
  - reliable
  - understandable
  - comparable
- Defines assets, liabilities, gains and losses, ownership interest and contributions and distributions to owners

Corporate reporting
- Provide information about performance and resources of an entity to its users
- Financial information is historic, but there are many online companies providing up-to-date information
- Non-financial information is widely distributed with the annual report including environmental and social reports
- Future developments and strategies can be reported in the management commentary

IFRS 13 fair value measurement
- Provides single source of guidance where FV measurment is required
- Initial recognition
  - recurring basis
  - non-recurring basis
- Based upon exit value
- Fair value hierachy - 3 levels

Performance reporting

Chapter learning objectives

Upon completion of this chapter you will be able to:

- prepare reports relating to corporate performance for external stakeholders
- discuss the issues relating to the recognition of revenue
- evaluate recent changes to reporting financial performance.

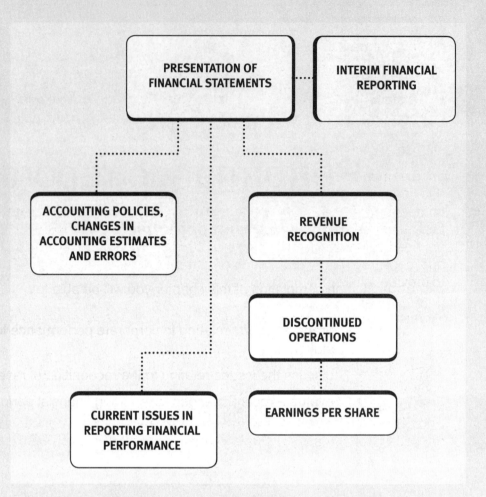

1 Presentation of financial statements (IAS 1 revised)

IAS 1 was amended in June 2011 to clarify the accounting disclosures for items of other comprehensive income. This is considered in more detail within Expandable Text content in this chapter.

Components of financial statements

The IASB first revised IAS 1 in September 2007. The intention of this revision was to aggregate information in the financial statements on the basis of shared characteristics and so improve the information provided to users of those financial statements.

Components of financial statements

A complete set of financial statements has the following components:

• a statement of financial position at the end of the reporting period

• a statement of profit or loss and other comprehensive income (or statement of profit or loss with a separate statement of other comprehensive income)

- a statement of changes in equity for the period

- a statement of cash flows for the period

- accounting policies note and other explanatory notes.

- a statement of financial position at the beginning of the earliest comparative period when an entity applies an accounting policy retrospectively or corrects an error retrospectively

Improvements to IFRS 2009-11 issued in May 2012 specifies that additional comparative information required by IAS 1, usually for the immediately preceding accounting period, need not also be presented for earlier periods. If it is provided, it should comply with IFRS. If provided voluntarily (rather than required by other reporting standards or applicable regulatory requirements), it would not result in a requirement to provide a full set of financial statements.

When there is a retrospective restatement of the financial statements, (e.g due to a change in accounting policy) which had a material impact on the statement of financial position at the beginning of the preceding period, the statement of financial position should be presented at the end of the current period, together with at the beginning and end of the preceding reporting period.
Additional comparative disclosures may be made in accordance with previous GAAP to assist in understanding in the first set of IFRS financial statements.

The titles used by IAS 1 are not mandatory. An entity may continue to use the previous title of balance sheet and cash flow statement.

Other reports and statements in the annual report, e.g. a financial review, an environmental report, a social report, etc, are outside the scope of this reporting standard.

Statement of financial position

The statement of financial position is largely the same as the balance sheet presented in the previous version of IAS 1, with one exception:

- Reserves other than share capital and retained earnings are now referred to as 'other components of equity'.

Statement of comprehensive income

Total comprehensive income is the realised profit or loss for the period plus all items of other comprehensive income for the period.

Other comprehensive income (OCI) is income and expenses that are not recognised in profit or loss, but instead recognised directly in equity (reserves).

Amendments to IAS 1 on Presentation of Items of Other Comprehensive Income was issued by the IASB in June 2011, and is effective for accounting periods commencing on or after 1 July 2012, with early adoption permitted.

The amendments change **how** items of OCI are presented in the financial statements – they do not change **which** items should be presented on OCI. Items of OCI must be classified into two groups as follows:

- items that might be reclassified (or recycled) to profit or loss in subsequent accounting periods:
    - foreign exchange gains and losses arising on translation of a foreign operation (IAS 21)
    - effective parts of cash flow hedging arrangements (IAS 39)

- items that will not be reclassified (or recycled) to profit or loss in subsequent accounting periods:
    - changes in revaluation surplus (IAS 16 & IAS 38)
    - remeasurement components on defined benefit plans (IAS 19)
    - remeasurement of equity instruments designated to be classified as fair value through OCI (IFRS 9)

Entities can prepare one combined statement for total comprehensive income for the year, with profit or loss for the year, followed by OCI which should be clearly identified. Alternatively, an entity can prepare two separate statements, given equal prominence, with the profit or loss statement, immediately followed by the statement of OCI. The statement of OCI should begin with profit or loss for the year, so that there is no duplication or confusion as to which items are included within each statement.

The primary reasons for introducing the amendments are:

- to achieve improved consistency and clarity in the way that OCI is presented, particularly as more items may be accounted for through OCI as new reporting standards are introduced or existing reporting standards are revised – e.g. IFRS 9 re financial assets and IAS 19 in respect of how returns on financial assets are dealt with when accounting for defined benefit pension schemes per IAS19.
- to ensure that items of profit or loss and OCI are presented together with equal prominence
- to enhance convergence with US GAAP, following changes made by US FASB

Format one: statement of comprehensive income

For illustration, one of the recommended formats is as follows (previous year comparative would normally be included).

XYZ Group – Statement of comprehensive income for the year ended 31 December 20X3

	$000
Revenue	X
Cost of sales	(X)
Gross profit	X
Other operating income	X
Distribution costs	(X)
Administrative expenses	(X)
Other operating expenses	(X)
Profit from operations	X
Finance costs	(X)
Share of profit of associates	X
Profit before tax	X
Income tax expense	(X)
Profit or loss for the period	X

Other comprehensive income

Items that will not be reclassified to profit or loss:

Gains on property revaluation	X
Remeasurement or actuarial gains and losses on defined benefit pension plans	(X)
Financial assets designated to be accounted for through OCI	X
Income tax relating to items that will not be reclassified	(X)

Total – items that will not be reclassified to profit or loss net of tax: **X**

Items that may be reclassified subsequently to profit or loss:

Cash flow hedges	X
Exchange differences on translating foreign operations	X
Income tax relating to items that may be reclassified	(X)

Total – items that may be reclassified to profit or loss net of tax: **X**

Total – other comprehensive income net of tax for the year **(X)**

Total comprehensive income for the year **X**

Profit attributable to:

	$000
Owners of the parent	X
Non-controlling interest	X
	X

Total comprehensive income attributable to:

Owners of the parent	X
Non-controlling interest	X
	X

Other comprehensive income and related tax

IAS 1 requires an entity to disclose income tax relating to each component of OCI. This may be achieved by either

- disclosing each component of OCI net of any related tax effect, or

- disclosing other OCI before related tax effects with one amount shown for tax (as shown in the above examples).

The purpose of this is to provide users with tax information relating to these components, as they often have tax rates different from those applied to profit or loss.

Statement of changes in equity

The previous version of IAS 1 required items of income or expense not recognised in profit or loss, such as revaluation gains, to be presented in the statement of changes in equity together with owner changes in equity.

IAS 1 now requires all changes in equity arising from transactions with owners in their capacity as owners to be presented separately from non-owner changes in equity.

The statement of changes in equity presents changes to equity arising from transactions with owners in their capacity as owners, in particular:

• Issues of shares

• Dividends.

Total comprehensive income is shown in aggregate only for the purposes of reconciling opening to closing equity.

XYZ Group – Statement of changes in equity for the year ended 31 December 20X3

	Equity capt'l	Ret'd earng's	Transl'n of for'gn operations	Financial assets thru' OCI	Cash flow hdg's	Reval'n surplus	Total
	$000	$000	$000	$000	$000	$000	$000
Balance at 1 Jan 20X3	X	X	(X)	X	X	–	X
Changes in accounting policy	–	X	–	–	–	–	X
Restated balance	X	X	X	X	X	X	X
Changes in equity for 20X3							
Dividends	–	(X)	–	–	–	–	(X)
Issue of equity capital	X	–	–	–	–	–	X
Total comprehensive income for year	–	X	X	X	X	X	X
Transfer to retained earnings	–	X	–	–	–	(X)	–
Balance at 31 December 20X3	X	X	X	X	X	X	X

In addition to these six columns, there should be columns headed:

(a) Non-controlling interest

(b) Total equity

A comparative statement for the prior period must also be published.

Overall considerations

Overall considerations

(a) Going concern

Once management's assessment is that there are no material uncertainties as to the ability of an entity to continue for the foreseeable future, financial statements should be prepared on the assumption that the entity will in fact continue; i.e. prepared on a going concern basis.

(b) **Accruals basis of accounting**

The accruals basis of accounting means that transactions and events are recognised when they occur, not when cash is received or paid for them. IFRS in general, and IAS 1 in particular, approach things from a matching viewpoint.

(c) **Consistency of presentation**

The presentation and classification of items in the financial statements should be retained from one period to the next unless:

– it is clear that a change will result in a more appropriate presentation

– a change is required by a Standard (IAS or IFRS) or an Interpretation (SIC or IFRIC). The application of new or revised accounting treatments is a major reason for changing a current accounting treatment; this may require a prior period adjustment in accordance with IAS 8 to ensure that prior periods are fairly stated in accordance with the new accounting policy to provide consistency of presentation.

(d) **Materiality and aggregation**

An item is material if its omission or misstatement could influence the economic decisions of users taken on the basis of the financial statements. Financial statements should therefore show material items separately, but immaterial items may be aggregated with amounts of a similar nature.

(e) **Offsetting**

Assets and liabilities, and income and expenses, should not be offset except when required or permitted by a Standard or an Interpretation.

(f) **Comparative information**

Comparative information for the previous period should be disclosed, unless a Standard or an Interpretation permits or requires otherwise.

(g) **Compliance with IFRS**

An entity whose financial statements comply with IFRS should make an explicit and unreserved statement of such compliance in the notes.

Accounting policies

The accounting policies note should describe:

- the measurement basis (or bases) used in preparing the financial statements (e.g. historical cost, fair value, etc)
- each significant accounting policy.

Sources of uncertainty

An entity should disclose information about the key sources of estimation uncertainty that may cause a material adjustment to assets and liabilities within the next year, e.g. key assumptions about the future.

Reclassification adjustments

Reclassification adjustments are amounts reclassified to profit or loss in the current period that were recognised in other comprehensive income in the current or previous periods. This is sometimes referred to as 'recycling'.

IAS 1 requires that reclassification adjustments should be disclosed, either on the face of the statement of comprehensive income or in the notes.

This is necessary to inform users of amounts that are included as other comprehensive income in previous periods and in profit or loss in the current period, so that they can assess the effect of such reclassifications on profit or loss.

Dividends

Unlike the previous version of the standard, IAS 1 revised does not permit the disclosure of dividends recognised as distributions to equity holders on the face of the statement of profit or loss and other comprehensive income.

Instead, these must be disclosed in the statement of changes in equity or in the notes.

This requirement is in line with separate disclosure of owner and non-owner changes in equity discussed earlier.

KAPLAN PUBLISHING

Accounting policies (IAS 8)

Where a Standard or Interpretation exists in respect of a transaction, the accounting policy is determined by applying the Standard or Interpretation.

- Where there is no applicable standard or interpretation, management must use its judgement to develop and apply an accounting policy. The accounting policy selected must result in information that is relevant and reliable.

- Management should refer to the following:
    - first, Standards and Interpretations dealing with similar and related issues; then
    - the Framework.

- Provided they do not conflict with the sources above, management may also consider:
    - the most recent pronouncements of other standard-setting bodies that use a similar conceptual framework (e.g. the UK ASB and the US FASB)
    - other accounting literature and accepted industry practices.

- An entity must select and apply its accounting policies consistently for similar transactions.

Changes in accounting policies

An entity should only change its accounting policies if the change is required by a Standard or Interpretation; or it results in reliable and more relevant information.

- New accounting standards normally explain how to deal with any resulting changes in accounting policy (through transitional requirements).

- Otherwise, the new policy should be applied retrospectively. The entity adjusts the opening balance of each affected component of equity, and the comparative figures are presented as if the new policy had always been applied.

- Where a change is applied retrospectively, IAS 1 revised requires an entity to include in its financial statements a statement of financial position at the beginning of the earliest comparative period. In practice this will result in 3 statements of financial position
    - at the reporting date
    - at the start of the current reporting period
    - at the start of the previous reporting period

Changes in accounting estimates

Making estimates is an essential part of the preparation of financial statements. For example, preparers may have to estimate allowances for receivables, inventory obsolescence or the useful lives of non-current assets.

- A change in an accounting estimate is not a change in accounting policy.

- The effect of a change in an accounting estimate must be recognised prospectively, by including it in the statement of profit or loss and other comprehensive income for the current period and any future periods that are also affected.

Correction of prior period errors

Prior period errors are omissions from, and misstatements in, the entity's financial statements for one or more prior periods arising from a failure to use reliable information that was available when the financial statements were authorised for issue, and could reasonably be expected to have been taken into account.

- They include mistakes in applying accounting policies, oversights and the effects of fraud.

- Material prior period errors should be corrected retrospectively in the first set of financial statements authorised for issue after their discovery. Opening balances of equity, and the comparative figures, should be adjusted to correct the error.

- IAS 1 revised also requires that where a prior period error is corrected retrospectively, a statement of financial position is provided at the beginning of the earliest comparative period

2 Revenue recognition (IAS 18)

Revenue

Revenue is the gross inflow of economic benefits during the period arising from the ordinary activities of the entity (IAS 18 Revenue).

- Revenue results from the sale of goods, the rendering of services and from the receipt of interest, royalties and dividends.

- 'Revenue' presented in the statement of profit or loss and other comprehensive income should not include items such as proceeds from the sale of its non-current assets. Although IAS 18 does not specifically prohibit this, IAS 16 prohibits any gain on the disposal of property, plant and equipment from being classified as revenue. 'Ordinary activities' here means normal trading or operating activities.

- IAS 18 does not apply to rental and lease agreements (see IAS 17), associates (see IAS 28) or construction contracts (see IAS 11).

Measurement of revenue

Revenue should be measured at the fair value of the consideration received or receivable.

- For a cash sale, the revenue is the immediate proceeds of sale.

- For a credit sale, the revenue is the anticipated cash receivable.

- If the effect of the time value of money is material, the revenue should be discounted to present value.

- Revenue excludes sales taxes and similar items (these are not economic benefits for the reporting entity).

Further detail

Allowances for irrecoverable debts and returns are usually calculated and disclosed separately. Irrecoverable debts are charged as an expense, not as a reduction in revenue.

If the goods are sold on extended credit, then there may be two transactions: a sale and the provision of finance. The sale (and trade receivable) is then measured at the discounted present value of the future cash flows. Future cash receipts are split between the repayment of capital and interest income.

Revenue from the sale of goods

The following conditions must be satisfied before revenue from the sale of goods can be recognised:

- the seller transfers the significant risks and rewards of ownership to the buyer

- the seller does not retain management or control over the goods sold

- the amount of revenue can be measured reliably

- the transaction's economic benefits will probably flow to the seller
- the costs incurred or to be incurred can be measured reliably.

Revenue from services

Revenue from services is recognised according to the stage of completion. The following conditions must be met:

- the revenue can be measured reliably
- the transaction's economic benefits will probably flow to the provider
- the stage of completion at the reporting date can be measured reliably
- the costs incurred and the costs to complete can be measured reliably.

If these conditions are not met, then revenue should be restricted to any recoverable costs incurred.

Interest, royalties and dividends

Revenue from these sources should be recognised when the receipt is probable and the revenues are measurable. Revenue should be recognised as follows:

- interest is recognised on a time proportion basis, taking into account the effective yield on the asset
- royalties are accrued in accordance with the relevant contract
- dividends are recognised when the shareholder's right to receive payment is established.

Illustration 1 – Car dealer revenue recognition

A car dealer sells a car on credit terms. When should the revenue be recognised?

Solution

This transaction gives rise to two different types of revenue – the trading profit and the finance income from the sale on credit. If the credit agreement is such that the user of the car becomes the legal owner either immediately or at some time in the future, then the risks and rewards are transferred to the user and the trading profit can be regarded as earned when the credit agreement is signed. However the finance income must be spread over the time period of the credit agreement.

Problem areas

Area	Guidance
Long-term contractual performance	Recognise in accordance with the performance of contractual obligations.
Separation or linking of contractual arrangements (e.g. the sale of goods with a maintenance contract)	Where the two components operate independently of each other, then recognise as separate transactions. Otherwise recognise as a single transaction.
Bill and hold arrangements	Recognise revenue if the substance of the arrangement is that the goods represent an asset of the customer.
Sale with right of return	Exclude the sales value of estimated returns from revenue. Continue to monitor the accuracy of estimates with any changes reported within revenue.
Presentation of turnover as principal or agent	The issue is whether in a transaction on behalf of a third party a seller should record total turnover or merely the commission received from the third party (e.g. the on-line retailer of holidays through a website). The IAS states that the substance of the arrangement needs to be examined.

Specific situations

IAS 18 includes an Appendix which gives guidance on specific situations:

(a) **Bill and hold arrangements**

This is a contract for the supply of goods, where the buyer accepts title to the goods but does not take physical delivery of them until a later date. Provided the goods are available for delivery, the buyer gives explicit instructions to delay delivery and there are no alterations to the terms on which the seller normally trades with the buyer, revenue should recognise when the buyer accepts title.

(b) **Payments for goods in advance (e.g. deposits)**

Revenue should be recognised when delivery of the goods to the buyer takes place. Until then, any payments in advance should be treated as liabilities.

(c) Payments for goods by instalments

Revenue is recognised when the significant risks and rewards of ownership have been transferred, which is usually when delivery is made. If the effect of the time value of money is material, the sale price should be discounted to its present value.

(d) Sale or return

Sometimes goods are delivered to a customer but the customer can return them within a certain time period. Revenue is normally recognised when the goods are delivered.

Revenue should then be reduced by an estimate of the returns. In most cases, a seller can estimate returns from past experience. For example, a retailer would know on average what percentage of goods were returned after the year end and could adjust revenue by the amount of expected returns.

(e) Presentation of revenue as a principal or as agent

The principal supplies goods or services on its own account, whilst the agent receives a fee or commission for arranging provision of goods or services by the principal. The principal is exposed to the risks and rewards of the transaction and therefore records revenue as the gross amount receivable. The agent only records the commission receivable on the transaction as revenue. An example would be a cosmetics agent who earns commission on the number of cosmetics sold. The agent owns no inventory, so is not exposed to obsolescence and therefore could only record commission as its revenue. The cosmetics company is exposed to inventory obsolescence and selling price changes, so would record the gross amount of the sale as revenue.

(f) Separation and linking of contractual arrangements

Sometimes businesses provide a number of different goods or services to customers as a package. For example, a customer might purchase software together with regular upgrades for one year. The problem here is whether the sale is one transaction or two separate transactions.

A 'package' such as this can only be treated as more than one separate transaction if each product or service is capable of being sold independently and if a reliable fair value can be assigned to each separate component. Using the example above, if the support service is an optional extra and the software can be operated without it, the sale is two (or more) separate transactions. If the software cannot operate successfully without the upgrades, then the sale is one transaction and the amount of revenue recognised depends on the extent to which the seller has performed at the reporting date.

Disclosure requirements

An entity should disclose:

- It's accounting policies for revenue including the methods adopted to determine the stage of completion of service transactions

- the amount of each significant category of revenue recognised during the period

- the amount of revenue arising from exchanges of goods or services.

Aggressive earnings management

Since IAS 18 was originally issued, businesses and transactions have become much more complex. For example, computer companies frequently enter into barter transactions. Transactions may include options, for example, to buy shares or to return goods within a specified time.

Some entities have exploited the weaknesses in IAS 18 in order to artificially enhance revenue (a practice sometimes called **'aggressive earnings management'**). For example, some software companies recognise sales when orders are made, well before it is reasonably certain that cash will be received.

The main issue is one of timing. At what point in a transaction should an entity recognise revenue?

Three questions can be helpful in dealing with an unusual transaction or situation:

- When is the 'critical event'? This is the point at which most or all of the uncertainty surrounding a transaction is removed.

- Has the seller actually performed? Transactions that give rise to revenue are legally contractual arrangements, regardless of whether a formal contract exists. Revenue can only be recognised when an entity has performed its obligations under the contract. For example, an entity cannot recognise revenue at the time that it receives payment in advance.

- Has the transaction increased the entity's net assets/equity? For example, when an entity makes a sale, its assets increase, because it has receivables (access to future economic benefits in the form of cash). Therefore it recognises a gain. This is one of the main principles in the Framework.

Asset and liability model for revenue recognition

The revenue recognition requirements in IAS 18 focus on the occurrence of critical events rather than changes in assets and liabilities. Some believe that this approach leads to debits and credits that do not meet the definition of assets and liabilities being recognised in the statement of financial position.

The Board has developed two approaches to implement the asset and liability model:

- The fair value (measurement) model, in which performance obligations are initially measured at fair value

- The customer consideration model, in which performance obligations are initially measured by allocating the customer consideration amount.

It is likely that neither of these will be the final model and the final standard is expected to be drawn from both of them.

Contracts providing more than one good or service

A practical weakness of IAS 18 is that it gives insufficient guidance on contracts that provide more than one good or service to the customer. It is unclear when contracts should be divided into components and how much revenue should be attributed to each component. The IFRIC receives frequent requests for guidance on the application of IAS 18.

Test your understanding 1 – Revenue recognition

Explain how much revenue should be recognised in each of the following situations.

(a) **Tuition provider**

A company trades as a tuition provider and charges a price of $5,000 for a course of tuition together with material. Fees are non refundable. An invoice is raised at the commencement of the course. The course length is 20 classes which are held weekly. At the commencement of the course each customer is also issued with course material which can be separately purchased for $1,000. At the current year end the company has ten customers enrolled on the course, six of whom have fully paid and four of whom have been credit checked and agreed credit terms. At the reporting date these customers have only paid $2,000 each and the company has delivered 5 of the 20 classes.

(b) **Magazine publisher**

A company publishes a magazine and on 1 July, sold annual subscriptions totalling $200,000. The monies have been received and are non-refundable. The financial year-end of the company is 31 December.

(c) **Internet travel agent**

An internet travel agent receives $1,000 for arranging a hotel booking, and will pass on $900 in due course to the hotel.

(d) **Furniture retailer**

A furniture retailer offers two-year 0% finance on furniture offered for sale at $10,000.

Required:

Calculate the revenue that can be recognised in the current year for each of the situations outlined above.

Discontinued operations (IFRS 5)

Definition

A discontinued operation is a component of an entity that either has been disposed of, or is classified as held for sale, and:

- represents a separate major line of business or geographical area of operations
- is part of a single co-ordinated plan to dispose of a separate major line of business or geographical area of operations
- is a subsidiary acquired exclusively with a view to resale.

A component of an entity may be a business, geographical, or reportable segment, a cash-generating unit, or a subsidiary.

If the component/operation has not already been sold, then it will only be a discontinued operation if it is held for sale.

An operation is **held for sale** if its carrying amount will not be recovered principally by continuing use. To be classified as held for sale (and therefore to be a discontinued operation) at the reporting date, it must meet the following criteria.

- The operation is available for immediate sale in its present condition.
- The sale is highly probable and is expected to be completed within one year.
- Management is committed to the sale.
- The operation is being actively marketed.
- The operation is being offered for sale at a reasonable price in relation to its current fair value.
- It is unlikely that the plan will change or be withdrawn.

KAPLAN PUBLISHING

Presentation

Presentation

Users of the financial statements are more interested in future profits than past profits. They are able to make a better assessment of future profits if they are informed about operations that have been discontinued during the period.

IFRS 5 requires information about discontinued operations to be presented in the financial statements.

- **On the face of the statement of profit or loss and other comprehensive income** a single amount comprising:
    - the total of the post-tax profit or loss of discontinued operations
    - the post-tax gain or loss on the measurement to fair value less costs to sell or on the disposal of the discontinued operation.

- **Either on the face of or in the notes to the statement of profit or loss and other comprehensive income** an analysis of the single amount described above into:
    - the revenue, expenses and pre-tax profit or loss of discontinued operations
    - the related tax expense
    - the gain or loss recognised on the measurement to fair value less costs to sell or on the disposal of the discontinued operation
    - the related tax expense.

- **Either on the face of or in the notes to the statement of cash flows** the net cash flows attributable to the operating, investing and financing activities of discontinued operations.

- If a decision to sell an operation is taken after the year-end but before the accounts are approved, this is treated as a non-adjusting event after the reporting date and disclosed in the notes. The operation does **not** qualify as a discontinued operation at the reporting date and separate presentation is not appropriate.

- In the comparative figures the operations are also shown as discontinued (even though they were not classified as such at the end of the previous year).

Example presentation

Statement of profit or loss (showing discontinued operations as a single amount, with analysis in the notes)

	20X2	20X1
	$m	$m
Revenue	100	90
Operating expenses	(60)	(65)
Operating profit	40	25
Interest expense	(20)	(10)
Profit before tax	20	15
Income tax expense	(6)	(7)
Profit from continuing operations	14	8
Discontinued operations		
Loss from discontinued operations*	(25)	(1)
Profit/(loss) for the year	(11)	7

The entity did not recognise any components of other comprehensive income in the periods presented.

* The analysis of this loss would be given in a note to the accounts.

Discontinued operations illustration

During the year ended 30 June 20X5, Glendale, a company with a number of subsidiary companies, sold a subsidiary, Janus for $4.6 million.

The net assets of Janus totalled $5 million at the date of sale. During the year ended 30 June 20X5, Janus had sales revenue of $940,000, operating expenses of $580,000 and an expected tax charge of $100,000.

KAPLAN PUBLISHING

The draft consolidated statement of profit or loss for the remainder of the Glendale group is as follows:

	$000
Revenue	3,240
Operating expenses	(2,057)
Profit from operations	1,183
Finance cost	(58)
Profit before tax	1,125
Income tax expense	(293)
Profit for the year	832

There were no items of other comprehensive income in the year.

Required:

Show how the consolidated statement of profit or loss would appear based upon the requirements of IFRS 5.

Solution

Consolidated statement of profit or loss for the year ended 30 June 20X5

Continuing operations	$000
Revenue	3,240
Operating expenses	(2,057)
Operating profit	1,183
Interest expense	(58)
Profit before tax	1,125
Income tax expense	(293)
Profit for the year from continuing operations	832
Loss from discontinued operation (working)	(140)
Profit for the year	692

Working

	$000
Revenue	940
Operating expenses	(580)
Loss on disposal (4,600 – 5,000)	(400)
Income tax expense	(100)
Loss for the year	(140)

Example presentation 2

ABC Group – Statement of comprehensive income for the year ended 31 December 20X7

	20X7	20X6
	$000	$000
Revenue	1,000,000	800,000
Cost of sales	(600,000)	(500,000)
Gross profit	400,000	300,000
Other income	10,000	10,000
Distribution costs	(100,000)	(80,000)
Administrative expenses	(200,000)	(160,000)
	110,000	70,000
Finance costs	(30,000)	(20,000)
Share of profits of associates	20,000	15,000
Share of profits of joint venture entities	10,000	8,000
Profit before tax	110,000	73,000
Income tax expense	(35,000)	(25,000)
Profit for the year from continuing operations	75,000	48,000
Loss for the year from discontinued operations	(15,000)	(10,000)
PROFIT FOR THE YEAR	60,000	38,000

Other comprehensive income:

Items that will not be reclassified to profit or loss in future periods:

Gains on property revaluation	40,000	10,000
Share of other comprehensive income of associates	4,000	–
Actuarial gains / (losses) on defined benefit pension plans	(30,000)	(15,000)
Financial assets at fair value through OCI	(1,000)	2,000
Income tax relating to the above items of other comprehensive income	(4,500)	(500)

Items that may be reclassified to profit or loss in future periods:

Cash flow hedges	(4,000)	5,000
Exchange differences on translating foreign operations	5,000	4,000
Income tax relating to the above items of other comprehensive income	(500)	(1,500)
	———	———
Other comprehensive income for the year, net of tax	9,000	4,000
	———	———
TOTAL COMPREHENSIVE INCOME FOR THE YEAR	69,000	42,000
	———	———

Profit for the period attributable to:

Owners of the parent

From continuing operations	57,000	40,000
From discontinued operations	(12,000)	(8,000)
	———	———
	45,000	32,000

Non-controlling interest

From continuing operations	18,000	8,000
From discontinued operations	(3,000)	(2,000)
	———	———
	15,000	6,000
	———	———
	60,000	38,000
	———	———

Total comprehensive income attributable to:

Owners of the parent		
From continuing operations	62,000	43,000
From discontinued operations	(12,000)	(8,000)
	50,000	35,000
Non-controlling interest		
From continuing operations	22,000	9,000
From discontinued operations	(3,000)	(2,000)
	19,000	7,000
	69,000	42,000

Portugal group re IFRS 5

The Portugal group of companies has a financial year-end of 30 June 20X4. The financial statements are signed off three months later. The group is disposing of many of its subsidiaries, each of which is a separate major line of business or geographical area.

- Subsidiary England was sold on 1 January 20X4.

- On 1 January 20X4, an announcement was made that there were advanced negotiations to sell subsidiary Switzerland, and subject to regulatory approval, this is expected to be completed by 31 October 20X4.

- The board has also decided to divest the independent cash-generating unit known as France. Agents have been appointed to find a suitable buyer but so far none has yet emerged. The agent's advice is that potential buyers are deterred by unquantified potential environmental damages and the expected price that Portugal hopes to achieve.

- On 10 July 20X4, an announcement was made that geographical segment Croatia was for sale and indeed it was sold by 10 September 20X4.

Explain whether these are discontinued operations as defined by IFRS 5.

Portugal group re IFRS 5 answer

The issue is whether or not these qualify as discontinued operations.

England has been sold during the year. It is a discontinued operation per IFRS 5. The results will be consolidated up to the date of disposal.

Switzerland is a discontinued operation per IFRS 5. There is clear intention to sell, and completion will occur within 12 months.

France is not a discontinued operation per IFRS 5. There are problems with the condition of the asset, the price being asked and there is no indication that it will be completed within 12 months.

Croatia is not a discontinued operation per IFRS 5 because it was after the year-end that it met the conditions for classification as held for sale.

3 Earnings per share (IAS 33)

Earnings per share (IAS 33)

Scope and definitions

IAS 33 applies to entities whose equity shares are publicly traded. Private entities must also follow IAS 33, if they disclose an earnings per share figure.

An **equity share** is an equity instrument that is subordinate to all other classes of equity instruments.

A potential equity share is a financial instrument or other contract that may entitle its holder to equity shares.

The basic calculation

The actual earnings per share (EPS) for the period is called the **basic EPS** and is calculated as:

$$\frac{\text{Profit or loss for the period attributable to equity shareholders}}{\text{Weighted average number of equity shares outstanding in the period}}$$

Basic earnings is profit after tax less NCI and preference dividends (if any). If an entity prepares consolidated financial statements, then EPS will be based on the consolidated results.

The weighted average number of shares takes into account when shares were issued during the year.

Basic illustration

An entity issued 200,000 shares at full market price ($3.00) on 1 July 20X8.

Relevant information

	20X8	20X7
Profit attributable to the ordinary shareholders for the year ending 31 Dec	$550,000	$460,000
Number of ordinary shares in issue at 31 Dec	1,000,000	800,000

Calculation of earnings per share

20X7 = $460,000 / 800,000 = 57.50c

20X8 = $550,000 / 800,000 + (½ × 200,000) = 61.11c

Since the additional 200,000 shares were issued at full market price but have only contributed finance for half a year, then only half their number is used. The earnings figure is not adjusted.

Bonus issues

Bonus issues

If an entity makes a bonus issue, share capital increases, but no cash is received and there is no affect on earnings. Therefore, a bonus issue reduces EPS.

The new shares are treated as if they have always been in issue. Comparative EPS is also adjusted

Bonus issue illustration

An entity made a bonus issue of one new share for every five existing shares held on 1 July 20X8.

Relevant information

	20X8	20X7
Profit attributable to the ordinary shareholders for the year ending 31 Dec	$550,000	$460,000
Number of ordinary shares in issue at 31 Dec	1,200,000	1,000,000

Calculation of earnings per share in 20X8 accounts

20X7 = $460,000 / 1,200,000 = 38.33c
(the comparative figure presented in the 20X8 accounts)

20X8 = $550,000 / 1,200,000 = 45.83c

In the 20X7 accounts, the EPS for the year would have appeared as 46c ($460,000 ÷ 1,000,000).

In 20X8, the EPS for 20X7 can be recalculated (as above), or the original EPS of 46c can be adjusted for the bonus issue as follows:

Original EPS of 46c × 1,000,000 / 1,200,000 = 38.33c

Rights issues

Rights issues

Because rights issues are normally made at less than the full market price, a rights issue combines the characteristics of an issue at full market price with those of a bonus issue.

The weighted average includes the bonus element for the full year plus the full price element on a time-apportioned basis.

Rights issue illustration

An entity issued one new share for every two existing shares held by way of rights at $1.50 per share on 1 July 20X8. The pre-issue market price was $3.00 per share.

Relevant information

	20X8	20X7
Profit attributable to the ordinary shareholders for the year ending 31 Dec	$550,000	$460,000
Number of ordinary shares in issue at 31 Dec	1,200,000	800,000

Solution

Step 1: Calculate the bonus element

This is done by multiplying the original number of shares by the following:

Actual cum rights price / Theoretical ex rights price

The actual cum rights price is the market value before the rights issue. The theoretical ex rights price is what each share should be worth immediately after the rights issue. It can be calculated as follows:

	Shares in issue	Price per Share	Market capitalisation $
Before the rights issue	800,000	300c	2,400,000
Rights issue	400,000	150c	600,000
After the rights issue	1,200,000	**250c**	3,000,000

The bonus adjustment can now be calculated:

800,000 shares × 300/250 = 960,000 shares

Step 2: Calculate the full-price element

The total number of shares after the rights issue is 1,200,000. We have just calculated that there were 960,000 shares after the bonus element adjustment. Therefore, there must have been 240,000 shares issued at full price (1,200,000 – 960,000).

Step 3: Calculate the weighted average number of shares

	Shares	Time	Average
Original shares	800,000	12/12	800,000
Bonus element of the rights issue	160,000	12/12	160,000
Full market price element of the rights issue	240,000	6/12	120,000
	1,200,000		1,080,000

Step 4: Calculate the earnings per share for the current year

$$\frac{\text{Earnings}}{\text{Equity shares in issue}} = \frac{\$550,000}{1,080,000 \text{ shares}} = \textbf{50.93 cents}$$

Step 5: Re-calculate or restate the EPS for the prior year.

Last year's earnings of $460,000 is divided by the number of shares in issue after the bonus element of this year's issue.

Earnings / Equity shares in issue = $460,000 / 960,000 shares = **47.92 cents**

or

$460,000 / 800,000 =

57.5 cents × Theoretical ex rights price/Actual cum rights price = 250c/300c = **47.92 cents**

Diluted earnings per share

Diluted earnings per share

Many companies issue convertible instruments, options and warrants that entitle their holders to purchase shares in the future at below the market price. When these shares are eventually issued, the interests of the original shareholders will be diluted. The dilution occurs because these shares will have been issued at below market price.

The Examiner has indicated that diluted earnings per share will not be examined in detail; however, students should have awareness of the topic as summarised below:

- Shares and other instruments that may dilute the interests of the existing shareholders are called potential ordinary shares.

- Examples of potential ordinary shares include:
  - debt and other instruments, including preference shares, that are convertible into ordinary shares. This includes partly-paid shares

  - share warrants and options (instruments that give the holder the right to purchase ordinary shares)

  - employee plans that allow employees to receive ordinary shares as part of their remuneration and other share purchase plans

  - contingently issuable shares (i.e. shares issuable if certain conditions are met).

- Where there are dilutive potential ordinary shares in issue, the diluted EPS must be disclosed as well as the basic EPS. This provides relevant information to current and potential investors.

- Diluted EPS is calculated using current earnings but assuming that the worst possible dilution has already happened.

- The profit used in the basic EPS calculation is adjusted for any expenses that would no longer be paid if the convertible instrument were converted into shares, e.g. preference dividends, loan interest.

- The weighted average number of shares used in the basic EPS calculation is adjusted for the conversion of the potential ordinary shares. This is deemed to occur at the beginning of the period or the date of issue, if they were not in existence at the beginning of the period.

Presentation

An entity should present basic and diluted earnings per share on the face of the statement of profit or loss and other comprehensive income for each class of ordinary shares that has a different right to share in the net profit for the period.

- An entity should present basic and diluted earnings per share with equal prominence for all periods presented.
- If an entity has discontinued operations, it should also present basic and diluted EPS from continuing operations.
- An entity that reports a discontinued operation must disclose the basic and diluted EPS for the operation, either on the face of the statement of profit or loss or in the notes.
- IAS 33 also requires basic and diluted losses per share to be disclosed.
- In most cases, if basic EPS is a loss, then the diluted EPS will be the same as the basic EPS. This is because the loss per share will be diluted, and therefore reduced. Diluted EPS only relates to factors that decrease a profit or increase a loss.

Disclosure

An entity should disclose the following.

- The earnings used for basic and diluted EPS. These earnings should be reconciled to the net profit or loss for the period.
- The weighted average number of ordinary shares used for basic and diluted EPS. The two averages should be reconciled to each other.
- An entity may disclose an alternative EPS in addition to the IAS 33 requirements provided that:
  - the earnings figure is reconciled back to the statement of profit or loss and other comprehensive income
  - the same weighted average number of shares is used as for the IAS 33 calculations
  - basic and diluted EPS is disclosed
  - the alternative figure is shown in the notes, not on the face of the statement of profit or loss and other comprehensive income.

EPS as a performance measure

The EPS figure is used to compute the major stock market indicator of performance, the Price/Earnings ratio (P/E ratio). Rightly or wrongly, the stock market places great emphasis on the earnings per share figure and the P/E ratio. IAS 33 sets out a standard method of calculating EPS, which enhances the comparability of the figure.

However, EPS has limited usefulness as a performance measure.

*   An entity's earnings are affected by its choice of accounting policies. Therefore, it may not always be appropriate to compare the EPS of different companies.

*   EPS does not take account of inflation. Apparent growth in earnings may not be true growth.

*   EPS does not provide predictive value. High earnings and growth in earnings may be achieved at the expense of investment, which would have generated increased earnings in the future.

*   In theory, diluted EPS serves as a warning to equity shareholders that the return on their investment may fall in future periods. However, diluted EPS as currently required by IAS 33 is not intended to be forward-looking but is an additional past performance measure. Diluted EPS is based on current earnings, not forecast earnings. Therefore, diluted EPS is only of limited use as a prediction of future EPS.

*   EPS is a measure of profitability. Profitability is only one aspect of performance. Concentration on earnings per share and 'the bottom line' arguably detracts from other important aspects of an entity's affairs, for example, cash flow and stewardship of assets.

Interim reporting (IAS 34)

*   Condensed financial statements should include all of the headings and sub-totals used in the most recent annual financial statements.

*   If an entity publishes a complete set of financial statements in its interim report, then they should comply with IAS 1 in full.

*   Basic and diluted EPS should be presented on the face of interim statements of comprehensive income for those entities within the scope of IAS 33.

Interim financial reports are prepared for a period shorter than a full financial year. Entities may be required to prepare interim financial reports under local law or listing regulations.

- IAS 34 does not require the preparation of interim reports, but sets out the principles that should be followed if they are prepared and specifies their minimum content.

- An interim financial report should include, as a minimum, the following components:
  - condensed statement of financial position as at the end of the current interim period, with a comparative statement of financial position as at the end of the previous financial year

  - condensed statement of comprehensive income for the current interim period and cumulatively for the current financial year to date (if, for example the entity reports quarterly), with comparatives for the interim periods (current and year to date) of the preceding financial year

  - condensed statement showing changes in equity. This statement should show changes in equity cumulatively for the current year with comparatives for the corresponding period of the preceding financial year

  - condensed statement of cash flows cumulatively for the year to date, with a comparative statement to the same date in the previous year

  - selected explanatory notes

  - Improvements to IFRS issued May 2010 emphasises that there should be appropriate disclosures and reconciliation of events and transactions in interim statements with the most recent annual report. This could even be the first set of IFRS annual financial statements following adoption of IFRS for the first time. This requirement is effective for accounting periods commencing on or after 1 January 2011, with earlier application permitted.

- Improvements to IFRS 2009-11 published in May 2012 specifies that total assets and liabilities for a reportable segment should only be separately disclosed in the interim statements if those amounts are regularly provided to the chief operating decision maker and there has been a material change from the amounts disclosed in the last annual financial statements for that reportable segment.

- Condensed financial statements should include all of the headings and sub-totals used in the most recent annual financial statements.

- If an entity publishes a complete set of financial statements in its interim report, then they should comply with IAS 1 in full.

- Basic and diluted EPS should be presented on the face of interim statements of comprehensive income for those entities within the scope of IAS 33.

Current issues in performance reporting

Revenue from contracts with customers

Introduction:

As part of a joint project between the IASB and US FAS, a revised ED dealing with revenue from contracts with customers was published in November 2011 (original ED published June 2010) with the objective to create a common revenue recognition standard for IFRS and US GAAP.

The reasons for developing a new reporting standard are as follows:

(a) to increase the extent of convergence between IFRS and US GAAP,

(b) to improve comparability of revenue recognition practices between entities, across industries and capital markets,

(c) to reduce complexity of revenue recognition principles and therefore simpler to prepare financial statements, and

(d) to enhance user benefits by improved disclosure requirements.

The current reporting standards dealing with revenue recognition (IAS 11 and IAS 18) are regarded as deficient as they do not provide a comprehensive framework for revenue recognition. Equally, simply amending either or both of these reporting standards will not achieve convergence between IFRS and US GAAP.

Revenue recognition proposals:

The ED proposes a five-step approach to revenue recognition as follows:

(1) Identify the contract(s) with the customer. This would enable identification of enforceable rights and obligations within a contract. It may be possible to combine contracts and account for them as one set of enforceable rights and obligations.

(2) Identify the separate enforceable obligations in a contract. The various promises within a contract to transfer goods or services are referred to as performance obligations; where they are distinct, they should be accounted for separately. This will be the case if the goods or services are regularly sold separately. If a good or service is not sold separately, or is a part of in interrelated bundle, it is not regarded as distinct.

(3) Determine the transaction price. This is defined as the amount to which an entity expects to be entitled in exchange for transferring promised goods or services to a customer. The time value of money need not be taken into account if, at inception of the contract, the period between transfer of the promised goods or services and payment is expected to be within one year. Additionally, the transaction price will not include any allowance for risk of non-collection of the amount due.

(4) Allocate the transaction price. It is expected that revenue would be allocated to each separate performance obligation, based upon the relative selling prices of each distinct good or service. If there are no observable selling prices available, it would need to be estimated.

(5) Recognise revenue when a performance obligation is satisfied. Revenue should be recognised only when a performance obligation has been satisfied, with the amount required to satisfy the performance condition being the revenue recognised.
Where performance conditions are satisfied over time, as with the provision of services, there needs to be an appropriate measure of progress or provision to determine the extent to which a performance obligation has been satisfied and revenue recognised accordingly.

There would also be a limit on the cumulative amount of revenue that could be recognised to date to the amount to which an entity is reasonably assured it is entitled.

Other proposals:

(1) Where performance obligations are to be satisfied over a period of time, and that time period exceeds one year, then any performance obligations regarded as onerous should result in recognition of a liability. In this context, onerous is defined as the lowest cost of settling a performance obligation exceeds the transaction price for that obligation.

(2) Where goods are transferred to a customer at a loss, this is an indication of impairment, and an impairment review should be performed. Where contracts are regarded as onerous, IAS 37 would continue to apply and provision for losses should be made.

(3) An asset may be recognised where costs have been incurred to obtain or fulfil a contract; such costs must:

　(a) relate to a specific contract,

　(b) generate or enhance resources that would be used in satisfying performance obligations relating to that contract, and

　(c) the costs are expected to be recovered.

(4) Enhanced qualitative and quantitative disclosures, particularly regarding significant judgements in applying the requirements of the standard, together with disclosures relating to recognition of assets

Conclusion:

The revised ED provides the basis for a framework for revenue recognition that overcomes the current weaknesses of IAS 11 and IAS 18. This should result in similar transactions being accounted for on a consistent basis, irrespective of the entity applying the standard, the nature of the industry it operates in and whether IFRS or US GAAP is applied. It is expected that a new reporting standard will be issued during the latter part of 2013.

Earnings per share

The amendments to IAS 33 expected as a result of this project will change the existing treasury stock method of calculating the effects of dilutive options and warrants on EPS. The proposed amendments to IAS 33 are in line with those proposed to the equivalent US standard. The proposal would:

- Amend the treasury stock method to include as assumed proceeds the end-of-period carrying value of a liability that is assumed to be settled in shares and use the end-of-period market price in the computation of incremental shares.

- Adopt a new 'fair value method' for all instruments that can be settled in cash or shares, are classified as liabilities and are measured at fair value (with changes to this shown in profit or loss.

- Include options and warrants with a nominal exercise price in the computation of basic EPS if
  - The instruments are currently exercisable or convertible into ordinary shares for little or no cost to the holder, or
  - The option or warrant currently participates in earnings with ordinary shareholders.

Current status of the project

This project was deferred in April 2009 and is now paused. Any further decisions regarding progress of this project will be confirmed at a later date.

Financial statements presentation project

In April 2004, the IASB and the FASB decided to combine their projects on the reporting and classification of revenue, expenses, gains and losses. The joint project was undertaken to establish a common, high quality standard for presentation of information in the financial statements.

The objective of the project is to present information in the financial statements that improves the ability of the users of the financial statement to understand the financial position, change in position and cash flows of an entity. Specifically, this means users will be able to:

* understand the entity's present and past financial position

* understand the past operating, financing and other activities that caused the financial position to change and

* use the financial statement information amongst other sources of information to assess an entity's future cash flows.

The standard that is developed from this project will initially only apply to business entities and not to not-for-profit entities.

Phases of the project

* Phase A deals with the question of what constitutes a complete set of financial statements and the requirement to present comparative information. This was completed with the issue of IAS 1 revised in September 2007.

* Phase B addresses the more fundamental issue of the presentation of information on the face of the financial statements which will lead to replacement of IAS 1 and IAS 7.

* Phase C will address the reporting of interim financial information in US GAAP. This may lead to the IASB reviewing the content of IAS 34 Interim financial reporting.

The current status of the project can be considered by reviewing each of the separate components.

Replacement of IAS 1 and IAS 7 (phase B)

The IASB and the US FASB are undertaking a project to develop a joint standard for financial statement presentation.
In IFRSs, the new proposals will replace the existing standards on financial statement presentation, IAS 1 Presentation of Financial Statements and IAS 7 Statement of Cash Flows.

The objective of the financial statement presentation project is to establish a global standard that will guide the organisation and presentation of information in the financial statements. The standard would directly affect how the management of an entity communicates financial statement information to the users of its financial statements, such as existing and potential equity investors, lenders and other creditors. The boards' goal is to improve the usefulness of the information provided in an entity's financial statements to help those users in their decision-making.

The IASB and the US FASB initiated the joint project on financial statement presentation to address users' concerns that existing requirements permit too many alternative types of presentation, and that information in financial statements is highly aggregated and inconsistently presented, making it difficult to understand fully the relationship between an entity's financial statements and its financial results.

The project's main proposals are:

- cohesive financial statements that share a common structure, separately presenting operating, investing and financing activities as well as income tax and discontinued operations;

- disaggregation in each financial statement, considering its function, nature and measurement basis, with some disaggregation included in the notes

- more disaggregation of operating cash receipts and payments, and reconciliation of profit or loss from operating activities to cash flows from operating activities;

- analyses of changes in asset and liability line items (including net debt – IASB only);

- and disclosure of remeasurement information.

The proposals would improve the comparability and understandability of information presented in financial statements, by imposing some degree of standardisation in the way that information is presented in the financial statements, particularly regarding how information is classified, and the degree to which it is disaggregated.

Whilst there have been amendments to IAS 1 in respect of how other comprehensive income is presented, the project is now paused with no indication that this situation will change in the forseeable future.

Discontinued operations

There is a joint project between IASB and FASB develop a common definition of discontinued operations and require common disclosures related to disposals of components of an entity. The project commenced in 2008, with an ED issued in September of that year. There was no change to the definition and measurement of non-current assets held for sale.

The objective of this project is to develop, jointly with the FASB, a common definition of discontinued operations, and to require common disclosures related to disposals of components of an entity. As a result of this joint project, the IASB expects to amend IFRS 5 Non-current Assets Held for Sale and Discontinued Operations, and the FASB expects to amend its equivalent reporting requirements.

In their joint project on financial statement presentation, the IASB and the US FASB decided to develop a common definition of a discontinued operation, and to require common disclosures about components of an entity that have been (or will be) disposed of. The boards decided to address these issues separately from the main financial statement presentation project (the replacement of IAS 1 and IAS 7).

Whilst there have been amendments to IAS 1 in respect of how other comprehensive income is presented, the project is now paused with no indication that this situation will change in the forseeable future.

UK syllabus focus

The ACCA UK syllabus contains a requirement that candidates should be able to discuss and apply the key differences between UK GAAP and IFRS GAAP. The accounting requirements of UK GAAP and IFRS GAAP are similar in this area, but there are some differences including the following:

UK FRS 3 – discontinued activities: there is a more restrictive definition of what constitutes a discontinued activity in comparison with the requirements of IFRS 5. Consequently, it is likely to disclose the discontinuance later than under IFRS GAAP. Per UK FRS 3 the definition of discontinued activities comprises those operations of the reporting entity that are sold or terminated and that satisfy all of the following conditions:

- The sale or termination is completed either in the period or before the earlier of three months after the commencement of the subsequent period and the date on which the financial statements are approved.

- If a termination, the former activities have ceased permanently.

- The sale or termination has a material effect on the nature and focus of the reporting entity's operations and represents a material reduction in its operating facilities resulting either from its withdrawal from a particular market (whether class of business or geographical) or from a material reduction in turnover in the reporting entity's continuing markets.

- The assets, liabilities, results of operations and activities are clearly distinguishable, physically, operationally and for financial reporting purposes.

Operations not satisfying all these conditions are classified as continuing.

As well as **disclosing** turnover, cost of sales and operating expenses of both continuing and discontinued operations **on the face of the profit and loss account**, an entity discloses profits or losses on the sale or termination of an operation on the face of the profit and loss account.

UK FRS 3 – exceptional items: Exceptional items are material items arising from an entity's ordinary activities. Because of their size or unusual nature they need to be disclosed if the financial statements are to give a true and fair view. Three types of item are shown separately on the face of the profit and loss account after operating profit and before interest:

- profits or losses on the sale or termination of an operation

- costs of a fundamental reorganisation or restructuring

- profits or losses on the disposal of fixed assets.

All other exceptional items should normally be included under the statutory format headings to which they relate and disclosed in the notes to the financial statements. They may be disclosed separately on the face of the profit and loss account if this is necessary to give a true and fair view.

4 Chapter summary

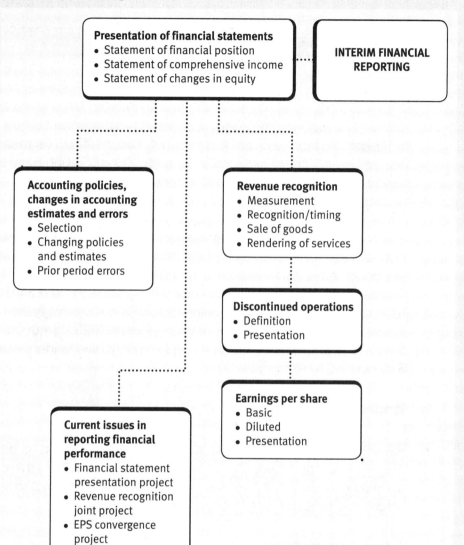

Presentation of financial statements
- Statement of financial position
- Statement of comprehensive income
- Statement of changes in equity

INTERIM FINANCIAL REPORTING

Accounting policies, changes in accounting estimates and errors
- Selection
- Changing policies and estimates
- Prior period errors

Revenue recognition
- Measurement
- Recognition/timing
- Sale of goods
- Rendering of services

Discontinued operations
- Definition
- Presentation

Current issues in reporting financial performance
- Financial statement presentation project
- Revenue recognition joint project
- EPS convergence project

Earnings per share
- Basic
- Diluted
- Presentation

Test your understanding answers

Test your understanding 1 – Revenue recognition

(a) Tuition provider

It is not relevant that the some customers have paid and others not in determining the revenue to be recognised, as it can be measured with reliability. Whilst invoices of 10 x $5,000 = $50,000 have been raised this is not the trigger for the recognition of revenue in the financial statements.

The company is selling both goods and services. All of the revenue from the sale of the goods (course materials) can be recognised as the goods have been delivered 10 x $1,000 = $10,000.
The services for tuition have a value of $4,000 ($5,000 – $1,000) and have only been partially delivered (5/20). Accordingly the revenue from tuition that can be recognised is 5/20 x $4,000 x 10 = $10,000. The total revenue that can be recognised is therefore $10,000 + $10,000 = $20,000.

(b) Magazine publisher

Revenue earned is only $100,000, as this is recognised as each magazine is published. The balance is deferred income; there is an obligation to publish the remaining magazines, even if not to actually refund the subscriptions in advance.

(c) Internet travel agent

The travel agent is an agent, so it only recognises commission received for arranging the transaction on behalf of the hotel. Revenue is $100. The $900 would be recognised as a liability until such time as it is paid over to the hotel.

(d) Furniture retailer

The furniture dealer has sold furniture on credit to the customer. The total of $10,000 should be divided into two elements comprising the sale of furniture and also the present value of the receipt of interest at an appropriate rate of return over two years. The revenue on the sale of furniture can be recognised immediately, presumably on sale or delivery as the risks and rewards have been transferred to the customer at that point. The interest receivable for two years should be recognised at a constant rate over the two-year period.

Employee benefits

Chapter learning objectives

Upon completion of this chapter you will be able to:

- apply and discuss the accounting treatment of defined contribution plans
- apply and discuss the accounting treatment of defined benefit plans
- account for gains and losses on settlements and curtailments
- apply and discuss the reporting of remeasurement gains and losses and the 'Asset Ceiling' test
- apply and discuss the accounting for short-term employee benefits
- apply and discuss the accounting for termination benefits
- apply and discuss the accounting for long-term employee benefits.

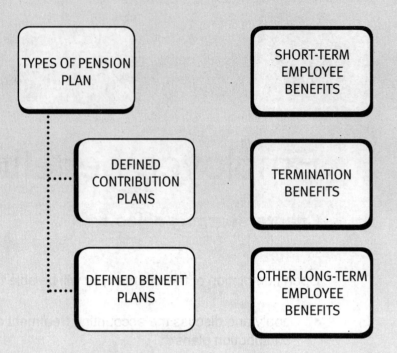

1 Introduction

IAS 19 Employee Benefits was issued in 1983 with the objective of specifying the accounting treatment and associated disclosure requirements when accounting for employee benefits. The original standard permitted a degree of choice when accounting for employee benefits, which consequently resulted in a lack of comparability between the financial statements of different entities.

IAS 19 has been subject to periodic amendment, with the most recent significant amendments dated June 2011. The objectives of these amendments are to improve users' understanding of how defined benefit obligations and assets are reported, together with improving comparability of reported information by eliminating some accounting treatment choices and standardising supporting disclosures. The revised version of IAS 19 is effective for accounting periods commencing on or after 1 January 2013, and is to be applied retrospectively in accordance with IAS 8 (i.e. account for a prior period adjustment as required if this results in a change of accounting policy), with early adoption permitted.

Types of employee benefit

IAS 19 identifies four types of employee benefit as follows:

*   **Post-employment benefits**. This normally relates to retirement benefits, which will typically take the form of either a defined contribution plan or a defined benefit plan (sometimes referred to as a defined benefit scheme).

- **Short-term employee benefits**. This includes wages and salaries, bonuses and other benefits.

- **Termination benefits**. Termination benefits arise when benefits become payable upon employment being terminated, either by the employer or by the employee accepting terms to have employment terminated.

- **Other long-term employee benefits**. This comprises other items not within the above classifications and will include long-service leave or awards, long-term disability benefits and other long-service benefits.

Each will be considered within this chapter, with particular emphasis upon post-employment defined benefit schemes.

2 Post-employment benefit plans

Introduction

A pension plan (sometimes called a post-employment benefit plan or scheme) consists of a pool of assets, together with a liability for pensions owed to employees. Pension plan assets normally consist of investments, cash and (sometimes) properties. The return earned on the assets is used to pay pensions.

There are two main types of pension plan:

- defined contribution plans
- defined benefit plans.

Defined contribution plans

The pension payable on retirement depends on the contributions paid into the plan by the employee and the employer:

- The employer's contribution is usually a fixed percentage of the employee's salary. The employer has no further obligation after this amount is paid.

- Therefore, the annual cost to the employer is reasonably predictable.

- Defined contribution plans present few accounting problems, other than ensuring that an accrual is made, where required, for contributions due, but not yet paid, at the reporting date.

In this situation, the employee bears the uncertainty regarding the value of the pension that will be paid upon retirement.

Defined benefit plans

The pension payable on retirement normally depends on either the final salary or the average salary of the employee during their career.

- The employer undertakes to finance a pension income of a certain amount,
    - e.g. 2/3 × final salary × (years of service / 40 years)

- The employer has an ongoing obligation to make sufficient contributions to the plan to fund the pensions.

- An actuary calculates the amount that must be paid into the plan each year in order to provide the promised pension. The calculation is based on various estimates and assumptions including:
    - life expectancy
    - investment returns
    - wage inflation.

- Therefore, the cost of providing defined benefit pensions will vary year-by-year over the working life of employees due to changes in circumstances, estimates and assumptions.

The actual contribution paid by the employer into a plan during an accounting period does not usually represent the true cost to the employer of providing pensions in that period. The financial statements must reflect the true cost of providing pensions, rather than accounting only for the cash contributions made into the pension plan.

Multi-employer plans

Often a small entity does not have the resources to run a pension plan in-house, so it pays pension contributions over to an insurance company which runs a multi-employer plan. Such a plan can be either of a defined contribution nature or a defined benefit nature. Alternatively, a group may operate a plan for the employees of all subsidiaries within the group.

KAPLAN PUBLISHING

3 Accounting for post-employment benefit plans

Defined contribution plans

The expense of providing pensions in the period is normally the same as the amount of contributions paid.

- The entity should charge the agreed pension contribution to profit or loss as an employment expense in each period.

- An asset or liability for pensions only arises if the cash paid does not equal the value of contributions due for the period.

- IAS 19 requires disclosure of the amount recognised as an expense in the period.

Test your understanding 1 – Defined contribution scheme

An entity makes contributions to the pension fund of employees at a rate of 5% of gross salary. The contributions made are $10,000 per month for convenience with the balance being contributed in the first month of the following accounting year. The wages and salaries for 20X6 are $2.7m.

Required:

Calculate the pension expense for 20X6, and the accrual/ prepayment at the end of the year.

Defined benefit plans: the basic principles

The entity recognises both the liability for future pension payments, together with the plan assets.

- If the liability exceeds the assets, there is a plan deficit (the usual situation) and a liability is reported in the statement of financial position.

- If the plan assets exceed the liability, there is a surplus and an asset is reported in the statement of financial position.

- In simple terms, the movement in the net liability (or asset) from one reporting date to the next is reflected in the statement of comprehensive income for the year.

Within the statement of total comprehensive income for the year, the movement is separated into three components as follows:

- **Service cost component**, which includes current and past service costs, together with any gains or losses on curtailments and settlements. This is charged to profit or loss for the year.

- **Net interest component**, which is computed by applying the discount rate to measure the plan obligation to the net defined benefit liability or asset. This is charged (or credited) to profit or loss for the year.

- **Remeasurement component** comprises actuarial gains and losses during the reporting period, including the returns on plan assets less any amount taken to profit or loss as part of the net interest component. This is taken to other comprehensive income for the year and identified as an item which will not be reclassified to profit or loss in future periods.

Measuring the liability and the assets

In practice, the actuary measures the plan assets and liabilities by applying carefully developed estimates and assumptions relevant to the defined benefit pension plan.

- The plan liability is measured at the present value of the defined benefit obligation, using the Projected Unit Credit Method. This is an actuarial valuation method.

- Discounting is necessary because the liability will be settled many years in the future and, therefore, the effect of the time value of money is material. The discount rate used should be determined by market yields on high quality corporate bonds at the start of the reporting period, and applied to the net liability or asset at the start of the reporting period.

- Plan assets are measured at fair value. This is normally market value. Where no market value is available, fair value is estimated (for example, by calculating the present value of expected future cash flows). Note that IFRS 13 Fair Value measurement (issued in May 2011) now provides a framework for determining how fair value should be established.

- Valuations should be carried out with sufficient regularity to ensure that the amounts recognised in the financial statements do not differ materially from actual fair values at the reporting date. In other words, IAS 19 does not prescribe a maximum time interval between valuations.

- Where there are unpaid contributions at the reporting date, these are not included in the plan assets. Unpaid contributions are treated as a liability; they are owed by the entity/employer to the plan.

Recognising the amounts in the financial statements

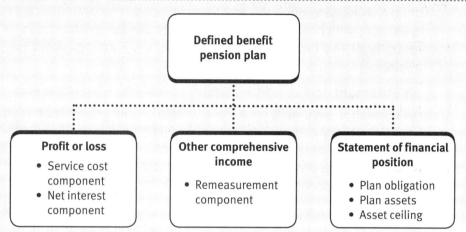

 Explanation of the terms used.

- **Current service cost** is the increase in the present value of the defined benefit obligation resulting from employee service in the current period. This is part of the service cost component.

- **Past service cost** is the change in the present value of the defined benefit obligation for employee service in prior periods, resulting from a plan amendment or a curtailment. In this context, a plan amendment is defined as the introduction of, or withdrawal of, or changes to a post-employment benefit plan. It may either increase or decrease present value of the defined benefit obligation. Past service costs could arise, for example, when there has been an improvement in the benefits to be provided under the plan. This will apply whether or not the benefits have vested (i.e. whether or not employees are immediately entitled to those enhanced benefits), or whether they are obliged to provide additional work and service to become eligible for those enhanced benefits.

  Past service costs are part of the service cost component for the year and are recognised at the earlier of three possibilities:

  - when the related restructuring costs are recognised, where it is part of a restructuring, **or**

  - when the related termination benefits are recognised, where it is linked to termination benefits, **or**

  - when the curtailment occurs; this is a matter of judgement – it could be, for example, when the change is announced, or when it is implemented.

- **A curtailment** occurs when there is a significant reduction in the number of employees covered by the plan. This may be a consequence of an individual event such as plant closure or discontinuance of an operation, which will typically result in employees being made redundant. Any gain or loss on curtailment is part of the service cost component.

- **A settlement** occurs when an entity enters into a transaction to eliminate the obligation for part or all of the benefits under a plan. For example, an employee may leave the entity for a new job elsewhere, and a payment is made from that pension plan to the pension plan operated by the new employer. Any gain or loss on settlement is part of the service cost component.

- **Net interest component** relates to the change in measurement in both the plan obligation and plan assets arising from the passage of time. It is computed by applying the discount rate used to measure the plan obligation to the net liability (or asset) at the start of the reporting period, irrespective of whether this results in net interest expense (or interest income) for the year. Net interest is charged (or credited) as a separate component to profit or loss for the year. In practical terms, the discount rate will be used when reconciling the movements in the plan obligation and plan assets for the year, whether this is done separately, or on a combined net basis. This is because the principal issue when accounting for defined benefit schemes is how to account for what is effectively a long-term liability and how it is funded.

- **Remeasurement component** comprises actuarial gains and losses arising during the reporting period, including the actual returns on plan assets less any amount taken to profit or loss as part of the net interest component. Actuarial gains and losses are increases and decreases in the net pension asset or net liability that occur either because the actuarial assumptions have changed or because of differences between the previous actuarial assumptions and what has actually happened (experience adjustments). This component is recognised in other comprehensive income for the year and will not be recycled or reclassified to profit or loss in future periods.

Note that this treatment of actuarial gains and losses is one of the key points of the revisions made to IAS 19 in 2011. The revised standard eliminates the choice of three possible accounting treatments for actuarial gains and losses which was permitted under the original standard. This will help to improve consistency and comparability of reported results.

Illustration 1 – Defined benefit plan – Celine

The following information is provided in relation to a defined benefit plan operated by Celine. All transactions are assumed to occur at the reporting date of the relevant year. At 1 January 20X4, the present value of the obligation was $140 million and the fair value of the plan assets amounted to $80 million.

	20X4	20X5
Discount rate at start of year	4%	3%
Current and past service cost ($m)	30	32
Benefits paid ($m)	20	22
Contributions into plan ($m)	25	30
Present value of obligation at 31 December ($m)	200	230
Fair value of plan assets at 31 December ($m)	120	140

Required:

Reconcile the movement for the year in the plan asset and obligation; determine the amounts to be taken to profit or loss and other comprehensive income for the year, together with the net plan obligation or asset at 31 December 20X4 and 20X5.

Solution

Celine – Solution

Step 1: Determine the amount of the remeasurement component on the assets and liabilities for the period.

This is done by analysing the change in the plan obligation and plan assets for the period; the remeasurement components are balancing figures. The current and past service cost increases the plan obligation. The benefits paid during the year reduce both the plan obligation and plan assets. The contributions into the scheme increase the plan assets. The net interest return or charge reflects the growth in the plan assets and obligation due to the passage of time.

Assets – stated at fair value

	20X4	20X5
	$m	$m
Balance b/fwd at 1 Jan	80.0	120.0
Interest return (4% 20X4; 3% 20X5)	3.2	3.6
Benefits paid	(20.0)	(22.0)
Contributions into plan	25.0	30.0
Remeasurement component on assets (bal fig)	31.8	8.4
Balance c/fwd at 31 December	120.0	140.0

Obligation – stated at present value

	20X4	20X5
	$m	$m
Balance b/fwd at 1 January	140.0	200.0
Interest charge (4% 20X4; 3% 20X5)	5.6	6.0
Current and past service cost	30.0	32.0
Benefits paid	(20.0)	(22.0)
Remeasurement (gain) loss on plan obligation (balancing figure)	44.4	14.0
Balance c/fwd at 31 December	200.0	230.0

Note that the interest return on the plan assets uses the same rate as used for the plan obligation. This means that any difference between interest return and actual return is included within the remeasurement component.

Step 2: Determine the net obligation or asset to be included in the statement of financial position at the reporting date

	20X4	20X5
	$m	$m
PV of plan obligation	200.0	230.0
FV of plan assets	(120.0)	(140.0)
Closing net liability	80.0	90.0

Step 3: Calculate the charge to profit or loss, together with other comprehensive income for the year

Both the current service cost and the net interest cost are charged to profit or loss for the year. The remeasurement component, which comprises actuarial gains and losses, together with returns on plan assets to the extent that they are not included within the net interest component, is taken to other comprehensive income.

	20X4	20X5
Profit or loss:	$m	$m
Service cost component:		
Current and past service cost	30.0	32.0
Net interest component:		
4% × $60m	2.4	
3% × $80m		2.4
	32.4	34.4
Other comprehensive income		
Net remeasurement component (W1)	12.6	5.6
Total comprehensive income charge for year	45.0	40.0

Step 4: Reconcile the movement in the net obligation or asset for the year:

	20X4	20X5
	$m	$m
Obligation bal b/fwd 1 January	140.0	200.0
Asset bal b/fwd at 1 January	(80.0)	(120.0)
Net obligation b/fwd at 1 January	60.0	80.0
Current and past service cost	30.0	32.0
Net interest charge		
4% × $60m	2.4	
3% × $80m		2.4
Contributions into plan	(25.0)	(30.0)
Net remeasurement component on obligation (W1)	12.6	5.6
Net obligation c/fwd at 31 December	80.0	90.0

(W1) **Summary of remeasurement components for the year**

This statement reconciles the figures in the statement of financial position using the charges to profit or loss.

	20X4 $m	20X5 $m
Remeasurement component on obligation – loss	44.4	14.0
Remeasurement component on assets – gain	(31.8)	(8.4)
Net remeasurement component	12.6	5.6

Solution - further information

Rather than prepare a separate reconciliation of the movement in the plan assets and the plan obligation for the year, it is usually possible to prepare a reconciliation of the movement in the net obligation for the year as follows:

Net obligation – stated at present value

	20X4 $m		20X5 $m
Net bal b/fwd at 1 January (140 - 80)	60.0	(200 - 120)	80.0
Net interest charge (4% 20X4; 3% 20X5)	2.4		2.4
Current and past service cost	30.0		32.0
Contributions into the plan	(25.0)		(30.0)
Net remeasurement (gain) loss on plan (bal fig) (44.4 - 31.8)	12.6	(14.0 - 8.4)	5.6
Net bal c/fwd at 31 December (200 - 120)	80.0	(230 - 140)	90.0

Note that benefits paid are excluded from the reconciliation when it is prepared on a net basis as they reduce both the pension obligation and pension assets.

Note also that this approach still provides the information required for inclusion in the financial statements as identified ealier within the answer to the illustration.

Test your understanding 2 – Fraser

The following information is provided relating to a defined benefit plan operated by Fraser. All transactions are assumed to occur at the reporting date. At 1 January 20X1, the present value of the obligation was $1,000,000 and the fair value of the plan assets amounted to $900,000.

	20X1	20X2	20X3
Discount rate at start of year	10%	9%	8%
Current and past service cost ($000)	125	130	138
Benefits paid ($000)	150	155	165
Contributions paid into plan ($000)	90	95	105
PV of obligation at 31 December ($000)	1,350	1,340	1,450
FV of plan assets at 31 December ($000)	1,200	1,150	1,300

Required:

Show how the defined benefit plan would be shown in the financial statements for each of the years ended 31 December 20X1, 20X2 and 20X3 respectively.

The impact of revisions to IAS 19

The revisions made to IAS 19 in 2011 have gone some way to overcoming weaknesses of the previous version of IAS 19 as follows:

- The classification of amounts to be included in profit or loss for the year have been standardised into two components; the service cost component and the net interest component.

- The net interest charge is recognition of the time value of money for what is essentially a long-term net obligation. Any returns on plan assets earned due to factors other than the time value of money are accounted for as part of other comprehensive income.

- The choice of three possible accounting treatments of actuarial gains and losses has now been removed. Actuarial gains and losses on the plan obligation and plan assets are now referred to as remeasurement components, and are accounted for as part of other comprehensive income.

- Accounting for past service costs has been simplified, in that any such costs incurred during an accounting period, which result in amendments to the defined benefit plan which increase or decrease the future obligation, are now immediately recognised either when the related restructuring costs or termination benefits are recognised, or when the plan amendment occurs. Previously, any such costs would have been spread and recognised over the vesting period which employees had to provide additional work and service to become entitled to the enhanced benefits.

- Accounting for a curtailment gives rise to a gain or loss which is included as part of past service cost.

- There should be improved consistency and comparability of information as a consequence of the increased standardisation and simplification of accounting treatments introduced by IAS 19 (revised).

Commentary

Retirement benefit accounting continues to be a controversial area. Commentators have perceived the following problems with the IAS 19 approach.

- Fair values of plan assets may be volatile, or even difficult to measure reliably depending upon the nature of the plan assets; consequently there may be significant fluctuations in the statement of financial position. This will now be reported as part of other comprehensive income each year.

- IAS 19 requires plan assets to be valued at fair value (normally market value). Fair values of plan assets are not relevant to the economic reality of most pension schemes. Under the requirements of IAS 19, assets are valued at short-term amounts, but most pension scheme assets and liabilities are held for the long term. The actuarial basis of valuing plan assets would better reflect the long-term costs of funding a pension scheme. However, such a move would be a departure from IFRS 13 Fair Value Measurement which seeks to standardise the application of fair value measurement when it is required by a particular reporting standard.

- The treatment of pension costs in the statement of profit or loss and other comprehensive income is complex and may not be easily understood by users of the financial statements. It has been argued that all the components of the pension cost are so interrelated that it does not make sense to present them separately. However, the revised standard categorises the amounts to be included in profit or loss, or other comprehensive income, which may help with consistency and comparability of reported information.

- Where there is a net pension plan surplus (rather than net obligation) at a reporting date, then IAS 19 treats it as if it 'belongs' to the employer. However, in practice, the situation is that the surplus perhaps 'belongs' to the members of the plan and must be applied for their benefit. IAS 19 may not reflect the legal and economic reality of this situation, unless the employer makes a statement to confirm that there will be enhanced future benefits paid to employees as a result of past service during which time the surplus would have accumulated, or that any surplus can be recovered by way of reduced future contributions and/or refunds. Where enhanced future benefits are to be paid, this would require acknowledgement by the employer of the increased obligation, which would effectively reduce the net plan surplus as currently reported.

Multi-employer plans

Multi-employer plans

Multi-employer plans are classified as either defined contribution plans or defined benefit plans.
Defined contribution multi-employer plans do not pose a problem because the employer's cost is limited to the contributions payable.

Defined benefit multi-employer plans expose participating employers to the actuarial risks associated with the current and former employees of other entities. There are also potential problems because an employer may be unable to identify its share of the underlying assets and liabilities.

IAS 19 states that where a multi-employer plan is a defined benefit plan, the entity accounts for its proportionate share of the obligations, benefits and costs associated with the plan in the same way as usual. However, where sufficient information is not available to do this, the entity accounts for the plan as if it were a defined contribution plan and discloses:

- the fact that the plan is a defined benefit plan

- the reason why sufficient information is not available to account for the plan as a defined benefit plan.

In this situation, the revised standard requires additional disclosures to be made regarding the defined benefit plan, some of which may be quite onerous for preparers of financial statements.

Past service costs

Past service costs arise either where a new retirement benefit plan is introduced, or where the benefits under an existing plan are improved. Where a new plan is introduced, employees are often given benefit rights for any years of service before commencement of the plan.

- If employees have the right to receive benefits under the plan immediately, the benefits are said to be 'vested' and the cost must be recognised immediately.

- If employees become entitled to benefits only at some later date, the benefits become vested at that later date, with the costs still recognised immediately following revision of IAS 19 in June 2011.

Illustration 2 – Accounting for pension plans

An entity operates a pension plan that provides a pension of 2% of final salary for each year of service. The benefits become vested after five years of service. On 1 January 20X5, the entity improves the pension to 2.5% of final salary, for each year of service starting from 1 January 20X1. At the date of the improvement, the present value of the additional benefits for service from 1 January 20X1 to 1 January 20X5, is as follows:

	$000
Employees with more than five years' service at 1.1.X5	150
Employees with less than five years' service at 1.1.X5 (average period until vesting: three years)	120
	270

Required:

Explain how the additional benefits are accounted for in the financial statements of the entity.

Solution

The entity recognises all $270,000 immediately as an increase in the defined benefit obligation following the amendment to the plan on 1 January 20X5. Whether or not the benefits have vested at that date is not relevant to their recognition as an expense in the financial statements.

Curtailments and settlements

A **curtailment** occurs when there is a significant reduction in the number of employees covered by a defined benefit plan. This may occur when there is closure of a plant or discontinuance of an operation. A curtailment gives rise to a past service cost which is recognised at the earlier of three possible dates:

- when the related restructuring costs are recognised, if it is part of a restructuring, or

- when the related termination benefits are recognised, if it is linked to termination, or

- when the curtailment occurs.

A **settlement** is a transaction that eliminates all further legal or constructive obligations for part or all of the benefits provided under a defined benefit plan.

For example, an employee leaves the entity for a new job elsewhere, and a payment is made on behalf of the employee into the defined benefit plan of the new employer.

The gain or loss arising on a curtailment or settlement should be recognised when the curtailment or settlement occurs.

The gain or loss comprises the difference between the fair value of the plan assets paid out and the reduction in the present value of the defined benefit obligation.

Curtailments and settlements do not affect profit or loss if they have already been allowed for in the actuarial assumptions; any impact would be considered part of the remeasurement component.

AB decides to close a business segment. The segment's employees will be made redundant and will earn no further pension benefits after being made redundant. Their plan assets will remain in the scheme so that the employees will be paid a pension when they reach retirement age (i.e. this is a curtailment without settlement).

Before the curtailment, the scheme assets had a fair value of $500,000, and the defined benefit obligation had a present value of $600,000. It is estimated that the curtailment will reduce the present value of the future obligation by 10%, which reflects the fact that employees will have fewer years of work and service with AB before retirement, and therefore be entitled to a smaller pension than previously estimated or accounted for.

Required:

What is net gain or loss on curtailment and how will this be treated in the financial statements?

Solution

The obligation is to be reduced by 10% x $600,000 = $60,000, with no change in the fair value of the assets as they remain in the plan. The reduction in the obligation represents a gain on curtailment which should be included as part of the service cost component and taken to profit or loss for the year. The net position of the plan following curtailment will be:

	Before	On curtailment	After
	$000	$000	$000
Present value of obligation	600	(60)	540
Fair value of plan assets	(500)	–	(500)
Net obligation in SOFP	100	(60)	40

The gain on curtailment is $60,000 and this will be included as part of the service cost component in profit or loss for the year.

Test your understanding 3 – TC

TC has a defined benefit pension plan and prepares financial statements to 31 March each year. The following information is relevant for the year ended 31 March 20X3:

- The net pension obligation at 31 March 20X3 was $55 million. At 31 March 20X2, the net obligation was $48 million, comprising the present value of the plan obligation stated at $100 million, together with plan assets stated at fair value of $52 million.

- The discount rate relevant to the net obligation was 6.25% and the actual return on plan assets for the year was $4 million.

- The current service cost was $12 million.

- At 31 March 20X3, TC granted additional benefits to those currently receiving benefits that are due to vest over the next four years and which have a present value of $4 million at that date. They were not allowed for in the original actuarial assumptions.

- During the year, TC made pension contributions of $8 million into the scheme and the scheme paid pension benefits in the year amounting to $3 million.

Required:

Prepare a summary of the movement in the net obligation for the year to 31 March 20X3, together with supporting explanation.

4 The asset ceiling

Sometimes the deduction of plan assets from the pension obligation results in a negative amount: i.e. an asset. IAS 19 states that pension plan assets (surpluses) are measured at the lower of:

- the amount calculated as normal per earlier examples and illustrations. or

- the total of the present value of any economic benefits available in the form of refunds from the plan or reductions in future contributions to the plan.

Applying the 'asset ceiling' means that a surplus can only be recognised to the extent that it will be recoverable in the form of refunds or reduced contributions in future. This would make it compatible with the definition of an asset as included within the 2010 Conceptual Framework for Financial Reporting.

Illustration 4 – The asset ceiling

The following information relates to a defined benefit plan:	$000
Fair value of plan assets	950
Present value of pension liability	800
Present value of future refunds and reductions in future contributions	70

Required:

What is the value of the asset that recognised in the financial statements?

Solution

The amount that can be recognised is the lower of:

	$000
Present value of plan obligation	800
Fair value of plan assets	(950)
	–––––
	(150)
	–––––

	$000
PV of future refunds and/or reductions in future contributions	(70)
	–––––

Therefore the amount of the asset recognised is restricted to $70,000.

Test your understanding 4 – Arc

The following information relates to the defined benefit plan operated by Arc for the year ended 30 June 20X4:

	$m
FV of plan assets b/fwd at 30 June 20X3	2,600
PV of obligation b/fwd at 30 June 20X3	2,000
Current service cost for the year	100
Benefits paid in the year	80
Contributions into plan	90
FV of plan assets at 30 June 20X4	3,100
PV of plan obligation at 30 June 20X4	2,400

Discount rate for the defined benefit obligation – 10%

Arc has identified that the asset ceiling at 30 June 20X3 and 30 June 20X4, based upon the present value of future refunds from the plan and/or reductions in future contributions amounts to $200m at 30 June 20X3 and 30 June 20X4.

Required:

(a) **Reconcile the movement in the plan assets and obligation, to determine what is charged in the statement of comprehensive income for the year ended 30 June 20X4, together with identification of the balance reported on the statement of financial position at 30 June 20X4.**

(b) **Explain the purpose of the asset ceiling, together with its impact upon accounting for the defined benefit plan operated by Arc.**

IFRIC 14 – Limit on defined benefit asset

IFRIC 14 – The limit on a defined benefit asset, minimum funding requirements and their interaction

The subject matter of IFRIC 14 was not incorporated into the 2011 revisions of IAS 19, and therefore is still relevant where there may be a net asset for the defined benefit plan at the reporting date. Although IFRICs are not examinable documents for the ACCA P2 syllabus, the principles applied by IFRIC 14 are consistent with the Framework for Financial Reporting 2010 and are therefore considered relevant to your studies in that context.

IFRIC 14 addresses areas of IAS 19 where detailed guidance is lacking, namely:

- How to determine the asset ceiling

- The effect of a minimum funding requirement (MFR) on that calculation

- When an MFR creates an onerous obligation that should be recognised as a liability.

It therefore only applies to those entities which have a plan surplus or are subject to minimum funding requirements.

IAS 19 states that pension plan surpluses are limited to the total of the present value of any economic benefits available in the form of refunds from the plan or reductions in future contributions to the plan. IFRIC 14, together with a subsequent amendment dated 26 November 2009, clarifies this by defining 'available' as having an unconditional right to realise the benefit at some point during the life of the plan or when the plan is settled, even if the benefit is not realisable immediately at the reporting date. If such a right is conditional, then no asset in respect of refunds or reductions in contributions can be recognised.

In many countries, laws or contractual terms require employers to make minimum funding payments (MFR) for their pension or other employee benefit plans. This enhances the security of the retirement benefit promise made to members of an employee benefit plan. A liability is recognised for MFR contributions to cover existing plan shortfalls in respect of services already received if the contribution payable is not expected to be available after it is paid into a plan.

In the specific situation where there is a MFR in place, and there has been early payment of contributions to cover the MFR, the amendment to IFRIC 14 enables the benefits of that early payment to be recognised as an asset.

Disclosure requirements

IAS 19 has extensive disclosure requirements, which were added to when it was revised in 2011. In summary, an entity should disclose the following information about defined benefit plans:

- explanation of the regulatory framework within which the plan operates, together with explanation of the nature of benefits provided by the plan

- explanation of the nature of the risks the entity is exposed to as a consequence of operating the plan, together with explanation of any plan amendments, settlements or curtailments in the year

- the entity's accounting policy for recognising actuarial gains and losses, together with disclosure of the significant actuarial assumptions used to determine the net defined benefit obligation or assets. Although there is no longer a choice of accounting policy for actuarial gains and losses, it may still be helpful to users to explain how they have been accounted for within the financial statements.

- a general description of the type of plan operated

- a reconciliation of the assets and liabilities recognised in the statement of financial position

- a reconciliation showing the movements during the period in the net liability (or asset) recognised in the statement of financial position

- the charge to total comprehensive income for the year, separated into the appropriate components

- analysis of the remeasurement component to identify returns on plan assets, together with actuarial gains and losses arising on the net plan obligation

- sensitivity analysis and narrative description of how the defined benefit plan may affect the nature, timing and uncertainty of the entity's future cash flows.

Other employee benefits

IAS 19 covers a number of other issues in addition to post-employment benefits as follows:

Short-term employee benefits – This includes a number of issues including:

- **Wages and salaries and bonuses and other benefits**. The general principle is that wages and salaries costs are expenses as they are incurred on a normal accruals basis, unless capitalisation is permitted in accordance with another reporting standard, such as IAS 16 or IAS 38. Bonuses and other short-term payments are recognised using normal criteria of establishing an obligation based upon past events which can be reliably measured.

- **Compensated absences**. This covers issues such as holiday pay, sick leave, maternity leave, jury service, study leave and military service. The key issue is whether the absences are regarded as being accumulating or non-accumulating:

  - accumulating benefits are earned over time and are capable of being carried forward. In this situation, the expense for future compensated absences is recognised over the period services are provided by the employee. This will typically result in the recognition of a liability at the reporting date for the expected cost of the accumulated benefit earned but not yet claimed by an employee. An example of this would be a holiday pay accrual at the reporting date where unused holiday entitlement can be carried forward and claimed in a future period.

  - for non-accumulating benefits, an expense should only be recognised when the absence occurs. This may arise, for example, where an employee continues to receive their normal remuneration whilst being absent due to illness or other permitted reason. A charge to profit or loss would be made only when the authorised absence occurs; if there is no such absence, there will be no charge to profit or loss.

- **Benefits in kind**. Recognition of cost should be based on the same principles as benefits payable in cash; it should be measured based upon the cost to the employer of providing the benefit and recognised as it is earned.

Termination benefits

The definition of what constitutes termination benefits, and how they should be accounted for, was included in the revised edition of IAS 19 issued in June 2011. Termination benefits may be defined as benefits payable as a result of employment being terminated, either by the employer, or by the employee accepting voluntary redundancy. Such payments are normally in the form of a lump sum; entitlement to such payments is not accrued over time, and only become available in a relatively short period prior to any such payment being agreed and paid to the employee. The obligation to pay such benefits is recognised either when the employer can no longer withdraw the offer of such benefits (i.e. they are committed to paying them), or when it recognises related restructuring costs (normally in accordance with IAS 37). Payments which are due to be paid more than twelve months after the reporting date should be discounted to their present value.

Other long-term employee benefits

This comprises other items not within the above classifications and will include long-service leave, long-term disability benefits and other long-service benefits. These employee benefits are accounted for in a similar manner to accounting for post-employment benefits, typically using the projected unit credit method, as benefits are payable more than twelve months after the period in which services are provided by an employee.

UK syllabus focus

The ACCA UK syllabus contains a requirement that candidates should be able to discuss and apply the key differences between UK GAAP and IFRS GAAP. The accounting requirements of UK GAAP and IFRS GAAP are very similar in this area, particularly so following the revisions made to IAS 19 during 2011; the key issues associated with UK reporting standard requirements are as follows:

- UK FRS 17 requires that the accounting treatment for **actuarial gains and losses** is that they are taken to the STRGL (i.e. reserves). The rationale for this treatment is that any gains or losses are recognised as part of overall performance, but without distortion of reported profits. In addition, having only one accounting treatment improves comparability of reported results. Following revision of IAS 19 in June 2011, IAS 19 is now substantially consistent with this accounting treatment as **remeasurement component gains and losses** are taken to other comprehensive income for the year. Previously, IAS 19 contained three permitted methods of accounting for actuarial gains and losses; this was perceived to be a weakness as it undermined comparability of reported results.

- IAS 19 previously permitted deferral of recognition of actuarial gains and losses. Following revision of IAS 19, this is no longer permitted and this is consistent with UK FRS 17 which does not permit deferral of actuarial gains and losses.

- UK FRS 17 covers only retirement benefits, whereas IAS 19 covers other short-term and long-term employee benefits, such as termination benefits.

5 Chapter summary

```
                    ┌──────────────────────────────────┐
                    │   Post-employment benefit plans   │
                    └──────────────────────────────────┘
```

Defined contribution plans
- Normal accruals accounting

Defined benefit plans
- SOFP
  - Plan obligation at PV
  - Plan assets at FV
  - Asset ceiling
- Profit or loss
  - Service cost component
  - Current and past service cost
  - Curtailments and settlements
  - Net interest component
- Other comprehensive income
  - Remeasurement component

Other long-term employee benefits
- Account for in similar way to defined benefit pension plans – spread cost over service period

Short-term employee benefits
- Normal accruals accounting
- Cumulating or non-cumulating

Termination benefits
- Recognise when an obligation or when related restructuring costs recognised

Test your understanding answers

Test your understanding 1 – Defined contribution scheme

This appears to be a defined contribution scheme.

The charge to income should be:

$2.7m × 5% = $135,000

The statement of financial position will therefore show an accrual of $15,000, being the difference between the $135,000 and the $120,000 paid in the year.

Test your understanding 2 – Fraser

Step 1 – Calculate remeasurement gains and losses on the net obligation

	20X1 $000	20X2 $000	20X3 $000
Net obligation at start of the year	100	150	190
Interest charge (10% X1/ 9% X2/ 8% X3)	10	14	15
Current and past service cost	125	130	138
Contributions into plan	(90)	(95)	(105)
Net remeasurement component (gain) loss – bal.fig	5	(9)	(88)
Net obligation at end of the year	150	190	150

Step 2 – The statement of financial position

	20X1 $000	20X2 $000	20X3 $000
Net pension (asset) liability	150	190	150

Step 3 – Profit or loss and other comprehensive income for the year

	20X1	20X2	20X3
Service cost component	$000	$000	$000
Current and past service cost	125	130	138
Net interest component	10	14	15
Charge to profit or loss	135	144	153
Other comprehensive income:			
Net remeasurement component	5	(9)	(88)
Total charge to comprehensive income	140	135	65

Step 4 – Reconcile the movement in the net obligation or asset for the year

	20X1	20X2	20X3
	$000	$000	$000
Obligation bal b/fwd at 1 January	1,000	1350	1,340
Asset bal b/fwd at 1 January	(900)	(1,200)	(1,150)
Net obligation at 1 January	100	150	190
Net interest:			
10% × 100	10		
9% × 150		14	
8% × 190			15
Current and past service cost	125	130	138
Contributions into plan	(90)	(95)	(105)
Net remeasurement component	5	(9)	(88)
Net obligation at reporting date	150	190	150

Note: This may not always be required, depending upon what is required when answering a particular question.

Test your understanding 3 – TC

		$m
Net obligation brought forward		48
Net interest component @ 6.25%		3
Service cost component:		
Current service cost	12	
Past service cost	4	16
	────	
Contributions into the plan		(8)
Remeasurement component (bal fig)		(4)
		────
Net obligation carried forward		55
		────

Explanation:

- The discount rate is applied to the net obligation brought forward and will be charged to profit or loss for the year as the net interest component.

- The current year service cost, together with the past service cost forms the service cost component which is charged to profit or loss for the year. Past service cost is charged in full, usually when the scheme is amended, rather than when the additional benefits vest.

- To the extent that there has been a return on assets in excess of the amount identified by application of the discount rate to the fair value of plan assets, this is part of the remeasurement component (i.e. $4m – $3.25m ($52m x 6.25%) = $0.75m).

- Contributions paid into the scheme during the year will reduce the net obligation.

- Benefits paid of $3 million will reduce both the scheme assets and the scheme obligation, so will have no impact on the net obligation.

Test your understanding 4 – Arc

(a)

	PV obligation	FV assets	Ceiling adjust*	Net defined benefit asset	Note
	$m	$m	$m	$m	
Balance b/fwd	2,000	(2,600)	400	(200)	1
Interest @10%	200	(260)	40	(20)	2
Service cost	100			100	3
Benefits paid	(80)	80			4
Contributions in		(90)		(90)	5
Sub-total:	2,220	(2,870)	440	(210)	
Remeasurement component:					
Obligation – loss	180		(180)		
Asset – gain		(230)	230		
			10	10	6
Balance c/fwd	2,400	(3,100)	500	(200)	

* note that this is effectively a balancing figure.

A separate reconciliation of assets and liabilities has been shown for reference only. It is often quicker and simpler to deal with movements in the net obligation for the year.

Explanation:

(1) The asset ceiling adjustment at the previous reporting date of 30 June 20X3 measures the net defined benefit asset at the amount recoverable by refunds and/or reduced future contributions, stated at $200m. In effect, the value of the asset was reduced for reporting purposes at 30 June 20X3.

(2) Interest charged on the obligation or earned on the plan assets is based upon the discount rate for the obligation, stated at 10%. This will then require adjustment to agree with the net return on the net plan asset at the beginning of the year. Net interest earned is taken to profit or loss for the year

(3) The current year service cost increases the plan obligation, which therefore reduces the net plan asset. The current year service cost is taken to profit or loss for the year.

(4) Benefits paid in the year reduce both the plan obligation and the plan assets by the same amount.

(5) Contributions into the plan increase the fair value of plan assets, and also the net plan asset during the year.

(6) The remeasurement component, including actuarial gains and losses for the year, is identified to arrive at the present value of the plan obligation and the fair value of the plan assets at 30 June 20X4. As there is a net asset of $700m ($3,100m – $2,400m) for the defined benefit pension plan, the asset ceiling test is applied to restrict the reported asset to the expected future benefits in the form of refunds and/or reduced future contributions, which is stated in the question to be $200m. To the extent that an adjustment is required to the net asset at the reporting date, this is part of the net remeasurement component.

(b) The asset ceiling test is designed to ensure that any net pension asset is not overstated on the statement of financial position. If it can be reliably measured based upon the present value of future economic benefits to be received, either in the form of reduced future contributions or refunds of contributions already paid, this will comply with the definition of an asset from the 2010 Conceptual Framework for Financial Reporting.

If the asset ceiling test was not applied, at 30 June 20X4, there would be a net asset for the defined benefit plan amounting to $700m ($3,100 – $$2,400). However, this amount would not be fully represented by the right to receive future economic benefits in the form of refunds of amounts already paid or reductions in future contributions into the plan. Consequently, the asset would be overstated as, even though the plan assets are stated at fair value, they are held to meet future payments in respect of a long-term obligation.

Share-based payment

Chapter learning objectives

Upon completion of this chapter you will be able to:

- apply and discuss the recognition and measurement criteria for share-based payment transactions
- account for modifications, cancellations and settlements of share-based payment transactions.

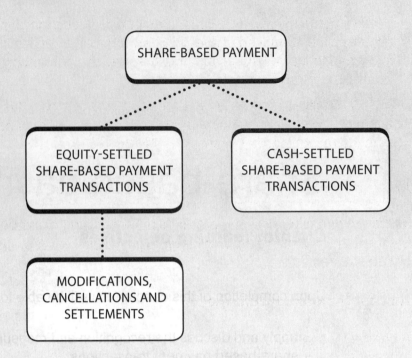

1 Share-based payment

Introduction

Share-based payment has become increasingly common. Share-based payment occurs when an entity buys goods or services from other parties (such as employees or suppliers), and settles the amounts payable by issuing shares or share options to them.

- Part of the remuneration of directors is often in the form of shares or options. Employees may also be granted share options.

- Many new 'e-businesses' do not expect to be profitable in their early years, so try to attract quality staff by offering to employees share schemes rather than high cash salaries.

The problem

If a company pays for goods or services in cash, an expense is recognised in profit or loss. If a company 'pays' for goods or services in share options, there is no cash outflow and under traditional accounting, no expense would be recognised.

- But when a company issues shares to acquire an investment in another entity, it is accepted that the acquirer has incurred a cost that should be recognised in the financial statements at fair value. Issuing shares to acquire goods or services is arguably no different.

- When a company issues shares to employees, a transaction has occurred; the employees have provided a valuable service to the entity, in exchange for the shares/options. It is illogical not to recognise this transaction in the financial statements.

- IFRS 2 **Share-based payment** was issued to deal with this accounting anomaly. IFRS 2 requires that all share-based payment transactions must be recognised in the financial statements.

Arguments not to recognise share-based payments

There are a number of arguments for **not** recognising share-based payment. IFRS 2 rejects them all, arguing in favour of recognising share-based payment.

No cost therefore no charge

A charge for shares or options should not be recognised because the entity does not have to sacrifice cash or other assets. There is no cost to the entity.

This argument ignores the fact that a transaction has occurred. The employees have provided valuable services to the entity in return for valuable shares or options. If this argument were accepted, the financial statements would fail to reflect the economic transactions that had occurred.

Earnings per share would be hit twice

The charge to profit for the employee services consumed reduces the entity's earnings. At the same time there is an increase in the number of shares issued (or to be issued).

However, the double impact on earnings per share simply reflects the two economic events that have occurred: the entity has issued shares, thus increasing the denominator of the EPS calculation, and it has also consumed the resources it received for those shares, thus reducing the numerator. Issuing shares to employees, instead of paying them in cash, requires a greater increase in the entity's earnings in order to maintain its earnings per share. Recognising the transaction ensures that its economic consequences are reported.

Adverse economic consequences

Recognition of employee share-based payment might discourage entities from introducing or continuing employee share plans.

If this were the case, this might be because the requirement for entities to account properly for employee share plans had revealed the economic consequences of such plans. This would correct the economic distortion, whereby entities are able to obtain and consume resources by issuing valuable shares or options without having to account for such transactions.

Types of transaction

IFRS 2 applies to all types of share-based payment transaction. There are two main types:

- in an **equity-settled share-based payment transaction**, the entity receives goods or services in exchange for equity instruments of the entity (e.g. shares or share options)
- in a **cash-settled share-based payment transaction**, the entity acquires goods or services in exchange for amounts of cash measured by reference to the entity's share price.

The most common type of share-based payment transaction is where share options are granted to employees or directors as part of their remuneration.

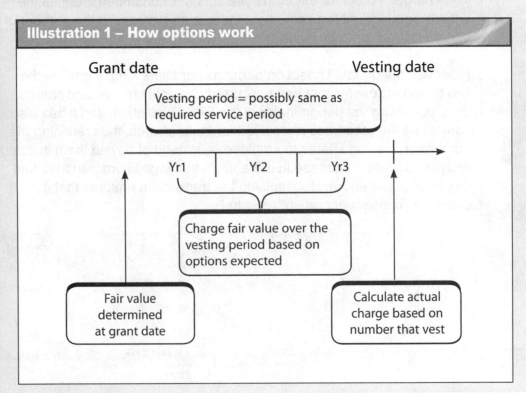

Illustration 1 – How options work

The basic principles

When an entity receives goods or services as a result of a share-based payment transaction, it recognises either an expense or an asset.

*   If the goods or services are received in exchange for equity (e.g., for share options), the entity recognises an increase in equity.
    *   The double entry is: Dr Expense/Asset; Cr Equity (normally a special reserve).

*   If the goods or services are received or acquired in a cash-settled share-based payment transaction, the entity recognises a liability.
    *   The double entry is: Dr Expense/Asset; Cr Liability.

All share-based payment transactions are measured at fair value.

2 Equity-settled share-based payment transactions

Measurement

The basic principle is that all transactions are measured at fair value.

Fair value is the amount for which an asset could be exchanged, a liability settled, or an equity instrument granted could be exchanged, between knowledgeable, willing parties in an arm's length transaction.

How fair value is determined:

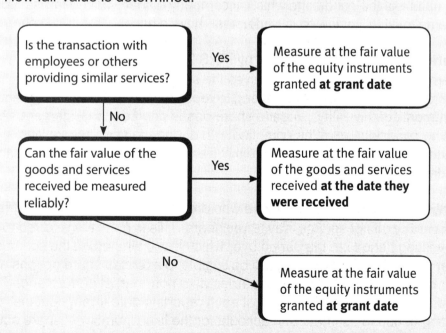

The **grant date** is the date at which the entity and another party agree to the arrangement.

Conditions attaching to share-based payment transactions

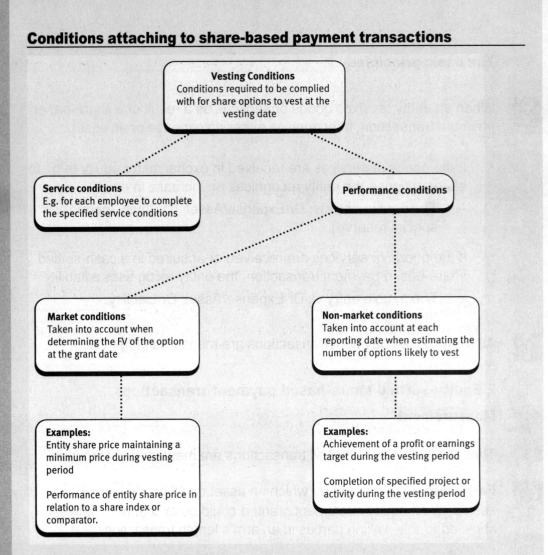

 The nature of the conditions which accompany a share-based transaction or scheme must be reviewed to understand how to account for such schemes.

Vesting conditions are defined by IFRS 2 as "...the conditions that determine whether the entity receives the services that entitle the counterparty (i.e. scheme members) to receive cash, other assets or equity instruments of the entity , under a share-based payment arrangement." All vesting conditions must be complied with during the specified vesting period; they can be classified as either service conditions or performance conditions.

Service conditions require those who are scheme members to complete a specified period of service, say, three years. This is normally referred to as the vesting period i.e. the period over which those who are in the scheme must provide work and service to be eligible to exercise share options at a later date. Such a condition is regarded as a non-market performance condition and must be evaluated at each reporting date throughout the vesting period to estimate and account for the likely number of share options that will vest.

If any individual scheme members leave their employment at any point during the vesting period, they forfeit any entitlement under the scheme. At each reporting date, the entity will estimate the number of scheme members who are likely to remain in employment at the vesting date as a basis for accounting for the annual expense of the scheme.

Performance conditions require those who are members of the scheme to meet specified performance conditions; they may be either market conditions or non-market conditions. Performance conditions are not wholly within the control of the employee; otherwise they would be regarded as service conditions.

- A **market condition** is defined by IFRS 2 as "...one that is related to the market price of the entity's equity instruments." Market conditions are taken into account when the fair value of the option is established at the grant date. An example of a market condition is that the entity must attain a minimum share price by the vesting date for scheme members to be eligible to participate in the share-based payment scheme. It does not affect the annual accounting for the share-based payment scheme during the vesting period.

- **Non-market performance conditions** are taken into consideration when estimating the number of share options that will vest at a later date. Consequently, they must be evaluated at each reporting date throughout the vesting period and will affect the expense recognised in profit or loss each year. Examples of non-market performance conditions include EPS or profit targets.

Determining fair value

Where a share-based payment transaction is with parties other than employees, it is assumed that the fair value of the goods and services received can be measured reliably, at their cash price for example.

Where shares or share options are granted to employees as part of their remuneration, it is not usually possible to arrive at a reliable value for the services received in return. For this reason, the entity measures the transaction by reference to the fair value of the equity instruments granted.

The fair value of equity instruments is market value, if this is available. Where no market price is available (for example, if the instruments are unquoted), a valuation technique is used.

The fair value of share options is harder to determine. In rare cases there may be publicly quoted traded options with similar terms, whose market value can be used as the fair value of the options we are considering. Otherwise, the fair value of options must be estimated using a recognised option-pricing model. IFRS 2 does not require any specific model to be used. The most commonly used is the Black-Scholes model.

Allocating the expense to reporting periods

Some equity instruments granted vest immediately, meaning that the holder is unconditionally entitled to the instruments. In this case, the transaction should be accounted for in full on the grant date.

The **vesting date** is the date on which the counterparty (e.g., the employee) becomes entitled to receive the cash or equity instruments under the arrangement.

- Note the difference in meaning between the grant date of options and the vesting date.

However, when share options are granted to employees as part of their remuneration package, the employees usually have to meet specified conditions before actually becoming entitled to the shares. For example, they may have to complete a specified period of service or to achieve particular performance targets.

- For this reason, the transaction normally has to be recognised over more than one accounting period.

IFRS 2 states that an entity should account for services as they are rendered during the vesting period.

- The vesting period is the period during which all the specified vesting conditions are satisfied.

Accounting after vesting date

IFRS 2 states that no further adjustments to total equity should be made after vesting date. This applies even if some of the equity instruments do not vest (for example, because some of the employees do not exercise their right to buy shares).

- But for those who do not vest, a transfer may be made from shares to be issued to retained earnings.

Equity-settled share-based payment transactions

On 1 January 20X1, A awards 1,000 share options to an employee, on condition that he is still working for the company in two years' time. The grant date is 1 January 20X1. The vesting period is from 1 January 20X1 to 31 December 20X2. The vesting date is 31 December 20X2.

The entity should recognise an amount for the goods or services received during the vesting period based on the best available estimate of the number of equity instruments expected to vest.

- Each year it should revise that estimate of the number of equity instruments expected to vest if subsequent information indicates that this number differs from previous estimates.

- On vesting date, the entity should revise the estimate to equal the number of equity instruments that actually vest.

- Sometimes one of the vesting conditions is a 'market condition', for example, where the share price must be above a certain amount on the vesting date. Market conditions are taken into account when estimating the fair value of the option at the grant date. Failure to satisfy a market condition is not taken into account when subsequently calculating the amounts recognised in profit and loss and equity over the vesting period.

Before the shares vest, the amount recognised in equity is normally credited to a special reserve called (for example) 'shares to be issued'.

- After the share options vest and the shares are issued, the relevant amount is usually transferred to share capital.

Equity-settled share-based payment

On 1 January 20X1 an entity grants 100 share options to each of its 500 employees. Each grant is conditional upon the employee working for the entity until 31 December 20X3. At the grant date the fair value of each share option is $15.

During 20X1, 20 employees leave and the entity estimates that a total of 20% of the 500 employees will leave during the three-year period.

During 20X2, a further 20 employees leave and the entity now estimates that only a total of 15% of its 500 employees will leave during the three-year period.

During 20X3, a further 10 employees leave.

Calculate the remuneration expense that will be recognised in respect of the share-based payment transaction for each of the three years ended 31 December 20X3.

Solution

The entity recognises the remuneration expense as the employees' services are received during the three-year vesting period. The amount recognised is based on the fair value of the share options granted at the grant date (1 January 20X1).

Assuming that no employees left, the total expense would be $750,000 ($100 \times 500 \times 15$) and the expense charged to profit or loss for each of the three years would be $250,000 ($750,000/3$).

In practice, the entity estimates the number of options expected to vest by estimating the number of employees likely to leave. This estimate is revised at each year end. The expense recognised for the year is based on this re-estimate. On the vesting date (31 December 20X3), it recognises an amount based on the number of options that actually vest.

A total of 50 employees left during the three-year period and therefore 45,000 options ($500 - 50 \times 100$) vested.

The amount recognised as an expense for each of the three years is calculated as follows:

	Expense for year (change in cumulative)	Cumulative expense at year-end
	$	$
20X1 $100 \times (500 \times 80\%) \times 15 \times 1/3$	200,000	200,000
20X2 $100 \times (500 \times 85\%) \times 15 \times 2/3$	225,000	425,000
20X3 $45,000 \times 15$	250,000	675,000

The financial statements will include the following amounts:

Statement of profit or loss	20X1	20X2	20X3
	$	$	$
Staff costs	200,000	225,000	250,000

Statement of financial position	Year 1	Year 2	Year 3
	$	$	$
Included with equity	200,000	425,000	675,000

Test your understanding 1 – Beginner

The fair value of the shares Beginner offered directors an option scheme based on a three-year period of service. The number of options granted to each of the ten directors at the inception of the scheme was 1 million. The options were exercisable shortly after the end of the third year. Upon execrcise of the share options, those directors eligible would be required to pay $2 for each share of $1 nominal value.

The fair value of the options and the estimates of the number of options expected to vest were:

Year	Rights expected to vest	Fair value of the option
Start of Year One	8m	30c
End of Year One	7m	33c
End of Year Two	8m	37c
End of Year Three	9m	74c

Required:

(a) **Show how the option scheme will affect the financial statements for each of the three years of the vesting period.**

(b) **Show the accounting treatment at the vesting date for each of the following situations:**

  (i) **The fair value of a share was $5 and all eligible directors exercised their share options immediately.**

  (ii) **The fair value of a share was $1.50 and all eligible directors allowed their share options to lapse.**

Test your understanding 2 – Asif

Asif has set up an employee option scheme to motivate its sales team of ten key sales people. Each sales person was offered 1 million options exercisable at 10c, conditional upon the employee remaining with the company during the vesting period of 5 years. The options are then exercisable three weeks after the end of the vesting period.

This is year two of the scheme. At the end of year one, two sales people suggested that they would be leaving the company during the second year. However, although one did leave, the other recommitted to the company and the scheme. The other employees have always been committed to the scheme and stated their intention to stay with the company during the 5 years. Relevant market values are as follows:

Date	Share price	Option price
Grant date	10c	20c
End of Year One	24c	38c
End of Year Two	21c	33c

The option price is the market price of an equivalent marketable option on the relevant date.

Show the effect of the scheme on the financial statements of Asif for Year Two.

Illustration: Equity-settled share-based payment transactions

JJ grants 100 share options to each of its 20 employees providing they meet performance targets for each of the next two years. At the end of the first year, it was estimated that 80% of the employees would meet the targets over both years. Improved performance meant that at the end of the second year it turned out that 85% of employees had done so.

The fair value of the option at the grant date was $10.

Calculate the charge to profits for each year.

Solution

At the end of year 1, 16 employees are eligible for the shares (20 × 80%).

The fair value of the options is: 100 × 16 × $10 = $16,000

This is spread over the two-year vesting period, so the charge to profits $8,000 ($16,000/2).

Dr Staff costs (profit or loss)	$8,000
Cr Equity	$8,000

At the end of the second year, 17 employees are eligible for shares (20 × 85%). This is the vesting date, so these 17 employees will receive share options.

The fair value of the options is: 100 × 17 × $10 = $17,000

$8,000 has already been charged to profits in the previous year, so to increase the charge and the corresponding equity balance, the charge for the second year is $9,000.

Dr Staff costs	$9,000
Cr Equity	$9,000

Test your understanding 3 - Blueberry

On 1 January 20X4 an entity, Blueberry, granted share options to each of its 200 employees, subject to a three-year vesting period, provided that the volume of sales increases by a minimum of 5% per annum throughout the vesting period. A maximum of 300 share options per employee will vest, dependent upon the increase in the volume of sales throughout each year of the vesting period as follows:

- If the volume of sales increases by between 5% and up to 10% each year, each eligible employee will receive 100 share options.
  If the volume of sales increases by from over 10% up to 15% each year, each eligible employee will receive 200 share options.

- If the volume of sales increases over 15% each year, each eligible employee will receive 300 share options.

At the grant date, Blueberry estimated that the fair value of each option was $10 and that the increase in the volume of sales each year would be between 10% and 15%. It was also estimated that a total of 22% of employees would leave prior to the end of the vesting period. At each reporting date within the vesting period, the situation was as follows:

Reporting date	Employees leaving in year	Further leavers expected prior to vesting date	Annual increase in sales volume for the year	Expected rate of future increase in sales volume over remaining vesting period	Average annual increase in sales volume to date
31 Dec X4	8	18	14%	14%	14%
31 Dec X5	6	4	18%	16%	(14% +18%)/2 = 16%
31 Dec X6	2		16%		(14% +18% +16%)/3 = 16%

Required:

Identify the annual charge to profit or loss, together with the amount and classification of the amount included on the statement of financial position for each reporting date within the vesting period.

3 Cash-settled share-based payment transactions

Examples of cash-settled share-based payment transactions include:

- share appreciation rights (SARs), where employees become entitled to a future cash payment based on the increase in the entity's share price from a specified level over a specified period of time

- those where employees are granted a right to shares that are redeemable. This gives them a right to receive a future payment of cash.

The basic principle is that the entity measures the goods or services acquired and the liability incurred at the **fair value of the liability**.

- Until the liability is settled, the entity remeasures the fair value of the liability at each reporting date until the liability is settled up to the date of settlement. (Notice that this is different from accounting for equity share-based payments, where the fair value is fixed at the grant date.)

- Changes in the fair value of the liability are recognised in profit or loss for the period. The fair value of a SAR comprises the intrinsic value (cash amount payable based upon the share price) together with the time value of money.

- Where services are received, (for example in return for SARs) these are recognised over the period that the employees render the services i.e the vesting period. (This is the same principle as for equity-settled transactions).

- The expense recognised in each accounting period has a double entry to a provision/liability account. On the vesting date, the amount of the provision/liability should equal the cash expected to be paid.

- When SARs are exercised, they are accounted for as an expense based upon their intrinsic value at the exercise date. i.e the amount of cash that is actually paid. Note that the fair value of a SAR could exceed the intrinsic value at any specific date during the exercise period as this reflects the rights of SARs holders to participate in future gains.

- At the end of the exercise period, any SARs not yet exercised must be exercised. At that date, the intrinsic value of the SAR will equal fair value of a SAR which will comprise wholly of its intrinsic value. The liability will be cleared, with any remaining balance taken to profit or loss.

Illustration 2 – Cash-settled share-based payment transactions

On 1 January 20X1 an entity grants 100 cash share appreciation rights (SAR) to each of its 300 employees, on condition that they continue to work for the entity until 31 December 20X3.

During 20X1, 20 employees leave. The entity estimates that a further 40 will leave during 20X2 and 20X3.

During 20X2, 10 employees leave. The entity estimates that a further 20 will leave during 20X3.

During 20X3, 10 employees leave.

The fair values of one SAR for each year are shown below.

	Fair value
	$
20X1	10.00
20X2	12.00
20X3	15.00

Calculate the amount to be recognised as an expense for each of the three years ended 31 December 20X3 and the liability to be recognised in the statement of financial position at 31 December for each of the three years.

Solution

Year	Liability at year-end $000	Expense for year $000
20X1 ((300 – 20 – 40) × 100 × 10 × 1/3)	80	80
20X2 ((300 – 20 – 10 – 20) × 100 × 12 × 2/3)	200	120
20X3 ((300 – 20 – 10 – 10) × 100 × 15)	390	190

Test your understanding 4 – Growler

On 1 January 20X4 Growler granted 200 cash share appreciation rights (SARs) to each of its 500 employees, on condition that they continue to work for the entity for four years. At 1 January 20X4, the entity expects that, based upon past experience, 5% of that number is expected to leave each year.

During 20X4, 20 employees leave, and the entity expects that this number will leave in each future year of the scheme.

During 20X5, 24 employees leave, and the entity expects that a total of 44 employees will leave over the remaining two-year period of the scheme.

During 20X6, eighteen employees leave, with a further 20 expected to leave in the final year. During 20X7, only 10 employees leave

The fair value and intrinsic value of each SAR was as follows:

Reporting date	FV per SAR	Intrinsic value per SAR
31 December 20X4	$5	
31 December 20X5	$7	
31 December 20X6	$8	
31 December 20X7	$9	
31 December 20X8	$12	$10
31 December 20X9	$11	$11

Required:

(a) **Calculate the amount to be recognised as a remuneration expense in the statement of profit or loss and other comprehensive income, together with the liability to be recognised in the statement of financial position for each of the four years of the scheme, commencing with the reporting date 31 December 20X4.**

(b) **Calculate the amount to be recognised as a remuneration expense and reported as a liability in the financial statements for each of the two years ended 31 December 20X8 and 20X9.**

Hybrid transactions

Some share-based payment transactions give either the reporting entity or the other party the choice of settling in cash or in equity instruments.

IFRS 2 states that if the entity has incurred a liability to settle in cash or other assets, the transaction should be accounted for as a cash-settled share-based payment transaction. Otherwise, it should be accounted for as an equity-settled share-based payment transaction.

Group cash-settled share-based payment transactions

In June 2009, the IASB issued a clarification of accounting for group cash-settled share-based payment transactions. The amendments respond to requests the IASB received to clarify how an individual subsidiary in a group should account for some share-based payment arrangements in its own financial statements.

In these arrangements, the subsidiary receives goods or services from employees or suppliers but its parent or another entity in the group must pay those suppliers.

The amendments issued today clarify:

- the scope of IFRS 2. An entity that receives goods or services in a share-based payment arrangement must account for those goods or services no matter which entity in the group settles the transaction, and no matter whether the transaction is settled in shares or cash.

- the interaction of IFRS 2 and other standards. The Board clarified that in IFRS 2 a 'group' has the same meaning as in IAS 27 Consolidated and Separate Financial Statements, that is, it includes only a parent and its subsidiaries.

The amendments to IFRS 2 also incorporate guidance previously included in IFRIC 8 Scope of IFRS 2 and IFRIC 11 IFRS 2 – Group and Treasury Share Transactions. As a result, the IASB has withdrawn IFRIC 8 and IFRIC 11.

Disclosures

Entities should disclose information that enables users of the financial statements to understand the nature and extent of share-based payment arrangements that existed during the period. The main disclosures are as follows:

- a description of each type of share-based payment arrangement that existed at any time during the period

- the number and weighted average exercise prices of share options:
    - (i) outstanding at the beginning of the period
    - (ii) granted during the period
    - (iii) forfeited during the period
    - (iv) exercised during the period
    - (v) expired during the period
    - (vi) outstanding at the end of the period
    - (vii) exercisable at the end of the period.

- for share options exercised during the period, the weighted average share price at the date of exercise

- for share options outstanding at the end of the period, the range of exercise prices and weighted average remaining contractual life.

IFRS 2 also requires disclosure of information that enables users of the financial statements to understand how the fair value of the goods or services received, or the fair value of the equity instruments granted, during the period was determined.

Entities should also disclose information that enables users of the financial statements to understand the effect of share-based payment transactions on the entity's profit or loss for the period and on its financial position, that is:

- the total expense recognised for the period arising from share-based payment transactions

- for liabilities arising from share-based payment transactions:
  - the total carrying amount at the end of the period
  - the total intrinsic value at the end of the period of liabilities for which the counterparty's right to cash or other assets had vested by the end of the period.

Modifications, cancellations and settlements

Modifications to the terms on which equity instruments are granted

An entity may alter the terms and conditions of share option schemes during the vesting period.

- For example, it might increase or reduce the exercise price of the options, which makes the scheme less favourable or more favourable to employees.

- It might also change the vesting conditions, to make it more likely or less likely that the options will vest.

The general rule is that, apart from dealing with reductions due to failure to satisfy vesting conditions, the entity must **always** recognise at least the amount that would have been recognised if the terms and conditions had not been modified (that is, if the original terms had remained in force).

- If the change reduces the amount that the employee will receive, there is no reduction in the expense recognised in profit or loss.

- If the change increases the amount that the employee will receive, the difference between the fair value of the new arrangement and the fair value of the original arrangement (the incremental fair value) must be recognised as a charge to profit. The extra cost is spread over the period from the date of the change to the vesting date.

Illustration: Modifications

An entity grants 100 share options to each of its 500 employees, provided that they remain in service over the next three years. The fair value of each option is $20.

During year one, 50 employees leave. The entity estimates that a further 60 employees will leave during years two and three.

At the end of year one the entity reprices its share options because the share price has fallen. The other vesting conditions remain unchanged. At the date of repricing, the fair value of each of the original share options granted (before taking the repricing into account) was $10. The fair value of each repriced share option is $15.

During year two, a further 30 employees leave. The entity estimates that a further 30 employees will leave during year three.

During year three, a further 30 employees leave.

Calculate the amounts to be recognised in the financial statements for each of the three years of the scheme.

Solution

The repricing means that the total fair value of the arrangement has increased and this will benefit the employees. This in turn means that the entity must account for an increased remuneration expense. The increased cost is based upon the difference in the fair value of the option, immediately before and after the repricing. Under the original arrangement, the fair value of the option at the date of repricing was $10, which increased to $15 following the repricing of the options, for each share estimated to vest. The additional cost is recognised over the remainder of the vesting period (years two and three).

The amounts recognised in the financial statements for each of the three years are as follows:

	Amount included in equity	Expense
	$	$
Year one Original (500 – 50 – 60) × 100 × 20 × 1/3	260,000	260,000
Year two Original (500 – 50 – 30 – 30) × 100 × 20 × 2/3	520,000	260,000
Incremental (500 – 50 – 30 – 30) × 100 × 5 × 1/2	97,500	97,500
	617,500	357,500
Year three Original (500 – 50 – 30 – 30) × 100 × 20	780,000	260,000
Incremental (500 – 50 – 30 – 30) × 100 × 5	195,000	97,500
	975,000	357,500

Further illustration

An entity grants 100 share options to each of the 15 employees in its sales team, on condition that they remain in service over the next three years. There is also a performance condition: the team must sell more than 40,000 units of a particular product over the three-year period. At the grant date the fair value of each option is $20.

During Year 2, the entity increases the sales target to 70,000 units. By the end of Year 3, only 60,000 units have been sold and the share options do not vest.

All 15 employees remain with the entity for the full three years.

Calculate the amounts to be recognised in the financial statements for each of the three years of the scheme.

Solution

IFRS 2 states that when a share option scheme is modified, the entity must recognise, as a minimum, the services received, measured at the fair value at the grant date. The employees have not met the modified sales target, but **did** meet the original target set on grant date.

This means that the entity must recognise the expense that it would have incurred had the original scheme continued in force.

The total amount recognised in equity is $30,000 (15 × 100 × 20). The entity recognises an expense of $10,000 for each of the three years.

Cancellations and settlements

An entity may also cancel or settle a share option scheme before vesting date. In a settlement, the employees receive compensation because the scheme is cancelled.

- If the cancellation or settlement occurs during the vesting period, the entity immediately recognises the amount that would otherwise have been recognised for services received over the vesting period (an acceleration of vesting).

- Any payment made to employees up to the fair value of the equity instruments granted at cancellation or settlement date is accounted for as a deduction from equity (repurchase of an equity interest).

- Any payment made to employees in excess of the fair value of the equity instruments granted at cancellation or settlement date is accounted for as an expense.

IFRS 2 specified the accounting treatment when an entity cancels a grant of equity instruments. However, it did not state how cancellations by a party other than the entity should be accounted for. The standard was amended in 2008 and clarifies that all cancellations, whether by the entity or by other parties, should receive the same accounting treatment.

UK syllabus focus

The ACCA UK syllabus contains a requirement that candidates should be able to discuss and apply the key differences between UK GAAP and IFRS GAAP. UK FRS 20 and IFRS 2 essentially use the same definitions and apply the same accounting requirements.

4 Chapter summary

Share-based payment
- What it is
- Types of transaction
- Basic principles

Equity-settled share-based payment transactions
- Measurement
- Allocating the expense to reporting periods

Cash-settled share-based payment transactions
- Measurement
- Accounting treatment

Modifications, cancellations and settlements
- Accounting treatment of modifications
- Accounting treatment of cancellations and settlements

Test your understanding answers

Test your understanding 1 – Beginner

Year		Expense	Amount included in equity
		$000	$000
Rep date year 1	(7m × 30c × 1/3)	700	700
Rep date year 2	(8m × 30c × 2/3)	900	1,600
Rep date year 3	(9m × 30c)	1,100	2,700

Note: the expense is measured using the fair value of the option at the grant date, i.e. the start of year one.

Part b(i) - all eligible directors exercised their options:

	$m	Satisfied by:	$m
Cash paid (9m × $2)	18.0	NV of shares (9m × $1)	9.0
Use of equity reserve	2.7	Share premium (balancing figure)	11.7
	–––––		–––––
	20.7		20.7
	–––––		–––––

Part b(ii) - no options are exercised

The equity reserve remains on the statement of financial position. An entity can choose whether or not it wants to make a transfer to retained earnings for the amount of the equity reserve.

Test your understanding 2 – Asif

The expense is measured using the fair value of the option at the grant date, i.e. 20c.

At the end of year two the amount recognised in equity should be $720,000 (1m × (10 – 1) × 20c × 2/5).

At the beginning of year two the amount recognised in equity would have been $320,000 (1m × 8 × 20c × 1/5).

The charge to profit for Year Two is the difference between the two: $400,000 (720 – 320).

Test your understanding 3 - Blueberry

Reporting date	Estimate of eligible employees	calculation of equity reserve	SOFP equity reserve	PorL expense	Note
			$	$	
31 Dec X4	(200 – 8 – 18) = 174	(174 × 200 × $10) × 1/3	116,000	116,000	1
31 Dec X5	(200 – 8 – 6 – 4) = 182	(182 × 300 × $10) × 2/3	364,000	248,000	2
31 Dec X6	(200 – 8 – 6 – 2) = 184	(184 × 300 × $10) × 3/3	552,000	188,000	3

Notes:

(1) At 31/12/X4 a total of 26 employees are expected to leave by the vesting date and Blueberry estimates that average annual growth in sales volume will be 14%. Consequently, it is estimated that eligible employees would each receive 200 share options at the vesting date

(2) At 31/12/X5, a total of 18 employees are expected to leave by the vesting date and Blueberry estimates that the average growth in sales volume will be 16%. Consequently, it is estimated that eligible employees will each receive 300 share options at the vesting date.

(3) A t 31/12/X65, it is known that total of 16 employees have left at some point during the vesting period, leaving 184 eligible employees. As average annual growth in sales volume over the vesting period was 16%, eligible employees are entitles to 300 share option each.

Test your understanding 4 – Growler

Part (a)

The liability is remeasured at each reporting date, based upon the current information available relating to known and expected leavers, together with the fair value of the SAR at each date. The remuneration expense recognised is the movement in the liability from one reporting date to the next as summarised below:

Reporting date	Workings	SOFP – liability	Change in liability	SOCI – expense
		$	$	$
31/12/20X4	(500 – 20 – 20 – 20 – 20) = 420 × 200 × $5 × 1/4	105,000		105,000
31/12/20X5	(500 – 20 – 24 – 44) = 412 × 200 × $7 × 2/4	288,400	288,400 – 105,000	183,400
31/12/20X6	(500 – 20 – 24 – 18 – 20) = 418 × 200 × $8 × 3/4	501,600	501,600 – 288,400	213,200
31/12/20X7	(500 – 20 – 24 – 18 – 10) = 428 × 200 × $9 × 4/4	770,400	770,400 – 501,600	268,800

Part (b)

The liability is measured at each reporting date, based upon the current information available at that date, together with the fair value of each SAR at that date. Any SARs exercised are reflected at their intrinsic value at the date of exercise.

Reporting date	Workings	SOFP	SOCI
		$	$
31/12/20X7	Bal b/fwd from part (a) above	770.400	
31/12/20X8	Bal c/fwd: (428 × 50% ×200 × $12)	513,600	
			(256,800)
	SARs exercised (428 × 50% ×200 × $10)		428,000
	Charge to profit or loss		172,000
31/12/20X9	Bal b/fwd from 31 December 20X8	513,600	
	Liability extinguished	Nil	
			(513,600)
	SARs exercised (428 × 50% ×200 × $11)		470,800
	Released to profit or loss		(42,800)

Related parties

Chapter learning objectives

Upon completion of this chapter you will be able to:

- determine the parties considered to be related to an entity
- identify the implications of related party relationships and the need for disclosure.

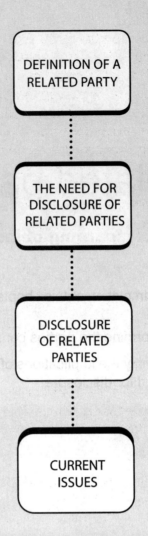

 1 Definition of a related party

 IAS 24 **Related party disclosures**, as revised in November 2009, states that a party (an individual or an entity) is related to another entity if it:

- controls, is controlled by, or is under common control with the entity
- has significant influence over the entity
- has joint control over the entity
- is an associate of the entity
- is a joint venture of the entity
- is a member of the key management personnel of the entity or its parent
- is a close family member of anyone with control, joint control or significant influence over the entity or of any members of key management personnel
- is controlled, jointly controlled or significantly influenced by any individual referred to above
- is a post-employment benefit plan for the benefit of employees of the entity or any of its other related parties.

IAS 24 was revised in November 2009. Previously, if a government controlled, or significantly influenced, an entity, that entity was required to disclose information about all transactions with other entities controlled, or significantly influenced by the same government. The revised standard still requires disclosures that are important to users of financial statements but eliminates requirements to disclose information that is costly to gather and of less value to users. It achieves this balance by requiring disclosure about these transactions only if they are individually or collectively significant.

Similarly, the revised definition introduces symmetry in the definition to either identify two entities as either being related or not related, from whichever perspective is considered. The main amendments to the definition are:

(1) The inclusion of:

   –   the relationship between a subsidiary and an associate of the same parent, in the individual financial statements of both the subsidiary and the associate.

   –   two entities where one is an investee of a member of key management personnel (KMP) and the other is the entity managed by the person that is a member of KMP.

(2) The removal of:

   –   situations in which two entities are related to each other because a person has significant influence over one entity and a close member of the family of that person has significant influence over the other entity.

The most common related party relationship occurs where one entity controls or has significant influence over the other.

Related parties

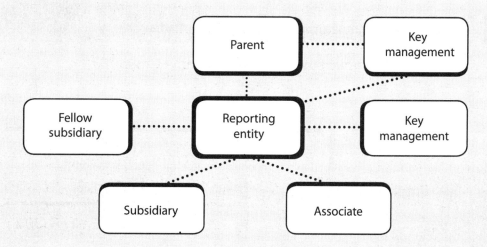

Further detail on definitions

IAS 24 adopts the updated definitions of control, joint control and significant influence as contained within IFRS 10, IFRS 11 and IAS 28 (revised) respectively.

Note that control and significant influence can be:

- direct, where an entity owns the majority of equity shares in a subsidiary, or

- indirect, where an entity owns the majority of equity shares in subsidiary 1 which, in turn, owns the majority of equity shares in subsidiary 2, Through its direct control of subsidiary 1, which itself has direct control over subsidiary 2, parent has 'indirect' control over subsidiary 2.

Key management personnel are those persons having authority and responsibility for planning, directing and controlling the activities of the entity. They include executive and non-executive **directors**.

In many situations it is easy to identify a related party relationship. For example, a subsidiary is clearly a related party of its parent. In more complicated situations it may be necessary to consider whether the parties are included in the list in the definition; and to consider the basic principle of control and influence.

What actually happens in practice within a relationship is often important. For example, two entities that have a single director in common are not necessarily related parties. A related party relationship only exists if it can be shown that the director is able to influence the policies of both entities in their mutual dealings.

Test your understanding 1 Group structures

The following group structure relates to the A Group:

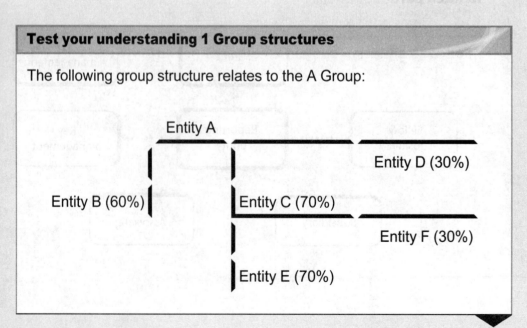

Required:

Identify the related party relationships for each of the entities within the group structure.

Test your understanding 2 – Individual shareholdings

Consider each of the following situations:

(A)

Entity A (70%)   Entity B (30%)

Mr P controls entity A and is able to exert significant influence over entity B.

(B)

Mr P

Entity A (25%)   Entity B (30%)

Mr P is able to exert significant influence over entity A and entity B.

Required:

For each situation explain whether or not entity A and entity B are related parties.

Test your understanding 3 - Key management personnel

Consider the following situation:

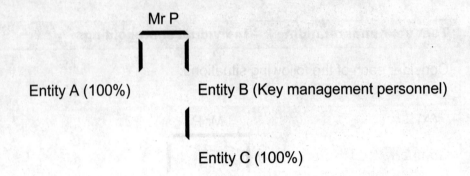

Mr P owns all of the issued share capital of entity A. He also is a member of the key management personnel of entity B which, in turn, owns all of the issued share capital of entity C.

Required:

Identify the related parties within the above structure.

Test your understanding 4 - Family members

Consider the following situation:

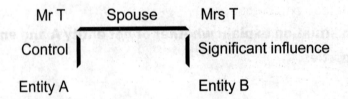

Mr T controls entity A and his spouse Mrs T exercises significant influence over entity B.

Required:

Determine whether entity A and entity B are related parties.

2 The need for disclosure of related parties

A **related party transaction** is the transfer of resources, services or obligations between related parties, regardless of whether a price is charged.

- Transactions between related parties are a normal feature of business.
- However, a related party relationship can affect the performance and financial position of an entity as shown by its financial statements.

Illustration

Company A owns 75% of the equity shares of B. B supplies goods to A at prices significantly below market rate. As a result, the profit of B is less than it would have been if it had been free to sell all its goods to a third party.

The performance of B is not comparable with that of a similar company which is not subject to the same restrictions.

- Users of the financial statements need to be made aware of any related party transactions that have occurred.
- They also need to be made aware of the existence of related party relationships even where there have been no transactions during the period.

Examples of related party transactions

Related party transactions could include:

- purchases or sales of goods
- purchases or sales of non-current assets
- giving or receiving of services e.g. accounting or management services
- leasing arrangements, e.g. allowing the use of an asset
- transfers of research and development
- financing arrangements (including loans)
- provision of guarantees or collateral
- settlement of liabilities on behalf of the entity.

Directors may not want to disclose related party relationships and transactions. Sometimes this is because they believe that disclosure will give users of the financial statements the impression of poor stewardship or wrong-doing The reason why transactions and relationships must be disclosed is that users need to be made aware of them. If they are not disclosed, users may assume that the entity has entered into all its transactions on the same terms that it could have obtained from a third party (on an arms' length basis) and that it has acted in its own interests throughout the period. They will then assess the entity's results and position on this basis and may be misled as a result.

A related party relationship can affect the financial position and operating results of an entity in a number of ways, particularly in a group situation.

- An entity may enter into transactions which may not have occurred if the relationship did not exist, e.g. a subsidiary may sell most of its production to its parent, where it might have found an alternative customer if the parent company had not purchased the goods.

- An entity may enter into transactions on different terms from those with an unrelated party, e.g. a subsidiary may lease equipment to another group company on terms imposed by the parent, possibly at a low rent or for no rent.

- Transactions with third parties may be affected by the existence of the relationship, e.g. a parent could instruct a subsidiary to sell goods to a particular customer or to close down a particular operation.

3 Disclosure of related parties

Disclosure of related parties

IAS 24 requires that relationships between parents and subsidiaries, together with joint arrangements and associates and joint ventures, are disclosed including the:

- name of the parent
- name of the ultimate controlling party (if different)
- nature of the relationship.

This will apply regardless of whether or not any transactions have taken place between the parties during the period.

Note that an entity must disclose the name of its parent and, if different, the ultimate controlling entity that prepares financial statements available to the public.

KAPLAN PUBLISHING

Note also that there are no exemptions from disclosure of related parties, and any transactions between those parties in the individual financial statements of an entity. There is some exemption from disclosure permitted in respect of information included in group financial statements. Typically, the nature and extent of any transactions undertaken by entities under common control are cancelled upon consolidation and would not require disclosure.

IAS 24 does contain an exemption from making disclosure of related party transactions where the related party is a local, national or international government, government agency or similar body. The intention of this exemption is to avoid having to make excessive disclosure of transactions which are likely to be of little value to users of financial statements. However, the existence of the related party relationship should still be disclosed.

Note that entities which are controlled or subjected to joint control or significant influence as defined by IFRS 10, IFRS 11 and IAS 28 (revised) respectively are now subject to the extended disclosure requirements of IFRS 12 Disclosure of interests in other entities. IFRS 12 requires disclosure of the significant judgements and assumptions made in determining whether an investor has control, joint control or significant influence over an investee. This should include sufficient information to enable users of financial statements properly understand the nature of any relationship and how it has been accounted for in the group financial statements.

Disclosure of the relationship is also required in the separate financial statements of each of the related parties.

Note that where control, joint control or significant influence is exercised by an individual (rather than an entity), the same principles apply regarding identification and disclosure of related parties, together with disclosure of any transactions and associated information.

Disclosure of management compensation

Any compensation granted to key management personnel should be disclosed in total and for each of the following categories:

- short-term employee benefits
- post-employment benefits
- other long-term benefits
- termination benefits
- share-based payment.

Disclosure of transactions and balances

If there have been transactions between related parties, and/or there are balances outstanding between the parties, the following should be disclosed, where material:

- the nature of the related party relationship
- a description of the transactions
- the amounts of the transactions
- the amounts and details of any outstanding balances
- allowances for receivables in respect of the outstanding balances
- the irrecoverable debt expense in respect of outstanding balances.

Disclosure should be made whether or not a price is charged.

IAS 1 states that specific information or disclosure need not be provided by a reporting entity where it is considered not to be material. Materiality may be evaluated based upon the size and nature of any potential omission or misstatement that may be contained in the financial statements. Where the related party under consideration is a person, it may be that materiality should also be considered from the perspective of the individual to determine whether there should also be disclosure of transactions that are material to an individual, but not to the reporting entity.

For example, the purchase of lunch by a director at the office refractory may be considered not to be material for disclosure from the perspective of both the director and the reporting entity. However, the purchase of several cars by a director from the reporting entity during the year, whether on fair value terms or not, may be considered to be material from the perspective of the director and disclosed in the financial statements. If any such transaction was on less than fair value terms, it is more likely to be considered to be material and worthy of disclosure in the financial statements.

IAS 24 does not specify that disclosure of the profit or loss arising on one or more related party transactions must be made. However, this may be necessary in certain circumstances in order to enable users of financial statements to gain a full understanding of the nature of any related party relationship, the transactions entered into and their impact upon the financial statements.

Further detail on disclosures

The existence of a parent/subsidiary relationship should be disclosed even where transactions have been entered into on normal commercial terms or where there have been no transactions at all. This information alerts users to the possibility that the entity's performance and position could be affected by related party transactions in future.

Further detail

All the disclosures required must be made separately for each of the following categories:

- the parent
- entities with joint control or significant influence over the entity
- subsidiaries
- associates
- joint ventures in which the entity is a venturer
- key management personnel
- other related parties.

Intra-group transactions

Transactions between a parent and a subsidiary are disclosed in their separate financial statements. Intra-group transactions are eliminated from the consolidated financial statements and therefore no disclosure is necessary in the group accounts.

IAS 24 is silent on what should happen where a related party relationship existed for only part of the year but transactions between the parties occurred throughout the year. For example, suppose that a group sells a subsidiary part way through the year. Transactions that take place after the sale are not eliminated on consolidation. Should they be disclosed?

The answer is probably yes. For ethical reasons it is advisable to disclose the information. This means that there is no possibility that users of the financial statements could be misled.

Arm's length transactions

IAS 24 states that related party transactions should be described as being made 'at arm's length' only if this can be substantiated, i.e. the transactions were carried out in all respects on the same terms as if they had been with independent third parties. By definition, related party transactions cannot be made at arm's length. Instead, the expressions 'at normal selling prices' or 'on normal commercial terms' should be used where appropriate.

Exemptions

Relationships and transactions with the following do not have to be disclosed since they are deemed not to be related parties in the course of their normal dealings with the entity:

- providers of finance

- trade unions

- utility companies

- government departments and agencies

- customers, suppliers, franchisers, distributors and general agents with whom the entity transacts a significant volume of business.

Test your understanding 5 – Ace

Ace

The objective of IAS 24 **Related party disclosures** is to ensure that an entity's financial statements contain the disclosures necessary to draw attention to the possibility that its financial position and profit or loss may have been affected by the existence of related parties and by transactions and outstanding balances with such parties

On 1 April 20X7, Ace owned 75% of the equity share capital of Deuce and 80% of the equity share capital of Trey. On 1 April 20X8, Ace purchased the remaining 25% of the equity shares of Deuce. In the two years ended 31 March 20X9, the following transactions occurred between the three entities:

(i) On 30 June 20X7 Ace manufactured a machine for use by Deuce. The cost of manufacture was $20,000. The machine was delivered to Deuce for an invoiced price of $25,000. Deuce paid the invoice on 31 August 20X7. Deuce depreciated the machine over its anticipated useful life of five years, charging a full year's depreciation in the year of purchase.

(ii) On 30 September 20X8, Deuce sold some goods to Trey at an invoiced price of $15,000. Trey paid the invoice on 30 November 20X8. The goods had cost Deuce $12,000 to manufacture. By 31 March 20X9, Trey had sold all the goods outside the group.

(iii) For each of the two years ended 31 March 20X9, Ace provided management services to Deuce and Trey. Ace did not charge for these services in the year ended 31 March 20X8 but in the year ended 31 March 20X9 decided to impose a charge of $10,000 per annum to each entity. The amounts of $10,000 are due to be paid by each entity on 31 May 20X9.

Required:

(a) **Explain why related party disclosures are needed.**

(6 marks)

(b) **Summarise the related-party disclosures which will be required in respect of transactions (i) to (iii) above for BOTH of the years ended 31 March 20X8 and 31 March 20X9 in the financial statements of Ace, Deuce and Trey.**

(14 marks)

You may assume that Ace presents consolidated financial statements for BOTH of the years dealt with in the question.

(Total: 20 marks)

UK syllabus focus

The ACCA UK syllabus contains a requirement that candidates should be able to discuss and apply the key differences between UK GAAP and IFRS GAAP. The accounting requirements of UK GAAP and IFRS GAAP are very similar in this area; the key issues associated with UK reporting standard requirements are as follows:

FRS 8 – Related party disclosures. Improvements to FRS 2010, which apply to accounting periods beginning on or after 1 January 2011, has amended FRS 8 to apply the same definition of a related party as contained within IAS 24.

IFRS 8 requires disclosure of related parties, typically group members, and others that are subject to joint control or significant influence. In addition, disclosure is required of **material transactions** – i.e. those which may be reasonably expected to influence decisions by the users of that information. Materiality is considered from the perspective of both the reporting entity and the related party, where the related party is a member of the key management personnel or someone connected to them (FRS 8 para 8).

IAS 24 does not directly address the issue of materiality, although it can be presumed that material related party transactions must be disclosed if the financial statements are to present a true and fair view. This would suggest that materiality is considered from the perspective of the reporting entity only; however, there is an implied requirement to consider materiality from the perspective of both the reporting entity and the related party as disclosure of such transactions is likely to be of interest to some users of financial statements.

FRS 8 requires **disclosure of the name** of any related party where a transaction has occurred. IAS 24 does not require disclosure of the name of the related party, although this may be required by local law or corporate governance regulations, or may even be required to convey a full understanding of the nature of the relationship and any disclosed transaction(s).

FRS 8 **exempts wholly-owned subsidiaries** from making related party transaction disclosures in its own accounts in respect of transactions with the parent company. Also, a parent company is exempt from making any related party disclosures in its own accounts, provided that the disclosures are included in the group financial statements. There are no such exemptions contained within IAS 24.

There is no **exemption for state-controlled entities** from disclosure of related party transactions and associated information within FRS 8, whereas there is exemption for such entities within IAS 24.

During 2008, amendments were made to FRS 8 following the introduction of the Companies Act 2006. Key management personnel are defined as: "Those persons having authority and responsibility for planning, directing, and controlling the activities of the entity, directly or indirectly, including any director (whether executive or otherwise) of that entity.

4 Chapter summary

Reporting not-for-profit entities
- These entities are in the public sector or are charities
- The objectives of these entities is to achieve their aims, not to make a profit
- Guidance is provided in SORP 2005 and the ASB's don't Statement of Principles for public benefit entities

The need for disclosure of related parties
- Users need to be aware of related party relationships
  - Users need to know which transactions have not been made at arm's length

Disclosure of related parties
- Parent/subsidiary relationships
- Disclosure of transactions and balances
- Key management compensation

Current issues
Amended standard expected in 2008 which clarifies existing requirements

Test your understanding answers

Test your understanding 1 Group structures

Related party relationships are defined by IAS 24 s9 and are typically characterised by being one party being able to exercise control or significant influence over another. Where a related party relationship exists it should be disclosed in the individual financial statements of an entity, and also the group accounts where applicable.

If each entity is considered in turn:

Entity A:

Entities which are under common control are related parties of entity A; this identifies entities B, C and E as being related to entity A. Entity A is also able to exert significant influence over entities D and F; this identifies entities D and F as being related to entity A. All of these related parties should be disclosed in the individual financial statements of entity A.

Entities B, C and E are consolidated into the group accounts of entity A and do not require disclosure as related parties in the group accounts. Entities D and F which are subject to significant influence from members of the same corporate group should be disclosed as related parties in the group financial statements,

Entity B:

Entities which are under common control are related parties of entity B; this identifies entities A, C and E as being related to entity B. Entities D and F which are subject to significant influence from an entity within the same corporate group are also identified as being a related party of entity B.

Entity C:

Entities which are under common control are related parties of entity C; this identifies entities A, B and E as being related to entity C. Entities D and F which are subject to significant influence from an entity within the same corporate group are also identified as being a related party of entity C.

Entity D:

Entity A is able to exercise significant influence over entity D and is therefore a related party of entity D. Entity A is part of the same corporate group as entities B, C and E and consequently they are also identified as related parties of entity D. As an associate of entity C, entity F is not subject to control or influence from entity D, nor is it able to exercise control or influence over entity D; entity F is not a related party of entity D,

Entity E:

Entities which are under common control are related parties of entity E; this identifies entities A, B and C as being related to entity E. Entities D and F which are subject to significant influence from an entity within the same corporate group are also identified as being a related party of entity E.

Entity F:

Entity C is able to exercise significant influence over entity F and is therefore a related party of entity F. Entity C is part of the same corporate group as entities A, B and E and consequently they are also identified as related parties of entity F. As an associate of entity C, entity F is not subject to control or influence from entity D, nor is it able to exercise control or influence over entity D; entity D is not a related party of entity F,

Note that IFRS 12 Disclosure of interests in other entities requires disclosure of the nature and extent of shareholdings in other entities, together with recognition and measurement criteria.

Test your understanding 2 – Individual shareholdings

Situation A:

Mr P is a related party of both entity A and entity B as he is able to exercise either control or significant influence over each entity. Consequently, entities A and B are also related parties. The financial statements of each entity should therefore disclose the existence of the related party relationship with the other entity, and also with Mr P. Having disclosed each of the related party relationships, details of any transactions undertaken during the reporting period should also be disclosed.

Situation B:

Mr P is a related party of both entity A and entity B as he is able to exercise significant influence over each entity. The financial statements of each entity should therefore disclose the existence of the related party relationship with Mr P. Having disclosed each of the related party relationship, details of any transactions undertaken during the reporting period should also be disclosed. Note that entities A and B are not related solely due to the same investor having significant influence in each entity.

Test your understanding 3 - Key management personnel

Entity A:

Mr P is able to control entity A - Mr P is therefore a related party of entity A. Entity B is also a related party of entity A due to the fact that Mr P controls one entity and is also one of the key management personnel of the other entity. Entity C is also a related party of entity A as it is controlled by an entity which includes Mr P as one of its key management personnel.

Entity B:

Mr P is able to exercise significant influence over entity B - Mr P is therefore a related party of entity B. Entity A is also a related party of entity B due to the fact that Mr P controls one entity and is also one of the key management personnel of the other entity. Entity C is also a related party of entity B as it is controlled by an entity which includes Mr P as one of its key management personnel.

Entity B must also prepare group financial statements as it has a subsidiary. For the group financial statements, entity A is a related party.

Entity C:

Entity A is a related party as it is controlled by Mr P, who is also one of the key management personnel who controls entity B, which controls entity C.

Test your understanding 4 - Family members

Answer:

Entities A and B are related as they are under the control of, or subject to significant influence from, two connected persons. There should be disclosure of the related party relationship in the financial statements of both entity A and entity B.

Test your understanding 5 – Ace

Answer – Ace

(a) The financial statements would be very difficult to understand if readers were not informed of any related party relationships and transactions. For example, cost or selling prices could be distorted by the fact that goods are being purchased from or sold to a related party. In extreme cases, this might be part of a deliberate strategy to manipulate the apparent profitability of one or other party. For example, one person might own two businesses and might have one sell to the other at a premium or a discount. This could make one business appear more profitable if the owner ever decides to sell it. There could also be tax advantages to making one generate a profit and the other a loss.

Related party disclosures may be enough to enable a reader to adjust for the effects of any mispricing or other concessions and thereby obtain a better insight into the true profitability of the entity. Even if this is impossible, it is useful to know that such an adjustment might be necessary.

The fact that a business has a related party could be enough in itself to require some disclosure. For example, the fact that a business can be compelled to enter into an agreement that may be contrary to its interests is potentially relevant to a reader who presumes or expects that the reported profit or loss for an accounting period is a fair reflection of overall profitability in the absence of any information to the contrary.

Knowledge of the related parties could also be important from a stewardship perspective. Shareholders might want to raise questions about these transactions at the annual general meeting.

IAS 24 requires consideration of the substance of any possible related party relationship, not merely its legal form, to determine whether or not there is a related party relationship that warrants disclosure. Other than for parent and subsidiary relationships, IAS 24 does not specifically require disclosure of the name of any related party. However, IFRS 12 Disclosure of interests in other entities has extensive disclosure requirements regarding the assumptions and judgements used to determine the status of any investment in another entity and how it has been accounted for within the group financial statements. IFRS 12 also requires disclosure of the name of principal subsidiaries, associates and joint arrangements accounted for within the group financial statements.

(b) **Disclosure of related party transactions**

The first step is to determine whether related party relationships existed between the three entities during each of the two accounting periods.

Year ended 31 March 20X8

Ace owns 75% of the equity share capital of Deuce and 80% of the equity share capital of Trey. This means that both subsidiaries are related parties of Ace, as it controls both of them. (An entity is regarded as a related party of another entity if it is able to exercise control joint control or significant influence over that other entity.)

Deuce and Trey are also related parties of each other as they are under common control. In the financial statements of Deuce, it should disclose both Trey and Ace as related parties, and also disclose that Ace is the parent entity that prepares group financial statements for publication. In the financial statements of Trey, it should disclose both Deuce and Ace as related parties, and also disclose that Ace is the parent entity that prepares group financial statements.

Year ended 31 March 20X9

From 1 April 20X8, Ace owns 100% of the equity share capital of Deuce and 80% of the equity share capital of Trey. Therefore all three entities are still related parties of each other. Each entity should again disclose the other two entities as related parties in the same way as in the financial statements for the year ended 31 March 20X8.

KAPLAN PUBLISHING

For both years Ace, as a parent entity, would not normally publish separate entity financial statements; it would publish group financial statements only. Consequently the following sets of financial statements are relevant for each year:

– the group financial statements of Ace

– the individual financial statements of Deuce

– the individual financial statements of Trey.

Related party disclosures

The following details of each related party transaction are required:

– description of the relationship between the parties

– description of the transaction and the amounts involved (including the fair value of the transaction if this is different from the actual value)

– any amounts due to or from related parties at the year end (including any doubtful debts)

– any amounts written off related party receivables

– any other information necessary for an understanding of the transaction and its effect on the financial statements.

It is assumed that all the related party transactions are material, although it is possible to aggregate identical or similar transactions, provided that this does not obscure a full understanding of the nature of any related party relationship or transaction.

The transactions are summarised in the following table:

Year ended 31 March 20X8

	Ace: group financial statements	Deuce	Trey
(i) Sale of machine by Ace to Deuce on 30 June 20X7.	Transaction and profit eliminated on consolidation. No disclosure of transaction required.	Disclose purchase of machine from parent at $25,000. No balance outstanding at the reporting date to disclose.	
(ii) Sale of goods by Deuce to Trey on 30 September 20X8			
(iii) Management services provided by Ace to both Deuce and Trey	Transactions would be eliminated on consolidation if there was a charge made. No disclosure of transactions required.	Disclose purchase of management services from parent at no charge.	Disclose purchase of management services from parent at no charge.

Note that IAS 24 does not specifically require disclosure of the profit or loss arising on any related party transaction, although it may be necessary to provide this information to enable users to understand the potential impact of the relationship on the financial statements.

Year ended 31 March 20X9

		Ace: group financial statements	Deuce	Trey
(i)	Sale of machine by Ace to Deuce on 30 June 20X7.	No disclosure as transaction completed.		
(ii)	Sale of goods by Deuce to Trey on 30 September 20X8.	Transaction eliminated on consolidation. No disclosure of transaction required.	Disclose sale of goods to fellow subsidiary for $15,000. No balance outstanding at the reporting date to disclose.	Disclose purchase of goods from fellow subsidiary for $15,000. No balance outstanding at the reporting date to disclose.
(iii)	Management services provided by Ace to both Deuce and Trey	Transaction eliminated on consolidation. No disclosure of transactions required.	Disclose purchase of management services from parent for $10,000. Disclose $10,000 due to parent at the reporting date.	Disclose purchase of management services from parent for $10,000. Disclose $10,000 due to parent at the reporting date.

Note that IAS 24 does not specifically require disclosure of the profit or loss arising on any related party transaction, although it may be necessary to provide this information to enable users to understand the potential impact of the relationship on the financial statements.

Segment reporting

Chapter learning objectives

Upon completion of this chapter you will be able to:

- determine the nature and extent of reportable segments
- specify and discuss the nature of segment information to be disclosed.

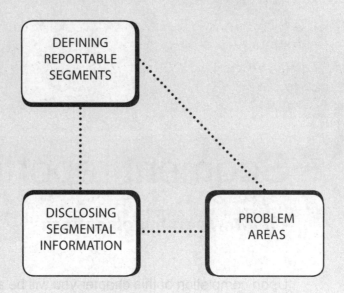

1 Defining reportable segments

Development of IFRS 8

- IFRS 8 was issued in November 2006 and forms part of the joint project between the IASB and the US standards setter, the FASB (Financial Accounting Standards Board).

- IFRS 8 largely adopts the US standard on segment reporting, FASB 131 **Disclosures about segments of an enterprise and related information**. The objective was to reduce differences in segment reporting between IFRS and US GAAP.

Introduction

IFRS 8 **Operating segments** requires an entity to disclose information about each of its operating segments.

- The purpose is to enable users of the financial statements to evaluate the nature and financial effects of the business activities in which it engages and the economic environments in which it operates.

IFRS 8 defines an **operating segment** as a component of an entity:

- that engages in business activities from which it may earn revenues and incur expenses

- whose operating results are regularly reviewed by the entity's chief operating decision maker to make decisions about resources to be allocated to the segment and assess its performance

- for which discrete financial information is available.

Segmental reports are designed to reveal significant information that might otherwise be hidden by the process of presenting a single statement of profit or loss and other comprehensive income and statement of financial position for an entity.

How to define reportable segments

Under IFRS 8 segment information reflects the way that the entity is actually managed. An entity's reportable segments (its operating segments) are those that are used in its internal management reports. Therefore management identifies the operating segments.

- Start-up operations may be operating segments even before they begin to earn revenue.

- A part of an entity that only sells goods to other parts of the entity is a reportable segment if management treats it as one.

- Corporate headquarters and other similar departments do not earn revenue and are therefore not operating segments. An entity's pension plan is not an operating segment.

- Management may use more than one set of segment information. For example, an entity can analyse information by classes of business (different products or services) and by geographical areas.

- If management uses more than one set of segment information, it should identify a **single** set of components on which to base the segmental disclosures. The basis of reporting information should be the one that best enables users to understand the business and the environment in which it operates.

- Operating segments can be combined into one reportable segment provided that they have similar characteristics.

Quantitative thresholds

An entity must separately report information about an operating segment that meets any of the following quantitative thresholds:

- its reported revenue, including both sales to external customers and inter-segment sales, is ten per cent or more of the combined revenue of all operating segments

- its reported profit or loss is ten per cent or more of the greater, in absolute amount, of:
  - the combined reported profit of all operating segments that did not report a loss and
  - the combined reported loss of all operating segments that reported a loss.

- its assets are ten per cent or more of the combined assets of all operating segments.

At least 75% of the entity's external revenue should be included in reportable segments. So if the quantitative test results in segmental disclosure of less than this 75%, other segments should be identified as reportable segments until this 75% is reached.

Information about other business activities and operating segments that are not reportable are combined into an 'all other segments' category.

There is no precise limit to the number of segments that can be disclosed, but if there are more than ten, the resulting information may become too detailed.

 Although IFRS 8 defines a reportable segment in terms of size, size is not the only criterion to be taken into account. There is some scope for subjectivity.

Illustration defining reportable segments

Diverse carries out a number of different business activities. Summarised information is given below.

	Revenue	Profit before tax	Total assets
	$m	$m	$m
Manufacture and sale of computer hardware	83	23	34
Development and supply of bespoke software:			
to users of the company's hardware products	22	12	6
to other users	5	3	1
Technical support and training	10	2	4
Contract work on information technology products	30	10	10
	150	50	55

Which of the company's activities should be identified as separate operating segments?

Illustration solution

Manufacture and sale of computer hardware and contract work on information technology products are clearly reportable segments by virtue of size. Each of these two operations exceeds all three 'ten per cent thresholds'.

On the face of it, it appears that development of bespoke software is a third segment. It would make logical sense for both parts of this operation to be reported together, as supply to users of other hardware forms only three per cent of total revenue and six per cent of total profit before tax.

Although technical support and training falls below all three 'ten per cent thresholds', it should be disclosed as a fourth reportable segment if (as seems likely) management treat it as a separate segment because it has different characteristics from the rest of the business.

Approaches to identify reportable segments

There are two main approaches to identifying reportable segments:

- the 'risks and returns' approach
- the 'managerial' approach.

The 'risks and returns' approach identifies segments on the basis of different risks and returns arising from different lines of business and geographical areas. Broadly speaking, this was the approach adopted by IAS 14 **Segment reporting**, which has been replaced by IFRS 8.

The 'managerial' approach identifies segments corresponding to the internal organisation structure of the entity. This is the approach adopted by IFRS 8.

The 'risks and returns' approach

The 'risks and returns' approach is believed to have the following advantages:

- it produces information that is more comparable between companies and consistent over time than the 'managerial' approach
- it assists in the assessment of profitability and the risks and returns of the component parts of the entity
- it reflects the approach taken in the financial statements for external reporting.

The main disadvantage of the approach is that defining segments can be difficult in practice and also subjective. This affects comparability.

The 'managerial' approach

The 'managerial' approach bases both the segments reported and the information reported about them on the information used internally for decision making. This means that management defines the reportable segments.

Arguments for the 'managerial approach' include the following.

- Segments based on an entity's internal structure are less subjective than those identified by the 'risks and returns' approach.
- It highlights the risks and opportunities that management believes are important.

- It provides information with predictive value because it enables users of the financial statements to see the entity through the eyes of management.

- The cost of providing the information is low (because it should already have been provided for management's use).

- It will produce segment information that is consistent with the way in which management discuss their business in other parts of the annual report (e.g. in the Chairman's Statement and the Operating and Financial Review).

Arguments against the 'managerial approach' include the following.

- Segments based on internal reporting structures are unlikely to be comparable between entities and may not be comparable from year to year for an individual entity. (For example, organisation structures, or the way in which they are perceived, may change as a result of new managers being appointed.)

- The information is likely to be commercially sensitive (because entities are organised strategically).

- In theory, segmental information could be given other than by products or services or geographically. This might be more difficult to analyse.

- Using the managerial approach could lead to segments with different risks and returns being combined.

- Analysts define their area of expertise by industry segment, usually based on product or service. The IAS 14 version of segmental reporting is more likely to reflect these.

However, it should be remembered that for many entities, the risks and returns approach and the managerial approach will probably identify exactly the same reportable segments.

2 Disclosing reportable segments

General information

IFRS 8 requires disclosure of the following.

- Factors used to identify the entity's reportable segments, including the basis of organisation (for example, whether segments are based on products and services, geographical areas or a combination of these).

- The types of products and services from which each reportable segment derives its revenues.

Information about profit or loss and other segment items

For each reportable segment an entity should report:

- a measure of profit or loss
- a measure of total assets
- a measure of total liabilities (if such an amount is regularly used in decision making).

IFRS 8 does not define segment revenue, segment result (profit or loss) or segment assets.

- Therefore, the following amounts must be disclosed if they are included in segment profit or loss:
  - revenues from external customers
  - revenues from inter-segment transactions
  - interest revenue
  - interest expense
  - depreciation and amortisation
  - material items of income and expense (exceptional items)
  - interests in the profit or loss of associates and joint ventures accounted for by the equity method
  - income tax expense
  - material non-cash items other than depreciation or amortisation.
- Interest revenue can be disclosed net of interest expense only if a majority of the segment's revenues are from interest and net interest revenue is used in decision making.
- The following amounts must be disclosed if they are included in segment assets:
  - investments in associates and joint ventures accounted for by the equity method
  - amounts of additions to non-current assets other than financial instruments.
- An entity must provide reconciliations of the totals disclosed in the segment report to the amounts reported in the financial statements as follows:
  - segment revenue
  - segment profit or loss (before tax and discontinued operations unless these items are allocated to segments)

- segment assets

- segment liabilities (if reported)

- any other material item of segment information disclosed.

Entity wide disclosures

IFRS 8 also requires the following disclosures about the entity as a whole, even if it only has one reportable segment.

- The revenues from external customers for each product and service or each group of similar products and services.

- Revenues from external customers split between the entity's country of domicile and all foreign countries in total.

- Non-current assets split between those located in the entity's country of domicile and all foreign countries in total.

- Revenue from a single external customer which amounts to ten per cent or more of an entity's revenue. The identity of the customer does not need to be disclosed.

Measurement

IFRS 8 requires segmental reports to be based on the information reported to and used by management, even where this is prepared on a different basis from the rest of the financial statements.

Therefore, an entity must provide explanations of the measurement of segment profit or loss, segment assets and segment liabilities, including:

- the basis of accounting for any transactions between reportable segments

- the nature of differences between the measurement of segment profit or loss, assets and liabilities and the amounts reported in the financial statements. Differences could result from accounting policies and/or policies for the allocation of common costs and jointly used assets to segments

- the nature of any changes from prior periods in measurement methods

- the nature and effect of any asymmetrical allocations to segments (for example, where an entity allocates depreciation expense but not the related non-current assets).

Preparing segmental reports

The illustration provides a useful format to follow when preparing a segmental report.

Illustration

	Segment A	Segment B	Segment C	Segment D	All other	Totals
	$000	$000	$000	$000	$000	$000
Revenues from external customers	5,000	9,500	12,000	5,000	1,000	32,500
Revenues from inter-segment transactions	–	3,000	1,500	–	–	4,500
Interest revenue	800	1,000	1,500	1,000	–	4,300
Interest expense	600	700	1,100	–	–	2,400
Depreciation and amortisation	100	50	1,500	900	–	2,550
Exceptional costs	–	–	–	200	–	200
Segment profit	70	900	2,300	500	100	3,870
Impairment of assets	200	–		–	–	200
Segment assets	5,000	3,000	12,000	57,000	2,000	79,000
Additions to non-current assets	700	500	800	600	–	2,600
Segment liabilities	3,000	1,800	8,000	30,000	–	42,800

Notes

(1) The 'all other' column shows amounts relating to segments that fall below the quantitative thresholds.

(2) Impairment of assets is disclosed as a material non-cash item.

(3) Comparatives should be provided. These should be restated if an entity changes the structure of its internal organisation so that its reportable segments change, unless the information is not available and the cost of preparing it would be excessive.

3 Problem areas in segmental reporting

Segmental reports can provide useful information, but they also have important limitations.

- IFRS 8 states that segments should reflect the way in which the entity is managed. This means that segments are defined by the directors. Arguably, this provides too much flexibility. It also means that segmental information is only useful for comparing the performance of the same entity over time, not for comparing the performance of different entities.

- Common costs may be allocated to different segments on whatever basis the directors believe is reasonable. This can lead to arbitrary allocation of these costs.

- A segment's operating results can be distorted by trading with other segments on non-commercial terms.

- These limitations have applied to most systems of segmental reporting, regardless of the accounting standard being applied. IFRS 8 requires disclosure of some information about the way in which common costs are allocated and the basis of accounting for inter-segment transactions.

Further problem areas

IFRS 8 was issued relatively recently (November 2006) and will only be fully effective from 2009. Presently, at January 2010, it is too early to say whether it will be more successful than its predecessor, IAS 14. There are some potential problem areas, which are briefly discussed below.

Determining reportable segments

IAS 14 required an entity to prepare two segmental reports: one based on business segments and one based on geographical segments. IFRS 8 only requires one segmental report. If management uses more than one set of segment information, it should identify a single set of components on which to base the segmental disclosures. In practice, this may be both difficult to do, and subjective. For example, some entities adopt a 'matrix' form of organisation in which some managers are responsible for different products worldwide, while others are responsible for particular geographical areas.

Disclosure of segment information

Some information (for example, segment liabilities) is only required if it is regularly provided to the chief operating decision maker. In theory, it would be possible to avoid disclosing 'bad news' or other sensitive information on the grounds that the information was not used in decision making.

Measurement of segment results and segment assets

IFRS 8 does not define segment results and segment assets. Although the standard requires disclosure of certain figures if these are included in the totals, the amounts will not necessarily be measured on the same basis as the amounts in the main financial statements. This may be a particular issue in countries such as the UK, where the consolidated financial statements are prepared using IFRSs but internal financial information may still follow local GAAP. Totals must be reconciled to the main financial statements, but users may still find it difficult to understand the disclosures.

IAS 14 required segmental information to conform with the accounting policies used in the main financial statements.

Changes to the way in which an entity is organised

One of the disadvantages of the IFRS 8 approach is that if a company changes the way in which it is organised, its reportable segments may also change. IFRS 8 requires an entity to restate its comparative information for earlier periods unless the information is not available and the cost of developing it would be excessive. If an entity does not restate its comparative figures, segment information for the current period must be disclosed both on the old basis and on the new basis. The disclosures should help users to understand the effect of the change, but some users may find it difficult to analyse the information, particularly where an entity undergoes frequent restructurings.

Test your understanding 1 – Segments

An entity has prepared the following segmental report:

Operating segments

	Fruit grow'g		Canning		Other		Group	
	20X2	20X1	20X2	20X1	20X2	20X1	20X2	20X1
	$000	$000	$000	$000	$000	$000	$000	$000
Total revenue	13,635	15,188	20,520	16,200	5,400	4,050	39,555	35,438
Less inter-segment revenue.	3,485	1,688	2,970	3,105			6,455	4,793
External. revenue	10,150	13,500	17,550	13,095	5,400	4,050	33,100	30,645
Segment. profit	3,565	3,375	4,725	3,600	412	540	8,702	7,515
Seg. assets	33,750	32,400	40,500	33,750	18,765	17,563	93,015	83,713
Unallocated (common) assets							13,500	11,003
Total assets							106,515	94,716

Required:

Identify areas in which the segmental report provided below does not necessarily result in the disclosure of useful information.

Test your understanding 2 – Tab

Tab has recently acquired four large overseas subsidiaries. These subsidiaries manufacture products which are totally different from those of the holding company. The holding company manufactures paper and related products whereas the subsidiaries manufacture the following:

	Product	**Location**
Subsidiary 1	Car products	Spain
Subsidiary 2	Textiles	Korea
Subsidiary 3	Kitchen utensils	France
Subsidiary 4	Fashion garments	Thailand

The directors have purchased these subsidiaries in order to diversify their product base but do not have any knowledge on the information which is required in the financial statements, regarding these subsidiaries, other than the statutory requirements. The directors of the company realise that there is a need to disclose segmental information but do not understand what the term means or what the implications are for the published accounts.

Required:

(a) Explain to the directors the purpose of segmental reporting of financial information.

(4 marks)

(b) Explain to the directors the criteria which should be used to identify the separate reportable segments (you should illustrate your answer by reference to the above information).

(6 marks)

(c) Advise the directors on the information which should be disclosed in financial statements for each segment.

(7 marks)

(d) Critically evaluate IFRS 8 Operating segments, setting out the major problems with the standard.

(8 marks)

(Total: 25 marks)

UK syllabus focus

The ACCA UK syllabus contains a requirement that candidates should be able to discuss and apply the key differences between UK GAAP and IFRS GAAP. The accounting requirements of UK GAAP and IFRS GAAP are similar in principle, but there are some differences as follows:

SSAP 25 – Segment reporting. UK GAAP requires that reportable segments are identified using a **"risks and rewards"** approach, rather than the "managerial approach" adopted under the equivalent regulation of IFRS 8 under IFRS GAAP. In addition, SSAP 25 requires **more extensive disclosure** of information; for both different classes of **business and also geographical analysis**. A class of business may comprise the provision of an individual, or group of related or distinguishable, products or services. A geographical segment could be an individual country or group of related countries (e.g. such as the European Union), in which an entity operates or to which it supplies goods or services.

The analysis prepared in accordance with SSAP 25 is **prepared in accordance with accounting policies**, whereas the information prepared in accordance with IFRS 8 is based upon management information for internal decision-making purposes. This form of information may not comply with accounting policies used for published information.

Note that SSAP 25 contains an exemption from the disclosure requirements where the disclosures would be **seriously prejudicial** to the entity's interests. There is no equivalent exemption contained in IFRS 8.

The main argument in favour of IFRS 8 is that identification of segments, together with supporting disclosures, is based upon the operational managerial structure of the business, thus making it relatively easy to prepare such information for the annual report and accounts. By comparison, UK GAAP disclosures based upon risks and rewards are unlikely to be on the same lines as managerial decision-making, therefore resulting in additional time and cost to compile information to include in the financial statements. There is also the issue of whether or not this information is of any value to users of financial statements, although the argument in favour of this approach is that is that it highlights the business segments and geographical segments where risks and/or returns differ from other segments of the business.

Both reporting standards use a "10% rule" as a rule of thumb for identification of segments, and have similar deficiencies regarding issues such as how to account for common costs, and intra-segment trading within the same reporting entity.

4 Chapter summary

Defining reportable segments
- Managerial approach
- Ten per cent thresholds

Disclosing segmental information
- General information
- Information about profit or loss and other segment items
- Entity wide disclosures
- Measurement
- Reconciliations

Problem areas
- Subjectivity
- Common costs
- Inter-segment sales

Test your understanding answers

Test your understanding 1 – Segments

Your answer may have included some of the following.

(i) **Definition of segments:** It would be helpful to know whether there are any other classes of business included within the three operating segments supplied by the company which are material. This is particularly important when one looks at the Canning segment and notices that it comprises 50% of the total sales to customers outside the group.

(ii) **Inter-segment sales:** The inter-segment sales for fruit growing are a relatively high percentage (at around 25% ($3,485/13,635)) of its total revenue. In assessing the risk and economic trends it might well be that those of the receiving segment are more useful in predicting future prospects than those of the segment from which the sale originated.

(iii) **Analysis of assets:** Users often need to calculate a return on capital employed for each segment. Therefore, it is important to ensure that the segment profit and assets are appropriately defined, so that segment profit can be usefully related to the assets figure to produce a meaningful ratio. This means that both the operating profit and assets figure need to be precisely defined. If, for example, the assets are the gross assets, then the operating profits should be before deduction of interest. This means that the preparer of the segmental report needs to be aware of the reader's information needs.

(iv) **Unallocated items:** The information provided includes unallocated assets that represent around 12% of the total assets. It is not clear what these assets represent.

(v) **Treatment of interest:** It would be useful to know if there has been any interest charge incurred and to ascertain whether it is material and whether it can be reasonably identified as relating to any particular segment. As mentioned in (iii) above, it is not clear how segment profit is defined or how it has been derived.

Test your understanding 2 – Tab

(a) The purpose of segmental information is to provide users of financial statements with sufficient details for them to be able to appreciate the different rates of profitability, different opportunities for growth and different degrees of risk that apply to an entity's classes of business and various geographical locations.

The segmental information should enable users to:

(i) appreciate more thoroughly the results and financial position of the entity by permitting a better understanding of the entity's past performance and thus a better assessment of its future prospects

(ii) be aware of the impact that changes in significant components of a business may have on the business as a whole.

(b) IFRS 8 defines an operating segment as a component of an entity:

– that engages in business activities from which it may earn revenues and incur expenses (including revenues and expenses relating to transactions with other components of the same entity)

– whose operating results are regularly reviewed by the entity's chief operating decision-maker to make decisions about resources to be allocated to the segment and assess its performance

– for which discrete financial information is available.

These qualitative criteria are supplemented by quantitative:

– reported revenue, including both sales to external customers and intersegment sales or transfers, is 10% or more of the combined revenue, internal and external, of all operating segments

– the absolute amount of its reported profit or loss is 10% or more of the greater, in absolute amount, of (i) the combined reported profit of all operating segments that did not report a loss and (ii) the combined reported loss of all operating segments that reported a loss

– assets are 10% or more of the combined assets of all operating segments.

(c) An entity shall disclose the factors used to identify the entity's reportable segments and types of products and services from which each reportable segment derives its revenues.

The following information will be reported about profit or loss, assets and liabilities for each segment:

An entity shall report a measure of profit or loss and total assets for each reportable segment:

- a measure of liabilities for each reportable segment if such an amount is regularly provided to the chief operating decision-maker.

- An entity shall also disclose the following about each reportable segment if the specified amounts are included in the measure of segment profit or loss reviewed by the chief operating decision-maker, or are otherwise regularly provided to the chief operating decision-maker, even if not included in that measure of segment profit or loss:
    - revenues from external customers;
    - revenues from transactions with other operating segments of the same entity;
    - interest revenue;
    - interest expense;
    - depreciation and amortisation;
    - material items of income and expense disclosed in accordance with IAS 1 **Presentation of financial statements**;
    - the entity's interest in the profit or loss of associates and joint ventures accounted for by the equity method;
    - income tax expense or income and
    - material non-cash items other than depreciation and amortisation.

TAB could classify on a geographical basis under the headings 'Europe' and 'The Far East'.

TAB has five types of products and more information is really required on the commonality of any of these five. A product split could thus be for five segments.

Likely candidates for grouping together are textiles and fashion garments, perhaps under the heading 'textiles' or 'textiles and clothing'. In addition it may be reasonable to group car products and kitchen utensils under the heading 'domestic products'.

(d) IFRS 8 lays down some very broad and inclusive criteria for reporting segments. Unlike earlier attempts to define segments in more quantitative terms, segments are defined largely in terms of the breakdown and analysis used by management. This is, potentially, a very powerful method of ensuring that preparers provide useful segmental information.

There will still be problems in deciding which segments to report, if only because management may still attempt to reduce the amount of commercially sensitive information that they produce.

The growing use of executive information systems and data management within businesses makes it easier to generate reports on an ad hoc basis. It would be relatively easy to provide management with a very basic set of internal reports and analyses and leave individual managers to prepare their own more detailed information using the interrogation software provided by the system. If such analyses became routine then they would be reportable under IFRS 8, but that would be very difficult to check and audit.

There are problems in the measurement of segmental performance if the segments trade with each other. Disclosure of details of inter-segment pricing policy is often considered to be detrimental to the good of a company. There is little guidance on the policy for transfer pricing.

Differing internal reporting structures could lead to inconsistent and incompatible segmental reports, even from companies in the same industry.

14

Non-current assets and inventories

Chapter learning objectives

Upon completion of this chapter you will be able to:

- apply and discuss the timing of the recognition of non-current assets and the determination of their carrying amounts including impairment and revaluations

- apply and discuss the treatment of non-current assets held for sale

- apply and discuss the accounting treatment of investment properties including classification, recognition and measurement issues

- apply and discuss the accounting treatment of intangible assets including the criteria for recognition and measurement subsequent to acquisition and classification

- apply and discuss the accounting treatment of inventories.

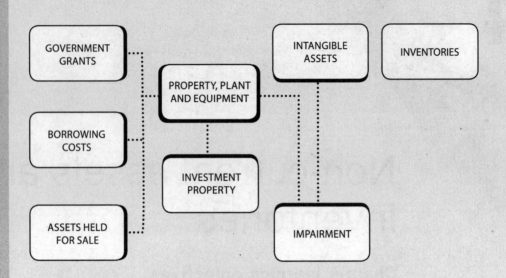

PP&E IAS 16 – recognition and measurement

Property, plant and equipment are tangible items that:

* are held for use in the production or supply of goods or services, for rental to others, or for administrative purposes
* are expected to be used during more than one period.

Tangible items have physical substance and can be touched.

* An item of property, plant and equipment should be recognised as an asset when:
  – it is probable that future economic benefits associated with the asset will flow to the entity
  – the cost of the asset can be measured reliably.

Improvements to IFRS 2009-11 published in May 2012 specifies that spare parts, stand-by equipment and servicing equipment should be classified in accordance with IAS 16 when they meet the definition; otherwise, IAS 2 will apply.

Measurement on initial recognition

A tangible non-current asset should initially be measured at its cost. Its cost comprises:

* its purchase price
* any costs directly attributable to bringing the asset to the location and condition necessary for it to be capable of operating in the manner intended by management, i.e. it is ready for use (whether or not it is actually in use)

- the initial estimate of the costs of dismantling and removing the item and restoring the site on which it is located. This might apply where, for example, an entity has to recognise a provision for the cost of decommissioning an oil rig or a nuclear power station.

Directly attributable costs include commissioning costs (e.g. sea trials for a ship, testing a computer system before it goes live).

The following costs, specifically identified, should never be capitalised:

- administration and general overheads
- abnormal costs (repairs, wastage, idle time)
- costs incurred after the asset is physically ready for use
- costs incurred in the initial operating period (e.g. initial operating losses and any further costs incurred before a machine is used at its full capacity)
- costs of opening a new facility, introducing a new product (including advertising and promotional costs) and conducting business in a new location or with a new class of customer (including training costs)
- costs of relocating/reorganising an entity's operations.

Subsequent cost

Where additional costs are incurred after the asset becomes operational, the entity applies the normal recognition principle for assets: is it probable that future economic benefits will flow to the entity?

The costs of day-to-day servicing (repairs and maintenance) should not be capitalised; rather than increasing economic benefits, they protect those expected at the time of the initial capitalisation. Instead, they should be recognised in profit or loss as they are incurred.

In contrast, the cost of replacing parts of items of property, plant and equipment is normally capitalised as it meets the recognition criteria. Examples:

- a furnace may require relining after a specified number of hours of use
- the interior walls of a building may need to be replaced.

so they can adjust their account – Revaluation Reserve

Measurement after initial recognition

IAS 16 allows a choice between the cost model and the revaluation model.

- Under the **cost model**, property, plant and equipment is valued at cost less accumulated depreciation.

- Under the **revaluation model**, property, plant and equipment is carried at fair value less any subsequent accumulated depreciation.

- Fair value is normally open market value (not existing use value). Depreciated replacement cost may be used where there is no reliable market value (for example, because the asset is specialised or rare).

- Revaluations must be made with 'sufficient regularity' to ensure that the carrying amount does not differ materially from the fair value at each reporting date.

- If an item is revalued, the entire class of assets to which the item belongs must be revalued.

- If a revaluation increases the value of an asset, the increase is disclosed as other comprehensive income and credited to other components of equity under the heading 'revaluation surplus' unless it reverses a previous decrease in value of the same asset that has been recognised as an expense. It should then be recognised in profit or loss. Note that IAS 1 now requires that such items included within other comprehensive income are classified as items which will not be recycled or reclassified to profit or loss in subsequent periods.

- If a revaluation decreases the value of the asset, the decrease should be recognised immediately in profit or loss, unless there is a revaluation reserve representing a surplus on the same asset.

Depreciation

All assets with a finite useful life must be depreciated.

Depreciation is the systematic allocation of the depreciable amount of an asset over its useful life.

The depreciable amount of an asset is its cost less its residual value. /scrap value .

The residual value is the amount that the entity would **currently** obtain from disposal, net of selling costs, if the asset were already of the age and in the condition expected at the end of its useful life.

- IAS 16 does not prescribe a depreciation method, but the method used must reflect the pattern in which the asset's future economic benefits are expected to be consumed.

- Depreciation begins when the asset is available for use and continues until the asset is derecognised, even if it is idle.

- If an asset is measured at historical cost, the depreciation charge is based on historical cost.

- If an asset has been revalued, then the depreciation charge is based on the revalued amount.

- The residual value and the useful life of an asset should be reviewed at least at each financial year-end and revised if necessary. Depreciation methods should also be reviewed at least annually.

- Any adjustments are accounted for as a change in accounting estimate under IAS 8 **Accounting policies, changes in accounting estimates and errors**, rather than as a change in accounting policy. This means that they are reflected in the current and future statements of profit or loss and other comprehensive income.

Illustration: Change in depreciation estimates

An asset was purchased for $100,000 on 1 January 20X5 and straight line depreciation of $20,000 per annum was charged (five year life, no residual value). A general review of asset lives is undertaken and for this particular asset, the remaining useful life as at 31 December 20X7 is seven years.

What should the annual depreciation charge be for 20X7 and subsequent years?

Solution

CV as at 31 December 20X6 (60% × $100,000)	$60,000
Remaining useful life as at 1 January 20X7 (7+1)	8 years
Annual depreciation charge	$7,500

 Note that the estimated remaining life is seven years from 31 December 20X7, but this information is used to compute the current year's charge as well.

Depreciation of separate components

Certain large assets are in fact a collection of smaller assets, each with a different cost and useful life. For example, an aeroplane consists of an airframe (which may last for 40 years or so) plus engines, radar equipment, seats, etc. all of which have a relatively short life. Instead of calculating depreciation on the aeroplane as a whole, depreciation is charged on each component (airframe, engines, etc.) instead.

For example, an entity buys a ship for $12m. The ship as a whole should last for 25 years. The engines, however, will need replacing after 7 years. The cost price of $12m included about $1.4m in respect of the engines.

The annual depreciation charge will be $624,000 made up as follows:

    engines: $1.4m over seven years = $200,000 pa, plus

    the rest of the ship: $10.6m over 25 years = $424,000 pa.

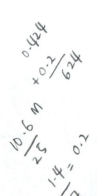

Derecognition

Assets are derecognised either on disposal; or when no future economic benefits are expected from their use or disposal.

- The gain or loss on derecognition of an asset is the difference between the net disposal proceeds, if any, and the carrying amount of the item.
- When a revalued asset is disposed of, any revaluation surplus may be transferred directly to retained earnings, or it may be left in equity under the heading revaluation surplus. The transfer to retained earnings should not be made through the statement of comprehensive income.

Disclosures

The following should be disclosed for each class of property, plant and equipment:

cost / revaluation method

- the measurement bases used for determining the gross carrying amount
- the depreciation methods used
- the useful lives or the depreciation rates used
- the gross carrying amount and the accumulated depreciation (aggregated with accumulated impairment losses) at the beginning and end of the period
- a reconciliation of the carrying amount at the beginning and end of the period showing: additions; disposals; increases or decreases resulting from revaluations and from impairment losses; depreciation; and other changes.

If items of property, plant and equipment are stated at revalued amounts, information about the revaluation should also be disclosed.

1 Impairment of assets (IAS 36)

When to carry out an impairment review

Definition

Impairment is a reduction in the recoverable amount of an asset or cash-generating unit below its carrying amount.

An entity should carry out an impairment review at least annually if:

- an intangible asset is not being amortised because it has an indefinite useful life
- goodwill has arisen on a business combination.

Otherwise, an impairment review is required only where there is evidence that an impairment may have occurred.

Indications of impairment

Indications that an impairment might have happened can come from external or internal sources.

- **External sources of information**:
    - unexpected decreases in an asset's market value
    - significant adverse changes have taken place, or are about to take place, in the technological, market, economic or legal environment
    - increased interest rates have decreased an asset's recoverable amount
    - the entity's net assets are measured at more than its market capitalisation.

- **Internal sources of information**:
    - evidence of obsolescence or damage
     – there is, or is about to be, a material reduction in usage of an asset
    - evidence that the economic performance of an asset has been, or will be, worse than expected.

Calculating an impairment loss

An impairment occurs if the carrying amount of an asset is greater than its recoverable amount.

The **recoverable amount** is the higher of fair value less costs to sell and value in use.

Fair value less costs to sell is the amount obtainable from the sale of an asset in an arm's length transaction between knowledgeable, willing parties, less the costs of disposal.

Value in use is the present value of future cash flows from using an asset, including its eventual disposal.

Carrying out an impairment test

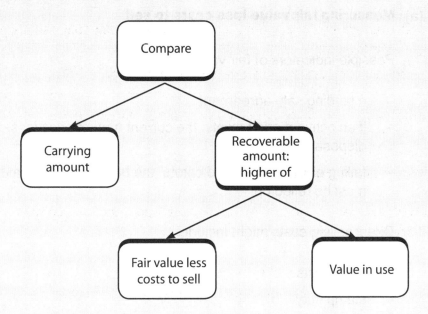

- If fair value less costs to sell is higher than the carrying amount, there is no impairment and no need to calculate value in use.

Illustration 1 – Impairment of item of plant (IAS 36)

An item of plant is included in the financial statements at a carrying amount of $350,000. The present value of the future cash flows from continuing to operate the plant is $320,000. Alternatively, the plant could be sold for net proceeds of $275,000.

What is the recoverable amount?

Is the plant impaired?

Solution

The recoverable amount is determined taking the greater of net selling costs and value in use. Net selling costs are $275,000 and value in use is $320,000 so the recoverable amount is $320,000.

To determine whether the plant is impaired, the carrying amount is compared to the recoverable amount. The carrying amount at $350,000 is greater than the recoverable amount, so the asset must be written down to its recoverable amount. Therefore, the impairment loss is $30,000.

Measurement of recoverable amount

(a) Measuring fair value less costs to sell

Possible indicators of fair value are:

– a binding sale agreement

– if an active market exists, the current market price less costs of disposal

– failing either of these indicators, the best information available must be relied on.

Direct selling costs might include:

– legal costs

– stamp duty

– costs relating to the removal of a sitting tenant (in the case of a building).

Redundancy and reorganisation costs (e.g. following the sale of a business) are not direct selling costs.

(b) Measuring value in use

Value in use is calculated by estimating future cash inflows and outflows from the use of the asset and its ultimate disposal, and applying a suitable discount rate to these cash flows.

Therefore, there are two steps to the calculation.

(1) Estimate future cash flows.

(2) Discount them to arrive at their present value.

Where possible, value in use should be estimated for individual assets. However, it may not always be possible to identify cash flows arising from individual assets. If this is the case, value in use is calculated for cash-generating units (groups of assets that produce independent income streams).

Test your understanding 1 – Impaired asset

Information about an asset is given below.

	$000
Carrying amount	500
Fair value less costs to sell	300
Future cash flows (per annum) for 2 years	200
Discount rate	10%

Required:

Determine the outcome of the impairment review.

Recognising impairment losses in the financial statements

An impairment loss is normally charged immediately in the statement of profit or loss and other comprehensive income to the same heading as the related depreciation (e.g. cost of sales or administration).

- If the asset has previously been revalued upwards, the impairment is recognised as comprehensive income and is debited to the revaluation reserve until the surplus relating to that asset has been exhausted. The remainder of the impairment loss is recognised in the profit or loss.

- The recoverable (impaired) amount is then depreciated over its remaining useful life.

Illustration 2 – Impairment of asset previously revalued (IAS 36)

At 1 January 20X7 a non-current asset had a carrying amount of $20,000, based on its revalued amount, and a depreciated historical cost of $10,000. An impairment loss of $12,000 arose in the year ended 31 December 20X7.

How should this loss be reported in the financial statements for the year ended 31 December 20X7?

Solution

A loss of $10,000 ($20,000 – $10,000) is recognised as other comprehensive income and debited to the revaluation surplus within other components of equity. The remaining loss of $2,000 is recognised as an expense in the period.

rating units

ly possible to identify cash flows relating to particular assets.
a factory production line is made up of many individual
but the revenues are earned by the production line as a whole.
This means that value in use must be calculated (and the impairment review performed) for groups of assets, rather than individual assets.

- These groups of assets are called cash-generating units (CGUs).

Cash-generating units are segments of the business whose income streams are largely independent of each other.

- In practice they are likely to mirror the strategic business units used for monitoring the performance of the business.

- It could also include a subsidiary or associate within a corporate group structure.

Test your understanding 2 – Cash generating units

An entity comprises three stages of production, A (growing and felling trees), B (creating parts of wooden furniture) and C (assembling the parts from B into finished goods). The output of A is timber that is partly transferred to B and partly sold in an external market. If A did not exist, B could buy its timber from the market. The output of B has no external market and is transferred to C at an internal transfer price. C sells the finished product in an external market and the sales revenue achieved by C is not affected by the fact that the three stages of production are all performed by the entity.

Required:

Identify the cash-generating unit(s).

Allocating assets to cash-generating units

The net assets of the business (including capitalised goodwill, but excluding tax balances and interest-bearing debt) are allocated to cash-generating units. There are two particular problem areas.

- Corporate assets: assets that are used by several cash-generating units (e.g. a head office building or a research centre). They do not generate their own cash inflows, so do not themselves qualify as cash-generating units.

- Goodwill, which does not generate cash flows independently of other assets and often relates to a whole business.

It may not be possible to allocate corporate assets and/or goodwill over other cash-generating units on a reasonable basis.

A cash-generating unit to which goodwill has been allocated must be tested for impairment at least annually.

If no reasonable allocation of corporate assets or goodwill is possible, then a group of cash-generating units must be tested for impairment together in a two-stage process.

Illustration 3 – Impairment of CGU including goodwill

An entity acquires a business comprising three cash-generating units, D, E and F, but there is no reasonable way of allocating goodwill to them. After three years, the carrying amount and the recoverable amount of the net assets in the cash-generating units and the purchased goodwill are as follows:

	D	E	F	Goodwill	Total
	$000	$000	$000	$000	$000
Carrying amount	240	360	420	150	1,170
Recoverable amount	300	420	360		1,080

Solution

Step 1: Review the individual units for impairment.

F is impaired. A loss of $60,000 is recognised and its carrying amount is reduced to $360,000.

Step 2: Compare the carrying amount of the business as a whole, including the goodwill, with its recoverable amount.

The total carrying amount of the business is now $1,110,000 (1,170,000 – 60,000). A further impairment loss of $30,000 must then be recognised in respect of the goodwill (1,110,000 – 1,080,000).

Allocation of an impairment to the unit's assets

If an impairment loss arises in respect of a cash-generating unit, it is allocated among the assets in the unit in the following order:

- any individual assets that are obviously impaired
- goodwill
- other assets pro rata to their carrying amount.

However, the carrying amount of an asset cannot be reduced below the highest of:

- its fair value less costs to sell (if determinable)
- its value in use (if determinable)
- zero.

Illustration 4 – Impairment allocation within CGU

Tinud has identified an impairment loss of $41m for one of its cash-generating units. The carrying amount of the unit's net assets was $150m, whereas the unit's recoverable amount was only $109m.

The draft values of the net assets of the unit are as follows:

	$m
Goodwill	13
Property	20
Machinery	49
Vehicles	35
Patents	14
Net monetary assets	19
	———
	150
	———

The net selling price of the unit's assets were insignificant except for the property, which had a market value of $35m. The net monetary assets will be realised in full.

How is the impairment loss allocated to the assets?

Solution

Firstly, the goodwill is reduced to zero.

No impairment loss can be set against the property because its net selling price is greater than its carrying amount.

Likewise, no impairment loss can be set against the net monetary assets (receivables, cash, etc.) because they will be realised in full.

The balance of $28m ($41m – $13m) is apportioned between the remaining assets on a pro rata basis (so (49/(49 + 35 + 14)) × 28 to machinery, and so on).

The table below shows how the impairment will be allocated.

	Draft values	Impairment loss	Impaired value
	$m	$m	$m
Goodwill	13	(13)	–
Property	20	–	20
Machinery	49	(14)	35
Vehicles	35	(10)	25
Patents	14	(4)	10
Net monetary assets	19	–	19
	150	(41)	109

Test your understanding 3 – Factory explosion

There was an explosion in a factory. The carrying amounts of its assets were as follows:

	$000
Goodwill	100
Patents	200
Machines	300
Computers	500
Buildings	1,500
	2,600

The factory operates as a cash-generating unit. An impairment review reveals a net selling price of $1.2m for the factory and value in use of $1.95m. Half of the machines have been blown to pieces but the other half can be sold for at least their book value. The patents have been superseded and are now considered worthless.

Required:

Show the effect of the explosion on the asset values.

2 Impairment of goodwill

IAS 36 **Impairment of assets** requires that once recognised according to IFRS 3 revised, goodwill is tested for impairment annually or more frequently if circumstances indicate it might be impaired.

Goodwill must not be amortised.

Accounting for an impairment

An **impairment loss** is the amount by which the carrying amount of an asset or a cash generating unit exceeds its recoverable amount.

Recoverable amount is the higher of fair value less costs to sell and value in use.

Key points:

- As goodwill does not generate cash flows of its own, its impairment is tested within the cash-generating unit to which the goodwill belongs.

- The goodwill is allocated to a specific cash-generating unit (CGU), or multiple cash generating units where the goodwill cannot be allocated to a single CGU, and the impairment test is carried out on the group of assets including the goodwill.

- Any impairment loss is allocated in the following order:
    - to goodwill allocated to the CGU
    - to other assets in the CGU on a pro rata basis. No asset can be written down below its net realisable value.

- A reversal of an impairment loss can occur if the conditions that caused the original impairment have improved. This reversal is recognised as income in profit or loss.

- If the reversal relates to a cash generating unit, the reversal is allocated to the assets of the unit on a pro rata basis according to their carrying value except goodwill which cannot be rewritten into the books.

- IFRIC 10, issued in 2006, confirms that, where impairment of goodwill has been recognised in interim financial statements, it cannot subsequently be written back or reversed in the next annual financial statements.

Test your understanding 4 – Cedar

The following information relates to a 60% subsidiary, Cedar:

Net assets at acquisition	Net assets at reporting date	Fair value of NCI at acquisition	Cost of investment at acquisition	Recoverable amount at reporting date
$m	$m	$m	$m	$m
500	600	250	800	1,000

Required:

Determine the outcome of the impairment review at the reporting date.

Test your understanding 5 – Homer

The following information relates to an 80% subsidiary, Homer.

Net assets at acquisition	Net assets at reporting date	Fair value of NCI at acquisition	Cost of investment at acquisition	Recoverable amount at reporting date
$m	$m	$m	$m	$m
100	150	25	200	255

Required:

Determine the outcome of the impairment review at the reporting date.

Accounting for an impairment with a non-controlling interest

Full method of valuing NCI

- The accounting treatment above also applies where there is a non-controlling interest valued using the full method.

- In this case goodwill shown in the group statement of financial position represents full goodwill, and so together with the rest of the CGU it can be compared to recoverable amount of the CGU on a like for like basis.

- Any impairment of goodwill is therefore allocated between the group and the NCI based upon their respective shareholdings. Note - this could result in the NCI share of impairment exceeding their share of goodwill upon acquisition.

Proportion of net assets method of valuing NCI

- Where this method is adopted, the NCI share of goodwill is not reflected in the group accounts.

- Therefore any comparison between the carrying value of a CGU (including goodwill) and its recoverable amount will not be on a like for like basis.

- In order to address this problem, goodwill must be grossed up to include goodwill attributable to the NCI prior to conducting the impairment review.

- This grossed up goodwill is known as 'total notional goodwill'.

- Once any impairment loss is determined, it should be allocated firstly to the total notional goodwill and then to the CGU's assets on a pro rata basis.

- As only the parent's share of the goodwill is recognised in the group accounts, only the parent's share of the impairment loss should be recognised.

Illustration 5 – Impairment of full value goodwill

A owns 80% of B. At 31 October 20X6 the carrying amount of B's net assets is $60 million, excluding goodwill of $8 million that arose on the original acquisition. The non-controlling interest is valued using the fair value method.

Calculate the impairment loss if the recoverable amount of B is:

(a) $64 million

(b) $50 million

Solution

Solution (a)

	Goodwill	Net assets	Total
	$m	$m	$m
Carrying amount	8	60	68
Recoverable amount			64
Impairment	(4)		4

The impairment loss relates only to goodwill. This will be charged to income, with the effect that it will be borne by the group and the NCI based upon their respective shareholdings.

Solution (b)

	Goodwill	Net assets	Total
	$m	$m	$m
Carrying amount	8	60	68
Recoverable amount			50
Impairment	(8)	(10)	18

The impairment loss relates first to goodwill, with the remainder set against other assets on a pro-rata basis, unless there is further information available regarding the recoverable amount of other individual assets. The impairment of $18m is charged to income, with the effect that it will be borne by the group and NCI based upon their respective shareholdings.

Illustration 6 – NCI on proportionate basis

A owns 80% of B. At 31 October 20X6 the carrying amount of B's net assets is $60 million, excluding goodwill of $8 million that arose on the original acquisition. The non-controlling interest is valued using the proportion of net assets method.

Calculate the impairment loss if the recoverable amount is:

(a) $64 million

(b) $50 million

Solution

Solution (a)

	Goodwill $m	Net assets $m	Total $m
Carrying amount	8	60	68
Notional NCI (20/80)	2		2
Notionally adjusted carrying amount	10	60	70
Recoverable amount			64
Impairment			6

The impairment loss only relates to goodwill. Only the proportion relating to the recognised goodwill is recognised in the financial statements, so 80% of $6m, i.e. $4.8 million.

Solution (b)

	Goodwill $m	Net assets $m	Total $m
Carrying amount	8	60	68
Notional NCI (20/80)	2		2
Notionally adjusted carrying amount	10	60	70
Recoverable amount			50
Impairment			20

The impairment loss is allocated as follows: $8 million to recognised goodwill (as before) and the remaining $10 million (20 – 10) to other net assets.

Test your understanding 6 – Happy

On 1 January 20X5, Lucky group purchased 80% of Happy for $500,000. The net assets of Happy at the date of acquisition amounted to $560,000. It is Lucky Group policy to value the non-controlling interest at its proportionate share of the fair value of the subsidiary's identifiable net assets.

The carrying amount of Happy's assets at 31 December is $520,000. Happy is a cash-generating unit on its own.

At 31 December 20X5 the recoverable amount of Happy is $510,000.

Required:

Calculate the impairment loss in Happy and explain how this would be dealt with in the financial statements of the Lucky group.

Reversal of an impairment loss

The calculation of impairment losses is based on predictions of what may happen in the future. Sometimes, actual events turn out to be better than predicted. If this happens, the recoverable amount is re-calculated and the previous write-down is reversed.

- Impaired assets should be reviewed at each reporting date to see whether there are indications that the impairment has reversed.

- A reversal of an impairment loss is recognised immediately as income in profit or loss. If the original impairment was charged against the revaluation surplus, it is recognised as other comprehensive income and credited to the revaluation reserve.

- The reversal must not take the value of the asset above the amount it would have been if the original impairment had never been recorded. The depreciation that would have been charged in the meantime must be taken into account.

- The depreciation charge for future periods should be revised to reflect the changed carrying amount.

An impairment loss recognised for goodwill cannot be reversed in a subsequent period.

Indications that an impairment has reversed

Indications of a reversal are the opposite of the indicators of impairment.

- External indicators
    - (i)   Increases in the asset's market value.
    - (ii) Favourable changes in the technological, market, economic or legal environment.
    - (iii) Decreases in interest rates.
- Internal indicators
    - (i)   Favourable changes in the use of the asset.
    - (ii) Improvements in the asset's economic performance.

Reversing the impairment of a cash-generating unit: If the reversal relates to a cash-generating unit, the reversal is allocated to assets other than goodwill on a pro rata basis. The carrying amount of an asset must not be increased above the lower of:

- its recoverable amount (if determinable)
- the carrying amount that would have been determined (net of amortisation or depreciation) had no impairment loss been recognised for the asset in prior periods.

The amount that would otherwise have been allocated to the asset is allocated pro rata to the other assets of the unit, except for goodwill.

Reversals and goodwill: Impairment losses relating to goodwill can never be reversed. The reason for this is that once purchased goodwill has become impaired, any subsequent increase in its recoverable amount is likely to be an increase in internally generated goodwill, rather than a reversal of the impairment loss recognised for the original purchased goodwill. Internally generated goodwill cannot be recognised.

Test your understanding 7 – Boxer

Boxer purchased a non-current asset on 1 January 20X1 at a cost of $30,000. At that date, the asset had an estimated useful life of ten years and nil residual value at the end of that period. Boxer does not revalue this type of asset, but accounts for it on the basis of depreciated historical cost. At 31 December 20X2, the asset is subject to an impairment review and has a recoverable amount of $16,000.

At 31 December 20X5, the circumstances which caused the original impairment to be recognised have reversed and are no longer applicable, with the result that recoverable amount is now $40,000.

Required:

Explain, with supporting computations, the impact on the financial statements of the two impairment reviews.

IAS 36 disclosure requirements

IAS 36 requires extensive disclosures about impairments, but the main ones are:

- losses recognised during the period, and where charged in the statement of profit or loss and other comprehensive income

- reversals recognised during the period, and where credited in the statement profit or loss and other comprehensive income

- for each material loss or reversal:
    - the amount of loss or reversal and the events causing it
    - the nature of the asset (or cash-generating unit) and its reportable segment
    - whether the recoverable amount is the fair value less costs to sell or value in use
    - basis used to determine the fair value less costs to sell
    - the discount rate(s) used in estimating the value in use.

Government grants IAS 20 – definitions

Government grants are transfers of resources to an entity in return for past or future compliance with certain conditions. They exclude assistance that cannot be valued and normal trade with governments.

Government refers to government, government agencies and similar bodies whether local, national or international.

Government assistance is government action designed to provide an economic benefit to a specific entity. It does not include indirect help such as infrastructure development.

General principles

Grants should not be recognised until the conditions for receipt have been complied with and there is reasonable assurance that the grant will be received.

- Grants should be recognised in profit or loss so as to match them with the expenditure towards which they are intended to contribute.

- Income grants given to subsidise expenditure should be matched to the related costs.

- Income grants given to help achieve a non-financial goal (such as job creation) should be matched to the costs incurred to meet that goal.

Grants related to assets

Grants for purchases of non-current assets should be recognised over the expected useful lives of the related assets. There are two acceptable accounting policies for this:

- deduct the grant from the cost of the asset and depreciate the net cost

- treat the grant as deferred income. Release the grant to profit or loss over the life of the asset. This is the method most commonly used.

Other grants and repayment

Purpose of grant	Recognise in profit/loss
To give immediate financial support	When receivable
To reimburse previously incurred costs	When receivable
To finance general activities over a period	In relevant period
To compensate for a loss of income	In relevant period

Repayment of government grants

A government grant that becomes repayable is accounted for as a revision of an accounting estimate.

(a) **Income-based grants**

Firstly, debit the repayment to any liability for deferred income. Any excess repayment must be charged to profits immediately.

(b) **Capital-based grants deducted from cost**

Increase the cost of the asset with the repayment. This will also increase the amount of depreciation that should have been charged in the past. This should be recognised and charged immediately.

(c) **Capital-based grants treated as deferred income**

Firstly, debit the repayment to any liability for deferred income. Any excess repayment must be charged against profits immediately.

Government assistance

As implied in the definition set out above, government assistance helps businesses through loan guarantees, loans at a low rate of interest, advice, procurement policies and similar methods. It is not possible to place reliable values on these forms of assistance, so they are not recognised.

Disclosure

The disclosure requirements of IAS 20 are:

- the accounting policy adopted for government grants, including the methods of presentation adopted in the financial statements

- the nature and extent of government grants recognised in the financial statements and other forms of government assistance received

- unfulfilled conditions and other contingencies attaching to government assistance that has been recognised.

Borrowing costs IAS 23 – general principle

As part of the short-term convergence project, the IASB issued IAS 23 revised in March 2007.

The revised standard removes the option to expense all borrowing costs as incurred (the benchmark treatment of the previous version of IAS 23).

Instead it requires that an entity capitalise borrowing costs directly attributable to the acquisition or construction of a qualifying asset as part of the cost of that asset. This was a permitted alternative treatment under the previous version of IAS 23.

Rules for capitalising interest

Accounting rules for capitalising interest

Interest should only be capitalised if it relates to the acquisition, construction or production of a qualifying asset, i.e. an asset that necessarily takes a substantial period of time to get ready for its intended use or sale.

- The interest capitalised should relate to the costs incurred on the project and the cost of the entity's borrowings.

- The total amount of finance costs capitalised during a period should not exceed the total amount of finance costs incurred during that period.

Capitalisation period

Interest should only be capitalised while construction is in progress.

* Capitalisation of borrowing costs should commence when:
    - expenditure for the asset is being incurred
    - borrowing costs are being incurred
    - activities that are necessary to get the asset ready for use are in progress.

* Capitalisation of finance costs should cease when substantially all the activities that are necessary to get the asset ready for use are complete.

* Capitalisation of borrowing costs should be suspended during extended periods in which active development is interrupted.

* When construction of a qualifying asset is completed in parts and each part is capable of being used while construction continues on other parts, capitalisation of finance costs relating to a part should cease when substantially all the activities that are necessary to get that part ready for use are completed.

How to calculate the interest cost

Where a loan is taken out specifically to finance the construction of an asset, the amount to be capitalised is the interest payable on that loan, less any investment income on the temporary investment of the borrowings.

Arriving at the interest cost is more complicated when the acquisition or construction of an asset is financed from an entity's general borrowings. In this situation it is necessary to calculate the finance cost by applying a notional rate of interest (the capitalisation rate) to the expenditure on the asset.

* The capitalisation rate is the weighted average of rates applicable to general borrowings outstanding in the period.

* General borrowings do not include loans for other specific purposes, such as constructing other qualifying assets.

IAS 23 is silent on how to arrive at the expenditure on the asset, but it would be reasonable to calculate it as the weighted average carrying amount of the asset during the period, including finance costs previously capitalised.

Disclosure requirements

The financial statements should disclose:

- the accounting policy adopted for borrowing costs
- the amount of borrowing costs capitalised during the period
- the capitalisation rate used.

3 Non-current assets held for sale (IFRS 5)

Classification as 'held for sale'

A non-current asset or disposal group should be classified as 'held for sale' if its carrying amount will be recovered principally through a sale transaction rather than through continuing use.

A **disposal group** is a group of assets (and possibly liabilities) that the entity intends to dispose of in a single transaction.

- IFRS 5 applies to disposal groups as well as to individual non-current assets that are held for sale.
- A disposal group may include goodwill acquired in a business combination if the group is a cash-generating unit to which goodwill has been allocated (IAS 36).
- Subsidiaries acquired exclusively with a view to resale are classified as disposal groups held for sale if they meet the conditions below.

IFRS 5 requires the following conditions to be met before an asset or disposal group can be classified as 'held for sale'.

- The item is available for immediate sale in its present condition.
- The sale is highly probable.
- Management is committed to a plan to sell the item.
- An active programme to locate a buyer has been initiated.
- The item is being actively marketed at a reasonable price in relation to its current fair value.
- The sale is expected to be completed within one year from the date of classification.
- It is unlikely that the plan will change significantly or be withdrawn.

Assets that are to be abandoned or wound down gradually cannot be classified as held for sale (although they may qualify as discontinued operations once they have been abandoned), because their carrying amounts will not be recovered principally through a sale transaction.

Measurement of assets and disposal groups held for sale

Items classified as held for sale should be measured at the lower of their carrying amount and fair value less costs to sell.

- Where fair value less costs to sell is lower than carrying amount, the item is written down and the write down is treated as an impairment loss.

- Where a non-current asset has been previously revalued and is now classified as being held for sale, it should be revalued to fair value immediately before it is classified as held for sale. It is then revalued again at the lower of the carrying amount and the fair value less costs to sell. The difference is the selling costs and these should be charged against profits in the period.

- When a disposal group is being written down to fair value less costs to sell, the impairment loss reduces the carrying amount of assets in the order prescribed by IAS 36 – that is write down goodwill first, then allocate the remaining loss to the assets pro rata based on their carrying amount.

- A gain can be recognised for any subsequent increase in fair value less costs to sell, but not in excess of the cumulative impairment loss that has already been recognised, either when the assets were written down to fair value less costs to sell or previously under IAS 36.

- An asset held for sale is not depreciated, even if it is still being used by the entity.

Illustration 7 – Non-current assets held for sale (IFRS 5)

On 1 January 20X1 AB acquires a building for $200,000 with an expected life of 50 years. On 31 December 20X4 AB puts the building up for immediate sale. On that date the building has a market value of $220,000 and expenses of $10,000 and tax of $5,000 will be payable on the sale. Describe the accounting for this building.

Solution

Until 31 December 20X4 the building is a normal non-current asset governed by IAS 16, being depreciated at $200,000 / 50 = $4,000 pa. The carrying amount at 31 December 20X4 is therefore $200,000 / (4 × $4,000) = $184,000.

On 31 December 20X4 the building is reclassified as a non-current asset held for sale. It is measured at the lower of carrying amount ($184,000) and fair value less costs to sell ($220,000 − $10,000 = $210,000). Note that any applicable tax expense is excluded from the determination of costs to sell.

The building will therefore be measured at 31 December 20X4 at $184,000.

Changes to a plan of sale

If a sale does not take place within one year, an asset (or disposal group) can still be classified as held for sale if:

- the delay has been caused by events or circumstances beyond the entity's control
- there is sufficient evidence that the entity is still committed to the sale.

If the criteria for 'held for sale' are no longer met, then the entity must cease to classify the assets or disposal group as held for sale. The assets or disposal group must be measured at the lower of:

- its carrying amount before it was classified as held for sale adjusted for any depreciation, amortisation or revaluations that would have been recognised had it not been classified as held for sale
- its recoverable amount at the date of the subsequent decision not to sell.

Any adjustment required is recognised in profit or loss as a gain or loss from continuing operations.

Presentation in the statement of financial position

IFRS 5 states that assets classified as held for sale should be presented separately from other assets in the statement of financial position. The liabilities of a disposal group classified as held for sale should be presented separately from other liabilities in the statement of financial position.

- Assets and liabilities held for sale should not be offset and presented as a single amount.
- The major classes of assets and liabilities classified as held for sale must be separately disclosed either on the face of the statement of financial position or in the notes.

KAPLAN PUBLISHING

- Where an asset or disposal group is classified as held for sale after the reporting date, but before the issue of the financial statements, details should be disclosed in the notes (this is a non-adjusting event after the reporting date).

Illustration 8 – Non-current assets held for sale (IFRS 5)

Statement of financial position (showing non-current assets held for sale)

	20X2 $m	20X1 $m
ASSETS		
Non-current assets		
Property, plant and equipment	X	X
Goodwill	X	X
Financial assets	X	X
	X	X
Current assets		
Inventories	X	X
Trade receivables	X	X
Cash and cash equivalents	X	
Non-current assets classified as held for sale	X	X
	X	X
Total assets	X	X

Disclosures in notes to the accounts

In the period in which a non-current asset or disposal group has been either classified as held for sale, or sold, the notes to the accounts must include:

- a description of the non-current asset (or disposal group)

- a description of the facts and circumstances of the sale or expected sale

- any impairment losses or reversals recognised

- if applicable, the segment in which the non-current asset (or disposal group) is presented in accordance with IFRS 8 **Operating segments**.

Test your understanding 8 – Hyssop

Hyssop is preparing its financial statements for the year ended 31 December 20X7.

(a) On 1 December 20X7, the entity became committed to a plan to sell a surplus office property and has already found a potential buyer. On 15 December 20X7 a survey was carried out and it was discovered that the building had dry rot and substantial remedial work would be necessary. The buyer is prepared to wait for the work to be carried out, but the property will not be sold until the problem has been rectified. This is not expected to occur until summer 20X8.

Can the property be classified as 'held for sale'?

(b) A subsidiary entity, B, is for sale at a price of $3 million. There has been some interest by prospective buyers but no sale as of yet. One buyer has made an offer of $2 million but the Directors of Hyssop rejected the offer as they were hoping to achieve a price of $3 million. The Directors have just received advice from their accountants that the fair value of the business is $2.5 million. They have decided not to reduce the sale price of B at the moment.

Can the subsidiary be classified as 'held for sale'?

Investment property IAS 40 – definition

Definition of investment property

Investment property is property (land or a building – or part of a building – or both) held (by the owner or by the lessee under a finance lease) to earn rentals or for capital appreciation or both.

Examples of investment property are a:

- land held for long-term capital appreciation
- land held for undecided future use
- building leased out under an operating lease
- vacant building held to be leased out under an operating lease.

The following are **not** investment property:

- property held for use in the production or supply of goods or services or for administrative purposes (IAS 16 **Property, plant and equipment** applies)

- property held for sale in the ordinary course of business or in the process of construction of development for such sale (IAS 2 **Inventories** applies)

- property being constructed or developed on behalf of third parties (IAS 11 **Construction contracts** applies)

- owner-occupied property (IAS 16 applies)

- property that is being constructed or developed for use as an investment property (IAS 16 currently applies until the property is ready for use, at which time IAS 40 starts to apply – see note below)

- property leased to another entity under a finance lease (IAS 17 **Leases** applies).

Measurement

On recognition, investment property shall be recognised at cost, measured along the lines of the principles in IAS 16.

After recognition an entity may choose either:

- the fair value model
- the cost model.

The policy chosen must be applied to all investment properties.

Change from one model to the other is permitted only if this results in a more appropriate presentation. IAS 40 notes that this is highly unlikely for a change from the fair value model to the cost model.

The cost model is the normal accounting treatment set out in IAS 16. Properties are held at historical cost less depreciation without any revaluation.

The fair value model

Under the fair value model, the entity remeasures its investment properties at fair value each year. There is no depreciation charge.

Fair value is defined as the amount for which the property could be exchanged between knowledgeable, willing parties in an arm's length transaction.

- Fair value is normally the active market price. There should be no deduction for transaction costs. Where there is no market for similar properties, the following values may be considered:
  - current prices in an active market for properties of a different nature, condition or location, adjusted to reflect those differences
  - recent prices in less active markets
  - discounted cash flow projections based on reliable estimates of future cash flows.

If in exceptional circumstances, it is impossible to measure the fair value of an individual investment property reliably, then the cost model should be adopted.

- All gains and losses on revaluation are reported in as part of the profit for the period.
- The profit or loss on disposal of an investment property is the difference between the net disposal proceeds and the then carrying amount in the statement of financial position.

Operating leases

A property interest that is held by a lessee under an operating lease may be classified as an investment property, if, and only if, the property would meet the definition if it were not held under an operating lease.

- This classification is available on a property-by-property basis.
- The lessee accounts for the property as if it were a finance lease.
- Once the classification has been made for such property interest, the fair value model must be used for all investment properties held by the entity.

KAPLAN PUBLISHING

Transfers

Transfers to or from investment property can only be made if there is a change of use. There are several possible situations in which this might occur and the accounting treatment for each is set out below.

Transfer from investment property to owner-occupied property

Use the fair value at the date of the change for subsequent accounting under IAS 16.

Transfer from investment property to inventory

Use the fair value at the date of the change for subsequent accounting under IAS 2 Inventories.

Transfer from owner-occupied property to investment property to be carried at fair value

Normal accounting under IAS 16 (cost less depreciation) will have been applied up to the date of the change. On adopting fair value, there is normally an increase in value. This is recognised as other comprehensive income and credited to the revaluation surplus in equity in accordance with IAS 16. If the fair valuation causes a decrease in value, then it should be charged to profits.

Transfer from inventories to investment property to be carried at fair value

Any change in the carrying amount caused by the transfer should be recognised in profit or loss.

Illustration: Investment property

Lavender owns a property, which it rents out to some of its employees. The property was purchased for $40 million on 1 January 20X2 and had a useful life of 30 years at that date. On 1 January 20X7 it had a market value of $50 million and its remaining useful life remained unchanged. Management wish to measure properties at fair value where this is allowed by accounting standards.

How should the property be treated in the financial statements of Lavender for the year ended 31 December 20X7.

(a) Carrying amount $32 million (original cost less 6 years' depreciation).

(b) Carrying amount $48 million (revalued amount less 1 year's depreciation); gain on revaluation in other components of equity.

(c) Carrying amount $50 million (revalued amount); gain on revaluation in other components of equity.

(d) Carrying amount $50 million (revalued amount); gain on revaluation in profit or loss.

Solution

The answer is B. Because the property is rented out to employees, it is owner-occupied, and cannot be classified as an investment property.

Management wish to measure the property at fair value, so Lavender adopts the fair value model in IAS 16 **Property, plant and equipment**, depreciating the asset over its useful life and recognising the revaluation gain in other components of equity (revaluation surplus).

4 Intangible assets (IAS 38)

Intangible assets IAS-38 definition

Definition and recognition criteria

An **intangible asset** is an identifiable non-monetary asset without physical substance.

An intangible asset should be recognised if all the following criteria are met.

separable

- It is identifiable. < *arises from contractual / legal rights*

- It is controlled by the entity (the entity has the power to obtain economic benefits from it).

- It is expected to generate future economic benefits for the entity.

- It has a cost that can be measured reliably.

These recognition criteria apply whether an intangible asset is acquired externally or generated internally.

- An intangible asset is identifiable when it:
  - is separable (capable of being separated and sold, transferred, licensed, rented, or exchanged, either individually or as part of a package)
  - it arises from contractual or other legal rights, regardless of whether those rights are transferable or separable from the entity or from other rights and obligations.
- If an intangible asset does not meet the recognition criteria, then it should be charged to profits as it is incurred. Once the expenditure has been so charged, it cannot be capitalised at a later date.

Definition and recognition criteria

An **intangible asset** is an identifiable non-monetary asset without physical substance.

An intangible asset should be recognised if all the following criteria are met.

- It is identifiable.
- It is controlled by the entity (the entity has the power to obtain economic benefits from it).
- It is expected to generate future economic benefits for the entity.
- It has a cost that can be measured reliably.

These recognition criteria apply whether an intangible asset is acquired externally or generated internally.

- An intangible asset is identifiable when it:
  - is separable (capable of being separated and sold, transferred, licensed, rented, or exchanged, either individually or as part of a package)
  - it arises from contractual or other legal rights, regardless of whether those rights are transferable or separable from the entity or from other rights and obligations.
- If an intangible asset does not meet the recognition criteria, then it should be charged to profits as it is incurred. Once the expenditure has been so charged, it cannot be capitalised at a later date.

Examples of intangible assets

Examples of possible intangible assets include:

- goodwill acquired in a business combination
- computer software
- patents
- copyrights
- motion picture films
- customer list
- mortgage servicing rights
- licences
- import quotas
- franchises
- customer and supplier relationships
- marketing rights.

The following **internally generated intangible assets** are not capable of being recognised as assets and IAS 38 prohibits their recognition:

- start-up, pre-opening, and pre-operating costs
- training costs
- relocation costs
- advertising cost
- goodwill
- brands
- mastheads — headline, name, logu s/k habar.
- publishing titles
- customer lists and items similar in substance.

Meeting the recognition criteria

(a) Identifiability

Intangible assets such as customer relationships cannot be separated from goodwill unless they:

- arise as a result of a legal right, if there are ongoing supply contracts, for example

- are separable, i.e. can be sold separately. This is unlikely unless there are legal contracts in existence, in which case they fall under the previous bullet point.

If they cannot be separated, then in a business combination such assets would become part of goodwill. – not as intangible assets.

(b) Control

The knowledge that the staff have is an asset. It can be possible for the entity to control this knowledge. Patents, copyrights and restraint-of-trade agreements will give the entity legal rights to the future economic benefits and prevent other people from obtaining them. Therefore copyrights and patents can be capitalised.

(c) Probable future economic benefits

An intangible asset can generate future economic benefits in two ways. Owning a brand name can boost revenues, while owning the patent for a production process may help to reduce production costs. Either way, the entity's profits will be increased.

When an entity assesses the probability of future economic benefits, the assessment must be based on reasonable and supportable assumptions about conditions that will exist over the life of the asset.

for asset obtained
from bus. combination
cost = FV

FV is the price
of similar asset in
active market.

Active market
– items are homogenous
– willing buyers & sellers
at any time.
– there are frequent
transactions.
– prices are available
to public

(d) Reliable measurement

If the asset is acquired separately then this is straightforward. For example, the purchase price of a franchise should be capitalised, along with all the related legal and professional costs.   cost = FV

If the asset is acquired as part of a business combination, then its cost will equal its fair value at the date of acquisition. The best measure of fair value is the quoted price of similar assets on an active market. In an active market, the items traded are homogenous, willing buyers and sellers can be found at any time, there are frequent transactions and prices are available to the public.

Measurement

When an intangible asset is initially recognised, it is measured at cost. After recognition, an entity must choose either the cost model or the revaluation model for each class of intangible asset.

*   The cost model measures the asset at cost less accumulated amortisation and impairment.

*   The revaluation model measures the asset at fair value less accumulated amortisation and impairment.

The revaluation model can only be adopted if fair value can be determined by reference to an **active market**. An active market is one where the products are homogenous, there are willing buyers and sellers to be found at all times, and prices are available to the public.

Active markets for intangible assets are rare. They may exist for assets such as:

*   milk quotas

*   European Union fishing quotas

*   stock exchange seats.

Active markets are unlikely to exist for brands, newspaper mastheads, music and film publishing rights, patents or trademarks.

Revaluations should be made with sufficient regularity such that the carrying amount does not differ materially from actual fair value at the reporting date.

Revaluation gains and losses are accounted for in the same way as revaluation gains and losses of tangible assets under IAS 16.

Amortisation

An entity must assess whether the useful life of an intangible asset is finite or indefinite.

- An asset with a finite useful life must be amortised on a systematic basis over that life. Normally the straight-line method with a zero residual value should be used. Amortisation starts when the asset is available for use.

- An asset has an indefinite useful life when there is no foreseeable limit to the period over which the asset is expected to generate net cash inflows. It should not be amortised, but be subject to an annual impairment review.

Research and development expenditure

Research is original and planned investigation undertaken with the prospect of gaining new scientific or technical knowledge and understanding.

Development is the application of research findings or other knowledge to a plan or design for the production of new or substantially improved materials, devices, products, processes, systems or services before the start of commercial production or use.

- Research expenditure cannot be recognised as an intangible asset. (Tangible assets used in research should be recognised as plant and equipment).

- Development expenditure should be recognised as an intangible asset if an entity can demonstrate that:
  - the project is technically feasible
  - the entity intends to complete the intangible asset, and then use it or sell it

- it is able to use or sell the intangible asset

- the intangible asset will generate future economic benefits. There must either be a market for the product or an internal use for it

- the entity has adequate technical, financial and other resources to complete the project

- it can reliably measure the attributable expenditure on the project.

Computer intangibles

Computer software

Some computer software is an integral part of the related hardware, for example the computer programme in a production-line robot or the operating system on a PC. The hardware will not work without the software, and so the software is capitalised as part of the hardware. This type of software is a tangible non-current asset subject to IAS 16.

Stand-alone computer software (for example an accounts package) is an intangible asset subject to IAS 38.

Illustration: Intangible assets

Rue has developed a software programme during the year to 30 November 20X2. The cost of developing the software was $5 million. The software is used by the rest of the group and sold to third parties. Net revenue of $4 million is expected from sales of the software, which has quickly become a market leader in its field. The software is expected to generate revenue for four years, after which an upgraded version will be developed.

Should Rue recognise the software as an intangible asset?

Solution

IAS 38 **Intangible assets** prohibits the recognition of internally generated brands, mastheads, publishing titles, customer lists and similar items as intangible assets. It could be argued that the software is a similar asset.

However, IAS 38 also requires internally generated intangibles to be recognised, provided that they meet certain criteria. An entity must demonstrate the technical feasibility of the asset, the ability to complete and use or sell the asset, the probable future economic benefits of the asset and the availability of adequate technical, financial and other resources before it can be recognised. It must also be possible to measure the expenditure attributable to the asset reliably and it should be capable of generating cash inflows in excess of cash outflows.

Because the software is generating external revenue, these criteria appear to be met. It is not clear how the cost of $5 million is made up, but it is possible that it includes items such as staff training and overheads that may not be capitalised under IAS 38.

It is also not clear when the cost of $5 million was incurred, relative to the date when the development met the criteria set out above. Only expenditure incurred after that date should be capitalised.

More information is therefore required about the components of the cost and when it was incurred. Any asset that is recognised should be amortised over its expected useful life of four years.

Inventories (IAS 2)

Inventories are measured at the lower of cost and net realisable value.

Cost includes all purchase costs, conversion costs and other costs incurred in bringing the inventories to their present condition and location.

- **Purchase costs** include the purchase price (less discounts and rebates), import duties, irrecoverable taxes, transport and handling costs and any other directly attributable costs.

- **Conversion costs** include all direct costs of conversion (materials, labour, expenses, etc), and a proportion of the fixed and variable production overheads. The allocation of production overheads must be based on the normal level of activity.

- Abnormal wastage, storage costs, administration costs and selling costs must be excluded from the valuation and charged as expenses in the period in which they are incurred.

Net realisable value is the expected selling price less the estimated costs of completion and sale.

- IAS 2 **Inventories** allows three methods of arriving at cost:
  - actual unit cost
  - first-in, first-out (FIFO)
  - weighted average cost (AVCO).

- Actual unit cost must be used where items of inventory are not ordinarily interchangeable.

- The same method of arriving at cost should be used for all inventories having similar nature and use to the entity. Different cost methods may be justified for inventories with different nature or use.

- Entities should disclose:
  - their accounting policy and cost formulas
  - total carrying amount of inventories by category
  - details of inventories carried at net realisable value.

Valuation of inventories

How should the following be valued?

(a) Materials costing $12,000 bought for processing and assembly for a profitable special order. Since buying these items, the cost price has fallen to $10,000.

(b) Equipment constructed for a customer for an agreed price of $18,000. This has recently been completed at a cost of $16,800. It has now been discovered that, in order to meet certain regulations, conversion with an extra cost of $4,200 will be required. The customer has accepted partial responsibility and agreed to meet half the extra cost.

Solution

(a) Value at $12,000. The $10,000 is irrelevant. The rule is lower of cost or net realisable value, not lower of cost or replacement cost. Since the materials will be processed before sale there is no reason to believe that net realisable value will be below cost.

(b) Value at net realisable value, i.e. $15,900 (contract price $18,000 – constructor's share of modification cost $2,100), because this is below cost.

KAPLAN PUBLISHING

Current issues

Rate-regulated activities

An ED was issued on this topic in July 2009 and seeks to clarify in what circumstances regulated entities should recognise assets or liabilities as a result of rate regulation. The proposed IFRS defines regulatory assets and regulatory liabilities, sets out criteria for their recognition, specifies how they should be measured and requires disclosures about their financial effects.

Rate regulation is a restriction in the setting of prices that can be charged to customers for services or products. Generally, it is imposed by regulatory bodies or governments when an entity has a monopoly or a dominant market position that gives it excessive market power. In the United Kingdom for example, this could apply to the provision of electricity and gas.

In December 2008, the IASB added a project on Rate-regulated Activities to its agenda. The project objective was to develop a standard on rate-regulated activities that clarifies whether regulated entities could or should recognise an asset or a liability as a result of rate regulation.

The proposed IFRS addresses only those rate-regulated activities that meet the following two criteria:

- an authorised body is empowered to establish rates that bind customers; and

- the price established by regulation(the rate) is designed to recover the specific costs the entity incurs in providing the regulated goods or services and to earn a specified return.

The following definition are applied within the ED:

- A regulatory asset exists because the entity obtains from the regulator the present right to set rates at a level that will ensure the entity recovers its previously incurred costs by receiving cash flows from its aggregate customer base.

- A regulatory liability arises from a present obligation enforced by the regulator to return previously collected amounts to the aggregate customer base by reducing rates.

This form of regulation is often referred to as 'cost-of-service' or 'return on rate base' regulation

Although a specific standard on accounting for the effects of rate regulation exists in the United States, it has no counterpart in IFRSs. However, rate regulation is widespread and significantly affects the economic environment of rate-regulated entities. Many billions of dollars of 'regulatory' assets and liabilities are currently recognised in jurisdictions that refer to US GAAP. Some of these jurisdictions are already converging to IFRSs. Clarifying whether assets and liabilities arise from rate regulation in IFRSs and if so, how to account for them is therefore important.

Following expiry of the comment period for the ED in February 2010, the IASB decided to continue research and analysis on this project and to focus on the key issue of whether regulatory assets and regulatory liabilities exist in accordance with the current Framework for the Preparation and Presentation of Financial Statements and whether they are consistent with other current IFRSs.

At September 2012, development work had focussed upon whether regulatory assets and liabilities exist, and whether they should be recognised in accordance with the Framework, and whether they are consistent with other reporting standards. However, there has been little tangible progress over the previous two years as the technical issues involved cannot be easily resolved.

Emission Trading Schemes

The objective of the project is to develop comprehensive guidance on the accounting for emissions trading schemes, including (but not limited to) the following issues:

- Are emissions allowances assets? Is this conclusion affected by how the allowance is acquired? What is the nature of the allowance (e.g. licence to emit or form of emission currency)? If allowances are assets, should they be recognised and, if so, how should they be measured initially?

- What is the corresponding entry for an entity that receives allowances from government free of charge? Does a liability exist? If so, what is the nature of the liability and how should it be measured both initially and subsequently?

- How should allowances be accounted for subsequently? Is the existing model in IAS 38 Intangible Assets or IAS 9 Financial Instruments appropriate? If not, what is the appropriate accounting?

- When should an entity recognise its obligations in emissions trading schemes and how should they be measured? How does IAS 37 Provisions, Contingent Liabilities and Contingent Assets apply?

- What are the overall financial reporting effects of the above decisions?

Among the reasons for adding the topic to the agenda, the Board noted in particular the increasing international use (or planned use) of schemes designed to achieve reduction of greenhouse gases through the use of tradable permits. It also noted that there was a risk of diverse accounting practices for such schemes following the withdrawal of IFRIC 3 Emission Rights and that this would impair the comparability and usefulness of financial statement information.

In November 2010, discussion and progress on this issue was deferred due to other work priorities and a decision regarding whether this topic should remain on the IASB agenda will be at a date still to be determined.

UK syllabus focus

The ACCA UK syllabus contains a requirement that candidates should be able to discuss and apply the key differences between UK GAAP and IFRS GAAP. The accounting requirements of UK GAAP and IFRS GAAP are very similar in this area; the relevant UK reporting standards are as follows:

SSAP 4 – Government grants. There are no significant differences in accounting treatment in comparison with IAS 20.

SSAP 9 – Stock. There are no significant differences between SSAP 9 and IAS 2 under IFRS GAAP. Note that the P2 syllabus excludes accounting for construction or long-term contracts.

SSAP 13 – Research and development. There are no significant differences in accounting treatment in comparison with IAS 38. Note that **development costs** must be capitalised where they meet defined criteria under IFRS GAAP. Under UK GAAP, development costs can either be capitalised and amortised, or written off as incurred.

SSAP 19 – Investment property. The definition of an investment property is the same under both accounting frameworks. Under UK GAAP, investment property **must** be carried at market value, and not subject to depreciation, unless it is a leasehold property with twenty years or less remaining. Any change in carrying value is taken to separate investment property revaluation reserve. In accordance with IAS 40, there is a **choice of accounting treatment**, based upon either cost or fair value. In effect, the cost model applies the accounting requirements equivalent to IAS 16 (Property, plant and equipment), with depreciation charged if the investment property has a finite useful life. However, if the fair value model is used, IAS 40 requires that no depreciation charge is made and that any change in carrying value is taken to profit or loss. SSAP 19 requires that any revaluation gains and losses are taken to revaluation reserve, unless the diminution in value is regarded as permanent, in which case it is charged to profit or loss.

UK FRS 10 – Goodwill and intangible assets. There are similar recognition criteria for intangible assets under both frameworks. Under UK GAAP, FRS 10 permits only separable **intangible assets** to be capitalised upon acquisition; IAS 38 requires intangibles to be recognised which are identifiable. Identifiable is defined by IAS 38 as either separable or that arise from contractual or legal rights.

Under IFRS GAAP, IFRS 3 permits a choice of accounting treatment for **goodwill** on an acquisition-by-acquisition basis. In effect, goodwill can be calculated either on a full basis, or on a proportionate basis. The former recognises goodwill on acquisition for the subsidiary as a whole; the latter basis recognises goodwill only on the controlling company's interest in the subsidiary. Within this publication, any group accounts questions which require goodwill (or non-controlling interest) to be calculated on a proportionate basis are suitable for UK GAAP accounting.

However, under UK GAAP, UK **FRS 10 requires goodwill on acquisition to be computed based upon the controlling company's holding only**; this is essentially the proportionate basis under IFRS GAAP. Upon calculation of goodwill, FRS 10 requires that goodwill would normally be amortised on a systematic basis over its expected useful life, with a rebuttable presumption of a maximum of twenty years, rather than accounted for as a permanent non-current intangible asset as required by IFRS 3.

Another distinction between UK FRS 10 and IFRS 3 relates to accounting for **negative goodwill**, which arises when the fair value of consideration paid to acquire control of a subsidiary is less than the fair value of net assets acquired. Under UK FRS 10, negative goodwill is accounted for as a 'negative asset' and released to profit or loss based on the expected useful life of the non-monetary assets acquired. In effect, the gain is recognised on the same period over which the related non-monetary assets are used in the business. IFRS 3 effectively treats negative goodwill as a bargain purchase and any such gain arising is taken to profit or loss immediately.

UK FRS 11 – Impairment of fixed assets and goodwill. Impairment treatment of tangible assets and most intangible assets are similar under both frameworks. For impairment of goodwill, under UK GAAP, only impairment on the controlling company's investment is accounted for. Under IFRS GAAP, under the full goodwill basis, any impairment would be for the subsidiary as a whole, with any impairment borne by the group and non-controlling interest (i.e. minority interest) based upon their respective shareholdings. Under IFRS GAAP, where goodwill has been calculated on a proportionate basis, accounting for impairment would be similar to accounting for impairment under UK GAAP.

The **order of allocation of impairment** arising on an IGU under UK GAAP is that it is specifically allocated to damaged assets(s) then to goodwill, then intangibles, and then to tangible assets. Under IFRS GAAP, IAS 36 dealing with impairment does not distinguish between tangible and intangible assets for allocation of impairment arising on an IGU.

Any impairment due to consumption of economic benefits is taken to profit and loss, irrespective of whether or not it has been revalued in the past.

Reversal of impairment of goodwill and intangibles is only possible if there is an external event which clearly demonstrates reversal of the impairing event. In practical terms, impairment of goodwill will not be reversed, whereas IAS 36 specifically disallows reversal of goodwill impairment losses.

UK FRS 15 – Tangible fixed assets. There are no significant differences in accounting for tangible fixed assets under UK GAAP and the equivalent requirements of IAS 16. One distinction is that under FRS 15, a company has the choice to either capitalise or write off **finance costs** in relation to construction of an asset; under IAS 23, it is compulsory to capitalise such costs if the criteria have been met.

Both frameworks permit accounting for fixed assets under the cost or fair value basis, provided they are appropriate and properly disclosed. However, UK FRS 15 contains specific guidance regarding the basis and frequency of valuation as follows:

	Non-specialised properties	**Specialised properties**	**Other tangible fixed assets**
Frequency of valuation	Full valuation every five years; interim valuation in year three or full valuation on a rolling basis over five-year cycles.	Full valuation every five years with interim valuation in year three.	Annual revaluation if market comparisons or appropriate indices available, otherwise every five years.
	But revaluation is required whenever it is likely that there has been a material change in value.		

Basis of valuation	Existing use value plus directly attributable acquisition costs if material. Disclose open market value where this is materially different.	Depreciated replacement cost.	Market value where obtainable, otherwise use depreciated replacement cost.
	For properties surplus to requirements use open market value, less expected direct selling costs where these are material.		

The normal accounting treatment for any revaluation gain is to credit it to revaluation reserve (i.e. equity) and report it in the statement of total recognised gains and losses (STRGL). The only time it may be taken to profit and loss is when it reverses a decrease in the value of an asset which was previously taken to profit and loss.

Where there is an upward revaluation on a fixed asset with a definite useful life, the annual depreciation charge should be re-calculated based upon the new carrying value of the asset and the remaining estimated useful life of that asset. There will then be an increased annual charge to profit and loss for the year. Best practice would be to also make an annual reserves transfer from revaluation reserve to profit and loss reserve for increase in the depreciation charge due solely to the revaluation. Note however, that this annual reserves transfer is optional – it is not compulsory.

- If a revaluation loss is caused by a consumption of economic benefits (e.g. physical damage), the loss must be recognised immediately in profit and loss as this reflects additional depreciation, rather than a change in valuation.

- Where there is no consumption of economic benefits, any decrease in the value of an asset is normally taken to profit or loss, unless there is a revaluation reserve representing a surplus on the same asset, in which case this is used as far as depreciated historical cost of that asset. Any further revaluation loss between depreciated historical cost and recoverable amount is taken to profit and loss; any further losses represented by a difference between recoverable amount and the revalued amount are taken to STRGL.

- Gains and losses on individual assets cannot be netted off against each other to reduce the loss recognised in profit and loss for the year.

- For a full valuation, the name and professional qualifications of the valuer should be stated, together with the date of the valuation. If the valuation is done by an officer, director or employee of the entity, this fact should be stated, together with the valuation being subject to review by an external valuer.

Revaluation illustration per FRS 15

A property costing $500,000 was purchased on 1 January 20X4 and was depreciated over its useful economic life of 10 years. It has no estimated residual value. At 31 December 20X4 the property was valued at $540,000 and at 31 December 20X5 it was valued at $350,000.

Required:

How should these revaluations be treated in the accounts for the years ended 31 December 20X4 and 31 December 20X5 if:

(a) **the recoverable amount at 31 December 20X5 was $350,000?**

(b) **the recoverable amount at 31 December 20X5 was $380,000?**

Revaluation illustration – solution

Year ended 31 December 20X4: a revaluation gain of $90,000 (W) is reported in the statement of total recognised gains and losses (i.e. other comprehensive income).

Year ended 31 December 20X5: a revaluation loss of $130,000 (W) occurs and is dealt with as follows:

(a) **Recoverable amount $350,000**

	$000
Statement of total recognised gains and losses (480 – 400)	80
Profit or loss	50
	——
	130
	——

(b) Recoverable amount $380,000

	$000
Statement of total recognised gains and losses	
Net book value less depreciated historical cost (480 – 400)	80
Recoverable amount less revalued amount (380 – 350)	30
	110
Profit and loss account	
Depreciated historical cost less recoverable amount (400 – 380)	20
	130

(W1)

	$000
Cost at 1 January 20X4	500
Depreciation (500 ÷ 10)	(50)
	450
Revaluation gain	90
Carrying value at 1 January 20X5	540
Less: depreciation (540 ÷ 9)	(60)
	480
Revaluation loss	(130)
Valuation at 31 December 20X5	350
Depreciated historical cost at 31 December 20X5:	
(500 – (500/10 × 2))	400

KAPLAN PUBLISHING

UK syllabus illustration Q&A – FRS 11

An entity, Trendy Clothes, owns a number of businesses which operate in different sectors of the clothing industry. One business unit within Trendy Clothes, which operates under the name of Kids Klobber, has experienced growing competition from importers who are able to manufacture and sell their clothing at cheaper prices.

At the reporting date of 31 December 20X7, Trendy Clothes estimate that the Kids Klobber, which is regarded as an income generating unit has a value in use of $2.2 million, and a net realisable value of $2.1 million.

The carrying values of the net assets at the reporting date were as follows:

	$000
Goodwill	175
Intangible non-current assets	150
Land and buildings	1,500
Plant and machinery	800
	–––––
	2,625
	–––––

Required:

Perform an impairment review at 31 December 20X7 on Kids Klobber, and allocate any impairment in the order specified by FRS 11.

Solution:

Impairment review of IGU:	$000
Carrying value	2,625
Recoverable amount: higher of:	
value in use – 2,200	2,200
net realisable value – 2,100	
	–––––
Impairment of income generating unit	425
	–––––

Allocation of impairment:

	Initial CV $000	Impaired $000	Revised CV $000
Goodwill	175	(175)	nil
Intangible non-current assets	150	(150)	nil
Land and buildings	1,500	(65)	1,435
Plant and machinery	800	(35)	765
	2,625	(425)	2,200

Notes on order of impairment allocation:

(1) Goodwill is written-off in full first.

(2) Intangible assets are next to be written-off in full.

(3) To the extent that the impairment has not yet been fully allocated, any remaining amount is allocated pro-rata against the tangible assets, based upon their current carrying values, as follows:

Land and buildings: 1,500 / 2,300 ×100 = 65
Plant and machinery: 800 / 2.300 ×100 = 35

UK syllabus illustration Q&A – FRS 10

Negative goodwill illustration per FRS 10

P acquired a wholly-owned subsidiary, S, on 1 July 20X8 at a cost of $1,000,000. The fair value of the net assets acquired were as follows:

	$000
Tangible fixed assets (remaining estimated useful fife – 5 years)	900
Stocks (disposed of within 1 year)	300
Net monetary assets (receivables less creditors)	400

Required:

Calculate goodwill on acquisition and identify the amounts to be included in profit and loss and the balance sheet at the year end of 30 June 20X9.

KAPLAN PUBLISHING

Negative goodwill illustration – solution

	$000
Fair value of consideration paid	1,000
Less: Fair value of net assets acquired (900 + 300 + 400)	(1,600)
Negative goodwill	(600)

Negative goodwill arising is recognised in profit and loss on the same basis as non-monetary assets are recognised in profit and loss as follows:

	$000
Amounts written off to profit and loss in the year relating to non-monetary assets ((900 ÷ 5) + 300)	480
Total of non-monetary assets at date of acquisition (900 + 300)	1,200
Proportion recognised in the year to 30 June 20X9: (480/1,200) =	2/5
Release of negative goodwill to profit and loss for the year to 30 June 20X9: ($600 × 2/5)	$240
Summary of movement in negative asset – negative goodwill	$000
Negative goodwill on acquisition	600
Released to profit and loss for the year	(240)
Negative goodwill carried forward at 30 June 20X9	360

5 Chapter summary

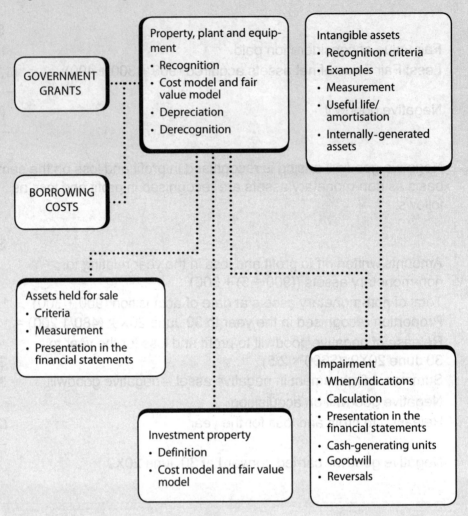

GOVERNMENT GRANTS

BORROWING COSTS

Property, plant and equipment
- Recognition
- Cost model and fair value model
- Depreciation
- Derecognition

Intangible assets
- Recognition criteria
- Examples
- Measurement
- Useful life/ amortisation
- Internally-generated assets

Assets held for sale
- Criteria
- Measurement
- Presentation in the financial statements

Investment property
- Definition
- Cost model and fair value model

Impairment
- When/indications
- Calculation
- Presentation in the financial statements
- Cash-generating units
- Goodwill
- Reversals

Inventories
- Cost
- NRV
- Valuation methods

Test your understanding answers

Test your understanding 1 – Impaired asset

Net selling price is lower than carrying amount, so it is necessary to calculate value in use:

	$000
Cash flow Year 1 (200 × 0.909)	182
Cash flow Year 2 (200 × 0.826)	165
	–––
	347
	–––
Carrying amount	500
Recoverable amount (value in use)	347
	–––
Impairment loss	153
	–––

Test your understanding 2 – Cash generating units

A forms a cash-generating unit and its cash inflows should be based on the market price for its output. B and C together form one cash-generating unit because there is no market available for the output of B. In calculating the cash outflows of the cash-generating unit B + C, the timber received by B from A should be priced by reference to the market, not any internal transfer price.

Test your understanding 3 – Factory explosion

As the value in use is higher than the net selling price, the impairment loss is £650,000 (£2.6m – 1.95m). It is allocated:

- first to goodwill, leaving $550,000 to be dealt with

- then to patents (200) and half the machines (150), leaving $200,000 to be dealt with

- then pro rata to computers ((500/(500 + 1,500) × 200) and buildings (note that because they can be sold for at least their book value, the remaining machines are not included in this pro rata exercise).

	Opening	Impairment	Closing
	$000	$000	$000
Goodwill	100	(100)	Nil
Patents	200	(200)	Nil
Machines	300	(150)	150
Computers	500	(50)	450
Buildings	1,500	(150)	1,350
	2,600	(650)	1,950

Test your understanding 4 – Cedar

Impairment of gross goodwill – 60% subsidiary Cedar

The gross goodwill at acquisition is:

	$m
Parent investment	800
FV of NCI	250
	1,050
Less: FV of net assets at acquisition	(500)
Gross goodwill	550

KAPLAN PUBLISHING

Impairment review of gross goodwill at reporting date:

	$m
CV of net assets	600
CV of unimpaired goodwill	550
	1,150
Recoverable amount	1,000
Impairment loss	150

The impairment loss on the gross goodwill will be allocated between the parent and the NCI in the normal proportion that profits and losses are shared (i.e. their respective shareholdings) – so 40% x 150 = $60m of the impairment loss will be charged against the NCI, and the remaining 60% = $90m will be charged against the retained earnings. The goodwill asset reported on the group statement of financial position will be $550m less $150m = $400m. Note that recoverable amount of a subsidiary is normally for the entity as a whole.

Test your understanding 5 – Homer

Impairment of gross goodwill – Homer 80% subsidiary

The gross goodwill at acquisition is:

	$m
Parent investment	200
FV of NCI	25
	225
Less: FV of net assets at acquisition	(100)
Gross goodwill at acquisition	125

Impairment review of gross goodwill at reporting date:

	$m
CV of net assets	150
CV of unimpaired goodwill	125
	275
Recoverable amount	255
Impairment loss	20

The impairment loss on the gross goodwill will be allocated between the parent and the NCI in the normal proportion that profits and losses are shared (i.e. based upon respective shareholdings in the subsidiary) – so 20% x 20 = $4m of the impairment loss will be charged against the NCI, and $16m will be charged against the retained earnings. The goodwill asset reported on the group statement of financial position will be $125m less $20m = $105m. Note that recoverable amount of a subsidiary is normally for the entity as a whole.

Test your understanding 6 – Happy

Goodwill:

	$
Fair value of consideration paid	500
NCI share of net assets at acquisition (20% × $560,000)	112
	612
Less: fair value of net assets at acquisition	(560)
Proportionate goodwill	52

Gross up goodwill:

Total notional goodwill 52 × 100/80 = $65,000

The carrying amount of Happy at 31 December 20X5 is:

	$000
Assets	520
Total notional goodwill	65
	585

The recoverable amount is $510,000, which means there is an impairment loss of $75,000.

This loss is allocated to total notional goodwill first, writing off the entire balance of $65,000. As $13,000 is attributable to the non-controlling interest, only $52,000 of the loss is charged to profit or loss relating to the parent's goodwill.

The remaining $10,000 impairment loss is allocated to the other assets. They would be written down on a pro-rata basis according to their carrying values.

Test your understanding 7 – Boxer

Solution:

Year ended 31 December 20X2

	$
Asset carrying value ($30,000 × 8/10)	24,000
Recoverable amount	16,000
Impairment loss	8,000

The loss is charged to income, the asset written down and in future the depreciation per annum will be 16,000 × 1/8 = 2,000 rather than before the impairment review when it was based on the historical cost of $30,000 × 1/10 = $3,000.

Year ended 31 December 20X5

	$
Asset carrying value ($16,000 × 5/8)	10,000
Recoverable amount	40,000
	———
Impairment loss	nil
	———

There has been no impairment loss; rather a complete reversal of the first impairment loss. The asset can be reinstated to its depreciated historical cost i.e. to the carrying value at 31 December 20X5 if there never had been an earlier impairment loss.

Year 5 depreciated historical cost (30,000 × 5/10) = $15,000

Carrying value: $10,000

Reversal of the loss: $5,000

The reversal of the loss is now recognised – by a CR to income (as that is where the original impairment loss was charged) and a DR to the asset so the asset is now $15,000. In future the annual depreciation will be 15,000 x 1/5 = $3,000 which is of course the same as the original depreciation based on the historical cost.

It should be noted that in reversing back the original impairment loss we cannot take the whole $8,000 that was originally charged, rather only $5,000 due to the depreciation difference of $1,000 per annum for each of the three years. The impairment can only be reversed to a maximum amount of depreciated historical cost, based upon the original cost and estimated useful life of the asset.

Test your understanding 8 – Hyssop

(a) IFRS 5 states that in order to be classified as 'held for sale' the property should be available for immediate sale in its present condition. The property will not be sold until the work has been carried out; this demonstrates that the facility is not available for immediate sale. Therefore the property cannot be classified as 'held for sale'.

(b) The subsidiary B does not meet the criteria for classification as 'held for sale', because while actions to locate a buyer are in place, the subsidiary is not for sale at a price that is reasonable compared with its fair value. The fair value of the subsidiary is $2.5 million, but it is up for sale for $3 million. It cannot be classified as held for sale' until the sale price is reduced.

15

Leases

Chapter learning objectives

Upon completion of this chapter you will be able to:

- apply and discuss the classification of leases and accounting by lessors and lessees

- account for and discuss the accounting for sale and leaseback transactions.

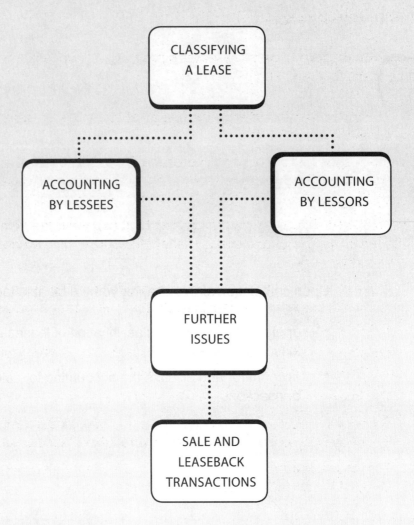

1 Classifying a lease

Definitions

Leases are classified as either finance leases or operating leases at inception (normally the date of the lease agreement).

A **finance lease** transfers substantially all the risks and rewards incident to ownership of an asset.

An **operating lease** is a lease other than a finance lease.

Whether a lease is a finance lease or an operating lease depends on the substance of the agreement.

- A finance lease (as its name suggests) is basically a way of financing the use of an asset (by spreading the payment over the life of the asset, instead of paying the full amount all at once).

- An operating lease is similar to a rental agreement. The entity normally rents the asset for only part of its useful life.

How to classify a lease

IAS 17 Leases explains that a lease is probably a finance lease if one or more of the following apply.

- Ownership is transferred to the lessee at the end of the lease (as in hire purchase agreements).

- The lessee has the option to purchase the asset for less than its expected fair value at the date the option becomes exercisable (so it is reasonably certain that the option will be exercised).

- The lease term is for the major part of the economic life of the asset, even if title is not transferred. The length of the lease includes any secondary period.

- At the inception of the lease, the present value of the minimum lease payments amounts to at least substantially all of the fair value of the leased asset.

- The leased assets are of a specialised nature so that only the lessee can use them without major modifications being made.

- The lessee will compensate the lessor if the lease is cancelled.

- Gains or losses from fluctuations in the fair value of the residual fall to the lessee (for example, by means of a rebate of lease payments).

- The lessee has the ability to continue the lease for a secondary period at a rent that is substantially lower than market rent.

How to classify a lease

In most cases, it should be fairly easy to tell whether or not any of the above situations apply. The exception is the fourth item, comparing the present value of the minimum lease payments with the fair value of the leased asset. The present value of the minimum lease payments normally has to be calculated, using an appropriate discount rate.

Illustration 1 – Classifying a lease

A company can buy an asset for cash at a cost of $5,800 or it can lease the asset on the following terms:

(1) the lease term is for four years from 1 January 20X2, with a rental of $2,000 pa payable on the 31 December each year

(2) the interest rate implicit in the lease is 15%.

Is the lease a finance lease?

The minimum lease payments are $8,000 (4 × 2,000)

Present value of minimum lease payments:

From discount tables, the present value at 15% of four annual sums first payable at the end of the first year is:

$2,000 × 2.855 = $5,710

The fair value of the asset is $5,800.

Therefore, the minimum lease payments are 98% of the fair value of the asset.

This strongly suggests that the lease is a finance lease.

Problem areas

IAS 17 does not define 'substantially all', but in practice this is often taken to mean 'more than 90%'.

IAS 17 defines minimum lease payments:

Minimum lease payments are the payments over the lease term that the lessee is, or can be required, to make (excluding contingent rent, costs for services and taxes to be paid by and reimbursed to the lessor), together with:

- in the case of the lessee, any amounts guaranteed by the lessee
- in the case of the lessor, any residual value guaranteed to the lessor by the lessee.

Contingent rent is that portion of the lease payments that is not fixed in amount but is based on a factor other than just the passage of time (for example, percentage of sales, amount of usage, price indices, market rates of interest).

Leases of land and buildings

Land and buildings are often leased together, but IAS 17 requires the land and buildings elements to be classified separately.

- The land element is normally classified as an operating lease unless title passes to the lessee at the end of the lease term.

- The buildings element may be classified as either a finance or an operating lease depending upon the nature of the lease contract.

- The minimum lease payments are allocated between the land and buildings elements in proportion to their relative fair values.

Note, however, that IAS 17 has been amended to require that leases of land and buildings are evaluated based upon the commercial substance of the whole transaction. This may result, for example, in a long-term lease of land and buildings (e.g. for 900 years) being accounted for as a finance lease as substantially all of the risks and rewards associated with the lease have been transferred.

2 Accounting by lessees

Finance leases

IAS 17 requires the accounting treatment to report the substance of the transaction: the lessee controls an asset and has a liability for the outstanding rentals.

- At the beginning of the lease term, the lessee recognises the leased asset and the obligation to make lease payments as an asset and a liability in the statement of financial position.

- The asset and the liability are measured at the lower of:
  - the fair value of the asset

  - the present value of the minimum lease payments (discounted at the interest rate implicit in the lease, if practicable, or else at the entity's incremental borrowing rate).

- The lease payments are split between the finance charge and the repayment of the outstanding liability.

- The finance charge is allocated so as to produce a constant periodic rate of interest on the remaining balance of the liability. The actuarial method gives the most accurate charge, but the sum of the digits is normally a reasonable approximation.

- The leased asset is depreciated over the shorter of:
  - its useful life

  - the lease term (including secondary period).

Illustration 2 – Lease classification

Wrighty acquired use of plant over three years by way of a lease. Instalments of $700,000, are paid six monthly in arrears on 30 June and 31 December. Delivery of the plant was on 1 January 20X0 so the first payment of $700,000 was on 30 June 20X0. The present value of minimum lease payment is $3,000,000. Interest implicit in the above is 10% per six months. The Plant would normally be expected to last three years. Wrighty is required to insure the plant and cannot return it to the lessor without severe penalties.

Required:

(a) **Describe whether the above lease should be classified as an operating or finance lease.**

(b) **Calculate the effect of the above on the statement of profit or loss and statement of financial position for the year ended 31 December 20X0.**

Solution

(a) Risks and rewards of ownership of the machine are with Wrighty; so this is a finance lease.

(b) Extracts of financial statements:

Statement of profit ofr loss (extract)

Depreciation (3000 / 3 years)	1,000
Interest (W1) (300 + 260)	560

Statement of financial position (extract)

Non-current assets:finance lease asset (3,000 - 1,000)	2,000
Long-term liabilities (W1)	1,144
Current liabilities (W1) (2160 – 1144)	1,016

(W1) **Leasing table**

Period	Opening loan	Interest (10%)	Instalment	Closing loan
	$000	$000	$000	$000
1	3,000	300	(700)	2,600
2	2,600	260	(700)	2,160
3	2,160	216	(700)	1,676
4	1,676	168	(700)	1,144

Operating leases

The substance of the transaction is that the lessee uses an asset, but does not own or control it.

- The lessee does not recognise the leased asset in its statement of financial position.

- Rentals are charged as an expense on a straight line basis over the term of the lease unless another systematic and rational basis is more appropriate.

- Any difference between amounts charged and amounts paid should be adjusted to prepayments or accruals.

Leases: off-balance sheet finance

If an entity leases a lot of its assets, accounting for them as finance leases can have a significant impact on the financial statements.

- Return on capital employed decreases, because of the additional assets.

- Earnings (and earnings per share) may decrease, because of the additional depreciation.

- Gearing increases, because of the additional liabilities (obligations to pay future rentals).

Therefore, management may have incentives to try to keep lease assets and liabilities out of the statement of financial position ('off balance sheet'). For example, the entity may already have a high level of long-term debt, or need to raise additional finance, or may be in danger of breaching loan covenants (agreements). Loan covenants often include a clause stating that the gearing ratio or the ratio of assets to liabilities must not exceed a certain figure.

However, the classification of leases is subjective. It is possible to structure a lease agreement so that technically the lease appears to be an operating lease when it is actually a finance lease.

This is a form of 'creative accounting'. IAS 17 requires that the classification of a lease should always reflect the **substance** of the agreement.

3 Accounting by lessors

Finance leases

Here, the lessee, not the lessor, has control of the asset.

- The lessor recognises the lease as a receivable. The carrying value is the lessor's net investment in the lease.

- The net investment in the lease equals:
  - the present value of the minimum lease payments receivable; plus
  - the present value of any unguaranteed residual value accruing to the lessor (e.g. the residual value of the leased asset when it is repossessed at the end of the lease).

- In practice, the lessor's net investment in the lease is the same as the lessee's lease liability.

- The lease receipts are split between finance income and a repayment of the principal. The finance income is calculated using a constant periodic rate of interest.

Accounting by lessors illustration

Vache leases machinery to Toro. The lease is for four years at an annual cost of $2,000 payable annually in arrears. The normal cash price (and fair value) of the asset is $5,900. The present value of the minimum lease payments is $5,710. The implicit rate of interest is 15%.

Show how the net investment in the lease is presented in Vache's statement of financial position at the end of Year 1.

Solution

Vache recognises the net investment in the lease as a receivable. This is the present value of the minimum lease payments: $5,710.

Vache receives lease rentals each year. These are split between finance income and a repayment of the principal.

Total finance income is $2,290 ($8,000 – $5,710). This is allocated as follows:

Year	Opening balance	Finance income @ 15%	Cash received	Closing balance
	$	$	$	$
1	5,710	856	(2,000)	4,566
2	4,566	685	(2,000)	3,251
3	3,251	488	(2,000)	1,739
4	1,739	261	(2,000)	–
		2,290		

Extract from the statement of financial position at the end of Year 1

	$
Current assets:	
Net investment in finance leases (see note)	1,315
Non-current assets:	
Net investment in finance leases	3,251

Note: the current asset is the next instalment less next year's interest, so $2,000 – 685 = $1,315. The non-current asset is the remainder, so $4,566 – 1,315 = $3,251.

Operating leases

If a lessor has an operating lease, it continues to recognise the leased asset.

- Assets held under operating leases are recognised in the statement of financial position as non-current assets. They should be presented according to the nature of the asset and depreciated in the normal way.

- Rental income from operating leases is recognised in profit or loss on a straight-line basis over the term of the lease, unless another systematic and rational basis is more appropriate.

- Any difference between amounts charged and amounts paid should be adjusted to receivables or deferred income.

Accounting by lessors illustration

Oroc hires out industrial plant on long-term operating leases. On 1 January 20X1, it entered into a seven-year lease on a mobile crane. The terms of the lease are $175,000 payable on 1 January 20X1, followed by six rentals of $70,000 payable on1 January 20X2 – 20X7. The crane will be returned to Oroc on 31 December 20X7. The crane cost $880,000 and has a 25-year useful life with no residual value.

(a) **Calculate the annual rental income that will be recognised by Oroc.**

(b) **Prepare extracts from the statement of profit or loss and statement of financial position of Oroc for 20X1 and 20X2.**

Solution

(a) Rental income must be recognised on a straight line basis. Therefore annual rental income is $85,000 (595,000 ÷ 7).

(b) Oroc recognises the crane in its statement of financial position and depreciates it over its useful life. The annual depreciation charge is $35,200 (880,000 ÷ 25).

The statement of financial position also includes a liability for deferred income (allocated between current liabilities and non-current liabilities). This is the difference between rental income received and rental income recognised in profit or loss.

Working for deferred income

Year	Cash Received	Income claimed	Difference	Cumulative difference
	$	$	$	$
20X1	175,000	85,000	90,000	90,000
20X2	70,000	85,000	(15,000)	75,000
				Deferred income

Extracts from the statement of profit or loss and statement of financial position for 20X1 and 20X2

	20X1	20X2
Profit or loss	$	$
Operating income: Rentals receivable	85,000	85,000
Operating expenses: Depreciation	(35,200)	(35,200)
	49,800	49,800

Statement of financial position

	20X1	20X2
Non-current assets		
Equipment held for use in operating leases	$	$
Cost	880,000	880,000
Depreciation	(35,200)	(70,400)
Carrying amount	844,800	809,600
Non-current liabilities Deferred income	75,000	60,000
Current liabilities Deferred income	15,000	15,000

Summary

Finance lease

- Substance = lessee has the asset

- Substance = financing agreement

- Lessee recognises asset in SFP

- Lessee recognises liability for future rentals

- Lessor recognises net investment in lease (a receivable)

- Interest accrues on outstanding amount and is paid by lessee/received by lessor

- Lease receivable/liability is reduced by lease rentals over the term of the lease

Operating lease

- Substance = lessor has the asset

- Substance = rental agreement

- Lessor recognises asset in SFP

- Lessor recognises lease rentals as income

- Lessee recognises lease rentals as an expense

Further issues in accounting for leases

Initial direct costs

Initial direct costs are costs that are directly attributable to negotiating and arranging a lease, for example, commissions, legal fees and premiums. Both lessees and lessors may incur these costs. The treatment is summarised below.

	Costs incurred by lessee	Costs incurred by lessor
Finance lease	Add to amount recognised as an asset; depreciate over asset's useful life	Include in initial measurement of receivable; reduce income receivable over lease term
Operating lease	Treat as part of lease rentals; expense over lease term on straight line basis	Add to carrying amount of leased asset; expense over lease term on same basis as lease income

- Exclude general overheads (these are not directly attributable to arranging the lease).

- Special rules apply to manufacturer or dealer lessors.

Operating leases: incentives

An operating lease agreement may include incentives for the lessee to sign the lease. Typical incentives include an up-front cash payment to the lessee (a reverse premium), rent-free periods, or contributions by the lessor to the lessee's relocation costs.

- Any incentives given by the lessor should be recognised over the life of the lease on a straight line basis. (SIC 15 Operating Leases – Incentives).

- This applies in the accounts of both the lessee and the lessor.

Depreciation of leased assets

Leased assets should be depreciated on the same basis as similar assets that the entity owns. This applies in the accounts of both the lessee (under a finance lease) and the lessor (under an operating lease).

Manufacturer or dealer lessors

Finance leases can be arranged with a third party, such as a bank, or they can be provided by the manufacturer or dealer of the goods. A manufacturer or dealer may offer customers the option to lease an asset as a way of encouraging sales.

A finance lease results in two transactions:

- a sale on normal terms (see below) giving rise to sales income and a profit or loss

- the provision of finance, giving rise to finance income.

The sales proceeds are measured at the lower of:

- fair value (i.e. the normal sales price)

- the present value of the minimum lease payments discounted at a commercial rate of interest (regardless of the rate of interest quoted to the customer). The requirement to use a commercial rate of interest prevents companies inflating the value of their sales and their profits by claiming to offer low rates of finance.

The cost of sales is the cost (or carrying amount) of the asset sold, less the present value of any unguaranteed residual value. All initial direct costs are charged when the sale is made.

Determining whether an arrangement contains a lease

Sometimes transactions or arrangements do not take the legal form of a lease but convey rights to use assets in return for a payment or series of payments. Examples of such arrangements include:

*   outsourcing arrangements

*   telecommunication contracts that provide rights to capacity

*   take-or-pay contracts, in which purchasers must make specified payments whether or not they take delivery of the contracted products or services.

4 Sale and leaseback transactions

Introduction

Under a sale and leaseback transaction an entity sells one of its own assets and immediately leases the asset back.

*   This is a common way of raising finance whilst retaining the use of the related assets. The buyer and lessor is normally a bank.

*   There are two key questions to ask when assessing the substance of these transactions:
    *   is the new lease a finance lease or an operating lease
    *   if the new lease is an operating lease, was the original sale at fair value or not?

*   The leaseback is classified in accordance with the usual criteria set out in IAS 17.

Sale and leaseback under a finance lease

In accordance with IAS 17, a sale and finance leaseback arrangement is, in essence, a financing arrangement. The substance of the arrangement is that the asset has been used as security for a loan. The accounting treatment required by IAS 17 is as follows:

*   The lessee defers any gain or loss on disposal of the asset, which is amortised over the lease term.

*   The lessee recognises both a finance lease asset and a finance lease obligation.

- The finance lease asset is depreciated over the lease term.

- The recognition of an annual finance cost, based upon the effective or implicit rate.

- The finance lease payments are split between a finance cost (based upon the effective or implicit rate) and capital repayment.

Sale and finance leaseback illustration

Lash sold an item of machinery and leased it back on a five-year finance lease. The sale took place on 1 January 20X4, and it has a reporting date of 31 December each year. The details of the scheme are as follows:

	$
Proceeds of sale at fair value	1,000,000
Carrying amount at the time of sale:	
Cost	1,500,000
Depreciation	(750,000)
	750,000

The remaining useful life of the machine at the time of sale is five years.

There are five annual lease payments of $277,409 each, commencing on 31 December 20X4. The implicit rate of interest is 12%.

Required:

Prepare relevant extracts from Lash's income statement and statement of financial position for each of the years ended 31 December 20X4 to 31 December 20X8 inclusive.

Solution

Statement of financial position:

	20X4 $	20X5 $	20X6 $	20X7 $	20X8 $
Non-current assets					
Finance lease asset	1,000,000	1,000,000	1,000,000	1,000,000	1,000,000
Accumulated depreciation	(200,000)	(400,000)	(600,000)	(800,000)	(1,000,000)
Carrying value	800,000	600,000	400,000	200,000	nil
Liabilities:					
Finance lease obligations:	1.000,000	842,591	666,293	468,839	247,691
Finance cost @12%	120,000	101,111	79,955	56,261	29,723
Repayment in arrears	(277,409)	(277,409)	(277,409)	(277,409)	(277,409)
	842,591	666,293	468,839	247,691	5
Comprising:					
Non-current liabilities:	666,293	468,839	247,691	247691	
Current liabilities	176,298	197,454	221,148		
Deferred gain on disposal	250,000	200,000	150,000	100,000	50,000
Recognised in year	(50,000)	(50,000)	(50,000)	(50,000)	(50,000)
	200,000	150,000	100,000	50,000	nil
Comprising:					
Due for release after one year	150,000	100,000	50,000	nil	nil
Due for release within one year	50,000	50,000	50,000	50,000	nil

Income statement

	20X4	20X5	20X6	20X7	20X8
	$	$	$	$	$
Deferred income	(50,000)	(50,000)	(50,000)	(50,000)	(50,000)
Depreciation charge	200,000	200,000	200,000	200,000	200,000
Finance cost	120,000	101,111	79,955	56,261	29,723

The accounting treatment should result in adjusting the overall charge to profit or loss to be consistent with writing off the carrying value of the asset immediately prior to the sale and leaseback arrangement over the lease term, together with recognition of a finance cost. The carrying value of $750,000 written off over five years would result in an annual charge of $150,000 – i.e. depreciation charge of $200,000 less release of deferred income $50,000.

Value of sales proceeds

The accounting treatment of a sale and finance leaseback is not affected if the sales proceeds are above or below the carrying value of the asset. The asset is only being used as security for the loan, and so it is up to the lender as to whether they are prepared to lend more or less than the value of the security.

However, if the sales proceeds are significantly lower than the asset's carrying amount, this suggests that the entity needs to carry out an impairment review. Alternatively, if sales proceeds are significantly higher than carrying amount, the entity may consider revaluing the asset. These adjustments are dealt with in the normal way and they do not affect the substance of the sale and leaseback transaction itself.

Sale and leaseback under an operating lease

A sale and operating leaseback transfers the risks and rewards incident to ownership to the buyer/lessor. Therefore it is treated as a sale.

- The asset is removed from the seller's statement of financial position.
- Operating lease rentals are recognised as an expense in profit or loss.

Summary

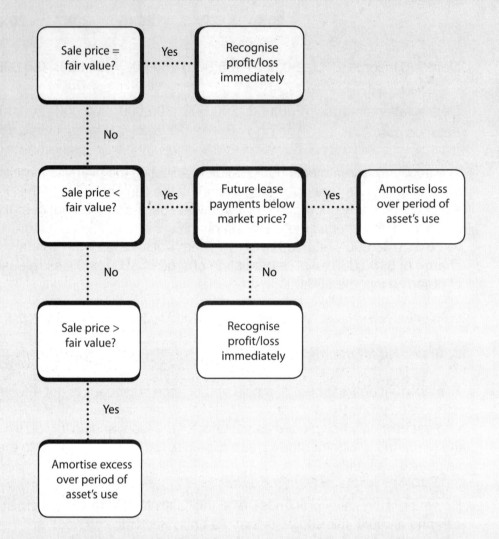

Sale and operating leaseback illustration

On 1 January 20X4, Crash sold its freehold office premises and leased them back on a 20-year operating lease. The details of the scheme are as follows:

Proceeds of sale	$8,000,000
Fair value of the asset at the time of sale	$15,000,000
Carrying amount at the time of sale	$12,000,000
Annual operating lease rentals (on a 20 year lease)	$650,000

Prepare all relevant extracts from Crash's statement of profit or loss and statement of financial position for the year ending 31 December 2004, assuming:

(a) the future rentals are at market rate

(b) the future rentals are at below market rate, and that the reduced rate will fully compensate Crash for the loss suffered on disposal.

Solution

(a) Future rentals at market rate

If the rentals are at market rate (or above), then the loss must be recognised immediately and no asset is carried forward in the statement of financial position.

Statement of profit or loss for the year ended 31 December 20X4

		$
Loss on disposal	$8m proceeds less $12m CV	4,000,000 Dr
Operating lease rentals	Amount paid	650,000 Dr

(b) Future rentals at below market rate

If the rentals are below market rate, the loss is deferred and amortised over the life of the lease.

Statement of profit or loss for the year ended 31 December 20X4

	$	$
Loss on disposal		Nil
Operating lease rentals		
Amount paid	650,000	
Plus: amortisation of deferred loss $4m / 20 years	200,000	
Amount charged to the income statement		850,000

Statement of financial position as at 31 December 20X4

Assets	$
Deferred loss on disposal	
Brought forward	–
Arising during the year	4,000,000
Amortised	(200,000)
Carried down	3,800,000

$3,600,000 of this loss would be separately disclosed as being recoverable after more than 12 months.

Sale price less than fair value

If a loss on disposal arises because the proceeds are less than the fair value of the asset, then the loss can only be deferred if the future operating lease rentals are also at below the market rate. This is because deferring a loss gives rise to an asset in the statement of financial position, and assets can only be recognised if there are future economic benefits. The economic benefits that will justify deferring this loss are reduced rentals.

If a loss is deferred.

- The loss should be amortised over the period the asset is expected to be used.

- It would be wise to conduct regular impairment reviews on such assets, because changes in market rentals and/or interest rates could easily impair the benefit of the reduced rent. For instance, if the lease rentals were $650,000 per year and the market rate for a property fell to $600,000 per year, then there would no longer be any benefit to be had from an agreed rent of $650,000. If there are no future benefits, then there is no asset to recognise.

If the sale proceeds are less than the fair value, and the fair value is less than the carrying value of the asset, then only the difference between the proceeds and the fair value can be deferred. The difference between the fair value and the carrying value must be recognised as a loss immediately.

For example, if a building with a carrying value of $9m and a fair value of $7m was sold for $4m, then a loss of $2m would be recognised on disposal, and the $3m difference between the proceeds and the fair value would be deferred.

Sale and operating leaseback illustration

Ash sells its freehold office premises and leases them back on a 20-year operating lease. The sale took place on 1 January 20X4, and the company has a 31 December year-end.

The details of the scheme are as follows:

Proceeds of sale	$10,000,000
Fair value of the asset at the time of sale	$9,000,000
Carrying amount at the time of sale	$3,500,000
Lease payments (annual rental)	$480,000
Market rate for similar premises (annual rental)	$410,000

(a) **Calculate the profit on disposal that Ash should claim in 20X4.**

(b) **Calculate the annual rental that Ash will charge in its statement of profit or loss.**

(c) **Prepare all relevant extracts from Ash's statement of profit or loss and statement of financial position for the year ending 31 December 20X4.**

Solution

(a) Ash can only claim a profit on disposal based upon the fair value of the asset. This will give a profit on disposal of $5,500,000 ($9,000,000 fair value less $3,500,000 CV).

(b) The $1m difference between the proceeds and the fair value is credited to deferred income and released over the life of the lease on a straight line basis. The annual release will be $50,000 ($1m / 20 years). This reduces the rent charged to $430,000.

(c) **Statement of profit or loss for the year ended 31 December 20X4**

	$	$
Profit on disposal at fair value		5,500,000 Cr
Operating lease rentals	480,000 Dr	
Less: release of deferred income	50,000 Cr	
		430,000 Dr

Statement of financial position as at 31 December 20X4

		$
Deferred income	Brought forward	–
	Arising during the year	1,000,000
	Released to profit or loss	(50,000)
	Carried down	950,000

$900,000 of this liability is non-current.

Sale price more than fair value

Where the proceeds of a sale and operating leaseback are greater than the fair value of the asset, it is usual for the lessor to recoup the excess proceeds by charging an above market rent. IAS 17 states that the excess profit should be spread forward over the period of the lease to match the additional rentals.

However, it is possible to view the agreement as two transactions: a sale of the asset at its fair value and the receipt of a loan. The logical accounting treatment would then be to recognise the liability to repay the loan immediately. The lease rentals would be treated as partly an operating expense (the rental of the asset), partly the capital repayment of the loan and partly the finance charge on the loan.

Many would argue for this accounting treatment because it recognises the substance of the transaction, whereas the treatment required by IAS 17 does not.

SIC 27 Evaluating the substance of transactions involving the legal form of a lease

This SIC refers to situations where an entity (A) leases an asset to another entity (B), and then immediately leases it back again on the same terms and conditions. Sometimes the leaseback is shorter than the original lease, but A will then have an option to repurchase the asset at the end of the lease. These transactions are designed to minimise tax liabilities or to obtain cheaper sources of finance.

When all the transactions are considered (the lease and the leaseback), there has obviously been no change to the risks and rewards that A is exposed to. Therefore, the legal form of the lease is ignored, and A continues to recognise the asset in the same way as before the leases were entered into.

Test your understanding 1 – Sale and leaseback

Details of several sale and leaseback transactions are shown below.

Description proceeds	Sale value	Fair value	Carrying amount
	$000	$000	$000
(i) Sale and finance lease back	10,000	10,000	8,000
(ii) Sale at fair value with an operating lease back	10,000	10,000	8,000
(iii) Sale at under value and operating lease back	10,000	15,000	12,000
(iv) Sale in excess of fair value and operating lease back	15,000	10,000	8,000

Required:

Explain how the seller accounts for each sale and lease back transaction.

Technical article

The P2 Examiner, Graham Holt, wrote an article discussing the accounting treatment of leases 'Lease - operating or finance?' dated September 2012 for the Student Accountant magazine. You can access this article from the ACCA website (www.accaglobal.com).

The aim of the project is to develop a new single approach to lease accounting that would ensure that all assets and liabilities arising under lease contracts are recognised in the statement of financial position. The project was added to the IASB's agenda in July 2006 and is a joint project with US FASB leading towards convergence of reporting standards.

In March 2009 a DP was published: Leases: Preliminary Views and was followed by an ED in August 2010. In July 2011, the IASB and US FASB agreed to re-expose their revised proposals for a common leases standard. This is because the revised proposals include significant changes to those included in the 2010 ED. The revised ED is expected to be issued during the final quarter of 2012 or early 2013.

The main areas of change include the lessee accounting model - specifically, how the lessee recognises lease expense in its statement of comprehensive income for some leases, the lessor accounting model, the accounting for variable lease payments and renewal options, and the definition of a lease. The key developments to date include the following:

Exclusions - the following would be excluded from the scope of a new leasing standard:

- Rights to explore for or use natural resources
- Biological assets
- Service concession arrangements

Accounting model - for all leases except short-term leases, a right-of-use model should be used.

Definition of a lease - a contract should be considered to be a lease if fulfilment of the contract depends on the use of a specified asset and the contract conveys the right to control the use of a specified asset for a period of time. The asset should be explicitly or implicitly identified in the contract.

Typically, the customer (i.e. party having use of the asset) should be able to control and direct its' use. If the supplier is able to control or direct use of the asset, then the contract may need to be separated into elements of (a) service provision and (b) lease of an asset. In circumstances where it is not practical to separate the elements, the contract would be regarded as a contract for services and not a lease. Note that a lease may comprise a physically distinctive part of a larger asset, such as one storey of a larger building.

Lease term - this is defined as the non-cancellable term plus any option to extend the lease where there is a significant economic incentive for an entity to extend the lease or for an entity not to exercise an option to terminate the lease.

Contracts including purchase or sale - the revised ED is likely to include any contract which meets the definition of a lease and also includes a bargain purchase option or automatically transfers title at the end of the lease term. This would include hire purchase agreements, for example. Where this is the case, the right-of-use asset would be amortised over the estimated useful life of the asset, rather than over the lease term. This would also require that the lessor's receivable and the lessee's payable should include any bargain purchase option; other forms of purchase option would be excluded from initial recognition.

Short-term leases - such leases are defined as those with a maximum lease term of twelve months from the date of commencements including any options to renew or extend. Therefore, no evaluation needs to be performed on whether any option to renew or extend such as lease would be taken up.
Short-term leases would not be recognised on the statement of financial position of lessees. Lease payments would be recognised on a straight-line basis, unless there was another basis that was more representative.

Lessee accounting - excluding short-term leases, there are two approaches, depending upon whether the lease term uses up more than an insignificant part of the leased asset over the lease term as follows:

- Straight-line approach – should be used for leases of land and/or buildings unless the lease term is for the major part of the economic life of the asset or the present value of the minimum lease payments accounts for substantially all of the value of the leased asset.

- Accelerated expense approach – should be used in all other cases, unless the lease term is an insignificant part of the life of the leased asset or the present value of the lease payments is insignificant in relation to the fair value of the leased asset. The liability would incur a finance cost based upon the effective rate of the lease and the asset would be amortised over the lease term.

Lessor accounting - excluding short-term leases, there are two approaches, depending upon whether the lease term uses up more than an insignificant part of the leased asset over the lease term and is symmetrical with the approach used by lessees to determine the accounting treatment for the lease as follows:

- Receivable and residual approach – the receivable would be recognised based the present value of lease receipts discounted at the effective rate. The residual asset initially recognised is the estimated present value of the leased asset at the end of the lease term. The carrying value of this will grow over the lease term.

- Other leases excluded from the receivable and residual approach – in effect, the lessor is deemed to have sold an insignificant portion of the asset to the lessee. In this situation, it should be accounted for as under the current IAS 17 when accounting for operating leases.

UK syllabus focus

The ACCA UK syllabus contains a requirement that candidates should be able to discuss and apply the key differences between UK GAAP and IFRS GAAP. The accounting requirements of UK GAAP and IFRS GAAP are very similar in this area; the relevant UK reporting standard requirements are as follows:

SSAP 21 – Leases. The accounting treatment is essentially the same under UK GAAP and IAS 17. There is distinction between finance leases and operating leases under both accounting frameworks; finance leases are capitalised and operating leases are recognised as an expense spread over the lease term.

One distinction is in the criteria used to determine whether or not a lease is a finance lease. UK GAAP includes **a "90% test", when comparing the present value of the minimum lease payments with the fair value of the leased asset**. If this is 90% or more then, unless there is clear evidence to the contrary, it is assumed that substantially the risks and rewards have been transferred – i.e. it is a finance lease. Even if the "90% test" is failed, it could still be classified as a finance lease if substantially the risks and rewards have been transferred. There is no "90%" test under IFRS GAAP; lease classification is determined based upon an assessment of whether substantially the risks and rewards have been transferred under the lease.

A further distinction arises when dealing with **sale and finance leaseback arrangements**. The preferred accounting treatment under SSAP 21 accounts for such arrangements based upon their commercial substance which would involve continuing to recognise the asset and depreciating it as normal, with the cash receipt recorded as receipt of a secured loan. The difference between the apparent disposal value and carrying value of the asset would be released to profit or loss over the shorter of either the lease term or the estimated useful life of the asset. Under IAS 17, the accounting treatment would be to recognise a finance lease asset and obligation, with any gain or loss on disposal of the disposed asset being released to profit or loss over the lease term.

Also, where there is a **lease of land and buildings**, SSAP 21 normally regards this as one lease and there is no requirement to split it into separate elements for evaluation of its substance, although this is permitted. IAS 17 normally requires that they are split into separate elements; the land element will be an operating lease, with the buildings element either a finance lease or an operating lease, depending upon the lease terms. However, an amendment to IAS 17 now requires that long-term leases for land and buildings are now evaluated based upon the substance of the whole transaction to determine whether or not most of the risks and rewards have been transferred.

Finally, where there are **incentives offered in return for entering into an operating lease**, such as receipt of a reverse premium from the lessor or a rent-free period, the incentive is recognised on a straight-line basis over the shorter period of either the lease term or the date on which the prevailing market rental will be payable. IAS 17 spreads the benefit of the incentives over the lease term.

UK syllabus illustration Q&A

Details of several sale and leaseback transactions are shown below.

Description	Sale proceeds	Fair value	Carrying amount
	$000	$000	$000
(i) Sale and finance leaseback	10,000	10,000	8,000
(ii) Sale at fair value with an operating leaseback	10,000	10,000	8,000
(iii) Sale at under value and operating leaseback	10,000	15,000	12,000
(iv) Sale in excess of fair value and operating leaseback	15,000	10,000	8,000

Required:

Explain how the seller accounts for each sale and lease back transaction.

(i) **Sale and finance leaseback**

Here, although the entity has given up legal title to the asset it immediately re-acquires the risks and rewards of ownership. In such circumstances there has not in substance been a sale. This transaction represents a secured loan and should be accounted for accordingly. No profit can be reported and the 'sale proceeds' are accounted for as a liability. In effect, the asset continues to be recognised and depreciated as normal. The finance lease rentals are accounted for partly as a capital repayment of the loan and partly as a finance charge in the income statement.

It would be possible to revalue the asset and to recognise a gain of $2 million through the statement of total recognised gains and losses (a revaluation reserve) but this is a separate issue from the treatment of the lease.

(ii) **Sale at fair value with an operating leaseback**

Here there has been an actual sale (as a result of the transfer of the risks and rewards of ownership). Because the sale is at fair value, the profit on the transaction is recognised immediately. The asset is derecognised and the operating lease rentals expensed in the income statement.

(iii) **Sale at under value and operating leaseback**

Again, the asset is derecognised and operating lease rentals recognised in the income statement. The treatment of the loss on sale depends on the circumstances. If it is a bad bargain, e.g. the sale was made in desperation for the cash then the loss is recognised immediately. If, however, the lease payments are also at undervalue, then the loss is deferred and amortised over the period until the end of the lease.

(iv) **Sale in excess of fair value and operating leaseback**

Again, there really has been a sale and the asset is derecognised. The profit on the disposal of the asset must be restricted to the difference between the fair value of the asset and its carrying amount ($2 million). Assuming that the buyer/lessor will charge lease rentals above the market rate to compensate for the loss, FRS 5 requires that the excess profit ($5 million) is treated as a loan. The lease rentals are then split between operating expenses (the normal market rental for the asset), repayment of the capital portion of the loan and interest on the loan.

5 Chapter summary

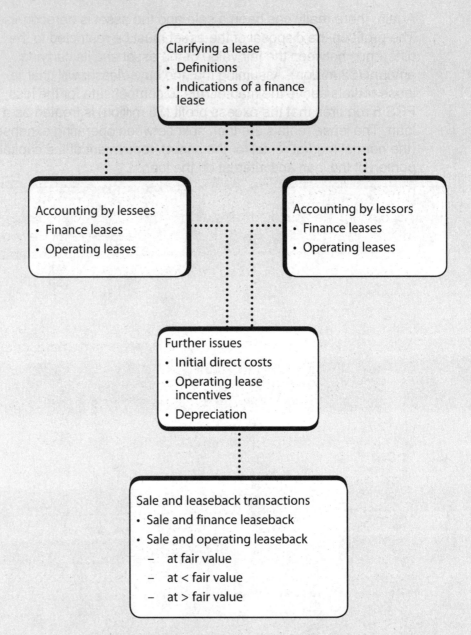

Clarifying a lease
- Definitions
- Indications of a finance lease

Accounting by lessees
- Finance leases
- Operating leases

Accounting by lessors
- Finance leases
- Operating leases

Further issues
- Initial direct costs
- Operating lease incentives
- Depreciation

Sale and leaseback transactions
- Sale and finance leaseback
- Sale and operating leaseback
  - at fair value
  - at < fair value
  - at > fair value

Test your understanding answers

Test your understanding 1 – Sale and leaseback

(i) Sale and finance leaseback

Here, although the entity has given up legal title to the asset it immediately re-acquires the risks and rewards of ownership. In such circumstances, the substance of the arrangement is a secured loan and should be accounted for accordingly.

Account for the gain on disposal of ($10m – $8m) $2m as deferred income and release to profit or loss over the lease term. Recognise a finance lease asset and a finance lease obligation for the amount received of $10m. Depreciate the finance lease asset over the lease term.

Split each finance lease repayment between a finance cost element (based upon the effective or implicit rate in the agreement) and a capital repayment element.

It would be possible to revalue the asset and to recognise a gain of $2 million as other comprehensive income (a revaluation reserve) but this is a separate issue from the treatment of the lease.

(ii) Sale at fair value with an operating leaseback

Here there has been an actual sale (as a result of the transfer of the risks and rewards of ownership). Because the sale is at fair value, the profit on the transaction is recognised immediately. The asset is derecognised and the operating lease rentals expensed in profit or loss.

(iii) Sale at under value and operating leaseback

Again, the asset is derecognised and operating lease rentals recognised in profit or loss. The treatment of the loss on sale depends on the circumstances. If it is a bad bargain, e.g. the sale was made in desperation for the cash, then the loss is recognised immediately. If, however, the lease payments are also at undervalue, then the loss is deferred and amortised over the period until the end of the lease.

(iv) Sale in excess of fair value and operating leaseback

Again, there really has been a sale and the asset is derecognised. The profit on the disposal of the asset must be restricted to the difference between the fair value of the asset and its carrying amount ($2 million). IAS 17 requires that the excess profit ($5 million) is deferred and amortised over the period of the lease. This treatment assumes that the buyer/lessor will charge lease rentals above the market rate to compensate for the loss.

Financial instruments

Chapter learning objectives

Upon completion of this chapter you will be able to:

- apply and discuss the recognition and derecognition of a financial asset or financial liability

- apply and discuss the classification of a financial asset or financial liability and their measurement

- apply and discuss the treatment of gains and losses arising on financial assets and financial liabilities

- apply and discuss the treatment of impairment of financial assets

- record the accounting for derivative financial instruments, and simple embedded derivatives

- outline the principle of hedge accounting, and account for fair value hedges and cash flow hedges including hedge effectiveness.

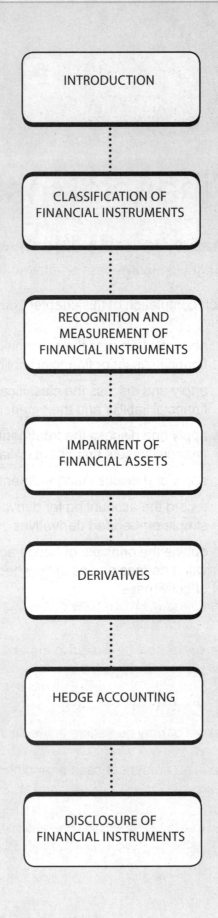

INTRODUCTION

CLASSIFICATION OF
FINANCIAL INSTRUMENTS

RECOGNITION AND
MEASUREMENT OF
FINANCIAL INSTRUMENTS

IMPAIRMENT OF
FINANCIAL ASSETS

DERIVATIVES

HEDGE ACCOUNTING

DISCLOSURE OF
FINANCIAL INSTRUMENTS

1 Introduction

Definitions

 A **financial instrument** is any contract that gives rise to a financial asset of one entity and a financial liability or equity instrument of another entity.

 A **financial asset** is any asset that is:

- cash

- an equity instrument of another entity

- a contractual right to receive cash or another financial asset from another entity

- a contractual right to exchange financial instruments with another entity under conditions that are potentially favourable

- a contract that will or may be settled in the entity's own equity instruments, and is a non-derivative for which the entity is or may be obliged to receive a variable number of the entity's own equity instruments

- a contract that will or may be settled in the entity's own equity instruments, and is a derivative that will or may be settled other than by the exchange of a fixed amount of cash or another financial asset for a fixed number of the entity's own equity instruments.

 A **financial liability** is any liability that is a contractual obligation:

- to deliver cash or another financial asset to another entity

- to exchange financial instruments with another entity under conditions that are potentially unfavourable

- a contract that will or may be settled in the entity's own equity instruments, and is a non-derivative for which the entity is or may be obliged to deliver a variable number of the entity's own equity instruments

- a contract that will or may be settled in the entity's own equity instruments, and is a derivative that will or may be settled other than by exchange of a fixed amount of cash or another financial asset for a fixed number of the entity's own equity instruments.

 An **equity instrument** is any contract that evidences a residual interest in the assets of an entity after deducting all of its liabilities.

Reporting standards

There are four reporting standards that deal with financial instruments:

- IAS 32 **Financial instruments: presentation**
- IAS 39 **Financial instruments: recognition and measurement**
- IFRS 7 **Financial instruments: disclosures**
- IFRS 9 **Financial instruments**

IAS 32 deals with the classification of financial instruments and their presentation in financial statements.

IAS 39 deals with how financial instruments are measured and when they should be recognised in financial statements. Most of IAS 39 has been replaced by IFRS 9, but parts of IAS 39 dealing with impairments, derivatives and hedging continue to apply.

IFRS 7 deals with the disclosure of financial instruments in financial statements.

IFRS 9 was issued in November 2009 and will eventually replace IAS 39. Upon publication, it was to be effective for accounting periods commencing on or after 1 January 2013; however, this has now been deferred to accounting periods commencing on or after 2015, although earlier adoption is permitted. Where early adoption is taken up, to the extent that IFRS 9 has not yet been fully updated, the provisions of the earlier standards continue to apply. IFRS 9 was updated in October 2010 to include accounting for financial liabilities. IAS 39 will be withdrawn in due course following further additions to IFRS 9 dealing with impairment and derivatives.

Entities applying IFRS 9 for the first time therefore have a choice as to when to apply the standard as follows:

- For accounting periods commencing **before 1 January 2015**:
    - IAS 39 can continue to be applied in full, or
    - IFRS 9 (2009) dealing only with financial assets can be applied, together with the remaining provisions of IAS 39 not yet replaced, or
    - IFRS 9 (2010) dealing with both financial assets and financial liabilities can be applied, together with the remaining provisions of IAS 39 not yet replaced.

- For accounting periods commencing **on or after 1 January 2015**, IFRS 9 must be applied in full, together with any remaining provisions of IAS 39 not yet replaced.

It is therefore possible that the provisions of IFRS 9 relating to financial assets may be applied in one accounting period, with application relating to financial liabilities applied in a subsequent accounting period. Note that the transition requirements of IFRS 9 can only be applied once at the date of initial application. This may lead to a lack of comparability between the reported results of entities who choose to apply the requirements of IFRS 9 relating to financial assets and/or liabilities for accounting periods ending any time prior to 31 December 2014.

2 Classification of financial instruments

IAS 32 **Financial instruments: presentation** provides the rules on classifying financial instruments as liabilities or equity. These are detailed below.

Presentation of liabilities and equity

The issuer of a financial instrument must classify it as a financial liability, financial asset or equity instrument on initial recognition according to its substance.

Financial liabilities

The instrument will be classified as a liability if the issuer has a contractual obligation:

- to deliver cash (or another financial asset) to the holder
- to exchange financial instruments on potentially unfavourable terms.

A redeemable preference share will be classified as a liability, because the issuer has the contractual obligation to deliver cash to the holders on the redemption date.

Equity instruments

A financial instrument is only an equity instrument if both of the following conditions are met:

(a) The instrument includes no contractual obligation to deliver cash or another financial asset to another entity; or to exchange financial assets or liabilities with another under conditions that are potentially unfavourable to the issuer.

(b) If the instrument will or may be settled in the issuer's own equity instruments, it is a non-derivative that includes no contractual obligation for the issuer to deliver a variable number of its own equity instruments; or it is a derivative that will be settled only by the issuer exchanging a fixed amount of cash or another financial asset for a fixed number of its own equity shares.

Interest, dividends, losses and gains

- The accounting treatment of interest, dividends, losses and gains relating to a financial instrument follows the treatment of the instrument itself.

- For example, dividends paid in respect of preference shares classified as a liability will be charged as a finance expense through profit or loss.

- Dividends paid on shares classified as equity will be reported in the statement of changes in equity.

Offsetting a financial asset and a financial liability

IAS 32 states that a financial asset and a financial liability may only be offset in very limited circumstances. The net amount may only be reported when the entity:

- has a legally enforceable right to set off the amounts
- intends either to settle on a net basis, or to realise the asset and settle the liability simultaneously.

Improvements to IFRS 2009-11 issued in May 2012 specifies that income tax relating to distributions to holders of equity instruments, and transactions costs associated with equity instruments, should be accounted for in accordance with IAS 12.

> ### Classification of rights issues
>
> This amendment to IAS 32 addresses the accounting for rights issues (rights, options or warrants) that are denominated in a currency other than the functional currency of the issuer. Previously such rights issues were accounted for as derivative liabilities. However, the amendment requires that, provided certain conditions are met, such rights issues are classified as equity regardless of the currency in which the exercise price is denominated.
>
> The global financial crisis has led to an increase in the number of such rights issues as entities seek to raise additional capital. The IASB has therefore moved swiftly to address this issue.
>
> Entities are required to apply the amendment for annual periods beginning on or after 1 February 2010, but earlier application is permitted.

3 Recognition and measurement of financial assets

Initial recognition of financial assets

IFRS 9 deals with recognition and measurement of financial assets. An entity should recognise a financial asset on its statement of financial position when, and only when, the entity becomes party to the contractual provisions of the instrument.

Examples of this principle are as follows:

- Unconditional receivables are recognised when the entity becomes a party to the contract. At that point the entity has a legal right to receive cash.

- Normal trading commitments to buy or sell goods etc are not recognised until one party has fulfilled its part of the contract. For example, a sales order will not be recognised as revenue and a receivable until the goods have been delivered.

- Forward contracts are accounted for as derivative financial assets and are recognised on the commitment date, not on the date when the item under contract is transferred from seller to buyer. (A forward contract is a commitment to buy or sell a financial instrument or a commodity at a later date.)

- Option contracts are accounted for as derivative financial assets and are recognised on the date the contract is entered into, not on the date when the item subject to the option is acquired if the option is exercised at a later date,

The four classifications of financial assets previously recognised under IAS 39 no longer apply.

Initial measurement of financial assets

At initial recognition, all financial assets are measured at fair value. This is likely to be purchase consideration paid to acquire the financial asset and will normally exclude transactions costs.

Subsequent measurement of financial assets

Subsequent measurement then depends upon whether the financial asset is a debt instrument or an equity instrument as follows:

Debt instruments:

Debt instruments would normally be measured at fair value through profit or loss (FVTPL), but could be measured at amortised cost if the entity chooses to do so, provided the following two tests are passed:

- the business model test, and
- the contractual cash flow characteristics test.

The **business model test** establishes whether the entity holds the financial asset to collect the contractual cash flows or whether the objective is to sell the financial asset prior to maturity to realise changes in fair value. If it is the former, it implies that there will be no or few sales of such financial assets from a portfolio prior to their maturity date. If this is the case, the test is passed. Where this is not the case, it would suggest that the assets are not being held with the objective to collect contractual cashflows, but perhaps may be disposed of to respond to changes in fair value. In this situation, the test is failed and the financial asset cannot be measured at amortised cost.

Where an entity changes its business model, it may be required to reclassify its financial assets as a consequence, but this is expected to be infrequent occurrence. If reclassification does occur, it is accounted for from the first day of the accounting period in which reclassification takes place.

The **contractual cash flow characteristics test** determines whether the contractual terms of the financial asset give rise to cash flows on specified dates that are **solely** payments of principal and interest based upon the principal amount outstanding. If this is not the case, the test is failed and the financial asset cannot be measured at amortised cost. For example, convertible bonds contain rights in addition to the repayment of interest and principal (the right to convert the bond to equity) and therefore would fail the test and must be accounted for as fair value through profit or loss.

In summary, for a debt instrument to be measured at amortised cost, it will therefore require that:

- the asset is held within a business model whose objective is to hold the assets to collect the contractual cashflows, and

- the contractual terms of the financial asset give rise, on specified dates, to cash flows that are solely payments of principal and interest on the principal outstanding.

Even if a financial instrument passes both tests, it is still possible to designate a debt instrument as FVTPL if doing so eliminates or significantly reduces a measurement or recognition inconsistency (i.e. accounting mismatch) that would otherwise arise from measuring assets or liabilities or from recognising the gains or losses on them on different bases. Therefore, it is now possible to have financial assets that meet the criteria above and which will now be measured at amortised cost, even if they are quoted in an active market.

Equity instruments

Equity instruments are measured at either:

- fair value either through profit or loss, or
- fair value through other comprehensive income.

The normal expectation is that equity instruments will have the designation of **fair value through profit or loss**, with the price paid to acquire the financial asset initially regarded as fair value. This could include unquoted equity investments, which may present problems in arriving at a reliable fair value at each reporting date. However, IFRS 9 does not include a general exception for unquoted equity investments to be measured at cost; rather it provides guidance on when cost may, or may not, be regarded as a reliable indicator of fair value.

It is possible to designate an equity instrument as **fair value through other comprehensive income**, provided specified conditions have been complied with as follows:

- the equity instrument cannot be held for trading, and
- there must be an irrevocable choice for this designation upon initial recognition.

In this situation, initial recognition will also include directly attributable transactions costs. This may apply, for example, to strategic investments to be held on a continuing basis which are not held to take advantage of changes in fair value. Equity derivatives are excluded from adopting this designation.

Dividends on financial assets through other comprehensive income must be taken to profit or loss, unless they represent a recovery of part of the investment. Changes in fair value will be recognised in other comprehensive income.

If an equity instrument has been designated as fair value through other comprehensive income, the requirements in IAS 39 to undertake an assessment of impairment no longer apply as all fair value movements now remain in equity. Note that there is no recycling or reclassification to profit or loss in subsequent periods of any gains and losses taken to other comprehensive income, although upon derecognition there may be a transfer within equity. Consequently, in accordance with IAS 1, amended in 2011, any amounts in other comprehensive income relating to remeasurement of financial assets should be clearly identified as items which will not be subject to recycling or reclassification in future periods.

Overview of recognition and measurement of financial assets

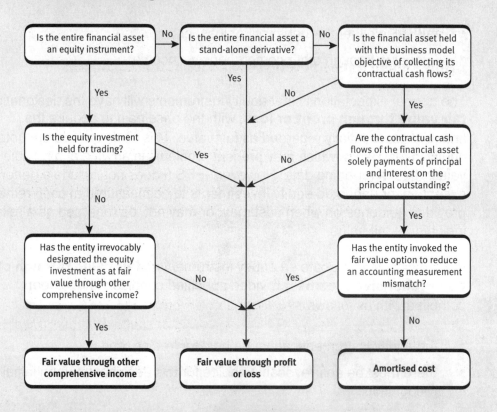

Test your understanding 1 – Ashes financial assets and liabilities

Ashes holds the following financial assets:

(1) Trade receivables

(2) Investments in ordinary shares that are held for short-term speculation

(3) Investments in ordinary shares that from the outset are intended to be held for the long term?

Ashes has issued the following financial instruments

(1) Ordinary shares

(2) Debentures

(3) Cumulative redeemable preference shares

(4) Convertible loan stock where the holder has the option to require conversion into equity shares

(5) Redeemable non-cumulative preference shares issued to directors for their period of office

Required

How should Ashes classify and account for its financial instruments

4 Recognition and measurement of financial liabilities

IFRS 9 was updated in October 2010 to include accounting for financial liabilities. In principle, the recognition and measurement criteria contained in IAS 39 have been retained within IFRS 9.

IFRS 9 has two classes of financial liability as follows:

(1) Financial liabilities at fair value through profit or loss. This classification will apply to liabilities incurred for trading or speculative purposes, including derivatives.

(2) Other financial liabilities. This is the default classification for financial liabilities if they are not required to be measured at fair value through profit or loss and are measured at amortised cost. Borrowings would normally be acounted for under this classification.

Note that it is possible to opt to measure a liability (FV option") at fair value when it would normally be measured at amortised cost. This would be applicable, for example, to eliminate or reduce an accounting mismatch. When this applies, the fair value of the liability is established by discounting the outstanding cashflows to their present value using the current market rate of interest at each reporting date.

Financial instrument	Measurement at recognition	Subsequent measurement	Recognition in statement of comprehensive income
Financial liabilities at fair value through profit or loss	Fair value	Measured at fair value with changes in value taken through profit or loss	Fair value gains and losses recognised in profit or loss.
Other financial liabilities	Amortised cost	Measured at amortised cost using the effective interest rate	The interest calculated using the effective rate is charged to profit or loss as a finance cost

Two forms of financial instrument which need to be considered are deep discounted bonds and compound instruments.

Deep discounted bonds measured at amortised cost

- One common form of financial instrument for many entities will be loans payable. These will be measured at amortised cost. The amortised cost of a liability equals: initial cost plus interest less repayments. (We will also use this method with compound instruments.)

- The interest will be charged at the effective rate or level yield. This is the internal rate of return of the instrument.

An example of a loan that uses an effective rate of interest is a deep discount bond.

It has the following features.

- This instrument is issued at a significant discount to its par value.

- Typically it has a coupon rate much lower than market rates of interest, e.g. a 2% bond when market interest is 10% pa.

- The initial carrying amount of the bond will be the net proceeds of issue.

- The full finance cost will be charged over the life of the instrument so as to give a constant periodic rate of interest.

- The full cost will include:
  - issue costs
  - deep discount on issue
  - annual interest payments
  - premium on redemption.

The constant periodic rate of interest (sometimes called the effective rate) can be calculated in the same way that the internal rate of return is calculated. In questions, the effective rate of interest will normally be given.

Illustration 1 – Deep discount bond

On 1 January 20X1 James issued a deep discount bond with a $50,000 nominal value.

The discount was 16% of nominal value, and the costs of issue were $2,000.

Interest of 5% of nominal value is payable annually in arrears.

The bond must be redeemed on 1 January 20X6 (after 5 years) at a premium of $4,611.

The effective rate of interest is 12% p.a.

Required:

How will this be reported in the financial statements of James over the period to redemption?

Solution

Firstly, we must establish at what amount the bond will be initially recognised in the statement of financial position. The calculation set out below also works out the total finance cost to be charged to profits.

	$	$
Net proceeds		
Face value	50,000	
Less: 16% discount	(8,000)	
Less: Issue costs	(2,000)	
	———	40,000

Initial recognition of liability

Repayments

Capital	50,000
Premium on redemption	4,611
Principal to be redeemed	54,611
Interest paid: $50,000 × 5% × 5 years	12,500
	67,111
Total finance cost	27,111

Secondly, we set up a table (similar to that used for compound instruments) to work out the balance of the loan at the end of each period.

Year	Opening balance	Effective interest rate 12%	Payments 5%	Closing balance
	$	$	$	$
1	40,000	4,800	(2,500)	42,300
2	42,300	5,076	(2,500)	44,876
3	44,876	5,385	(2,500)	47,761
4	47,761	5,731	(2,500)	50,992
5	50,992	6,119	(2,500)	54,611
		27,111	(12,500)	
		To: Profit or loss	To: Statement of cash flows	To: SOFP

The finance charge taken to profit or loss is greater than the actual interest paid, and so the balance shown as a liability increases over the life of the instrument until it equals the redemption value at the end of its term.

In Years 1 to 4 the balance shown as a liability is less than the amount that will be payable on redemption. Therefore the full amount payable must be disclosed in the notes to the accounts.

Test your understanding 2 – Hoy

Hoy raised finance on 1 January 20X1 by the issue of a two-year deep discounted 2% bond with a nominal value of $10,000 that is issued at a discount of 5% and is redeemable at a premium of $1,075. Issue costs can be ignored. The bond has an effective rate of interest of 10%..

Wiggins raised finance by issuing $20,000 6% four-year loan notes on 1 January 20X4. The loan notes are issued at a discount of 10%, and will be redeemed after three years at a premium of $1,015. The effective rate of interest is 12%. The issue costs were $1,000.

Cavendish raises finance by issuing zero coupon bonds at par on 1 January 20X5 with a nominal value of $10,000. The bonds will be redeemed after two years at a premium of $1,449. Issue costs can be ignored. The effective rate of interest is 7%.

Boardman issued three-year 5% $30,000 loan notes on 1 January 20X6 at nominal value when the effective rate of interest was also 5%. The loan notes will be redeemed at par. The liability is held for trading purposes and so has been classified at FVTPL. At 31 December 20X6 market interest rates increased to 6%. At 31 December 20X7 market interest increased to 7%.

The reporting date for each entity is 31 December.

Required:

Illustrate and explain how these financial instruments should be accounted for by each company.

Presentation of compound instruments

The issuer of a financial instrument must classify it as a financial liability or equity instrument on initial recognition according to its substance.

- A **compound instrument** is a financial instrument that has characteristics of both equity and liabilities, for example debt that can be converted into shares.

- The bondholder has the prospect of acquiring cheap shares in an entity, because the terms of conversion are normally quite generous. Even if the bondholder wants cash rather than shares, the deal may still be good. On maturity the cash-hungry bondholder will accept the conversion, and then sell the shares on the market for a tidy profit.

- In exchange though, the bondholders normally have to accept a below-market rate of interest, and will have to wait some time before they get the shares that form a large part of their return. There is also the risk that the entity's shares will under-perform, making the conversion unattractive.

- IAS 32 requires compound financial instruments be split into their component parts:
    - a financial liability (the debt)
    - an equity instrument (the option to convert into shares).

- These must be shown separately in the financial statements.

Examples of compound instruments

Convertible loan stock contains elements of both a liability and equity. The proceeds raised are allocated between the two elements upon initial recognition. The present value of the future obligation is regarded as a liability, with the residual amount recognised as an equity element. Any requirement to pay an annual dividend would also be classed as an obligation. When an obligation is recognised, any returns on the liability element are recognised as part of the finance cost, which is based upon the effective rate of interest for an equivalent liability withoout conversion rights.

Normally, the accounting treatment of any return on a financial instrument is based upon whether it has been classified as equity or as a liability. There are occasions when this may not be quite so straightforward

Irredeemable preference share would normally be regarded as equity as there is no obligation to repay or redeem them. However, if there is a requirement (i.e an obligation) to pay an annual dividend, then the irredeemable preference share would be regarded as a compound instrument which must be split between liability and equity elements. The annual compulsory dividend would be regarded as part of the liability element.

Redeemable equity shares would normally be regarded as a liability as there is an obligation to redeem them at a later date. The accounting treatment of any dividends paid will depend upon whether the dividends are compulsory (i.e. an obligation) or discretionary; if the dividends are compulsory, the payment would be regarded as a finance cost. If the dividends are discretionary, they are regarded as a distribution of profit or loss from equity.

Illustration 2 – Compound instruments

On 1 January 20X1 Daniels issued a $50m three-year convertible bond at par.

- There were no issue costs.

- The coupon rate is 10%, payable annually in arrears on 31 December.

- The bond is redeemable at par on 1 January 20X4.

- Bondholders may opt for conversion. The terms of conversion are two 25-cent equity shares for every $1 owed to each bondholder on 1 January 20X4.

- Bonds issued by similar entities without any conversion rights currently bear interest at 15%.

- Assume that all bondholders opt for conversion in full.

How will this be accounted for by Daniels?

Solution

On initial recognition, the method of splitting the bond between equity and liabilities is as follows.

- Calculate the present value of the debt component by discounting the cash flows at the market rate of interest for an instrument similar in all respects, except that it does not have conversion rights.

- Deduct the present value of the debt from the proceeds of the issue. The difference is the equity component.

(1) Splitting the proceeds

The cash payments on the bond should be discounted to their present value using the interest rate for a bond without the conversion rights, i.e. 15%.

Date		Cash flow	Discount factor @ 15%	Present value
		$000		$000
31-Dec-X1	Interest	5,000	$1/1.15$	4,347.8
31-Dec-X2	Interest	5,000	$1/1.15^2$	3,780.7
31-Dec-X3	Interest	5,000	$1/1.15^3$	3,287.6
1-Jan-X4	Principal	50,000	$1/1.15^3$	32,875.8

Present value (the liability component)	A		44,291.9
As the net proceeds of issue were	B		50,000.0
So the equity component is	B – A		5,708.1

(2) The annual finance costs and year end carrying amounts

	Opening balance	Effective interest rate 15%	Payments	Closing balance
	$000	$000	$000	$000
20X1	44,291.9	6,643.8	(5,000)	45,935.7
20X2	45,935.7	6,890.4	(5,000)	47,826.1
20X3	47,826.1	7,173.9	(5,000)	50,000.0

(3) The conversion of the bond

The carrying amounts at 1 January 20X4 are:

	$000
Equity	5,708.1
Liability – bond	50,000.0
	55,708.1

The conversion terms are two 25-cent equity shares for every $1, so $50m × 2 = 100m shares, which have a nominal value of $25m. The remaining $30,708,100 should be classified as the share premium, also within equity. There is no remaining liability, because conversion has extinguished it.

Test your understanding 3 – Craig

Craig issues a $100,000 4% three-year convertible loan on 1 January 20X6. The market rate of interest for a similar loan without conversion rights is 8%. The conversion terms are one equity share ($1 nominal value) for every $2 of debt. Conversion or redemption at par takes place on 31 December 20X8.

Required:

How should this be accounted for:

(a) **if all holders elect for the conversion?**

(b) **no holders elect for the conversion?**

FVO for financial liabilities

Own credit risk definition:

Own credit risk can be considered to be similar to the risk of default on a liability – it is the risk that an entity will be unable to discharge a particular liability. It will not necessarily be the same for all liabilities incurred by an entity. For example, if an entity issues both secured and unsecured debt, the risk of default on the secured debt is likely to be low and relatively stable, particularly if the loan agreement includes performance and other criteria which protect the position of the lender. However, the risk of default attaching to the unsecured debt will certainly be higher and will almost certainly vary over time, due to trading performance and other factors, until the liability is settled.

Accounting treatment:

IFRS 9 permits entities to opt to designate liabilities which would normally fall to be measured at amortised cost, to be designated at fair value through profit or loss (Fair value Option (FVO)). This designation, if made, must be made upon initial recognition and is irrevocable. Where an entity opts for this treatment, any change in fair value of the liability must be separated into two elements as follows:

- Changes in fair value due to own credit risk, which are taken to other comprehensive income, and

- Other changes in fair value, which are taken to profit or loss.

One possible approach to identifying the two elements is to separate the interest rate charged on the financial liability into a benchmark rate (e.g. such as LIBOR) and an instrument-specific rate. Any change in the fair value of the liability which is not wholly due to the change in the benchmark rate must therefore be due to a change on own credit risk. The movement in fair value can then be split into the two separate elements.

Note that IFRS 9 does not define what a "benchmark" interest rate is, nor does it specify a required basis for separating the two elements of the change in fair value; entities are therefore able to use an alternative basis from that which is included in the guidance to IFRS 9 which they believe provides a better representation of the change in fair value due to changes in own credit risk. If there is no standard basis for accounting for own credit risk, this may lead to problems of inconsistency and lack of comparability in reported information.

It is possible that the FVO may be appropriate to financial institutions, rather than other entities generally. Accordingly, most entities will continue to account for financial liabilities in accordance with IFRS 9 with no practical change from the requirements of IAS 39. The FVO is not available if it will create or enlarge an accounting mismatch or for financial liabilities that are held for trading; any change in the fair value of such liabilities will be taken to profit or loss as before.

FVO for liabilities illustration

On 1 January 20X8 an entity issues a 7 year bond at par value of $300,000 and annual fixed coupon rate of 9%, which is also the market rate, when LIBOR is 6%. Therefore the instrument-specific element of IRR = (9% - 6%) is 3%.

At 31 December 20X8, LIBOR has moved to 5.5%, thus making the benchmark interest rate (5.5% + 3%) 8.5% (i.e. LIBOR plus the instrument-specific element of IRR). If the fair value of the liability is consistent with a market interest rate of, say, 8.3%, then any change in the fair value of the liability from the benchmark rate to fair value must be due to something other than the change in the benchmark rate – i.e. it must be due to the change in the liability's credit risk.

Required:

Calculate the amounts to be included within the financial statements for the year ended 31 December 20X8.

Solution

It can be quantified by calculating the present value (PV) of the liability using the benchmark rate and comparing it with the PV of the liability using the market rate as follows:

PV at benchmark rate 8.5%	Cash flow	Factor	PV
Year	$		$
1 – 6	27,000	4.5533	122,939
6	300,000	0.6129	183,870
			306,809

PV at market rate 8.3%	Cash flow	Factor	PV
Year	$		$
1 – 6	27,000	4.5811	123,690
6	300,000	0.6197	185,910
			309,600

Therefore, the change in the fair value of the liability which is not due to the change in the benchmark rate must be due to the change in the liability's credit risk.

	$
PV of liability at market rate of 8.3% (on SOFP at reporting date)	309,600
PV of liability at benchmark rate of 8.5%	306,809
Other comprehensive income	2,791

IFRS 9 requires that this change in fair value relating to the change in the liability's credit risk is taken to Other Comprehensive Income. In the above situation, it will be reflected by a reduction in equity as the carrying value of the liability is increased.

There are likely to be different models or bases of determination adopted by different entities as they prepare annual financial statements to implement fully the requirements relating to both financial assets and financial liabilities. From a corporate reporting perspective, perhaps the best way to consider the total movement in the fair value of financial liabilities from one reporting date to the next, is to split it into two elements:

- to the extent that the change in fair value relates to a change in own credit risk, this is taken to OCI, and

- to the extent that the change in fair value is related to anything else, this is recognised in profit or loss for the year.

The only exception to this accounting treatment arises where the outcome would create or enlarge an accounting mismatch in profit or loss. If this is the case, then an entity will present all changes in fair value on that liability in profit or loss.

5 Derecognition of financial instruments

The derecognition requirements of IAS 39 have been transferred to IFRS 9. Derecognition is currently part of the IASB work plan for the development of reporting standards, which includes a continuing commitment to convergence of IFRS with US GAAP. These requirements may be changed at some future date, as practical issues associated with derecognition of financial assets and financial liabilities become apparent.

A **financial asset** should be derecognised if one of the following criteria occur:

- the contractual rights to the cash flows of the financial asset have expired, e.g. when an option held by the entity has expired worthless

- the financial asset has been sold and the transfer qualifies for derecognition because substantially all the risks and rewards of ownership have been transferred from the seller to the buyer.

The analysis of where the risks and rewards of ownership lie after the transaction is critical. For example if an entity sells an investment in shares and enters into a total return swap with the buyer, the buyer will return any increases in value to the entity or the entity will pay the buyer for any decrease in value. In this case the entity has retained substantially all of the risks and rewards of the investment, which therefore should not be derecognised.

A **financial liability** should be derecognised when, and only when, the obligation specified in the contract is discharged, cancelled or expires.

On derecognition, the difference between the carrying amount of the asset or liability and the amount received or paid for it should be recognised in the profit or loss for the period.

Test your understanding 4 – Ming

Ming has two receivables that it has factored to a bank in return for immediate cash proceeds of less than the face value of the invoices. Both receivables are due from long standing customers who are expected to pay in full and on time. Ming has agreed a three-month credit period with both customers.

The first receivable is for $200,000 and in return for assigning the receivable Ming has just received from the factor $180,000. Under the terms of the factoring arrangement this the only money that Ming will receive regardless of when or even if the customer settles the debt, i.e. the factoring arrangement is said to be "without recourse ".

The second receivable is for $100,000 and in return for assigning the receivable Ming has just received $70,000. Under the terms of this factoring arrangement if the customer settles the account on time then a further $5,000 will be paid by the factoring bank to Ming, but if the customer does not settle the account in accordance with the agreed terms then the receivable will be reassigned back to Ming who will then be obliged to refund the factor the original $70,000 plus a further $10,000. This factoring arrangement is said to be "with recourse".

Required:

Discuss Ming's accounting treatment of the monies received under the terms of the two factoring arrangements.

Test your understanding 5 – Jones

Jones bought an investment for $40 million plus associated transaction costs of $1 million. The asset was designated upon initial recognition as fair value through other comprehensive income. At the reporting date the fair value of the financial asset had risen to $60 million. Shortly after the reporting date the financial asset was sold for $70 million.

Required:

(1) **How should this be accounted for?**

(2) **How would the answer have been different if the investment had been classified as at fair value through profit and loss?**

6 Impairment of financial assets

Impairment of financial assets will, in due course, be included within updated requirements of IFRS 9. Until that occurs, impairment requirements are as specified in IAS 39, subject to minor amendment following the publication of IFRS 9 containing revised classification of financial assets. Current developments relating to impairment of financial assets are considered elsewhere in this chapter.

The current situation is as follows:

* Financial assets that are measured at fair value through profit or loss are not subject to an impairment review. Remeasurement of fair value at each reporting date will automatically take account of any impairment.

* Similarly, financial assets measured at fair value through other comprehensive income are not subject to an impairment review. Any changes in fair value, including those which may relate to impairment, are recognised in other comprehensive income. There is no recognition or recycling of impairment to profit or loss.

* For financial assets measured at amortised cost, IAS 39 requires that an assessment be made, at every reporting date, as to whether there is any objective evidence that a financial asset is impaired, i.e. whether an event has occurred that has had a negative impact on the expected future cash flows of the asset.

- The event causing the negative impact must have already happened. An event causing an impairment in the future shall not be anticipated.
  - For example, on the last day of its financial year a bank lends a customer $100,000. The bank has consistently experienced a default rate of 5% across all its loans. The bank is **not** permitted immediately to write this loan down to $95,000 based on its past experience, because no default has occurred at the reporting date.

Impairment review of financial assets measured at amortised cost

Examples of objective evidence of impairment at the reporting date include: significant financial difficulty of the borrower, and the failure of the borrower to make interest payments on the due date.

An impairment loss on financial assets measured at amortised cost is determined as follows:

	$
Carrying value of the asset per the financial statements	X
Less:	
PV of the estimated future cash flows discounted at the original effective interest rate	(X)
	—
Impairment loss	X
	—

Any impairment loss is recognised as an expense in profit or loss. If recoverable amount exceeds carrying value, the asset is not impaired.

Accounting for impairment of financial assets is a controversial issue. One school of thought is that impairment losses could be evaluated by using an 'expected loss' approach. This approach would be likely to result in earlier recognition of impairment losses but it would be a more subjective approach than currently applied by the requirements of IAS 39.

Illustration 3 – Impairment of financial assets

On 1 February 20X6, Eve makes a four-year loan of $10,000 to Fern. The coupon rate on the loan is 6%, the same as the effective rate of interest. Interest is received at the end of each year.

During February 20X9, it becomes clear that Fern is in financial difficulties. This is the necessary objective evidence of impairment. At this time the current market interest rate is 8%.

It is estimated that the future remaining cash flows from the loan will be only $6,000, instead of $10,600 (the $10,000 principal plus interest for the fourth year of $600).

Solution

Because the coupon and the effective interest rate are the same, the carrying amount of the principal will remain constant at $10,000.

On 1 February 20X9, the carrying amount of the loan should be restated to the present value of the estimated cash flows of $6,000, discounted at the original effective interest rate of 6% for one year.

6,000 × 1/1.06 = $5,660

The result is an impairment loss of $4,340 ($10,000 – $5,660).

The impairment loss is recognised as an expense in profit or loss.

The asset will continue to be accounted for using amortised cost, based on the revised carrying amount of the loan. In the last year of the loan, the interest income of $340 (5,660 × 6%) will be recognised in profit or loss.

Test your understanding 6 – Pendleton

Pendleton is a lender and as such holds a portfolio of financial assets. These loans require the interest only to be paid during the term of the loan and are eventually redeemed at par. At the start of the year the company lent a total of $100,000 and the financial assets were classified and accounted for at amortised cost, having been properly designated upon initial recognition and meet both the business model and cash flow tests. Each loan has a coupon rate of 20% as well as an effective rate of 20%. In the first accounting period no lenders have actually defaulted; however, it is felt that a proportion of loans will default over the loan period and, in the long run, the rate of return from the portfolio will be approximately 6%.

Required

Discuss the impairment review of these assets in the first accounting period using the incurred loss and the expected loss model.

Reversals of impairment losses

Reversal of an impairment loss is only permitted as a result of an event occurring after the impairment loss has been recognised. An example would be the credit rating of a customer being revised upwards by a credit rating agency.

Reversal of impairment losses in respect of financial assets measured at amortised cost are recognised in profit or loss.

7 Derivatives

Definitions

A derivative is a financial instrument with the following characteristics:

(a) Its value changes in response to the change in a specified interest rate, security price, commodity price, foreign exchange rate, index of prices or rates, a credit rating or credit index or similar variable (called the 'underlying').

(b) It requires little or no initial net investment relative to other types of contract that have a similar response to changes in market conditions.

(c) It is settled at a future date.

The problems of derivatives

- Derivatives were originally designed to hedge against fluctuations in agricultural commodity prices on the Chicago Stock Exchange. A speculator would pay a small amount (say $100) now for the contractual obligation to buy a thousand units of wheat in three months' time for $10,000. If in three months time one thousand units of wheat costs $11,000, then the speculator would make a profit of $900 (11,000 – 100 – 10,000). This would be a 900% return on the original investment over 3 months, which is one of the attractions of derivatives to speculators. But if the price had dropped to $9,000, then the trader would have made a loss of $1,100 (100 + 1,000) despite the initial investment only having been $100.

- This shows that losses on derivatives can be far greater than the historical cost-carrying amount of the related asset. Therefore, shareholders need to be given additional information about derivatives in order to assess the entity's exposure to loss.

- In most cases, entering into a derivative is at a low or nil cost. Therefore it is important that derivatives are recognised and disclosed in the financial statements as they have very little initial outlay but can expose the entity to significant gains and losses.

Typical derivatives

Typical derivatives

Derivatives include the following types of contracts:

Forward contracts

- The holder of a forward contract is obliged to buy or sell a defined amount of a specific underlying asset, at a specified price at a specified future date.

- For example, a forward contract for foreign currency might require £100,000 to be exchanged for $150,000 in three months time. Both parties to the contract have both a financial asset and a financial liability. For example, one party has the right to receive $150,000 and the obligation to pay £100,000.

- Forward currency contracts may be used to minimise the risk on amounts receivable or payable in foreign currencies.

Forward rate agreements

- Forward rate agreements can be used to fix the interest charge on a floating rate loan.

- For example, an entity has a $1m floating rate loan, and the current rate of interest is 7%. The rates are reset to the market rate every six months, and the entity cannot afford to pay more than 9% interest. The entity enters into a six-month forward rate agreement (with, say, a bank) at 9% on $1m. If the market rates go up to 10%, then the bank will pay them $5,000 (1% of $1m for 6 months) which in effect reduces their finance cost to 9%. If the rates only go up to 8% then the entity pays the bank $5,000. The forward rate agreement effectively fixes the interest rate payable at 9% for the period.

Futures contracts

- Futures contracts oblige the holder to buy or sell a standard quantity of a specific underlying item at a specified future date.

- Futures contracts are very similar to forward contracts. The difference is that futures contracts have standard terms and are traded on a financial exchange, whereas forward contracts are tailor-made and are not traded on a financial exchange. Also, whereas forward contracts will always be settled, a futures contract will rarely be held to maturity.

Swaps

- Two parties agree to exchange periodic payments at specified intervals over a specified time period.

- For example, in an interest rate swap, the parties may agree to exchange fixed and floating rate interest payments calculated by reference to a notional principal amount.

- This enables companies to keep a balance between their fixed and floating rate interest payments without having to change the underlying loans.

Options

- These give the holder the right, but not the obligation, to buy or sell a specific underlying asset on or before a specified future date.

Measurement of derivatives

- On recognition, derivatives should initially be measured at fair value. Transaction costs may not be included.

- Subsequent measurement depends on how the derivative is categorised. In many cases, this will involve the derivative being measured at fair value with changes in the fair value recognised in profit or loss. However if the derivative is used as a hedge (see later in this chapter), then the changes in fair value should be recognised in equity.

Illustration 4 – Derivatives

Entity A enters into a call option on 1 June 20X5, to purchase 10,000 shares in another entity on 1 November 20X5 at a price of $10 per share. The cost of each option is $1. A has a year end of 30 September.

By 30 September the fair value of each option has increased to $1.30 and by 1 November to $1.50, with the share price on the same date being $11. A exercises the option on 1 November and the shares are classified as at fair value through profit or loss.

Solution

On 1 June 20X5 the cost of the option is recognised:

Debit	Call option (10,000 × $1)	$10,000
Credit	Cash	$10,000

On 30 September the increase in fair value is recorded:

Debit	Call option (10,000 × ($1.30 – 1))	$3,000
Credit	Profit or loss	$3,000

On 1 November the option is exercised, the shares recognised and the call option derecognised. As the shares are financial assets at fair value through profit or loss, they are recognised at $110,000 (10,000 × the current market price of $11)

Debit	Investment in shares at fair value	$110,000
Debit	Expense – loss on call option	$3,000
	((10,000 + 3,000 + 100,000) – 110, 000)	
Credit	Cash (10,000 × $10)	$100,000
Credit	Call option (10,000 + 3,000 carrying amount)	$13,000

Test your understanding 7 – Hoggard

Hoggard buys a call option on 1 January 20X6 for $5 per option that gives the right to buy 100 shares in Rowling on 31 December at a price of $10 per share.

Required:

How should this be accounted for, given the following outcomes?

(a) **The options are sold on 1 July 20X6 for $15 each.**

(b) **On 31 December 20X6, Rowling's share price is $8 and Hoggard lets the option lapse unexercised.**

(c) **The option is exercised on 31 December when Rowling's share price is $25. The shares are classified as held for trading.**

Further points

Embedded derivatives

IAS 39 required separation of certain embedded derivates. IFRS 9 removes this requirement when the host contract is a financial asset within the scope of IAS 39.

As a result, embedded derivatives that would have been separately accounted for at fair value through profit or loss under IAS 39 because they were not closely related to the financial asset host will no longer be separated. Instead, the contractual cash flows of the financial asset are assessed as a whole and the asset is measured as fair value through profit or loss if any of its cash flows do not represent payments of principal and interest as outlined in IFRS 9.

For example:

An entity has an investment in a convertible bond, which can be converted into a fixed number of equity shares at a specified future date. Normally, under IAS 39, the convertible bond is bifurcated (i.e. separated) into the host debt instrument and the conversion option which is the embedded derivative. This was required as risks attaching to the conversion option were not closely matched to those of the debt instrument. They were also measured differently as the debt instrument under IAS 39 would normally be measured at amortised cost with the conversion option measured at fair value through profit or loss.

IFRS 9 now requires that embedded derivatives, such as the convertible bond, are evaluated for correct classification in their entirety due to the presence of the conversion option. In practical terms it would mean that the bond would fail the contractual cash flow characteristics test and would therefore be measured at fair value through profit or loss.

The need for a financial reporting standard

Derivatives can be easily acquired, often for little or no cost, but their values can change very rapidly, exposing holders to the risk of large profits or losses. Because many derivatives have no cost, they may not appear in a traditional historical cost statement of financial position, even if they represent substantial assets or liabilities of the entity. Gains and losses have traditionally not been recorded until cash is exchanged. Gains and losses can be easily realised, often simply by making a telephone call. If gains and losses are recognised on a cash basis, then management can choose when to report these gains and losses.

Derivatives can rapidly transform the position, performance and risk profile of an entity. Consequently, there is great debate regarding the accounting for derivatives, together with ensuring that there are adequate disclosures for users to fully understand and appreciate their impact upon the reported financial performance and position of an entity. Current developments relating to financial instruments are dealt with elsewhere in this chapter.

Measurement of derivatives

Under IAS 39, derivatives should initially be measured at fair value in the statement of financial position (usually cost); and subsequent measurement will involve the derivative being measured at fair through profit or loss. However if the derivative is used as a hedge (see later) then the changes in fair value should be recognised as other comprehensive income.

The arguments for using fair value for these items rather than historical cost are as follows.

(a) Sometimes these items have no historical cost, and so they are ignored by conventional accounting.

(b) Fair valuation reports gains and losses as they arise, not just when they are realised in cash. This gives a better and more objective indication of a entity's performance.

(c) Fair valuation reports the way in which risks are being managed.

(d) Fair valuation promotes comparability. All derivatives will be carried at their fair value at the reporting date, rather than at out-of-date historical costs. Different entities will also be using the same up-to-date fair values.

(e) Fair values have more predictive value.

(f) It is practical, because many derivatives are traded on active markets and are therefore easy to value.

However, some people still disagree with using fair values. Some of the arguments against fair values are as follows.

(a) Reporting changes in fair value will result in volatile profits. (However, as these profits reflect real changes in value, some would say that they must be reported.)

(b) Some of the changes in fair value might never be realised. Therefore, the profit or loss will include losses that never arise and profits that are never realised.

(c) It may not always be possible to value all derivatives reliably.

8 Hedge accounting

Definitions

Hedging is a method of managing risk by designating one or more hedging instruments so that their change in fair value is offset, in whole or in part, to the change in fair value or cash flows of a hedged item.

A **hedged item** is an asset or liability that exposes the entity to risks of changes in fair value or future cash flows (and is designated as being hedged).

A **hedging instrument** is a designated derivative whose fair value or cash flows are expected to offset changes in fair value or future cash flows of the hedged item.

So the **item** generates the risk and the **instrument** modifies it.

Introduction

As at August 2010, IFRS 9 does not contain any specific requirements relating to hedge accounting; this constitutes the third phase of the project to replace IAS 39 with IFRS 9. Accordingly, the requirements specified in IAS 39 continue to apply until withdrawn.

- Hedging is a means of reducing risk.

- One simple hedge is where an entity takes out a foreign currency loan to finance a foreign currency investment. If the foreign currency strengthens, then the value of the asset and the burden of the liability will increase by the same amount. Any gains or losses will be cancelled out.

- Hedge accounting recognises symmetrically the offsetting effects, on net profit or loss, of changes in the fair values of the hedging instrument and the related item being hedged.

- The hedging instrument will often be a derivative.

- Hedge accounting is allowed under IAS 39 provided that the hedging relationship is clearly defined, measurable, and actually effective.

IAS 39 identifies three types of hedge, two of which are within the P2 syllabus:

(1) Fair value hedge – This hedges against the risk of changes in the fair value of a recognised asset or liability. For example, the fair value of fixed rate debt will change as a result of changes in interest rates.

(2) Cash flow hedge – This hedges against the risk of changes in expected cash flows. For example, a UK entity may have an unrecognised contractual commitment to purchase goods in a year's time for a fixed amount of US dollars.

Accounting for a fair value hedge

Under IAS 39 hedge accounting rules can only be applied to a fair value hedge if the hedging relationship meets four criteria.

(1) At the inception of the hedge there must be formal documentation identifying the hedged item and the hedging instrument.

(2) The hedge is expected to be highly effective.

(3) The effectiveness of the hedge can be measured reliably (i.e. the fair value/cash flows of the item and the instrument can be measured reliably).

(4) The hedge has been assessed on an on-going basis and is determined to have been effective.

Accounting treatment

*   The hedging instrument will be remeasured at fair value, with all gains and losses being reported in profit or loss for the year.

*   The hedged portion of the hedged item will be remeasured at fair value, with all gains and losses being reported in profit or loss for the year.

One consequence of introducing redefined classifications of financial assets under IFRS 9 is that some financial assets, previously measured at amortised cost, would now be measured at fair value through profit or loss under IFRS 9. If this is the case, both the hedged item and the hedging instrument would fall to be measured at fair value through profit or loss. Any change in fair value would therefore be matched in profit or loss and hedge accounting would be discontinued.

It is possible for a financial asset measured at amortised cost to be part of a fair value hedge. If this is the case, it would be measured at fair value, with any change in fair value taken to profit or loss as part of the hedge arrangement as identified above.

A further issue arises with the designation of items as fair value through other comprehensive income under IFRS 9. This designation must be made at initial recognition and is irrevocable. Similarly, any hedging arrangement must also be clearly designated at the point of inception. One reason for designation as fair value through other comprehensive income is to eliminate an accounting mismatch, where assets and liabilities are recognised or measured on different bases. It would appear possible that a fair value hedge arrangement could include a financial asset at fair value through other comprehensive income, with the remeasurement of both the hedged item and the hedging instrument both reported in either profit or loss (the current situation under IAS 39) or in other comprehensive income. This may arise following the elimination of the available-for-sale category of financial asset identified under IAS 39.

It is expected that eligibility conditions for the fair value option will be reconsidered again as the hedge accounting phase of the project to replace IAS 39 is progressed.

Hedge accounting illustration

On 1 January 20X8 an entity purchased an equity instrument at a fair value of $900,000. As it was not acquired with the intention of taking advantage of short-term changes in fair value, it would normally be designated upon initial recognition to be classified as fair value through other comprehensive income.

Due to the exposure to risk of changes in fair value of the equity instrument, the entity entered into an option contract, identifying the option contract as a hedging instrument as part of a fair value hedging arrangement. The fair value hedge has been correctly documented and designated upon initial recognition and is expected to be an effective hedging arrangement. Consequently, changes in fair value to both the equity instrument (hedged item) and the option contract (hedge instrument) will be matched in profit or loss, rather than accounted for separately.

At the reporting date 31 December 20X8, the fair value of the equity instrument has fallen to $800,000, and there has been an increase in the fair value of the option contract of $90,000.

Required:

Illustrate and explain the accounting treatment for the fair value hedge arrangement based upon the available information.

Solution

The fall in fair value of the equity interest of $100,000 is taken to profit or loss. This is matched with the increase in fair value of the option contact of $90,000, resulting in a small net loss of $10,000.

The effectiveness in the hedge arrangement (see later within section in Complete Text) can be evaluated by comparing the change in the hedged item and the hedged instrument as follows:

Change in hedged item $100,000
Change in hedging instrument $90,000

Either: 100,000/90,000 = 111%

Or: 90,000/100,000 = 90%

As long as either one of the two measures above falls within the range 80% – 125%, the hedge is regarded as effective.

The above fair value hedge arrangement would therefore be regarded as effective.

Note that the hedge documentation would normally specify the basis upon which the hedge arrangement is measured to evaluate whether or not it is effective.

Test your understanding 8 – Ennis

During the year an entity, Ennis, entered into three derivatives at no cost. No entry has been made in the draft financial statements. At the reporting date all three derivatives represent assets with a fair value of $10m. The first derivative was entered into for speculation purposes. The second derivative was entered into as a fair value hedge; the risk that this derivative was hedging has resulted in a loss of $9m which has been recognised in profit or loss. The third derivative was entered into as cash flow hedge.

Required:

Explain and illustrate how the three derivatives should be accounted for.

Accounting for a cash flow hedge

Before the IAS 39 hedge accounting rules can be applied to a cash flow hedge, the hedging relationship must meet five criteria. These are the four listed for a fair value hedge, plus:

- the transaction giving rise to the cash flow risk is highly probable and will ultimately affect profitability.

Accounting treatment

- The hedging instrument will be remeasured at fair value. The gain (or loss) on the portion of the instrument that is deemed to be an effective hedge will be taken to equity and recognised in the statement of changes in equity.

- The ineffective portion of the gain or loss will be reported immediately in the statement of profit or loss and other comprehensive income.

- If the hedged item eventually results in the recognition of a non-financial asset or liability, the gain or loss held in equity must be recycled in one of the two following ways
  - the gain / loss goes to adjust the carrying amount of the non-financial assets/liability.
  - the gain / loss is transferred to profit and loss in line with the consumption of the non-financial assets / liability.

Test your understanding 9 – Farah

Farah has entered into three transactions as follows:

Transaction A is concerned with the price of raw materials which Farah expects to rise in the medium term. Accordingly last year it entered into derivatives with a view to fixing the price in five years time. At the start of the current accounting period the price of raw materials had in fact risen, resulting in the derivatives being an asset with a fair value of $5m. During the current accounting period no new raw material derivative contracts were entered into and at the year-end the fair value of the derivatives had fallen to $3m.

Transaction B comprises a number of derivative contracts entered into during the year relating to foreign currency in the expectation of generating a profit. There were no such derivatives held at the start of the year. During the year realised losses on such derivative trading amounted to $4m. In addition, at the year-end, there were further foreign currency derivative contracts measured as a liability with a fair value of $6m.

Transaction C is an overseas investment and Farah is concerned that the value of this asset may fall, so has taken out a derivative to act as a hedge against any fall in the fair value. At the start of the year the asset had a fair value of $100m and at the year-end it has indeed fallen to $90m. At the start of the year the derivative had a fair value of $20m and at the year-end $29m.

Required:

Explain and illustrate how the three transactions dealing with derivatives should be accounted for.

Test your understanding 10 – Grayton

Grayton (whose functional currency is the $) decided in January that it will need to buy an item of plant in one year's time for KR 200,000. As a result of being risk averse, it wishes to hedge the risk that the cost of buying KRs will rise and so enters into a forward rate agreement to buy KR 200,000 in one year's time for the fixed sum of $100,000. The fair value of this contract at inception is zero and is designated as a hedging instrument.

At Grayton's reporting date on 31 July, the KR has depreciated and the value of KR 200,000 is $90,000. It remains at that value until the plant is bought.

Required:

How should this be accounted for?

Hedge effectiveness

One of the requirements of IAS 39 is that to use hedge accounting, the hedge must be effective. IAS 39 describes this as the degree to which the changes in fair value or cash flows of the hedged item are offset by changes in the fair value or cash flows of the hedging instrument.

A hedge is viewed as being highly effective if actual results are within a range of 80% to 125%. Note that the hedge documentation would normally specify the basis upon which the hedge arrangement is measured when considering its effectiveness.

Joseph uses hedging transaction to minimise the risk of exposure to foreign exchange fluctuations. He buys goods from overseas and takes out forward contracts to fix the price of his inputs.

The gain on his forward contract for November was $570. The loss on a foreign currency creditor was $600.

The effectiveness of the hedge is determined by dividing 570 by 600 or 600 by 570.

This gives an effectiveness percentage of 95% and 105% respectively. The hedge meets the criteria of 80 – 125% and is effective.

9 Disclosure of financial instruments

IFRS 7 **Financial instruments: disclosures** provides the disclosure requirements for financial instruments. A summary of the requirements is detailed below.

The two main categories of disclosures required are:

(1) Information about the significance of financial instruments.

(2) Information about the nature and extent of risks arising from financial instruments.

The disclosures made should be made by each class of financial instrument.

Significance of financial instruments

- An entity must disclose the **significance** of financial instruments for their financial position and performance. The disclosures must be made for each class of financial instruments.

- An entity must disclose items of income, expense, gains, and losses, with separate disclosure of gains and losses from each class of financial instrument.

Nature and extent of risks arising from financial instruments

Qualitative disclosures

The qualitative disclosures describe:

- risk exposures for each type of financial instrument
- management's objectives, policies, and processes for managing those risks
- changes from the prior period.

Quantitative disclosures

The quantitative disclosures provide information about the extent to which the entity is exposed to risk, based on information provided internally to the entity's key management personnel. These disclosures include:

- summary quantitative data about exposure to each risk at the reporting date
- disclosures about credit risk, liquidity risk, and market risk as further described below
- concentrations of risk.

IFRS 7 Disclosures

Introduction

IFRS 7 was issued in August 2005 and replaced the disclosure elements of IAS 32. The presentation elements of IAS 32 remain the same. It adds to the disclosures that were required by IAS 32 and includes both quantitative and qualitative disclosures. IFRS 7 was also amended in October 2010 to require enhanced disclosures dealing with aspects of derecognition and off-balance sheet activities.

Additionally, some of the disclosure requirements have been amended following the introduction of IFRS 9. In principle, there should be sufficient information to enable users of financial statements to fully understand:

- how financial assets and liabilities have been designated
- the date, reason and effect of any reclassification of financial assets

The two main categories of disclosures required are:

(1) Accounting policies applied in respect of accounting for financial instruments

(2) Information about the significance of financial instruments upon the financial performance and position of the entity.

(3) Information about the nature and extent of risks arising from financial instruments.

(4) Detailed disclosures relating to the nature and extent of accounting for fair value and cash flow hedging arrangements.

Types of risk

There are four types of financial risk:

(1) **Market risk** – This refers to the possibility that the value of an asset (or burden of a liability) might go up or down. Market risk includes three types of risk: currency risk, interest rate risk and price risk.

   (a) **Currency risk** is the risk that the value of a financial instrument will fluctuate because of changes in foreign exchange rates.

   (b) Fair value **interest rate risk** is the risk that the value of a financial instrument will fluctuate due to changes in market interest rates. This is a common problem with fixed interest rate bonds. The price of these bonds goes up and down as interest rates go down and up.

   (c) Price risk refers to other factors affecting price changes. These can be specific to the enterprise (bad financial results will cause a share price to fall), relate to the sector as a whole (all Tech-Stocks boomed in the late nineties, and crashed in the new century) or relate to the type of security (bonds do well when shares are doing badly, and vice versa).

   Market risk embodies not only the potential for a loss to be made but also a gain to be made.

(2) **Credit risk** – The risk that one party to a financial instrument fails to discharge its obligations, causing a financial loss to the other party. For example, a bank is exposed to credit risk on its loans, because a borrower might default on its loan.

(3) **Liquidity risk** – This is also referred to as funding risk. This is the risk that an enterprise will be unable to meet its commitments on its financial instruments. For example, a business may be unable to repay its loans when they fall due.

(4) **Cash flow interest rate risk** – This is the risk that future cash flows associated with a monetary financial instrument will fluctuate in amount due to changes in market interest rates. For example, the cash paid (or received) on floating rate loans will fluctuate in line with market interest rates.

Offsetting financial assets and financial liabilities

Following a joint project between the IASB and US FASB, IFRS 7 was amended in December 2011.

The initial objectives, as reflected in the ED issued in January 2011, were to agree a common offsetting model, agree presentation in the statement of financial position and to agree supporting disclosures.

The use of different offsetting models, together with amounts presented in the statement of financial position made it difficult for users of financial statements to compare the financial performance and position of entities. This was compounded by less than full disclosure of amounts which had been offset together with their associated accounting treatment. In addition, the application of offsetting can significantly reduce the values of assets and liabilities reported in the statement of financial position.

Although a common offsetting model could not be agreed between IASB and US FASB, and is therefore excluded from the approved amendments, there was agreement on common disclosures required in the financial statements which should enable users of those financial statements to better compare the financial position and performance of entities.

In principle, the following must be disclosed:

* gross amounts before offsetting,

* gross amounts set-off,

* net amounts presented in the statement of financial position,

* other amounts not set off, and

* net amounts

As the amounts set-off will depend upon the offsetting model, disclosure is required of the basis of offsetting, together with accounting treatment adopted.

The amendments are effective for accounting periods commencing on or after 1 January 2013, with retrospective application required.

In situations where the net cash flow hedge arrangement covers more than one accounting period, any gain or loss on cash flows to date at each reporting date must be taken to other comprehensive income and deferred. The deferred gain or loss will be reclassified (i.e. recycled) to profit or loss when the later cash flows affect profit or loss.

The hedge document should specify the volume and nature of items which constitute the net position, together with the reporting period(s) in which profit or loss is likely to be affected.

Discontinuance of a hedging relationship would occur when any of the following arise:

(1) when the risk management objective has changed,

(2) when the economic relationship between the hedged item and the hedging instruments no longer exists, or

(3) when credit risk dominates the changes in value that result from the economic relationship.

Voluntary discontinuance of a hedging relationship is not permitted if the risk management objective remains unchanged.As a further, but separate development, an ED on **macro-hedge accounting** is expected to be published at some future date. As at September 2012, this has been separated from the IFRS 9 project and will be developed as a separate project. IAS 39 will continue to apply to fair value hedge accounting requirements in relation to portfolio hedges of interest rate risk. A DP is expected in late 2012 or early 2013.

Financial instruments with the characteristics of equity

This is a long-term project dealing with particular aspects of accounting for financial instruments. IAS 32 provides the relevant guidance for distinguishing between asset and liability instruments (non-equity instruments) and equity instruments. The IASB is reviewing this guidance to address some practice issues, including eliminating current rules-based approaches, and to achieve convergence with US GAAP.

Following publication of a DP in February 2008 the IASB and US FASB decided to begin future deliberations using the principles underlying the perpetual and basic ownership approaches. They have developed a model where classification is based on the form of an instrument's settlement, assets (e.g. cash) or its own equity instruments (e.g. shares) as follows:

For instruments that the issuer settles with assets:

(1) Classify as equity if asset-settlement occurs because of the following reasons:

    (a) on distribution of all of its assets (such as bankruptcy)

    (b) the issuer chooses to pay a dividend or repurchase shares

    (c) redemption allows existing instrument holders to maintain control of the entity

    (d) the holder ceases to participate in the activities of the entity

(2) All other asset-settled instruments are classified as liabilities.

For instruments that the issuer settles with its own equity instruments:

(1) A contract for a specified number of its own equity instruments in exchange for a specified price are classified as equity

    – Specified number must be fixed or vary as an anti-dilution measure

    – Specified price must be in the functional currency of the reporting entity or shareholder

(2) All other equity-settled instruments are classified as liabilities

Instruments with both liability and equity features will be separated into liability and equity components. For example, equity shares with required dividend payments, debt convertible at the option of holder into a specified number of equity shares.

Following the issue of the DP, there have been no significant developments relating to this project. Work on the project was paused in 2010 as this project was assessed to be of relatively low priority.

Technical articles

Tony Sweetman of Kaplan Publishing wrote an article discussing financial instruments for the August 2011 edition of Student Accountant magazine. You can access this article from the ACCA website (www.accaglobal.com).

Tom Clendon of Kaplan Financial wrote a two-part article discussing the accounting treatment of financial assets and liabilities 'What is a financial instrument?' dated July 2012 for the Student Accountant magazine. You can access this article from the ACCA website (www.accaglobal.com).

10 Chapter summary

Classification of liabilities and equity:
- Liabilities include a contractual obligation to pay cash or exchange financial instruments
- Equity – no such obligation

Financial liabilities measured at either:
- Fair value through profit or loss, or
- Amortised cost
Note there is option to measure liabilities at FV to reduce accounting mismatch.

Derivatives (assets and liabilities):
- Include options, swaps, forward contracts and future contracts
- Categorised as fair value through profit or loss, unless used as a hedge
  - Fair value hedge
  - Cash flow hedge
- Embedded derivatives are included within another non-derivative contract – need to split from host contract

Financial assets:
- Initial recognition at fair value
- Subsequent measurement depends upon categorisation:
  - Fair value through profit or loss is the default categorisation
  - Fair value through other comprehensive income - elect upon recognition for equity instruments only
  - Amortised cost – elect upon initial recognition provided two tests passed:
- Business model test
- Cash flow characteristics test

Impairment of financial assets:
- Need to review annually for evidence of impairment
- If measured at FV, then impairment taken to profit or loss or other comprehensive income to follow categorisation
- If measured at amortised cost, then impairment taken to profit or loss.

Disclosure requirements:
- Significance of financial instruments
- Nature and extents of risks
- Qualitative and quantitative issues

Test your understanding answers

Test your understanding 1 – Ashes financial assets and liabilities

Financial assets:

(1) Trade receivables will be recognised until the cash that is due has been collected. As such they meet both the business model and cash flow characteristics tests specified by IFRS 9 to be classified and accounted for at amortised cost.

(2) Investments held for short-term speculative purposes must be classified and accounted for as FVTP&L. Consequently, they are recognised and measured on the statement of financial position at fair value and the gains and losses on remeasurement recognised in profit or loss.

(3) Investments that from the outset are going to be indefinitely may be irrevocably designated upon initial recognition as FVTOCI. They are recognised and measured on the statement of financial position at fair value and the gains and losses recognised in other comprehensive income (i.e. equity). Note that intention at the point of recognition is the key issue; it does not mean that the financial assets must be held for a minimum or specified period. If no such election on purchase is made then the investment must be classified and accounted for as FVTP&L.

Equity and liabilities

(1) Ordinary shares that are issued contain no obligation to be repaid and thus form part of the equity of the company. Equity is not subsequently remeasured. Any dividends paid are a reduction on equity found as movement in reserves in the SOCIE.

(2) The issue of debentures creates a debt instrument. This will be classified and accounted at amortised cost unless specifically designated as FVTP&L which would only be appropriate if it was held for trading purposes or to avoid an accounting mismatch. Amortised cost means that the effective rate is charged as a finance cost to profit or loss and that at the year-end the liability is not remeasured.

(3) Whilst the legal form of redeemable preference shares is that they are shares, in substance they are debt i.e. a liability as they are redeemable. Substance over form applies and will result with redeemable preference shares classified and accounted as a liability at amortised cost.

(4) Convertible loan stock is a hybrid financial instrument containing elements of both debt and equity. The option to convert the instrument into shares is the equity element. On initial recognition the proceeds need to be split between the debt element and the equity element. The debt element is measured as the present value of the future cash flows leaving the equity element as the balancing figure. Any issue costs are allocated between each element on a pro rata basis. The equity element will form a reserve and is not remeasured. The debt element will be accounted for at amortised cost thus creating a finance cost based on the effective rate of interest.

(5) Redeemable non-cumulative preference shares would normally be regarded as a liability as there is an obligation to redeem, presumably when the directors leave office. If there is a compulsory dividend payable, this would also be regarded as part of the liability. If dividends payable are discretionary, then these shares would be regarded as a compound instrument and must be split between liability and equity elements. When paid, any discretionary dividends would therefore be regarded as a distribution from equity.

Test your understanding 2 – Hoy

Hoy has a financial liability to be measured at amortised cost.

It is initially recorded at the fair value of the consideration received, i.e. net proceeds of issue. This amount is then increased each year to redemption by interest added at the effective rate and reduced by the interest actually paid, with the result that the carrying amount at the end of the first year is at amortised cost.

Hoy has no issue costs and the net proceeds are $10,000 less 5% = $9,500. The annual cash payment is the 2% coupon rate on the nominal value of the debt $10,000.

Rep date	Bal b/fwd $	Eff rate 10% $	Cash paid $	Bal c/fwd $
31 Dec X1	9,500	950	(200)	10,250
31 Dec X2	10,250	1,025	(200)	
			(11,075)	
		1,975		

Wiggins has a liability that will be classified and accounted for at amortised cost and thus initially measured at the fair value of consideration received less the transaction costs.

As there is a discount on issue and transaction costs to deal with, the first step is to calculate the initial measurement of the liability:

	$
Cash received ($20,000 × 90%)	18,000
Less the transaction costs	(1,000)
Initial recognition	17,000

The effective rate is used to determine the finance cost for the year - this is charged to profit or loss. The coupon rate applied to the nominal value of the loan notes to determine the cash paid to the holder of the loan notes.The workings for the liability accounted for at amortised cost can be summarised and presented as follows.

Rep date	Bal b/fwd $	Eff rate 12% $	Cash paid $	Bal c/fwd $
31 Dec X4	17,000	2,040	(1,200)	17,840
31 Dec X5	17,840	2,141	(1,200)	18,781
31 Dec X6	18,781	2,254	(1,200)	19,835
31 Dec X7	19,835	2,380	(1,200)	
			(21,015)	
		8,815		

Cavendish has a financial liability to be measured at amortised cost.

It is initially recorded at the fair value of the consideration received, i.e. net proceeds of issue. There is no discount on issue and nor is there any issue costs to deduct from the initial measurement.

The opening balance is then increased each year to redemption by interest added at the effective rate and reduced by the interest actually paid - which in this case is nil as it is a zero coupon bond.

In the final year there is a single cash payment which wholly discharges the obligation. The workings for the liability being accounted for at amortised cost can be summarised and presented as follows:

Rep date	Bal b/fwd $	Eff rate 7% $	Cash paid $	Bal c/fwd $
31 Dec X5	10,000	700	Nil	10,700
31 Dec X6	10,700	749	(11,449)	

Boardman

The initial measurement of the liability classified as FVTP&L is at fair value i.e. the $30,000 received. There are no transaction costs in this example but these would be expensed rather than taken into account in arriving at the initial measurement.

With both the effective rate of interest and the coupon rate at 5% during the year to 31 December 20X6, the carrying value of the liability will remain at $30,000. This is because the finance cost that will increase the liability is $1,500 (5% × $30,000 – the effective rate applied to the opening balance), and the cash paid reducing the liability is also $1,500 (5% × $30,000 – the coupon rate applied to the nominal value).

As the liability has been classified as FVTPL this carrying value at 31 December 20X6 must now be remeasured using the current market rate of interest. The fair value of the liability at this date will be the present value (using the new rate of interest of 6%) of the remaining two years' payments. This process will be repeated when the market rate of interest increases to 7% at 31 December 20X7.

The movement on the liability can be presented as follows:

Rep date	Bal b/fwd $	Mkt rate	Finance cost $	Cash paid $	(Gain) Loss	Bal c/fwd $
31 Dec X6	30,000	5%	1,500	(1,500)	(550)	(W1) 29,450
31 Dec X7	29,450	6%	1,767	(1,500)	(265)	(W2) 29,439
31 Dec X8	29,439	7%	2,061	(1,500)		
				(30,000)		

(W1) FV of liability at 31 Dec X6 using 6% discount factor: $
Payment due 31 Dec X7 - cash interest only ($1,500 × 0.943)   1,415
Payment due 31 Dec X8 - cash interest plus capital repaid   28,035
($31,500 × 0.890)

29,450

(W2) FV of liability at 31 Dec X7 using 7% discount factor:
Payment due 31/12/X8 cash interest plus capital repaid   29,439
(31,500 × (1/1.07))

As you may know from financial management studies, and as is demonstrated here, when interest rates rise so the fair value of bonds will fall and vice versa.

As Boardman has classified this liability as FVTPL, it is revalued to $29,450 at 31 December 20X6. The gain or loss on remeasurement is identified as a balancing amount. The reduction of $550 in the carrying value of the liability from $30,000 is regarded as a profit, and this is recognised in profit or loss. If however the higher discount rate used was not because general interest rates have risen but because the credit risk of the entity has risen, then the gain is recognised in other comprehensive income.

Test your understanding 3 – Craig

Up to 31 December 20X8, the accounting entries are the same under both scenarios.

(1) **Splitting the proceeds**

The cash payments on the bond should be discounted to their present value using the interest rate for a bond without the conversion rights, i.e. 8%.

Date		Cash flow	Discount factor @ 8%	Present value
		$		$
31-Dec-X6	Interest	4,000	1/1.08	3,704
31-Dec-X7	Interest	4,000	$1/1.08^2$	3,429
31-Dec-X8	Interest and principal	104,000	$1/1.08^3$	82,559

Present value (the liability component)	A	89,692
As the net proceeds of issue were	B	100,000
So the equity component is	B – A	10,308

(2) **The annual finance costs and year end carrying amounts**

	Opening balance	Effective interest rate 8%	Payments 4%	Closing balance
	$	$	$	$
20X6	89,692	7,175	(4,000)	92,867
20X7	92,867	7,429	(4,000)	96,296
20X8	96,296	7,704	(4,000)	100,000

(3) (a) **Conversion**

The carrying amounts at 31 December 20X8 are:

	$
Equity	10,308
Liability – bond	100,000
	———
	110,308
	———

If the conversion rights are exercised, then 50,000 ($100,000 ÷ 2) equity shares of $1 are issued and $60,308 is classified as share premium.

(b) **Redemption**

The carrying amounts at 31 December 20X8 are the same as under 3a. On redemption, the $100,000 liability is extinguished by cash payments. The equity component remains within equity, probably as a non-distributable reserve.

Test your understanding 4 – Ming

The principle at stake with derecognition or otherwise of receivables is whether, under the factoring arrangement, the risks and rewards of ownership pass from the trading company i.e. Ming. The principal risk with regard to receivables is the risk of bad debt.

In the first arrangement the $180,000 has been received as a one-off, non refundable sum. This is factoring without recourse for bad debts. The risk of bad debt has clearly passed from Ming to the factoring bank. Accordingly Ming should derecognise the receivable and there will be an expense of $20,000 recognised. No liability will be recognised.

In the second arrangement the $70,000 is simply a payment on account. More may be received by Ming implying that Ming retains an element of reward. The monies received are refundable in the event of default and as such represent an obligation. This means that the risk of slow payment and bad debt remains with Ming who is liable to repay the monies so far received. As such despite the passage of legal title the asset (i.e. receivable) should remain recognised in the accounts of Ming. In substance Ming has borrowed $70,000 and this loan should be recognised immediately. This will increase the gearing of Ming.

Test your understanding 5 – Jones

(1) On purchase the investment is recorded at the consideration paid including, as the asset is classified as fair value through other comprehensive income, the associated transaction costs:

		$m
Dr	Asset	41
Cr	Cash	41

At the reporting date the asset is remeasured and the gain is recognised in other comprehensive income and taken to equity:

Dr	Asset	19
Cr	Other components of equity	19

On disposal, the asset is derecognised, the gain or loss on disposal is determined by comparing disposal proceeds and carrying value, with the result taken to profit or loss.

Dr	Cash	70
Cr	Asset	60
Cr	Profit	10

Note that the any gains or losses previously taken to equity are **not** recycled upon derecognition, although they may be reclassified within equity.

(2) If Jones had designated the investment as fair value through profit and loss, the transaction costs would have been recognised as an expense in profit or loss. So on purchase:

Dr	Asset	40m
Cr	Cash	40m
Dr	Expense	1m
Cr	Cash	1m

Subsequent measurement – at fair value through profit or loss:

Dr	Asset	20m
Cr	Profit	20m

On disposal the asset is derecognised with the gain taken to income

Dr	Cash	70
Cr	Asset	60
Cr	Profit	10

Note that the reported profit on derecognition of $10 million is the same, whether designated as fair value through profit or loss or fair value through other comprehensive income. This is one change brought about by IFRS 9 as recycling of gains and losses previously recognised in other comprehensive income is no longer done.

Test your understanding 6 – Pendleton

Incurred loss model

The gross interest income that is initially recognised in income is $20,000 (as calculated using the effective rate of 20% on the initial carrying value of $100,000). With no defaults, cash of $20,000 will also be received (as calculated using the coupon rate of 20% on the nominal value). Thus, on an incurred loss model there is no impairment loss and the carrying value at the end of the first reporting period is $100,000.

Expected loss model

However, to recognise the impairment loss on an expected loss basis the actual net rate of return inclusive of expected defaults of 6% has to be considered. This gives a net $6,000 (6% × $100,000) to be recognised in income. Thus, there is an expected loss adjustment of $14,000 ($20,000 less $6,000) leaving the asset written down to $86,000 ($100,000 less $14,000).

Test your understanding 7 – Hoggard

In all scenarios the cost of the derivative on 1 January 20X6 is $500 ($5 × 100) and an asset is recognised in the statement of financial position.

Dr	Asset – option	$500
Cr	Cash	$500

Outcome A

If the option is sold for $1,500 (100 × $15) before the exercise date, it is derecognised at a profit of $1,000.

Dr	Cash	$1,500
Cr	Asset – option	$500
Cr	Profit	$1,000

Outcome B

If the option lapses unexercised, then it is derecognised and there is a loss to be taken to profit or loss:

Dr	Expense	$500
Cr	Asset – option	$500

Outcome C

If the option is exercised, the option is derecognised, cash paid upon exercise and the investment in shares is recognised at fair value. An immediate profit is recognised:

Dr	Asset – investment (100 × $25)	$2,500
Cr	Cash 100 × $10)	$1,000
Cr	Asset – option	$500
Cr	Profit	$1,000

Test your understanding 8 – Ennis

All derivatives must be recognised on the statement of financial position at their fair value. Each derivative has a fair value of $30m and will be reported as assets. As each derivative has a nil cost so there is also a corresponding gain arising of $10m on each.

The first derivative was entered into for trading / speculation purposes and as such the gain is recognised in profit or loss for the year.

The second derivative was entered into as a fair value hedge and as such it is matched in profit or loss with the loss arising that the derivative was covering. There is instant hedge accounting with the gain of $10m on the derivative being offset against the loss it was designed to cover of $9m. Consequently, a net gain of $1m is recognised in profit or loss for the year.

The third derivative was entered into as a cash flow hedge and the gain is recognised directly in other comprehensive income for the year and within other components of equity on the statement of financial position.

Test your understanding 9 – Farah

Transaction A Farah is risk adverse and is using the derivative to hedge / cover a risk concerning future cash flows. This is a cash flow hedge. The loss in the period of $2m ($5m - $3m) will be recognised in other comprehensive income and equity so that it can be subsequently recycled to income when indeed the transaction arises. There is an asset with a fair value of $3m that is recognised on the statement of financial position.

Transaction B Farah has engaged in speculation and lost! Such cumulative losses of $10m ($4m + $6m) are recognised in profit or loss. There is a liability with a fair value of $6m that is recognised on the statement of financial position.

Transaction C Farah is risk adverse and is using the derivative to hedge / cover the risk concerning the potential fall in the fair value of a recognised asset. This is a fair value hedge. The hedge has proved 90% effective, in that the loss of $10m on the asset is only covered by 90% as the derivative has generated a gain of $9m in the period. In profit or loss a net loss of $1m is reported after the offset of the loss on the asset and the gain on the fair value hedge.

Note that where a hedging arrangement is entered into, it must be formalised and documented at inception. It must also be reviewed regularly to ensure that the hedging arrangement is effective. If, for any reason, the hedging arrangement is no longer effective, hedge accounting must be discontinued and any individual financial assets and financial liabilities accounted for in accordance with IFRS 9 as applicable.

Test your understanding 10 – Grayton

This is a cash flow hedge.

Because the forward rate agreement has no fair value at its inception, the need to account for the derivative really first arises at the reporting date, when it has a value and the change in value has to be recorded.

Because it has been designated a cash flow hedge, the change in value is recognised as other comprehensive income and taken to a cash flow hedge reserve, to be carried forward to be matched against the future cash flow. The agreement is showing a loss of $10,000 at the reporting date because Grayton is locked into buying KR 200,000 for $100,000 when everyone else can buy them for $90,000.

In hindsight there was no need to have hedged, because the price of buying the foreign currency has come down, not gone up.

On 31 July, the derivative is recognised in the financial statements:

Dr Cash flow hedge reserve (other components of equity) $10,000
Cr Liability – derivative $10,000

(Had this not been designated a hedging instrument, the loss would have been recognised immediately in profit or loss.)

The forward contract will be settled and closed when the asset is purchased.

Although the loss on the derivative could be recognised in profit or loss as the plant is depreciated (effectively becoming additional depreciation), it will be more sensible for Grayton to use it to adjust the plant's carrying amount upwards on initial recognition (this has the same net effect over time).

This will result in the non-current asset being recognised at $100,000, which is what the hedging transaction was seeking to ensure.

Dr	Liability – derivative	$10,000
Dr	Plant	$90,000
Cr	Cash	$100,000
Dr	Plant	$10,000
Cr	Other components of equity	$10,000

Provisions

Chapter learning objectives

Upon completion of this chapter you will be able to:

- apply and discuss the recognition, derecognition and measurement of provisions, contingent liabilities and contingent assets including environmental provisions
- calculate and discuss the accrual of restructuring provisions
- apply and discuss accounting for events after the reporting date
- determine and report going concern issues arising after the reporting date

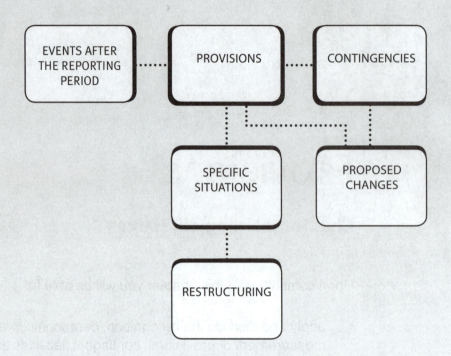

1 Provisions

Recognition

A **provision** is a liability of uncertain timing or amount.

A **liability** is a present obligation arising from past events, the settlement of which is expected to result in an outflow of economic benefits.

A provision can only be recognised if it meets the definition of a liability.

IAS 37 **Provisions, contingent liabilities and contingent assets** requires that a provision should be recognised when and only when:

- an entity has a present obligation (legal or constructive) as a result of a past event
- it is probable that a outflow of resources embodying economic benefits will be required to settle the obligation
- a reliable estimate can be made of the amount of the obligation.

An obligation is something that **cannot be avoided.**

- An entity has a **constructive obligation** if, by an established pattern of past practice, published policies or a sufficiently specific current statement, it has indicated to other parties that it will accept certain responsibilities; and as a result, it has created a valid expectation on the part of those other parties that it will discharge those responsibilities.

- A provision cannot be recognised unless there has been a past event, which is an **obligating event**. This is an event, which creates a legal, or constructive obligation and that results in an entity having no realistic alternative to settling that obligation. The obligating event is the past event that leads to the present obligation.

- An outflow of economic benefits is regarded as probable if it is **more likely than not** to occur.

- Where there are a number of similar obligations (for example product warranties), it is necessary to consider the class of obligations as a whole.

- Only in extremely rare cases is it impossible to make a reliable estimate of the amount of the obligation.

Derecognition

Provisions should be reviewed at the end of each reporting period.

- They should be reversed if it is no longer probable that an outflow of economic benefits will be required to settle the obligation.

- Provisions should be used only for expenditure that relates to the matter for which the provision was originally recognised.

Measurement

The amount recognised as a provision should be the best estimate of the expenditure required to settle the obligation that existed at the reporting date.

- The estimate should take into account:
  - risks and uncertainties associated with the cash flows
  - expected future events (for example, new technology or new legislation)
  - the time value of money, if it has a material effect.

- If the effect of the time value of money is material, then the provision should be discounted. The discount rate should be pre-tax and risk-specific.

- The unwinding of the discount is a finance cost, and it should be disclosed separately on the face of the statement of profit or loss.

- Provisions should be reviewed at each reporting date and adjusted to reflect the current best estimate.

Provisions and 'creative accounting'

Before IAS 37 was issued, provisions were recognised on the basis of prudence. Little guidance was given as to when a provision should be recognised and how it should be measured. This gave rise to inconsistencies, and also allowed profits to be manipulated.

In particular, provisions could be created when profits were high and released when profits were low, in order to smooth reported results. This was common where an entity made an acquisition. The acquirer would create excessive provisions for the cost of integrating a new subsidiary's operations into the group. When the provisions were released, the profits reported by the group as a whole would be artificially inflated.

As well as disguising poor performance in a particular year, profit smoothing can also create an impression that profits are less volatile (and therefore less risky), than they really are. This tends to boost share prices.

IAS 37 prevents entities from recognising excessive provisions by focusing on the statement of financial position and applying the definitions and recognition criteria in the Framework for the preparation and presentation of financial statements. A provision cannot be recognised unless it represents a genuine liability.

Offset

Sometimes an entity may be able to recover the costs required to settle a provision. For example, it may have an insurance policy to cover the costs of a law suit. In general, the liability and the recovery should be treated as a separate liability and a separate asset. This is because the entity remains liable for the full amount, regardless of whether it can recover expenditure from a third party.

Amounts should only be offset where the reporting entity no longer has an obligation for that part of the expenditure to be met by the third party.

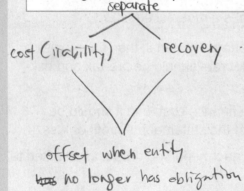

Contingent liabilities and contingent assets

Contingent liabilities

A **contingent liability** is

- a possible obligation that arises from past events and whose existence will be confirmed only by the outcome of one or more uncertain future events not wholly within the control of the entity

- a present obligation that arises from past events, but does not meet the criteria for recognition as a provision. This is either because an outflow of economic benefits is not probable; or (more rarely) because it is not possible to make a reliable estimate of the obligation.

A contingent liability should not be recognised.

- Instead, it should be disclosed, unless the possibility of a future outflow of economic benefits is remote.

- Contingent liabilities should be reviewed regularly. If an outflow of economic benefits becomes probable, then they must be reclassified as provisions.

Contingent assets

A **contingent asset** is a possible asset that arises from past events and whose existence will be confirmed only by the outcome of one or more uncertain future events, not wholly within the control of the entity.

A contingent asset should not be recognised.

- A contingent asset should be disclosed if the future inflow of economic benefits is probable.

- If the future inflow of benefits is virtually certain, then it ceases to be a contingent asset and should be recognised as a normal asset.

Summary

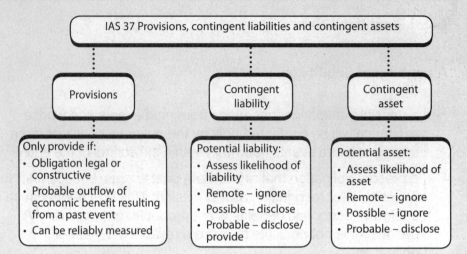

Problems in applying IAS 37

(a) Definition of contingent liability

The definition of a contingent liability gives particular problems, because 'possible' is not defined. However, IAS 37 says that 'probable' means 'more likely than not'. Because probable means 'more than 50% likely' it is reasonable to assume that 'possible' means 'less than 50% likely'.

Therefore, a contingent liability is often taken to be a liability whose existence is less than 50% likely or where the probability of an outflow of economic benefits is less than 50%.

(b) 'Virtually certain' and 'remote'

Contingent assets should be recognised if they are virtually certain and contingent liabilities should not be disclosed if they are remote. There is no definition of 'virtually certain' or 'remote'.

However, it is usually assumed that 'virtually certain' means more than 95% probable and 'remote' means less than 5% probable.

2 Specific situations

Future operating losses

In the past, provisions were recognised for future operating losses on the grounds of prudence. However, these should not be provided for the following reasons.

- They relate to future events.

- There is no obligation to a third party. The loss-making business could be closed and the losses avoided.

Onerous contracts

An **onerous contract** is a contract in which the unavoidable costs of meeting the contract exceed the economic benefits expected to be received under it.

- A common example of an onerous contract is a lease on a surplus factory. The leaseholder is legally obliged to carry on paying the rent on the factory, but they will not get any benefit from using the factory.

- If an entity has an onerous contract, a provision should be recognised for the present obligation under the contract. (The signing of the contract was the past event giving rise to the present obligation.)

- The provision is measured at the least net cost: the lower of the cost of fulfilling the contract or of terminating it and suffering any penalty payments.

- Some assets may have been bought specifically for use in fulfilling the onerous contract. These should be reviewed for impairment before any separate provision is made for the contract itself.

Illustration – specific situation

Droopers has recently bought all of the trade, assets and liabilities of Dolittle, an unincorporated business. As part of the takeover, all of the combined business's activities have been relocated to Droopers' main site. As a result Dolittle's premises are now empty and surplus to requirements.

Just before the acquisition, Dolittle had signed a three-year lease for its premises at $6,000 per month. At 31 December 20X3, this lease had 32 months left to run and the landlord had refused to terminate the lease. A sub-tenant has taken over part of the premises for the rest of the lease at a rent of $2,500 per month.

(a) Should Droopers recognise a provision for an onerous contract in respect of this lease?

(b) Show how this information will be presented in the financial statements for 20X3 and 20X4. Ignore the time value of money.

Solution

Despite not making any use of the premises, Droopers has a legal obligation to pay a further $192,000 ($6,000 × 32), to the landlord, as a result of a lease signed before the year-end (the obligating event). Therefore, an onerous contract exists and a provision must be recognised.

There is also an amount recoverable from the sub-tenant of $80,000 ($2,500 × 32). This is shown separately in the statement of financial position as an asset.

The $192,000 payable and the $80,000 recoverable can be netted off in profit or loss for the year.

Statements of profit or loss

	20X3	20X4
	$	$
Provision for onerous lease contract (net)	112,000 Dr	–

Statements of financial position

	20X3	20X4
Receivables		
Amounts recoverable from sub-tenants	80,000 Dr	50,000 Dr
Liabilities		
Amounts payable on onerous contracts	192,000 Cr	120,000 Cr

Future repairs to assets

Some assets need to be repaired or to have parts replaced every few years. For example, an airline may be required by law to overhaul all its aircraft every three years.

- Provisions cannot normally be recognised for the cost of future repairs or replacement parts.

- This is because the obligating event is the repair or purchase of the replacement part, which has not yet occurred.

- Even if the future expenditure is required by law, the entity has an alternative to incurring it; it could sell the asset.

- Instead, the expenditure should be capitalised and depreciated over its useful life (for example, the period until the next major overhaul is required).

Environmental provisions

Environmental provisions are often referred to as clean-up costs because they usually relate to the cost of decontaminating and restoring an industrial site, when production has ceased. The normal rules in IAS 37 apply.

- A provision is recognised if there is an obligation (legal or constructive) to repair environmental damage.

- Merely causing damage or intending to clean-up a site does not create an obligation.

- An entity may have a constructive obligation to repair environmental damage. This will be the case if (for example), an entity publicises policies that include environmental awareness or explicitly undertakes to clean up the damage caused by its operations.

There must have been a past obligating event. A provision can only be set up to rectify environmental damage that has **already happened.**

The **full cost** of an environmental provision should be recognised as soon as the obligation arises.

- Because it may be many years before the costs relating to the provision are paid out, the effect of the time value of money is usually material. Therefore, an environmental provision is normally discounted to its present value.

- If the expenditure results in future economic benefits an equivalent asset can be recognised. This is depreciated over its useful life, which is the same as the 'life' of the provision. (Note that IAS 37 is silent on whether an asset should be recognised at the same time as a provision. But IAS 16 **Property, plant and equipment** requires capitalisation of the provision if it relates to an item of property, etc.)

Illustration – specific situation

On 1 January 20X6, Scrubber paid the Government of Metallica $5m for a three-year licence to quarry gravel. At the end of the licence, Scrubber must restore the quarry to its natural state. This will cost a further $3m. These costs will be incurred on 1 January 20X9. Scrubber's cost of capital is 10%.

Explain how this expenditure is treated in the financial statements of Scrubber.

Solution

Scrubber has a legal obligation (the obligating event is the taking out of the licence). Therefore, it recognises a provision for $3m at 1 January 20X6. This provision is discounted to its present value.

Each year, the discount unwinds and the provision increases. The unwinding of the discount is charged to profit as a finance cost.

Movement on provision	20X6	20X7	20X8	20X9
	$000	$000	$000	$000
Opening balance	2,253	2,478	2,727	3,000
Finance cost at 10%	225	249	273	–
Release to profit	–	–	–	(3,000)
Closing balance	2,478	2,727	3,000	–

Scrubber could not carry out its quarrying operation without incurring the clean-up costs. Therefore, incurring the costs gives it access to future economic benefits. It includes the additional expenditure in the cost of the licence and recognises this as an asset. The licence is depreciated over the three years.

Cost of licence	$000
Cash paid 1 January 20X6	5,000
Present value of clean-up costs 1 January 20X9	2,253
Total	7,253

The effect on the financial statements is shown below:

Statements of profit or loss	20X6 $000	20X7 $000	20X8 $000	20X9 $000
Operating costs				
Depreciation (over 3 years)	2,418	2,418	2,417	–
Finance costs				
Unwinding of discount	225	249	273	–

Statement of financial position	$000	$000	$000	$000
Non-current assets				
Licence: Cost	7,253	7,253	7,253	–
Depreciation	(2,418)	(4,836)	(7,253)	–
Carrying value	4,835	2,417	–	–
Liabilities				
Clean-up provision	2,478	2,727	3,000	–

Test your understanding 1 – Situations

Consider each of the following situations to determine whether or not a provision is required.

(a) An entity has a policy of only carrying out work to rectify damage cause to the environment when it is required by local law so to do. For several years the entity has been operating an oil rig which causes such damage, in a country that did not have legislation in place, that required such rectification.

A new government has been elected in that country and at the reporting date, it is virtually certain the legislation will be enacted, that will require damage rectification; this legislation will have retrospective effect.

(b) Under a licence granted by a local government, an entity has constructed a rock-crushing plant to process material mined from the surrounding area. Mining activities have already started. Under the terms of the licence, the entity must remove the rock-crushing plant when mining activities have been completed and must landscape the mined area, so as to create a national park.

Required:

For each of the situations, explain whether a provision should be recognised.

3 Restructuring provisions

Definition

A **restructuring** is a programme that is planned and controlled by management and has a material effect on:

- the scope of a business undertaken by the reporting entity in terms of the products or services it provides
- the manner in which a business undertaken by the reporting entity is conducted.

A restructuring could include:

- sale or termination of a line of business
- the closure of business locations in a country or region or the relocation of business activities from one country or region to another
- changes in management structure, for example, eliminating a layer of management
- fundamental reorganisations that have a material effect on the nature and focus of the entity's operations.

When can a provision be recognised?

Before IAS 37 was issued, entities would often set up unnecessary 'restructuring provisions' that could then be used for profit smoothing in later periods. IAS 37 has prohibited this.

A restructuring provision can only be recognised where an entity has a **constructive obligation** to carry out the restructuring.

A constructive obligation exists **only** if:

- there is a detailed formal plan for restructuring. This must identify the businesses, locations and employees affected

- those affected have a valid expectation that the restructuring will be carried out. For example, the plan is already being implemented or it has been announced to those affected by it

- the constructive obligation must exist at the year-end. (An obligation arising after the year-end may require disclosure under IAS 10 **Events after the reporting period** as a non-adjusting event after the reporting date.)

- a board decision alone does not create a constructive obligation unless:
    - the plan is already being implemented. For example, assets are being sold, redundancy negotiations have begun
    - the plan has been announced to those affected by it. The plan must have a strict timeframe without unreasonable delays
    - the board itself contains representatives of employees or other groups affected by the decision. (This is common in mainland Europe.)

- an announcement to sell an operation does not create a constructive obligation. An obligation only exists when a purchaser is found and there is a binding sale agreement.

Accruing a provision

A restructuring provision should only include the direct costs of restructuring. These must be both:

- necessarily entailed by the restructuring

- not associated with the ongoing activities of the entity.

The following costs relate to future events and therefore, must **not** be included:

- retraining or relocating staff
- marketing
- investment in new systems and distribution networks
- future operating losses (unless these arise from an onerous contract)
- profits on disposal of assets (but losses on disposal may need to be included as a restructuring may trigger an impairment review under IAS 36)

The amount recognised should be the best estimate of the expenditure required and it should take into account expected future events. This means that expenses should be measured at their actual cost, where this is known, even if this was only discovered after the reporting date (this is an adjusting event after the reporting date per IAS 10).

Illustration 1 – Restructuring provisions

On 15 January 20X5, the Board of Directors of Shane voted to proceed with two reorganisation schemes involving the closure of two factories. Shane's financial year-end is 31 March, and the financial statements will be finalised and published on 30 June.

Scheme 1

The closure costs will amount to $125,000. The factory is rented on a short-term lease, and there will be no gains or losses arising on this property. The closure will be announced in June, and will commence in August.

Scheme 2

The costs will amount to $45,000 (after crediting $105,000 profit on disposal of certain machines). The closure will take place in July, but redundancy negotiations began with the staff in March.

For each of the two schemes:

(a) Should a provision be recognised?

(b) If so, what is the amount of the provision?

Solution

Scheme 1

The obligating event is the announcement of the plan, which occurs in June. This is after the year-end, so there can be no provision. However, the announcement in June should be disclosed as a non-adjusting event after the reporting date.

Scheme 2

Although the closure will not begin until July, the employees will have had a valid expectation that it would happen when the redundancy negotiations began in March. Therefore, a provision should be recognised. The provision will be for $150,000 because the expected profit on disposal cannot be netted off against the expected costs.

Test your understanding 2 – Delta

On 30 June 20X2, the directors of Delta decided to close down a division. This decision was announced to the employees affected on 15 July 20X2 and the actual closure occurred on 31 August 20X2, prior to the 20X2 financial statements being authorised for issue on 15 September.

Expenses and other items connected with the closure were as follows:

	$m
Redundancy costs (estimated)	22
Staff retraining (actual)	10
Operating loss for the 2 months to 31 August 20X2	
(estimated at 30 June)	12
Profit on sale of property	5

The actual redundancy costs were $20 million and the actual operating loss for the two months to 31 August 20X2, was $15 million.

Required:

What is the amount of the restructuring provision to be recognised in the financial statements of Delta plc, for the year ended 31 July 20X2?

Test your understanding 3 – Repairs

An entity has a reporting date of 31 December 20X7 and intends to repair an item of plant next year. The cost has been reliably estimated at the reporting date at $10,000. The repair is made in the following accounting period at a cost $12,000.

Required:

What provision (if any) should be recognised in the statement of financial position in the year ended 20X7?

Test your understanding 4 – Smoke filters

Under new legislation, an entity is required to fit smoke filters to its factories by 31 December 20X7. At the reporting date of 30 June 20X7, the entity has not fitted the smoke filters.

Required:

Should a provision be made at the reporting date for the estimated cost of fitting the filter?

Test your understanding 5 – Guarantee

An entity sells domestic appliances such as washing machines. These goods retail at $500 each and are sold with a one-year guarantee. Under the terms of the guarantee if the machine needs to be repaired then the entity will do so at no charge to the customer. In the entity's experience 20% of machines sold do require some form of repair at an average cost of $50. The entity has sold 200 machines. You may assume that the repairs are performed one year after the sale and that the relevant discount rate is 10%.

Required:

Calculate any provision required that arises under the guarantee.

Test your understanding 6 – Oil rig

An oil company has erected an oil rig in the North Sea. The installation costs are $50 million and the cost of construction $400 million. It is also estimated that it will cost $200 million to dismantle in twenty years time

Required:

When (if ever) should a provision be made for the decommissioning costs and how should this be accounted for?

Current issues: provisions & contingencies

Liabilities – amendments to IAS 37

IAS 37 addresses liabilities of uncertain timing or amount that are not within the scope of another standard. The objective of this project is to develop a new IFRS to replace IAS 37.

The proposed new IFRS would:

*   align of the requirements for recording costs of restructuring activities with those in US GAAP

*   align the criteria for recording liabilities with the criteria in other IFRSs

*   provide more specific requirements on measuring the liabilities within its scope.

In June 2005, the Board published an ED of the proposed amendments to IAS 37, and in January 2010 a second ED was published, setting out proposed new measurement guidance.

The revised ED proposes that the measurement should be the amount that the entity would rationally pay at the measurement date to be relieved of the liability. Normally, this amount would be an estimate of the present value of the resources required to fulfil the liability. The estimate would take into account the expected outflows of resources, the time value of money and the risk that the actual outflows might ultimately differ from the expected outflows.

For example:

- If the liability is to pay cash to a counterparty (for example to settle a legal dispute), the outflows would be the expected cash payments plus any associated costs, such as legal fees.

- If the liability is to undertake a service – for example to decommission plant – at a future date, the outflows would be the amounts that the entity estimates it would pay a contractor at the future date to undertake the service on its behalf.

As at August 2010, the expectation is that a new reporting standard will be issued in 2011.

Events after the reporting date IAS 10 – definitions

Definition

Events after the reporting period are those events, both favourable and unfavourable, that occur between the reporting date and the date on which the financial statements are authorised for issue.

There are two types of event:

- adjusting events
- non-adjusting events.

Financial statements are prepared on the basis of conditions existing at the reporting date.

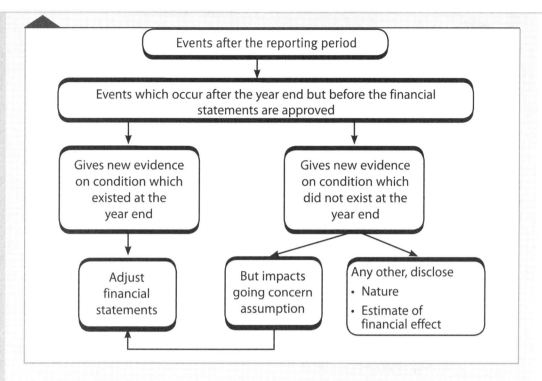

Further detail

Adjusting events

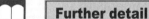

Adjusting events provide evidence of conditions that existed at the reporting date.

Examples include:

- the sale of inventory after the reporting date which gives evidence about its net realisable value at the reporting date

- the bankruptcy of a customer after the reporting date that confirms that an allowance is required against an outstanding balance at the reporting date

- the discovery of fraud or errors that show that the financial statements are incorrect

- the settlement after the reporting period of a court case that confirms that the entity had a present obligation at the reporting date. This would require a provision to be recognised in the financial statements (or an existing provision to be adjusted).

Adjusting events result in changes to the figures recognised in the financial statements.

Non-adjusting events

Non-adjusting events are those that are indicative of conditions that arose after the reporting period.

Examples include:

- a major business combination after the reporting date or the disposal of a major subsidiary

- announcing a plan to discontinue an operation

- major purchases and disposals of assets

- destruction of a major production plant by a fire after the reporting date

- announcing or commencing a major restructuring

- abnormally large changes after the reporting date in asset prices or foreign exchange rates.

Non-adjusting events do not affect any items in the statements of financial position or comprehensive income. However, if the events are material, then they must be disclosed, otherwise the financial statements could be misleading.

- The following should be disclosed for material non-adjusting events:
  - the nature of the event
  - an estimate of the financial effect, or a statement that such an estimate cannot be made.

- Equity dividends declared or proposed after the year-end are not a liability at the year-end (because no obligation to pay a dividend exists at that time). They should be disclosed in a note to the financial statements. This is a non-adjusting event.

Date of authorisation for issue

The date when the financial statements were authorised for issue, and who gave that authorisation, should be disclosed in the financial statements.

- If the entity's owners or others have the power to amend the financial statements after issue, this must also be disclosed.

- It is important that the authorisation date is disclosed as the financial statements do not reflect events occurring after this date.

Problems with events after the reporting date

(a) **'Window dressing'**

Window dressing is the practice of entering into certain transactions before the year-end and reversing those transactions after the year-end. The objective of window dressing a set of accounts is to artificially improve the view given by the accounts. Management may have a particular incentive to enter into window dressing transactions, where there is a need to boost year-end profitability and liquidity (for example, where loan agreements specify that the current ratio should not fall below a certain level, or where directors' remuneration depends upon meeting certain targets).

Typical examples include.

– Obtaining a long-term loan before the year-end on the understanding that it will be repaid soon after the year-end. This will boost the current ratio at the year-end.

– Selling goods before the year-end on the understanding that they will be returned (and a credit note raised) after the year-end. This will boost the profits for the year.

IAS 10 does not refer to window dressing. Some have argued that disclosure of window dressing should be explicitly required. If IAS 10 is applied correctly, users of the financial statements should be made aware of any unusual transactions that reverse after the year-end. In addition, IAS 1 and the Framework require that entities report the substance of their transactions, rather than the strict legal form.

(b) **Adjusting or non-adjusting?**

Sometimes it can be difficult to determine whether an event took place before the reporting date or whether or not it provides evidence of conditions existing at the reporting date.

For example, suppose that a non-current asset is valued shortly after the year-end and this valuation reveals a significant fall in value. It is probably reasonable to assume that the fall in value occurred over a period of several months beforehand. The loss would then be an adjusting event. However, there may be evidence that the fall in value occurred after the year-end (perhaps as a result of a particular event). It is important to look at all the circumstances surrounding an event after the reporting period.

IAS 10 Question

The following material events have occurred after the reporting period and prior to the date of approval of the financial statements by the directors.

	Adjusting	Non-adjusting
(i) Insolvency of a customer at the year-end.		
(ii) Uninsured loss of inventory in a fire.		
(iii) Detailed public announcement of any redundancies that had been decided by the board prior to the year-end.		
(iv) Proposal of a final equity dividend.		
(v) Change in foreign exchange rates.		

Required:

State whether the above events are adjusting or non-adjusting events.

IAS 10 Solution

(i) Adjusting.

(ii) Non-adjusting.

(iii) Non-adjusting.

(iv) Non-adjusting.

(v) Non-adjusting.

Going concern issues arising after the reporting date

There is one important exception to the normal rule that the financial statements reflect conditions at the reporting date. If, after the reporting date, management decides to liquidate the entity or cease trading (or decides that it has no realistic alternative to these actions), the financial statements cannot be prepared on a going concern basis.

- If operating results and financial position have deteriorated since the reporting date, management may need to assess whether the going concern assumption is still appropriate.

- If the going concern assumption is no longer appropriate, the effect is so pervasive that there must be a fundamental change in the basis of accounting.

- If the financial statements are not prepared on a going concern basis, that fact must be disclosed (IAS 1).

- Management must also disclose any material uncertainties relating to events or conditions that cast significant doubt upon an entity's ability to continue trading. This applies if the events have arisen since the reporting period (IAS 1).

Going concern considerations

IAS 1 states that management should assess whether the going concern assumption is appropriate. In many cases, it will be obvious that the entity is a going concern and no detailed analysis is necessary.

Where there is uncertainty, management should consider all available information about the future, including current and expected profitability, debt repayment finance and potential sources of alternative finance. If there is greater doubt or uncertainty, then more work will be required to evaluate whether or not the entity can be regarded as a going concern. Here, 'the future' means at least twelve months from the reporting date.

Current issues

Replacement of IAS 37

IAS 37 addresses liabilities of uncertain timing or amount that are not within the scope of another standard. The objective of this project is to develop a new IFRS to replace IAS 37.

The proposed new IFRS would:

*   align of the requirements for recording costs of restructuring activities with those in US GAAP

*   align the criteria for recording liabilities with the criteria in other IFRSs

*   provide more specific requirements on measuring the liabilities within its scope

In June 2005, the IASB published an ED of the proposed amendments to IAS 37 and. following feedback on the proposals, has tentatively decided to change some of the proposals in the light of comments received. Specifically, the IASB has decided to provide more guidance on applying the proposed measurement requirements. In January 2010 it published a second ED, setting out the proposed new measurement guidance. Work to date has consisted of focussing upon the following issues:

*   how the criteria for recording liabilities proposed in the working draft IFRS differ from those in the existing IAS 37

*   how the new criteria would apply to liabilities arising from lawsuits, and

*   why the IASB is changing the criteria.

In the two years to September 2012, there has been little tangible progress on this project due to the IASB focussing upon other priorities; however, the IASB is likely to return to this project at some later date, with progress to come thereafter.

UK syllabus focus

The ACCA UK syllabus contains a requirement that candidates should be able to discuss and apply the key differences between UK GAAP and IFRS GAAP. The accounting requirements of UK GAAP and IFRS GAAP are very similar in this area; the key issues associated with UK reporting standard requirements are as follows:

UK reporting standards FRS 12 and FRS 21 deal with accounting for provisions and post-balance sheet events respectively. There are no significant differences in the definitions and accounting treatments identified within the UK reporting standards and their international equivalents, IAS 37 and IAS 10 respectively.

4 Chapter summary

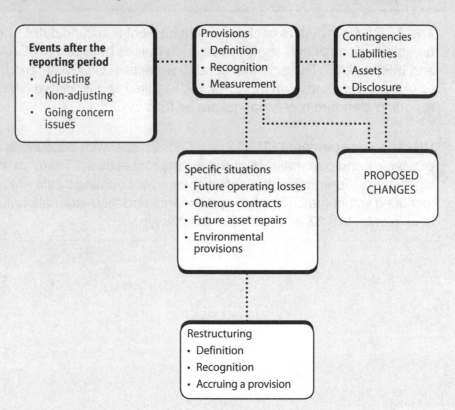

Events after the reporting period
- Adjusting
- Non-adjusting
- Going concern issues

Provisions
- Definition
- Recognition
- Measurement

Contingencies
- Liabilities
- Assets
- Disclosure

Specific situations
- Future operating losses
- Onerous contracts
- Future asset repairs
- Environmental provisions

PROPOSED CHANGES

Restructuring
- Definition
- Recognition
- Accruing a provision

Test your understanding answers

Test your understanding 1 – Situations

For each of the two situations, ask two questions.

(a) Is there a present obligation as the result of a past event?

(b) Is an outflow of economic benefits probable as a result?

Recognise a provision if the answer to both questions is yes. In the absence of information to the contrary, it is assumed that any future costs can be estimated reliably.

(a) Present obligation? Yes. Because the new legislation with retrospective effect is virtually certain to be enacted, the damage caused by the oil rig is the past event that gives rise to a present obligation.

Outflow of economic benefits probable? Yes.

Conclusion – Recognise a provision.

(b) Present obligation? Yes. There is a legal obligation under the licence to remove the rock-crushing plant and to make good damage caused by the mining activities to date (but not any that may be caused by these activities in the future, because mining activities could be stopped and no such damage caused).

Outflow of economic benefits probable? Yes.

Conclusion – Recognise a provision for the best estimate of the eventual costs of rectifying the damage caused up to the reporting date.

Test your understanding 2 – Delta

The only item which can be included in the provision is the redundancy costs, measured at their actual amount of $20 million.

IAS 37 prohibits the recognition of future operating losses, staff retraining and profits on disposals of assets.

Test your understanding 3 – Repairs

The standard clearly states that no provision should be made for future repairs despite it being probable and capable of being reliably measured. There has been no relevant past event and there is no obligation at the yearend. Repair expenditure has to be expensed as incurred.

Test your understanding 4 – Smoke filters

No provision should be made for this future expenditure despite it being probable and capable of being reliably measured. There has been no relevant past event and there is no obligation at the year end.

Test your understanding 5 – Guarantee

A provision is required. The relevant past event creating the present obligation to repair the machines is the sale. The liability can be measured with reliability, using expected values and discounting as follows.

$50 repair cost x 200 machines x 20% expected value x 0.909 discount factor = $1,818

Test your understanding 6 – Oil rig

A provision is only required if either there is a legal obligation (e.g. the licences granting permission to drill contains a requirement to dismantle the rig) or a constructive obligation (e.g. the company has published suitable and detailed environmental policies). The decommissioning costs should be provided for in full and measured at present value to reflect the time value of money. The provision is capitalised as an asset and then subject to amortisation.

KAPLAN PUBLISHING

Tax

Chapter learning objectives

Upon completion of this chapter you will be able to:

- apply and discuss the recognition and measurement of deferred tax liabilities and deferred tax assets including the exceptions to recognition

- determine the recognition of tax expense or income and its inclusion in the financial statements.

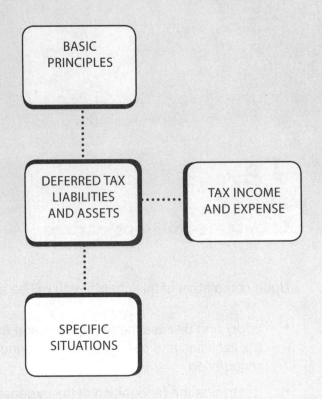

1 Basic principles of deferred tax

The need to provide for deferred tax

Taxable profits are nearly always different from accounting profits. Some differences are permanent; for example, fines, political donations and entertainment are normally disallowed for tax purposes. These items do not give rise to deferred tax. Some differences are temporary; for example, interest received and paid is normally taxed on a cash basis, whereas it is accounted for on an accruals basis.

- Temporary differences often mean that there is a delay between profits being reported for accounting purposes and tax being charged on those profits.

- They may also mean that tax is payable before profits are reported for accounting purposes.

- The tax effects of transactions should be reported in the same accounting period as the transactions themselves.

- As a result, there is a need to recognise a deferred tax liability or a deferred tax asset.

 A **temporary difference** is the difference between the carrying amount of an asset or liability and its tax base.

The **tax base** is the amount attributed to an asset or liability for tax purposes.

- .The most common example of a temporary difference relates to non-current assets. These attract tax relief (capital allowances or tax depreciation) at a different rate from the rate at which depreciation is charged to profits.

- Where there have been accelerated capital allowances, the carrying amount of the asset exceeds the tax base. This difference is the temporary difference on which deferred tax is provided.

Deferred tax is provided for on temporary differences in full, i.e. without any discounting.

Calculating a deferred tax liability

If tax allowances exceed the financial statements deductions, the net temporary differences at the yearend are multiplied by the current rate of tax. The result is the liability for deferred tax that is recognised in the statement of financial position.

The charge (or credit) to income is the difference between the deferred tax liability at the beginning of the year and the deferred tax liability at the end of the year.

Illustration 1 – Basic principles of deferred tax

Prudent prepares financial statements to 31 December each year. On 1 January 20X0, the entity purchased a non-current asset for $1.6 million that had an anticipated useful life of four years. This asset qualified for immediate tax relief of 100% of the cost of the asset.

For the year ending 31 December 20X0, the draft accounts showed a profit before tax of $2 million. The directors anticipate that this level of profit will be maintained for the foreseeable future.

Prudent pays tax at a rate of 30%. Apart from the differences caused by the purchase of the non-current asset in 20X0, there are no other differences between accounting profit and taxable profit or the tax base and carrying amount of net assets.

Required:

Compute the pre, and post-tax profits for Prudent for each of the four years ending 31 December 20X0–20X3 inclusive and for the period as a whole assuming:

(a) **that no deferred tax is recognised**

(b) **that deferred tax is recognised.**

No deferred tax

First of all, it is necessary to compute the taxable profits of Prudent for each period and the current tax payable:

	Year ended 31 December				Total
	20X0	**20X1**	**20X2**	**20X3**	
	$000	$000	$000	$000	$000
Accounting profit	2,000	2,000	2,000	2,000	8,000
Add back Depreciation	400	400	400	400	1,600
Deduct Capital allowances	(1,600)	–	–	–	(1,600)
Taxable profits	800	2,400	2,400	2,400	8,000
Current tax at 30%	240	720	720	720	2,400

The differences between the accounting profit and the taxable profit that occur from one year to another, cancel out over the four years as a whole.

The statements of profit or loss for each period and for the four years as a whole, are given below:

	Year ended 31 December				Total
	20X0	**20X1**	**20X2**	**20X3**	
	$000	$000	$000	$000	$000
Profit before tax	2,000	2,000	2,000	2,000	8,000
Current tax at 30%	(240)	(720)	(720)	(720)	(2,400)
Profit after tax	1,760	1,280	1,280	1,280	5,600

Ignoring deferred tax produces a performance profile that suggests a declining performance between 20X0 and 20X1.

In fact the decline in profits is caused by the timing of the current tax charge on them.

In 20X0, some of the accounting profit escapes tax, but the tax is only postponed until 20X1, 20X2 and 20X3, when the taxable profit is more than the accounting profit.

Deferred tax is recognised

The deferred tax figures that are required in the statement of financial position are given below:

	Year ended 31 December			
	20X0	20X1	20X2	20X3
	$000	$000	$000	$000
Carrying amount	1,200	800	400	Nil
Tax base	Nil	Nil	Nil	Nil
Temporary difference at year end	1,200	800	400	Nil
Closing deferred tax liability (30%)	360	240	120	Nil
Opening deferred tax liability	Nil	(360)	(240)	(120)
So charge/(credit) to income	360	(120)	(120)	(120)

The statements of profit or loss for the four year period including deferred tax are shown below:

	Year ended 31 December				Total
	20X0	20X1	20X2	20X3	
	$000	$000	$000	$000	$000
Profit before tax	2,000	2,000	2,000	2,000	8,000
Current tax	(240)	(720)	(720)	(720)	(2,400)
Deferred tax	(360)	120	120	120	Nil
Profit after tax	1,400	1,400	1,400	1,400	5,600

A more meaningful performance profile is presented.

Reasons for recognising deferred tax

If a deferred tax liability is ignored, profits are inflated and the obligation to pay an increased amount of tax in the future is also ignored. The arguments for recognising deferred tax are summarised below.

- The accruals concept requires tax to be matched to profits as they are earned.

- The deferred tax will eventually become an actual tax liability.

- Ignoring deferred tax overstates profits, which may result in:
  - over-optimistic dividend payments based on inflated profits
  - distortion of earnings per share and of the price/earnings ratio, both important indicators of an entity's performance
  - shareholders being misled.

Methods of accounting for deferred tax

There are two main methods of accounting for deferred tax – the deferral method and the liability method. The liability method may be subdivided into two – the income statement liability method and the balance sheet liability method.

(a) **The deferral method**

Under the deferral method, the original amount set aside for deferred tax is retained without alteration for subsequent changes in tax rate.

The deferral method does not keep the deferred tax amount up to date as tax rates change, and is thus generally held to be inferior to the liability method.

(b) **The liability method**

Using the liability method, the deferred tax balance is adjusted as tax rates change, thus maintaining the amount at the actual liability expected to arise.

(c) The income statement liability method and the statement of financial position liability method

The difference between these two methods is largely conceptual. The deferred tax figure will be the same. The income statement liability method focuses on the differences between taxable profit and accounting profit (timing differences), while under the statement of financial position method the calculation is made by reference to differences between statement of financial position values and tax values of assets and liabilities (temporary differences).

IAS 12 requires the use of the balance sheet liability method.

Examples of temporary differences

Examples of temporary differences include (but are not restricted to).

- Tax deductions for the cost of non-current assets that have a different pattern to the write-off of the asset in the financial statements, i.e. accelerated capital allowances.

- Pension liabilities that are accrued in the financial statements, but are allowed for tax only when the contributions are made to the pension fund at a later date.

- Intra-group profits in inventory that are unrealised for consolidation purposes yet taxable in the computation of the group entity that made the unrealised profit.

- A loss is reported in the financial statements and the related tax relief is only available by carry forward against future taxable profits.

- Assets are revalued upwards in the financial statements, but no adjustment is made for tax purposes.

- Development costs are capitalised and amortised to profit or loss in future periods, but were deducted for tax purposes as incurred.

- The cost of granting share options to employees is recognised in profit or loss, but no tax deduction is obtained until the options are exercised.

Calculating temporary differences

Deferred tax is calculated by reference to the tax base of an asset or liability. The tax base is the amount attributed to the asset or liability for tax purposes.

If the carrying amount of an asset exceeds the tax base, deferred tax must be provided for, and the temporary difference is said to be a **taxable** temporary difference (a liability).

If the tax base of an asset exceeds the carrying amount, the temporary difference is a **deductible** temporary difference (an asset).

Test your understanding 1 – Dive

An entity, Dive, provides the following information regarding its assets and liabilities.

ASSETS	Carrying amount	Tax base	Temporary difference
Machine cost $100,000 with depreciation to date $18,000 and capital allowances of $30,000			
Interest receivable in the statement of financial position is $1,000. The interest will be taxed when received.			
Trade receivables have a carrying amount of $10,000. The revenue has already been included in taxable profit.			
An entity writes down its inventory by $500 to a net realisable value of $4,500. The reduction is ignored for tax purposes until the inventory is sold.			
LIABILITIES			
Current liabilities include accrued expenses of $1,000. This is deductible for tax on a cash paid basis.			
Accrued expenses have a carrying amount of $5,000. The related expense has been deducted for tax purposes.			

Required:

Complete the following table to identify carrying amount, tax base and temporary difference for each of the assets and liabilities.

2 Deferred tax liabilities and assets

Recognition

IAS 12 Income taxes states that deferred tax liabilities should be provided on all taxable temporary differences, unless the deferred tax liability arises from:

- goodwill, for which amortisation is not tax deductible

- the initial recognition of an asset or liability in a transaction, which is not a business combination, and at the time of the transaction affects neither accounting profit nor taxable profit. An example is expenditure on a finite life intangible asset, which attracts no tax allowances. Accounting profit is only affected after the transaction (by subsequent amortisation), while taxable profit is never affected.

Deferred tax assets should be recognised on all deductible temporary differences unless the exceptions above also apply, provided that taxable profit will be available against which the deductible temporary difference can be utilised.

- It is appropriate to offset deferred tax assets and liabilities when presenting them in the statement of financial position as long as:
    - the entity has a legally enforceable right to set off **current** tax assets and **current** tax liabilities

    - the deferred tax assets and liabilities relate to tax levied by the same tax authority on either, the same taxable entity or different taxable entities, which settle **current** tax balances on a net basis.

Conceptual basis for recognition of deferred tax

The central principle behind accounting for deferred tax is that financial statements for a period should recognise the tax effects, whether current or deferred, of all transactions occurring in that period.

IAS 12 adopts the 'temporary difference' approach. Temporary differences are the differences between the carrying amounts of the assets and liabilities in the statement of financial position at the end of the period and the amounts that will actually be taxable or recoverable in respect of these assets and liabilities in the future. The temporary difference approach looks at the tax that would be payable, if the assets and liabilities were realised for the amounts at which they are stated in the statement of financial position. The reasoning behind this is that assets eventually generate cash flows at least equal to their carrying amount. The tax payable/receivable on these cash flows is a liability/asset of the entity and should be recognised.

The temporary difference approach focuses on the statement of financial position. The deferred tax charge (or credit) for the period, is the movement between the tax liability at the beginning of the period and the tax liability at the end of the period.

Temporary differences are similar to valuation adjustments, even though they may not be liabilities in their own right. A deferred tax liability is recognised in respect of accelerated capital allowances on a non-current asset, because that asset is carried at less than an otherwise equivalent asset that is still fully tax-deductible.

Problems with the temporary differences approach

Identifying and measuring temporary differences can be difficult in practice. For example, differences can arise where the financial statements of an overseas subsidiary are consolidated. These can be difficult to quantify, because some assets are eliminated on consolidation and others may or may not be taxable.

A more important disadvantage is that many believe that the 'temporary difference' approach is conceptually wrong. The framework for the preparation and presentation of financial statements defines a liability as an obligation to transfer economic benefits, as the result of a past event. In practice, a liability for deferred tax is often recognised before the entity actually has an obligation to pay the tax.

For example, suppose that an entity revalues a non-current asset and recognises a gain. It will not be liable for tax on the gain until the asset is sold. However, IAS 12 requires that deferred tax is recognised immediately on the revaluation gain, even if the entity has no intention of selling the asset (and realising the gain) for several years.

As a result, the IAS 12 approach could lead to the build-up of liabilities that may only crystallise in the distant future, if ever.

An important exception to the normal rule

In theory, a temporary difference arises as soon as an asset or a liability is recognised.

For example, say an entity acquires an asset for $100. This asset is subject to tax at 30%, but depreciation will not be allowable for tax. The asset's carrying amount is $100 and its tax base is nil and therefore, a deferred tax liability of $30 should be recognised.

However, this would effectively reduce the carrying amount of the asset in the financial statements. This is misleading. The entity would not have acquired the asset if its value had been less than its cost. To make the financial statements meaningful, the asset should still be recognised at its cost of $100.

For this reason, IAS 12 states that deferred tax liabilities and assets are not recognised if they result from the initial recognition of an asset or liability, which at the time of the transaction affects neither taxable nor accounting profit.

Timing differences: the alternative

An alternative approach to recognising deferred tax, focuses on timing differences rather than temporary differences.

Timing differences arise because some gains and losses are recognised in the financial statements in different accounting periods, from those in which they are assessed to tax. This results in differences between an entity's reported profit in the financial statements and its taxable profit. Timing differences originate in one period and may reverse in one or more subsequent periods.

The timing differences approach, focuses on profit and loss for the period and on the actual tax expense. It is normally simpler to apply than the temporary differences approach, as it is usually easy to identify timing differences from tax computations.

It is possible to argue that, like temporary differences, timing differences are a form of valuation adjustment. However, it is much more usual to think of timing differences as **incremental liabilities**.

Under the incremental liability approach, timing differences are recognised only if they represent rights or obligations at the reporting date, that is, only if the critical events that will cause their future reversal, have occurred by the reporting date. In other words, deferred tax is only recognised where it represents an asset or a liability in its own right.

For example, if an entity has capital allowances in excess of depreciation, it has an obligation to pay more tax in future. It cannot avoid this obligation. Therefore, it has a liability. In contrast, if an entity revalues a non-current asset, it will not have an obligation to pay more tax unless it enters into a binding agreement to sell the asset. Therefore, it does not have a liability and deferred tax is not provided.

Measurement

The tax rate in force (or expected to be in force) when the asset is realised or the liability is settled, should be used to calculated deferred tax.

- This rate must be based on tax rates and legislation that has been enacted or substantively enacted by the reporting date.

- Deferred tax assets and liabilities should not be discounted to present value.

Test your understanding 2 – Drown

An entity, Drown, has the following temporary differences:

	30 June 20X5	30 June 20X6
	$000	$000
Accelerated capital allowances	400	900
General provisions (disallowed for tax)	Nil	50
Accrued pension liabilities (tax relief is given on a cash basis)	60	40
Provision for unrealised profits	Nil	10
Loss relief being carried forward	Nil	100

Required:

Calculate the deferred tax provision required at each reporting date, together with the movement in the deferred tax provision for the year ended 30 June 20X6. The tax rate applicable for both reporting periods was 30%.

3 Specific situations

Revaluations

Deferred tax should be recognised on revaluation gains even if:

- there is no intention to sell the asset

- any tax due on the gain made on any sale of the asset can be deferred by being 'rolled over' against the cost of a replacement asset.

Test your understanding 3 – Dodge

An entity, Dodge, owns a non-current asset which cost $100,000 when purchased and depreciation totalling $40,000, has been charged up to the reporting date – 31 March 20X1. The entity has claimed total tax allowances on the asset of $50,000. On 31 March 20X1, the asset is revalued to $90,000. Assume that the tax rate is 30%.

Required:

Explain the deferred tax implications of this situation.

4 Investment property measured at fair value

An amendment to IAS 12, issued in December 2010, deals with how deferred tax should be measured in the specific situation when either an investment property is measured using the fair value model in accordance with IAS 40 or when the revaluation model is used in relation to a non-depreciable asset in accordance with IAS 16.

The issue is: will an entity recover value on an asset by selling it or by continued use in the business? The presumption made within the amendment to IAS 12 is that investment properties, or non-depreciable assets on which the IAS 16 revaluation model has been applied, will be recovered from sale, unless there is evidence to the contrary. This latter situation may arise, for example, when the relevant asset is included within a business model whose objective is to consume most of the economic benefits over time, rather than recovery of economic value through disposal.

In principle, the tax treatment will take into consideration how an asset is measured and accounted for in the financial statements, together with how an entity expects to recover value from it – usually from disposal proceeds.

IAS 40 illustration

Melbourne has an investment property, which is measured using the fair value model in accordance with IAS 40, comprising the following elements:

	Cost $000	Fair value $000
Land	800	1,200
Building	1,200	1,800
	2,000	3,000

Further information is as follows:

- Accumulated tax allowances claimed on the building to date are $600,000.

- Unrealised changes in the carrying value of investment property do not affect taxable profit.

- If an investment property is sold for more than cost, the reversal of cumulated depreciation will be included in taxable profit and taxed at the standard rate.

- The standard rate of tax is 30%, but for asset disposals in excess of cost, the tax rate is 20%, unless the asset has been held for less than two years, when the tax rate is 25%.

Required:

Calculate the deferred tax provision required if:

(a) **Melbourne expects to hold the investment property for more than two years.**

(b) **Melbourne expects to sell the investment property within two years.**

IAS 40 solution

A summary of cost, fair value, and accumulated allowances claimed to date, together with tax base and temporary difference is as follows:

	(a)	(b)		(c)	(a) - (c) = (d)	(b) - (d) = (e)
	Cost	**Fair value**	**Tax**	**allowances claimed**	**Tax base**	**Temp. diff**
	$000	$000		$000	$000	$000
Land	800	1,200		–	800	400
Building	1,200	1,800		(600)	600	1,200
	2,000	3,000		(600)	1,400	1,600

Note that the tax rate to apply in each situation will be the tax rate expected to apply when the investment property is sold.

(a) **If Melbourne expects to hold the investment property for more than two years:**

The reversal of the cumulated depreciation charged on the building element will be charged at the standard rate of 30%, whilst the proceeds in excess of cost will be charged at 20% as follows:

		$000
Cumulated depreciation	(600 × 30%)	180
Proceeds in excess of cost	(1,000 × 20%)	200
Deferred tax liability		380

(b) **If Melbourne expects to sell the investment property within two years:**

The reversal of the cumulated depreciation charged on the building element will be charged at the standard rate of 30%, whilst the proceeds in excess of cost will be charged at 25% as follows:

		$000
Cumulated depreciation	(600 × 30%)	180
Proceeds in excess of cost	(1,000 × 25%)	250
		–––
Deferred tax liability		430
		–––

Share option schemes

Accounting for share option schemes involves recognising an annual remuneration expense in profit or loss throughout the vesting period. However, tax relief is normally granted at a later date when the options are actually exercised, giving rise to a deferred tax asset until tax relief is obtained.

IFRS 2 requires that, at each reporting date, an estimate of the future tax relief available should be based upon the intrinsic value of the option, which is the difference between the fair value of the share and the exercise price of the option. Where the amount of the estimated future tax deduction exceeds the accumulated remuneration expense, this indicates that the tax deduction relates partly to the remuneration expense and partly to equity.

Test your understanding 4 – Splash

An entity, Splash, has established a share option scheme for its four directors, commencing 1 July 20X8. Each director will be entitled to 25,000 share options on condition that they remain with Splash for four years, from the date the scheme was introduced.

Information regarding the share options are as follows:

Fair value of option at grant date	$10
Fair value of option at 30 June 20X9	$12
Exercise price of option	$5

The market value (i.e. fair value) of the shares at 30 June 20X9 was $17 per share.

Tax allowances on any expense recognised for share options are only granted at the date when the options are exercised and will be based upon the intrinsic value of the options. Assume a tax rate of 30%.

Required:

Calculate and explain the amounts to be included in the financial statements of Splash for the year ended 30 June 20X9, including explanation and calculation of any deferred tax implications.

Business combinations

A business combination can have several deferred tax consequences.

* The assets and liabilities of the acquired business are revalued to fair value. The revaluation to fair value of the assets does not always alter the tax base, and if this is the case, a temporary difference will arise.

* The deferred tax recognised on this difference is deducted in measuring the net assets acquired and, as a result, it increases the amount of goodwill.

* The goodwill itself does not give rise to deferred tax as IAS 12 specifically excludes it.

* The acquirer may be able to utilise the benefit of its own unused tax losses against the future taxable profit of the acquiree. In such cases, the acquirer recognises a deferred tax asset, but does not take it into account in determining the goodwill arising on the acquisition.

Test your understanding 5 – Complex

On 30 June 20X1, the Complex group acquired a new subsidiary. At the date of acquisition the subsidiary had inventory that was shown in its financial statements at a carrying amount of $50,000. The group assessed the fair amount of the inventory at $55,000. Assume the tax rate is 30%.

Required:

Explain the deferred tax implications.

Unremitted earnings

A temporary difference arises when the carrying amount of investments in subsidiaries, branches, associates or joint ventures is different from the tax base.

- The carrying amount in consolidated financial statements is the investor's share of the net assets of the investee, plus purchased goodwill, but the tax base is usually the cost of the investment. Unremitted earnings (i.e. undistributed profits) in the accounts of subsidiaries, branches, associates or joint ventures, will lead to a temporary difference.

- Deferred tax should be recognised on these temporary differences except when:
  - the parent, investor or venturer is able to control the timing of the reversal of the temporary difference and
  - it is probable that the temporary difference will not reverse (i.e the profit will not be distributed) in the foreseeable future.

- An investor can control the dividend policy of a subsidiary, but not always that of other types of investment. This means that deferred tax does not arise on investments in subsidiaries, but may on investments in associates and joint ventures. Trade investments will not usually give rise to deferred tax unless they are revalued.

Test your understanding 6 – Domestic

An entity, Domestic, has a subsidiary located overseas in Taxland. Domestic's share of the retained earnings of the subsidiary is $40,000. If the retained earnings were remitted to the entity as a dividend, then under tax legislation in Taxland, the subsidiary would need to deduct withholding tax equivalent to $4,000, from the payment. It is likely that these profits will be remitted as a dividend in the next couple of years.

Required:

Explain the deferred tax implications.

Unused tax losses

Where an entity has unused tax losses, IAS 12 allows a deferred tax asset to be recognised only to the extent that it is probable that future taxable profits will be available against which the unused tax losses can be utilised.

IAS 12 advises that the deferred tax asset should only be recognised after considering:

- whether an entity has sufficient taxable temporary differences against which the unused tax losses can be offset.

- whether it is probable the entity will have taxable profits before the unused tax losses expire.

- whether the tax losses result from identifiable causes which are unlikely to recur (otherwise, the existence of unused tax losses is strong evidence that future taxable profits may not be available).

- whether tax planning opportunities are available to the entity that will create taxable profit in the period that the tax losses can be utilised.

Current tax expense and income

IAS 12 contains the following requirements relating to current tax.

- Unpaid tax for current and prior periods should be recognised as a liability. Overpaid current tax is recognised as an asset.

- Current tax should be accounted for in profit or loss unless the tax relates to an item that has been accounted for in equity.

- If the item was disclosed as an item of other comprehensive income and accounted for in equity, then the tax should be disclosed as relating to other comprehensive income and allocated to the equity.

- Tax is measured at the amount expected to be paid. Tax rates used should be those that have been enacted or substantively enacted by the reporting date.

Deferred tax

The deferred tax expense (or income) is the difference between the net liability at the beginning of the year and the net liability at the end of the year.

- If the item giving rise to the deferred tax is dealt with in the profit or loss, the related deferred tax should also be presented in profit or loss.

- If the item giving rise to the deferred tax is dealt with in other comprehensive income, the related deferred tax should be disclosed as relating to other comprehensive income and recorded in equity.

Illustration

During 20X3, Upward revalued some land from $50m to $100m. Its profit before tax for the year ended 31 December 20X3, was $40m, on which it pays tax at 30%.

The opening balance on the retained earnings reserve was $220m, and there were no deferred tax balances brought forward.

Prepare all relevant extracts from Upwards' financial statements for the year ended 31 December 20X3.

Solution

Statement of profit or loss and other comprehensive income for the year ended 31 December 20X3

	$000
Profit before tax	40,000
Income tax expense (at 30%)	(12,000)
Profit for the period	28,000
Other comprehensive income: items that will not be reclassified to profit or loss in future periods:	
Gain on revaluation	50,000
Tax relating to revaluation	(15,000)
Other comprehensive income net of tax	35,000
Total comprehensive income	63,000

Statement of financial position at 31 December 20X3

			$000
Non-current assets	Property	Cost	50,000
		Revaluation	50,000
		Revalued amount	100,000
Non-current liabilities	Deferred tax		15,000
Current liabilities	Current tax		12,000

Current issues

The IASB is currently undertaking a joint project with the US FASB to reduce the differences between IAS 12 and its US counterpart.

Although both standards take a balance sheet liability approach to deferred tax, differences arise because both standards have a number of exceptions to the basic principle. The approach to convergence in this project is not to reconsider the underlying approach, but rather to eliminate exceptions to the basic principle. The project is part of the short-term convergence project.

In December 2010, the IASB issued an amendment to IAS 12 dealing with accounting for deferred tax on investment property measured at fair value. This amendment is included within the content of this chapter.

Development of accounting for uncertain tax positions will only be progressed once revisions to IAS 37 have been finalised. Additionally, the IASB may consider whether a more fundamental review of IAS 12 is required as part of its normal consultation process during 2012.

The ACCA UK syllabus contains a requirement that candidates should be able to discuss and apply the key differences between UK GAAP and IFRS GAAP. The accounting requirements of UK GAAP and IFRS GAAP are very similar in this area; the key issues associated with UK reporting standard requirements are as follows:

UK FRS 16 Current tax and UK FRS 19 Deferred tax. UK GAAP has two reporting standards dealing with accounting for current tax and deferred tax respectively; IFRS GAAP has one reporting standard, **IAS 12 Income tax**, which deals with the issues covered by both of the UK reporting standards.

One difference is that of **terminology**; UK GAAP refers to current or corporation tax; IAS 12 refers to income tax charged against the profits of entities. UK GAAP refers to the tax written down value of an asset or liability; IFRS GAAP refers to the tax base of the asset or liability.

For deferred tax, UK GAAP adopts a profit and loss perspective to identification of **timing differences** upon which deferred tax is calculated. In principle, timing differences arise when the tax consequences of a transaction arise in one or more accounting periods different to the one in which the transaction is included in the financial statements. IAS 12 adopts a **temporary difference** approach which focuses upon a balance sheet approach to identification of temporary differences upon which deferred tax is calculated. Essentially, both approaches will provide a similar outcome in accounting for deferred tax.

Details which differ in accounting for deferred tax are as follows:

*   in respect of **revalued assets**, under UK GAAP, revaluation gains on land and buildings are excluded from deferred tax calculations, unless there is a binding agreement to dispose of the revalued asset by the reporting date. In effect, unless it is probable that a tax liability will be incurred, no provision is made. This allows for the situation that, even if there is likely to be a tax consequence as a result of a binding commitment to sell, deferred tax is not recognised if it is more likely than not that the taxable gain will be rolled over. In contrast, revaluation gains on land and buildings are included within deferred tax calculations under IAS12.

*   in respect of **fair value adjustments** upon acquisition of a subsidiary, UK GAAP does not recognise deferred tax on fair value adjustments when a subsidiary is consolidated for the first time, whereas IAS 12 does require recognition of deferred tax on fair value adjustments.

- UK FRS 19 gives a choice to entities as to **whether or not to discount** the deferred tax balance to reflect the time value of money. For many entities, the practical problems of discounting the deferred tax balance will be outweighed by possible benefits, and is unlikely to be done. In addition, it is inconsistent with IAS 12.

SSAP 5 accounting for value added tax confirms the basic principle that sales revenue should be accounted for excluding tax charged to customers (on outputs) and that expenses should be accounted for excluding such tax charged by suppliers (on inputs).

UK GAAP Illustration 1

Wasp has the following timing differences at the reporting date of 30 September 20X3:

	$000
Accelerated capital allowances	900
General provision disallowed for tax purposes as tax relief is given on actual expenditure	200
Capitalised development expenditure where tax relief is granted on expenditure	600
Tax losses being carried forward which are reasonably expected to be recovered in the near future	100

The timing differences relating to accelerated capital allowances are expected to reverse at $300,000 per annum. The timing difference relating to capitalised development expenditure relates to a product with a remaining estimated useful life of three years as at 30 September 20X3. A discount rate of 5% should be used to discount these timing differences.

The timing differences relating to the tax losses and the general provision are expected to reverse within one year, and are not required to be discounted.

The deferred tax provision at 30 September 20X2 (discounted where appropriate) was $180,000.

The tax rate is 30%.

Required:

Compute the deferred tax provision required at 30 September 20X3, together with the associated impact on profit or loss for the year ended 30 September 20X3.

UK GAAP Answer 1

Answer – Wasp

Timing differences at 30 September 20X3:	$000		$000
Accelerated capital allowances (W1)	816.6		
General provision	(200.0)		
Capitalised development expenditure (W2)	544.6		
Tax losses carried forward	(100.0)		
	———		
Provision at 30 September 20X3	1,061.2	@30%	318.36
			———
Less: provision at 30 September 20X2			180.00
			———
Net charge to profit or loss account			138.36
			———

(W1) Discounting timing differences – accelerated capital allowances:

Rep Date	$000	5% Discount factor	$000
30 Sept 20X4	300	0.952	285.6
30 Sept 20X5	300	0.907	272.0
30 Sept 20X6	300	0.864	259.0
			———
			816.6
			———

(W2) Discounting timing differences – capitalised development expenditure:

Rep Date	$000	5% Discount factor	$000
30 Sept 20X4	200	0.952	190.4
30 Sept 20X5	200	0.907	181.4
30 Sept 20X6	200	0.864	172.8
			———
			544.6
			———

UK GAAP Illustration 2

Revaluation of assets and deferred tax

Parker owns a property which has a carrying value at 1 January 20X6 of $3 million. At the reporting date of 31 December 20X6, the property is revalued to $3.6 million. The profit for the year was $8million, and there were no other amounts to be accounted for within the statement of recognised gains and losses for the year.

The tax rate is 30%;

Required:

Explain how this information will be included in the financial statements for the year ended 31 December 20X6 in each of the following situations:

(a) **At the reporting date, Parker has entered into a contract to dispose of the property for $3.6 million.**

(b) **At the reporting date, Parker has the intention to sell the property, but a buyer has not been found.**

UK GAAP Answer 2

Solution:

(a) In this situation, the revaluation must be accounted for, together with the deferred tax consequences as there is a binding commitment to sell, as follows:

Increase property, plant and equipment, and also the revaluation reserve, by $600,000 to reflect the revaluation of the asset ($3 million to $3.6 million). Account for deferred tax arising on the timing difference due to the imminent sale of the property amounting to $180,000 ($600,000 × 30%). This will increase the deferred tax provision and also reduce the revaluation reserve.

Statement of total recognised gains and losses (extract):	$000
Profit for the year	8,000
Unrealised surplus on property revaluation	600
Deferred tax on revaluation surplus	(180)
Total recognised gains and losses for the year	8,420

(b) In this situation, there is no binding commitment to sell; consequently, only the revaluation would be accounted for – there are no tax consequences as there is not yet a binding commitment to sell.

Increase property, plant and equipment, and also the revaluation reserve, by $600,000 to reflect the revaluation of the asset ($3 million to $3.6 million).

Statement of total recognised gains and losses (extract):	$000
Profit for the year	8,000
Unrealised surplus on property revaluation	600
Total recognised gains and losses for the year	8,600

5 Chapter summary

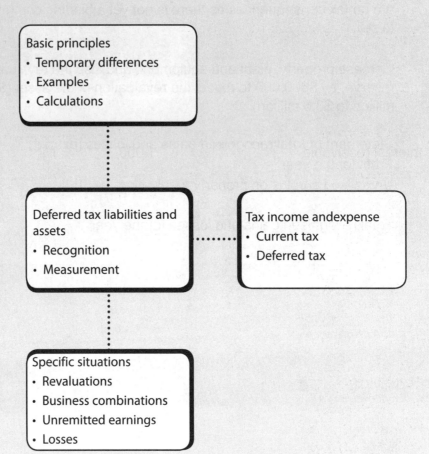

Basic principles
- Temporary differences
- Examples
- Calculations

Deferred tax liabilities and assets
- Recognition
- Measurement

Tax income andexpense
- Current tax
- Deferred tax

Specific situations
- Revaluations
- Business combinations
- Unremitted earnings
- Losses

Test your understanding answers

Test your understanding 1 – Dive

	Carrying value	Tax base	Temp. difference
	$	$	$
Non-current asset	82,000	70,000	12,000
Interest receivable	1,000	Nil	1,000
Receivables	10,000	10,000	Nil
Inventory	4,500	5,000	(500)
Accrual (cash basis for tax)	(1,000)	Nil	(1,000)
Accrual (already tax relief)	(5,000)	(5,000)	Nil

Test your understanding 2 – Drown

	30 June 20X5	30 June 20X6
Temporary differences	$000	$000
Accelerated capital allowances	400	900
General provision	Nil	(50)
Accrued pension liabilities	(60)	(40)
Provision for unrealised profits	Nil	(10)
Loss relief	Nil	(100)
	340	700
Deferred tax liability		
30% × 340 =	102	
30% × 700 =		210
Less b/f 30% × 340 =		(102)
Therefore charge to profit or loss		108

Test your understanding 3 – Dodge

- The carrying amount of the asset before revaluation is $60,000 ($100,000 – $40,000) and its tax base is $50,000($100,000 – $50,000). The difference between the carrying amount and its tax base is $10,000 and this difference is referred to in IAS 12 as a temporary difference. Under IAS 12 deferred tax is recognised on most temporary differences, so the liability will be $3,000 ($10,000 × 30%).

- Revaluing the asset increases its carrying amount without altering its tax base (since revaluations have no immediate tax consequences). Therefore, the revaluation creates an additional temporary difference of $30,000 ($90,000 – $60,000) and so additional deferred tax of $9,000 ($30,000 × 30%), would be recognised.

- The revaluation gain is disclosed as other comprehensive income and credited to the revaluation reserve (within other components of equity). In line with this treatment, the deferred tax expense must be disclosed as tax relating to other comprehensive income and debited to the revaluation reserve.

Test your understanding 4 – Splash

Share options should be recognised as a remuneration expense as they are part of the work and service provided by the directors throughout the four-year vesting period to earn entitlement to exercise the options at the vesting date. The entity should also recognise an equity reserve as this represents part of the consideration towards payment for the shares. This is calculated based upon the fair value of the option at the grant date at the start of the vesting period for each year of the share option scheme.

As this is the first year of the scheme, calculate the equity reserve required, and this will also provide the expense required to be recognised for the year as follows:

Year-ended 30 June 20X9
4 × 25,000 × $10 × 1/4 years $250,000

For each subsequent year, calculate the cumulative equity reserve required at that year-end; any increase in the equity reserve from the previous year will be the charge to recognise in the income statement as follows:

Year-ended 30 June 20X0 Equity reserve
4 × 25,000 × $10 × 2/4 years $500,000

Remuneration expense for the year will be the movement in the equity reserve:

$500,000 – $250,000 = $250,000

Notice that the entity uses the fair value of the option at the grant date throughout the vesting period.

For tax purposes, tax relief is allowed only at the time the options are exercised, which will be at the end of the vesting period. Until then, the entity will have recognised an expense, on which tax relief will be obtained at a later date. This is a temporary difference for the purposes of accounting for deferred tax, giving rise to a deferred tax asset. The intrinsic value of the option is the difference between the market value of the shares at the reporting date and the option exercise price, and this should also be spread over the vesting period as follows:

Year ended 30 June 20X9	Temporary difference
$4 \times 25,000 \times (\$17 - \$5) \times 1/4$	$300,000

The temporary difference is then multiplied by the tax rate to determine the deferred tax asset:

$300,000 × 30% = $90,000

If the deferred tax asset is to be recognised, it must be capable of reliable measurement and also be regarded as recoverable.

Test your understanding 5 – Complex

The carrying amount of the inventory in the consolidated accounts is $55,000, while its tax base is $50,000. Deferred tax is recognised on the temporary difference of $5,000. Since the tax rate is 30%, then the deferred tax liability is $1,500.

Test your understanding 6 – Domestic

The existence of a potential tax charge on the payment of a dividend, affects the tax base of the net assets of the subsidiary in the consolidated accounts. Deferred tax is recognised for the $4,000 potentially payable, because the earnings are likely to be remitted by way of dividend.

Non-financial reporting

Chapter learning objectives

Upon completion of this chapter you will be able to:

- discuss the increased demand for transparency in corporate reports, and the emergence of non-financial reporting standards

- discuss the progress towards a framework for environmental and sustainability reporting

- appraise the impact of environmental, social and ethical factors on performance measurement

- evaluate current reporting requirements in the area

- discuss why entities might include disclosures relating to the environment and society.

Non-financial reporting

Non-financial reporting

Non-financial information, in the form of additional information provided alongside the financial information in the annual report, has become more important in recent years.

While financial information remains important, stakeholders are interested in other aspects of an entity's performance.

For example:

- how the business is managed
- its future prospects
- the entity's policy on the environment
- its attitude towards social responsibility, and so on.

Many of these issues, whilst included within the financial statements to some extent, have not always been fully reported to meet the needs of users of financial statements. In recent years, there has been a growing demand for transparency of reported information covering both financial and non-financial information. This could include information relating to a number of issues such as:

- selection, application and appropriate disclosure of accounting policies adopted by an entity, so that users of financial statements fully understand the basis upon which financial statements have been prepared.

- the impact of the entity's activities on the environment – this could include waste management and recycling policies, use of renewable energy sources and pollution management policies.

- the interaction of the entity with society generally or particular communities within which it operates – this could include labour recruitment and development policies, charitable donations and activities and other contributions to the local community. Many organisations now actively participate within the communities within which they operate, perhaps by supporting or donating to local charities, with the intention of 'putting something back' into those communities. This may happen, for example, if an entity permits staff to take time away from their employment to provide work or service to a local charity or similar organisation for benevolent reasons.

Although these activities do have an impact upon financial position and performance, some users of financial statements may have a particular interest in these activities. For example, potential shareholders may be attracted to invest in a particular entity (or not), based upon their environmental or social policies, in addition to their financial performance. Regulators or consumer pressure groups may also have a particular interest in such policies and disclosures to manage their activities or monitor the effectiveness of their activities.

All of this information is reported in a number of ways.

- An operating and financial review (OFR) will assess the results of the period and discuss the future prospects of the business. In the UK, for example, it is a legal requirement for all entities listed on the London Stock Exchange to produce such a report. Many entities have embraced the spirit of the regulation, rather than merely complied with the legal requirements, as a means to improve stakeholder understanding and awareness, which could lead to competitive advantage.

- A report on corporate governance will report on how the entity is managed and directed. For example, entities which are listed on the London Stock Exchange, are required to comply with a code of best practice and to make disclosures regarding the extent of compliance or non-compliance with the code as appropriate.

- An environmental and social report will report upon entity policies and responsibilities towards the environment and society, or both of these issues could be combined in a report on sustainability. This may include policy statements, supported by narrative explanation together with both qualitative and quantitative disclosures to enable its evaluation by users of that information.

- Information may be provided in the form of a management commentary. The IASB has acknowledged that there is a growing demand for this form of reporting, and a willingness on the part of entities to provide it, with the publication of Practice Statement 1 (PS) Management Commentary in December 2010 (see later within chapter).

The additional reports and disclosures go some way towards providing transparency for evaluation of entity financial performance, position and strategy. Transparency fosters confidence in the information which is made available to investors and other stakeholders who may be interested in both financial and non-financial information.

Management Commentary

Purpose of the Management Commentary (MC)

The IFRS Practice Statement (PS) Management Commentary provides a broad, non-binding framework for the presentation of management commentary that relates to financial statements that have been prepared in accordance with International Financial Reporting Standards (IFRSs)

It is a narrative report that provides a context within which to interpret the financial position, financial performance and cash flows of an entity. Management are able to explain its objectives and its strategies for achieving those objectives. Users routinely use the type of information provided in management commentary to help them evaluate an entity's prospects and its general risks, as well as the success of management's strategies for achieving its stated objectives. For many entities, management commentary is already an important element of their communication with the capital markets, supplementing as well as complementing the financial statements.

This PS helps management to provide useful commentary to financial statements prepared in accordance with IFRS information. The users are identified as existing and potential members, together with lenders and creditors.

Framework for presentation of management commentary

The following principles should be applied when a management commentary is prepared:

- to provide management's view of the entity's performance, position and progress; and

- to supplement and complement information presented in the financial statements.

Consequently, the MC should include information which is both forward-looking and adheres to the qualitative characteristics of information as described in the 2010 Conceptual Framework for Financial Reporting (see chapter 8 of this publication).

The management commentary should provide information to help users of the financial reports to assess the performance of the entity and the actions of its management relative to stated strategies and plans for progress. That type of commentary will help users of the financial reports to understand, risk exposures and strategies of the entity, relevant non-financial factors and other issues not otherwise included within the financial statements.

Management commentary should provide management's perspective of the entity's performance, position and progress. Management commentary should derive from the information that is important to management in managing the business.

Elements of management commentary

Although the particular focus of management commentary will depend on the facts and circumstances of the entity, management commentary should include information that is essential to an understanding of:

- the nature of the business;

- management's objectives and its strategies for meeting those objectives;

- the entity's most significant resources, risks and relationships;

- the results of operations and prospects; and

- the critical performance measures and indicators that management uses to evaluate the entity's performance against stated objectives.

It can be adopted by entities, where applicable, any time from the date of publication in December 2010.

Sustainability

Definition

Sustainability is the process of conducting business in such a way that it enables an entity to meet its present needs without compromising the ability of future generations to meet their needs.

Introduction

In a corporate context, sustainability means that a business entity must attempt to reduce its environmental impact through more efficient use of natural resources and improving environmental practices.

More and more business entities are reporting their approach to sustainability in addition to the financial information reported in the annual report. There are increased public expectations for business entities and industries to take responsibility for the impact their activities have on the environment and society.

Reporting sustainability

- Currently, sustainability reporting is voluntary, although its use is increasing.

- Reports include highlights of non-financial performance such as environmental, social and economic reports during the accounting period.

- The report may be included in the annual report or published as a stand alone document, possibly on the entity's website.

- The increase in popularity of such reports highlights the growing trend that business entities are taking sustainability seriously and are attempting to be open about the impact of their activities.

- Reporting sustainability is sometimes called reporting the 'triple bottom line' covering environment, social and economic reporting.

Framework for sustainability reporting

- There is no framework for sustainability reporting in IFRS, so this reporting is voluntary.

- This lack of regulation leads to several potential problems:

  (a) Because disclosure is largely voluntary, not all businesses disclose information. Those that do tend to do so either because they are under particular pressure to prove their 'green' credentials (for example, large public utility companies whose operations directly affect the environment) or because they have deliberately built their reputation on environmental friendliness or social responsibility.

  (b) The information disclosed may not be complete or reliable. Many businesses see environmental reporting largely as a public relations exercise and therefore only provide information that shows them in a positive light.

  (c) The information may not be disclosed consistently from year to year.

  (d) Some businesses, particularly small and medium sized entities, may believe that the costs of preparing and circulating additional information outweigh the benefits of doing so.

- The most accepted framework for reporting sustainability is the Global Reporting Initiative's Sustainability Reporting Guidelines, the latest of which 'G3' – the third version of the guidelines – was issued in October 2006. As at August 2010, this is still the most recent version of the guidelines.

- The G3 Guidelines provide universal guidance for reporting on sustainability performance. They are applicable to all entities including SMEs and not-for-profit entities worldwide. The G3 consist of principles and disclosure items .The principles help to define report content, quality of the report, and give guidance on how to set the report boundary. Disclosure items include disclosures on management of issues, as well as performance indicators themselves.

The best way to understand sustainability is to look at some examples of sustainability reports in financial statements.

ACCA – ACCA hold annual awards for sustainability reporting. You can review sustainability reports of those companies commended by ACCA, and it will also provide you with an idea of the information typically used in these reports via the ACCA web site at: www.accaglobal.com.

Global Reporting Initiative

- You can also look at the Global Reporting Initiative website (www.globalreporting.org)
- The financial statements of companies that have applied the GRI guidelines are listed with a link to their reports.

The Global Reporting Initiative

Principles and guidance

This section of the G3 provides:

- Guidance for **defining report content**, by applying the principles of materiality, stakeholder inclusiveness, sustainability context and completeness.
- Principles for **ensuring report quality**, these being balance, comparability , accuracy, timeliness, reliability and clarity.
- Guidance for **report boundary setting** in terms of determining the range of entities to be included in the report.

Standard disclosures

There are three different types of measures that can be used to express strategic approach, management goals, and performance results:

- **Profile disclosures** set the overall context for understanding performance. This section of the report should include consideration of:

  Strategy and analysis:

  - statement from CEO explaining the relevance of sustainability to organisational strategy in the short, medium and long terms.
  - Description of organisation's key impacts on sustainability and impact of sustainability trends, risks and opportunities on the organisation.

Organisational profile:

- overview of the reporting entity in terms of products, organisational structure, location of operations and markets etc.

Report parameters:

- boundary of report
- specific exclusions
- basis for reporting on subsidiaries etc
- location of standard disclosures in the report

Governance

- committees and responsibilities
- mechanisms for stakeholders to provide recommendations to governance bodies
- internal codes of conduct and their application

Commitments to external initiatives

- external initiatives to which the entity subscribes
- strategic memberships, funding and participation in industry associations

Stakeholder engagement

- list of stakeholder groups engaged by entity
- approach to stakeholder engagement
- key topics and concerns of stakeholders

- **Management Approach disclosures** are intended to address the entity's approach to managing the sustainability topics associated with risks and opportunities. Disclosures may include:
  - Goals and performance
  - Policy
  - Organisational responsibility
  - Training and awareness
  - Monitoring and follow up
  - Additional contextual information

- **Performance Indicator disclosures** elicit comparable information on a number of areas, including:

  - Environmental, for example, level of materials, energy and water used, biodiversity, level of emissions and waste, impact of products and services and transport.

  - Human rights, for example number of suppliers who have undergone human rights screening, number of discrimination actions, measures taken to contribute to the elimination of child and forced and compulsory labour.

  - Labour practices, for example employment turnover, percentage of employees covered by collective bargaining agreements, rates of injury and occupational diseases, average hours training per employee per year, indicators of diversity.

  - Society, for example impact of operations on communities, number of corruption investigations, number of legal actions for anti-competitive behaviour, level of fines for non-compliance with legal requirements.

  - Product responsibility, for example results of customer satisfaction surveys, number of breaches of customer confidentiality and losses of personal data.

  - Economic, for example level of spending on local suppliers, number of senior management hired from local community.

International Integrated Reporting Committee (IIRC)

What is the purpose of the IIRC?

The IIRC is being created to respond to this need for a concise, clear, comprehensive and comparable integrated reporting framework structured around the organization's strategic objectives, its governance and business model and integrating both material financial and non-financial information. The objectives for an integrated reporting framework are to:

- support the information needs of long-term investors, by showing the broader and longer-term consequences of decision-making;

- reflect the interconnections between environmental, social, governance and financial factors in decisions that affect long-term performance and condition, making clear the link between sustainability and economic value;

- provide the necessary framework for environmental and social factors to be taken into account systematically in reporting and decision-making;

- rebalance performance metrics away from an undue emphasis on short-term financial performance; and

- bring reporting closer to the information used by management to run the business on a day-to-day basis.

What is the role of the IIRC?

At present a range of standard-setters and regulatory bodies are responsible for individual elements of reporting. No single body has the oversight or authority to bring together these different elements that are essential to the presentation of an integrated picture of an organization and the impact of environmental and social factors on its performance. In addition, globalisation means that an accounting and reporting framework needs to be developed on an international basis. At present, there is a risk that, as individual regulators respond to the risks faced, multiple standards will emerge.

The role of the IIRC is to:

- raise awareness of this issue and develop a consensus among governments, listing authorities, business, investors, accounting bodies and standard setters for the best way to address it;

- develop an overarching integrated reporting framework setting out the scope of integrated reporting and its key components;

- identify priority areas where additional work is needed and provide a plan for development;

- consider whether standards in this area should be voluntary or mandatory and facilitate collaboration between standard-setters and convergence in the standards needed to underpin integrated reporting; and

- promote the adoption of integrated reporting by relevant regulators and report preparers.

Who is behind this?

In December 2009, His Royal Highness The Prince of Wales convened a high level meeting of investors, standard setters, companies, accounting bodies and UN representatives. At the meeting it was agreed that the Prince's Accounting for Sustainability and the Global Reporting Initiative should work together with other organizations to establish an international body to oversee the creation of a generally accepted integrated reporting framework that would connect financial and sustainability reporting.
Who are the members?

The IIRC brings together a powerful cross section of representatives from the corporate, accounting, securities, regulatory, and standard-setting sectors. Membership will comprise international representation from the following stakeholder groups: companies, investors, regulators, standard-setters, intergovernmental organizations, non-governmental organizations, the accounting profession, civil society and academia.

Further information on the IIRC can be found at
www.integratedreporting.org

Other issues in sustainability reporting

The World Business Council for Sustainable Development (WBCSD)

The WBCSD was formed in 1991 in Norway and now consists of over 180 international companies in a shared commitment to sustainable development through economic growth, ecological balance and social progress.

Its members come from more than 30 countries and 20 major industrial sectors.

It aims to get businesses involved in the issue of sustainability and to promote sustainable development through economic growth, ecological balance and social progress.

Legal requirements

- Legal requirements for sustainability reporting are the responsibility of the governments of individual countries.

- In 2006, for the first time, the UK government passed legislation requiring mandatory reporting on business' social and environmental performance. This is the seen as a very positive step by the corporate social responsibility community.

- The revised Companies Act requires directors to report on what they are doing and, therefore, they will have to consider how it affects the community and environment. The Act makes it mandatory for business to report anything concerning the welfare of the employees, community, environment, suppliers and the company itself. It will also allow shareholders and the general public to judge companies' performances.

- The law will not make companies report on anything that is considered commercially sensitive or confidential.

Environmental accounting

Definition

Environmental reporting is the disclosure of information in the published annual report or elsewhere, of the effect that the operations of the business have on the natural environment.

As detailed in section 2, the sustainability report combines environmental, social and economic reporting in one report. Environmental reports were the first step in reporting an entity's impact on its environment.

This section details the contents of an environment report together with any accounting issues.

Environmental reporting in practice

There are two main vehicles that companies use to publish information about the ways in which they interact with the natural environment:

(a) The published annual report (which includes the financial statements)

(b) A separate environment report (either as a paper document or simply posted on the company website).

The IASB encourages the presentation of environmental reports if management believe that they will assist users in making economic decisions, but they are not mandatory.

IAS 1 points out that any statement or report presented outside financial statements is outside the scope of IFRSs, so there are no mandatory IFRS requirements on separate environmental reports.

Separate environmental reports

Many large public companies publish environmental reports that are completely separate from the annual report and financial statements. The environmental report is often combined in a sustainability report.

Most environmental reports take the form of a combined statement of policy and review of activity. They cover issues such as:

- waste management
- pollution
- intrusion into the landscape
- the effect of an entity's activities upon wildlife
- use of energy
- the benefits to the environment of the entity's products and services.

Generally, the reports disclose the entity's targets and/or achievements, with direct comparison between the two in some cases. They may also disclose financial information, such as the amount invested in preserving the environment.

Public and media interest has tended to focus on the environmental report rather than on the disclosures in the published annual report and financial statements. This separation reflects the fact that the two reports are aimed at different audiences.

Shareholders are the main users of the annual report, while the environmental report is designed to be read by the general public. Many companies publish their environmental and social reports on their websites, which encourages access to a wide audience.

The content of environment reports

The content of an environment report may cover the following areas.

(a) **Environmental issues pertinent to the entity and industry**

- The entity's policy towards the environment and any improvements made since first adopting the policy.

- Whether the entity has a formal system for managing environmental risks.

- The identity of the director(s) responsible for environmental issues.

- The entity's perception of the risks to the environment from its operations.

- The extent to which the entity would be capable of responding to a major environmental disaster and an estimate of the full economic consequences of such a future major disaster.

- The effects of, and the entity's response to, any government legislation on environmental matters.

- Details of any significant infringement of environmental legislation or regulations.

- Material environmental legal issues in which the entity is involved.

- Details of any significant initiatives taken, if possible linked to amounts in financial statements.

- Details of key indicators (if any) used by the entity to measure environmental performance. Actual performance should be compared with targets and with performance in prior periods.

(b) **Financial information**

- The entity's accounting policies relating to environmental costs, provisions and contingencies.

- The amount charged to profit or loss during the accounting period in respect of expenditure to prevent or rectify damage to the environment caused by the entity's operations. This could be analysed between expenditure that the entity was legally obliged to incur and other expenditure.

- The amount charged to profit or loss during the accounting period in respect of expenditure to protect employees and society in general from the consequences of damage to the environment caused by the entity's operations. Again, this could be analysed between compulsory and voluntary expenditure.

–   Details (including amounts) of any provisions or contingent liabilities relating to environmental matters.

–   The amount of environmental expenditure capitalised during the year.

–   Details of fines, penalties and compensation paid during the accounting period in respect of non-compliance with environmental regulations.

Accounting for environmental costs

Definitions

Environmental costs	include environmental measures and environmental losses.
Environmental measures	are the costs of preventing, reducing or repairing damage to the environment and the costs of conserving resources.
Environmental losses	are costs that bring no benefit to the business.

Environmental measures can include:

•   capital expenditure

•   closure or decommissioning costs

•   clean-up costs

•   development expenditure

•   costs of recycling or conserving energy.

Environmental losses can include:

•   fines, penalties and compensation

•   impairment or disposal losses relating to assets that have to be scrapped or abandoned because they damage the environment.

Accounting treatment

Environmental costs are treated in accordance with the requirements of current accounting standards.

(a) Most expenditure is charged to profit or loss in the period in which it is incurred. Material items may need to be disclosed separately in the notes to the accounts or on the face of the statement of profit or loss and other comprehensive income as required by IAS 1.

(b) Entities may have to undertake fundamental reorganisations or restructuring or to discontinue particular activities in order to protect the environment. If a sale or termination meets the definition of a discontinued operation, its results must be separately disclosed in accordance with the requirements of IFRS 5. Material restructuring costs may need to be separately disclosed on the face of the statement of profit or loss and other comprehensive income.

(c) Fines and penalties for non-compliance with regulations are charged to profit or loss in the period in which they are incurred. This applies even if the activities that resulted in the penalties took place in an earlier accounting period, as they cannot be treated retrospectively as prior period adjustments.

(d) Expenditure on non-current assets is capitalised and depreciated in the usual way as per IAS 16 **Property, plant and equipment**. Any government grants received for expenditure that protects the environment are treated in accordance with IAS 20 **Accounting for government grants and disclosure of government assistance**.

(e) Non-current assets (including goodwill) may become impaired as a result of environmental legislation or new regulations. IAS 36 **Impairment of assets** lists events that could trigger an impairment review, one of which is a significant adverse change in the legal environment in which the business operates.

(f) Research and development expenditure in respect of environmentally friendly products, processes or services is covered by IAS 38 **Intangible assets**.

Provisions for environmental liabilities

IAS 37 **Provisions, contingent liabilities and contingent assets** states that three conditions must be met before a provision may be recognised:

(a) the entity has a present **obligation** as a result of a past event

(b) it is **probable** that a transfer of economic benefits will be required to settle the obligation

(c) a **reliable estimate** can be made of the amount of the obligation.

IAS 37 is covered in detail in a later chapter, but some points are particularly relevant to provisions for environmental costs.

(a) The fact that the entity's activities have caused environmental contamination does not in itself give rise to an obligation to rectify the damage. However, even if there is no legal obligation, there may be a constructive obligation. An entity almost certainly has a constructive obligation to rectify environmental damage if it has a policy of acting in an environmentally responsible way and this policy is well publicised.

(b) The obligation must arise from a past event. This means that a provision can only be set up to rectify environmental damage that has already happened. If an entity needs to incur expenditure to reduce pollution in the future, it should not set up a provision. This is because in theory it can avoid the expenditure by its future actions, for example by discontinuing the particular activity that causes the pollution.

Capitalisation of environmental expenditure

If environmental expenditure provides access to future economic benefits, it meets the IASB's definition of an asset. It would normally be capitalised and depreciated over the useful life of the asset.

An asset may also arise as the result of recognising a provision. In principle, when a provision or change in a provision is recognised, an asset should also be recognised when, and only when, the incurring of the present obligation gives access to future economic benefits. Otherwise the setting up of the provision should be charged immediately to in the statement of profit or loss and other comprehensive income.

Test your understanding 1 – Two transactions

You are the chief accountant of Redstart and you are currently finalising the financial statements for the year ended 31 December 20X1. Your assistant (who has prepared the draft accounts) is unsure about the treatment of two transactions that have taken place during the year. She has written you a memorandum that explains the key principles of each transaction and also the treatment adopted in the draft accounts.

Transaction one

One of the corporate objectives of the enterprise is to ensure that its activities are conducted in such a way as to minimise any damage to the natural environment. It is committed in principle to spending extra money in pursuit of this objective but has not yet made any firm proposals. The directors believe that this objective will prove very popular with customers and are anxious to emphasise their environmentally friendly policies in the annual report.

Your assistant suggests that a sum should be set aside from profits each year to create a provision in the financial statements against the possible future costs of environmental protection. Accordingly, she has charged profit or loss for the year ended 31 December 20X1 with a sum of $100,000 and proposes to disclose this fact in a note to the accounts.

Transaction two

A new law has recently been enacted that will require Redstart to change one of its production processes in order to reduce the amount of carbon dioxide that is emitted. This will involve purchasing and installing some new plant that is more efficient than the equipment currently in use. To comply with the law, the new plant must be operational by 31 December 20X2. The new plant has not yet been purchased.

In the draft financial statements for the year ended 31 December 20X1, your assistant has recognised a provision for $5 million (the cost of the new plant). This has been disclosed as a separate item in the notes to the statement of profit or loss for the year.

The memorandum from your assistant also expresses concern about the fact that there was no reference to environmental matters anywhere in the published financial statements for the year ended 31 December 20X0. As a result, she believes that the financial statements did not comply with the requirements of International Financial Reporting Standards and therefore must have been wrong.

Required:

Draft a reply to your assistant that:

(a) **reviews the treatment suggested by your assistant and recommends changes where relevant. In each case your reply should refer to relevant International Accounting Standards**

(b) **replies to her suggestion that the financial statements for the year ended 31 December 20X0 were wrong because they made no reference to environmental matters.**

Social reporting

Definition

Corporate social reporting is the process of communicating the social and environmental effects of organisations' economic actions to particular interest groups within society and to society at large.

It involves extending the accountability of organisations (particularly companies) beyond the traditional role of providing a financial account to the owners of capital. Social and ethical reporting would seem to be at variance with the prevailing business. However, there are a number of reasons why entities publish social reports.

(a) They may have deliberately built their reputation on social responsibility (e.g. Body Shop, Traidcraft) in order to attract a particular customer base.

(b) They may perceive themselves as being under particular pressure to prove that their activities do not exploit society as a whole or certain sections of it (e.g. Shell International and large utility companies).

(c) They may be genuinely convinced that it is in their long-term interests to balance the needs of the various stakeholder groups.

(d) They may fear that the government will eventually require them to publish socially oriented information if they do not do so voluntarily.

Social responsibility

A business interacts with society in several different ways as follows.

* It employs human resources in the form of management and other employees.

* Its activities affect society as a whole, for example, it may:
    – be the reason for a particular community's existence
    – produce goods that are helpful or harmful to particular members of society
    – damage the environment in ways that harm society as a whole
    – undertake charitable works in the community or promote particular values.

If a business interacts with society in a responsible manner, the needs of other stakeholders should be taken into account and performance may encompass:

* providing fair remuneration and an acceptable working environment
* paying suppliers promptly
* minimising the damage to the environment caused by the entity's activities
* contributing to the community by providing employment or by other means.

Social reporting in practice

Social reporting in the financial statements

* Disclosures of social reporting matters in financial statements tend to be required by national legislation and by the stock exchange on which an entity is quoted. There is little mention of social matters in international accounting standards.

* IAS 1 requires disclosure of the total cost of employee benefits for the period. If the 'nature of expense' method is chosen for the statement of profit or loss, then the total charge for employee costs will be shown on the face of that statement. If the 'function of expense' method is chosen, then IAS 1 requires disclosure of the total employee costs in a note to the financial statements.

- IAS 24 **Related party disclosures** requires the benefits paid to key management personnel to be disclosed in total and analysed into the categories of benefits.

- Other possible disclosures (e.g. details of directors and corporate governance matters, employee policies, supplier payment policies, charitable contributions, etc.) are normally dealt with by local legislation and would only be required by IFRSs when such disclosure is necessary to present fairly the entity's financial performance.

Separate social reports

- Stand alone social and ethical reports do not have to be audited and there are no international regulations prescribing their content.

- There are some sets of non-mandatory guidelines and codes of best practice, for example, the standard AA1000, which has been issued by the Institute of Social and Ethical Accountability (ISEA).

- Some organisations have the data in their reports independently verified and include the auditor's report in their published document. The social report may or may not be combined with the environmental report.

It has been suggested that there should be three main types of information in the social report.

(a) **Information about relationships with stakeholders**, e.g. employee numbers, wages and salaries, provision of facilities for customers and information about involvement with local charities.

(b) **Information about the accountability of the entity**, e.g. sickness leave, accident rates, noise levels, numbers of disabled employees, compliance with current legal, ethical and industry standards.

(c) **Information about dialogue with stakeholders**, e.g. the way in which the entity consults with all stakeholders and provides public feedback on the stakeholders' perceptions of the entity's responsibilities to the community and its performance in meeting stakeholder needs.

Test your understanding 2 – Social and environmental

(a) **Explain why companies may wish to make social and environmental disclosures in their annual report. Discuss how this content should be determined.**

(b) Company B owns a chemical plant, producing paint. The plant uses a great deal of energy and releases emissions into the environment. Its by-product is harmful and is treated before being safely disposed of. The company has been fined for damaging the environment following a spillage of the toxic waste product. Due to stricter monitoring routines set up by the company, the fines have reduced and in the current year they have not been in breach of any local environment laws.

The company, is aware that emissions are high and has been steadily reducing them. They purchase electricity from renewable sources and in the current year have employed a temporary consultant to calculate their carbon footprint so they can take steps to reduce it.

Discuss the information that could be included in Company B's environmental report.

Social and HCM reporting

The social contract

The social contract is an expressed or implicit contract between individual entities and society as a whole.

Some academics believe that social and environmental accounting should develop in such a way that it reflects the existence of the 'social contract'.

Proponents of the social contract argue that every business is a social institution whose existence can only be justified in so far as it serves society in general and the particular groups from which it derives its power. Businesses are accountable to the communities in which they operate and to grow and survive they must demonstrate:

(a) that society requires their services

(b) that the groups benefiting from its rewards (e.g. earnings) have society's approval.

Corporate social reporting is one means by which an entity demonstrates its accountability.

The legitimacy of an organisation

Academics have developed theories to explain corporate social reporting practices.

Stakeholder theory views social reporting as a means by which organisations attempt to manage and negotiate their relationships with their stakeholders. The nature of the reporting reflects the importance that an organisation attaches to the various stakeholder groups.

Legitimacy theory views social reporting as a means by which organisations attempt to demonstrate that they reflect the same social value system as the society in which they operate.

Legitimacy theory is a development of stakeholder theory. It argues that organisations cannot continue to exist unless the society in which they are based perceives them as operating to the same values as that society. If an organisation feels that it is under threat (e.g. because there has been a financial scandal or a serious accident causing major pollution) it may adopt one or more legitimation strategies by attempting to:

(a) 'educate' stakeholders about its intentions to improve its performance

(b) change stakeholders' perceptions of the event (without changing its actual performance)

(c) distract attention away from the issue (by concentrating on positive actions not necessarily related to the event)

(d) manage expectations about its performance (e.g. by explaining that certain events are beyond its control).

Legitimacy theory can explain several aspects of social and environmental reporting as it exists in practice. For example, entities tend to report positive aspects of their behaviour and not to report negative ones.

Human capital management (HCM)

Definition:

Human capital management relates to the management of the recruitment, retention, training and development of employees. It views employees as a business asset, rather than just a cost.

HCM is a key resource of competitive advantage and, ultimately, profitability. Any business needs to ensure that its workforce has the right mix of people, with appropriate skills and experiences, allowing the business to compete effectively.

Accounting for People Task Force

In January 2003, the Accounting for People Task Force was set up by the UK government to look at ways in which organisations can measure the quality and effectiveness of their human capital management. Its brief was to:

- look at the performance measures currently used to assess investment in HCM

- consider best practice in human capital reporting, and the performance measures that are most valuable to stakeholders

- establish and champion the business case for producing such reports

- produce a final advisory report.

The Task Force believes that effective people policies and practices will benefit organisations and their stakeholders. Managers, investors, workers, consumers and clients all have an interest in knowing that an organisation is aiming for high performance by investing in their people.

The Task Force recommends that reports on HCM should have a strategic focus. They should communicate clearly, fairly and unambiguously the board's current understanding of the links between the HCM policies and practices, its business strategy and its performance.

They should include information on:

- the size and composition of the workforce

- retention and motivation of employees

- the skills and competences necessary for success, and training to achieve these

- remuneration and fair employment practices

- leadership and succession planning

- being balanced and objective, following a process that is susceptible to review by auditors

- providing information in a form that enables comparisons over time.

To take this further, the Task Force recommended that the UK's Accounting Standards Board develop guidelines on HCM reporting. They should undergo a consultation process with leading employers, investors, professional organisations and other relevant stakeholders. The ASB would then monitor the extent and depth of HCM reporting.

The response from the UK government was to agree that HCM reports should be included in the UK's Operating and Financial Review (the equivalent to the IASB's Management Commentary) and to review the area within a five year period.

In summary, this will become another area of corporate reporting alongside environmental and social reports that companies will be expected to produce. Already there is some guidance from the findings of the Task Force as to what should be included in such a report. It remains to be seen whether this requirement will become mandatory in the future. There is no doubt that by requiring companies to consider this area, the link between investment in employees and improved business performance will be made.

Impact on performance measures

The developments outlined above in the reporting of the environmental and social consequences of an entity's activities have identified a wide array of areas, over and above financial performance, in which management performance should be evaluated, such as:

- Environmental
- Social
- Management of customers
- Management of employees
- Ethics

(a) environmental:

- – use of energy, including proportion from renewable sources
- – efficiency of energy creation (for power generators)
- – CO2 emissions
- – waste management
- – accidents affecting environment
- – transport.

(b) social:

- investment in local community initiatives

- time off for employees involved in charitable work

- matching money raised by employees for charitable work

- employment opportunities for the disadvantaged

- ethnic balance in workforce

- equality, e.g. women in senior management positions

- accidents affecting the community.

To these can be added other headings, such as:

(c) customers:

- failures to supply on time and in good condition

- customer complaints, e.g. about direct selling techniques

- fair pricing

- help for the disadvantaged through special pricing schemes.

(d) employees:

- absenteeism rates

- sickness leave

- diversity

- equal opportunities

- investment in training

- number of industrial relations tribunals in respect of the entity.

(e) ethics:

- number and cost of incidents leading to fines and/or penalties

- number and cost of incidents leading to compensation:
  - to customers
  - to employees
  - to others

- non-penalisation of whistle blowers.

But for performance measurement in these areas to be useful, the result must be information which is helpful in the making of economic decisions, whether they relate to the choice of investment, employment or suppliers. The IASB Framework's characteristics for useful financial information are that it should be relevant, reliable and comparable. These characteristics can be applied to environmental, social and ethical areas as follows.

- **Relevance**: how much weight do/will investors, employees and consumers give to these factors, compared with that given to financial factors (so return on investment, employee benefits and price, respectively)?

- **Reliability**: how much can the performance measured in these areas be relied on? How sure can users of this information be that it is a faithful representation of what has occurred, as opposed to a selective view, focusing on the successes? Are there external assurance processes that can validate the information, perhaps using the GRI guidelines?

- **Comparability**: is the information produced by different entities pulled together on a comparable basis, using similar measurement policies, so that the users can make informed choices between entities? If not, all that can be measured is an entity's performance compared with its own performance in previous periods.

Even if the information is reliable and comparable, is it useful, i.e. will it change the behaviour of investors, employees and consumers?

The answers to these questions will determine whether entities take such reporting seriously or merely treat it as part of their promotional activities. And the answers in ten years' time will almost certainly be different from those of today.

1 Chapter summary

Non-financial reporting
- Important additional information provided by management
- Management commentary – assesses results of the period

Sustainability
- Method of conducting business to enable future generations to be able to meet their needs
- Organisations often produce a sustainability report which details their actions and policies towards the environment and society

Environmental reporting
- Details the effect of the business on the environment
- It is reported separately or as part of a sustainability report
- No mandatory guidelines, so Global Reporting Initiative guidelines tend to be used
- The effect of environmental provisions is reflected in the financial statements

Social reporting
- Details the organisation's approach to society
- This includes employees, local community, suppliers and customers
- It can be reported on a stand-alone basis or as part of a sustainability report

Impact on performance measures
- Can performance measures provide reliable and comparable information?
- Is this information relevant to needs of
  - investors?
  - employees
  - consumers?

Test your understanding answers

MEMORANDUM

To: Assistant Accountant

From: Chief Accountant

Subject: Accounting treatment of two transactions and disclosure of environmental matters in the financial statements

Date: 25 March 20X2

(a) **Accounting treatment of two transactions**

Transaction one

IAS 37 **Provisions, contingent liabilities and contingent assets** states that provisions should only be recognised in the financial statements if:

– there is a present obligation as a result of a past event

– it is probable that a transfer of economic benefits will be required to settle the obligation

– a reliable estimate can be made of the amount of the obligation.

In this case, there is no obligation to incur expenditure. There may be a constructive obligation to do so in future, if the board creates a valid expectation that it will protect the environment, but a board decision alone does not create an obligation.

There is also some doubt as to whether the expenditure can be reliably quantified. The sum of $100,000 could be appropriated from retained earnings and transferred to an environmental protection reserve within other components of equity, subject to formal approval by the board. A note to the financial statements should explain the transfer.

Transaction two

Again, IAS 37 states that a provision cannot be recognised if there is no obligation to incur expenditure. At first sight it appears that there is an obligation to purchase the new equipment, because the new law has been enacted. However, the obligation must arise as the result of a past event. At 31 December 20X1, no such event had occurred as the new plant had not yet been purchased and the new law had not yet come into effect. In theory, the company does not have to purchase the new plant. It could completely discontinue the activities that cause pollution or it could continue to operate the old equipment and risk prosecution under the new law. Therefore no provision can be recognised for the cost of new equipment.

It is likely that another effect of the new law is that the company will have to dispose of the old plant before it would normally have expected to do so. IAS 36 **Impairment of assets** requires that the old plant must be reviewed for impairment. If its carrying value is greater than its recoverable amount, it must be written down and an impairment loss must be charged against profits. This should be disclosed separately in the notes to the statement of profit or loss and other comprehensive income if it is material.

(b) **Reference to environmental matters in the financial statements**

At present, companies are not obliged to make any reference to environmental matters within their financial statements. Current international financial reporting practice is more designed to meet the needs of investors and potential investors, rather than the general public. Some companies choose to disclose information about the ways in which they attempt to safeguard the environment, something that is often carried out as a public relations exercise. Disclosures are often framed in very general terms and appear outside the financial statements proper. This means that they do not have to be audited.

Several companies publish fairly detailed 'environmental reports'. It could be argued that as Redstart's operations affect the wider community, it has a moral responsibility to disclose details of its activities and its environmental policies. However, at present it is not required to do so by IFRSs.

If a company has, or may have, an obligation to make good any environmental damage that it has caused, it is obliged to disclose information about this commitment in its financial statements (unless the likelihood of this is remote).

If it is probable (more likely than not) that the company will have to incur expenditure to meet its obligation, then it is also required to set up a provision in the financial statements.

In practice, these requirements are unlikely to apply unless a company is actually obliged by law to rectify environmental damage or unless it has made a firm commitment to the public to do so (for example, by promoting itself as an organisation that cares for the environment, as the directors propose that Redstart should do in future).

Test your understanding 2 – Social and environmental

(a) The way in which companies manage their social and environmental responsibilities is a high level strategic issue for management. Companies that actively manage these responsibilities can help create long-term sustainable performance in an increasingly competitive business environment.

Reports that disclose transparent information will benefit organisations and their stakeholders. These stakeholders will have an interest in knowing that the company is attempting to adopt best practice in the area. Institutional investors will see value in the 'responsible ownership' principle adopted by the company.

Although there is no universal 'best practice', there seems to be growing consensus that high performance is linked with high quality practice in such areas as recruitment, organisational culture, training and reduction of environmental risks and impact. Companies that actively reduce environmental risks and promote social disclosures could be considered to be potentially more sustainable, profitable, valuable and competitive. Many companies build their reputation on the basis of social and environmental responsibility and go to substantial lengths to prove that their activities do not exploit their workforce or any other section of society.

Governments are encouraging disclosure by passing legislation, for example in the area of anti-discrimination and by their own example in terms of the depth and breadth of reporting (also by requiring companies who provide services to the government to disclose such information). External awards and endorsements, such as environmental league tables and employer awards, encourage companies to adopt a more strategic approach to these issues. Finally, local cultural and social pressures are causing greater demands for transparency of reporting.

There is no IFRS that determines the content of an environmental and social report. While companies are allowed to include the information they wish to disclose, there is a lack of comparability and the potential that only the positive actions will be shown.

A common framework that provided guidelines on sustainability reporting would be useful for both companies and stakeholders.

The Global Reporting Initiative (GRI) provides guidelines on the content of a sustainability report, but these are not mandatory. However, a number of companies prepare their reports in accordance with the guidelines and the GRI is becoming the unofficial best practice guide in this area.

(b) Company B's environmental report should include the following information.

    (i)   A statement of the environmental policy covering all aspects of business activity. This can include their aim of using renewable electricity and reducing their carbon footprint – the amount of carbon dioxide released into the environment as a result of their activities.

    (ii) The management systems that reduce and minimise environmental risks.

    (iii) Details of environmental training and expertise.

    (iv) A report on their environmental performance including verified emissions to air/land and water, and how they are seeking to reduce these and other environmental impacts. Operating site reports for local communities for businesses with high environmental impacts. Company B's activities have a significant impact so it is important to show how this is dealt with. The emissions data could be graphed to show it is reducing. If they have the data, they could compare their carbon dioxide emissions or their electricity usage over previous periods. Presenting this information graphically helps stakeholders see how the business is performing in the areas it is targeting.

(v) Details of any environmental offence that resulted in enforcement action, fine, etc. and any serious pollution incident. They can disclose how fines have been reducing and state that there have not been any pollution incidents in the current period.

(vi) A report on historical trends for key indicators and a comparison with the corporate targets.

Specialised entities and specialised transactions

Chapter learning objectives

Upon completion of this chapter you will be able to:

- account for transactions and events occurring in not- for-profit and public sector entities

- outline the principal considerations in developing a set of accounting standards for SMEs

- discuss solutions to the problem of differential financial reporting

- identify when an entity may no longer be viewed as a going concern and outline circumstances when a reconstruction may be an alternative to corporate liquidation

- outline the appropriate accounting treatment required relating to reconstructions.

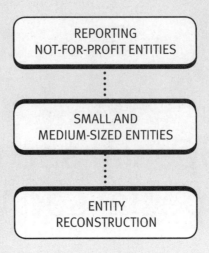

1 Not-for-profit entities

Reporting not-for-profit entities

Definition

A **not-for-profit entity** is one that does not carry on its activities for the purposes of profit or gain to particular persons, including its owners or members; and does not distribute its profits or assets to particular persons, including its owners or members.

The main types of not-for-profit entity are:

- clubs and societies

- charities

- public sector organisations (including central government, local government and National Health Service bodies).

The objectives of a not-for-profit entity

Key points

- The main objective of public sector organisations is to provide services to the general public. Their long-term aim is normally to break even, rather than to generate a surplus.

- Most public sector organisations aim to provide value for money, which is usually analysed into the three Es – economy, efficiency and effectiveness.

- Other not-for-profit entities include charities, clubs and societies whose objective is to carry out the activities for which they were created.

Assessing performance in a not-for-profit entity

- It can be difficult to monitor and evaluate the success of a not-for-profit organisation as the focus is not on a resultant profit as with a traditional business entity.

- The success of the organisation should be measured against the key indicators that reflect the visions and values of the organisation. The strategic plan will identify the goals and the strategies that the organisation needs to adopt to achieve these goals.

- The focus should be the measures of output, outcomes and their impact on what the charity is trying to achieve.

Accounting in a not-for-profit entity

The financial statements of a public sector entity or a charity are set out differently from those of a profit making entity, because their purpose is different. A public sector organisation is not reporting a profit; it is reporting on its income and how it has spent that income in achieving its aims.

The financial statements include a statement of financial position or balance sheet, but the statement of profit or loss and other comprehensive income is usually replaced with a statement of financial activities or an income and expenditure account showing incoming resources and resources expended.

Example of not-for-profit accounts

An example of a statement of financial activities for a charity is shown below.

The Toytown Charity, Statement of Financial Activities for the year ended 31 March 20X7

	$
Incoming resources	
Resources from generated funds	
Grants	10,541,000
Legacies	5,165,232
Donations	1,598,700
Activities for generating funds	
Charity shop sales	10,052,693
Investment income	3,948,511
	————
Total incoming resources	31,306,136

Resources expended
Cost of generating funds

Fund raising	(1,129,843)
Publicity	(819,828)
Charity shop operating costs	(6,168,923)
Charitable activities	
Supporting local communities	(18,263,712)
Elderly care at home	(4,389,122)
Pride in Toytown campaign	(462,159)
Total resources expended	(31,233,587)
Net incoming resources for the year	72,549
Funds brought forward at 1 March 20X6	21,102
Funds carried forward at 31 March 20X7	93,651

The statement of financial position or balance sheet of a not-for-profit entity only differs from that of a profit making entity in the reserves section, where there will usually be an analysis of the different types of reserve, as shown below.

Toytown Charity, Balance sheet as at 31 March 20X7

	$
Non-current assets	
Tangible assets	80,500
Investments	12,468
	92,968
Current assets	
Inventory	2,168
Receivables	10,513
Cash	3,958
	16,639
Total assets	109,607

KAPLAN PUBLISHING

Reserves	
Restricted fund	20,200
Unrestricted funds	73,451
	———
	93,651
Non-current liabilities	
Pension liability	9,705
Current liabilities	
Payables	6,251
	———
Total funds	109,607
	———

The reserves are separated into restricted and unrestricted funds.

- Unrestricted funds are funds available for general purposes.

- Restricted funds are those that have been set aside for a specific purpose or in a situation where an individual has made a donation to the charity for a specific purpose, perhaps to replace some equipment, so these funds must be kept separate.

Accounting guidance

There is no specific reporting standard accounting for non-profit making entities within IFRS GAAP. However, there is guidance in the U.K. where four Statements of Recommended Practice (SORPs) relevant to public benefit activities have been issued. SORPs are issued by an industry or sponsoring body, recognised by the UK Accounting Standards Board (ASB) as being an appropriate body for that purpose. The nature of the transactions, together with organisational, legal and other factors require that SORPs are individual in nature, to meet specific accounting and reporting requirements. A summary of the relevant SORPs is as follows:

(1) Accounting and Reporting by Charities – (2nd edition – May 2008)

(2) Accounting for Further and Higher Education (Issued July 2007)

(3) Accounting by Registered Social Landlords (Revised 2007)

(4) Code of Practice on Local Authority Accounting in the UK 2009 (May 2009)

In June 2007, the ASB published an Interpretation for Public Benefit Entities of the Statement of Principles for Financial Reporting. The Interpretation explains how the principles in the Statement apply for public benefit entities. The Interpretation will support the work of those bodies within the public benefit sector that are recognised by the ASB for the purpose of issuing SORPs. It will also be of interest to international work, including the conceptual framework project that is being taken forward by the International Public Sector Accounting Standards Board. It comprises eight chapters as follows:

(1) The objective of financial statements

(2) The reporting entity

(3) The qualitative characteristics of financial information

(4) The elements of the financial statements

(5) Recognition in the financial statements

(6) Measurement in the financial statements

(7) Presentation of financial statements

(8) Accounting for interests in other entities

These chapter headings, together with much of the detail within, will be familiar to those who have knowledge of the UK ASB Statement of Principles or the IASB Framework document.

As an additional issue, the new IFRS-based Code of Practice on Local Authority Accounting will apply to local authority accounts from 1 April 2010.

2 Small and medium sized entities

Definition:

A SME may be defined or characterised as follows:

- they are usually owner-managed by a relatively small number of individuals such as a family group, rather than having an extensive ownership base,

- they are usually smaller entities in financial terms such as revenues generated and assets and liabilities under the control of the entity,

- they usually have a relatively small number of employees, and

- they usually undertake less complex or difficult transactions which are normally the focus of a financial reporting standard.

By contrast, listed companies have an extended base of ownership, principally financial institutions and professional investors. They invariably enter into a broader range of transactions and arrangements in their business dealings, which may be complex and which may require direction to ensure they are accounted for in an objective and consistent manner. Consequently, there is a need for specific and detailed reporting standards to direct entities to provide financial information to users which is relevant, reliable and comparable with other entities.

If SMEs can be identified as distinct from other entities, then it may be worth evaluating whether the financial reporting requirements of such entities should also be distinct or different from other entities. After all, one of the underlying requirements for financial reporting is that the cost and burden of producing financial reporting information for shareholders and other stakeholders is that it the benefits should outweigh the costs of making that information available.

There is no definitive definition of a SME. However a SME may be defined, it would appear clear that that its shares will not be listed on a public exchange. There is still the issue of making a judgement, based upon a range of size or other criteria, as to what may be regarded as a SME. It is also possible to identify particular classes of business activity which could be excluded from the definition of a SME if considered desirable. If monetary values are used to determine SME status, there may be problems of comparability on an international basis.

The problem of accounting for SMEs

One possible source of confusion in developing a reporting standard for SME is that the European Union (EU) has passed Directives defining small and medium-sized companies (and groups). In the UK, as well as other countries, it is now possible to identify three distinct financial reporting groups:

- Listed entities, with an extensive ownership and which generate significant revenues and control assets and liabilities with monetary carrying values in the financial statements in the millions. They will also be major employers. Full IFRS GAAP compliance is required from these companies.

- Small and medium-size companies as defined by European Union (EU) law to reduce filing and publicity requirements for such companies. For example, implementation of relevant the EU Directive in the UK by the 2006 Companies Act defines a company as small or medium-sized if it meets any two out of three specified criteria based upon annual sales revenue, assets total from the statement of financial position and the total number of employees.

If an entity meets the definition of either a small or medium-sized company, it is eligible to file abbreviated or reduced financial reporting information at Companies House. Additionally, small companies can choose to exempt themselves from the requirement for an annual audit. However, in principle, they would still need to comply fully with relevant reporting standards unless specifically exempt from doing so. Some companies are excluded from taking advantage of the audit exemption and reduced filing and disclosure requirements if they are banks, building societies or others operating in the financial services industry. In the UK, the Financial Reporting Standard for Smaller Entities (FRSSE) identifies which UK Financial Reporting Standards are applicable to entities which meet the definition of a small company based upon UK company law.

EU member states may need to consider whether to eliminate the law-based definition of a small company and use a definition for SME which can then apply to all non-publicly listed entities. If this is done, it will have a two-tier financial reporting system, rather than a three-tier system which may result in confusion.

- SME's which are non-listed and which are non-publicly accountable; they may or may not also meet the definition of a small or medium-sized company based upon EU or other national law. There is now an IFRS for SMEs which identifies the extent to which IFRS should be applied by SMEs, together with underlying concepts and principles to apply if a topic is not covered within the IFRS for SME. In the UK, and probably throughout the EU, the potential application of IFRS for SME is greater than the FRSSE (or national equivalent) as the latter only applies to companies meeting the statutory definition of a small company, whereas potentially IFRS for SME may be applied by any non-publicly accountable entity, irrespective of any size criteria.

Another possible problem is the reporting and compliance burden placed upon SME when full compliance with IFRS GAAP is required, particularly when they may have relatively few transactions covered by an applicable reporting standard. For example, ensuring compliance with IFRS 5 (assets held for sale) or IFRS 8 (segmental reporting) may result in benefits of providing that information to users of financial statements not being exceeded by the costs of making that information available.

It could also be argued that there may be a comparability problem if some entities comply with IFRS GAAP in full, whilst others comply with IFRS for SME.

How are reporting requirement for SMEs to be identified and communicated?

Having considered whether there is a need for a different financial reporting regime for SME, it is then worth considering how the financial reporting requirements for SME should be identified and reported. One possible approach could be to include specific references within each reporting standard whether it was to be applied by SMEs, or the extent to which it was relevant or exempt. This would be quite a cumbersome method to introduce and would require detailed consideration each time a reporting standard was to be revised or replaced. An alternative approach would be to produce a self-contained, stand-alone, reporting standard applicable only to SMEs.

The approach used in the UK and some other countries was to produce a stand-alone reporting standard, the Financial Reporting Standard for Smaller Entities (FRSSE), the first of which was issued in 1997. The idea was to have was a one-stop shop for financial reporting requirements for those entities eligible to apply it. If a particular issue or transaction entered into was not covered within the requirements of the FRSSE, preparers of financial statements should refer to other reporting standards for guidance as to what may be regarded as current practice.

The IFRS for SME was issued in July 2009 and has adopted a similar approach to the UK. It is effective immediately, but note that it has been left for each country to determine which entities will be eligible to apply the IFRS for SME. On 13 August 2009, South Africa became the first country to adopt IFRS for SME. Initially, the UK ASB proposed to have a variant of IFRS for SME effective in the UK for accounting periods commencing on or after 1 January 2012, and this was subsequently deferred to 1 January 2013. It would now appear that the UK is preparing for a UK-focussed version of IFRS for SME to be effective for accounting periods commencing on or after 1 January 2015.

Although the IASB regards this standard as relevant and applicable to all non-publicly accountable entities, national governments may permit or restrict its application as they see fit.

What is the effect of introducing the IFRS for SME?

Instead of complying fully with IFRS, consisting of approximately 3,000 disclosure points within approximately 37 reporting standards (and additional IFRICs or UITF announcements as appropriate), compliance with IFRS for SME will comprise approximately 300 disclosure points all contained within the one document. This significantly reduces the burden and associated time and cost of producing financial statements. Similarly, the IFRS for SME will be updated approximately every three years, rather than having to manage the ever-present risk of reporting standards being amended, revised or withdrawn and replaced altogether.

The subject matter of several reporting standards has been **omitted from the IFRS for SME** as follows:

- Earnings per share (IAS 33)
- Interim reporting (IAS 34)
- Segmental reporting (IFRS 8)
- Assets held for sale (IFRS 5)

Omission of subject matter from the IFRS for SME is usually because the cost of preparing and reporting information exceeds the expected benefits which users would expect to derive from that information. This would perhaps be the case with the requirements of IAS 33 dealing with earnings per share. In addition, much of the content of the omitted standards is perceived not to be applicable to those entities who may apply the IFRS for SME, and consequently would result in additional time and effort to make minimal additional disclosures, which would provide little or no benefit to users of those financial statements. This would perhaps be the case with segmental reporting requirements where smaller entities tend to have only one or few distinct business or operating segments; the entity tends to be operated and managed as a whole.

The subject matter of other reporting standards has been **simplified for inclusion within the IFRS for SME**. In principle, many of the recognition and measurement principles have been simplified, resulting in the elimination of choice where that was possible within IFRS, to apply the most straight-forward treatment such as:

- R & D always expensed
- Goodwill amortised (10 years)
- No revaluation of property, plant and equipment
- No available-for-sale financial instruments (note that this category of financial asset has been eliminated by IFRS 9)
- Finance costs never capitalised

Simplification of accounting treatments permitted by the IFRS for SME is an attempt to minimise the cost of preparing and making information available for shareholders and other interested parties. It is also an attempt to improve consistency and comparability of information prepared by entities who are applying the requirements of the IFRS for SME. It could be argued that the simplified accounting treatments are a way of reducing judgement in the preparation of financial statements. For example, the judgement of whether research and development costs should be capitalised, and then the determination of the amortisation period for any capitalised expenditure, is avoided by the IFRS for SME. The time and cost incurred in obtaining and accounting for revaluations of property, plant and equipment has also been avoided by the IFRS for SME.

In countries where there is currently a Financial Reporting Standard for Smaller Entities (FRSSE) or equivalent, there may be differences between that national standard and the IFRS for SME. For example, one matter in which the IFRS for SME currently differs from the UK FRSSE is that the latter does not require a cash flow statement to be included as part of the annual financial statements. Additionally, there may be legal and regulatory differences between the IFRS for SME and a nationally-defined equivalent, such as:

- determination, and application of, any size criteria for defining a SME – which could be a comprise a combination of any or all of the following:
    - revenue generated in an accounting period
    - total or net assets at reporting date
    - number of employees
    - extent of indebtedness to financial institutions
    - whether particular trading activities are entered into, such as provision of investment and other financial services to the public
    - whether particular forms of transactions are entered into, such as hedging arrangements
    - whether there is any perceived public interest in excluding particular entities from identification, and therefore regulation, associated with a SME

- determination, and application of, any exemption or exclusion criteria, such as mandatory exclusion from SME for entities undertaking particular activities – perhaps those entities who handle cash and other assets on behalf of members of the public

- determination, and application of any ownership criteria – there would appear to be a general acceptance of the principle that a SME cannot have its' shares listed and traded on a recognised exchange; other than that, national regulators could apply ownership criteria appropriate to their circumstances. For example, until the 1960's, one of the defining criteria of a private limited-liability entity in the UK was that it had up to a maximum of fifty shareholders.

Benefits expected to accrue following adoption of IFRS for SMEs

Expected benefits may include the following:

- Provide improved comparability for users of accounts with other entities who also use IFRS

- Enhance the overall confidence in the accounts of SMEs if they are seen to be applying reporting requirements which have some degree of comparability with compliance with IFRS in full.

- Reduce the significant costs involved in maintaining standards on a national basis. Potentially, this may lead to the demise of national standard setters as listed entities in many countries have adopted IFRS. If SME move towards adoption of IFRS for SME, there may be little left for national standard setters to regulate.

- Facilitate subsequent adoption of full IFRS, for example, if a SME intends to seek a stock exchange listing at a later date.

Technical Article

The P2 Examiner, Graham Holt, wrote an article discussing the issue of IFRS for SME in the March 2010 Student Accountant magazine. You can access this article from the ACCA website (www.accaglobal.com).

Test your understanding 1 – SME

(1) **Describe the reasons a standard for SMEs is required.**

(2) **Describe the potential solutions to accounting for SMEs.**

(3) **What is the IASB's method of reporting for SMEs?**

3 Entity reconstruction schemes

Key reason for an entity reconstruction

Financial difficulties

If an entity is in financial difficulty it may have no recourse but to accept liquidation as the final outcome. However it may be in a position to survive, and indeed flourish, by taking up some future contract or opportunities. The only hindrance to this may be that any future operations may need a prior cash injection. This cash injection cannot be raised because the present structure and status of the entity may not be attractive to current and outside investors.

A typical corporate profile of an entity in this situation could be as follows:

- Accumulated trading losses
- Arrears of unpaid debenture and loan interest
- No payment of equity dividends for several years
- Market value of equity shares below their nominal value
- Lack of investor and market confidence in the entity.

To get a cash injection the entity will need to undergo a reorganisation or reconstruction.

To consider how a reconstruction may help the entity to survive, the rights and interests of the various stakeholders need to be considered.

Entity stakeholders

The capital structure of a corporate entity is designed to protect its principal stakeholders – normally identified as equity holders and providers of finance. Any changes to this structure are therefore restricted by corporate law in most countries to protect these stakeholders. Some of the ways in which this is achieved are explained below.

An entity with accumulated losses is normally prevented from paying equity dividends, usually until the accumulated losses have been recovered by trading profitably, which could take several years, because of corporate law restrictions on distributions to shareholders. This situation will not make the entity an attractive proposition for prospective equity investors.

Non-payment of equity dividends add to the problem for the following reasons:

- Current equity holders will find it difficult to sell their shares for what they may consider to be a satisfactory price; any potential purchase of their shares is likely to be at a low value.

- Potential investors will not be attracted by the poor dividend payment history, and the fact that this situation is unlikely to improve in the foreseeable future.

- If the market price of equity shares is below their nominal value, a new issue of equity shares is unlikely to be successful as potential investors will seek to pay only market value for the shares. Many countries have corporate law which prevent equity capital being issued at less than its nominal value.

In summary, there is likely to be a lack of confidence in the entity to attract new investors, or to encourage existing investors to retain or increase their investment.

Providers of loan finance are primarily concerned with recovery of their capital and interest. The operational performance and profitability is of secondary importance provided that they can recoup their capital and interest. Existing or threatened arrears of debenture or bank interest are a negative factor when trying to raise finance for the following reasons:

- They tie up any future resources for interest and capital payments which could otherwise be used for expansion.

- They tie up any future profits which could be used for distribution in the form of a dividend.

- They make it difficult to obtain new loan finance as past arrears will make any attempt to raise new finance unattractive to the market.

- Existing providers of loan finance may also have the right to enforce recovery of funds from the entity, perhaps by having security (i.e. collateral) for their loans.

- There may be few, if any, assets available within the entity for use as security (i.e. collateral) to support any future raising of finance.

A reconstruction of the entity's capital may help to alleviate these problems and may involve one or more of the following procedures:

- Write off the accumulated losses.

- Write off arrears of repayment of loan finance

- Write down the nominal value of the equity capital.

How is this achieved?

To do this the entity must ask all or some of its existing stakeholders to surrender existing rights and amounts owing in exchange for new rights under a new or reformed entity.

Why would stakeholders be willing to do this?

The main reason is that a reconstruction may result in an outcome preferable to any other alternative as follows:

- Providers of loan finance and other creditors may be left with little or no prospect of repayment.

- Providers of equity finance may be left with little or no prospect of a return (dividends and capital growth) on their investment.

- Corporate liquidation may provide some return to providers of loan finance, but is unlikely to provide any return to equity holders, depending upon the financial position of the entity.

How could this be agreed between the various stakeholders?

It may be helpful to review the situation faced by each group of stakeholders as follows:

Equity shareholders This is the last group to be allocated funds in a corporate liquidation, and therefore have a high chance of receiving no return at all. It would therefore seem appropriate that they should bear most of the losses from the present situation, in exchange for potential future benefits if the entity is profitable following reconstruction.

Trade creditors and payables may have some prospect of recovery of at least part of the amounts due to them as they rank ahead of equity holders for repayment upon corporate liquidation. Some trade creditors may also protect themselves from the risk of non-recovery by including the right to retain legal title or ownership of goods delivered to customers until they are paid for. In the event of non-recovery of amounts due to them, they will have the right to take repossession of their inventory.

Debenture holders often have a better chance of recovery of capital under liquidation than other stakeholders because such loans are often secured against entity assets. However, even in this situation, the full amount outstanding of such loans may not be recovered. In this case, any amount not recovered from the assets used as security (or collateral) would then normally be regarded as an unsecured creditor in the same way as trade payables.

There may be a situation where there is more than one debenture loan secured against entity assets. in this situation, the respective rights of each debenture holder would need to be examined to determine who would be paid off first in the event of there being insufficient assets to meet the claims of all secured loans. It could be, for example, that secured loans are paid off or settled in the order in which they were created; i.e. the oldest loans would be paid off first from available assets, then more recent loans would be paid off out of any available surplus.

It may therefore be in the best interests of all stakeholders to agree to a scheme of reconstruction. In effect, they give up existing rights and amounts owing (which are unlikely to be recovered) for the opportunity to share in the future profitability which may arise from the extra cash which can be generated as a consequence of their actions. This can only be achieved if all stakeholders are willing to compromise by waiving some or all of their existing rights, and if they can be convinced that there is an improved prospect of future returns as a result of a reconstruction scheme.

In examination questions, be alert to identify any information relating to the order in which liabilities are to be settled or paid off, and what happens to any amounts not paid due to inadequate security or collateral. This information should then be applied to ensure that liabilities are paid off in the correct order, having identified those liabilities secured by assets or collateral.

One additional factor is that there may be **professional fees** incurred as part of any reconstruction scheme. Carefully review the information in the question to determine whether:

- such creditors rank ahead of unsecured creditors for payment

- whether their fees are paid by any particular stakeholder group, depending upon who initiates the reconstruction scheme.

Capital reduction scheme

Using this scheme, an entity may:

- write off unpaid equity capital – this situation may arise, for example, if there are partly-paid shares in issue. The entity is effectively reducing the nominal value of its equity share capital by the amount not yet called up and paid by the equity holders. For example, partly paid equity shares with a nominal value of $1, may be reduced to the amount currently paid up, say, $0.75; in doing so, the equity holders will no longer be required to pay the amount still outstanding.

- write off any equity capital which is lost or not represented by available assets – in this situation, the entity has a deficit on retained earnings due to accumulated losses. This prevents payment of an equity dividend and also depresses the share price. In effect, the entity will write off this deficit against any other available components of equity to clear all or part of the deficit on retained earnings.

- write off any paid up equity capital which is in excess of requirements – in this situation, the entity uses surplus cash to repay its equity holders.

This scheme does not really affect creditors as the equity holders have reduced their capital stake in the entity, either by reducing the nominal value of the shares in issue, or by reducing the total number of shares in issue, or a combination of both.

This scheme is normally regulated by formalised procedures detailed in law, such as the Companies Act 2006 s641 in the United Kingdom, which may differ in other countries. **In examination questions**, it is unlikely that there will be questions set which require a specific and detailed knowledge of law from any particular jurisdiction; however, it is likely that students will be expected to have an understanding of the principles of when such a scheme may be appropriate and how it may be applied. It is also possible that a question could be set which provided the rules to apply in a given scenario.

Struggler has the following statement of financial position at 30 June 20X8:

	$000
Assets	500
	────
	500
	────

	$000
Equity and liabilities:	
Issued equity shares @ $1 each	600
Share premium	100
Retained earnings/(deficit)	(300)
Liabilities	100
	────
	500
	────

Struggler has the following problems:

- Accumulated losses which prevent payment of a dividend should the entity become profitable at some future date.

- Issued equity capital of $600,000 which is only backed by assets to the extent of $500,000.

- Difficulty in attracting new sources of equity and/or loan finance.

Required:

Apply a capital reduction scheme and restate the statement of financial position at 30 June 20X8.

Solution

Using the reduction of capital scheme, the deficit on retained earnings could be cleared by reducing both the share premium and issued equity capital accounts. Any balance on share premium account should be utilised first to minimise the reduction of equity capital as follows:

	$000	$000
Dr Share premium	100	
Dr Equity share capital	200	
Cr Retained earnings		300

The resulting statement of financial position would be:

	$000
Assets	500
	–––––
	500
	–––––

	$000
Equity and liabilities:	
Issued equity shares	400
Share premium	nil
Retained earnings/(deficit)	nil
Liabilities	100
	–––––
	500
	–––––

The equity holders have effectively recognised the financial reality of their situation by reducing the nominal value of the issued share capital. If the entity begins to make profits following the reconstruction, there is no longer a deficit on retained earnings to clear before a dividend can be paid. Potential equity and/or loan finance providers may also be encouraged by this situation.

The reduction in equity capital could be reflected by either a reduction in the nominal value per share (from $1 down to approximately (400/600) $0.67, or by converting and reducing shareholdings on a pro-rata basis. For example, if a person previously owned thirty shares with a nominal value of $1 each, following conversion and reduction, they would now own only twenty shares with a nominal value of $1 each. In either situation, the total equity share capital would be $400,000.

4 Reconstruction schemes

Reconstruction schemes extend the principles of the capital reduction schemes by including the various creditors within the scheme. In addition to reducing equity share capital, reconstruction schemes may also include:

- writing off debenture loan interest arrears
- replacement of debenture loans with new loans having different interest and capital repayment terms
- write off amounts owing to unsecured or trade payables.

Equity holders and creditors may be willing to do this if the entity is considered likely to survive and return to profitable trading in the future. They are effectively sacrificing their current legal and commercial rights for future legal and commercial rights which will hopefully bring them better financial returns than under their current position. Such reconstruction schemes may be subject to court or law-based formal approval procedures before they can be implemented.

In practical terms, this can only be achieved if all stakeholders agree to forego some of their current legal and commercial rights. For those in the weakest position, usually the equity holders, they would be expected to sacrifice more than others, such as secured debenture loan providers. Secured debenture loan providers could act in their own interest and enforce possession of the assets provided as security (i.e. collateral), but this would often be to the detriment of other stakeholders and could lead to the liquidation of the entity if it can no longer operate. Consequently, due to their stronger position, secured loan providers will be reluctant to sacrifice as much as the equity holders in any reconstruction scheme.

In the United Kingdom, these schemes are governed by the Companies Act 2006 s895. As with the capital reduction scheme considered earlier, it is unlikely that an examination question will be set which requires a detailed knowledge of specific law from any one jurisdiction. However, questions may be set on the application of the principles, possibly including rules to apply in a given situation.

Illustration 1 – Machin

Consider the statement of financial position of Machin at 30 June 20X9:

	$000
Non-current assets:	
Intangible – brand	50,000
Tangible	220,000
	270,000
Current assets:	
Inventory	20,000
Receivables	30,000
	320,000

	$000
Equity and liabilities:	
Equity share capital @ $1 shares	100,000
Share premium	75,000
Retained earnings	(100,000)
	75,000
Non-current liabilities: Debenture loan	125,000
Current liabilities:	
Bank overdraft	20,000
Trade payables	100,000
	320,000

The following reconstruction scheme is to be applied:

(1) The equity shares of $1 nominal value currently in issue will be written off and will be replaced on a one-for-one basis by new equity shares with a nominal value of $0.25.

(2) The debenture loan will be replaced by the issue of new equity shares – four new equity shares with a nominal value of $0.25 each for every $1 of debenture loan converted.

(3) Existing equity holders will be offered the opportunity to subscribe for three new equity shares with a nominal value of $0.25 each for every one equity share currently held. The shares are to be issued at nominal value. It is expected that all current equity holders will take up this opportunity.

(4) The share premium account is to be eliminated.

(5) The brand is considered to be impaired and must be written off.

(6) Retained earnings deficit is to be eliminated

Required:

Prepare the statement of financial position of Machin immediately after the scheme has been put into effect. Show any workings required to arrive at the solution.

Solution

Begin by opening a reconstruction account:

All adjustments to the statement of financial position as a result of the reconstruction scheme must be accounted for within this account. Any balance remaining on this account will be used to either write down assets or create a capital reserve.

Reconstruction account

	$000		$000
New equity shares (100,000 x $0.25) (Note 1)	25,000	Equity shares @ $1 (Note 1)	100,000
New equity shares (125,000 x 4 x $0.25) (Note 2)	125,000	Debenture loan (Note 2)	125,000
Brand impaired (Note 5)	50,000	Share premium (Note 4)	75,000
Retained earnings (Note 6)	100,000		
	_____		_____
	300,000		300,000
	_____		_____

The note references refer to the details of the reconstruction scheme.

The debenture holders may be prepared to sacrifice their rights as a creditor if they believe that Machin will trade profitably following the reconstruction scheme. They will forego the rights of a creditor in exchange for the rights of an equity holder – i.e. future dividends plus growth in the capital value of their equity shares.

The resulting statement of financial position for Machin will be:

	$000
Non-current assets:	
Intangible – brand	nil
Tangible	220,000
	_____
Current assets:	
Inventory	20,000
Receivables	30,000
Bank ((20,000) + 75,000) (Note 3)	55,000
	_____
	325,000
Share premium	nil
Retained earnings	nil
	_____
	225,000
Non-current liabilities: Debenture loan	nil
Current liabilities:	
Bank overdraft (eliminated by cash receipt from share issue)	nil
Trade payables	100,000
	_____
	325,000
	_____

(W1) Confirmation of equity share capital following reorganisation:

		No
Note 1	Issue of one new equity share for one old equity share	100,000
Note 2	Convert debenture loan into new equity shares: 125,000 x 4	500,000
Note 3	Issue of new equity shares for cash	300,000
		_____
		900,000
		_____

Illustration – Bentham

Bentham has been making losses for several years, principally due to severe competition, which has put downward pressure on revenues whilst costs have increased.

The statement of financial position for Bentham at 30 June 20X1 is as follows:

	$000
Non-current assets	7,200
Current assets	10,550
	———
	17,750
	———

Equity and liabilities	$000
Equity share capital @$1 shares	20,000
Retained earnings (deficit)	(17,250)
	———
	2,750
Non-current liabilities:	
11% debentures 20X3 (secured)	7,000
8% debentures 20X4 (secured)	5,000
Current liabilities	3,000
	———
	17,750
	———

The entity has changed its marketing strategy and, as a result, it is expected that annual profit before interest and tax will be $3,000,000 for the next five years. Bentham incurs tax at 25% on profit before tax.

The directors are proposing to reconstruct Bentham and have produced the following proposal for discussion:

(1) The existing $1 equity shares are to be cancelled and replaced by equity shares of $0.25.

(2) The 8% debentures are to be replaced by 8,000,000 equity shares of $0.25 each, regarded as fully paid up, plus $3,000,000 6% debentures 20X9.

(3) Existing shareholders will have their $1 equity shares replaced by 11,000,000 $0.25 equity shares, regarded as fully paid up.

(4) The 11% debentures are to be redeemed in exchange for:

   –   for:$6,000,000 6% debentures 20X9, and

   –   4,000,000 equity shares of $0.25, regarded as fully paid up.

In the event of a liquidation, it is estimated that the net realisable value of the assets would be $6,200,000 for the non-current assets and $10,000,000 for the current assets.

Required:

•   **Prepare a statement of financial position for Bentham at 1 July 20X1, immediately after the reconstruction scheme has been implemented.**

•   **Prepare computations to show the effect of the proposed reconstruction scheme on each of the equity shareholders, 11% debenture holders and 8% debenture holders.**

•   **Comment on the potential outcome of the scheme from the perspective of a shareholder who currently owns 10% of the equity share capital on whether to agree to the reconstruction scheme as proposed.**

Solution

Bentham – the revised statement of financial position at 1 July 20X1 following reconstruction would be:

	$000
Non-current assets	7,200
Current assets	10,550
	———
	17,750
	———

Equity and liabilities:	$000
Equity share capital (23 million shares @ $0.25)(W1)	5,750
Retained earnings (deficit)	nil
	――――
	5,750
Non-current liabilities:	
6% debentures 20X9 (W1)	9,000
Current liabilities	3,000
	――――
	17,750
	――――

(W1) The reconstruction account would be as follows:

Reconstruction account

	$000		$000
New 6% debentures	6,000	11% Debentures redeemed	7,000
New equity shares: 4m @ $0.25	1,000	8% Debenture redeemed	5,000
New equity shares: 11m @ $0.25	2,750	Equity cancelled	20,000
New equity shares: 8m @ $0.25	2,000		
New 6% debentures	3,000		
Deficit on retained earnings	17,250		
	――――		――――
	32,000		32,000
	――――		――――

If Bentham was to be put into liquidation, rather than undergo the reconstruction, the following could be the consequence:

	$000
Net realisable value of non-current assets	6,200
Net realisable value of current assets	10,000
	――――
	16,200
Repayment of 11% secured debenture loan	(7,000)
Repayment of 8% secured debenture loan	(5,000)
	――――

Available for unsecured creditors	4,200
Unsecured creditors	(3,000)
Available for equity holders	1,200

It can be seen that, whilst secured creditors will be paid off, and there should then be sufficient assets available for payment of unsecured creditors, equity shareholders would not fully recover the nominal value of their shareholding. The equity holders would receive only (1,200 / 20,000) $0.06 for each $1 equity share held. Note that this does not include any legal and professional fees that may be payable to implement such a scheme.

If the scheme is implemented, the debenture holders would forego part of their prior claim for repayment in exchange for equity shares. If they are to agree to this, they must be satisfied regarding the reliability of the profit forecast for future trading, so that they can receive future dividends and enjoy capital growth on the value of their shares. Additionally, they will have a significant equity holding of 12 million out of 23 million equity shares. This is just enough to give them a majority of the equity capital; they could then use their voting power to appoint or remove directors as they see appropriate.

If the reconstruction scheme is implemented, the revised capital structure results in significantly more equity shares in issue, with reduced long term liabilities in the form of secured debenture loans. It can be seen that the current debenture loan holders have deferred the repayment date of their loans from 20X3 and 20X4 respectively to 20X9, and accepted a reduced rate of interest on their loans. In addition, they have received some equity shares which will give them the opportunity to share in the future prosperity of Bentham if it becomes profitable following the reconstruction.

From the perspective of someone who holds 10% of the equity before the reconstruction takes place, the following comments can be made:

- The gearing ratio has reduced as follows:

Before:	$000		After:	$000	
Gearing ratio	$\dfrac{12,000}{14,750}$	= 81.3%		$\dfrac{9,000}{14,750}$	= 61.0%

The reduction in gearing will be regarded as a decrease in financial risk for the equity holders.

- If the forecast regarding expected profit before interest and tax is reliable, then the following will result:

		$000
Profit before interest and tax		3,000
Less: debenture interest	9,000 x 6%	540
		———
Profit before tax		2,460
Tax @ 25%		(615)
		———
Profit after tax available to equity holders		1,845

Potentially, there are retained profits available for payment of an equity dividend. Whilst it may not be advisable to distribute all profit after tax in the form of a dividend, it is a positive step to have retained earnings within the entity. Additionally, interest cover of (3,000 / 540) 5.5 may be regarded as reasonable in the circumstances.

- One further factor is the change in proportionate voting power if the reconstruction scheme is implemented. Previously, someone who owned 10% of the equity share capital would have 10% x 11 million = 1.1 million equity shares in the restructured entity out of 23 million equity shares – i.e. 4.7% of the equity shares. This is a significant dilution of voting power, but it may be a reasonable thing to give up in exchange for the future prospect of the continuation of Bentham, together with the potential receipt of a dividend if the forecast is realistic.

Test your understanding 2 – Wire

Wire has suffered from poor trading conditions over the last three years. Its statement of financial position at 30 June 20X1 is as follows:

	$	$
Non-current assets:		
Land and buildings		193,246
Plant and equipment		60,754
Investment in Cord		27,000
		————
		281,000
Current assets:		
Inventory	120,247	
Receivables	70,692	
	————	
		190,939
		————
		471,939
		————

		$
Equity and liabilities:		
Equity shares @$1		200,000
Retained earnings (deficit)		(39,821)
		————
		160,179
Non-current liabilities:		
8% debenture 20X4	80,000	
5% debenture 20X5	70,000	
	————	
		150,000
Current liabilities:		
Trade payables	112,247	
Interest payable	12,800	
Overdraft	36,713	
	————	
		161,760
		————
		471,939
		————

It has been difficult to generate revenues and profits in the current year and inventory levels are very high. Interest has not been paid to the debenture holders for two years. Although the debentures are secured against the land and buildings, the debenture holders have demanded either a scheme of reconstruction or the liquidation of Wire.

During a meeting of directors and representatives of the shareholders and debenture holders, it was decided to implement a scheme of reconstruction.

The following scheme has been agreed in principle:

(1) Each $1 equity share is to be redesignated as an equity share of $0.25.

(2) The existing 5% debenture is to be exchanged for a new issue of $35,000 9.5% loan stock, repayable in 20X9, plus 140,000 equity shares of $0.25 each. In addition, they will subscribe for $9,000 debenture stock, repayable 20X9, at par value. The rate of interest on this new debenture is 9.5%.

(3) The equity shareholders are to accept a reduction in the nominal value of their shares from $1 to $0.25 per share, and subscribe for a new issue on the basis of one-for-one at a price of $0.30 per share.

(4) The 8% debenture holders, who have received no interest for two years, are to receive 20,000 equity shares of $0.25 each in lieu of the interest payable. It is agreed that the value of the interest liability is equivalent to the fair value of the shares to be issued. In addition, they have agreed to defer repayment of their loan until 20X9, subject to an increased rate of interest of 9.5%.

(5) The deficit on retained earnings is to be written off.

(6) The investment in Cord has been subject to much speculation as Cord has just obtained the legal rights to a new production process. As a result, the value of the investment has increased to $60,000. This investment is to be sold as part of the reconstruction scheme.

(7) The bank overdraft is to be repaid.

(8) 10% of the receivables are regarded as non-recoverable and are to be written off.

(9) The remaining assets were independently valued, and should now be recognised at the following amounts:

	$
Land	80,000
Buildings	80,000
Equipment	30,000
Inventory	50,000

If the reconstruction goes ahead, the following is expected to happen:

(1) It is expected that, due to the refinancing, operating profits will be earned at the rate of $50,000 after depreciation, but before interest and tax.

(2) Wire will be subject to tax on its profit before tax at 25%.

Required:

- **Prepare the statement of financial position of Wire immediately after the reconstruction**

- **Advise the equity holders and debenture holders whether or not they should support the reconstruction scheme.**

5 External reconstructions

Such schemes normally involve the assets and liabilities of the current entity being transferred to a new entity on an agreed basis. Typically, this will require information regarding the following:

- details of purchase consideration to acquire the business as a whole, or specified assets and liabilities – this may give rise to goodwill for the purchaser.

- details of what will happen to assets and liabilities currently belonging to the entity which are to be sold, transferred, written off or realised as appropriate – this will lead to a profit or loss on realisation for the vendor.

- how repayment or settlement of capital of the selling entity is to be arranged.

Test your understanding 3 – Smith and Thompson

Smith has agreed to acquire the net assets, excluding the bank balance, and the debenture liability which is to be paid off in cash, of Thompson. The purchase consideration comprises the following:

	$000
50,000 equity shares @ $1 at a fair value of $1.04	52,000
$30,000 debenture loan issued at par value	30,000
Cash	18,000
	———
	100,000
	———

When determining the consideration to be paid, the directors of Smith valued the land and buildings of Thompson at $40,000, inventory at $15,000 and receivables at carrying value, subject to a 3% write off for bad debts.

After the sale, Thompson is liquidated.

The statement of financial position of Thompson immediately before the acquisition is as follows:

	$
Non-current assets:	
Land and buildings	24,000
Plant and machinery	22,000
	———
	46,000
Current assets:	
Inventory	19,000
Receivables	20,000
Bank	5,000
	———
	90,000
	———

	$
Equity and liabilities:	
Equity shares @ $1	30,000
Share premium	10,000
Retained earnings	16,000
	———
	56,000
Non-current liabilities:	
6% debentures	20,000
Current liabilities:	
Trade payables	14,000
	———
	90,000
	———

Required:

- **Prepare the closing entries for Thompson**
- **Prepare the opening statement of financial position for Smith**

Small and Medium-sized Entities

UK GAAP has had a reporting standard for smaller companies, the Financial Reporting Standard for Smaller Entities "FRSSE" since 1997. The FRSSE can be adopted by entities in the UK who meet the size criteria of being a small company as defined below. Note that if a UK entity does not apply the FRSSE must comply with all relevant elements of UK GAAP, such as reporting standards and UITF statements.

More recently, the IASB has developed an equivalent reporting framework for smaller entities, IFRS for SME which was published in July 2009. The content of this chapter includes comparison between the FRSSE and IFRS for SME. The UK has approved IFRS for SME and initially set the effective date as 1 January 2013, with comparatives required from 2012, subject to appropriate legal and regulatory issues to be dealt with, and to allow time for those companies who want to adopt the IFRS for SME to arrange compliance with its requirements. Note that the current timetable for implementation of revisions to UK GAAP (including adoption of the principles within IFRS for SME) proposes that changes will be approved during 2013 and be effective for accounting periods commencing on or after 1 January 2015. This issue is considered further within the current issues chapter of this publication.

The UK also has financial reporting and filing requirements based upon size criteria specified in the CA 2006 as follows:

	Small-sized	Medium-sized
Turnover max. (£m)	6.5	25.9
Balance sheet total max. (£m)	3.26	12.9
Number of employees max.	50	250

The size criteria exclude banks, building societies, insurance and financial services companies, regardless of their size. This also applies to members of a group containing any of these companies. The UK FRSSE applies to individual entities who meet the definition of being small per CA 2006; such entities are required only to publish a balance sheet and limited supporting disclosure notes. They can choose not to have an annual audit (s477–478 CA 2006), although it must be remembered that holders of 10% or more of any class of shares can request that an audit be performed.

One distinction between IFRS for SME and UK GAAP is that IFRS for SME requires a statement of cash flows to be included as part of the annual financial statements. Under UK GAAP, this is not required for entities that meet the definition of a small-sized company (whether or not they choose to apply the FRSSE).

Medium-sized entities disclose turnover whilst having limited disclosure relating to cost of sales, gross profit and other operating income, but there is very little further exemption from accounting and disclosure requirements.

Small Groups

Small groups are able to exempt themselves from audit provided the group includes no ineligible entities (see above) and that it qualifies as a small group for the entire year based upon the following size criteria:

	Before consolidation adjustments	After consolidation adjustments
Group aggregate turnover max. (£m)	7.8	6.5
Balance sheet total max. (£m)	3.9	3.26
Number of employees max.	50	250

Note that there is no equivalent exemption for medium-sized groups.

Entity reconstruction and insolvency issues

As part of the UK variant syllabus, students are required to have knowledge of the legal requirements associated with aspects of entity insolvency, reorganisation and reconstructions. Note that company administrators and liquidators must hold the appropriate qualifications to perform corporate administration and liquidation work.

Capital reduction scheme

Formalised procedures (s641 Companies Act 2006) detailed in law to reduce either the number of shares in issue, or the nominal value per share in issue, or both the number and nominal value of shares in issue. There is a simplified procedure for private companies, which does not require court approval, comprising a special resolution passed by the members, together with a statement of corporate solvency signed by the directors, which are filed at Companies House.

The equivalent scheme for a public company requires a special resolution passed by the members, together with an application to court. The court will not approve the scheme unless it is satisfied that all creditors have been notified and had time to object to the scheme; their amounts due are either paid or secured.

Administration

Administration involves the appointment of an insolvency practitioner, known as an administrator, to manage the affairs, business and property of a company. It was first introduced by Schedule 16 IA 1986, but has subsequently been amended by the Enterprise Act 2002. Administration is often used as an alternative to putting a company into liquidation, e.g. to:

- rescue a company in financial difficulty with the aim of allowing it to continue as a going concern, or

- achieve a better result for the creditors than would be likely if the company were to be wound up, or

- realise property to pay one or more secured or preferential creditors.

An administrator can be appointed by any of the following persons:

- the court, in response to a petition by, e.g. a creditor, the directors or the company itself, or

- the holder of a qualifying floating charge over the company's assets, or

- the company or its directors provided that winding up has not already begun.

Liquidation

This is the winding up of a limited company to bring its existence to an end. It may be a:

- compulsory liquidation (s122 Insolvency Act 1986) whereby a petition is presented to the court, and a winding up order is granted. The most frequently used grounds for use of these proceedings is where a judgement debt of £750 or more is unpaid after more than three weeks, or where the court considers that it is 'just and equitable' to wind up the company. A liquidator will be appointed to realise the assets and distribute then in accordance with the respective claims of the various classes of creditor, and also to the members if there is any surplus.

- voluntary liquidation, which identifies that, in the first instance, the members have passed a special resolution to wind up the company, which can be done for any reason, but normally it is a reflection of the company being in financial difficulties. In principle, a liquidator is appointed who then realises and distributes the assets based upon the respective rights of the different creditors, with the ordinary shareholders taking any surplus thereafter. It may either be:

  - a members' voluntary liquidation, where the company is solvent, which is supported by a declaration of solvency by the directors (s89 insolvency Act 1986) and a liquidator is appointed by the members (s91 Insolvency Act 1986). In principle, as creditors will be paid in full, they have no rights in respect of this process, other than being paid what is due to them, ; or

  - a creditors' voluntary liquidation where the company is insolvent, or is identified as being insolvent during a members' voluntary winding up, . A meeting of creditors will follow that of the members and they may choose to appoint a different liquidator (s100 Insolvency Act 1986). In this situation, not all creditors will be paid in full, normally unsecured creditors will not receive full payment, and equity shareholders will receive nothing.

6 Chapter summary

Reporting not-for-profit entities

- These entities are in the public sector or are charities
- The objective of these entities is to achieve their aims, not to make a profit
- Guidance is provided in SORP 2005 and the ASB's Statement of Principles for public benefit entities

Small and medium-sized entities

- These entities need exemptions from some of the requirements of IFRSs
- Two possible solutions: exemption or differential reporting

Entity reconstruction

- Going concern issues
- Possible alternative to liquidation
- Accounting treatment

Test your understanding answers

Test your understanding 1 – SME

(1) SMEs are very different entities from the large listed companies that typically apply IFRS. The content of many IFRSs is not relevant to the needs of these smaller unlisted entities and many of them would be put off adopting IFRS due to the large reporting burden.

Primarily, the users of the financial statements of smaller entities are often banking institutions who have loaned money to the business. In many cases, small businesses are owner-managed and their focus is on the profitability and cash generation of the business. It makes sense that these entities should have their own reporting requirements more attuned to the needs of their businesses.

(2) There are two potential solutions to reporting for SMEs.
  (a) Exemptions from IFRS. A case can be made for requiring a lower level of disclosure from small and medium-sized entities, and in some countries this already happens.

  (b) Differential reporting. This is where a completely new set of standards is developed for small companies.

The first option is better, because it does not require completely new standards to be written and keeps both large and small companies applying the same standards even though the smaller companies are applying abbreviated versions. this is the approach used in the UK with the issue of the Financial Reporting Standard for Smaller Entities ("FRSSE") which has then been updated periodically since it was first introduced in 1997.

(3) The IASB's method is a stand-alone standard for SMEs. The content of this will be a full IFRS that address transactions, events, or conditions commonly encountered by SMEs. It will provide a framework for the preparation of financial statements by a SME.

Those accounting requirements covered by reporting standards relating to transactions, events or conditions not generally encountered by SMEs are not included in the IFRS for SMEs. The goal is to minimise the circumstances in which an SME would need to fall back to full IFRS for guidance on how to account for a particular transaction or situation.

**Wire – statement of financial position at 30 June 20X1
(after reconstruction)**

	$
Non-current assets:	
Land and buildings at valuation	160,000
Equipment	30,000
Financial asset – investment in Cord	nil
	———
	190,000
Current assets:	
Inventory	50,000
Receivables (70,692 x 90%)	63,623
Bank (W2)	92,287
	———
	395,910
	———

	$
Equity and liabilities:	
Equity shares @ $0.25 (W3)	140,000
Share premium (W3)	17,800
Retained earnings	nil
Capital reserve (W1)	1,863
	———
	159,663
Non-current liabilities:	
9.5% debentures (W4)	124,000
Current liabilities:	
Trade payables	112,247
	———
	395,910
	———

Wire – workings:

(W1) Reconstruction account

	$	$
Carrying values:		
Land and buildings	193,246	
Equipment	60,754	
Investment in Cord	27,000	
Inventory	120,247	
Receivables written off (70,962 x 10%)	7,069	
Deficit on retained earnings written off	39,821	
Revised valuations:		
Land and buildings		160,000
Equipment		30,000
Investment in Cord		60,000
Inventory		50,000
Share capital reduced (200,000 @ $0.75)		150,000
Capital reserve (bal fig)	1,863	
	———	———
	450,000	450,000
	———	———

(W2) Bank account

		$
Overdraft		(36,713)
New equity share issue	200,000 @ $0.30	60,000
New debenture issue	9,000 at par value	9,000
Sale of investment – Cord		60,000
		———
		92,287
		———

(W3) Shareholdings

	Equity shares		Share premium
	Number	$	$
Redesignated existing shares @ $0.25 each	200,000	50,000	
New issue @ $0.30 each	200,000	50,000	10,000
Part-exchange of 5% debenture	140,000	35,000	
Debenture interest (12,800 – 5,000)**	20,000	5.000	7,800
	560,000	140,000	17,800

**8% deb interest on $80,000 p.a. for 2 years = $12,800 – $5,000 (20,000 @ $0.25) = $7,800 share premium.

(W4) Debenture loan

	$
8% debenture 20X4 deferred to 20X9 with 9.5% interest rate	80,000
New 9.5% debentures 20X9 – nominal value	9,000
New 9.5% debentures 20X9 – part conversion of 5% debenture	35,000
	124,000

Advice to equity and debt holders:

Based upon the situation at 30 June 20X1 before the reconstruction scheme was devised, the following can be ascertained:

(1) There are sufficient assets to repay the secured debentures and perhaps most of the arrears of interest.

(2) Unsecured creditors would be unlikely to receive payment in full for amounts owed.

(3) Equity shareholders are unlikely to receive anything upon liquidation.

If a reconstruction scheme is to be agreed between the various parties, those who are in the strongest position (secured creditors) would expect to give up the least. Those in the weakest position (unsecured creditors and equity holders), would be expected to sacrifice more of their current entitlement to have any chance of recovery in the future.

The position of Wire if it was to go into liquidation is as follows:

		$
Land and buildings		160,000
Plant and equipment		30,000
Investment		60,000
Inventory		50,000
Receivables (70,962 x 90%)		63,623
Assets available		363,263
Secured liabilities (80,000 + 70,000)		(150,000)
		213,623
Current liabilities:		
Overdraft	36,713	
Interest	12,800	
Trade payables	112,247	
		(161,760)
Available to equity holders		51,863

The above summary identifies the position of the various stakeholders if there was no reconstruction scheme and Wire was liquidated. The debenture holders would be sure to receive their loan repayment, together with probably all of the arrears of interest, depending upon realised values of the assets and no other significant liabilities being uncovered.

The equity holders would not receive a full return of the nominal value of their capital, receiving only approximately (51,863 / 200,000) $0.26 per share.

Consequently, if the reconstruction scheme is implemented:

(1) The debenture holders are to be offered an increased rate of interest, but must also accept extension of the lending period to 20X9. It continues to be secured against land and buildings. Their position is relatively strong and safe.

(2) Some of the debenture holders have exchanged some of their legal rights as creditors for rights as equity holders. They must hope that Wire becomes profitable so that they can receive dividends in future years and that the share price increases. In addition, they must hope that, even if Wire gets into financial difficulties at a later date, there are still sufficient assets available to repay them, after the secured creditors have been repaid.

(3) It would appear that Wire will make profit after tax if the reconstruction goes ahead and if the profit forecast is reliable as follows:

	$
Profit before tax and interest	50,000
Less: debenture interest (9.5% x $124,000)	11,780
Profit before tax	38,220
Tax @ 25%	(9,555)
Profit available to equity holders	28,665

Earnings per share would therefore be: $28,665 / 560,000 = 5.1 cents per share (i.e $0.051 per share)

Test your understanding 3 – Smith and Thompson

Closing accounting for Thompson

(W1) Realisation account

	$	$
Carrying values:		
Land and buildings	24,000	
Plant and equipment	22,000	
Inventory	19,000	
Receivables	20,000	
Creditors		14,000
Purchase consideration		100,000
Profit on realisation (bal fig) (W3)	29,000	
	———	———
	114,000	114,000
	———	———

(W2) Bank and cash

	$	$
Balance b/fwd	5,000	
Cash received for sale of business	18,000	
Debenture stock paid off		20,000
Cash to shareholders as part of winding up (W3)		3,000
	———	———
	23,000	23,000
	———	———

(W3) Capital settlement on winding up

	$	$
Equity shares received at FV	52,000	
Debenture received	30,000	
Cash return to equity holders (W2)	3,000	
Share capital		30,000
Share premium		10,000
Retained earnings		16,000
Profit on realisation (W1)		29,000
	———	———
	85,000	85,000
	———	———

(W4) **Receivable Account – Smith**

	$	$
Purchase consideration due		
Equity shares	100,000	
Shares at FV		52,000
Debenture loan		30,000
Cash		18,000
	100,000	100,000

Smith – Statement of Financial Position

Assets	$
Goodwill (balancing figure)	17,600
Land and buildings	40,000
Plant and equipment	22,000
	79,600
Current assets:	
Inventory	15,000
Receivables	19,400
	114,000

Equity and liabilities	$
Equity share capital @ $1	50,000
Share premium	2,000
Non-current liabilities: Debenture loan	30,000
Current liabilities:	
Trade payables	14,000
Bank overdraft	18,000
	114,000

Notes:

* Goodwill is identified as a residual amount as all other values are known for the SOFP.

** The fair value of equity shares issued = 50,000 @ $1.04 = $52,000

Of this: NV = $50,000, with share premium of $2,000.

Adoption of IFRS

Chapter learning objectives

Upon completion of this chapter you will be able to:

- apply and discuss the accounting implications of the first time adoption of a body of new accounting standards

- outline the issues in implementing a change to new accounting standards including organisational, behavioural and procedural changes within the entity

- evaluate the implications of worldwide convergence with International Financial Reporting Standards

- discuss the implementation issues arising from the convergence process

- identify the reasons for major differences in accounting practices, including culture

- discuss the influence of national regulators on international financial reporting.

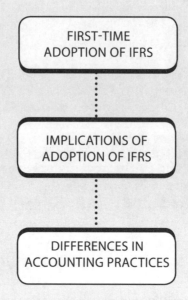

IFRS 1 First time adoption of IFRS

Due to the drive towards convergence of reporting standards between IAS/IFRS and US GAAP, and also national moves to harmonise national standards with IAS/IFRS, many of the historical differences between the different GAAPs have been reduced or eliminated. Where differences remain between IAS/ IFRS and a particular set of national reporting standards, they are not as significant as they may have been, say, 20 years ago. Consequently, the importance of first-time adoption of IFRS, and the application of IFRS 1, may be perceived to be less important than it has been in the past. However, it is still of importance for several reasons:

- Entities who expect to seek a listing for the first time still need guidance on how the adoption process should be managed, accounted for, and disclosed in the financial statements.

- Entities who have no expectation of seeking a listing may choose to adopt IFRS if they perceive that IFRS is more relevant to their situation.

- Unlisted multinational corporate groups may choose to adopt IAS/IFRS as the basis for financial reporting throughout the group. This may save time and resources in the preparation of management information throughout the group, and streamline group annual financial reporting requirements.

- Entities may believe that adoption of IFRS could assist in their efforts to raise capital; if potential capital providers are familiar with IFRS, it may ease their evaluation of any capital investment opportunity.

- Entities may believe that they are 'doing the right thing' by adopting IFRS as it is already used by other, usually listed and often larger entities.

The above commentary demonstrates the significant progress to date made by the IASB and FASB towards achieve their desired outcome of producing high quality, compatible accounting standards that are suitable for both domestic and cross-border financial reporting. While there is still some way to go, and numerous obstacles to be negotiated, there appears to be a momentum which will ensure that progress continues in the coming

Introduction

- IFRS 1 First-time adoption of international financial reporting standards sets out the procedures to follow when an entity adopts IFRS in its published financial statements for the first time.

- Before adopting IFRS it will have applied its own national standards. This is called previous GAAP.

Definition

A **first-time adopter** is an entity that, for the first time, makes an explicit and unreserved statement that its annual financial statements comply with IFRS.

There are five issues that need to be addressed when adopting IFRS.

(1) The date of transition to IFRSs.

(2) Which IFRSs should be adopted.

(3) How gains or losses arising on adopting IFRS should be accounted for.

(4) The explanations and disclosures to be made in the year of transition.

(5) What exemptions are available.

Date of transition

Definition

The **date of transition** is the beginning of the earliest period for which an entity presents full comparative information under IFRS in its first IFRS financial statements.

- IFRS should be applied from the first day of the first set of financial statements published in compliance with IFRS. This is called the opening IFRS statement of financial position.

- Because IFRS require comparative statements to be published, the opening IFRS statement of financial position for an entity adopting IFRS for the first time in its 31 December 2008 financial statements and presenting one year of comparative information will be 1 January 2007. This is the transition date – the first day of the comparative period.

- The opening IFRS statement of financial position itself need not be published, but it will provide the opening balances for the comparative period.

- If full comparative financial statements for preceding periods are published, then these too must comply with IFRS.

- If only selected information is disclosed about preceding periods, then these need not comply with IFRS. However, this non-compliance must be disclosed.

Which IFRS?

- The entity should use the same accounting policies for all the periods presented; these policies should be based solely on IFRS in force at the reporting date. (The term IFRS includes any IAS and Interpretations still in force.)

- A major problem for entities preparing for the change-over is that IFRSs themselves keep changing.

- Entities will have to collect information enabling them to prepare statements under previous GAAP, current IFRS and any proposed new standards or amendments.

- IFRS 1 states that the opening IFRS statement of financial position must:
  - recognise all assets and liabilities required by IFRS
  - not recognise assets and liabilities not permitted by IFRS
  - reclassify all assets, liabilities and equity components in accordance with IFRS
  - measure all assets and liabilities in accordance with IFRS.

Further points

Reporting gains and losses

Any gains or losses arising on the adoption of IFRS should be recognised directly in retained earnings, i.e. not recognised.

Explanations and disclosures

- Entities must explain how the transition to IFRS affects their reported financial performance, financial position and cash flows. Two main disclosures are required, which reconcile equity and profits.
  - The entity's equity as reported under previous GAAP must be reconciled to the equity reported under IFRS at two dates.
    - The date of transition. This is the opening reporting date.
    - The last statement of financial position prepared under previous GAAP.
  - The last annual reported under previous GAAP must be reconciled to the same year's total comprehensive income prepared under IFRS.

- Any material differences between the previous GAAP and the IFRS cash flows must also be explained.

- When preparing its first IFRS statements, an entity may identify errors made in previous years, or make or reverse impairments of assets. These adjustments must be disclosed separately.

Improvements to IFRS issued May 2010 clarified the following points:

- when an entity changes an accounting policy after issue of interim statements, but before the first set of IFRS annual statements, it must explain those changes and update reconciliations between previous GAAP applied and IFRS. IAS 8 relating to change of accounting policy does not apply to such changes.

- an entity adopting IFRS for the first time is able to use revaluation basis for deemed cost at the measurement date (usually the start of the accounting period) based upon measurement events that occurred at any point during the period covered by the first IFRS financial statements.

- an entity adopting IFRS for the first time may elect to use the previous GAAP carrying amount for items of property, plant and equipment or intangible assets that were used in operations subject to rate regulation.

The above three points are effective for accounting periods commencing on or after 1 January 2011, although earlier adoption is permitted.

Improvements to IFRS 2009-11 published in May 2012 confirms that it is possible for IFRS 1 to be applicable more than once. Where this is the case, if the most recent previous annual financial statements did not comply with IFRS, then either:

- IFRS 1may be applied, or

- IFRS must be applied retrospectively as if there had been no interruption in its application.

The following disclosures should be made:

- the reason application of IFRS was stopped,

- the reason IFRS application has been resumed, and

- the reason for electing not to apply IFRS 1, if applicable.

Borrowing costs capitalised under a previous GAAP before the date of transition to IFRS may be carried forward without adjustment at the date of transition. Borrowing costs incurred on or after the date of transition should be accounted for in accordance with IAS 23. A first-time adopter can choose to apply IAS 23 at a date earlier than the transition date.

Exemptions

IFRS 1 grants limited exemptions in situations where the cost of compliance would outweigh the benefits to the user. For example:

- Previous business combinations do not have to be restated in accordance with IFRS. In particular, mergers (pooling of interests) do not have to be re-accounted for as acquisitions, previously written off goodwill does not have to be reinstated and the fair values of assets and liabilities may be retained. However, an impairment test for any remaining goodwill must be made in the opening statement of financial position.

- ED 2009/11 Improvements to IFRS issued in August 2009 identifies that, if there are any changes to accounting policies in the first year of adoption of IFRS, but after the issue of the first interim statements, the changes need to be explained and reconciliations required should also be updated.

- ED 2009/11 also confirms that revaluations used as a basis for deemed cost may arise during the period covered by the first IFRS financial statements, rather than having been done in the period prior to this. Normally, deemed cost would be either fair value, determined in accordance with IAS 39, or the carrying value under previous national standards.

- An entity may elect to use fair values for property, plant and equipment, investment properties and intangibles as the deemed cost under IFRS. This fair value may have been a market-based revaluation or an indexed amount. This means that even if the cost model is used for these assets under IFRS, this valuation can be used to replace cost initially. Therefore, the entity can use fair value as the deemed cost but then not have to revalue the assets each year.

- Some actuarial gains and losses on pension schemes are left unrecognised under IAS 19 **Employee benefits**. A first-time adopter may find it easier to recognise all gains and losses at the date of transition and this option is given in IFRS 1.

- Past currency translation gains and losses included in revenue reserves need not be separated out into the currency translation reserve.

- Under IAS 32 **Financial instruments: presentation part of the proceeds of convertible debt** is classified as equity. If the debt had been repaid by the date of transition, no adjustment is needed for the equity component.

- If a subsidiary adopts IFRS later than its parent, then the subsidiary may value its assets and liabilities either at its own transition date or its parent's transition date (which would normally be easier).

There are also three situations where retrospective application of IFRS is prohibited. These relate to derecognition of financial assets and liabilities, hedging and estimates.

The IASB thought that it would be impractical to obtain the information necessary to restate past financial statements, and that restating past fair values and estimates was open to manipulation.

Implications of adoption of IFRS

There are a number of considerations to be made when adopting IFRS for the first time. The key factors on converting from local GAAP to IFRS are discussed below.

Factors to consider in implementing IFRS

Initial evaluation

The transition to IFRS requires careful and timely planning. Initially there are a number of questions that must be asked to assess the current position within the entity.

(a) Is there knowledge of IFRS within the entity?

(b) Are there any agreements (such as bank covenants) that are dependent on local GAAP?

(c) Will there be a need to change the information systems?

(d) Which IFRSs will affect the entity?

(e) Is this an opportunity to improve the accounting systems?

Once the initial evaluation of the current position has been made, the entity can determine the nature of any assistance required.

They may need to:

- engage IFRS experts for assistance. Such experts can provide staff training and assistance on the preparation of the opening statement of financial position and first set of accounts. They can inform the entity of the information that will be needed to ensure a smooth transition to IFRS. It is essential that the entity personnel understand the key differences between local GAAP and IFRS and in particular the IFRS that will most affect the entity

- inform key stakeholders of the impact that IFRS could have on reported performance. This includes analysts, bankers, loan creditors and employees. Head office personnel will not be the only staff to require training; managers of subsidiaries will need to know the impact on their finance functions as there will be budgeting and risk management issues

- produce a project plan that incorporates the resource requirements, training needs, management teams and timetable with a timescale that ensures there is enough time to produce the first IFRS financial statements

- investigate the effect of the change on the computer systems. Establish if the current system can easily be changed and, if not, what the alternatives will be. Potentially the IT cost could be significant if changes need to be made.

Other considerations

Aside from the practical aspect of implementing the move to IFRS, there are a number of other factors to consider:

(i) **Debt covenants**

– The entity will have to consider the impact of the adoption of IFRS on debt covenants and other legal contracts.

– Covenants based on financial position ratios (for example the gearing ratio) and profit or loss measures such as interest cover will probably be affected significantly by the adoption of IFRS.

– Debt covenants may need to be renegotiated and rewritten, as it would not seem to be sensible to retain covenants based on a local GAAP if this is no longer to be used.

(ii) **Performance related pay**

– There is a potential impact on income of moving to IFRS, which causes a problem in designing an appropriate means of determining executive bonuses, employee performance related pay and long-term incentive plans.

– With the increase in the use of fair values and the potential recycling of gains and losses under IFRS (e.g. IAS 21 **The effects of changes in foreign exchange rates**), the identification of relevant measures of performance will be quite difficult.

– If there are unrealised profits reported in profit or loss, the entity will not wish to pay bonuses on the basis of profits that may never be realised in cash.

– There may be volatility in the reported figures, which will have little to do with financial performance but could result in major differences in the pay awarded to a director from one year to another.

(iii) **Views of financial analysts**

– It is important that the entity looks at the way it is to communicate the effects of a move to IFRS with the markets and the analysts.

– The focus of the communication should be to provide assurance about the process and to quantify the changes expected. Unexpected changes in ratios and profits could adversely affect share prices.

– Presentations can be made to interested parties of the potential impact of IFRS. Analysts should have more transparent and comparable data about multinational entities once IFRS has been adopted.

> - Consistency over account classifications, formats, disclosures and measurement will assist the analyst's interpretation.
> - Analysts will be particularly concerned about earnings volatility that may affect how they discount future profits to arrive at a present fair value for the business.

Benefits of harmonisation

There are a number of reasons why the harmonisation of accounting standards would be beneficial. Businesses operate on a global scale and investors make investment decisions on a worldwide basis. There is thus a need for financial information to be presented on a consistent basis. The advantages are as follows.

(1) Multi-national entities

Multi-national entities would benefit from closer harmonisation for the following reasons.

(a) Access to international finance would be easier as financial information is more understandable if it is prepared on a consistent basis.

(b) In a business that operates in several countries, the preparation of financial information would be easier as it would all be prepared on the same basis.

(c) There would be greater efficiency in accounting departments.

(d) Consolidation of financial statements would be easier.

(2) Investors

If investors wish to make decisions based on the worldwide availability of investments, then better comparisons between entities are required. Harmonisation assists this process, as financial information would be consistent between different entities from different regions.

(3) International economic groupings

International economic groupings, e.g. the EU, could work more effectively if there were international harmonisation of accounting practices. Part of the function of international economic groupings is to make cross-border trade easier. Similar accounting regulations would improve access to capital markets and therefore help this process.

Reasons for differences in accounting practices

The reasons why, failing the introduction of a common set of international reporting standards, accounting practices may differ from one country to another, include the following.

- **Legal systems**. In some countries, financial statements are prepared according to a strict code imposed by the government. This is often because the accounts are being prepared primarily for tax purposes rather than for investment.

- **Professional traditions**. In contrast to countries where accounting standards are embedded in legislation, other countries have a strong and influential accounting profession and can rely on the profession to draft relevant standards.

- **User groups**. As mentioned above, in some countries the tax authorities are the main users of accounts, and so a standardised, rule-based approach to accounting emerges. Quite often, depreciation rates will be set by law rather than being based upon useful lives. In countries where businesses are generally financed by loans (rather than by equity) then financial statements will focus on a business' ability to service and pay back its debts. In the UK and the US, businesses are generally financed through equity. In these countries, the shareholders share the risks of profits and losses, and so they demand full disclosure of a business' financial affairs.

- **Nationalism**. Individual countries believe that their own standards are the best.

- **Culture**. Differences in culture can lead to differences in the objective and method of accounting.

Culture and local custom

Financial reporting practice may be influenced by cultural factors in a number of ways.

- Some nationalities are naturally conservative and this may affect their attitude to accounting estimates, particularly when it comes to providing for liabilities.

- Religion may affect accounting practices; for example, Islamic law forbids the charging or accepting of interest.

- Different nationalities have different attitudes to risk. For example, in Japan high gearing is usual and is a sign of confidence in an entity.

- Attitudes to disclosure also vary. Some cultures value openness while others have a strong tradition of confidentiality.

- In the UK and the USA, the main objective of management and shareholders is generally to maximise profit in the short term. However, in other countries, investors and management may have different or wider objectives, such as long-term growth, stability, benefiting the community and safeguarding the interests of employees.

Convergence of IFRS with US GAAP

In October 2002, the IASB and the US standard setter the Financial Accounting Standards Board (FASB) approved the Norwalk Agreement marking a step towards formalising their commitment to the convergence of international accounting standards. This led to a Memorandum of Understanding (MoU) in February 2006, subsequently updated in 2008, which provided the basis for both short-term and long-term projects to increase the extent of convergence between IFRS and US GAAP.

The objective of the updated MoU in 2008 was to enable companies to file annual financial statements, prepared in accordance with IFRS GAAP, to be accepted by the Securities and Exchange Commission (SEC) in the US. This followed on from an announcement in 2007 that the SEC would no longer require IFRS-compliant financial statements filed with the SEC to also include a reconciliation to US GAAP. Based on the 2008 MoU, a small group of companies began to prepare their financial statements using IFRS with effect from years starting 15 December 2009 onwards. Companies eligible must be one of the 20 largest in that industry (measured by market capitalisation), and financial reporting by those 20 major companies must have IFRS GAAP as the major basis for financial reporting.

This announcement was followed, in January 2009, by a SEC statement that a mandatory two-year dual-reporting period would begin for most companies in 2012, with IFRS only required by 2014. The SEC's decision reflects the increasing acceptance of IFRS as a widely used and high-quality financial reporting language.

Projects may be grouped as follows:

- financial crisis related - this includes the common control project which resulted in the publication of IFRS 10 and IFRS 12. It also includes work resulting in the publication of IFRS 13 fair value measurement and the on-going project to replace IAS 39 dealing with recognition and measurement of financial instruments. All of these projects form part of the MoU.

- Other MoU projects - this includes accounting for joint arrangements which resulted in the publication of IFRS 11 and post-employment benefits which resulted in revision of IAS 19.

- Other projects - this includes the annual improvements process and the management commentary project which resulted in the publication of PS 1. These projects generally are not part of the MoU.

A key driver towards convergence has been the global financial crisis. Whilst there were already proposals to harmonise accounting for financial instruments, this issue took on increased significance and priority. IFRS 9 Financial Instruments currently deals with recognition and measurement of financial assets and financial liabilities and is effective for accounting periods commencing on or after 1 January 2015. Work continues on other aspects of accounting for financial instruments, including impairment and hedging. IFRS 7 has also been updated to deal with related disclosures. Accounting for financial instruments is considered in detail within chapter 16 of this publication.

Currently, the IASB and FASB have completed work on the short-term convergence project. The scope of the short-term convergence project was limited to those differences between US GAAP and IFRS in which convergence around a high-quality solution appears achievable in the short term (by 2008). Because of the nature of the differences, it was expected that a solution could be achieved for a particular issue by choosing between either the existing US GAAP or the IFRS treatment, and then requiring the preferred treatment to be adopted by both IFRS and US GAAP.

Topics covered by the short-term convergence project which resulted in amendment of IFRS include:

- IAS 23 permitted borrowing costs on the construction of an asset to be either capitalised or written off, whereas US GAAP required such costs to be capitalised. IAS 23 was amended in March 2007 and is now in line with US GAAP; from 1 January 2009, entities have been required to capitalise borrowing costs when specified criteria have been met.

- IFRS 8 supersedes IAS 14 and deals with segmental reporting. IFRS 8 identifies reportable segments based on a 'managerial approach', which is consistent with the approach adopted under US GAAP, rather than the 'risk and returns' approach adopted by IAS 14. This is considered further in chapter 13 of this publication.

- IAS 1 was revised in September 2007, with the balance sheet renamed as the 'statement of financial position'. The income statement was renamed as the 'statement of comprehensive income', and now includes items of income and expense that are not recognised in profit or loss but were directly recognised in equity, such as revaluation gains. Note that IAS 1 has been further amended and suggests 'statement of profit or loss and other comprehensive income' as the performance statement title, although this not compulsory.

- IFRS 11 Joint arrangements established principles for entities that have entered into joint arrangements, whether they are a joint venture or a joint operation. This is considered further with chapter 1 of this publication.

Other short-term projects completed by amendment to US GAAP include inventory accounting, voluntary changes in accounting policy and research and development.

As at mid-2012, there are two short-term projects not yet completed – accounting for income tax which led to the issue of a joint discussion paper in 2008 but was subsequently evaluated as a low-priority project and accounting for investment property entities which is in the course of development to revise US GAAP.

Significant progress has also been made on longer-term projects as follows:

- IAS 27 and IFRS 3 were amended in January 2008. The new standards change the calculation of goodwill (and non-controlling interests) and also the treatment of piecemeal acquisitions. Along with changes to US GAAP, these amendments bring the accounting treatment for goodwill into line, although some differences still exist, such as the definition of control and fair value. A review is scheduled to commence in 2012, by which date the revised standards would have been applied for two years.

- IFRS 10 Consolidated financial statements and IFRS 12 Interests in other entities were published in May 2011. These standards provided more comprehensive guidance to determine whether control was exercised over another entity whilst also extending and standardising the associated disclosure requirements. These issues are considered further in chapter 1 of this publication.

- IFRS 13 fair value measurement was issued in May 2011 and provides a definition for what constitutes a fair value measurement, together with a single source of guidance on how it is determined. Fair value measurement is considered further in chapter 8 of this publication.

- IAS 19 post-employment benefits was revised in 2011 to require more standardised accounting treatment and presentation of amounts and disclosures relating to defined benefit retirement plans in particular. Post-employment benefits are considered further in chapter 10 of this publication.

- IAS 1 presentation of financial statements was amended in 2011 relating to presentation of items of other comprehensive income; in particular, items of other comprehensive income should now be grouped for disclosure as being either items that may be reclassified (i.e. recycled) to profit or loss in subsequent accounting periods, and those which will not be reclassified.

- IFRS 7 Financial instruments: disclosures was amended in October 2010 to include additional disclosures dealing with aspects of derecognition and off-balance sheet activities. US GAAP accounting requirements were amended to bring it more into line with IFRS requirements. Disclosure requirements between IFRS and US GAAP were also substantially aligned.

Two long-term projects remain to be completed – investment entities and financial instruments with the characteristics of equity. The IASB issued an ED in August 2011 which proposed a definition and accounting treatment for investment entities. Current developments relating to investment entities are considered further in chapter 1 of this publication. Following the publication of a joint DP in February 2008 'Financial instruments with the characteristics of equity' was reassessed to be a low-priority project.

There are three further projects from the MoU on which progress is ongoing: revenue recognition, leases and financial instruments. In respect of revenue recognition, a revised ED was published in June 2011 with the objective of increasing the extent of convergence of accounting treatments and disclosure requirements between IFRS and US GAAP. Current developments relating to revenue recognition are considered in chapter 9 of this publication.

With regard to leases, a revised ED is expected to be issued in late 2012 or early 2013, with an approved standard published later in 2013. Leases are considered further in chapter 15 of this publication.

The financial instruments project comprises several smaller projects. Classification and measurement of financial assets and financial liabilities is now incorporated into IFRS 9. However, there is still more to be done on classification and measurement to achieve convergence, with new or revised reporting standards expected in 2013, in particular dealing with financial assets eligible to be accounted for at amortised cost.

Project work on asset and liability offsetting resulted in approval of common disclosure requirements incorporated into IFRS 7.

Work on impairment of financial assets has focussed upon joint development of a common 'expected loss' impairment model. An ED is expected late in 2012 to be followed by publication of a reporting standard in 2013.

There are considerable differences between the IASB and US FASB regarding hedge accounting requirements and disclosures. The IASB published an ED in June 2010, with publication of a reporting standard scheduled for late 2012 in relation to general hedge accounting, with an ED expected in late 2012 on the subject of macro (i.e. portfolio) hedge accounting.

The IASB and FASB are also undertaking other joint projects which are not part of the MoU. Joint projects are those that the standard setters have agreed to conduct simultaneously in a coordinated manner, involving the sharing of staff resources, and every effort is made to keep joint projects on a similar time schedule at each board as follows:

- Earnings per share – this has involved both IASB and FASB reviewing proposed amendments to the calculation of diluted earnings per share. This project is currently paused.

- Conceptual framework – to date, this has focused on the objectives of financial reporting and the qualitative characteristics of financial reporting information. The Conceptual Framework for Financial Reporting 2010 is considered within chapter 8 of this Publication

Technical article

Tony Sweetman of Kaplan Publishing wrote an article discussing convergence between IFRS and US GAAP in the November 2009 issue of Student Accountant magazine. You can access this article from the ACCA website (www.accaglobal.com)

Differences in accounting treatment

Major differences between financial accounting practices in different countries

Introduction

In recent years, more and more countries are harmonising their accounting standards with IFRS. At the present time, the US standard setter, the Financial Accounting Standards Board (FASB), and the IASB are involved in a joint project to harmonise their accounting standards. The ASB in the UK has also adopted a number of international standards. However, some differences remain.

Goodwill	IASB	US GAAP	UK GAAP
Preferred treatment	Capitalise but do not amortise, subject to annual impairment review	Capitalise but do not amortise, subject to annual impairment review	Capitalise and amortise over economic useful life
Allowed alternative treatment	–	–	No need to amortise if life is indefinite and impairment is tested annually

Deferred tax	IASB	US GAAP	UK GAAP
Preferred treatment	Liability method, full provision based on temporary differences	Liability method, full provision based on temporary differences	Liability method, full provision based on timing differences

Valuation of property	IASB	US GAAP	UK GAAP
Preferred treatment	No preferred treatment	Cost	No preferred treatment
Allowed alternative	Cost or valuation	–	Cost or valuation
Not allowed	–	Valuation	–

Capitalisation of development costs	IASB	US GAAP	UK GAAP
Preferred treatment	Recognise such costs as assets when specified criteria are met and write off as expense when the criteria are not met	Write off as incurred	May recognise as assets when specific criteria are met; choice of immediate write off also permitted

Profits on long-term contracts	IASB	US GAAP	UK GAAP
Preferred treatment	Percentage of completion method	Percentage of completion or completed contract method	Percentage of completion method
Not allowed	Completed contract method	–	Completed contract method

Borrowing costs	IASB	US GAAP	UK GAAP
Preferred treatment	Capitalisation compulsory for certain assets	Capitalisation compulsory for certain assets	No preferred treatment
Allowed alternative treatment	–	–	Capitalise or write off immediately
Not allowed	Immediate write-off	Immediate write off for certain assets	–

Reconciliation statements

In some cases, an entity with a listing on more than one stock exchange may still be required to produce financial information that is expressed in terms of its domestic accounting policies.

A reconciliation statement reconciles the accounts prepared under domestic accounting policies with another GAAP, such as US GAAP or IFRS.

The role of national standard setters

- The harmonisation process has gathered pace in the last few years. From 2005 all European listed entities were required to adopt IFRS in their group financial statements. Many other countries including Australia, Canada and New Zealand decided to follow a similar process. National standard setters are committed to a framework of accounting standards based on IFRS.

- Additionally, the US are committed to harmonise with IFRS and the FASB and the IASB are aiming for convergence over the next few years.

- In Europe, the EU has adopted IFRS for use in member countries, with the exception of part of IAS 39 Financial Instruments: recognition and measurement.

- In Japan, until the 1990s, financial reporting was not transparent and while the economy prospered, there was little pressure for change. However, the Asian economic crisis changed the situation, and Japan has committed itself to developing new accounting standards more in line with the IASC model.

- In Russia, large-scale adoption of IFRS has been planned since 1998. It is expected that this will be achieved by 2010.

- India announced in 2007 that it has decided to fully converge with IFRS for accounting periods commencing on or after April 1 2011. In line with other countries, this decision will initially be applied to listed companies and public service entities.

- The overall impact of the above is that the trend towards closer international harmonisation of accounting practices is now set. Currently, 102 countries require or permit use of IFRS in the preparation of financial statements in their countries. By 2011, this figure is expected to reach 150. It will become increasingly difficult for domestic standard setters to justify domestic standards at odds with IFRSs.

The role of accounting standard setters and the IASB

- In February 2005, the IASB issued a memorandum setting out the responsibilities of the IASB and national standard setters. It is most relevant to those who have adopted or converged with IFRSs'. It deals with the responsibilities of national standard setters to facilitate adoption or convergence with IFRS.

- It includes the responsibilities of the IASB to ensure that it makes information available on a timely basis so that national standard setters can be informed of the IASB's plans. Sufficient time should be allowed in relation to consultative documents so that national standard setters have sufficient time to prepare the information in their own context and to receive comments from their own users.

- The national standard setters should deal with domestic barriers to adopting or converging with IFRS. They should avoid amending an IFRS when adopting it in their own jurisdiction, so that the issue of non-compliance with the IFRS does not arise. They should encourage their own constituents to communicate their technical views to the IASB and they themselves should respond with comments on a timely basis. They should also make known any differences of opinion that they have with a project as early as possible in the process.

Test your understanding 1 – Pailing

Pailing

Pailing, a public limited entity, is registered in Erehwon. Under the local legislation, it is allowed to prepare its financial statements using IFRS or local GAAP and it uses local GAAP.

Klese, a UK registered entity who has adopted IFRS, is considering buying the entity but wishes to restate Pailing's group financial statements so that they are consistent with IFRS before any decision is made.

The Pailing group's net profit for the period drawn up utilising local GAAP is $89 million for the year ending 31 March 20X1 and its group net assets under local GAAP is $225 million as at 31 March 20X1.

The following accounting practices under local GAAP have been determined.

(a) A change in accounting policies has been dealt with by a cumulative catch up adjustment that is included in the current year's income. During the year, the accounting policy for the capitalisation of interest was changed from capitalisation as part of the cost of non-current assets to charging directly to profit or loss for the year.

The total interest included in non-current assets was $30 million, of which only $3m relates to the current year.

(b) Pailing had acquired 100% of a subsidiary entity, Odd, on 31 March 20X1. The assets stated in the statement of financial position were based on the carrying value of the net assets of the subsidiary before any fair value adjustments. The fair value and the carrying value of the net assets of Odd at the date of acquisition were $28 million and $24 million respectively.

(c) Pailing had paid $32 million for the subsidiary, Odd, on 31 March 20X1. There is an agreement to pay contingent consideration of $2 million in a year's time if Odd makes a net profit of $1 million. In the current year, Odd has made losses of $2 million. Pailing has made a provision in the financial statements for this amount, charging it to profit or loss for the year.

(d) Pailing had spent $6 million during the period on development expenditure on a project that started commercial production on 28 February 20X1. So far, sales have been in excess of the forecast. Pailing writes off development expenditure as an expense in the period it is incurred.

Required:

Restate the Pailing group's net profit for the year ending 31 March 20X1 and net assets as at 31 March 20X1 in accordance with IFRS, commenting on your adjustments.

Current issues

The objective of this project is to amend IFRS 1 First-time Adoption of International Financial Reporting Standards to address potential challenges for entities and jurisdictions adopting IFRSs at some future date. In October 2011 ED/2011/5 Government Loans (Proposed amendments to IFRS 1) was published. The proposed amendment sets out how a first-time adopter would account for a government loan with a below-market rate of interest when they transition to IFRSs.

If adopted, this amendment would provide the same relief to first-time adopters as is granted to existing preparers of IFRS financial statements when applying IAS 20 Accounting for Government Grants and Disclosure of Government Assistance.

IAS 20 requires entities to measure government loans with a below-market rate of interest at fair value on initial recognition. A first-time adopter applying IAS 20 retrospectively to existing government loans at the date of transition to IFRSs would be required to identify a fair value at an earlier date. The proposed amendment would require that first-time adopters apply this requirement in IAS 20 prospectively to loans entered into on or after the date of transition to IFRSs. However, if an entity obtained the information necessary to apply these requirements to a government loan as a result of a past transaction at the time of initially accounting for that loan, then it may choose to apply IAS 20 retrospectively to that loan. The proposed amendment would add an exception to the retrospective application of IFRSs and in doing so would provide the same relief to first-time adopters as was granted to existing preparers of IFRS financial statements when the requirement was first incorporated into IAS 20 in 2008.

Chapter summary

First time adoption of IFRS

- Five points to consider are:
  - the date of transition to IFRS
  - which IFRS should be adopted
  - how gains or losses arising on adopting IFRS should be accounted for
  - the explanations and disclosures to be made in the year of transition
  - what exemptions are available

Implications of adoption of IFRS

- Consider practical implications – training, IT systems, planning project
- Also consider terms in debt covenants, calculation of performance-related pay and anything that is based on the profit figure
- Communicate with analysts on the expected changes to the financial statements

---

Differences in accounting practices

- There are historical reasons for differences in accounting systems such as legal, professional, culture
- Some accounting differences remain, but the harmonisation process is taking place
  Many countries are adopting IFRS
- The IASB is aiming to converge with the US standard-setter the FASB to harmonise IFRS with US GAAP

Test your understanding answers

Test your understanding 1 – Pailing

Restatement

	Net profit	Net assets (i.e. equity)
	$	$
Per local GAAP	**89**	**225**
(a) Under IFRS, qualifying borrowing costs should be capitalised as part of the cost of non-current assets. The $27m adjustment and $3m current year cost should be added back to profit and will increase non-current assets in the SFP.	30	30
(b) The assets should be stated at fair value so the carrying amount of the assets will increase by $4m and goodwill will decrease by $4m. Profit is unaffected. There is no effect on net assets.	–	–
(c) It is unlikely that Odd will make a profit given the large losses in the current year so there is no need to make a provision at the year end. In any event, it should not have been charged against profit but added on to the cost of investment. The provision must be reversed.	2	2
(d) Under IFRS, development expenditure on a feasible project must be capitalised. This project appears feasible given the strong sales so the expenditure must be removed from profit or loss and capitalised as a non-current asset.	6	6
	127	263

Current issues

Chapter learning objectives

Upon completion of this chapter you will be able to:

- discuss current issues in corporate reporting
- identify the issues and deficiencies that have led to a proposed change to an accounting standard
- apply and discuss the implications of a proposed change to an accounting standard on the performance and statement of financial position of an entity

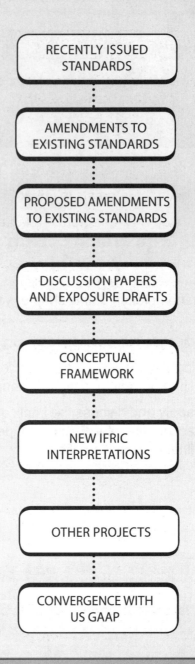

RECENTLY ISSUED
STANDARDS

AMENDMENTS TO
EXISTING STANDARDS

PROPOSED AMENDMENTS
TO EXISTING STANDARDS

DISCUSSION PAPERS
AND EXPOSURE DRAFTS

CONCEPTUAL
FRAMEWORK

NEW IFRIC
INTERPRETATIONS

OTHER PROJECTS

CONVERGENCE WITH
US GAAP

Introduction

The IASB is continually engaged in projects to update and improve existing standards and introduce new ones.

At any time there are a number of discussion papers (DPs) and exposure drafts (EDs) in issue as part of these projects.

In addition, the IFRIC continues to issue interpretations addressing newly identified reporting issues not covered in standards and issues where conflicting interpretations have arisen.

A good source of up to date information is the current projects page of the IASB website at www.iasb.org.

Recently issued and revised standards

The most recently issued reporting standards, examinable in 2012 examinations and thereafter, are as follows:

- IFRS 10 Consolidated Financial Statements – chapter 1
- IFRS 11 Joint Arrangements – chapter 1
- IFRS 12 Disclosure of Interests in Other Entities – chapter 1
- IFRS 13 Fair Value Measurement – chapter 8

Recently revised or amended reporting standards, examinable in 2012 examinations and thereafter, are as follows:

- IAS 27 Single Financial Statements – chapter 1
- IAS 28 Associates and Joint Ventures – chapter 1
- IAS 1 amendment in accounting for presentation of other comprehensive income – chapter 9
- IAS 19 revised accounting for defined benefit retirement plans – chapter 10
- IFRS 9 Financial Instruments – revised to include accounting for financial liabilities – chapter 16
- IAS 12 revised accounting for deferred tax on investment properties measured at fair value – chapter 18

Other examinable documents recently published include:

- Conceptual Framework for Financial Reporting 2010 – chapter 8
- Management Comentary (PS1) – chapter 19

During the year to 30 September 2012, no new or significantly revised reporting standards were issued. Note, however, that development of new and revised standards continues and this is likely to result in new or revised standards on several technical issues, including revenue recognition and leases, in 2013.

Proposed amendments to existing standards

You should refer to the current issues section within each chapter as appropriate to identify current developments in the form of published Discussion Papers (DP) and Exposure Drafts (ED) and other documents. Examples (not an exhaustive list) of current developments included within this publication are:

Topic	Chapter
Investment Entities	1
Transition Guidance, proposed amendments to IFRS 10	1
Conceptual Framework for Financial Reporting 2010	8
Revenue recognition in contracts with customers (ED)	9
Preliminary views on financial statement presentation – replacement of IAS 1 and IAS 7	9
Preliminary views on financial statement presentation – discontinued operations	9
Earnings per share	9
Rate regulated activities (ED)	14
Emissions trading schemes	14
Leases (ED)	15
Financial instruments – impairment (ED)	16
Financial instruments – hedging	16
Liabilities – IAS 37 amendment (ED)	17
First-time adoption of IFRS – re government loans	21

Annual improvements process

- The IASB has adopted an annual process to deal with non-urgent minor amendments to existing standards. These amendments tend to focus on areas of inconsistency in IFRSs or where clarification of wording is required. It is not part of the convergence project with FASB, but may include elements of harmonisation with US GAAP.

- Each year the IASB discusses and decides on proposed improvements to IFRSs as they arise throughout the year. In the third quarter of the year, an omnibus ED of the collected proposals is published for public comment, with a comment period of 90 days. After the IASB has considered the comments received, it aims to issue the amendments in final form in the following second quarter, with an effective date of 1 January of the subsequent year.

- Progress on the Annual Improvements cycle 2009–11 to September 2011 is that an ED was issued in June 2011 with proposed amendments to five reporting standards. Following expiry of the comment period in October 2011, an Annual Improvements Standard was issued in May 2012, with amendments to individual reporting standards effective for accounting periods commencing on or after 1 January 2013.

- The Annual improvements cycle 2010–12 commenced in May 2012 with the issue of ED/2002/1; the objective is that, following availability for comment, the approved amendments will be effective for accounting periods commencing on or after 1 January 2014.

Improvements to IFRS

The most recently issued ED Improvements to IFRSs (2009/2011 cycle) was published in May 2012 and contains relatively minor technical amendments to five reporting standards as follows:

IFRS	Subject of amendment
IFRS 1 First-time Adoption of IFRSs	Repeated application of IFRS 1 when the most recent previous financial statements did not contain an unreserved statement of compliance with IFRS. Borrowing costs capitalised in accordance with previous GAAP before transition to IFRS may carry forward the previous amount capitalised without amendment.
IAS 1 Presentation of Financial Statements	Clarification of requirements for comparative information when an entity provides more than the minimum comparative information.

Minor amendments to ensure consistency with the Conceptual Framework for Financial Reporting 2010 |
IAS 16 Property Plant & Equipment	Servicing equipment should be classified and accounted for as property, plant and equipment when it is used for more than one accounting period; if this is not the case, it should be classified as inventory.
IAS 32 Financial Instruments: Presentation	Clarification that income tax relating to distributions to holders of equity instruments should be accounted for in accordance with IAS12.
IAS 34 Interim Financial Reporting	Total assets for a reportable segment needs to be disclosed only when amounts are regularly provided to chief operating decision-makers, or where there has been a material change in total assets for that segment from that reported in the last annual financial statements. This amendment will enhance consistency with the requirements of IFRS 8.

The amendments are effective for annual periods beginning on or after 1 January 2013, with early adoption permitted.

IFRIC 19 Extinguishing Financial Liabilities with Equity was issued on 26 November 2009. IFRIC 19 is effective for annual periods beginning on or after 1 July 2010 with earlier application permitted. Recognising that entities would face practical difficulties in determining the fair value of the equity instruments previously issued, retrospective application is required only from the beginning of the earliest comparative period presented.

At September 2011, IFRIC 19 was the most recently issued interpretation statement.

Convergence with UK GAAP

This is a continuing process, and has resulted in co-operation between the IASB and US FASB to converge reporting standards. There is more specific information regarding this process in chapter 21 of this publication. In addition, other countries are undertaking a similar process to converge their national GAAP with IFRS.

The situation in the UK

In August 2009, following publication of IFRS for SME by the IASB, the UK ASB issued a Consultation Paper 'Policy Proposal: the future of UK GAAP' which set out proposals for the future reporting requirements of UK and Irish entities. The Consultation Paper was followed by an ED in October 2010 which proposed a three-tier structure for financial reporting in the UK. This proposal has been abandoned and revised proposals were issued in January 2012. As at September 2012, responses to the revised proposals are currently under review.

Although this content has a UK focus for illustrative purposes, other countries that have their own national GAAP are likely to be going through a broadly similar process. They will be considering to what extent they want to converge with IFRS, and how this should be managed, including national circumstances which may not be well-suited to application of IFRS. The time taken to develop and approve proposals in the UK reflects the range of issues to be considered, together with their complexity, which is likely to be mirrored in other countries.

UK syllabus focus

In October 2010 the UK ASB issued an ED 'Accounting Standards in the UK: an overview'. The ED proposed a three-tier structure for financial reporting in the UK as detailed in FREDs 43, 44 and 45. Tier 1 entities would apply IFRS GAAP and would comprise listed entities, together with other entities which met the definition of being publicly accountable. Tier two entities would apply the IFRS for SME, as adapted for use in the UK. Tier three entities would apply UK FRSSE.

Following public consultation, this proposal was dropped and revised proposals contained in the consultation document 'The Future of Financial Reporting in the United Kingdom and Republic of Ireland' which contained FREDs 46, 47 and 48 was issued in January 2012 by UK ASB. The effect of the revised proposals, if implemented, would mean that no additional entities would be required to apply full IFRS GAAP than is currently the case and that the three-tier approach to financial reporting in the UK proposed by FREDs 43, 44 and 45 would be abandoned.

The revised proposals are summarised as follows:

FRED 46 Application of Financial Reporting Requirements (draft FRS 100) – FRED 46 provides the proposed accounting framework for eligible entities to prepare financial statements as follows:

Currently applying	Revised structure alternatives	Reduced disclosures
UK FRSSE	No change, but can opt to either apply draft FRS 102 or IFRS	
UK FRS	Apply draft FRS 102 or can opt to apply IFRS	Available for qualifying entities - apply draft FRS 101
Opted to apply IFRS	Either continue with IFRS or can opt to apply draft FRS 102	Available for qualifying entities - apply draft FRS 101
Required to apply IFRS	No change	

FRED 47 Reduced Disclosures Framework (FRS 101) – Qualifying entities can choose to adopt the reduced disclosures framework proposed by FRED 47 whilst applying recognition and measurement requirements of IFRS. A qualifying entity is either a subsidiary or an ultimate parent company (not a group). There would be reduced disclosures applicable to individual eligible entities whether they were preparing financial statements in accordance with IFRS or proposed standard FRS 102. Examples of the reduced disclosures include no requirement for a statement of cash flows and related party transactions between parent and wholly-owned subsidiaries need not be disclosed.

FRED 48 The Financial Reporting Standard applicable in the UK and Republic of Ireland (draft FRS 102) – all SSAPs and FRSs currently effective would be replaced by a single, consistent international framework. This standard would be based upon IFRS for SME and would be subject to tailored amendments to make it suitable for the UK. Once introduced, it would be updated every three years. It would also include a choice of accounting treatment for some issues such as capitalisation of development costs, capitalisation of borrowing costs and revaluation of property, plant and equipment. Other accounting treatments would be simplified, such as amortisation of goodwill on acquisition over its finite useful life.

It is anticipated that the new regime will be approved during 2013 so that it will be effective for accounting periods commencing on or after 1 January 2015.

Chapter summary

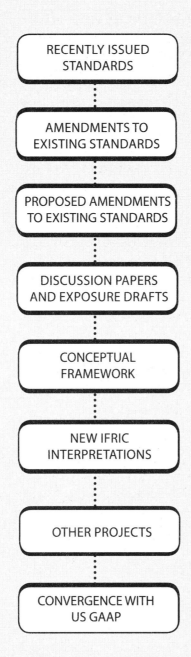

RECENTLY ISSUED
STANDARDS

AMENDMENTS TO
EXISTING STANDARDS

PROPOSED AMENDMENTS
TO EXISTING STANDARDS

DISCUSSION PAPERS
AND EXPOSURE DRAFTS

CONCEPTUAL
FRAMEWORK

NEW IFRIC
INTERPRETATIONS

OTHER PROJECTS

CONVERGENCE WITH
US GAAP

Assessing financial performance and position

Chapter learning objectives

Upon completion of this chapter you will be able to:

- develop accounting policies for an entity that meet the entity's reporting requirements

- identify accounting treatments adopted in financial statements and assess their suitability and acceptability

- select and calculate relevant indicators of financial and non-financial performance

- identify and evaluate significant features and issues in financial statements

- highlight inconsistencies in financial information through analysis and application of knowledge

- make inferences from the analysis of information taking into account the limitation of the information, the analytical methods used and the business environment in which the entity operates.

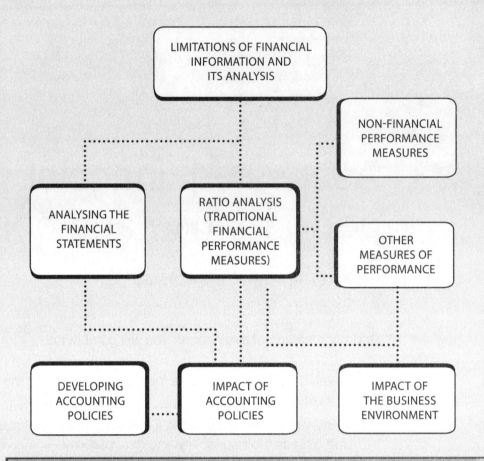

IAS 8

IAS 8 **Accounting policies, changes in accounting estimates and errors** states that where a Standard or Interpretation exists in respect of a transaction, the accounting policy is determined by applying the Standard or Interpretation.

- Where there is no applicable Standard or Interpretation, management must use its judgement to develop and apply an accounting policy.

- The accounting policy selected must result in information that is both relevant to the needs of users and reliable, in that the financial statements:

    - represent faithfully the financial position, financial performance and cash flows of the entity

    - reflects the economic substance of transactions, other events and conditions, and not merely the legal form

    - are neutral, i.e. free from bias

    - are prepared on a prudent basis

    - are complete in all material respects.

IAS 8 provides a 'hierarchy' of sources that the management should use to develop an appropriate accounting policy in the absence of a Standard or Interpretation that specifically applies. These sources should be used in the following order:

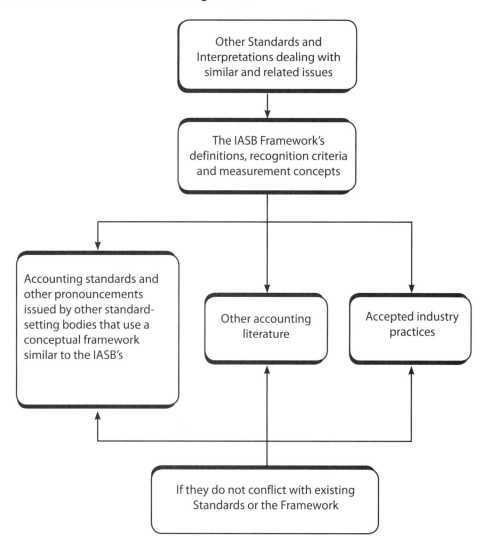

An entity must select and apply accounting policies consistently for similar transactions.

An entity should only change its accounting policies if the change:

- is required by a Standard or Interpretation
- results in reliable and more relevant information.

Overtrading

Overtrading is the term used to describe the situation where an entity expands its sales rapidly without securing additional long-term capital adequate for its needs. The symptoms of overtrading are:

*   inventories increasing, possibly more than proportionately to sales

*   receivables increasing, possibly more than proportionately to sales

*   cash and liquid assets declining at a fairly alarming rate

*   payables increasing rapidly.

These symptoms imply that the entity has expanded without giving proper thought to the necessity to expand its capital base. It has consequently continued to rely on its suppliers and probably its bank overdraft to provide the additional finance required. It will reach a stage where suppliers will withhold further deliveries and bankers will refuse to honour further cheques until borrowings are reduced. The problem is that borrowings cannot be reduced until sales revenue is earned, which in turn cannot be achieved until production is completed, which in turn is dependent upon materials being available and wages paid. Overall result – deadlock and rapid financial collapse!

Interpreting financial obligations

As well as calculating and interpreting liquidity ratios, it is important to be aware of other potential obligations that may affect liquidity and cash flow. These may not necessarily be recognised in current liabilities or even included in the statement of financial position at all.

(a) **Earn out arrangements**

Where one company acquires another, part of the consideration may be deferred to a later date because it is dependent (contingent) on the performance of the acquired entity. If this deferred consideration is recognised in the financial statements, the amount is likely to be based on an estimate. Alternatively, the acquirer's management may not have provided for the obligation because they believe that it is unlikely to become payable.

(b) **Redeemable debt**

A company may have raised finance by issuing loan notes that it is committed to redeem or repurchase, possibly at a premium.

(c) **Contingent liabilities**

Contingent liabilities are not recognised in the financial statements but must normally be disclosed in the notes.

(d) **Interpretation**

In all cases such as these, the obligation may involve a material cash outflow in the near future.

Where there are either provisions based on estimates or contingent liabilities, it is possible that the situation may have changed since the reporting date (for example, a contingent liability could have become an actual liability). It is necessary to use whatever information is available (e.g. selected notes to the financial statements, details of events since the publication of the latest financial statements) to determine the likelihood of the cash outflow occurring, its timing and whether the entity is likely to be able to meet the obligation in practice.

Non-financial performance measures

Non-financial performance measures are measures of performance based on non-financial information. They are becoming increasingly important both to management and to shareholders and other interested parties external to an entity.

Ratio analysis and other interpretation techniques based on the financial statements cannot measure all aspects of performance. For example, the effect of a business on the environment cannot be measured using financial criteria, but is increasingly regarded as an important aspect of performance.

- Where an entity presents an Operating and Financial Review or a Management Discussion and Analysis it may include Key Performance Indicators (KPIs) based on non-financial information.

- KPIs may also be included in an environmental or social report. Reports prepared in accordance with the Global Reporting Initiative (GRI) Sustainability Guidelines should contain economic indicators, environmental indicators and social indicators.

- Examples of non-financial performance measures are:
  - trend in market share
  - number of customers at the year end
  - sales per square foot of floor space (for a retailer)
  - percentage of revenue from new products
  - number of new products being developed at the year end
  - number of instances of environmental spillage per year
  - reduction in CO_2 emissions during the year
  - amount of waste (kg) arising from packaging on each $1,000 of products
  - employee turnover
  - training time per employee
  - lost time injury frequency rate (relating to employees).

- Non-financial performance measures are likely to be particularly relevant to 'not for profit' organisations, because these organisations need to measure the effectiveness with which services have been provided. Examples of non-financial performance indicators for public sector bodies could include:
  - pupil-teacher ratios
  - population per police officer
  - serious offences per 1,000 of the population
  - proportion of trains arriving on time
  - number of patients who wait more than one year for treatment.

- Where an entity presents non-financial measures:
  - the definition and calculation method should be explained
  - the purpose of the measure should be explained
  - the source of the data on which the measure is based should be disclosed
  - the measure should be presented and calculated consistently over time (and ideally, there should be comparative figures for the previous year)
  - any changes in the measures or in the way they are calculated should be disclosed and explained.

Illustration: non-financial measures

Verdant is an entity that manufactures hazardous substances. There have been several escapes of toxic gases from its plant over the last few years and the directors are concerned that this will damage the entity's reputation.

The directors decide to publish a key performance indicator to assess the effectiveness of the management of hazardous substances (and to demonstrate that the entity is taking steps to reduce the problem).

The measure is the number of significant incidents during the year. Significant incidents are defined as escapes of gas exceeding 10,000 cubic feet.

The data is taken from all Verdant's manufacturing plants.

In 20X6 there were 15 significant incidents compared with 21 gas escapes in 20X5.

Other measures of performance

In recent years, investment analysts have developed a number of new financial performance measures. These attempt to overcome the limitations of traditional ratios, such as earnings per share and return on capital employed.

- Earnings before interest, tax, depreciation and amortisation (EBITDA) is an approximation to operating cash flow and is therefore believed to be a better point of comparison between entities than earnings per share.

- Free cash flow is calculated as cash revenues less cash expenses, taxes paid, cash needed for working capital and cash required for routine capital expenditure. Analysts attach importance to this measure because cash is essential for an entity's survival and it is also less easy to manipulate than profit.

Shareholder value is created by generating future returns for equity investors that exceed the returns that those investors could expect to earn elsewhere.

- Many entities are adopting the enhancement of shareholder value, rather than the generation of profit, as their primary objective.

- A number of ways to measure shareholder value have been developed. The most important of these is probably Economic Value Added (EVA).

- EVA = adjusted net operating profit after tax – (weighted average cost of capital × adjusted invested capital). It is a variation on return on capital employed that adjusts the numerator and the denominator to remove the effects of accruals accounting and some of the effects of the entity's choice of accounting policies.

Alternative measures of performance

A number of ways of measuring shareholder value have been developed as follows. Measures of shareholder value have a number of common features.

- They focus on cash flow rather than on profit.

- They emphasise the 'whole' business. The idea behind the concept of shareholder value is that there are several 'drivers' within a business that can be managed to create value, e.g. growth in sales, increase in the operating profit margin, reduction in the cash tax rate. These are summarised into a single performance measure.

- They are essentially forward looking. In particular, calculating SVA involves estimating future performance.

(a) **Shareholder value analysis (SVA)**

SVA calculates a value for the entity that is based on projected future cash flows, discounted to their present value at the entity's cost of capital. The market value of debt is deducted from this figure to give shareholder value.

(b) **Market value added (MVA)**

MVA is the additional value that is added to an entity by its management in excess of the actual value of the funds invested by the shareholders.

MVA = Market value of entity – capital employed

The market value of the entity is the market share price multiplied by the number of shares in issue. Performance can be measured by calculating the yearly change in MVA.

(c) Economic value added (EVA)

EVA is calculated as follows:

EVA = adjusted net operating profit after tax – (WACC × adjusted invested capital)

EVA was developed as a sophisticated version of return on capital employed and similar methods of measuring the return on an investment. It can be argued that the normal calculation is distorted by the following factors:

– the effect of accruals based bookkeeping, which tends to hide the true 'cash' profitability of a business

– the effect of prudence, which often leads to a conservative bias and affects the relevance of reported figures (although this is less of a problem following the issue of IAS 37 **Provisions, contingent liabilities and contingent assets**)

– the effect of 'successful efforts accounting' whereby entities write off costs associated with unsuccessful investments. This tends to understate the 'true' capital of a business and subject profit or loss to 'one off' gains and losses.

Therefore adjustments are made to operating profit and asset values. These can include the following:

– removing non-recurring gains and losses such as restructuring costs

– capitalising intangible assets such as research and development expenditure

– adding back 'unnecessary' provisions (such as deferred tax)

– capitalising the net present value of future operating lease payments.

A positive EVA for a single year does not necessarily mean that value has been created and a negative EVA for a single year does not necessarily mean that value has been destroyed. EVA is probably most helpful when it is used to interpret an entity's performance over a period of several years.

Analysing the financial statements

The best way to start to analyse the financial statements is by observation. This can often tell a reader more, more quickly, than calculating ratios (and it does not depend on selecting the correct ratios).

Analysis should take into account:

- the nature of the entity's business

- any particular concerns of the users of the information (for example, a shareholder may suspect that the financial statements have been manipulated)

- any important issues facing the business

- the accounting policies adopted by management (if these are known).

The statement of financial position

The main areas of interest in the statement of financial position are set out below.

Non-current assets	• Significant additions/disposals ?
	• Evidence of business expanding ?
	• Any unusual items (e.g. intangibles) ?
	• Revaluations ?
	• How are assets valued ?
	• Depreciation/amortisation/useful lives?
	• Any associates or joint ventures (equity accounting)?
Current assets/current liabilities	• Significant movements?
	• In line with revenue and cost of sales?
	• Any unusual items?
	• Cash position?
	• Financial instruments: accounting policy?
Equity	• Share issues in the year?
	• Reason (e.g. to finance asset purchases/ acquisitions)?
	• Any significant/unusual movements on reserves?
	• Increases/decreases in minority interest?

Non-current liabilities
- Increase/decrease in year?
- When do loans fall due?

The statement of comprehensive income and statement of changes in equity

The main areas of interest in the statement of comprehensive income and statement of changes in equity are set out below.

Revenue	• Increase/decrease? How significant?
Cost of sales/ Gross profit	• Movement in line with revenue? • Sales growth v profit growth?
Operating expenses/ Operating profit	• In line with revenue (especially selling costs)? • Any unusual items?
Finance costs	• Reasonable given level of loans/overdraft? Movement? Interest cover?
Profit before tax	• Any investment income, interests in associates, joint ventures?
Income tax expense/ Profit for the period	• Effective rate of tax? (This should be reasonably constant from year to year).
Dividends	• Trend, level, cover? A fall is usually a very bad sign.
Other comprehensive income	• revaluations?

Operating expenses may include various items that affect the analysis, for example:

- one-off unusual items
- depreciation and profits or losses on disposal of non-current assets
- research and development expenditure
- advertising expenditure
- staff costs that may have risen in line with inflation (rather than sales)
- pension costs including any surpluses or deficiencies (dealt with according to IAS 19 **Employee benefits**)

- amortisation of intangibles

- impairment losses (including goodwill)

- directors' emoluments (including share-based payment).

Trend analysis

Comparative figures for one or more years provide information about the way in which the performance and financial position of a business has changed over a period. Published accounts give comparative information in two main areas:

- the corresponding amounts for items shown in the statements of financial position, comprehensive income, cash flows and changes in equity and notes. Such amounts are required by IAS 1 **Presentation of financial statements** for virtually all items disclosed in the accounts

- historical summaries of information covering several years.

It may be possible to predict future performance from trend information, particularly if the figures are very stable.

- The extent to which amounts and ratios are stable or volatile can reveal a great deal. Figures that are very volatile, or sudden changes in trends, may indicate that the company will experience problems in the future, even if performance is apparently improving.

- Trend information should be interpreted with caution because it does not take account of the effect of inflation.

Impact of accounting policies and choices

Introduction

Accounting policies can significantly affect the view presented by financial statements, and the ratios computed by reference to them, without affecting a business's core ability to generate profits and cash.

The potential impact of accounting policies is especially important where:

- accounting standards permit a choice (e.g. cost v fair value)

- judgement is needed in making accounting estimates (e.g. inventory valuation, depreciation, doubtful receivables, provisions)

- there is no accounting standard (e.g. some forms of revenue recognition).

Asset valuation

A key area is the measurement of non-current assets. Measuring assets at fair value rather than historic cost has the following effects (assuming fair value is increasing each year):

- earnings reduce (profits decrease due to the additional depreciation)

- return on capital employed reduces (capital employed increases while profits decrease)

- gearing reduces (capital employed /equity increases, while debt remains the same)

- another effect of fair value accounting is that profits and trends in ratios may become more volatile and therefore harder to interpret.

Illustration: impact of accounting policies

Three entities are identical in all respects, except for the way they finance the major productive capacity they need. The following information has been extracted from the financial statements of the three entities for the year ended 30 September 20X4:

	A	B	C
Profit or loss	$000	$000	$000
Revenue	200	200	200
Operating costs	(160)	(190)	(170)
Profit from operations	40	10	30
Statement of financial position			
Share capital	50	50	50
Retained earnings	90	60	50
Revaluation reserve	–	210	–
Capital employed	140	320	100
Operating profit margin	20%	5%	15%
Asset utilisation	1.43	0.63	2
Return on capital employed	28.6%	3.1%	30%

Entity A

A obtained the capacity needed by purchasing a non-current asset costing $200,000 four years ago. The asset is being depreciated on the straight-line basis over 10 years. Therefore, $20,000 of depreciation has been charged to this year's profit and the asset has a carrying value of $120,000 in the statement of financial position.

Entity B

B also purchased a non-current asset four years ago for the same price but revalued it to its fair value of $350,000 at the start of the current year. As a result, a revaluation gain of $210,000 has been recognised within other comprehensive income. With seven years, life remaining, the depreciation charge has been increased to $50,000 per annum.

The revaluation has caused the operating profit margin to fall due to the extra depreciation. Asset utilisation has also fallen due to the revaluation reserve being included in capital employed.

Hence the entity appears to be generating a lower return.

Entity C

C has obtained the capacity needed under an operating lease agreement, paying an annual rental of $30,000, which has been charged to operating expenses.

This causes its operating profit margin to be lower than A's, because the lease payments are higher than A's depreciation charges. However, the asset utilisation is higher than A's since the non-current asset is not recognised in the statement of financial position.

Recognition of assets and liabilities

Another key area is the recognition (or non-recognition) of assets and liabilities. IAS 1, IAS 8 and the IASB's Framework set out the general principle that an entity should report the substance of a transaction rather than its strict legal form.

- There is no accounting standard that specifically deals either with specific types of transaction (e.g. sale and repurchase agreements, debt factoring) or with substance in general.

- It is still possible for a company to account for complex transactions so that significant assets and liabilities are not recognised on in the statement of financial position.

- Non-recognition of assets normally improves ROCE while non-recognition of liabilities normally improves gearing. For example, leasing obligations increase debt and therefore increase gearing.

- Management may seek to keep liabilities off the balance sheet in order to manipulate the gearing ratio.

Illustration: impact of accounting policies

The following ratios have been calculated for Laxton, based on its financial statements for the year ended 31 December 20X4:

Return on capital employed	$45m/$160m	= 28%
Gearing	$80m/$160m	= 50%

During the year, Laxton sold a property with a carrying value of $40 million to a bank for $50 million. Laxton has treated this transaction as a sale, even though it continues to occupy the property and has agreed to repurchase it for $55 million on 31 December 20X9.

The substance of the transaction is that it is not a sale, but a secured loan. The difference between the sale proceeds and the amount at which the property will eventually be repurchased represents interest.

If the agreement is treated correctly, the effect is:

- profit before interest and tax is reduced by $10m (the profit on disposal)

- capital employed increases by $40m (the property continues to be recognised at its carrying value)

- debt increases by $50m (the amount received from the bank).

(Depreciation is ignored).

The ratios now become:

Return on capital employed	$35m/$200m = 17.5%
Gearing	$130m/$200m = 65%

Illustration: choice of accounting treatment

Below are examples where reporting standards permit a choice of accounting treatment:

Goodwill on acquisition of a subsidiary – IFRS 3 permits goodwill on acquisition to be accounted for using the full goodwill method or the proportionate goodwill method.

Actuarial gains and losses on defined benefit pension plans – IAS 19 prior to its revision in 2011 permitted a choice from three methods of accounting for actuarial gains and losses arising on defined benefit pension plans as follows:

- immediate write off to profit or loss for the year, or

- accounted for as part of other comprehensive income for the year, or

- deferred and only accounted for if regarded as excessive by reference to application of the "10% corridor test".

Revised IAS 19 now requires that actuarial gains and losses arising on defined benefit pension plans are accounted for in other comprehensive income.

Joint ventures – IAS 31 Interests in joint ventures permitted either proportional consolidation or equity accounting for jointly controlled entities, until it was superseded in 2011. IFRS 12 now requires that any joint arrangements which meet the definition of a joint venture are accounted for using the equity method.

Property plant and equipment – IAS 16 permits property, plant and equipment to be measured using the cost model or the valuation model.

Required:

Briefly explain how choices may affect the financial statements and the main performance measures: earnings per share, ROCE and gearing.

Briefly explain why many of the more recently-issued new and revised reporting standards reduce or eliminate the extent of choice of accounting treatment available to those who prepare financial statements.

Solution

Earnings per share is not affected by the choice of accounting treatment. The venturer's share of profit recognised in profit or loss is the same whichever method is used.

If the equity method is used, the interest in the joint venture appears as one line under non-current assets. Both ROCE and gearing will probably be lower than under proportionate consolidation, because this recognises the venturer's share of individual assets and liabilities. One of the limitations of the equity method is that it enables the venturer's share of any significant liabilities not to be disclosed, so that the venturer's financial position can appear better than it actually is.

When goodwill has been accounted for using the full goodwill method, there will be recognition of an asset at a greater carrying value in comparison with goodwill calculated on a proportionate basis. This may give rise to possible sources of inconsistency in making comparisons between reported information from two separate groups as follows:

- one group may have prepared financial statements where goodwill for all subsidiaries has been calculated using the full goodwill method; the other may have applied the proportionate goodwill method upon acquisition of subsidiaries

- the carrying value of non-controlling interest in the group financial statements will be affected by the choice of goodwill accounting policy

- any subsequent write-off for impairment of goodwill in the group financial statements is likely to be greater under the full goodwill method.

When property, plant and equipment (or any single class of asset under this heading) is measured by valuation, this will lead to a greater carrying value in comparison with being measured at cost. There will be a consequent impact upon equity on the statement of financial position, which will impact upon net assets and gearing. Profitability will also be affected as any depreciation charge based upon a revalued amount will lead to a greater charge in profit or loss for the year.

IAS 19 permitted three methods of accounting for actuarial gains and losses before it was revised in 2011. By taking such items to profit or loss in the year, this would have a direct impact upon profitability and earnings per share. This accounting treatment was not favoured by entities when preparing their financial statements as such items were volatile and there was little, if anything management could do to control them.

Deferral of recognition of these items arguably was not desirable as this could be argued to lead to less than full financial reporting, which could lead to mis-stated results for the year (including reported EPS), mis-stated net assets and the consequent impact upon other accounting ratios.

Accounting for these items as part of other comprehensive income has the benefit of reporting the information, but which does not directly impact upon reported profit or loss for the year.

However, it can be appreciated that if entities applied different, even if permitted, accounting treatments for actuarial gains and losses, this would undermine comparability of financial statements.

The key reason for recently issued new and revised reporting standards to eliminate or reduce choice of accounting treatment is to enhance consistency of reported information. This should assist preparers of financial statements as they will have a clearer understanding of what is required when preparing financial statements. This should also assist users of reported information as there will be a greater degree of comparability between the financial statements of different entities.

Intangible assets and intellectual property

A traditional manufacturing business generates profits mainly from the use of property, plant and equipment. Its financial statements can be interpreted fairly easily because there is a clear relationship between the plant and equipment and working capital in the statement of financial position and the statement of profit or loss and other comprehensive income.

Business practice has changed very significantly over the last 20 years. Many businesses now depend on assets such as copyrights, patents, customer databases and the technical or interpersonal skills of their staff.

These assets are not normally recognised in the statement of financial position, and there are important implications for analysis of the financial statements. Key ratios, such as ROCE and gearing may be virtually meaningless. Interpretations of performance have to be based on profit margins and sales growth. It can be much harder to predict future performance because this is more likely to be significantly affected by unpredictable events than in a business such as manufacturing or retailing. For example, in some situations it could be disastrous if several key members of staff left the company.

Creative accounting

Creative accounting is a form of accounting which, while complying with all regulations, nevertheless gives a biased impression (usually favourable) of the company's performance.

Management may have strong incentives to present the financial statements in the best possible light. For example:

- the directors want to sell the company in the near future

- the company is going through a difficult period (e.g. falling profits, lack of shareholder confidence, a possible takeover)

- directors' remuneration is strongly linked to performance (e.g. bonuses if earnings per share exceeds a certain amount or share based payment that depends on the entity's share price)

- the company is in danger of breaching loan covenants (for example, if the current/quick ratio or the gearing ratio falls below or above a certain figure).

There are a number of ways in which creative accounting can take place.

- **Off balance sheet finance**: transactions are deliberately constructed to allow the non-recognition of assets and (particularly) liabilities for loans. Examples include sale and repurchase agreements and the use of special-purpose entities (quasi-subsidiaries). Note that the issue of IFRS 10, IFRS 11 and IFRS 12 dealing with aspects of accounting for investments in other entities could be seen to be an attempt to close apparent loopholes in how investments in other entities are accounted for.

- **Aggressive earnings management**: recognising revenue before it has been earned. Note that there are current developments which consider how revenue recognition for goods and services provided can be more consistently reported, which may have the benefit of reducing the extent of variation or earnings management which may happen in practice.

- **Unusual assets**: an attempt to recognise an asset which, strictly speaking, is not an asset but an expense. Examples include marketing or advertising costs and recruitment costs (particularly where these have been incurred to recruit staff with essential skills or technical knowledge).

- **Unjustified changes to accounting policies or accounting estimates**: for example, extending the useful lives of assets with the object of reducing the depreciation expense and increasing earnings.
- **Profit smoothing:** manipulating the profit figure by setting up assets or liabilities in the statement of financial position and releasing these amounts to profit over time.

Question

Egremont, a mining company, has been fined for environmental pollution of the area in which it operates. The fine has been treated as an intangible asset and is being amortised over 15 years, the estimated remaining useful life of the quarry in which the pollution incident took place. The directors argue that this treatment is logical because operating the quarry brings them economic benefits in the form of revenues.

Required:

Comment on this accounting treatment.

Solution

An intangible asset is a resource controlled by the company as a result of past events and from which future economic benefits are expected to flow (IAS 38 **Intangible assets**).

The directors seem to be trying to argue that the fine is an unavoidable cost of operating the quarry and that economic benefits result from it. But the fine is avoidable and therefore it is an expense and not an asset.

The fine should be recognised in the profit or loss in the current year and possibly disclosed as a material item under IAS 1 **Presentation of financial statements**.

Limitations of financial information and its analysis

Limitations of financial information

During the last few years, users of traditional financial statements have become increasingly aware of their limitations.

- Preparing financial statements involves a substantial degree of classification and aggregation. There is always a risk that essential information will either not be given sufficient prominence or will be lost completely.

- Financial statements focus on the financial effects of transactions and other events and do not focus to any significant extent on their non-financial effects or on non-financial information in general.

- They provide information that is largely historical. They do not reflect future events or transactions, nor do they anticipate the impact of potential changes to an entity. This means that it is not always possible to use them to predict future performance.

- There is often a time interval of several months between the year-end and the publication of the financial statements. Most financial information is out of date by the time it is actually published.

Limitations of financial analysis

Ratio analysis and other types of analysis such as trend analysis are a useful means of identifying significant relationships between different figures, but they have many limitations, including the following.

- Profit and capital employed are arbitrary figures. They depend on the accounting policies adopted by an entity.

- Many businesses produce accounts to a date on which there are relatively low amounts of trading activity. As a result the items on a statement of financial position are not typical of the items throughout the accounting period.

- Ratios based on historical cost accounts do not give a true picture of trends from year to year. An apparent increase in profit may not be a 'true' increase, because of the effects of inflation.

- Comparing the financial statements of similar businesses can be misleading for a number of reasons, including the effect of size differences and of operating in different markets.

- There are particular problems in comparing the financial statements of similar businesses that operate in different countries. There can be significant differences in accounting policies, terminology and presentation.

Impact of the environment

The type of business

It can often be helpful to consider whether the statement of profit or loss and other comprehensive income and statements of financial position appear as they should for a particular type of business.

For example:

- Manufacturing industries are capital intensive, therefore they have relatively low asset turnover.

- Service industries depend mainly on people rather than capital assets, therefore asset turnover should be relatively high.

- A builder should have high inventories and work in progress, therefore inventory turnover is usually relatively low.

- A supermarket has perishable inventories, therefore inventory turnover should normally be high.

Question

Given below is information from the statements of financial position of five entities expressed as percentages of total assets less current liabilities.

The respective areas of activity of the companies are:

(a) Manufacturing

(b) Insurance brokers

(c) Housebuilding

(d) Retail stores

(e) Investment in properties for rental

The assets and liabilities shown as a percentage of net assets

	1	2	3	4	5
	%	%	%	%	%
Land and property	16	32	83	96	72
Other non-current assets	7	42	14	1	23
Inventory and work in progress	148	47	13	–	–
Trade receivables	31	41	4	1	436
Cash/short-term investments	1	11	6	4	91
	203	173	120	102	622
Trade payables	(36)	(60)	(11)	(2)	(509)
Bank overdraft	(67)	(13)	(9)	–	(13)
Total assets less current liabilities	100	100	100	100	100

Required:

State which statement of financial position belongs to each of the entities, giving your reasons for your opinion.

Solution

Company A (Manufacturing) – Statement of financial position No 2

Higher than average investment in other non-current assets (plant and equipment) together with relatively high inventories and work in progress and trade payables.

Company B (Insurance) – Statement of financial position No 5

No inventories and work in progress and comparatively small investment in other non-current assets, but very high proportions of receivables and payables.

Company C (Housebuilding) – Statement of financial position No 1

High investment in inventories and work in progress and relatively high payables.

Company D (Retail stores) – Statement of financial position No 3

High investment in land and property (shops). Low trade receivables. High cash.

Company E (Properties) – Statement of financial position No 4

High investment in land and property. Low other non-current assets and receivables. No inventories.

Groups and individual companies

Being part of a group can have quite a significant effect on the financial statements of an individual company. Intra-group transactions often take place on terms that are different (so more favourable to one of the entities, less favourable to the other) than between two independent companies trading at arms' length:

- Profit margins in the seller may be unusually high.

- The rate of Interest payable on intra-group loans may be unusually low.

- A group company may exist (for example) only to supply essential goods or services to another, so that it has a guaranteed market for its output.

- Services (e.g. administration) may be supplied free of charge.

Events taking place during the period

A significant event during the year often distorts the financial statements and accounting ratios for that year, particularly if it takes place near the year-end. This can make it harder for a user to predict future performance.

Illustration – events in the period

An entity increases its long-term borrowings from $40 million to $100 million just before the year end. Operating profit for the year is $25 million, interest for the year is $5 million and profit after tax for the year is $15 million. The average rate of interest on long-term borrowings is 10%.

Interest cover can be calculated as five times. However, the accounts do not include a full year's interest charge on the new borrowings.

Assuming that operating profit, tax charge and total long-term borrowings remain at the same level, interest cover for the next year will fall to approximately 2.5 times (25 ÷ (100 × 10%)) and profit after tax will fall to approximately $10 million (25 − ((100 × 10%) − 5 charged in current year)).

Significant events may include:

- acquisition or disposal of a subsidiary during the year

- management actions (e.g. price discounting to increase market share) or changes in the nature of the business (e.g. diversification or divestment)

- raising finance just before the year end

- significant asset sales or purchases just before the year end.

It can be useful to ask the following questions:

- What effect do these events have on performance (including cash flow) and key ratios for the current year?

- What effect might they be expected to have on performance and key ratios in the next period and in the longer term?

- What is the apparent or possible reason for the event? Has it taken place for a legitimate business reason, or is it a deliberate attempt to improve the appearance of the financial statements in the short term?

Other business factors

These may include the nature of the business, for example, whether it is highly seasonal or vulnerable to changes in fashion or the market. Other factors to consider are the quality of management and the state of the economy and market conditions.

- Better managed businesses are likely to be more profitable and have better working capital management than businesses where management is weak.

- If the market or the economy in general is depressed, this is likely to affect companies adversely and make most or all of their ratios appear worse. The impact may differ between market sectors.

Preparing a report

Preparing a report

An exam question may ask for a report.

REPORT

To

- The report should be focused on the reader(s) and their information needs.

From

Date

Subject

Introduction

- **Brief** introductory paragraph setting out the purpose of the report/terms of reference.

Discussion

This should:

- be structured with headings (usually the specific issues highlighted in the scenario)
- refer to calculations (including ratios) in an appendix (unless the question requires otherwise)
- (if required) interpret the information and any performance measures calculated (for example, possible reasons for a feature or a change)
- make connections between different areas, if the question asks for interpretation/analysis
- state what other information might be needed/would be useful (if appropriate or required by the question).

Conclusion

- Summarise findings and make a recommendation (if required).

Illustration: analysis of financial statements

The consolidated financial statements of TW for the year ended 30 April 20X4 are due to be published in June 20X4. The first draft of the 20X4 financial statements has just been prepared. Extracts from these statements are set out below:

Statement of comprehensive income – year ended 30 April:

	20X4 (draft)	20X3 (final)
	$m	$m
Revenue	3,600	3,400
Cost of sales	(2,300)	(2,250)
Gross profit	1,300	1,150
Other operating expenses	(700)	(600)
Profit from operations	600	550
Profit on sale of subsidiaries	350	Nil
Finance cost	(250)	(120)
Profit before tax	700	430
Income tax expense	(200)	(140)
Profit after tax	500	290

Other comprehensive income:

Item that will not be reclassified to profit or loss in future years:

	20X4 (draft)	20X3 (final)
Gain on property revaluation	800	–
Total comprehensive income	1,300	290

Profit attributable to:

	20X4 (draft)	20X3 (final)
Owners of the parent	440	235
Non-controlling interest	60	55
	500	290

Total comprehensive income attributable to			
Owners of the parent		1,200	235
Non-controlling interest		100	55
		1,300	290
Earnings per equity share		176 cents	94 cents

Statement of financial position at 30 April:

	20X4 (draft)		20X3 (final)	
	$m	$m	$m	$m
ASSETS				
Non-current assets:				
Property, plant and equipment	2,400		1,350	
Financial assets	180		250	
		2,580		1,600
Current assets:				
Inventories	430		400	
Trade receivables	600		550	
Deferred marketing costs	100		Nil	
Cash and cash equivalents	940		Nil	
		2,070		950
		4,650		2,550
EQUITY AND LIABILITIES				
Equity:				
Equity capital ($1 equity shares)	250		250	
Share premium	150		150	
Revaluation reserve	800		Nil	
Retained earnings	1,050		610	
		2,250		1,010
Non-current liabilities:				
Long-term borrowings	2,000		1,000	
Deferred tax	180		100	
		2,180		1,100

Current liabilities:

Trade payables	220	200
Short-term borrowings	Nil	240
	220	440
	4,650	2,550

Notes to the draft financial statements

(i) During the financial year, the group decided to change the nature and focus of its operations. Consequently, on 31 March 20X4, the group disposed of two subsidiaries for total cash proceeds of $1,000 million. In the year to 30 April 20X4, the two subsidiaries that were disposed of contributed $800 million to group revenue, $320 million to group gross profit and $175 million to group profit from operations.

(ii) During the last few months of the year ended 30 April 20X4 the group embarked on an extensive marketing campaign to underpin the new operational focus. Marketing costs are normally charged to cost of sales but, in the draft financial statements, the directors of TW have included them in the statement of financial position on the basis that the new operational focus is likely to generate future economic benefits for the group.

(iii) The revaluation reserve is caused by a group-wide revaluation of property, plant and equipment on 31 March 20X4, immediately after the disposal of the two subsidiaries. Depreciation was charged on the revalued amounts from 1 April 20X4. The average remaining useful lives of the revalued assets at 1 April 20X4 was eight years.

Ms A is a newly-appointed non-executive director of TW. She wishes to seek your advice prior to the board meeting and her request is set out below.

'The papers contain an assertion from the Chief Executive that the financial statements show a very pleasing financial performance and position. The Chief Executive highlights the increase in revenue, profits, earnings per share and cash balances as evidence to support this assertion. I would like you to evaluate this assertion and to highlight any relevant issues.'

Prepare a reply to the question Ms A has raised.

Solution

Financial performance and position of TW

It is true that the draft financial statements show that revenue, profits, earnings per share and cash balances have all increased. However, the notes to the financial statements reveal a number of issues that should be taken into account when interpreting the figures. The potential effect of these issues on the gross profit margin and the operating profit margin are illustrated in the Appendix.

Disposal of subsidiaries

The group has disposed of two subsidiaries during the year, but their results have not been separately presented within the statement of comprehensive income. In fact the two subsidiaries contributed 22% of total revenue (800 as a percentage of 3,600); 25% of total gross profit (320 as a percentage of 1,300); and nearly 30% of total profit from operations (175 as a percentage of 600). In other words, the discontinued operations appear to be more profitable than the rest of the group. This suggests that the group may be less profitable in future years.

Profit before tax has increased by nearly two-thirds in the year, but this includes the exceptional profit on disposal of $350 million. This profit will not recur and without it profit before tax would have fallen, due to the fact that finance costs have doubled as the group has also doubled its long-term borrowings.

The group has experienced a total cash net inflow of $1,180 million (940 + 240) for the year. However, most of this increase results from the sale proceeds of $1,000 million. The group's cash flow position does not appear to be as healthy as the Chairman suggests.

Marketing costs

The treatment of the marketing costs of $100 million is not justified. An asset can only be recognised if it is probable that the group will obtain future economic benefits from the expenditure as a result of past events or transactions and if these benefits can be measured reliably. It is impossible to measure the economic benefits attributable to specific marketing costs (rather than to other factors, such as the reputation built up over many years), so IAS 38 **Intangible assets** prohibits the capitalisation of marketing costs. Profits are overstated by $100 million.

Revaluation

When non-current assets are revalued, the depreciation charge must be calculated on the revalued amount. This means that depreciation charges increase and profits are reduced. Because the revaluation took place on 1 April 20X4, the financial statements show the increase in property, plant and equipment, but only reflect one month's additional depreciation. However, the full depreciation charge will be reflected in the statement of comprehensive income for the year to 30 April 20X5. The effect of this can be estimated from the increase in the revaluation reserve: there will be a reduction in profit of approximately $92 million $(800 \div 8 \times 11/12)$.

Conclusion

The potential impact of all these issues is significant, particularly in relation to reported profit. On the face of it, the group's results for the current year may be good, but this trend is unlikely to continue into the future. The financial statements should be interpreted with caution.

Appendix

	Gross profit margin	Operating profit margin
20X4 as reported	1,300/3,600 =36.1%	600/3,600 =16.7%
20X4 adjusted:		
Removal of discontinued operations	980/2,800 =35%	425/2,80 =15.2%
As above less marketing costs now charged to income	880/2,800 =31.4%	325/2,800 =11.6%
As above less additional depreciation now charged to cost of sales	788/2,800 =28.1%	233/2,800 = 8.3%

Chapter summary

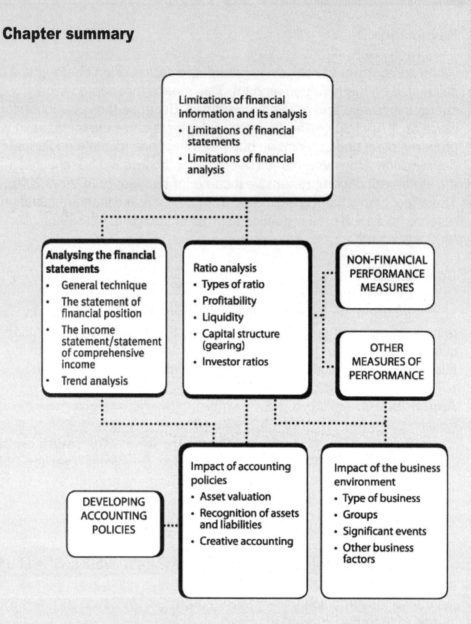

827

Questions & Answers

Test your understanding 1 - Exotic

The Exotic Group carries on business as a distributor of warehouse equipment and importer of fruit. Exotic is a listed entity and was incorporated over 20 years ago to distribute warehouse equipment. Since then the group has diversified its activities to include the import and distribution of fruit, and it expanded its operations by gaining control of two listed entities, Melon in 20X1 and Kiwi in 20X3, either directly or indirectly.

Accounts for all entities are prepared up to 31 December.

The draft statements of total comprehensive income for Exotic, Melon and Kiwi for the year ended 31 December 20X6 are as follows:

	Exotic	Melon	Kiwi
	$000	$000	$000
Revenue	45,600	24,700	22,800
Cost of sales	(18,050)	(5,463)	(5,320)
Gross profit	27,550	19,237	17,480
Distribution costs	(3,325)	(2,137)	(1,900)
Administrative expenses	(3,475)	(950)	(1,900)
Profit from operations	20,750	16,150	13,680
Finance costs	(325)	–	–
Profit before tax	20,425	16,150	13,680
Tax	(8,300)	(5,390)	(4,241)
Profit for the period	12,125	10,760	9,439

There were no items of other comprehensive income during the year.

Notes

	Exotic	Melon	Kiwi
Dividends paid in the year	9,500		
Retained earnings brought forward	20,013	13,315	10,459

The draft statements of financial position as at 31 December 20X6 are as follows:

	Exotic $000	Melon $000	Kiwi $000
Assets:			
Non-current assets (NBV)	35,483	24,273	13,063
Investments:			
Shares in Melon	6,650	–	–
Shares in Kiwi	–	3,800	–
Current assets	1,568	9,025	8,883
Total assets	43,701	37,098	21,946
Equity and liabilities:	$000	$000	$000
Equity shares ($1)	8,000	3,000	2,000
Retained earnings	22,638	24,075	19,898
Total equity	30,638	27,075	21,898
Sundry liabilities	13,063	10,023	48
Total equity and liabilities	43,701	37,098	21,946

The following information is available relating to Exotic, Melon and Kiwi:

(1) On 1 January 20X1 Exotic acquired 2,700,000 $1 equity shares in Melon for $6,650,000 at which date there was a credit balance on the retained earnings of Melon of $1,425,000. No shares have been issued by Melon since Exotic acquired its interest.

(2) On 1 January 20X3 Melon acquired 1,600,000 $1 equity shares in Kiwi for $3,800,000 at which date there was a credit balance on the retained earnings of Kiwi of $950,000. No shares have been issued by Kiwi since Melon acquired its interest.

(3) During 20X6, Kiwi had made inter-company sales to Melon of $480,000 making a profit of 25% on cost and $75,000 of these goods were in inventory at 31 December 20X6.

(4) During 20X6, Melon had made inter-company sales to Exotic of $260,000 making a profit of 33⅓% on cost and $60,000 of these goods were in inventory at 31 December 20X6.

(5) On 1 November 20X6 Exotic sold warehouse equipment to Melon for $240,000 from inventory. Melon has included this equipment in its non-current assets. The equipment had been purchased on credit by Exotic for $200,000 in October 20X6 and this amount is included in its liabilities as at 31 December 20X6.

(6) Melon charges depreciation on its warehouse equipment at 20% on cost. It is company policy to charge a full year's depreciation in the year of acquisition to be included in the cost of sales.

(7) It is group policy to account for non-controlling interest on a proportionate basis. Since acquisition, the goodwill of Melon has been fully written off as a result of an impairment review which took place two years ago. The goodwill of Kiwi has been impaired 60% by 31 December 20X5 and a further 50% of the remaining balance of goodwill was impaired in the year ended 31 December 20X6.

Required:

(a) **Prepare a consolidated statement of comprehensive income for the Exotic Group for the year ended 31 December 20X6 including a reconciliation of retained earnings for the year.**

(12 marks)

(b) **Prepare a consolidated statement of financial position as at that date.**

(13 marks)

(Total: 25 marks)

Test your understanding 2 - Howard

Howard, Sylvia and Sabrina are three entities preparing their financial statements under IFRSs. Their statements of financial position as at 30 September 20X5 are given below:

Statements of Financial Position	Howard	Sylvia	Sabrina
	$000	$000	$000
Non-current assets:			
Property, plant and equipment	160,000	60,000	64,000
Investments	80,000	–	–
	240,000	60,000	64,000

Current assets	65,000	50,000	36,000
	305,000	110,000	100,000

	$000	$000	$000
Equity capital ($1 shares)	50,000	20,000	15,000
Retained earnings	185,000	43,000	42,000
	235,000	63,000	57,000
Non-current liabilities	25,000	18,000	20,000
Current liabilities	45,000	29,000	23,000
	305,000	110,000	100,000

Note 1 – Investment by Howard in Sylvia

On 1 October 20X3, Howard acquired 70% of the equity share capital of Sylvia for $45 million in cash, when the balance on Sylvia's retained earnings was $28 million. It was determined that at this date, land with carrying value of $40 million had a fair value of $45 million.

On 30 September 20X5, Howard acquired a further 10% of the equity shares of Sylvia paying $10 million in cash.

Note 2 – Investment by Howard in Sabrina

On 1 January 20X2, Howard acquired 60% of the equity shares of Sabrina for $21 million in cash, when the balance on Sabrina's retained earnings was $15 million. It was determined that the book value of Sabrina's net assets on 1 January 20X2 were equal to their fair values.

On 30 September 20X5, Howard disposed of one quarter of its shareholding in Sabrina for $15 million cash. Howard's remaining 45% holding enabled Howard to exercise significant influence over the operating and financial policies of Sabrina. The fair value of the remaining 45% holding was $35 million at 30 September 20X5.

Howard have recorded the proceeds of $15 million by debiting cash and crediting investments, but no other entries have been made.

Note 3 – Intra-group trading

During the year ended 30 September 20X5, Howard sold goods to Sylvia for $8 million. These goods were sold at a profit margin of 25%. Half of these goods remain in Sylvia's inventory at the reporting date.

Note 4 – NCIs and goodwill

Howard's policy is to value NCIs at acquisition at fair value. The fair value of the non-controlling interest in Sylvia was $17.4 million and the fair value of the non-controlling interest in Sabrina was $13 million at the relevant dates of acquisition. No impairment losses have arisen on goodwill.

Required:

Prepare the consolidated statement of financial position of the Howard group as at 30 September 20X5.

Test your understanding 3 - Large & Little

Little was incorporated over 20 years ago, operating as an independent entity for 15 years until 1 April 20X0 when it was taken over by Large. Large's directors decided that the local expertise of Little's management should be utilised as far as possible, and since the takeover they have allowed the subsidiary to operate independently, maintaining its existing supplier and customer bases. Large exercises 'arms' length' strategic control, but takes no part in day-to-day operational decisions.

The statements of financial position of Large and Little at 31 March 20X4 are given below. The statement of financial position of Little is prepared in francos (F), its functional currency.

		Large		Little
	$000	$000	F000	F000
Non-current assets:				
Property, plant and equipment	63,000		80,000	
Investments	12,000		–	
		75,000		80,000
Current assets:				
Inventories	25,000		30,000	
Trade receivables	20,000		28,000	
Cash	6,000		5,000	
		51,000		63,000
		126,000		143,000

Equity:

Equity capital (50 cents/1 Franco shares)	30,000	40,000
Revaluation reserve	–	6,000
Retained earnings	35,000	34,000
	65,000	80,000

Non-current liabilities:

Long-term borrowings	20,000		25,000	
Deferred tax	6,000		10,000	
		26,000		35,000

Current liabilities:

Trade payables	25,000		20,000	
Tax	7,000		8,000	
Bank overdraft	3,000		–	
		35,000		28,000
		126,000		143,000

Notes to the SFPs

Note 1 – Investment by Large in Little

On 1 April 20X0 Large purchased 36 million shares in Little for 72 million francos. The retained earnings of Little at that date were 26 million francos. It is group accounting policy to account for goodwill on a proportionate basis. Goodwill has been impairment tested annually and, in the year to 31 March 20X4, had reduced in value by ten per cent.

Note 2 – Intra-group trading

Little sells goods to Large, charging a mark-up of one-third on production cost. At 31 March 20X4, Large held $1 million (at cost to Large) of goods purchased from Little in its inventories. The goods were purchased during March 20X4 and were recorded by Large using an exchange rate of $1 = 5 francos. (There were minimal fluctuations between the two currencies during March 20X4). On 29 March 20X4, Large sent Little a cheque for $1 million to clear the intra-group payable. Little received and recorded this cheque on 3 April 20X4.

Note 3 – Accounting policies

The accounting policies of the two entities are the same, except that the directors of Little have decided to adopt a policy of revaluation of property, whereas Large includes all property in its statement of financial position at depreciated historical cost. Until 1 April 20X3, Little operated from rented warehouse premises. On that date, the entity purchased a leasehold building for 25 million francos, taking out a long-term loan to finance the purchase. The building's estimated useful life at 1 April 20X3 was 25 years, with an estimated residual value of nil, and the directors decided to adopt a policy of straight line depreciation. The building was professionally revalued at 30 million francos on 31 March 20X4, and the directors have included the revalued amount in the statement of financial position. No other property was owned by Little during the year.

Note 4 – Exchange rates

Date	Exchange rate (francos to $1)
1 April 20X0	6.0
31 March 20X3	5.5
31 March 20X4	5.0
Weighted average for the year to 31 March 20X4	5.2
Weighted average for the dates of acquisition of closing inventory	5.1

Required:

(a) Explain (with reference to relevant accounting standards to support your argument) how the financial statements (statement of financial position, statement of profit or loss and other comprehensive income) of Little should be translated into $s for the consolidation of Large and Little.

(5 marks)

(b) Translate the statement of financial position of Little at 31 March 20X4 into $s and prepare the consolidated statement of financial position of the Large group at 31 March 20X4.

(20 marks)

Note: Ignore any deferred tax implications of the property revaluation and the intra-group trading. and assume that the Large Group uses the proportion of net assets method to value the non-controlling interest.

(Total: 25 marks)

Test your understanding 4 - Arc

Arc owns 100% of the ordinary share capital of Bend and Curve. All ordinary shares of all three entities are listed on a recognised exchange. The group operates in the engineering industry, and are currently struggling to survive in challenging economic conditions. Curve has made losses for the last three years and its liquidity is poor. The view of the directors is that Curve needs some cash investment. The directors have decided to put forward a restructuring plan as at 30 June 20X1. Under this plan:

(1) Bend is to purchase the whole of Arc's investment in Curve. The purchase consideration is to be $105 million payable in cash to Arc and this amount will then be loaned on a long-term unsecured basis to Curve; and

(2) Bend will purchase land and buildings with a carrying amount of $15 million from Curve for a total purchase consideration of $25 million. The land and buildings has a mortgage outstanding on it of $8 million. The total purchase consideration of $25 million comprises both ten million $1 nominal value non-voting shares issued by Bend to Curve and the $4 million mortgage liability which Bend will assume; and

(3) Curve had also entered into a finance lease obligation on 1 July 20X0. The present value of the minimum lease obligation at that date was $3 million, and the implicit rate of interest associated with the lease obligation was 10.2%. The lease required that annual payments in arrears of $700,000 must be made. No entries had been made in respect of the lease in the draft financial statements of Curve; and

(4) A dividend of $25 million will be paid from Bend to Arc to reduce the accumulated reserves of Bend.

The draft statements of financial position of Arc and its subsidiaries at 30 June 20X1 are summarised below:

	Arc $m	Bend $m	Curve $m
Non-current assets:			
Tangible non-current assets	500	200	55
Cost of investment in Bend	150		
Cost of investment in Curve	95		
Current assets	125	145	25
	870	345	80

Equity and liabilities			
Ordinary share capital	100	100	35
Share premium			8
Retained earnings	720	230	5
	820	330	48
Non-current liabilities:			
Long-term loan	5		12
Current liabilities:			
Trade payables	45	15	20
	870	345	80

As a result of the restructuring, some of Bend's employees will be made redundant. Based upon a detailed plan, the costs of redundancy will be spread over three years with $2.08 million being payable in one year's time, $3.245 million payable in two year's time and $53.375 million in three years' time. The market yield of high quality corporate bonds is 4%. The directors of Arc consider that, based upon quantification of relevant and reliable data at 30 June 20X1, it will incur additional restructuring obligations amounting to $3 million.

Required:

(a) **Prepare the individual entity statements of financial position after the proposed restructuring plan; (13 marks)**

(b) **Discuss the key implications of the proposed plans, in particular whether the financial position of each company has been improved as a result of the reorganisation. (5 marks)**

Professional marks will be awarded in part (b) for clarity and expression of your discussion. (2 marks)

(Total: 20 marks)

Test your understanding 5 - Kelly

Extracts from the consolidated financial statements of Kelly are given below:

Consolidated statements of financial position as at 31 March

	20X5		20X4	
	$000	$000	$000	$000
Non-current assets				
Property, plant and equipment	5,900		4,400	
Goodwill	85		130	
Investment in associate	170		140	
		6,155		4,670
Current assets				
Inventories	1,000		930	
Receivables	1,340		1,140	
Short-term deposits	35		20	
Cash at bank	180		120	
		2,555		2,210
		8,710		6,880
Equity and liabilities				
Equity capital	2,000		1,500	
Share premium	300		–	
Other components of equity	50		–	
Retained earnings	3,400		3,320	
		5,750		4,820
Non-controlling interests		75		175
Total equity		5,825		4,995
Non-current liabilities				
Interest-bearing borrowings	1,400		1,000	
Obligations under finance leases	210		45	
Deferred tax	340		305	
		1,950		1,350
Current liabilities				
Trade payables	885		495	
Accrued interest	7		9	

Income tax	28	21
Obligations under finance leases	15	10
	935	535
	8,710	6,880

Consolidated statement of comprehensive income for the year ended 31 March 20X5

	$000
Revenue	875
Cost of sales	(440)
Gross profit	435
Other operating expenses	(210)
Profit from operations	225
Finance cost	(100)
Gain on sale of subsidiary	30
Share of associate's profit	38
Profit before tax	193
Tax	(48)
Profit for the year	145

Other comprehensive income

Items that will not be reclassified to profit or loss in subsequent accounting periods

Gains on land revaluation	50
Total comprehensive income for the year	195

Profit attributable to:

Equity holders of the parent	120
Non-controlling interests	25
	145

Total comprehensive income attributable to:

Equity holders of the parent	170
Non-controlling interests	25
	195

Notes:

Dividends

Kelly paid a dividend of $40,000 during the year.

Property, plant and equipment

The following transactions took place during the year:

- Land was revalued upwards by $50,000 on 1st April 20X4.
- During the year, depreciation of $80,000 was charged to profit or loss.
- Additions include $300,000 acquired under finance leases.
- A property was disposed of during the year for $250,000 cash. Its carrying amount was $295,000 at the date of disposal. The loss on disposal has been included within cost of sales.

Gain on sale of subsidiary

On 1 January 20X5, Kelly disposed of a 80% owned subsidiary for $390,000 in cash. The subsidiary had the following net assets at the date of disposal:

	$000
Property, plant and equipment	635
Inventory	20
Receivables	45
Cash	35
Payables	(130)
Income tax	(5)
Interest-bearing borrowings	(200)
	400

This subsidiary had been acquired on 1 January 20X1 for a cash payment of $220,000 when its net assets had a fair value of $225,000 and the non-controlling interest had a fair value of $50,000.

Goodwill

The Kelly Group uses the full goodwill method to calculate goodwill. No impairments have arisen during the year.

Required:

Prepare the consolidated statement of cash flows of the Kelly group for the year ended 31 March 20X5 in the form required by IAS 7 Statement of cash flows. Show your workings clearly.

Test your understanding 6 - Bahzad

Bahzad has singled out the inventory control director for an employee option scheme. He has been offered 3 million options exercisable at 20c, conditional upon him remaining with the company for three years and improving inventory control by the end of that period. The proportion of the options that vest is dependent upon the inventory days on the last day of the three years. The schedule is as follows:

Inventory days	Proportion vesting
5	100%
6	90%
7	70%
8	40%
9	10%

The options also have a vesting criteria related to market value. They only vest if the share price is above 25c on the vesting day, i.e. at the end of the third year. This is the second of the three years. At the end of year one it was estimated that the inventory days at the end of the third year would be 7. However, during year two inventory control improved and at the end of the year the estimate of inventory days at the end of the third year was 6. The relevant market data is as follows:

Date	Share price	Option price
Grant date	20c	10c
End of Year One	19c	6c
End of Year Two	37c	19c

The option price is the market price of an equivalent marketable option on the relevant date.

Required:

(a) **Show the effect of the scheme on the financial statements of Bahzad for year two of the share option scheme.**

(b) **Explain the significance of any conditions attaching to the share option scheme and how they are dealt with in accounting for such a scheme.**

Test your understanding 7 - Splash

An entity, Splash, has established a share option scheme for its four directors, commencing 1 July 20X8. Each director will be entitled to 25,000 share options on condition that they remain with Splash for four years, from the date the scheme was introduced.

Information regarding the share options are as follows:

Fair value of option at grant date	$10
Fair value of option at 30 June 20X9	$12
Exercise price of option	$5

The market value (i.e. fair value) of the shares at 30 June 20X9 was $17 per share.

Tax allowances on any expense recognised for share options are only granted at the date when the options are exercised and will be based upon the intrinsic value of the options. Assume a tax rate of 30%.

Required:

Calculate and explain the amounts to be included in the financial statements of Splash for the year ended 30 June 20X9, including explanation and calculation of any deferred tax implications.

Test your understanding 8 - Fourkings

Fourkings is a marketing and public relations entity which provides a 'one-stop-shop' for all aspects of market research and product promotion activities, both domestically and abroad, including hire of staff, venues and marquees, and other associated requirements. In recent years, Fourkings has experienced significant expansion, fuelled mainly by the growth experienced by entities in the financial sector. More recently, the business environment has become more challenging as a result of the global financial crisis and Fourkings has requested advice on a number of financial reporting issues in respect of the financial statements for the year ended 31 October 2010 as follows:

(1) Fourkings requires clients to pay a 15% initial amount at the time of booking an event plus facilities required, with the balance payable by the date of the event. The initial amount is not refundable in the event of the client cancelling at any stage prior to the due date of the event. Currently, the initial amount is taken to revenue immediately upon receipt as Fourkings does not foresee any circumstances when it would need to cancel their service provision.

Required:

Advise Fourkings on the appropriateness of the accounting policy adopted.

(5 marks)

(2) Fourkings purchased a country manor house in extensive grounds to make available to potential clients as an event venue. The property cost $5 million (of which the grounds accounted for $1 million) on 1 November 2006. Both the manor house and the grounds require regular expenditure to keep them in excellent condition to attract clients and bookings. The expenditure has always been expensed but Fourkings now intends to capitalise this expenditure.

The number of bookings for the manor house and grounds for the current year fell in comparison with earlier years. For the year to 31 October 2010, the property was utilised for only 150 days, when the average annual utilisation in earlier years had been 200 days, with the average spend per client day also reduced from previous levels. Fourkings is currently reviewing alternative uses for the house and grounds, including disposal to a property developer who is willing to pay $4.5 million to purchase the manor house and grounds to convert it into a theme park.

Required:

Advise Fourkings on the accounting issues associated with this situation.

(8 marks)

(3) Fourkings spends a considerable amount of time and effort to recruit, train and retain staff. They regard this as a crucial element of their success to date as many competitor companies hire staff on a casual basis and pay minimum wages to keep costs as low as possible. Fourkings is considering capitalisation of recruitment and training costs as it believes that the benefits of staff training are received over several years. It introduced an employee share-option scheme on 1 November 2009 in an effort to retain staff loyalty. A pre-defined group of one hundred employees were selected to join the scheme on the following terms:

(a) Each employee eligible would be granted 500 share options, with a three-year vesting period; the options would become exercisable immediately thereafter.

(b) To be eligible to exercise the options, employees would be required to still be employed by the company at the vesting date. At the date the scheme was established, it was expected that ten employees would leave during the year; however, only five actually left during the year to 31 October 2010.

(c) Fourkings has provided the following information relating to the share option scheme:

Date	Number expected to leave in year	FV of option
1 Nov 2009		$6.00
31 Oct 2010		$7.50
31 Oct 2011	5	(est) $8.25
31 Oct 2012	7	(est) $9.95

Required:

Advise Fourkings on the accounting issues associated with this situation.

(6 marks)

(4) Fourkings has undertaken the organisation of several major product launches during the year. One such event required making payments to an exclusive venue to reserve, pay for the use of facilities and to meet catering and hospitality costs. Fourkings paid a deposit on 31 August 2010 for rental of a villa in the Seychelles on 31 December 2010 amounting to 100,000 Seychelles rupees. The terms of the agreement are that the villa rental can be cancelled at any time up to 31 December 2010 and the deposit returned without penalty. The balance outstanding for the villa rental is due on 1 February 2011 and amounts to 150,000 Seychelles rupees. The table below summarises the rates of exchange during the relevant period:

Date	Rupees per $
31 August 2010	1.25
31 October 2010	1.30
31 December 2010	1.20
1 February 2011	1.35

Additionally, Fourkings is considering opening a Euro currency bank account during 2011 to facilitate payments made to third parties within the Euro zone but is unsure about how this should be included within the financial statements for the year ended 31 October 2011.

Required:

Explain the accounting treatment for this situation and calculate the amounts to include in the financial statements for the year ended 31 October 2010 and explain how transactions passing through a Euro currency bank account should be treated in the financial statements for the year ending 31 October 2011.

(6 marks)

(Total: 25 marks)

Test your understanding 9 - Seejoy

Seejoy is a famous football club but has significant cash flow problems. The directors and shareholders wish to take steps to improve the club's financial position. The following proposals had been drafted in an attempt to improve the cash flow of the club. However, the directors need advice upon their implications.

(a) **Sale and leaseback of football stadium (excluding the land element)**

The football stadium is currently accounted for using the cost model in IAS 16 Property, plant, and equipment. The carrying value of the stadium will be $12 million at 31 December 20X6. The stadium will have a remaining life of 20 years at 31 December 20X6, and the club uses straight line depreciation. It is proposed to sell the stadium to a third party institution on 1 January 20X7 and lease it back under a 20-year finance lease. The sale price and fair value is $15 million which is the present value of the minimum lease payments. The agreement transfers the title of the stadium back to the football club at the end of the lease at nil cost. The rental is $1.2 million per annum in advance commencing on 1 January 20X7. The directors do not wish to treat this transaction as the raising of a secured loan. The implicit interest rate on the finance in the lease is 5.6%.

(9 marks)

(b) **Player registrations**

The club capitalises the unconditional amounts (transfer fees) paid to acquire players. The club proposes to amortise the cost of the transfer fees over ten years instead of the current practice that is to amortise the cost over the duration of the player's contract. The club has sold most of its valuable players during the current financial year but still has two valuable players under contract.

Player	Transfer fee capitalised $m	Amortisation to 31 December 20X6 $m	Contract commenced	Contract expires
A. Steel	20	4	1 January 20X6	31 December 20Y0
R. Aldo	15	10	1 January 20X5	31 December 20X7

If Seejoy win the national football league, then a further $5 million will be payable to the two players' former clubs. Seejoy are currently performing very poorly in the league.

(5 marks)

(c) **Issue of bond**

The club proposes to issue a 7% bond with a face value of $50 million on 1 January 20X7 at a discount of 5% that will be secured on income from future ticket sales and corporate hospitality receipts, which are approximately $20 million per annum. Under the agreement the club cannot use the first $6 million received from corporate hospitality sales and reserved tickets (season tickets) as this will be used to repay the bond. The money from the bond will be used to pay for ground improvements and to pay the wages of players.

The bond will be repayable, both capital and interest, over 15 years with the first payment of $6 million due on 31 December 20X7. It has an effective interest rate of 7.7%. There will be no active market for the bond and the company does not wish to use valuation models to value the bond.

(6 marks)

(d) **Player trading**

Another proposal is for the club to sell its two valuable players, Aldo and Steel. It is thought that it will receive a total of $16 million for both players. The players are to be offered for sale at the end of the current football season on 1 May 20X7.

(5 marks)

Required:

Discuss how the above proposals would be dealt with in the financial statements of Seejoy for the year-ending 31 December 20X7, setting out their accounting treatment and appropriateness in helping the football club's cash flow problems. (Candidates do not need knowledge of the football finance sector to answer this question.)

(Total: 25 marks)

Test your understanding answers

Key answer tips:

This is not a past exam question, but it is a great question to revise complex groups. If you can work your way through this, then you should be feeling comfortable with this topic and can attempt some of the more difficult questions.

(a) **Consolidated statement of comprehensive income for the year ended 31 December 20X6**

	Exotic $000	Melon $000	Kiwi $000	Adjusts $000	SOCI $000
Revenue	45,600	24,700	22,800	(980))	92,120
Cost of sales	(18,050)	(5,463)	(5,320)	740)	
Cost re equip't sale	200				) (27,915)
URPS made by M & K (W5)		(15)	(15)	)	
Excess dep'n adj (W6)		8		) ───────	
Gross profit					64,205
Distribution costs	(3,325)	(2,137)	(1,900)		(7,362)
Administration expenses	(3,475)	(950)	(1,900)		(6,325)
Goodwill impaired (W3)					(259)
					───────
Profit from operations					50,259
Finance costs	(325)				(325)
					───────
Profit before tax					49,934
Tax	(8,300)	(5,390)	(4,241)		(17,931)
		───────	───────		───────
Profit for the period		10,753	9,424		32,003
		───────	───────		───────
Attributable to:					
Equity holders of the parent (bal fig)					28,289
Non-controlling interests (W8)					3,714
					───────
					32,003
					───────

There were no items of other comprehensive income during the year.

Reconciliation of retained earnings:

Retained earnings brought forward (W9)	34,115
Profit for the period	28,289
Dividends paid	(9,500)
Retained earnings carried forward	52,904

(b) **Consolidated statement of financial position as at 31 December 20X6**

	$000
Assets:	
Non-current assets (35,483 + 24,273 + 13,063 – 32 (W6))	72,787
Goodwill (W3)	259
Current assets (1,568 + 9,025 + 8,883 – 15(W5) – 15(W5))	19,446
Total assets	92,492
Equity and liabilities:	
$1 equity shares	8,000
Group retained earnings (W7)	52,904
	60,904
Non-controlling interest (W4)	8,454
Total equity	69,358
Sundry liabilities:(13,063 + 10,023 + 48)	23,134
Total equity and liabilities	92,492

Workings

(W1) Group structure

$$\frac{2,700}{3,000} = 90\% \quad \text{Exotic}$$

	90%	Effective interest of Exotic in
		Kiwi (90% × 80%) = 72%
Melon		Effective NCI in Kiwi = 28%
	80%	

$$\frac{1,600}{2,000} = 80\% \quad \text{Kiwi}$$

(W2) Net assets

	At date of acquisition		At reporting date	
	$000	$000	$000	$000
Melon				
Equity capital		3,000		3,000
Retained earnings	1,425		24,075	
Excess depreciation (W6)			8	
Unrealised profit (W5)			(15)	
		1,425		24,068
		4,425		27,068

	At date of acquisition		At reporting date	
	$000	$000	$000	$000
Kiwi				
Equity capital		2,000		2,000
Retained earnings	950		19,898	
Unrealised profit (W5)			(15)	
		950		19,883
		2,950		21,883

(W3) Goodwill

	In Melon	In Kiwi
	$000	$000
Cost of investment to the group	6,650	
90% × 3,800		3,420
Melon: NCI% of CV of NA at acq'n (10% × 4,425)(W2)	442	
Kiwi: NCI% of CV of NA at acq'n (28% × 2,950)(W2)		826
	7,092	4,246
Fair value of all net assets at acquisition:		
Melon: (W2)	(4,425)	
Kiwi: (W2)		(2,950)
	2,667	1,296
Impairment – in previous years (100%) / 60%	(2,667)	(778)
	–	518
Impairment current year (50% × 518) (I/S)	–	(259)
Statement of financial position	–	259
Charged against retained earnings	2,667	1,037

(W4) Non-controlling Interest – proportionate basis for both subsidiaries

Melon

CV of NCI at acquisition (10% × 4,425) (W2)	442.5
Share of post-acq'n retained earnings (10% × (27,068 – 4,425)) (W2)	2264.3
(rounded)	2,707

Kiwi (use effective interest %)

CV of NCI at acquisition (28% × 2,950) (W2)	826
Share of post-acq'n retained earnings (28% × (21,883 – 2,950)) (W2)	5,301
Less: NCI share of cost of investment by Melon in Kiwi (10% × 3,800)	(380)
	8,454

(W5) **Unrealised profit in inventory**

Kiwi – Melon	$75{,}000 \times 25 \div 125$	= 15,000
Melon – Exotic	$60{,}000 \times 33.333$	= 15,000
	÷ 133.333	

(W6) **Inter-company transfers of non-current assets**

Exotic – Melon   240,000

Therefore Exotic has made an unrealised profit.

Debit group statement of comprehensive income	40,000
Credit group non-current assets	40,000

Total intra-group revenues (480 + 260 + 240) = $980,000

Total intra-group adjustment to cost of sales (480 + 260)
= $740,000

Total intra-group addition to NCA re equipt sold by Exotic to Melon
= $240,000 when original cost was $200,000.

Depreciation is charged on $240,000 at 20% on cost (i.e. $48,000 each year). This should be charged in the group accounts at 20% on $200,000 (i.e. $40,000).

Therefore $8,000 extra depreciation has been charged each year and must be added back.

Debit depreciation group	8,000
Credit statement of comprehensive income group	8,000
Therefore net impact $40,000 – $8,000 =	32,000
Net non-current assets credit	32,000
Statement of comprehensive income debit	32,000

(W7) Consolidated retained earnings carried forward

	$000
All of Exotic	
Per the question	22,638
Unrealised profit re equip't (W6)	(40)
	22,598
Share of Melon	
90% (24,068 – 1,425) (W2)	20,378
Share of Kiwi	
72% (19,883 – 950) (W2)	13,632
Goodwill impairment (2,667 + 1,037) (W3)	(3,704)
	52,904

(W8) Non-controlling interest in profit

Melon (10,753 × 10%)	1075
Kiwi's profit (9,424 × 28%)	2,639
	3,714

(W9) Consolidated retained earnings brought forward

	$000
All of Exotic	20,013
Share of Melon	
90% (13,315 – 1,425) (W2)	10,701
Share of Kiwi	
72% (10,459 – 950) (W2)	6,846
Goodwill impairment (2,667 + 778) (W3)	(3,445)
	34,115

Test your understanding 2 - Howard

Howard – Consolidated Statement of Financial Position at 30 September 20X5

Assets:		$000
Goodwill (W3)		9,400
Property, plant & equipment	(160,000 + 60,000 + 5,000(FVA))	225,000
Investments	(80,000 – 45,000(W3) – 10,000(W7) – 21,000(W3) + 15,000(W8))	19,000
Investment in associate		35,000
Current assets	(65,000 + 50,000 – 1,000(W6))	114,000
		402,400

Equity and liabilities:		$000
Equity Capital		50,000
Retained earnings (W5)		223,500
Other components of equity (W7)		(2,700)
Non-controlling interest (W4)		14,600
		285,400
Non-current liabilities	(25,000 + 18,000)	43,000
Current liabilities	(45,000 + 29,000)	74,000
		402,400

Workings:

(W1) Group structure

Howard

1 Oct X3	70%		1 Jan X2	60%
30 Sept X5	10%		30 Sept X5	(15%)
Rep date	80%		Rep date	45%
	Sylvia		Sabrina	

Note that Howard controls Sylvia from 1 October 20X3. The purchase of additional shares on 30 September 20X5 does not change this situation. An equity transfer is required between the group and NCI to reflect the purchase of additional shares.

Note that Howard controls Sabrina from 1 January 20X2. The sale of shares on 30 September 20X5 results in a loss of control, on which a group gain or loss disposal should be computed and included in the group statement of comprehensive income. The fair value of the residual holding should be included in the calculation of the group gain or loss on disposal and also as initial recognition of an associate as significant influence is exercised following the loss of control.

(W2) **Net assets**	**Sylvia**		**Sabrina**	
	Acq'n date	**Rep date**	**Acq'n date**	**Rep date**
	$000	$000	$000	$000
Share capital	20,000	20,000	15,000	15,000
Retained earnings	28,000	43,000	15,000	42,000
FVA – Land (45,000 – 40,000)	5,000	5,000		
	53,000	68,000	30,000	57,000

(W3) **Goodwill**

	Sylvia	Sabrina
	$000	$000
FV of cost of gaining control	45,000	21,000
FV of NCI at acquisition	17,400	13,000
	62,400	34,000
Less: FV of net assets at acq'n (W2)	(53,000)	(30,000)
Goodwill at acq'n - unimpaired at rep date/disposal date	9,400	4,000

(W4) **Non–controlling interest**

	Sylvia $000	Sabrina $000
NCI at acquisition date (W3)	17,400	13,000
NCI share of post-acq'n retained earnings (30% × ($68,000 – $53,000) (W2))	4,500	
NCI share of post-acq'n retained earnings (40% × ($57,000 – $30,000)(W2))		10,800
NCI before equity transfer	21,900	23,800
Equity transfer due to purchase of additional shares by group (W7)	(7,300)	N/A
NCI at reporting date/disposal date	14,600	23,800

(W5) **Retained earnings**

	$000
Howard	185,000
Provision for unrealised profit (W6)	(1,000)
Sylvia (70% × $15,000 (W2))	10,500
Sabrina (60% × $27,000 (W2))	16,200
Gain on disposal of Sabrina (W8)	12,800
	223,500

(W6) **Provision for unrealised profits**

	$000
Goods in inventory (1/2 × $8,000)	4,000
Provision for unrealised profit (25% × $4,000) made by Howard	1,000

(W7) Equity transfer between group and NCI

	$000
Cash paid by Howard to buy additional shares	10,000
Decrease in NCI (10/30 × $21,900(W4))	7,300
Net decrease in equity of the group	2,700
Dr NCI (W4)	7,300
Dr Equity	2,700
Cr Investments (reversal of original accounting for receipt of disposal proceeds)	10,000

(W8) Group gain/loss on disposal of Sabrina

	$000	$000
Proceeds		15,000
Fair value of residual interest		35,000
Less: interest in Sabrina disposed of:		
Net assets at disposal date (W2)	57,000	
Unimpaired goodwill at disposal date (W3)	4,000	
Gain on disposal of Sabrina (W8)		
	61,000	
Less: NCI at disposal date (W5)	(23,800)	(37,200)
Group gain on disposal to retained earnings (W5)		12,800

At the reporting date, the residual investment is accounted for as an associate at a deemed cost of $35 million.

Test your understanding 3 - Large & Little

Group accounting – foreign currency Large and Little

Answer 1

(1) It is clear from the information contained in the question that, on a day-to-day basis, Little operates as a relatively independent entity, with its own supplier and customer bases. Therefore, the cash flows of Little do not have a day-to-day impact on the cash flows of Large. The functional currency of Little is the Franco, rather than the dollar. For consolidation purposes, the financial statements of Little must be translated into a presentation currency: the dollar (the functional currency of Large, in which the consolidated financial statements of Large are presented). In these circumstances, IAS 21 The effects of changes in foreign exchange rates requires that the financial statements be translated using the closing rate (or net investment) method (the presentation currency method). This involves translating the net assets in the statement of financial position at the spot rate of exchange at the reporting date and income and expenses in the statement of profit or loss and other comprehensive income at the rate on the date of the transactions, or as an approximation, a weighted average rate for the year.

Exchange differences are reported as other comprehensive income as they do not impact on the cash flows of the group until the relevant investment is disposed of. Note that following amendments made to IAS 1, the exchange differences reported will be reported as within other comprehensive income as 'Items which may be reclassified to profit or loss in future periods'.

(b) **Group statement of financial position – Large Group**

Non-current assets:		$000
Intangibles - goodwill	(W3)	2,268
Property, plant and equipment	63,000 + ((80,000 – 6,000) / 5)	77,800
Current assets:		
Inventories	25,000 + ((30,000 – 1,250 (URP)) / 5)	30,750
Trade receivables	20,000 + (28,000 / 5) – 1,000 (CIT)	24,600
Cash	6,000 + (5,000 / 5) + 1,000 (CIT)	8,000
		143,418

Equity and liabilities		$000
Equity share capital		30,000
Revaluation reserve	(6,000 – 6,000)	–
Retained earnings	(W5)	35,926
Group foreign exchange reserve	(W7)	2,437
Non-controlling interest	(W4)	1,455
Total equity		69,818
Non-current liabilities	20,000 + (25,000 / 5)	25,000
Deferred tax	6,000 + (10,000 / 5)	8,000
Current liabilities		
Payables	25,000 + (20,000 / 5)	29,000
Tax	7,000 + (8,000 / 5)	8,600
Overdraft	3,000 + 0	3,000
		143,418

Workings

(W1) Group structure

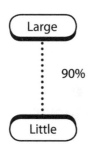

(W2) Net assets of subsidiary in functional currency

	Acq'n Date	Rep date
	F000	F000
Equity capital	40,000	40,000
Retained earnings	26,000	34,000
Revaluation reserve		6,000
Accounting policy adjustment		(6,000)
URPS		(1,250)
	66,000	72,750

*Calculation of unrealised profit on closing inventory sold by subsidiary:

	%age	F000
URPS on inventory sold by subsidiary		
Cost	100.0	3,750
Profit element	33.3	**1,250**
Selling price	133.3	5,000

**Accounting policy adjustment:

This arises due to the parent and subsidiary having different accounting policies relating to property. At the reporting date, the property has been owned by the subsidiary, and depreciated, for one year (F25m / 25 year = F1m per annum), giving a carrying value of F24m before the revaluation is accounted for at the reporting date. The revaluation reserve created is therefore (F30m – F24m) F6m. This needs to be removed from both non-current assets and revaluation reserve of the subsidiary.

(W3) **Goodwill on proportionate basis in subsidiary functional currency**

	F000
Cost	72,000
NCI at acquisition (10% × 66,000 (W2)	6,600
	78,600
Fair value of net assets at acquisition (W2)	(66,000)
Proportionate basis goodwill at acquisition	12,600
Impairment in year – 10%	(1,200)
Unimpaired goodwill at reporting date	11,340
Translated at closing rate @ 5 for SOFP	$2,268

Reconciliation of movement in goodwill:

		F000	Rate	$000
1 April 20X0 year to 31/03/X4	Goodwill at acquisition	12,600	6.0	2,100
	Impaired in year - include in (W5)	(1,260)	Ave rate	5.2 (242)
	Exchange gain on retranslation of goodwill	**Bal fig**		**410**
31 March 20X4		11,340	Cl rate	5.0 2,268

Note that the exchange gain (or loss) arising on retranslation of goodwill is an amount which changes year-by-year, depending upon movement in the rate of echange over time. It is included within other components of equity on the group statement of financial position.

Note also that, as goodwill has been calculated on a proportionate basis, all of the impairment is taken to retained earnings in (W5).

(W4) Non-controlling interest on proportionate basis

		F000	Rate	$000
NCI at acquisition (W3)		6,600	Acq'n 6.0	1,100
NCI % of profit for the year	10% × (72,750 - 66,000) (W2)	675	Ave 5.2	130
NCI % of goodwill impairment (if appropriate)			Ave 5.2	N/A
NCI % of exchange gain (loss) on retranslation of net assets	(W6)			225
To group SOFP				1,455

(W5) **Group retained earnings**

		F000	Rate	$000
Large				35,000
Group% of profit for year	90% × (72,750 - 66,000) (W2)	6,075	5.2	1,168
Goodwill impaired in year (W3)		(1,260)	5.2	(242)
				36,095

(W6) **Exchange gain (loss) on retranslation of net assets**

	F000		Rate	$000
Net assets at acquisition	66,000	Acq'n	6.0	11,000
Post-acq'n change in NA (exclude g'will impairment) (W2)	6,750	Ave	5.2	1,298
Exchange gain (loss) on retranslation of net assets			bal fig	**2,252**
Closing NA at rep date	72,750			14,550

The exchange gain (loss) arising on retranslation of net assets is then allocated between the group and NCI based upon their respective shareholdings as follows:

		$000
Group (90% × 2,252)	(W7)	2,027
NCI (10% × 2,252)	(W4)	225
		2,252

(W7) **Group foreign exchange reserve**

	$000
Arising on retranslation of goodwill (W3)	410
Arising on retranslation of net assets (W6)	2,027
To Group SOFP	2,437

Test your understanding 4 - Arc

Answer (a)

Arc - restatement	Initial $m	Adjusts $m	Notes	Final $m
Non-current assets:				
Tangible non-current assets	500			500
Cost of investment in Bend	150			150
Cost of investment in Curve	95	(95)	(1)	
Loan to Curve		105	(2)	105
Current assets	125	105	(1)	150
		(105)	(2)	
		25	(3)	
	870	345		905
Equity and liabilities:				
Ordinary share capital	100			100
Retained earnings	720	10	(1)	755
		25	(3)	
	870	35		855
Non-current liabilities:				
Long-term loan	5			5
Current liabilities:				
Trade payables	45			45
	870	35		905

Notes:

(1) Disposal of investment in Curve for $105m, resulting in a profit of $10m.

(2) Long-term loan made to Curve.

(3) Dividend due from Bend.

KAPLAN PUBLISHING

Answer (a)

Bend restatement	Initial $m	Adjusts Notes $m	Final $m
Non-current assets:			
Tangible non-current assets	200	25 (3)	225
Cost of investment in Curve		105 (1)	105
Current assets	145	(105)(1)	40
	345	25	370
Equity and liabilities:			
Ordinary share capital	100	10 (3)	110
Share premium		11 (3)	11
Retained earnings	230	(25)(2)	205
	330	(4)	326
Non-current liabilities:			
Long-term loan		4 (3)	4
Current liabilities:			
Trade payables	15		15
	345	25	370

Notes:

(1) Purchase of investment in Curve for $105m.

(2) Dividend due to Arc.

(3) Purchase of land and buildings from Curve – comprising:

	$m
Non-voting shares of $1 each	10
Share premium (bal fig)	11
Mortgage liability taken over	4
	25

Answer (a)

Curve - restatement	Initial $m	Adjusts Notes $m	Final $m
Non-current assets:			
Tangible non-current assets	55	(15.0)(2	40.0
Finance lease assets		3.0(3)	2.5
		(0.5)(3	
Cost of investment in Bend		21.0	21.0
Current assets	25	105.0(1)	129.3
		(0.7)(3)	
	80	112.8	192.8
Equity and liabilities:			
Ordinary share capital	35		35.0
Share premium	8		8.0
Retained earnings	5	10.0(2)	14.2
		(0.5)(3)	
		(0.3)(3)	
	48	9.2	57.2
Non-current liabilities:			
Long-term loan	12	(4.0)	8.0
Loan from Arc		105.0(1)	105.0
Finance lease obligation		3.0(3)	2.2
		0.3(3)	
		(0.7)(3)	
		(0.4)(3)	
Current liabilities:			
Finance lease obligation		(0.4)(3)	0.4
Trade payables	20		20.0
	80	112.8	192.8

Notes:

1 – Loan from Arc of $105m.

	$m
2 – Sale of land and buildings to Bend as follows:	
Disposal proceeds (Mort tfr at + shares at FV $21m)	25
CV of land and buildings	15
Profit on disposal	10

KAPLAN PUBLISHING

3 – Finance lease obligation as follows:

	Bal b/fwd	Int @ 10.2%	Cash paid	Bal c/fwd
	$000	$000	$000	$000
Y/end 30/06/X1	3,000	306	(700)	2,606
Y/end 30/06/X2	2,606	266	(700)	2,172

Current liability element = $2,606,000 – $2,172,000 = $434,000

Answer (b)

The plan has no impact on the group financial statements as all of the internal transactions will be eliminated on consolidation but does affect the individual accounts of the companies. The reconstruction only masks the problem facing Curve. It does not solve or alter the business risk currently being faced by the group.

A further issue is that such a reorganisation may result in further costs and expenses being incurred. Note that any proposed provision for restructuring must meet the requirements of IAS 37 Provisions, Contingent Liabilities and Contingent Assets before it can be included in the financial statements. A constructive obligation will arise if there is a detailed formal plan produced and a valid expectation in those affected that the plan will be carried out. This is normally crystallised at the point when there is communication by the company with those who are expected to be affected by the plan.

The transactions outlined in the plans are essentially under common control and must be viewed in this light. This plan overcomes the short-term cash flow problem of Curve and results in an increase in the accumulated reserves. The plan does show the financial statements of the individual entities in a better light except for the significant increase in long-term loans in Curve's statement of financial position. The profit on the sale of the land from Curve to Bend will be eliminated on consolidation.

In the financial statements of Curve, the investment in Bend should be accounted for under IFRS 9. There is now cash available for Curve and this may make the plan attractive. However, the dividend from Bend to Arc will reduce the accumulated reserves of Bend but if paid in cash will reduce the current assets of Bend to a critical level.

The purchase consideration relating to Curve may be a transaction at an overvalue in order to secure the financial stability of the former entity. A range of values are possible which are current value, carrying amount or possibly at zero value depending on the purpose of the reorganisation.

Another question which arises is whether the sale of Curve gives rise to a realised profit. Further, there may be a question as to whether Bend has effectively made a distribution. This may arise where the purchase consideration was well in excess of the fair value of Curve. An alternative to a cash purchase would be a share exchange. In this case, local legislation would need to be reviewed in order to determine the requirements for the setting up of any share premium account.

Test your understanding 5 - Kelly

Consolidated statement of cash flows for the year ended 31 March 20X5

	$000	$000
Cash flows from operating activities		
Profit before tax		193
Gain on sale of subsidiary		(30)
Share of associate's profit		(38)
Finance costs		100
Adjust for non-cash items dealt with in arriving at operating profit:		
Depreciation		80
Loss on disposal of property (250 – 295)		45
		――――
Operating profit before working capital changes		350
Increase in inventory (1,000 – (930 – 20))		(90)
Increase in receivables (1,340 – (1,140 – 45))		(245)
Increase in payables (885 – (495 – 130))		520
		――――
		535
Finance costs paid (W2)		(102)
Tax paid (W3)		(1)
		――――
		432

Cash flows from investing activities

Sale of property	250	
Purchases of property, plant and equipment (W4)	(2,160)	
Dividends received from associate (W5)	8	
Net proceeds from sale of subsidiary (390 – 35)	355	
		(1,547)

Cash flows from financing activities

Repayments of finance leases (W6)	(130)	
Cash raised from interest-bearing borrowings (W7)	600	
Issue of shares (500 + 300)	800	
Dividends paid to equity shareholders of parent	(40)	
Dividends paid to non-controlling interests (W8)	(40)	
		1,190
Increase in cash and cash equivalents		75
Opening cash and cash equivalents (120 + 20)		140
Closing cash and cash equivalents (180 + 35)		215

(1) Goodwill

Goodwill on acquisition of subsidiary disposed of during the year

	$000
Fair value of consideration paid	220
Fair value of NCI	50
	270
Less: Fair value of net assets at acquisition	(225)
Full goodwill at acquisition	45

Goodwill

	$000		$000
Bal b/d	130	Disposal of sub (as above)	45
		Bal c/d	85
	———		———
	130		130
	———		———

(2) Finance

Finance

	$000		$000
Cash (bal fig)	102	Bal b/d	9
Bal b/d	7	SCI	100
	———		———
	109		109
	———		———

(3) Tax paid

Tax

Disposal of sub	5	Bal b/d – IT	21
Tax paid (bal fig)	1	Bal b/d – DT	305
Bal c/d – IT	28	SCI – group	48
Bal c/d – DT	340		
	———		———
	374		374
	———		———

(4) Purchase of non-current assets

Property, plant and equipment

Bal b/d	4,400	Depreciation	80
Revaluation	50	Disposal –property	295
Finance leases (W6)	300	Disposal – sub	635
Cash (bal fig)	2,160	Bal c/d	5,900
	———		———
	6,910		6,910
	———		———

(5) Dividend from associate

Associates

Bal b/d	140	Divi received (bal fig)	8
Share of profit for the year	38	Bal c/d	170
	178		178

(6) Repayment of finance leases

Finance leases

Lease repayments (bal fig)	130	Bal b/d (10 + 45)	55
Bal c/d (15 + 210)	225	New leases (W4)	300
	355		355

(7) Cash raised from borrowings

Interest-bearing borrowings

Disposal of sub	200	Bal b/d	1,000
Bal b/d	1,400	Cash (bal fig)	600
	1,600		1,600

(8) Dividend paid to non-controlling interests

Non-controlling interests

NCI in sub disposed (W9)	85	Bal b/d	175
Dividends paid (bal fig)	40	Share of profits	25
Bal c/d	75		
	———		———
	200		200
	———		———

(W9) NCI in sub at disposal date

		$000
FV of NCI at acquisition		50
NCI share of increase in post-acquisition retained earnings	(20% × (400 – 225))	35
		———
		85
		———

Test your understanding 6 - Bahzad

Part (a)

At the end of year two the amount recognised in equity is $180,000 (3m × 10c × 90% × 2/3).

At the end of year one the amount recognised in equity should have been $70,000 (3m × 10c × 70% × 1/3).

Therefore the charge to profit or loss for year two is $110,000 (180,000 – 70,000).

Part (b)

Conditions attaching to a share option scheme may be either service conditions or performance conditions. An example of a **service condition** is that each member of a share option scheme must remain employed by the entity throughout the vesting period. If an individual member of the scheme is no longer employed by the entity at any time prior to the vesting date, they will lose their eligibility to remain as a member of the scheme. Service conditions are regarded as non-market conditions (see below) and are taken into account when estimating the number of options that are likely to vest at the end of the vesting period.

A **performance condition** relates to specified service conditions and/or specified performance targets which should be complied with if a scheme member is to become eligible to exercise their options at some point following the vesting date performance conditions may be either market or non-market conditions.

Market conditions are taken into account when arriving at the fair value of a share option at the grant date. The fair value of an option could be determined by on option pricing model such as Black-Scholes, although other models could be used. This would include, for example, attainment of a minimum share price by the vesting date, or growth in the share price in relation to a specified index. Within this question, one of the conditions of vesting is a 'market condition' (the share price must be above 25c on the vesting day). This should already have been taken into account when the option price was fixed and it does not affect the calculations required to determine amounts included in the financial statements at each reporting date.

Non-market conditions are relevant at each reporting date to estimate the number of options which are likely to vest at the vesting date. Examples of non-market conditions include achievement of a profit or earnings target by the vesting date.

Test your understanding 7 - Splash

Share options should be recognised as a remuneration expense as they are part of the work and service provided by the directors throughout the four-year vesting period to earn entitlement to exercise the options at the vesting date. The entity should also recognise an equity reserve as this represents part of the consideration towards payment for the shares. This is calculated based upon the fair value of the option at the grant date at the start of the vesting period for each year of the share option scheme.

As this is the first year of the scheme, calculate the equity reserve required, and this will also provide the expense required to be recognised for the year as follows:

Year-ended 30 June 20X9
$4 \times 25,000 \times \$10 \times 1/4$ years $250,000

For each subsequent year, calculate the cumulative equity reserve required at that year-end; any increase in the equity reserve from the previous year will be the charge to recognise in profit or loss as follows:

Year-ended 30 June 20X0 Equity reserve
$4 \times 25,000 \times \$10 \times 2/4$ years $500,000

Remuneration expense for the year will be the movement in the equity reserve:

$500,000 − $250,000 = $250,000

Notice that the entity uses the fair value of the option at the grant date throughout the vesting period.

For tax purposes, tax relief is allowed only at the time the options are exercised, which will be at the end of the vesting period. Until then, the entity will have recognised an expense, on which tax relief will be obtained at a later date. This is a temporary difference for the purposes of accounting for deferred tax, giving rise to a deferred tax asset. The intrinsic value of the option is the difference between the market value of the shares at the reporting date and the option exercise price, and this should also be spread over the vesting period as follows:

Year ended 30 June 20X9   Temporary difference
$4 \times 25,000 \times (\$17 − \$5) \times 1/4$ $300,000

The temporary difference is then multiplied by the tax rate to determine the deferred tax asset:

$300,000 × 30% = $90,000

> If the deferred tax asset is to be recognised, it must be capable of reliable measurement and also be regarded as recoverable.

Test your understanding 8 - Fourkings

Revenue recognition

IAS 18 deals with revenue recognition. The principles which underpin the basis on which revenue is recognised are as follows;

- The revenue earned should be capable of reliable measurement
- Economic benefits will probably flow to the provider of services
- The costs incurred can be measured reliably.

If a contract, including the terms of service provision and a price has been agreed, it would appear that the first condition has been met. Similarly, if the contract cannot be cancelled by the client, this would go some way towards regarding the flow of economic benefits to Fourkings as being probable.

Ideally, the deposit should only be released to revenue at the point when the service is provided. However, this principle should be examined more closely, even though Fourkings cannot foresee any circumstances when it may need to cancel attendance or provision for an event, there could be circumstances when it may have no practical alternative. For example, any of the following circumstances could occur which would result in the accounting treatment used by Fourkings being inappropriate:

(a) The venue for an event (whether or not at their own property) could be closed by court or other public order announcement, such as travel and other restrictions imposed during an outbreak of foot and mouth disease. Such an eventuality may be beyond the control of Fourkings.

(b) Illness of Fourkings staff, such as swine fever where staff must stay away from work to prevent the spread of an infection.

(c) The venue could become unavailable due to a freak natural disaster, such as flooding or subsidence due to unusual weather conditions.

In these circumstances, there would be a failure to supply the service or support for an event which would not be the fault of either the client or Fourkings. Consequently, it may be that the deposit should either be returned, or retained pending provision of the service at an alternative date or location. Fourkings may have done little, if anything, to justify recognising the revenue under such circumstances. Where some cost has been incurred, for example ordering catering supplies, it would seem reasonable to recognise some revenue to offset those costs.

Reliable measurement of costs would appear to be a straightforward issue. The principal elements of cost will typically include staff hire, ordering of catering supplies and hire of external premises etc should be capable of reliable measurement.

Fourkings should undertake a thorough review of the risk that deposits may need to be refunded or deferred to other dates if the service is not provided when the client is not responsible. It is possible that this could be challenged by an unhappy client and there may need to be a provision recognised in accordance with IAS 37 for refund of deposit.

If revenue was to be recognised only at the point of service provision, it would mean that deposits would be released to revenue only when earned. This may reduce revenue in the first accounting period the practice was applied. It is unlikely to be material or significant enough to require a prior period adjustment, but the change of revenue recognition policy should be disclosed in the financial statements.

Manor house and grounds

One issue to consider is the nature of the expenditure to maintain the manor house and grounds in excellent condition. Any expenditure which is purely repairs and maintenance should be expensed in accordance with the current accounting policy. If there are any elements of improvement, such as expanding the car park, improving access to or from the property, improving drainage etc, it would be reasonable to capitalise these items. In accordance with IAS 16, any capitalised expenditure should be depreciated over their expected useful life to the business.

A further issue is the nature of any cyclical or periodic repairs; IAS 37 prevents building up a reserve in advance of incurring such expenditure or recognition of a provision where no legal or constructive obligation exists. If expenditure is incurred which may help to generate economic benefits over a number of years, it may be possible to capitalise and depreciate this expenditure. One example of this could be periodic replacement of the hobs and ovens in the kitchen, perhaps every ten years.

The fall in business activity and profitability is an indication of possible impairment. Based upon the available information, there could be impairment if the possible sale proceeds (less selling costs) is less than the carrying value. The question identifies initial cost of $5 million and an offer from a potential purchaser amounting to $4.5 million before selling costs. Further information regarding the carrying value of the land and depreciated building would be necessary to make more specific comment on any impairment review. Fourkings should also consider value in use when doing an impairment review. Value in use would comprise the net revenues expected from continued use of the manor house and grounds as currently used.

However, it should consider alternative uses (such as opening as a hotel or using the premises as a conference centre); it may also be possible to generate revenue from the sub-letting of part of the property to a third party. Any impairment recognised should be charged in full immediately to profit or loss. If, however, the property had previously been revalued, it would be possible to apply part of the impairment against the revaluation reserve.

If the decision is made to dispose of the property, it may need to be classed as held for sale in accordance with IFRS 5. For this to apply there must be a commitment to sell the property in its current condition at a realistic price. It would also be expected that disposal would be completed within twelve months and that there was little chance of the management reversing the decision to dispose of the property. If the criteria applied, the property would be removed from non-current assets and measured at the lower of carrying value and recoverable amount and presented separately on the statement of financial position.

Staff issues

The capitalisation of recruitment and training costs requires careful consideration. These costs should only be capitalised if there is a reporting standard which requires such treatment, or if it meets the definition of an asset in accordance with the Framework.

Whilst it would be accepted that entities employee staff to help them to generate future economic benefits, the key issue is whether there is a right to receive such benefits and, even if there is, can this be reliably measured for inclusion in the financial statements. Another issue would be that employees may resign after receiving training, and therefore no economic benefits would accrue to Fourkings. Whilst it may be possible to reliably measure both internal and external costs associated with recruitment and training, the problem arises of how benefits are to be identified and quantified. Capitalisation would also require amortisation – over what time period should such costs be amortised?

In conclusion, it would appear inappropriate to capitalise recruitment and training costs; such costs should be expensed as incurred.
The introduction of an employee share option scheme should be accounted for in accordance with IFRS 2. The fair value of the share option at the grant date is used, together with the number of employees who are expected to remain as employees at the vesting date. This information is applied to the number of share options and the costs spread over the three-year vesting period. The accounting treatment creates an equity reserve and also a remuneration expense.

For the year ended 31 October 2010 the amounts are as follows:

Year ended 31 October 2010	SOFP	SOCI
	equity reserve	payroll expense
	$000	$000
$(100 – 5 – 5 – 7) \times 500 \times \$6.00 \times 1/3$	83	83

Foreign currency

IAS 21 requires transactions designated in foreign currency are translated using the exchange rate ruling at the date of the transaction. The payment made on 31 August will be translated at the rate 1.25 Seychelles rupees to the $, giving a value of $80,000. As the payment made is a refundable deposit, it will be accounted for as a receivable. The risks and rewards associated with the payment have not yet been transferred as the event could be cancelled at any time up to 31 December 2010 and the deposit refunded in full.

At the reporting date, the receivable of 100,000 Seychelles rupees should be retranslated at the rate ruling at that date – i.e. 1.3 rupees to the $. This will be the best estimate of the dollar value of the receivable as at the year end at an amount of $76,923. The difference in the carrying value of the receivable $3,077 is an exchange loss which is taken to profit or loss.

Whether or not the event is cancelled after the reporting date and prior to the date on which the financial statements are approved by the directors will not be relevant. It would be a non-adjusting event per IAS 10, as would the dollar value of the deposit refunded. If considered to be material, a non-adjusting event could be disclosed by note in the financial statements for the year ended 31 October 2010.

If a euro-denominated bank account was to be opened, any dollar transfers in would be translated at the rate ruling at the date of the transaction. Similarly, any transfers out of the euro bank account into dollars would be translated at the rate ruling at the date of the transaction. At the year-end, the balance on the euro bank account would be translated at the closing rate at that date for inclusion in the financial statements within either current assets or current liabilities as appropriate.

Marking Scheme

(i)	Revenue recognition	5.0
(ii)	Manor house issues	8.0
(iii)	Staff issues	6.0
(iv)	Foreign currency transaction	6.0
		———
		25
		———

Test your understanding 9 - Seejoy

(a) Sale and leaseback

A sale and leaseback agreement releases capital for expansion, repayment of outstanding debt or repurchase of share capital. The transaction releases capital tied up in non liquid assets. There are important considerations. The price received for the asset and the related interest rate/rental charge should be at market rates. The interest rate will normally be dependent upon the financial strength of the 'tenant' and the risk/reward ratio which the lessor is prepared to accept. There are two types of sale and leaseback agreements, one utilising a finance lease and the other an operating lease.

The accounting treatment is determined by IAS 17 Leases. The substance of the transaction is essentially one of financing as the title to the stadium is transferred back to the club. Thus a sale is not recognised. The excess of the sale proceeds over the carrying value of the assets is deferred and amortised to profit or loss over the lease term. The leaseback of the stadium is for the remainder of its economic and useful life, and therefore under IAS 17, the lease should be treated as a finance lease. The stadium will remain as a non-current asset and will be depreciated. The finance lease loan will be accounted for under IFRS 9 Financial instruments in terms of the derecognition rules in the standard.

The transaction will be recognised by the club as follows in the year to 31 December 20X7:

	Dr $m	Cr $m
Receipt of cash 1 January 20X7		
Cash received	15	
Stadium		12
Deferred income		3
Assets held under finance lease	15	
Finance lease payable		15
Depreciation (15 ÷ 20 years)	0.75	
Assets held under finance lease		0.75

Statement of profit or loss and other comprehensive income:

		$000
Deferred income	($3m / 20 yrs)	150
Depreciation		(750)
Finance charge	($15m − $1.2m) × 5.6%	(773)

Statement of financial position:

		$000
Non-current assets - stadium	($15m − $0.75m)	14,250
Non-current liabilities:		
Deferred income	($3m − $0.15m)	2,850
Long-term borrowings	(($15m − ($1.2m ×2) + 0.773)	13,373
Current liabilities - rental payment		1,200

This form of sale and leaseback has several disadvantages. The profit for the period may decrease because of the increase in the finance charge over the deferred income. Similarly the gearing ratio of the club may increase significantly because of the increase in long term borrowings although the short term borrowings may be reduced by the inflow of cash.

Unsecured creditors may have less security for their borrowings after the leasing transaction. It may be worth considering a sale and leaseback involving an operating lease as in this case the profit on disposal can be recognised immediately because the sale price is at fair value. The stadium will be deemed to be sold and will be removed from the statement of financial position. Similarly no long-term liability for the loan will be recognised in the statement of financial position, and the sale proceeds could be used to repay any outstanding debt. This form of sale and leaseback would seem to be preferable than the one utilising a finance lease although any increase in the residual value of the stadium would be lost. However the secured loan approach which the directors do not wish to use may better reflect substance over form.

(b) **Player registrations**

The players' transfer fees have been capitalised as intangible assets under IAS 38 Intangible assets because it is probable that expected future benefits will flow to the club as a result of the contract signed by the player and the cost of the asset can be measured reliably, being the transfer fee. The cost model would be used because the revaluation model has to use an active market to determine fair value and this is not possible because of the unique nature of the players. IAS 38 requires intangible assets such as the player contracts to be amortised over their useful life. Intangible assets with indefinite useful lives should not be amortised and should be impairment tested annually. If the player is subsequently 'held for sale' i.e., becomes available for sale to other clubs and satisfies the criteria in IFRS 5 Non-current assets held for sale and discontinued operations, then amortisation ceases.

The amortisation method should reflect the pattern of the future economic benefits. The amortisation of the contracts over ten years does not fit this criterion. IAS 38 recommends an amortisation method that reflects the useful life of the asset and the pattern of economic benefits and, therefore, the proposed method over ten years cannot be used as an accounting policy. The current amortisation level should be maintained and a charge of $9 million $((20 \div 5) + (15 \div 3))$ would be shown in the statement of comprehensive income for the year-ending 31 December 20X7. This proposal in any event would only mask the poor financial state of the club. It is a book entry which may help prevent negative equity but will not give a cash benefit. The fundamental strategy for the club should be to contract players which it can afford and to spend at levels appropriate to its income.

There does not appear to be any probability that the contingent liability will crystallise. Under IAS 37 Provisions, contingent liabilities and contingent assets, a contingency is a possible obligation arising out of past events and whose existence will be confirmed only by the occurrence or non-occurrence of one or more uncertain future events not wholly within the control of the entity. At present the club is performing very poorly in the league and is unlikely to win the national league. Therefore, the contingent liability will not become a present obligation but will still be disclosed in the financial statements for the year-ending 31 December 20X7.

(c) Issue of bond

This form of financing a football club's operations is known as securitisation. Often in these cases a special purpose vehicle is set up to administer the income stream or assets involved. In this case, a special purpose vehicle has not been set up. The benefit of securitisation of the future corporate hospitality sales and season ticket receipts is that there will be a capital injection into the club and it is likely that the effective interest rate is lower because of the security provided by the income from the receipts. The main problem with the planned raising of capital is the way in which the money is to be used. The use of the bond for ground improvements can be commended as long term cash should be used for long term investment but using the bond for players' wages will cause liquidity problems for the club.

This type of securitisation is often called a 'future flow' securitisation. There is no existing asset transferred to a special purpose vehicle in this type of transaction. The bond is shown as a long term liability and is accounted for under IAS 39 Financial instruments: recognition and measurement. There are no issues of derecognition of assets as there can be in other securitisation transactions. In some jurisdictions there are legal issues in assigning future receivables as they constitute an unidentifiable debt which does not exist at present and because of this uncertainty often the bond holders will require additional security such as a charge on the football stadium.

The bond will be a financial liability and it will be classified in one of two ways:

- Financial liabilities at fair value through profit or loss include financial liabilities that the entity either has incurred for trading purposes or, where permitted, has designated to the category at inception. Derivative liabilities are always treated as held for trading unless they are designated and effective as hedging instruments. An example of a liability held for trading is an issued debt instrument that the entity intends to repurchase in the near term to make a gain from short-term movements in interest rates. It is unlikely that the bond will be classified in this category.

- The second category is financial liabilities measured at amortised cost. It is the default category for financial liabilities that do not meet the criteria for financial liabilities at fair value through profit or loss. In most entities, most financial liabilities will fall into this category. Examples of financial liabilities that generally would be classified in this category are account payables, note payables, issued debt instruments, and deposits from customers. Thus the bond is likely to be classified under this heading. When a financial liability is recognised initially in the statement of financial position, the liability is measured at fair value. Fair value is the amount for which a liability can be settled between knowledgeable, willing parties in an arm's length transaction. Since fair value is a market transaction price, on initial recognition fair value will usually equal the amount of consideration received for the financial liability. Subsequent to initial recognition financial liabilities are measured using amortised cost or fair value. In this case the company does not wish to use valuation models nor is there an active market for the bond and, therefore, amortised cost will be used to measure the bond.

The bond will be shown initially at $50 million × 95%, i.e. $47.5 million as this is the consideration received. Subsequently at 31 December 20X7, the bond will be shown as follows:

	$m
Initial recognition	47.5
Interest at 7.7%	3.7
Cash payment	(6.0)
Amount owing at 31 December 20X7	45.2

(d) **Player trading**

The sale of the players will introduce cash into the club and help liquidity. The contingent liability will be extinguished as the players will no longer play for Seejoy. The club, however, is not performing well at present and the sale of the players will not help their performance. This may result in the reduction of ticket sales and, therefore, cause further liquidity problems. The proceeds from the sale of players may be difficult to estimate at present as the date of sale is significantly into the future. (The players will not constitute held for sale non-current assets under IFRS 5 Non-current assets held for sale and discontinued operations at 31 December 20X6 as the players are not available for immediate sale. As a loss on sale is anticipated on the players, an impairment review should be undertaken at 31 December 20X6.) If the sale proceeds are $16 million, then a loss on sale will be recorded of $2 million if the players are sold on 1 May 20X7.

	Transfer fee $m	Amortisation $m	Carrying amount $m
A. Steel	20	4 + 4/12 of 4	14.7
R. Aldo	15	10 + 4/12 of 5	3.3
			────
			18.0
Sale proceeds (estimated)			16.0
			────
Loss			2.0
			────

If the players are not sold by 31 December 20X7, they may constitute non-current assets held for sale, if the conditions of IFRS 5 are met. Immediately before the initial classification of the asset as held for sale, the carrying amount of the asset will be measured in accordance with applicable IFRSs and the non-current assets if deemed to be held for sale will be measured at the lower of carrying amount and fair value less costs to sell. Impairment must be considered both at the time of classification as held for sale and subsequently. Non-current assets that are classified as held for sale are not depreciated. Thus amortisation of the transfer fees will stop if the non-current assets are held for sale. Assets classified as held for sale must be presented separately on the face of the statement of financial position at 31 December 20X7.

```
┌─────────────────────────────────────────────────────────────┐
│                        Marking Scheme                          │
│    (i)     Sale and leaseback                          9.0    │
│    (ii)    Player registrations                        5.0    │
│    (iii)   Bond                                        6.0    │
│    (iv)    Player trading                              5.0    │
│                                                       ─────   │
│                                                        25     │
│                                                       ─────   │
└─────────────────────────────────────────────────────────────┘
```

Index

Index

Index